Crafting the LANDSCAPE PHOTOGRAPH

with Lightroom Classic and Photoshop

Techniques for Realizing the Full Potential of Your Photography

BEN WILLMORE

The Experts Agree...

"If you want to push your images to the next level, you've got the right book! Ben Willmore is a modern-day Michelangelo of Photoshop and his books bring you a classic apprenticeship of learning which sets you on your way to becoming a master yourself."
—**Russell Preston Brown**: Senior Creative Director at Adobe for 32+ years, www.russellbrown.com

"For decades, Ben has been one of my go-to sources for Photoshop information at the highest level. Few people give more 'I didn't know you could do that' moments than Ben."
—**John Paul Caponigro**: photographer, artist, author, educator, www.johnpaulcaponigro.art

"Ben has always been at the cutting edge of post-processing in Adobe Lightroom and Photoshop. His ability to convey the latest technology, while including his wisdom from years of teaching, makes his lessons extremely valuable."
—**Marc Muench**: third-generation photographer, author, www.marcmuench.com

"From my first days into the digital darkroom, Ben has inspired and taught me the craft of finishing! The love he has for photography, teaching, and the digital darkroom comes out in every sentence!"
—**Moose Peterson**: photographer, author of 29 photography books, www.moosepeterson.com

"I've had the honor of working with Ben Willmore over many years while I helped lead the Lightroom product team at Adobe. During that time, I've learned that Ben has that rare combination of great artistic talent, an understanding of the underlying craft and technology, and the unique ability to distill that knowledge in a way that unlocks the potential of the broader community of photographers. Ben has always had a front row seat and understanding of how Lightroom has grown in relation to Photoshop over the years to create unlimited opportunities for photographers who want to create that next great image or pull the best out of a digital negative they've already captured."
—**Tom Hogarty**: Former Senior Director of Product Management, Photoshop & Lightroom

"This is a valuable, comprehensive resource for anyone serious about improving both the efficiency of their digital editing workflow and the quality of their photographs. Ben is not only a great photographer, but a wonderful, straightforward instructor. I'm happy to recommend this book to my students and professional colleagues alike."
—**Craig Blacklock**: photographer, author of 19 photography books, www.blacklockgallery.com

"Ben has always had a gift for making complex topics simple and understandable without over-explaining the concepts, and I've always loved that about his teaching. In this book, I feel he's taken that technique up another notch. His writing here is so wonderfully succinct and to the point, making it so approachable and a joy to read. Highly recommended for any serious landscape photographer."
—**Scott Kelby**: founder KelbyOne.com, publisher of *Photoshop User* magazine, author of 60+ books

"Not only is Ben a fabulous artist, but he is the best Photoshop teacher ever. He is unmatched at teaching the techniques that create incredible images."
—**Russell Williams**: Principal Scientist of Photoshop at Adobe for 25+ years

"The great landscape photographer Ansel Adams used to say, 'The negative is the equivalent of the composer's score, and the print the performance.' In today's digital world, the raw capture is the score, and the processed image is the performance. Ben Willmore is the perfect guide to sharing processing techniques that will take your score and make it a master performance!"
—**Lewis Kemper**: photographer, author, educator, www.lewiskemper.com

"As an exceptional Photoshop and Lightroom guru, Ben Willmore has led the way with a gift
and enviable ability to break down and make clear the most advanced concepts and
techniques, so that a novice as well as an advanced photographer can understand."
—**Tony Sweet**: photographer, author, Nikon Legend Behind the Lens, www.tonysweet.com

"Ben is a true master of his craft. He sees things the rest of us don't see and the magic
he performs makes my mind melt."
—**Trey Ratcliff**: worlds #1 travel photography blogger, author, www.stuckincustoms.com

"Ben Willmore is the most knowledgeable master I have ever met. Not only does he have the
answers, but he can explain his technique in a way anyone can understand. This is a book
I will be coming back to often."
—**Andy Katz**: 1st Sony Artisan of Imagery, author 14 photo books, www.andykatzphotography.com

"If you are looking to step up your landscape photography, Ben is the guy to pay attention to.
His skills in the digital darkroom are unsurpassed, and his creative process is like no one else's.
Following the techniques outlined in this book is a sure way to elevate your art."
—**Juan Pons**: photographer, educator, www.juanpons.org

"Well Ben has done it again! Created an absolutely gorgeous resource for everyone who has ever
taken (or been taken by) a photo of Mother Nature! Whether pro or enthusiast, everyone will
be empowered by Ben's incredible depth of expertise, as well as his amazing ability to convey
that in practical, easy-to-understand prose using his award-winning photography! Crafting
the Landscape is a must buy for everyone wanting to take their photography to a new level
of quality!"
—**Jack Davis**: photographer, co-author *How to Wow: Photoshop for Photography*

"Ben's books are like getting all the answers before you even know what the questions are."
—**Vincent Versace**: photographer, author, www.versacephotography.com

"Ben Willmore has a remarkable talent for explaining even the most complex subjects in a way
that makes the concepts easy to grasp. With his in-depth knowledge, extensive experience,
and clear communication style, Ben is an excellent resource for any photographer who wants
to learn to truly realize their photographic vision."
—**Tim Grey**: photographer, digital imaging expert, author of 12+ books, www.timgreyphoto.com

"I've known Ben a long time and have always learned useful tips and techniques from him
when it comes to Photoshop and Lightroom. Ben is great at explaining how to do things in
a way that makes it easy for photographers of all skill levels to understand."
—**Brenda Tharp**: photographer, author of 4 photography books, www.brendatharp.com

CRAFTING THE **LANDSCAPE** PHOTOGRAPH

WITH LIGHTROOM CLASSIC AND PHOTOSHOP

Techniques for Realizing the Full Potential of Your Photography

Ben Willmore

Project editor: Jocelyn Howell
Project manager: Lisa Brazieal
Marketing coordinator: Katie Walker
Initial copy editing: Karen Willmore
Design and layout: Ben Willmore
Cover design: Aren Straiger

ISBN: 978-1-68198-989-1
1st Edition (1st printing, October 2023)
© 2023 Ben Willmore
All images © Ben Willmore unless otherwise noted

Rocky Nook Inc.
1010 B Street, Suite 350
San Rafael, CA 94901 USA
www.rockynook.com

Distributed in the UK and Europe by Publishers Group UK
Distributed in the U.S. and all other territories by Publishers Group West

Library of Congress Control Number: 2022950235

Dedication

This book is dedicated to all the amazing photographers who have played a role in shaping my photographic evolution.

Those who have devoted their lives to mastering the art of photography and generously share their knowledge with others who share a passion for that art.

Their selfless generosity was the spark that ignited my desire to write this book.

My greatest hope is for this book to inspire others in a way that is similar to how this amazing group of photographers has served to inspire me.

About the Author

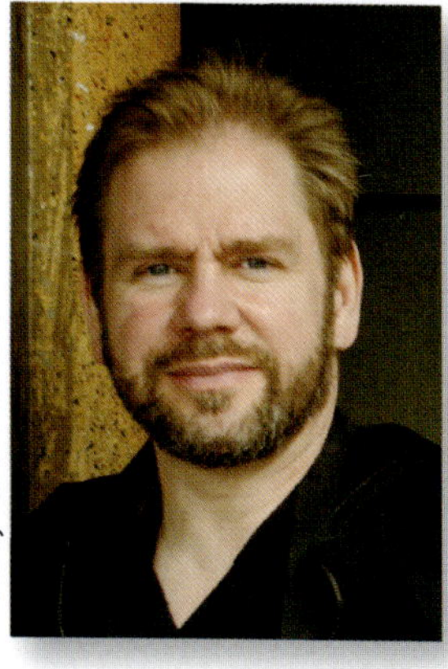

In the late 1970s, Ben Willmore developed an obsession with computers. At the time, his only access to one was at a local computer store, where he spent as much of his free time as possible. He even taught the store's salespeople how to use their new Commodore PET computer.

Once his mother became convinced that his interest in computers was not just a passing fad, she bought him an Apple][computer. Then, at the age of fourteen, she fed his obsession by sending him to Compu-Camp, where he created his first digital images using a graphics tablet.

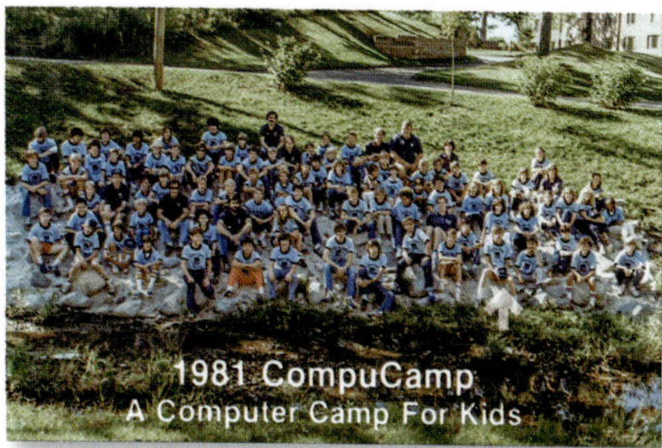

Ben developed a passion for photography after hand-building his first camera out of a kit while attending middle school. It was a 110-format film camera that came as a box full of parts with an instruction manual, much like the way miniature car models were packaged.

High school was not a pleasant time for Ben, as he lost his mother to cancer and subsequently showed little interest in learning topics he was not passionate about. As a result, his school allowed him to end his school day early to work part-time at a well-paying job. With the money he earned, he bought a Macintosh computer in 1984, the same year it was launched.

One of the first Mac programs he tried was called MacPaint, which had many of the same features that would later be found in Photoshop. Within a year, Ben figured out how to capture photographs on his Mac using a special piece of hardware called MacVision, which connected to a video camera and took 22 seconds to capture an image. He also hacked his dot matrix printer and transformed it into a scanner by replacing its ink ribbon with a scanning device known as Thunderscan. That setup enabled him to scan an 8.5x11" page at 144ppi in 10 minutes!

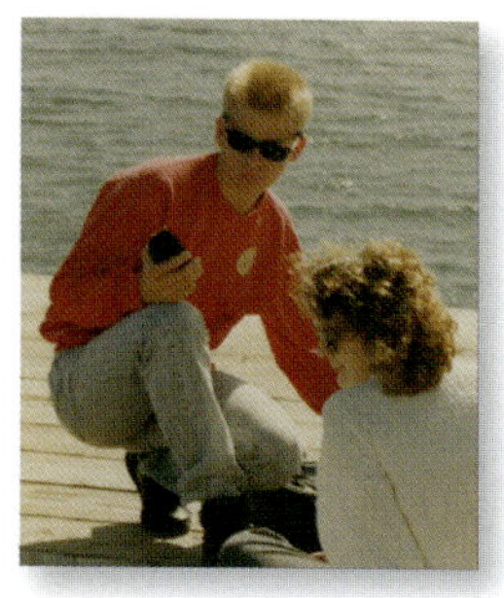

He got into 35mm and 4x5" film photography during high school and college, producing both B&W and color prints in the darkroom. He also experimented with liquid photographic emulsions in order to make prints on unique substrates, such as the surface of an egg.

Ben shifted his attention to graphic design in 1985 when the first laser printer that could incorporate text and images was released. To learn the skills of the trade, he got a job at the *Minnesota Daily* newspaper. That's where he learned to lay out pages the old-school way, which involved cutting out blocks of text with an X-acto knife, securing them to a page with wax, and putting borders around advertisements using a roll of black tape.

By day, he used the newspaper's expensive typesetting system, stat camera, and wax to lay out pages; by night, he learned to do the same digitally on his Mac. To test his capabilities, he partnered with an antique dealer to create the *Midwest States Collector* –

a newspaper dedicated to antiques. Once he was confident in his newfound skills, he used them to help transition his college's newspaper to a digital workflow.

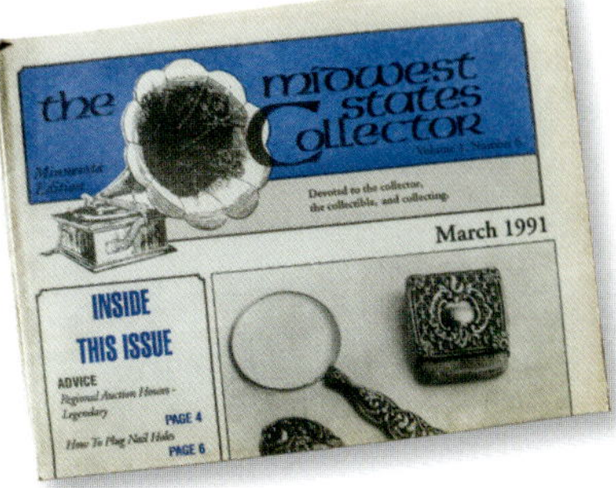

After college, Ben worked as a graphic designer for newspapers, magazines, and design firms. During that time, he hired photographers instead of using his own camera. Ben still enjoys the graphic design process and designed and produced the pages of the book you are reading. Ben likes to write and arrange the pages interactively.

In the late 1980s, Ben started experimenting with what would eventually became known as Photoshop. In 1994 he quit his job and presented his first Photoshop seminar, just a few short months before the concept of layers was added to the program. Since then, he has spoken at hundreds of events across 29 US states and 17 countries.

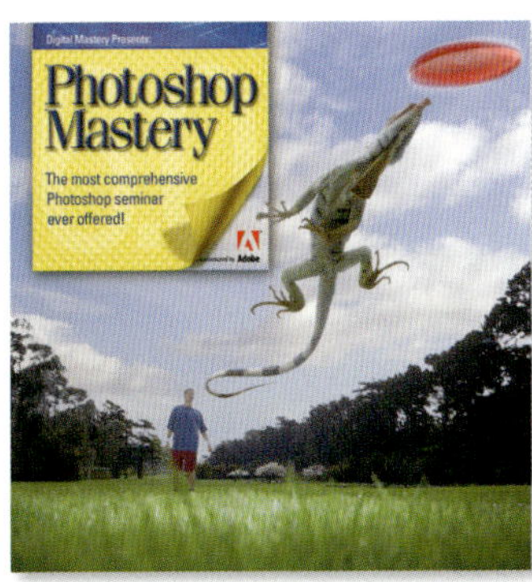

In 1997, Adobe asked Ben to write a Photoshop book for Adobe Press, which sparked a successful writing career. He has since written a dozen books and hundreds of magazine articles, which have been published in eight languages. His impact on the industry was acknowledged in 2004 when he was inducted into the Photoshop Hall of Fame.

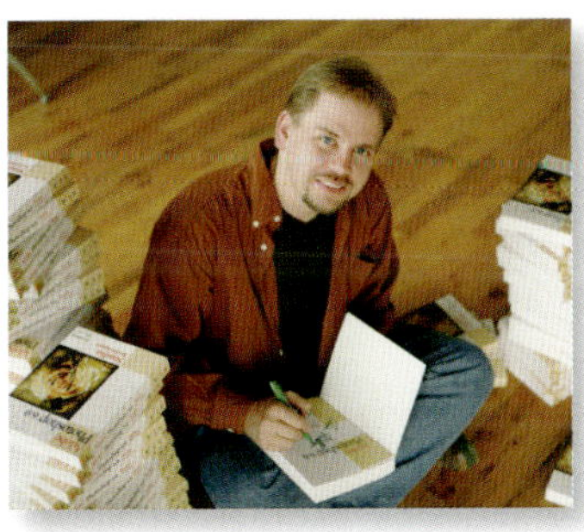

Ben's love for photography was reignited by the travel associated with giving seminars. In 1994, he bought a Casio QV-10 digital camera, but its tiny 320x240 images weren't enough to replace his film camera. The 2001 launch of the Canon D30 enabled Ben to stop shooting film altogether. Then, when full-frame mirrorless cameras were introduced in 2013, he made the switch within a year. He's since used full-frame and medium-format digital cameras from Canon, Nikon, Olympus, Phase One, and Sony.

Ben accumulated an expansive list of locations he wanted to photograph across the USA. In 2006, he realized he wouldn't have time to visit them all if he didn't make a radical lifestyle change. That's when he decided to sell his home and spend the next decade living a fully nomadic lifestyle aboard a 40' motorcoach.

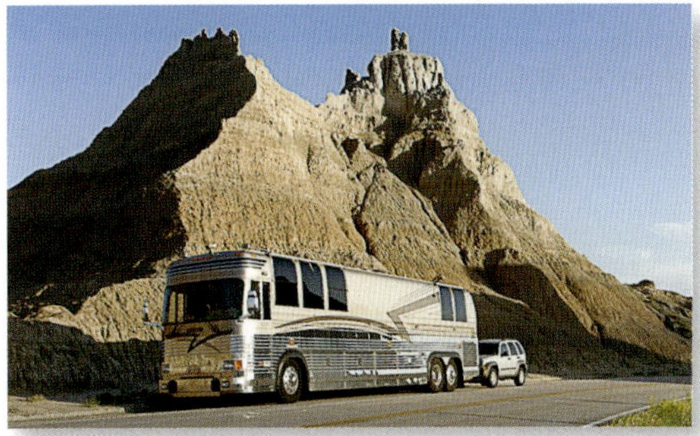

He has since explored all 50 US states and over 85 countries on all seven continents. These days, he regularly leads groups of photographers on workshops to the Galapagos Islands, Africa, Iceland, Thailand, Laos, and Cambodia, as well as somewhat less exotic places across the USA.

In 2016, Ben finished restoring a vintage bus, which contains so many high-tech features that it was featured on the Extreme RVs TV show.

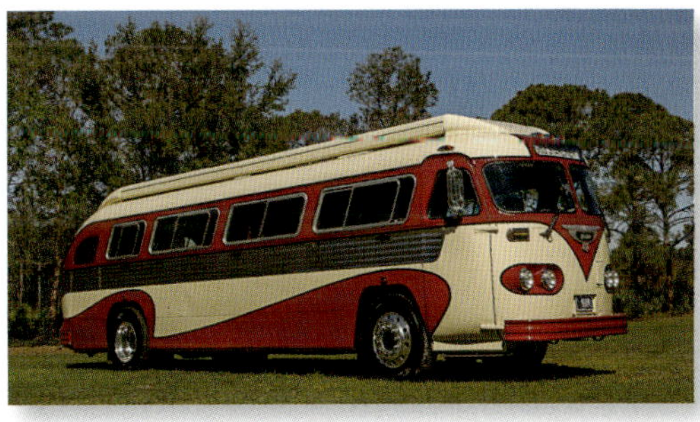

Over the last seven years, Ben has been building a comprehensive resource for learning photography, Photoshop, and Lightroom. Over 275 hours of video tutorials and 4,500 pages of PDF companion guides are available at MastersAcademy.com.

Just before COVID put a halt to all travel, Ben and his wife Karen purchased a home in Clearwater, Florida. Their vintage bus now serves as their escape pod which allows them to explore the country and avoid the hot Florida summer.

CONTENTS

Fundamental Concepts

Quality Considerations

Crafting a Photograph

Foreword

Landscape photography is both experiential and artistic. When a scene, or something within it, speaks to us loudly enough that we want to stop to interact with it, then we as photographers also want to capture that experience and share it with others through our imagery. But the technology of photography is constantly advancing, and the technical knowledge required to positively apply it to our photographs must be continually refreshed.

Equally transformative, however, is the post-capture processing software that takes our landscape photographs to the next level of perfection in quality and character. It's this combination of technical skill and artistic interpretation—from capture to final rendition—that Ben Willmore has mastered and shares with us in this beautiful and educational book.

While some photographers might argue that new photographic technology creates images that aren't "real," that's a bit like arguing that only a camel is a "real" form of transportation. In fact, landscape photography began with black-and-white capture on glass plates. Since nature rarely presents itself in black and white, we will have to conclude that method was not offering accurate renditions of the subject.

With the advent of film, improvement of chemical processing, and print media that further softened or sharpened the image, photographers began to have more control over their resulting images. One of the best-known examples of the perpetual reinterpretation of an image is Ansel Adams's iconic *Moonlight Over Hernandez*, the original of which was quite flat, but which after dodging, burning, and contrast control, emerged from Adams's darkroom as a masterpiece that he repeatedly revised over the following decades.

Similar adjustments were constantly adapted by photographers who embraced color transparency film with all its uncertainties, including color renditions that varied by film type and processing. While color photography represented a huge advancement, photographers still had negligible control over the color palette in the final print, although results could be influenced slightly by direct printing or using an internegative derived from the original film. Nonetheless, the era of color film produced groundbreaking landscape renditions and, towards its end, printing and media technology that made the long-lasting color print a reality.

But why are such "last century" techniques still relevant? Because they remind us that the truly great photographers are also innovators who recognize technological advancement, understand how it will improve the accuracy and/or artistic rendition of their work, and learn to use it and apply it effectively.

Around the turn of the 21st century, computers and software programs became available to photographers, enabling digitization of their analog film (B&W and color) and printing on early color printers. But it wasn't until the introduction of digital cameras, both small- and medium-format, that photographers had a complete system to control all aspects of their photography, from capture to processing to print. Those of us who had always embraced—and sometimes invented—breakthroughs that helped us to achieve better photographic expression were immediately on board with the digital revolution. But alongside these innovative new cameras, a new set of experts emerged to drive the development of post-capture technology, explore and apply its potentials, and explain these new processes to the rest of us.

This is where I, and many other photographers, sought the expertise of Ben Willmore. From early on in the digital era, photographers understood that while they might know their cameras and have excellent photographic technique, mastering computer technology and software—most significantly Photoshop—demanded a whole new knowledge base. I first met Ben at Photoshop World, where he was a knowledgeable and articulate presenter with a gift for making complex software understandable and applicable to my photographic aspirations. Ben quickly became my go-to source for information on post-processing programs. I avidly consumed his books, CDs, videos, and online classes, and attended his in-person seminars whenever possible. I later taught alongside Ben at Photoshop World; my emphasis was on digital capture, and his was on the optimization software, which gave me a chance to observe and participate in his programs.

Recognizing the great demand for photographic education in the new era, I established a school, the Lepp Institute of Digital Imaging (LIDI), which brought photographers to the California coast to learn digital photography skills amongst its magnificent landscapes, then to work in a computer- and printer-equipped classroom setting to learn post-processing and printing.

Ben was one of LIDI's most effective and popular guest instructors. One aspect of Ben's teaching that makes him a standout is that he is also an excellent photographer, producing the examples that demonstrate his knowledge base. He works in a real world where he experiences and solves the everyday problems of digital photography. I observed Ben's enthusiasm for digital capture when he would arrive at LIDI a week before his own scheduled classes at the school so that he could participate in my field photography sessions. He was always enthusiastic and always generous with his knowledge.

Fifteen years later, Ben Willmore is still leading us with clarity and passion as we continue to visualize, learn, and apply the constantly evolving advances in photographic capture and processing, particularly as they relate to landscape subjects. As with his seminars given all over the world and in excellent online venues such as Creative Live, in this book you will find easy-to-understand, well-illustrated, practical, and through information that you can use to take your landscape photography to the next level.

I am a frequent judge of international nature photography contests where the highest ethical, artistic, and technical standards are applied. I often see unrealized potential in so many of the submitted images; the photographer has witnessed and captured an extraordinary natural event, only to fail in the competition because the image has not been properly processed post-capture.

Whether you are a beginning or advanced photographer, the state-of-the-art information found in this book will give you the opportunity to take control of your digital landscape images and optimize the results to achieve the photograph you had hoped for when the capture was made, overcoming the still-there limitations of the camera to render and share the scenario you envisioned and experienced. And that is what outstanding landscape photography is all about.

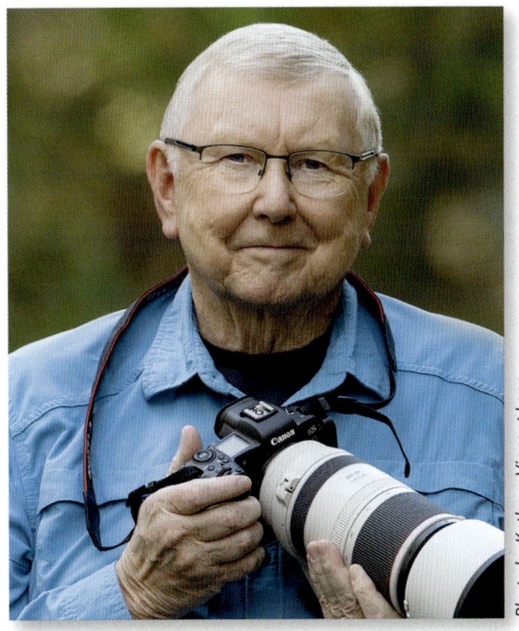

—George D. Lepp

One of North America's best-known contemporary outdoor and nature photographers and a leader in the field of digital imaging, George Lepp is the author of many books and hundreds of nationally and internationally published articles about the creative, ethical, and technical aspects of nature photography. An original member of Canon USA's Explorers of Light program, featuring the industry's most influential photographers, Lepp is now a Canon Legend and field editor of **Outdoor Photographer** *magazine. His photography is extensively published and exhibited, and is represented by Getty Images, Corbis, and Photo Researchers. He has presented hundreds of lectures and led workshops all over the world, and often serves as a judge of international photography competitions. A founder and fellow of the North American Nature Photographers Association (NANPA), Lepp has won many awards for his work, including Photo Media's Photography Person of the Year, the Photographic Society of America's prestigious Progress Award, and NANPA's Lifetime Achievement Award. First trained in wildlife and wildlands management, Lepp later earned a BA and honorary MSc from Brooks Institute of Photography. George and his wife and collaborator, Kathryn Vincent Lepp, live in Bend, Oregon, and can be contacted at www.GeorgeLepp.com.*

Introduction

LET ME BE honest. I am not the greatest photographer out there. Yet my images have somehow made their way onto the covers of multiple magazines, they have been used in photography-related advertisements, and have received regular praise from the photographic community. What's my secret? Well, my true superpower lies in my ability to transform an average image into something that will knock your socks off. It all comes down to truly understanding and knowing how to fully harness the power of Lightroom Classic and Photoshop. If you want to realize the full potential of your photographs, then you've come to the right place. I've been pushing Photoshop to its limits for over thirty years and have used Lightroom since the first day it was available. In the pages that follow, I will show you how to transform the images you capture into stunning works of art.

We'll start by ensuring you have a firm foundation of knowledge on the most essential concepts in working with Lightroom and Photoshop. It's only once you understand how those programs take fundamentally different approaches to working with images that you can develop a strategy to maximize your effectiveness and take full advantage of both.

You'll then learn how to fix all the issues that are inherent in the image your camera produced. You'll learn how to compensate for under- and overexposed images, reduce noise, fix optical issues, and much more. After that, you'll discover how to go beyond the limitations of your camera by combining multiple exposures. This will allow you to extend the dynamic range and depth of field in order to produce images that could never be achieved with a single shot.

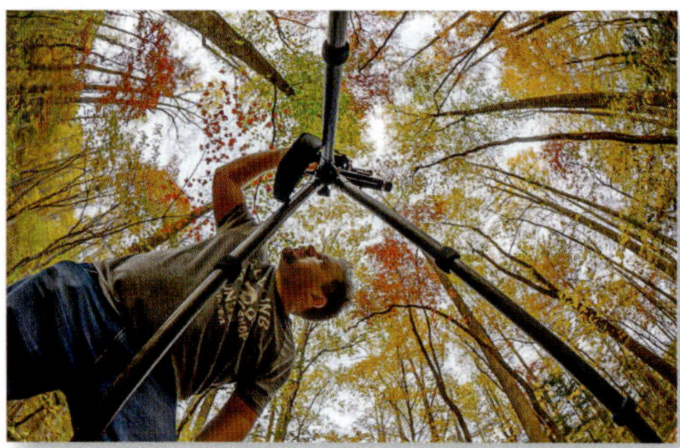

Once you have developed an ideal image to serve as the base for further enhancement, you'll learn how to craft that image into something truly amazing. It will feature engaging color, a heightened sense of dimension, a captivating focal point, and a path that seems to magnetically lead your eye through the image. Then, just when you think you're finished, we'll become critical, zooming up and eliminating any undesirable artifacts that were caused by all the enhancements you've performed. The result will be a breathtaking image that you can be proud of.

Develop a Critical Eye

Along the way, I will also help you develop an eye for recognizing unrealized potential in your images. You may find that the images you thought were hopeless just needed some simple tweaks to transform them into something special. That way, fewer images will end up in the trash and your percentage of keepers will increase.

I feel it's also my job to show you how to recognize when you've gone overboard and compromised the quality of your results through over-processing. That can happen any time you learn a new technique and then push it a bit too far. The novelty of learning a new skill makes it impossible to see your results from the perspective of someone who has used the technique for years. But revisit images that you processed years ago and compare them to what you're producing today, and you'll usually see more subtlety and refinement in your results once that novelty wears off. I'll show you how to recognize over-processing, teach you what causes it, and, more importantly, show you how to prevent it from compromising the quality of your images.

Producing an image that looks amazing on your screen is one thing, but delivering such an image will place your work before the critical eye of others. For that reason, we'll need look behind the magic curtain and learn a bit about how images are constructed behind the scenes. This will ensure you know how to maintain quality when exporting and sharing your images.

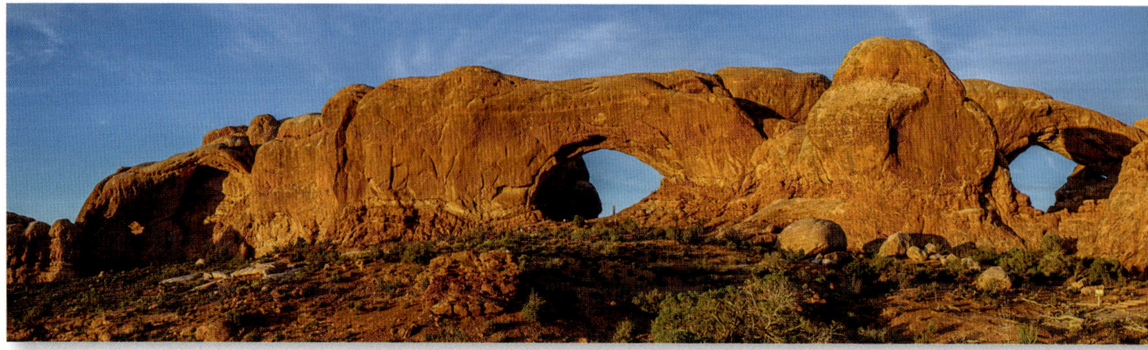

Efficient Use of Your Time

Throughout the nine chapters that follow, I promise to be concise and focus exclusively on techniques that are useful for landscape photographers. The idea is to make the time you spend with this book a concentrated learning experience that is jam-packed with useful information and zero fluff.

To prevent fluff from creeping onto these pages, I'm going to assume that you've at least installed both Lightroom Classic and Photoshop and spent some time fumbling around with them. Therefore, I'm not going to show you how to do things like open or save a file, but I will teach you about what matters most. The vast majority of basic stuff that I don't cover can be learned with a simple Google search or a quick visit to YouTube.

By confining the subject matter to landscapes, I am able to keep the concepts as focused as possible. Also, the settings used for optimizing a landscape image will be different than those used to optimize a portrait or sports image. Therefore, a more generalized approach would lead to more generic advice. That's not what I want for your photography.

Conventions Used In the Book

There are multiple versions of Lightroom available from Adobe. I'll be using the one that has the official name of Adobe Photoshop Lightroom Classic. That's the version that expects you to store your images locally, on normal hard drives. There is another version called Adobe Photoshop Lightroom, which is designed for storing your images on Adobe's servers. Just be aware that anytime I mention Lightroom, I'm always referring to Lightroom Classic.

As you're working your way through the book, you'll notice that many passages of text will be in **bold**. These terms represent the names of the actual tools, menu commands, and adjustment sliders you'll be interacting with and the settings that I'd like you to dial into each one. I do that to make it easier for you to scan a paragraph and determine exactly what you should be doing in Lightroom or Photoshop.

Getting Help when You Get Stuck

If you get stuck when working through a technique, consider joining my free Facebook group. Here, you'll get responses from others who have read the book or have attended one of my seminars. Just be aware that, just like this book, my group does not contain any fluff, so be sure to get to the point and ask or answer a question. The group is not designed for showing off your images, for asking overly vague questions, or for asking questions that could be answered with a simple Google search. You can join the group at **www.facebook.com/groups/BenWillmore**

Also visit **www.craftingthelandscape.com** where I may post associated information, such as corrections or updates to the techniques found in this book.

Let's Get Started

Capturing a moment in time is not just about pressing the camera's shutter button. The resulting photograph's success is determined by a series of intentional decisions made by the photographer. Those decisions start well before the shutter is released and continue until the resulting image is displayed for others to see. The pages that follow aim to equip you with the necessary skills to truly realize the full potential of your photography.

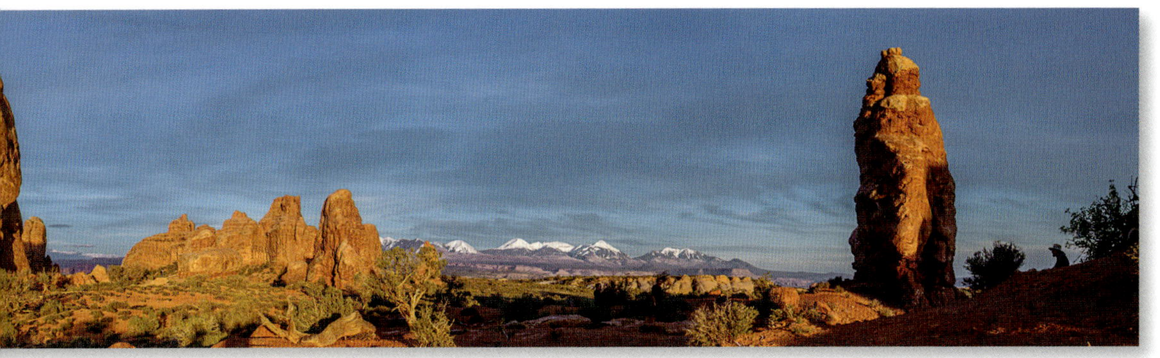

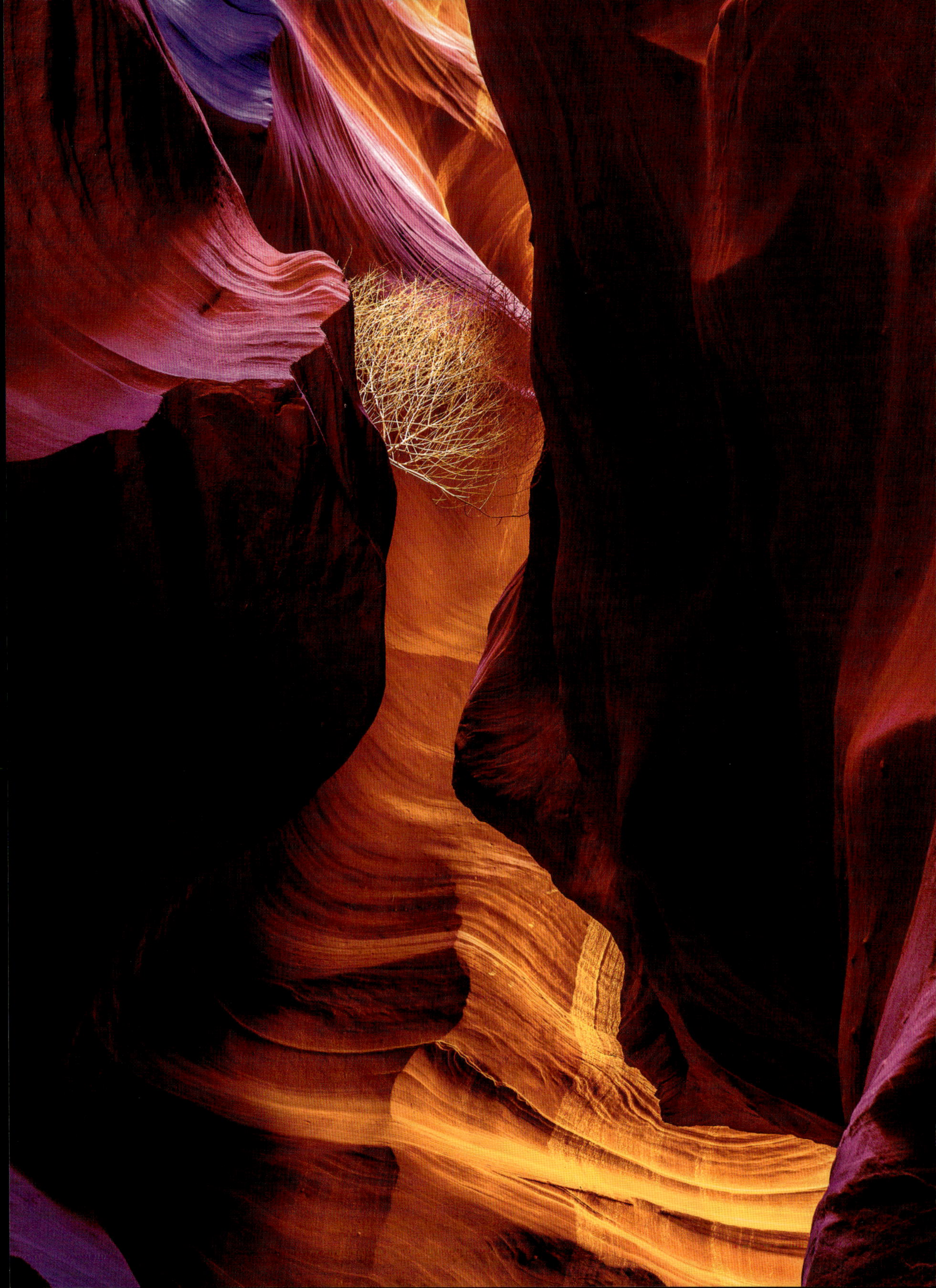

Section I

Fundamental Concepts

BEFORE WE GET into techniques that are specific to optimizing landscape images, I need to make sure you understand the fundamental concepts that we'll rely on to enhance our images. This section attempts to do that in the fewest number of pages possible. I find that the majority of Lightroom and Photoshop users have gaping holes in their knowledge, even at the most basic level. This makes it difficult to dive deep into learning how to make your landscapes look their best, as you risk compromising the quality of your images or misusing key tools. So, let's jump in and skim the most essential concepts to make sure you have a good foundation to build upon.

Chapter 1

Develop a Lightroom + Photoshop Mindset

THE GOAL OF this chapter is to ensure that you understand that Lightroom Classic and Photoshop take fundamentally different approaches to working with images.

We'll start by looking at the processing pipeline all images must go through between the moment they are captured and the stage at which they can be worked on in Lightroom or Photoshop. In the process, you should realize that Lightroom has a distinct advantage when working on raw files.

We'll then look at specific strengths and weaknesses of each program so you can develop an idealized workflow that utilizes the best of both programs.

In-Camera versus Post-Processing

All images captured digitally must go through a complex pipeline of adjustments before they can be viewed on a screen or saved in a universally accepted file format.

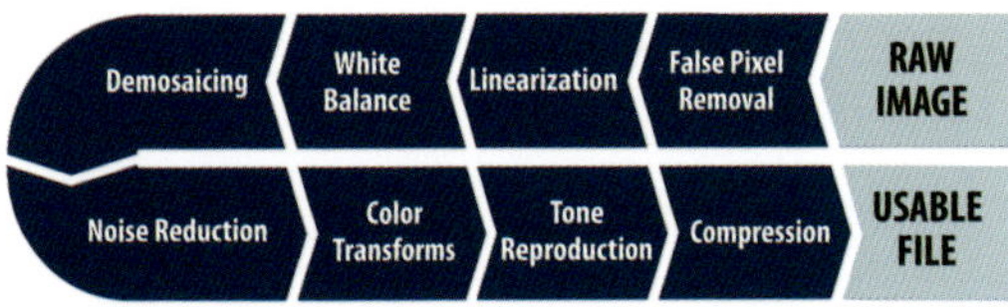

In-camera processing pipeline from capture to final image.

Capturing Color

Camera sensors are made up of a grid of squares, one for each pixel that will make up the resulting image. Each square contains a sensor that measures the brightness of the light falling on the square.

To capture color, a mosaic of red, green, and blue filters is added above the squares so only one of those three colors is allowed to pass through to each sensor. A full range of colors can be captured using only three colors because your eye contains just three types of color receptors: one type is most sensitive to red light, a second type is most sensitive to green light, and the third type is most sensitive to blue light.

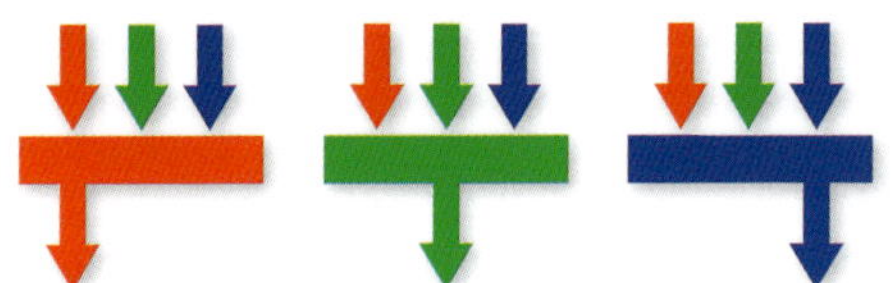

Color-absorbing filters limit the color of light being measured.

Essential Processing Steps

After you press the shutter button, the information captured goes through the following adjustments to compensate for issues that were discovered when that specific camera was manufactured:

False-Pixel Removal: It is rare for a camera sensor to be manufactured that is completely free of defects. A few of the squares that make up the sensor will likely fail to react to changes in brightness and will instead output a fixed brightness value. To avoid rejecting the entire sensor due to a few

"stuck" squares, the location of those pixels are noted in the camera's firmware and the camera conceals the defect by substituting an average of the readings of the surrounding squares that were measuring the same color.

Linearization: Camera sensors do not react proportionally to changes in light. A 10% increase in light would ideally cause a corresponding 10% increase in the measurement produced by the sensor. If it instead only causes an 8% increase, then this must be compensated for to produce a linear response to the amount of light falling on the sensor.

At this point, all adjustments that are unique to your exact camera have been performed. Any further steps do not require information that is stored in the camera firmware, and therefore do not have to be performed by the camera.

Save Raw or Continue to Rendered JPEG

The image hasn't had enough processing to be viewable at this stage and the steps listed below will need to be applied before a usable image is produced. For raw files, those steps will be performed in Lightroom where the user can move around adjustment sliders to influence the results. For JPEG files, all the steps below will be applied in-camera based on the settings in the camera's menu system at the time of capture.

White Balance: You may have noticed that photographs taken indoors under artificial light often appear more yellow/orange than what you remember experiencing with your own eyes at the time the photo was taken. That's because your brain adjusts to the color of the light sources you experience throughout the day in an attempt to maintain consistency in how you perceive the color of recognizable objects. Your brain adjusts to make it appear as if your surroundings are being lit by the white light of the midday sun.

When you view a photograph, your brain is adjusted to the environment where the photo is being viewed. For that reason, photos tend to be preceived as natural when the scene appears to be lit by white light, and that's why someone came up with the idea of adjusting white balance.

The brightness of the red, green, and blue light that was captured can be adjusted to make a scene appear to be lit by white light regardless of

the color of light that it was actually captured under. That's due to the fact that areas containing a
perfectly balanced amount of red, green, and blue
light will always be rendered as a neutral shade
of gray when an image is displayed or printed.
White balance can alternatively be used to make
an image feel warm or cool.

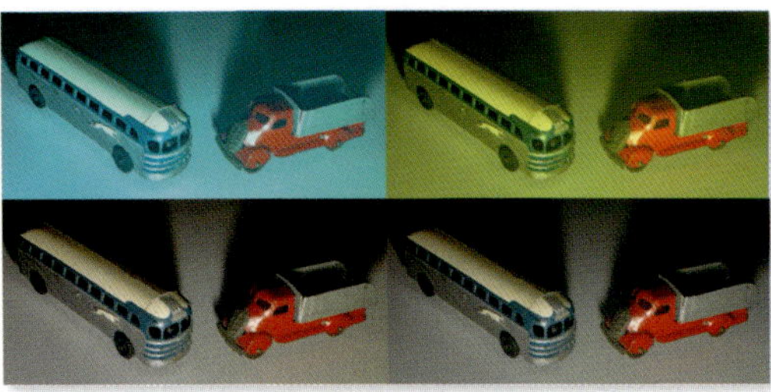

Top: The same scene lit by two different light sources.
Bottom: Result of neutralizing color cast with white balance.

A wider brightness range is captured by the sensor than is rendered in the resulting image to
leave some headway for white balance adjustments. This ensures that the brightest area in
the image will have proper information for red,
green, and blue without encountering clipping.
That extra headroom is discarded before the
image-processing pipeline is complete.

Demosaicing: To display an image in color, each
square that makes up the image needs to contain
brightness measurements for all three colors:
red, green, and blue. Since the camera only recorded a single color reading for each square,
the missing colors will be created by averaging
surrounding squares that were measuring the
needed color.

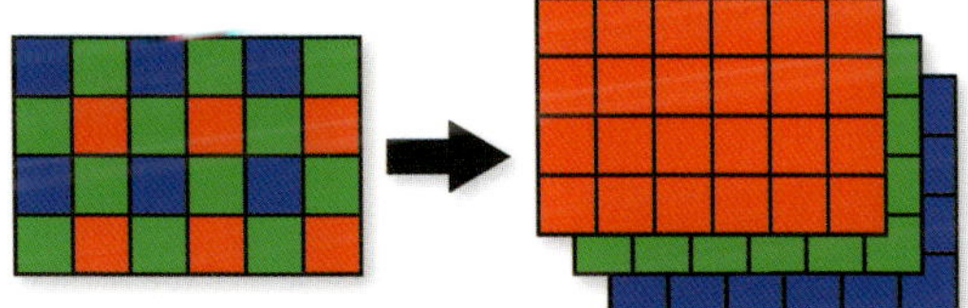

*Each pixel must contain red, green, AND blue before the
image can be saved in a universally accepted file format.*

Noise Reduction: The process of capturing a
digital image always generates noise, so noise
reduction is necessary to produce a usable image.
This is why Lightroom's default setting for noise
reduction varies, with raw files receiving a good
amount and JPEG files defaulting to zero since
they were likely processed in-camera.

Color Transforms: The exact colors of red, green,
and blue filters used varies between camera man-
ufacturers, so a color conversion is applied to
convert the colors into a more standard color
space such as sRGB or Adobe RGB.

Tone Reproduction: The brightness of the captured scene is adjusted, which brightens the dark
areas of the image and lowers the contrast of the
bright areas. This process was originally done
to compensate for how old-school vacuum-
tube-based displays caused images to appear
overly dark. It is still applied today because it
causes adjustments to better align with how our
brains perceive differences in brightness levels
(doubling the amount of light does not make
something look twice as bright to a human), and
it helps to increase the amount of detail stored
in the dark regions of an image when saved at a
lower bit depth than the raw capture. Any processing steps that are based on how the physics
of light works in the real world need to be applied
before this step. Otherwise, they will produce unnatural-looking results.

Compression: Modern digital cameras capture a
minimum of 4,096 brightness levels (also known
as 12 bits), and some can capture as many as
16,384 levels (16 bits), which allows for radical
image adjustments while maintaining a smooth
transition across all brightness levels. To reduce
file size, the number of brightness levels is reduced to only 256 (8 bits), which is just enough to
produce a smooth-looking image for display and
printing, but not enough to allow for future adjustments without producing banding. As a final
step, the image is separated into brightness and
color components. Then the color information
is degraded in such a way that further reduces
the file size.

Ultimately, choosing to capture raw images is
deciding to retain as much of the data the camera
captured as possible, with absolute minimal processing so you can have the most control when
those steps are applied later in Lightroom. For
instance, consider how many adjustments come
after the white balance stage in the in-camera
adjustment pipeline. This should give you a sense
for why adjusting white balance on JPEG files is
not as effective as it is on raw files. The in-camera
white balance adjustment and all the subsequent
adjustments have been baked into the image and
cannot be reversed.

Pixels versus Parameters

Photoshop and Lightroom Classic take radically different approaches to working with images. Photoshop takes an old-school approach because it was originally designed back when everyone was still shooting film. Lightroom, on the other hand, was designed about a decade after Photoshop, when digital photography was becoming the norm and raw files were becoming the preferred way to capture images.

What Makes Raw Different?

The following qualities define what it means to work with a raw file:

- Setting a digital camera to capture raw files signals the camera to retain as much of the information that the sensor captures as possible with absolute minimal processing.
- Each camera manufacturer has invented their own proprietary file format that they save raw data into. For that reason, different brands of cameras produce files with different file extensions that are collectively referred to as raw files. For instance, Canon cameras produce .crw or .cr2 files, while Nikon cameras produce .nef files and Sony makes .arw files, etc.
- A raw file, by definition, cannot be modified by Lightroom, Photoshop, or any other program. There is an option to change the capture time, but the data that makes up the actual image that was captured is locked.
- Raw files require extensive processing before they can be viewed, printed, or saved into a common file format.
- The in-camera previews, histograms and the initial view you may see in some programs are all based on a camera-generated JPEG image, which makes it only an approximation of what is contained in the raw file.
- By shooting raw, you will be forced to take the time to send your images through Lightroom or a similar raw processing program before you'll be able to produce a file that can be saved in a standard file format such as JPEG or TIFF.

Now that you understand some of the unique qualities of a raw file, let's look at how Photoshop and Lightroom approach them differently.

Photoshop Is a Pixel Editor

Photoshop is known as a pixel editor because it is limited to either directly modifying the pixels that make up an image, or stacking pixel-based changes (such as retouching) onto layers above the image. Sure, it has some fancy features that try to act like that's not the case (such as adjustment layers and smart objects), but in the end, everything you do will end up adding or altering pixels inside the file Photoshop produces.

Photoshop requires red, green, and blue (RGB) information for every pixel that makes up a color image. Raw files only contain a single color value for each pixel and must go through a process called demosaicing to end up with RGB pixels. That's why Photoshop always forces you into the Adobe Camera Raw plug-in (ACR for short) whenever it encounters a raw file. ACR handles all the processing necessary to get the image into a state that Photoshop can work with. The result can no longer be considered raw since it has been extensively processed and no longer resembles the original raw data the camera captured.

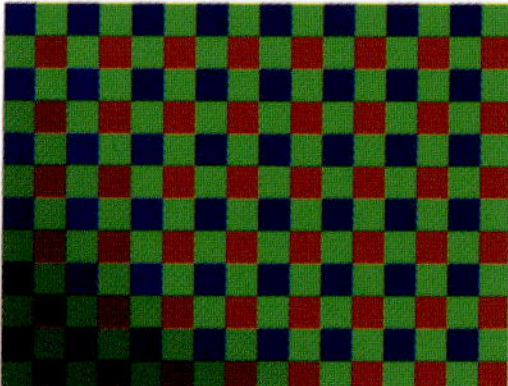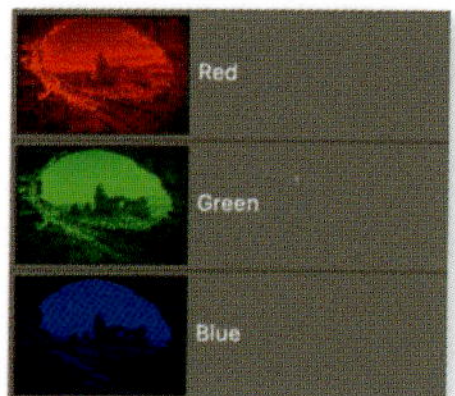

Raw = single color per pixel, which becomes RGB in Photoshop.

Pixel editors are notorious for producing massive files. For example, opening a 27.5MB raw file in Photoshop, adding a single empty layer, and then saving the result produced a 235.1MB file (TIFF or PSD)! Why is it so big? Well, the raw file contained a single brightness value for each pixel, and sending it through ACR resulted in three values (RGB) per pixel, which is 3x as much information. Then, when I added the layer, it forced Photoshop to include a second version of the image that had all the layers merged together (flattened) to make the file compatible with programs that are not designed to work with layers (like Lightroom), which doubled the file size again. Had I not added a layer, then the result would have been 126.2MB.

Using Photoshop is the old-school way of editing an image, which is sometimes necessary, but I'm sure glad it's not our only choice.

Lightroom Is a Parametric Editor

Lightroom Classic was designed from the ground up to be optimized for working on raw files. That's not the only type of image it can handle, but the fundamental concepts on which it is based are centered on the unique qualities of raw images.

When you adjust an image in Lightroom's Develop module, it keeps track of each change you make as a list of simple text instructions, such as **Contrast= +30, Saturation= +23,** and saves that information along with a screen-sized JPEG preview that reflects what the changes look like. That text description would only take up 8 kilobytes of space on a hard drive, which is about the size of a text email message. It's so small that it can be saved in real time as you move adjustment sliders, which is why there is no save button in Lightroom. The JPEG preview adds maybe a megabyte of additional space.

This is known as parametric editing since the adjustments could collectively be called parameters (contrast, exposure, saturation, etc.). Some people also refer to this approach as editing metadata. Metadata is information about a file that is not part of the actual image data that is contained within the file. Typical metadata would be capture date and time, shutter speed, aperture, ISO, camera model, etc.

It's only when you ask Lightroom to print, edit the image in Photoshop, or export to a standard file format that it looks for the original raw file, opens the image like a pixel editor would, applies the changes, and then delivers only what's requested without retaining a copy of the resulting image.

A more fundamental advantage of this approach is that Lightroom can take advantage of all the information contained within a raw file, which makes many adjustments more effective. For instance, noise reduction is much more effective if it's applied before demosaicing, and merging multiple exposures into a high dynamic range image will produce a more natural-looking result if done on linearized data before standard tone-reproduction processing is applied.

To fully grasp the difference between parametric and pixel editing, consider these two examples:

Retouching

Imagine that you performed time-consuming retouching, then discovered you had worked on an image that was over-sharpened and part of the sky was blown out to pure white.

Parametric Retouching: If you're working in Lightroom, this isn't a problem since all your edits were stored as a series of instructions that did not change the original raw file. All you'd need to do is change the sharpening setting in the Detail panel and lower the Highlights slider in the Basic panel and the image (as well as the retouching) would update to reflect the change.

Retouching Pixels: Performing the retouching in Photoshop would be a different story. First, any sharpening that was applied to the raw file would have been baked into the file the moment it was opened in Photoshop, and there would be no ability to recover blown-out highlight detail because Photoshop would not have access to all the info the camera captured. Sure, you could find the original raw file, make the needed adjustments, and use the results to replace the bottom layer of the Photoshop file, but that would not change the retouching, which would still be over-sharpened with blown-out highlights and not match the updated base image. You'd have to pretty much start over.

Multiple Adjustments

Next, think about how adjustments work. What if you make an initial adjustment that causes a large area to become solid black, and later try to lighten up the area with an additional adjustment?

Parametric Adjustments: In Lightroom, you can apply **Blacks -20** to the entire image via the Basic panel and then switch to a masked adjustment and brush in a **Black +20** adjustment just to the area where you don't like the results of the initial adjustment. The result is simple math: negative 20 combined with positive 20 equals zero, which cancels out the initial adjustment.

Adjusting Pixels: Adjustment layers in Photoshop do not work that way. Each adjustment can only work on the end result of previous adjustments and therefore the moment an area becomes solid black, any subsequent adjustments will be unable to bring back detail that was lost due to an earlier adjustment.

Browsing versus Cataloging

If you're accustomed to working with Photoshop, you might be thinking that Lightroom's approach to working with images sounds like how Adobe Camera Raw works... and you'd be right. But there are important differences that have to do with working with a file browser, such as Adobe Bridge, versus a cataloging program like Lightroom Classic.

Camera Raw Came before Lightroom

Adobe Camera Raw debuted four years before Lightroom and was Adobe's first attempt at parametric editing of raw files. In fact, the Develop module in Lightroom Classic shares the same base code as the Adobe Camera Raw plug-in. That means the adjustment choices are identical.

ACR + Bridge = Unmanaged File Browsing

The combination of Bridge for browsing images and ACR for adjusting them was a powerful one. But there were also many issues related to saving adjustments as metadata while allowing users to freely move their files around between programs without strict file management.

Since raw files cannot be modified, any changes made to such files in Adobe Camera Raw need to be saved separately in .xmp files that share a common base name with the original raw file.

What if you decide to rename a raw file using your computer's operating system and forget to rename the matching .xmp sidecar file? That would cause the image to revert to its original, unadjusted state when viewed in Bridge or ACR.

Adjustments made to non-raw files in ACR are saved directly into the metadata of the file and do not change the appearance of the original image.

So, what will happen if you adjust and crop a JPEG file and then post it on Facebook? The changes you make will be recorded as text attached to the image in the same way as the aperture and shutter speed was from the camera. Facebook would consider that unessential extra information that should be stripped out of the file to save space and you'd end up seeing the image as it looked before it was ever changed in ACR.

That means it's up to you to remember if the JPEG file sitting on your desktop has been modified in ACR. If it was, then you need save out a fresh JPEG file from ACR or Photoshop to get the changes to be "baked in" and hope you don't accidentally save over the original file in the process.

Then, what if you need four versions of an image, one cropped square, one rectangular, and each with both black-and-white and color versions because you need to experiment to see what works best for the image. With ACR, it's not going to be an elegant experience with either duplicate files, or snapshots that cannot be viewed side by side for comparison, etc.

Finally, what if you are like me and have over 200,000 photos and you want to find all the photos that were shot with an aperture setting of f/2.8 in an attempt to find an image that has shallow depth of field? Bridge can't even show the contents of more than one folder at a time (although they recently added the ability to show the contents of sub-folders). Bridge only keeps preview images for the last few hundred images you've browsed. If I want to search my whole photo archive, then it's going to take many hours to find those images shot at f/2.8.

That's because Bridge can only work with images that it can actively locate on a connected hard drive. That's what puts it into the category of being a file browser. It has the same limitation as a web browser, which requires an active internet connection to function. That means you cannot see images that are on a drive you left at home while you're traveling. Bridge only retains a small cache of previews for files you've recently browsed, which means it will need to open and produce new previews (a time-consuming process) for any images that it has not worked with in the recent past. That setup makes file browsers ideal for working with small batches of images that you will likely not need to work with far into the future.

Lightroom Catalogs

When you launch Lightroom Classic, you're really opening a Lightroom catalog file. If you don't have one already, then you'll have the option to either create one or quit Lightroom. The program cannot function without a catalog file to work with.

The process of importing an image causes a new record to be created in the current catalog file. That record includes all the camera metadata (such as shutter speed and capture date). The only thing that links this record to the original file is the exact file name and folder location.

At the same time, a preview image is produced and stored in a separate file within the same folder as your Lightroom catalog file. Having a preview of every image that you have ever imported allows you to browse and organize your images even when the original files are on a hard drive that is not currently attached to your computer.

Your Lightroom catalog file is where almost everything that Lightroom does to an image is recorded. It doesn't matter if you're optimizing the image in the Develop module, organizing a project using collections, or fine-tuning how an image will be printed. What you are doing is modifying the records in your catalog file.

When organizing your images, changes made in Lightroom's folder list are also made on your hard drive to ensure that everything remains in sync (as long as you make those changes using Lightroom). Therefore, it is important to commit to starting all file changes from within Lightroom to ensure it does not get out of sync with the contents of your hard drive.

Choose **File>Export** to create a derivative image that is based on the original but has all adjustments applied in a standard file format such as JPEG or TIFF. By removing you from your operating system and including convenient features such as export presets, Lightroom alleviates most of the file management issues that were common when using ACR and Bridge.

Now that you have a general idea of how Lightroom's catalog is used, let's take a look at some of the advantages of this approach over using ACR and Bridge.

Fast Browsing: The previews that were created at the time the images were imported allow you to scroll through tens of thousands of images with little or no lag (unlike Bridge, which would slow down for any images you have not browsed recently).

Browse Images Remotely: Lightroom's previews also allow you to browse your entire catalog of images even when you don't have access to the hard drive that contains the original images.

Adjust Images Remotely: If you create Smart Previews before disconnecting a hard drive, then you can even adjust images when the hard drive containing the original images is not available.

Instant Search Results: The metadata for every image is contained in your catalog file, which makes searching for images that were shot with a 200mm lens at f/2.8 take a fraction of a second. Bridge, on the other hand, would have to inspect each file individually to find such information and could only do so for images that are on hard drives that are currently connected to your computer.

Virtual Copies: These allow you to have multiple versions of an image without needing to create duplicate files on your hard drive. A virtual copy appears as if it's a separate image, but it is really just a separate entry in your catalog file that contains alternative adjustment settings and takes up very little space on your hard drive.

Persistent History: Lightroom maintains a history of every change you've made to an image so you can experiment without concern about the ability to return to a previous state of the image. This is in contrast to ACR, where clicking the **Cancel** button by accident would discard the changes you've made and you'd be unable to undo changes after clicking **Done** to save the changes to the image.

Adjust Layered Images: Lightroom (unlike Adobe Camera Raw) can even apply adjustments to layered TIFF and PSD files while retaining the ability to edit the individual layers in Photoshop.

The Best of Both Worlds

Now that we've explored the differences between Lightroom Classic and Photoshop, let's look at the most ideal way to use them together in a way that takes advantage of the unique strengths each program has to offer.

Start Workflow in Lightroom Classic

All images that are captured in raw format will benefit greatly from having initial optimizations performed in Lightroom since it will be able to take advantage of all the information your camera captured. You also have the ability to retouch out sensor dust spots on multiple images simultaneously as well as copy and paste settings between files. Smart Previews will even allow you to leave your hard drive at home and perform initial adjustments while traveling.

> **Tip:** *You can copy and paste settings between images using the options found in the **Photo>Develop** menu.*

The quality of the results that are produced by Lightroom and the Camera Raw filter in Photoshop are identical when working on files that do not contain raw data (such as JPEG or TIFF). I prefer to perform initial adjustments on all non-layered files in Lightroom Classic.

Bridge + Camera Raw for Fleeting Images

The only images I do not import into Lightroom are those that either I did not capture myself, or that I will not need to work with or organize on a long-term basis (such as images I've downloaded from the web, or might have captured to create a listing on Ebay).

HDR Merging in Lightroom

Both Photoshop and Lightroom have the ability to merge multiple exposures into a high dynamic range (HDR) image or panorama. When you create HDR images using Lightroom, the software starts with minimally processed raw files that are still in a form that aligns with the physics of how light works in the real world. Photoshop, on the other hand, cannot use the raw data and must start with RGB images that have gone through many color and tonal adjustments, which cause the results to often look somewhat unnatural.

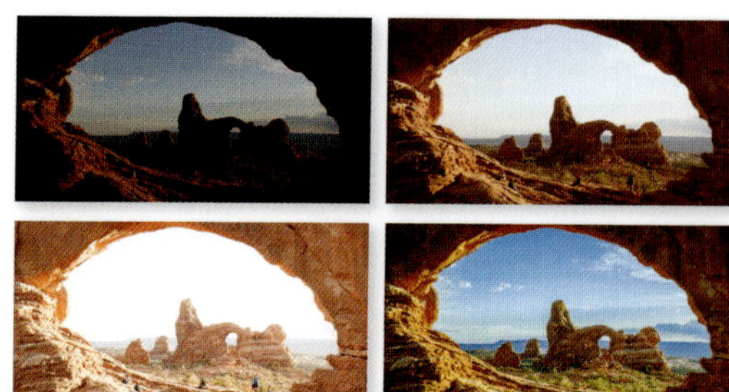

Three exposures and the result of merging into an HDR image.

Panorama Stitching in Lightroom

Panoramas that are stitched in Lightroom result in a .DNG file that retains many of the qualities of a raw file, such as the ability to adjust white balance and recover highlight detail, which would not be possible if the images were merged using Photoshop. I mainly use Photoshop as an alternative for HDR or Panoramas when I'm not satisfied with the results produced by Lightroom.

Sharpening in Both

To produce high-quality results, it is best to sharpen your images in three separate passes.

Compensate for Camera: Digital cameras produce soft-looking images because of two design choices. Most cameras have a low-pass filter in front of the sensor that effectively blurs the image slightly on purpose to prevent moire patterns when shooting fine structures such as fabric or bricks. The process of demosaicing an image into RGB pixels also causes the image to become soft. This is why the default settings for sharpening are not zero for raw files. Inital sharpening is best performed in concert with noise reduction and demosaicing in Lightroom.

Selective Sharpening and Blurring: Sharpening and/or blurring is a useful way to help attract the eye to areas in an image. This is best done in Photoshop because you have more options for how the sharpening is applied, but it can also be done in Lightroom for those images that don't require any additional work in Photoshop.

Compensate for Resizing and Output: The third pass of sharpening is needed to compensate for the final output process. This final sharpening is best done in Lightroom since all its export and print features offer settings that will vary depending on the final output size and do not affect what is opened in Photoshop.

Section I: **Fundamental Concepts**

Photoshop for Heavy Lifting

Lightroom's parametric editing approach is both its greatest strength and its greatest weakness. There are simply only so many things that can be done to an image without digging into the actual pixels that make up the image. When you run into a task that is either too difficult, inefficient, impractical, or literally impossible, then it's time to head to Photoshop.

Here are just a few of the things that can only be done in Photoshop:

- Controlling bright and dark sharpening halos separately.
- Combining multiple exposures that vary in focus point, focal length, capture time, or shutter speed to produce an idealized result.
- Retouching using source material from a separate document.
- Retouching that involves rotation, scaling, or flipping of source material.

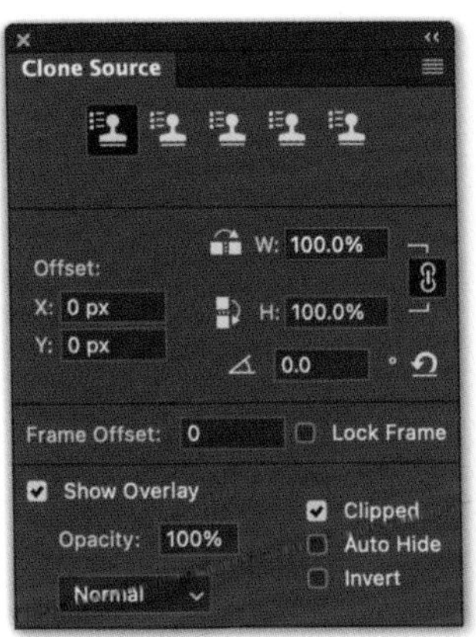

The Clone Source panel offers settings for rotating, flipping, and scaling the source image used by Photoshop's retouching tools.

Just don't head to Photoshop to do things that could easily be accomplished in Lightroom because Photoshop is only going to be able to work with a fraction of the information that was found in the original raw file, and you're going to end up with an additional file that is many times larger than what you started with. At least 30% of the images I work on never get opened in Photoshop.

I use Photoshop only when doing something would be inefficient, inconvenient, or impossible in Lightroom Classic. Although once an image has been opened in Photoshop, then continuing there is best, with the exception of finishing techniques such as cropping, sharpening (which might need different settings for different uses), and output-device-specific adjustments.

Final Adjustments & Printing in Lightroom

Lightroom's virtual copy feature is a blessing when you need to output an image to multiple devices and end up with mismatching results. By applying additional adjustments on top of a layered TIFF or PDF file, you can optimize an image for each output device without the need to duplicate the file. Printing is also a much more elegant and pain-free experience in Lightroom.

Switch Back and Forth as Much as Needed

As long as you were thoughtful enough to only switch to Photoshop after initial adjustments were complete using Lightroom, then you can go back and forth between them as often as needed. Here's how to make it work:

1) Start with a raw file in Lightroom, working until you are satisfied that you've taken the image as far as is practical using Lightroom's parametric adjustments.
2) If the image demands more than you could accomplish in Lightroom, then send the image to Photoshop, knowing that in the process you'll end up permanenty baking in your initial raw adjustments and transitioning from parametic to pixcl-based editing.
3) Get as fancy as you want, using layers and the almost endless possibilities that Photoshop offers. When done, save and close the image to produce the layered file that should, from this point forward, be considered your master working file.
4) Back in Lightroom, feel free to apply a second round of adjustments, this time to the layered file that Photoshop produced.
5) If needed, reopen the layered file into Photoshop and make additional changes. The moment you save the file and return to Lightroom, you should see your second round of Lightroom adjustments reapplied. (More on how this can be accomplished later.)
6) Print or export deliverable files from within Lightroom so that all output-specific resizing, sharpening, or adjustments do not affect the contents of your layered master file.

That's how to get the the best of both worlds when working in Lightroom and Photoshop.

Chapter 2

Working in Lightroom Classic

THIS CHAPTER IS designed to get you up to speed with the key concepts and tools for working in Lightroom Classic. I'll start by showing you how to get your images to appear in Lightroom. You'll then learn how to evaluate a set of images so that you can determine which is most worthy of further processing. Next, we'll venture into the Develop module and focus on the most essential tonal and color adjustments. You'll learn how the powerful masking features can be used to adjust select areas in a photo and how Lightroom's retouching tools can make it a breeze to remove unwanted objects. Finally, we'll explore how to most effectively take an image on a round-trip journey between Lightroom and Photoshop and then export it so you can share it with others.

Importing

Images must be imported before they can be viewed or edited in Lightroom Classic. If you're unfamiliar with the concept, be sure to review chapter 1, page 11, to get a feeling for what happens when an image is imported. A whole chapter could be written on this process, but I assume you've experimented with Lightroom in the past, so what follows is what I consider to be the essentials.

Accessing the Import Dialog Box
Below are the three methods I use most commonly to initiate the importation process.

Insert Memory Card: If the **Show import dialog when a memory card is detected** setting is enabled in Lightroom's preferences, then the act of inserting a memory card into a card reader is enough to prompt the import dialog box to appear with the card selected as the source.

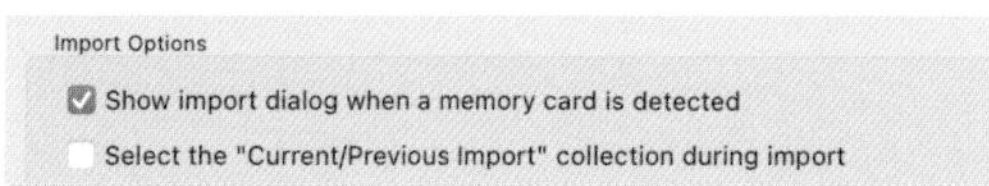

Drag Folder to Lightroom Icon: On a Mac, drag a folder containing images to the Lightroom icon in the dock at the bottom of your screen. This will open the import dialog box with the folder selected as the source for importation.

Click Import Button: Click the **Import** button that's found on the left-side panel of the Library module. You will then need to navigate to the folder that contains the images you wish to import from the **Source** area in the upper left of the import dialog box.

Choosing Action Options
At the top center of the import dialog box, choose **Add** if the images you wish to import are already located where you want them to reside on your hard drive. Choose **Copy** if the images reside in a temporary location (a memory card, for example) and you'd like to move a copy to a hard drive that is attached to your computer.

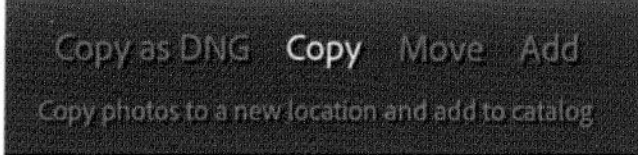

File Handling Options
I usually set the **Build Previews** pop-up menu to **Standard** in the upper right of the import dialog box to generate a preview that fits my screen. I enable **Build Smart Previews** so I'm able to make adjustments to the image even when its original source is not connected. I also enable **Don't Import Suspected Duplicates**, as I tend to wait until I've backed up my images before erasing a memory card. This way, I'm able to import from the same card multiple times and only import newly captured images.

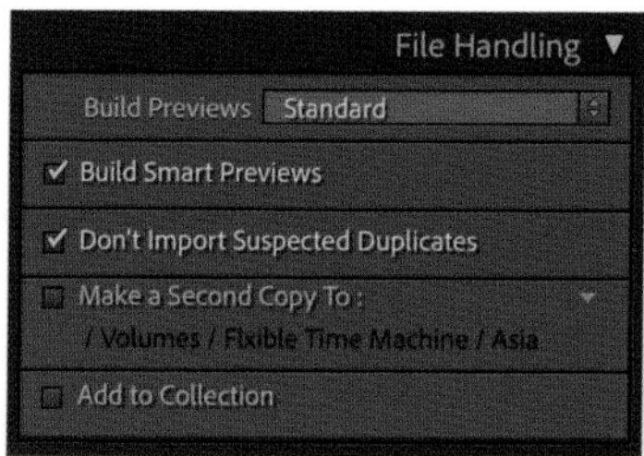

Using File Renaming Templates
To ensure my images have distinct names, I use a file-naming template when importing from a memory card. This method prevents confusion or duplicate names when moving images between folders.

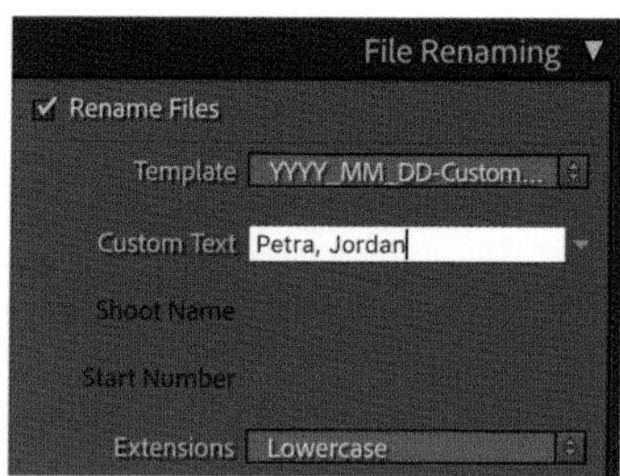

To build a custom file-name formula, enable the **Rename Files** option in the import dialog box (available when using the **Copy** or **Move** settings) and choose **Edit** from the **Template** pop-up menu. I generally start with the date, add the **Custom Text** option, and end with the image number that the camera assigned. Then, when applying the template, I enter a short description of the location or subject matter into the **Custom Text** field and Lightroom does the rest to construct a name for each file being imported. I avoid the **Shoot Name** option since it is not usable when renaming files after importing.

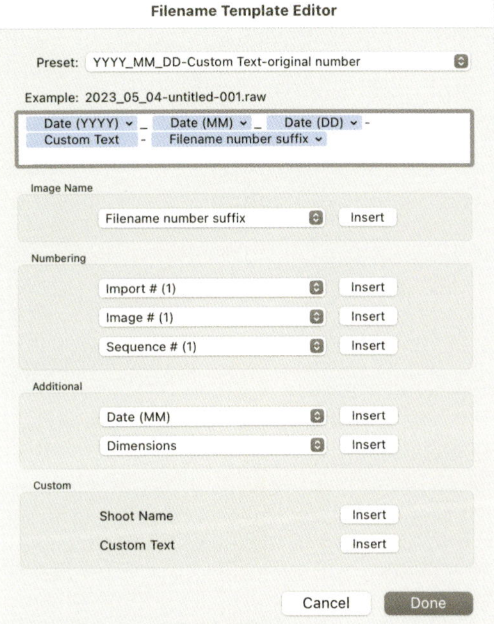

Renaming after Importing

The same template can be used to rename files after they have been imported by choosing **Library>Rename Photos**, or clicking the icon that is found to the right of the **File Name** field in the **Metadata** panel on the right side of the Library module **A**.

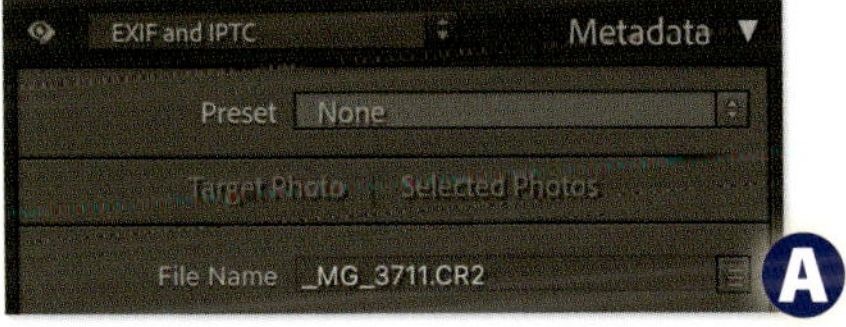

Note: *Editing images outside of Lightroom is the most frequent cause of issues for new users. Once an image is imported, any further changes must be made using Lightroom. Otherwise, Lightroom will become out of sync with the contents of your hard drive, which is like someone randomly reorganizing warehouse shelves and causing the inventory computer to get out of sync with the warehouse contents. After importing, never rename, move, or edit images without starting the process in Lightroom.*

Post-Importation Tips

The following ideas can help you prevent future issues or get your Lightroom catalog back on track when things get out of sync.

Rename File

You can change the file name of any file by selecting an image and changing the text found in the **File Name** field in the **Metadata** panel on the right side of the Library module. To rename multiple images, select them and then click the icon that is found to the right of the **File Name** field.

Rename Folder

To change the name of a folder, right-click it and select **Rename**.

Create Folder

To make a new sub-folder inside an existing folder, right-click the folder and select **Create Folder Inside**.

Move Files and Folders

You can move any file or folder to a new location on your hard drive by dragging it to another folder within the **Folder** list in the Library module.

Delete Images

To delete images, view them from the folder list in Lightroom and then press the **Delete** key to access the **Remove from Lightroom** or **Delete from Disk** options. If viewing a collection or search, right-click the image and select **Go To Folder in Library**.

Find Missing Folder

If you rename or move a folder outside of Lightroom, a question mark will appear on it in the Library module. To inform Lightroom of the change, right-click on the folder, select **Find Missing Folder**, and point to the folder's location.

Synchronize Folder

If you add a file to a folder outside of Lightroom, the image may not appear in the app. To import the added photo, right-click on the folder in the Library module and select **Synchronize Folder**.

Choosing an Ideal Image

It's important to start with the best capture you have available of a scene to ensure you end up with an image worthy of further development in Lightroom. Let's take a look at the process and considerations I find to be useful when choosing the best image to develop.

Finding the Best Composition

When you return from shooting in the field, you'll likely end up with dozens, if not hundreds, of images, yet there will only be a select few that are worthy of processing into a finished image.

Find and Remove Obvious Outtakes

My process for finding the keepers involves choosing a folder of images, clicking on the first image of the set, then pressing **spacebar** to make the image fill my screen. I will then do one of the following:

1) If the image is out of focus or has any other uncorrectable flaws, I type **X** to flag the image as a reject, which is my indication that I should never need to look at the image again.

2) If the image has any promise at all, then I type **1** to add a one-star rating to indicate that it has enough potential to call for further evaluation.

3) If the image leaves me undecided between the first two choices, then I type **right arrow** to move to the next image without making any changes.

After going through a full pass on a folder of images, I'll usually start to have a pretty good idea of what I have to work with. My next step is to isolate the rejected images into a sub-folder by choosing **Edit>Select By Flag>Rejected**. I'll then right-click on the folder they live in within the Folder list and choose **Create Folder Inside** from the pop-up menu. I'll name the folder "Outtakes," turn on the **Include Selected Photos** check box, and click **Create**.

Break Shoot into Sequences of Similar Images

With rejects out of the way, I mentally divide all the images into sequences of images that were taken from a similar vantage point and attempt to determine the best single image out of each sequence. This is done by clicking on the first

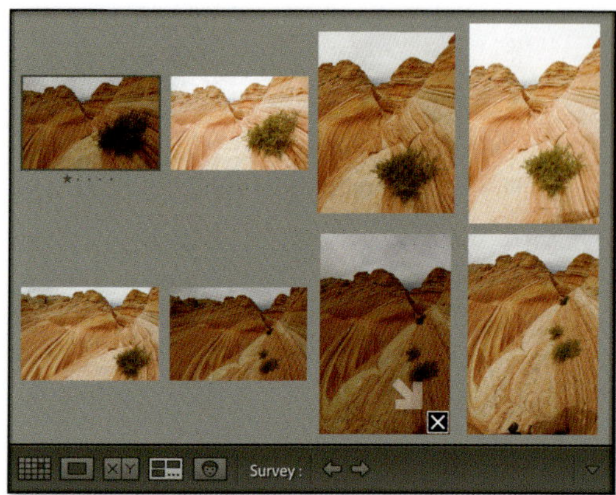

Hover over any image and click the X to remove it from the sequence of shots being viewed in Survey view.

image of the sequence, then holding **shift** and clicking on the last image before clicking the **Survey** view icon in the toolbar at the bottom of the window. I will then compare the images and remove the least desirable frames by clicking the **X** that appears in the lower-right corner when hovering over an image.

Narrow Each Sequence to a Single Image

Once I have narrowed it down to just a handful of good contenders, I then switch to the **Compare** view to see two images side by side. In this view, you can use the **right** and **left arrow** keys to cycle through the images that appear on the right side of the screen. Click the **X** in the lower right of the image to remove the current candidate from the group, or click the **left arrow** icon to move it to the select position. Once I've narrowed the group of images down to a single image, I type **G** to return to the grid view and drag the images that did not make the cut into the **Outtakes** folder.

> **Tip:** In **Compare** view, type / to remove the current candidate. Click within an image to zoom in and inspect the sharpness of the two images being compared. The **Zoom** slider in the toolbar at the bottom of your screen can then be used to adjust the magnification.

When evaluating a group of similar images to determine which is worthy of processing, I evaluate the following attributes to help me determine which image will be most likely to produce a quality result.

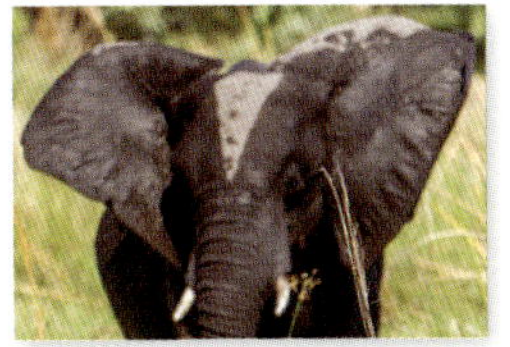 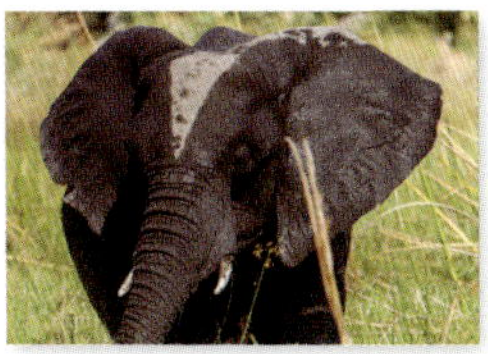

Evaluating Sharpness

The first thing that I evaluate is if an image is overly soft, out of focus, or has blurred content due to shooting hand-held without using a sufficiently high shutter speed. When that's the case, there is usually nothing that can be done, so the image is rejected.

Evaluating Exposure

When I have multiple images of the same composition that differ in exposure, I'll use the histogram that is available near the upper right of the Library or Develop module to determine which would be ideal for processing. Here are some of the things I look for when evaluating a histogram:

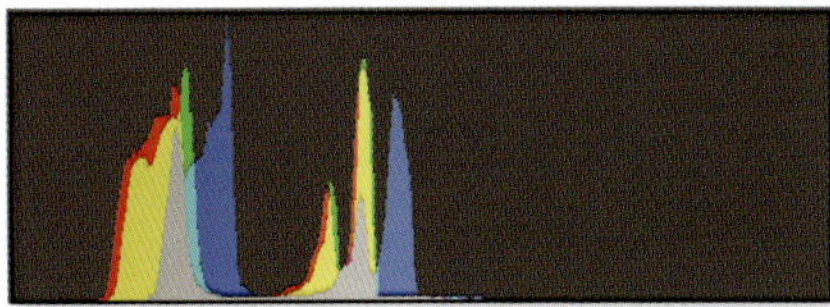

Large Gap on the Right: This indicates that nothing in the image is anywhere close to white and therefore the image is likely to be underexposed. Any attempts to brighten the image will likely cause the noise that is lurking in the dark areas to become obvious. If there is an alternative image of the same scene that is brighter and therefore has a smaller gap on the right, then it would likely contain less noise.

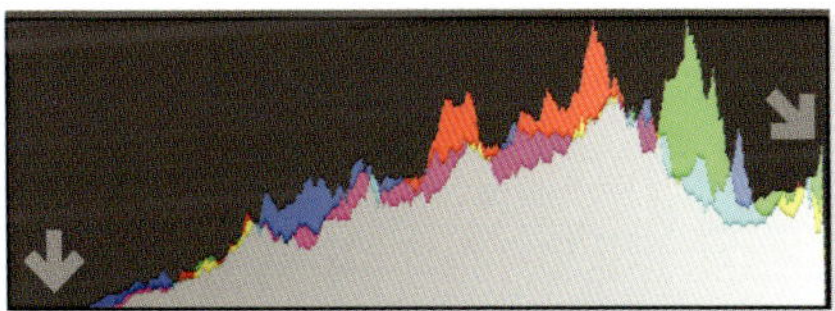

Gap on Left and Spike at Right: This indicates that white takes up a lot of space within the image and there was leeway to capture a darker exposure without causing the shadows to become solid black. Alternative images with a shorter or nonexistent spike on the right would likely be better options for adjustment. Ideally, there would only be a spike if the sun is large in the scene or if there are large reflections of the sun on water.

Spike on Both Ends: This indicates a high-contrast scene that contains large areas of both solid black and solid white, which is usually an indication that the scene would best be captured using multiple exposures that can be merged into an HDR image.

When inspecting a histogram, spikes are only significant if they appear directly above where white and black are represented, which is at the absolute extreme left and right edge of the rectangle that contains the histogram. A spike appears when the scene being photographed contained brightness levels that are being rendered as solid black or white. Just look at any histogram that does not extend to the end and you'll usually find a smooth and gentle transition to nothing instead of a cliff-like end, which is considered a spike.

Once you've isolated the images that are worthy of adjusting, it's time to head to the Develop module and apply basic adjustments.

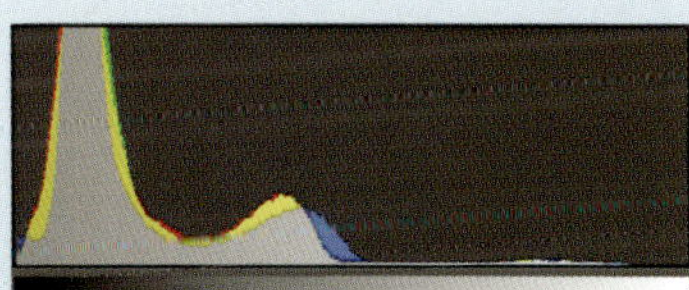

Note: *The key to understanding a histogram is to imagine a horizontal bar below it that contains black on the left edge, white on the right edge, and a transition between them filling the rest of the bar. Then, note where there are bars above (regardless of height or color) to determine which of the shades are found within the image. One of the bars will always extend all the way to the top and that represents the shade that is the most prevalent in the image. All the other bar heights are relative to the tallest. Therefore, a bar that is extending half way to the top is a shade that is half as prevalent as the tallest. The colors that appear in the histogram are of limited value, but can be helpful for troubleshooting color issues.*

Initial Adjustments

The process of optimizing an image usually begins with the choices available in the Basic panel within Lightroom's Develop module.

As we look at each adjustment choice, I'll show the result of moving each individual slider on a previously unadjusted image. You'll find tiny images and histograms that indicate the results achieved by moving the slider a bit to the left, leaving it centered, and moving it a bit to the right. The center image will always be the unadjusted version of the image.

Tonal Adjustments

The adjustments in this category are limited to altering the brightness of an image and are not intended to shift color.

Exposure: Brightens or darkens the entire image, which causes the histogram to swing wildly in the same direction you drag the slider. When you push it too far, you'll end up forcing large areas to white or black, which will result in a spike on one end of the histogram. A very small tweak to this slider can be useful to correct for exposures that are a little too bright or dark.

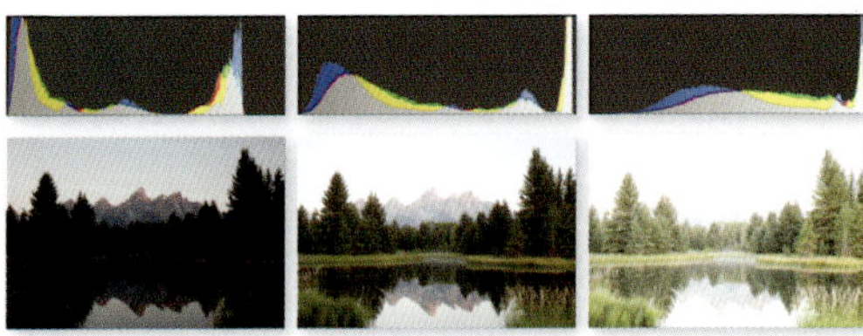

Contrast: Determines how large of a difference in brightness there will be between bright and dark areas. This has the effect of widening or compressing the histogram, while leaving the middle largely unchanged.

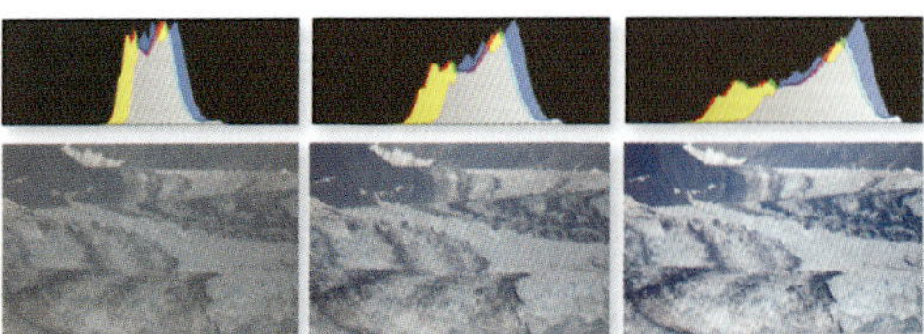

Highlights: Attempts to isolate and adjust the brightest 30ish percent of the image. This will usually only affect the right half of the histogram. If you ever push this slider as far as it can go to the left and wish you could push it even further, then slide the **Exposure** slider to the left until the bright area of the image is the way you'd like it. Then, to compensate for the fact that the **Exposure** slider darkened the entire image, slide the **Shadows** slider toward the right to brighten the dark areas back to what they looked like previously.

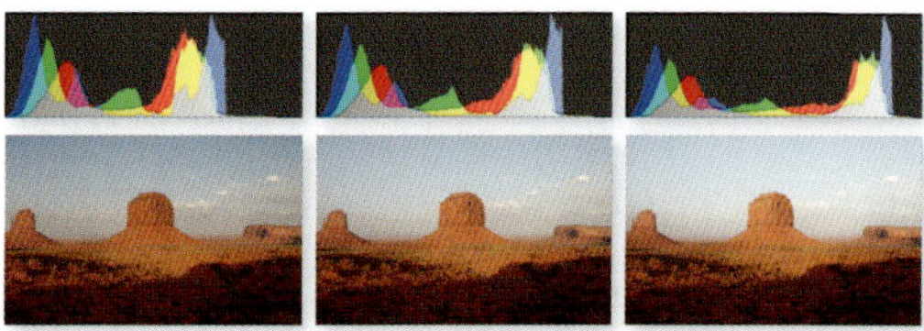

Shadows: Attempts to isolate and adjust the darkest 30ish percent of the image. This will usually only affect the left half of the histogram. When maxed out at +100 you can push it further using **Exposure** and **Highlights** in a similar fashion to what I mentioned above.

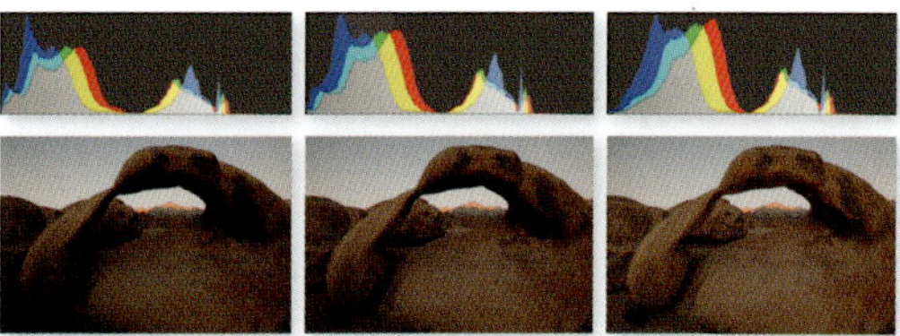

Whites: Changes the brightness of the absolute brightest area in an image. This will affect a wider area of the histogram than the **Highlights** slider, with the most pronounced change happening to the rightmost edge of the histogram.

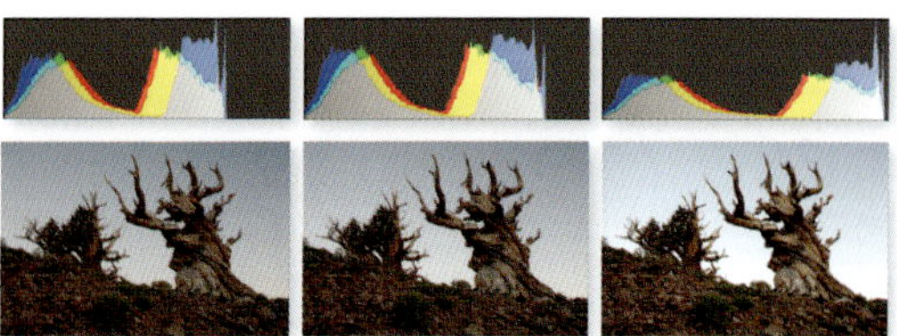

When adjusting the **Whites** slider, it can be useful to keep an eye on the right side of the histogram to see if you have space to push the histogram to the right before it runs out of room and turns into a spike of solid white. I often move the slider to the right until the gap goes away, and then inspect the image and back off until I like the brightness of the brightest area within the image.

Section I: Fundamental Concepts

Blacks: Changes the brightness of the absolute darkest area in an image. This will affect a wider area of the histogram than the **Shadows** slider, with the most pronounced change happening to the leftmost edge of the histogram.

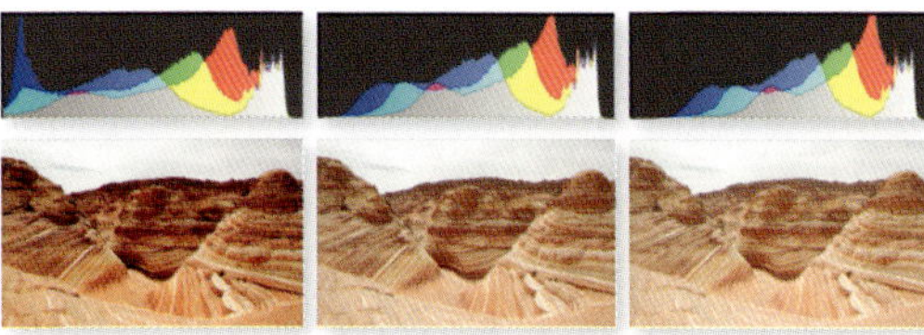

Real-World Tonal Adjustments

When performing an initial adjustment on most images, I find that I move the **Exposure** slider the least, often leaving it at zero. The **Highlights** and **Shadows** sliders often need to be moved radically to produce a satisfactory image and are the beginning step for most images. **Contrast** is occasionally useful when the result of the other sliders is not quite satisfactory. I mainly use the **Whites** and **Blacks** sliders at the end of my adjustment process to control how much of the image will end up containing solid black and how close the highlights should be allowed to get toward white. I generally reserve solid white for the sun or another light source or the reflections of those lights on shiny surfaces such as water.

Color Adjustments

The following adjustments will change the overall appearance of the colors within an image.

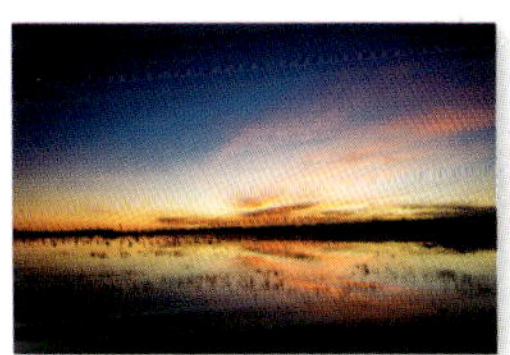 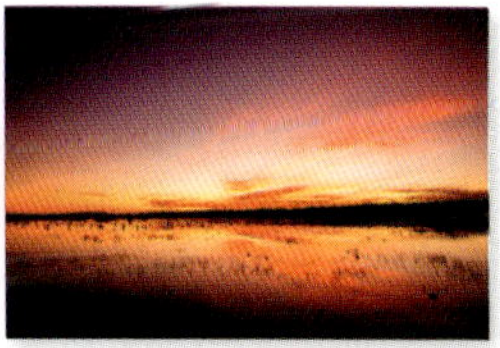

White Balance: The **Temp** (short for temperature) slider shifts the overall color of an image toward either blue or yellow, while the **Tint** slider shifts everything toward green or magenta. The two sliders are collectively known as white balance and can be changed in three ways.

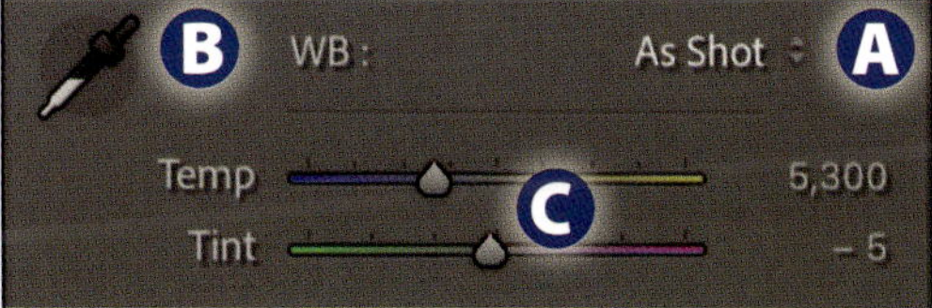

1) Choosing a preset from the pop-up menu located above the sliders **A** will correct for known lighting conditions by moving the sliders to preset positions.
2) The **White Balance Selector B** can be used to click within an image in an area that you would like to shift to become neutral gray. The area clicked upon must be darker than white to have any effect on the image.
3) Manually adjusting the **Temp** and **Tint** sliders **C**. To this end, this is what the other two methods are using to accomplish their results.

I almost always end up fine-tuning the results of the first two methods of setting white balance by manually adjusting the **Temp** and **Tint** sliders, as I rarely want something to look perfectly neutral and often prefer it to appear slightly warm or cool.

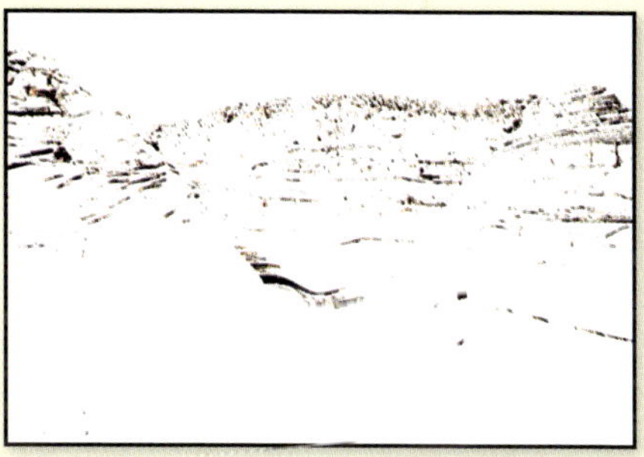

Saturation: Causes the colors within an image to become more colorful or less colorful. Moving the slider to -100 will produce an image with no color. Does not affect areas that are neutral gray.

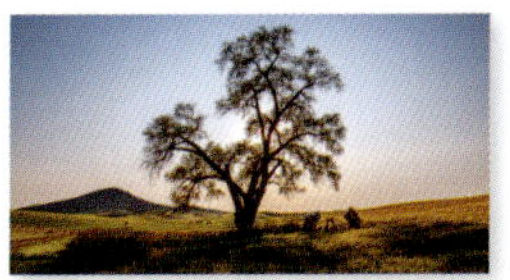 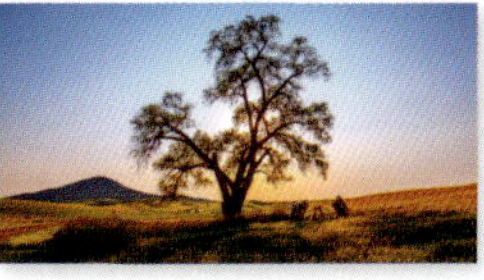

Vibrance: Similar to **Saturation**, but produces more pronounced changes to areas that are not all that colorful and less pronounced changes to areas that are nearing the limit of saturation. **Vibrance** was designed to avoid radical changes to skin tones, but is unable to distinguish between faces and similarly colored areas within a landscape. It also causes blue skies to become darker and more colorful, but will overdo adjustments on icebergs and other blue objects that will usually necessitate fine-tuning with other tools.

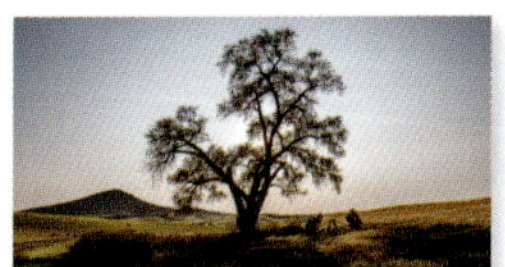 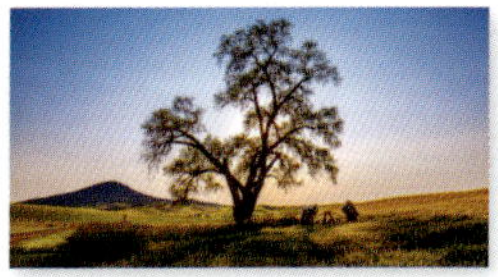

Real-World Color Adjustments

When obvious areas of gray are found within an image, such as clean snow, gray clouds, or a waterfall, then I might start with the **White Balance Selector** tool, clicking on various areas to find the best starting point. I then fine-tune the **Temp** and **Tint** sliders until I find the settings that produce the most pleasing color, often looking for the settings that produce the most pronounced difference in the colors found within the image.

I then try to determine which direction to move the **Vibrance** slider, moving it toward the right if I think the image would look better if the mellower colors became more prominent, or to the left if I'd rather not have those mellow colors

compete with the more vividly colored areas. I then fine-tune the results by adjusting the **Saturation** slider to end up with an appropriate level of saturation overall.

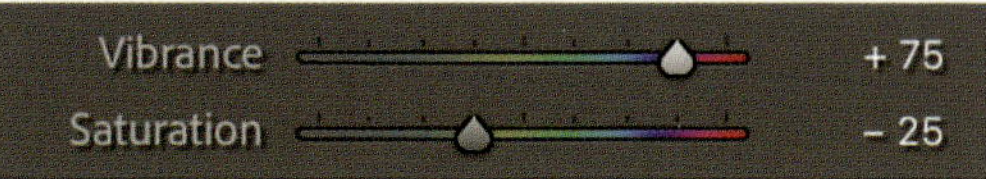

Presence Adjustments

The following adjustments can be used to change the perceived detail and contrast in an image.

Texture: Determines how pronounced the fine details should be within an image. This will affect areas that contain things like sand and the prominence of texture on boulders. It is best used while zoomed in to at least 100% view so you can see the subtle changes it produces.

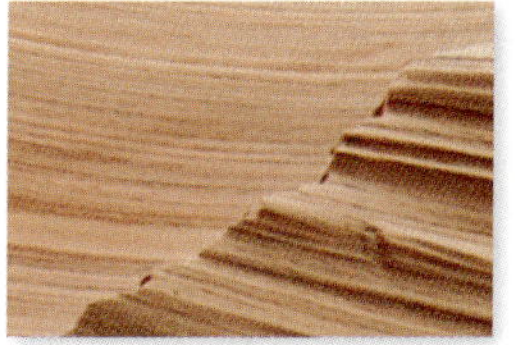 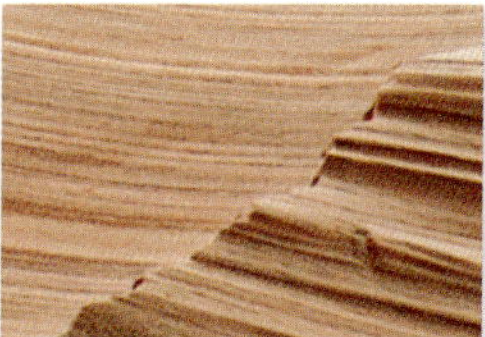

Clarity: Increases or reduces contrast around the edges of medium and large objects in an effort to make them more or less prominent.

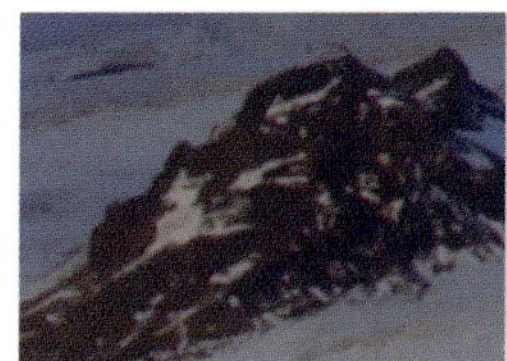 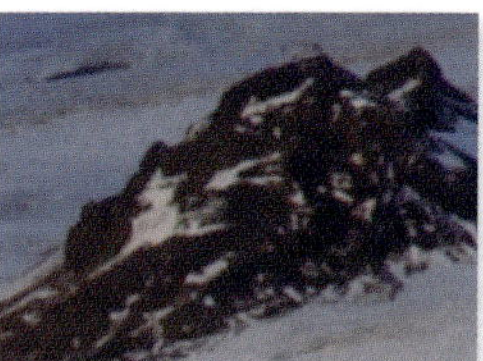

Dehaze: Moving this slider to the right will darken the darkest areas of an image in a similar fashion to the **Blacks** slider, but will usually cause more shadow detail to be retained. Moving it to the left will brighten the darkest areas and will lighten shadow areas to create a more aggressive change than the **Blacks** slider could create.

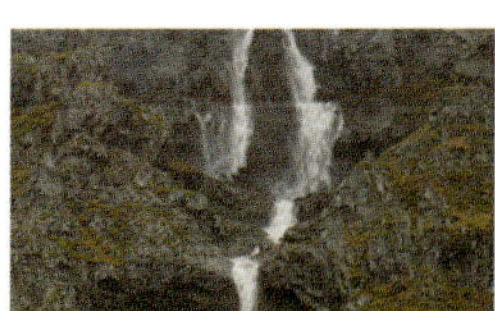 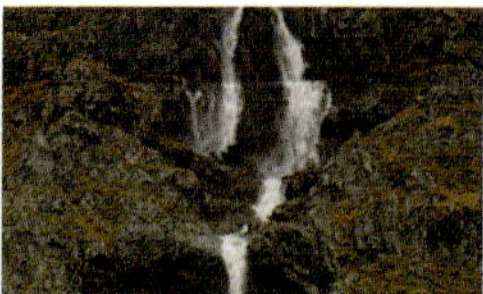

Section I: Fundamental Concepts

Example Optimization

Now let's take a look at how I used these basic adjustments to perform the initial optimization on an image. My general approach is to tackle the most obvious problem first and then repeat the process until there are either no issues remaining, or I run out of patience and decide it's good enough for Instagram.

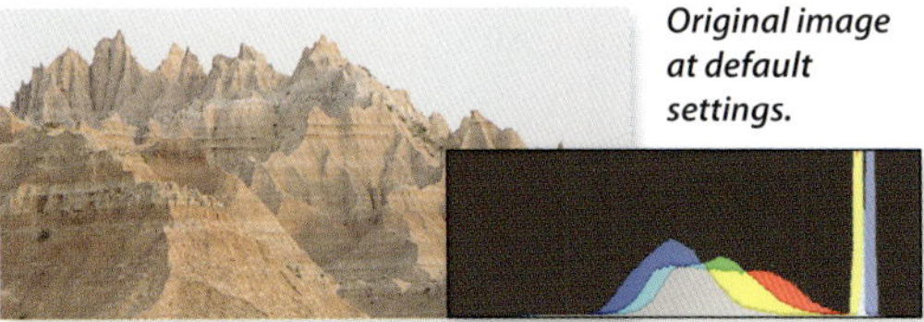

Original image at default settings.

My initial impression was that the image looked rather bland. I also glanced at the histogram and noticed it was not very wide. To widen the histogram, and therefore use more of the brightness range available, I increased **Contrast** to **+75**. I then boosted **Clarity** to **+30** in an effort to make the horizontal stripes stand out.

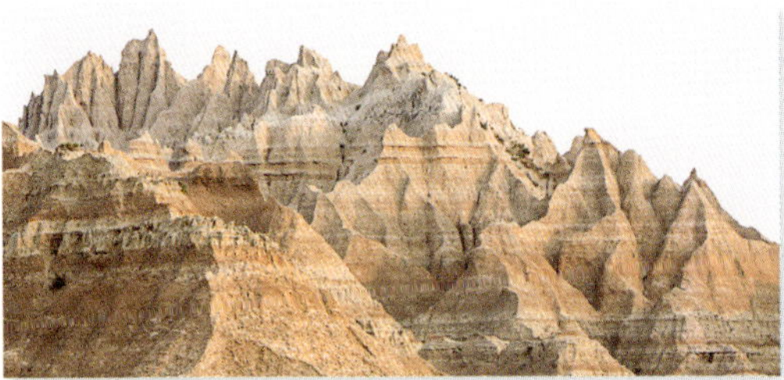

That brought my attention to the tip of the peaks, as they were brighter than most other areas and pulled my eye to the boring sky. I lowered the **Highlights** slider to **-75** to darken the tips and make them look more like the rest of the mountain. I then lowered **Exposure** to **-0.60**.

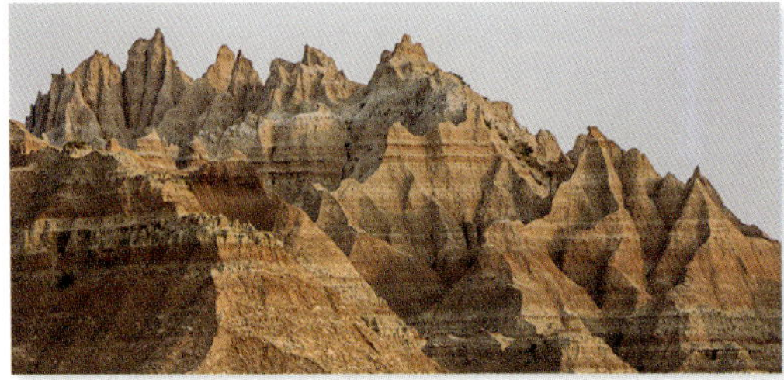

At this point, I noticed that nothing in the image was really bright. While watching the histogram, I moved the **Whites** slider to the right until the gap on the right was gone. I then glanced at the image, knowing that would be the highest I could go without losing detail, and then backed off to **+44** because this setting made the image look its best. I then held the **Option** key and lowered the **Blacks** setting until I saw a small blob of solid black appear.

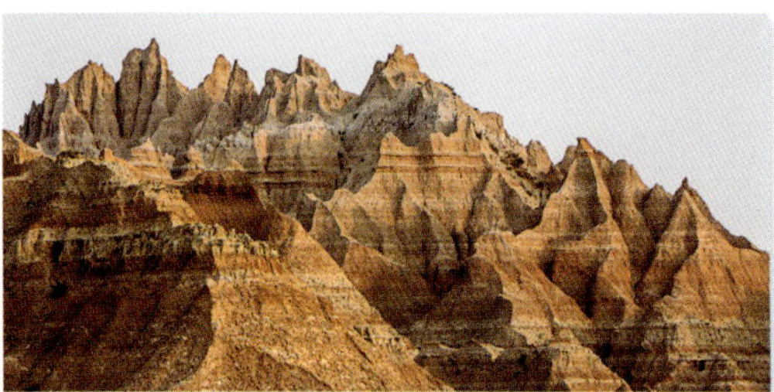

At this point, I did not like the colors so I spent quite a few minutes going back and forth between adjusting white balance and the **Vibrance** and **Saturation** sliders. I ultimately decided that I liked the result of having **Vibrance** at **-38** and **Saturation** at **+60**. After adjusting the color, I noticed that I wanted the dark areas to be just a little brighter, so I boosted **Shadows** to **+30**.

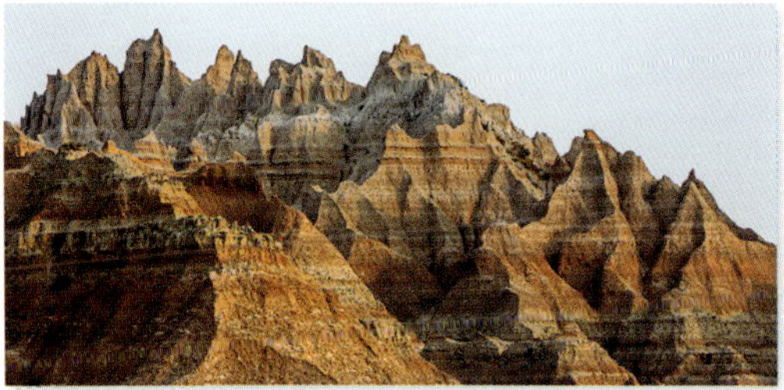

To finish things off, I zoomed up and boosted **Texture** to **+25** in order to breath new life into this decade-old capture. Lastly, I just couldn't resist tweaking the **HSL/Color** sliders that we'll cover in the "Selective Adjustments" section of chapter 8. At this point, I thought it was good enough for Instagram, so I called it quits.

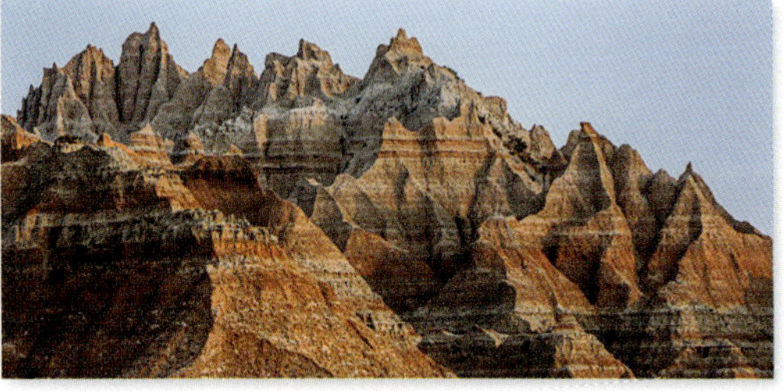

Masked Adjustments

The options found under the Mask icon just below the histogram in the Develop module allow you to adjust isolated areas within an image. The adjustment choices available are limited to a subset of the settings offered in the rest of the Develop module.

Let's start by looking at each method for creating a mask and then explore how to combine different mask types to produce more refined results.

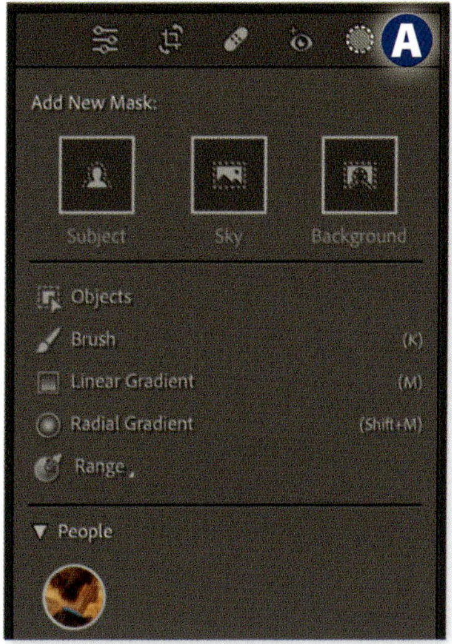

*Lightroom's Masks panel can be accessed by clicking the round masking icon **A** that is found just below the histogram in the Develop module.*

Artificial Intelligence–Generated Masks
Lightroom offers five choices that utilize artificial intelligence and machine learning to produce complex masks with little effort.

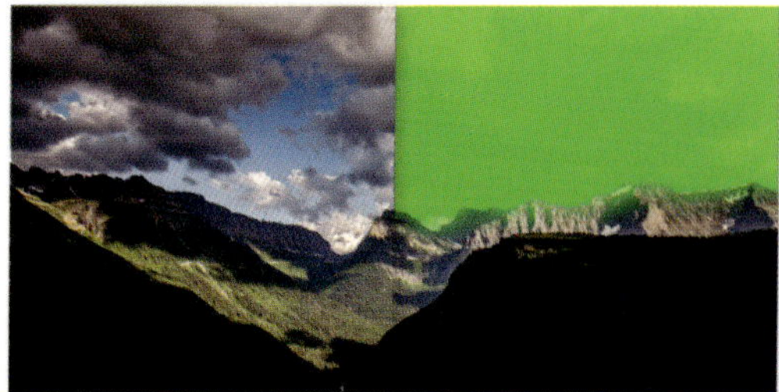

Sky
With a single click, this option will attempt to isolate the sky in an image but will often include areas near the sky that are similar in color and brightness.

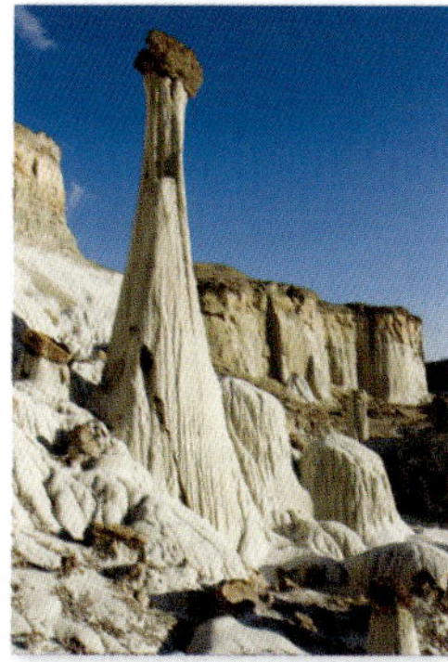
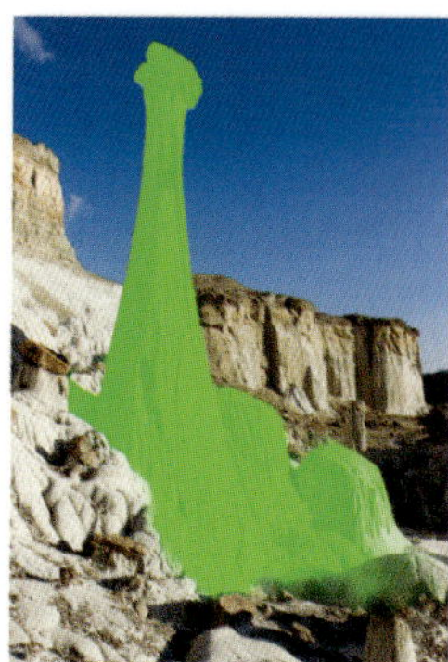

Subject
Lightroom will attempt to mask the subject of a photograph. This option is of limited use on landscape images since they usually don't have well-defined and obvious subjects.

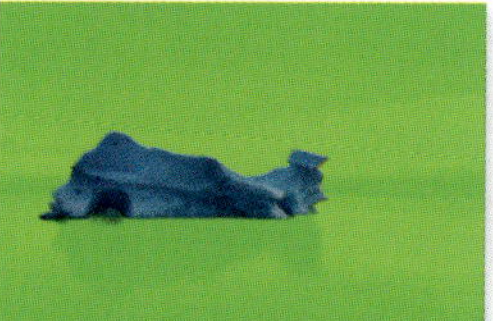

Background
This usually produces the exact opposite of the **Subject** option mentioned above.

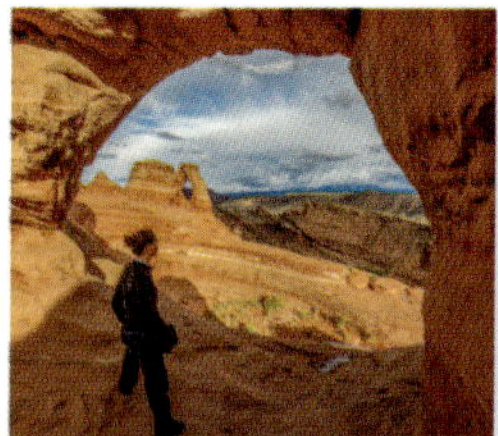
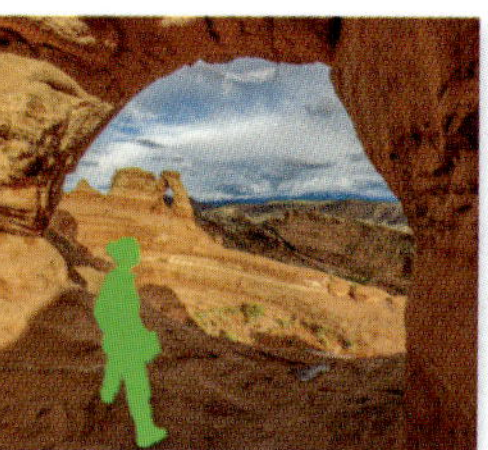

People
This option will only be available when people are prominent in an image. It offers many options that I will not cover here (such as isolating the whites of eyes) since people are rarely found in landscape photographs. For landscapes, I primarily find the **Entire Person** setting to be useful.

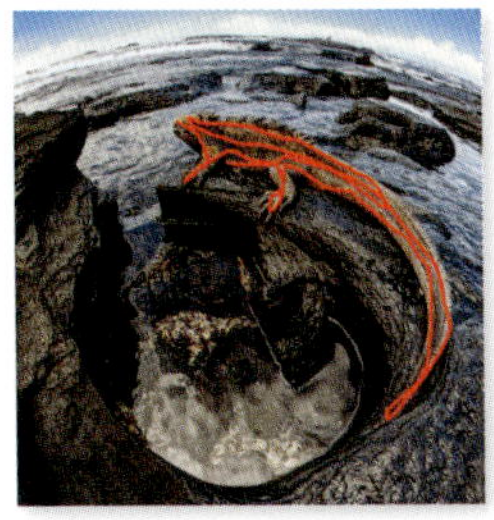 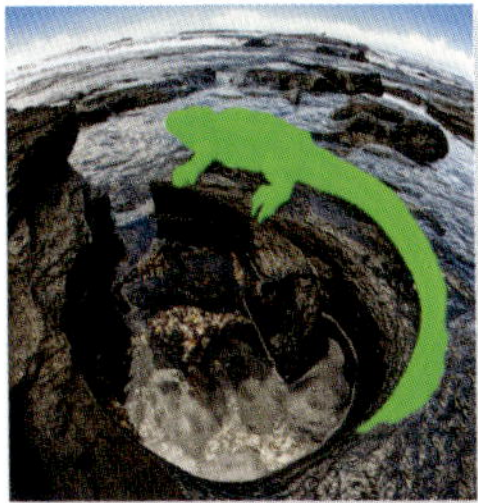

Objects

This allows you to paint across an area to indicate where an object is located using either a rectangle or a brush. The brush option is the most versatile because it allows for greater precision. I find it's usually essential to modify the resulting mask using the techniques covered later in this section.

Manual Masking

There is another set of masking tools that are useful for manually defining which area should be adjusted.

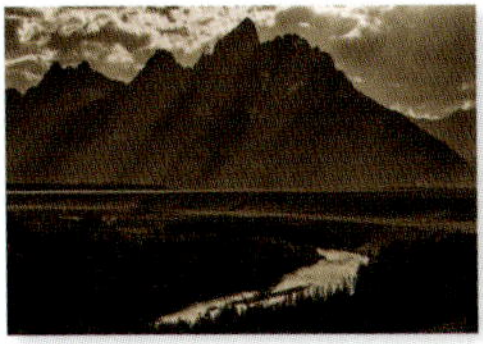 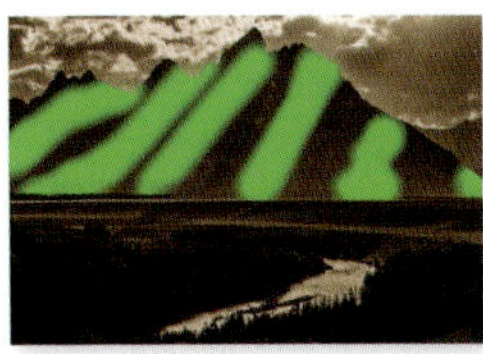

Brush

This tool allows you to manually paint over the area you'd like to adjust. The **Brush** tool offers the following settings:

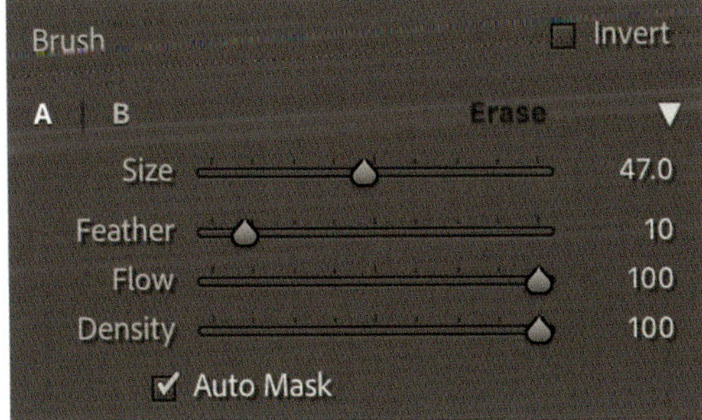

Size: Determines how large of an area you will affect when painting over the image. It can be adjusted via the slider, or by either rotating the screen wheel on a mouse (moving with two fingers on a laptop trackpad is usually equivalent), or pressing] or [on your keyboard.

Feather: Determines how soft the edge of the brush will be. Adding **Shift** to the shortcuts mentioned above will change the feather setting. The size of the brush also has a dramatic effect on the softness of the brush, with small brushes producing crisper edges and larger ones more pronounced softness.

Flow: Determines how much of the adjustment you've dialed in will be applied on the first paint stroke and subsequent passes thereafter. Starting with a very low **Flow** will allow you to paint across areas multiple times to build up a change.

Density: Allows you to paint with an absolute percentage of the adjustment that is consistent with every paint stroke and therefore does not change if you paint over the same area twice.

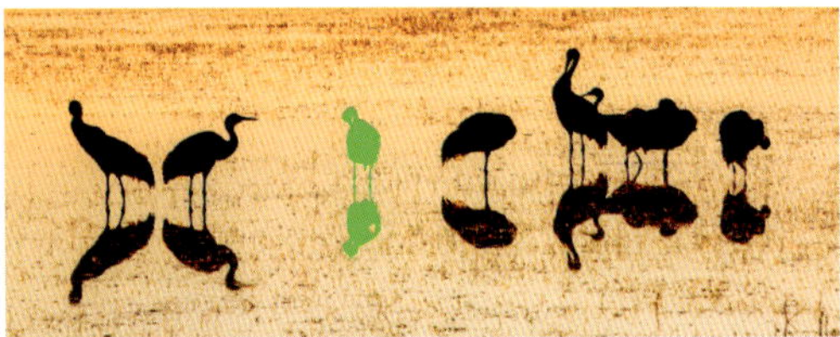

Auto Mask: Attempts to limit the area affected by the brush strokes to those that are similar to the colors found under the crosshair symbol in the center of your brush. Typing **A** will toggle this feature on or off.

A | B Brushes: Near the upper left of the brush settings, you can choose between two sets of brush settings, labeled A and B. This allows you to set up the A brush to be large and soft-edged, for example, and then quickly switch to the B brush, set up as a smaller, harder-edged brush for more detailed areas. That's just one example of how you can set them up. The main thing is that it will retain the settings of each of those brushes independently.

Erase: This option allows you to remove from the area that was previously masked. Its brush settings are independent of the **A** and **B** brushes, so don't be surprised if your brush suddenly changes in size or softness when switching between those three brushes. You can temporarily access the **Erase** brush by holding **Option** (Mac), or **Alt** (PC). You can also use the keyboard shortcuts mentioned earlier for changing the brush size while holding **Option** to use the **Erase** brush.

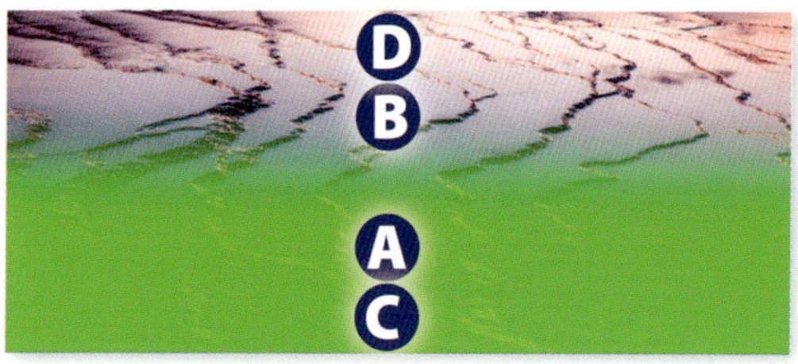

Linear Gradient

Start by clicking where you would like the adjustment to be applied at full strength **A**, then drag to where you'd like to stop applying the adjustment altogether **B**. The result will have a smooth transition along the length you dragged while making the area beyond your first click get full strength **C** and the area outside where you released to have no adjustment at all **D**.

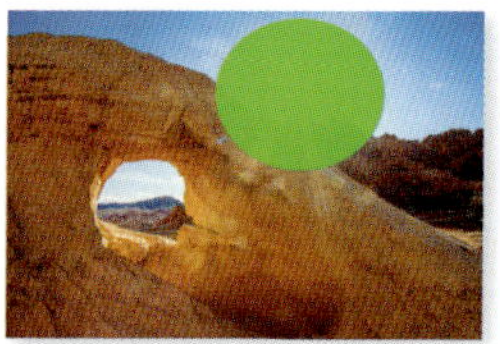 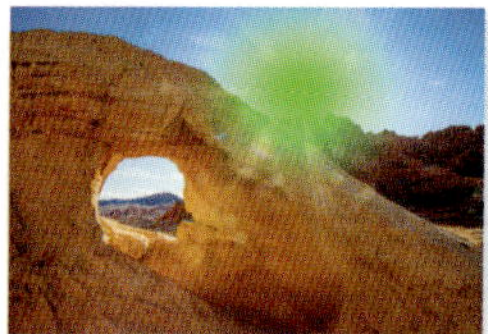

Radial Gradient

This allows you to isolate an oval-shaped area by clicking to define the center and releasing where you would like to stop applying the adjustment. The feather setting determines how soft of an edge you will produce.

Range

This option allows you to isolate an area based on brightness and/or color. Each choice offers a slightly different set of options.

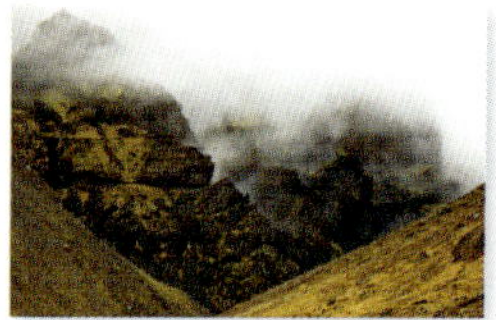 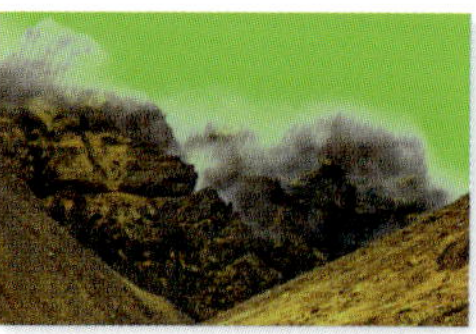

Luminance Range: After choosing this option, click and drag within the image to define the brightness range you'd like to isolate. There will then be controls in the Masks panel that can be used to fine-tune your results. The rectangular box **A** represents the shades that were present in the area you dragged across. You can drag on either edge of the rectangle to expand or condense the range, and then adjust the triangular

pointers to determine if the mask should fade out into brighter **B** or darker **C** regions of the image. The **Show Luminance Map** check box will display the image without color since the mask is based solely on the brightness of the image.

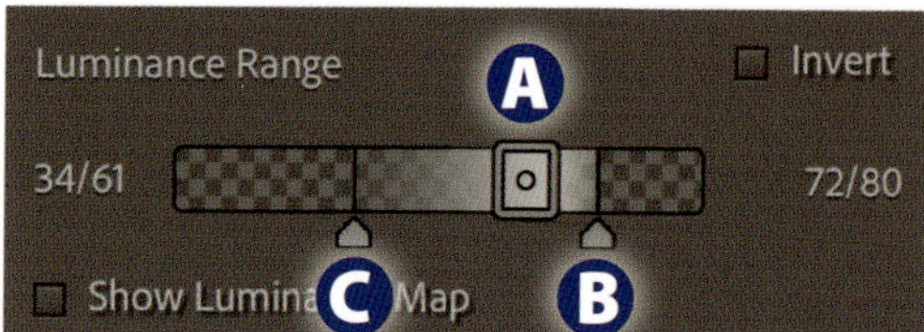

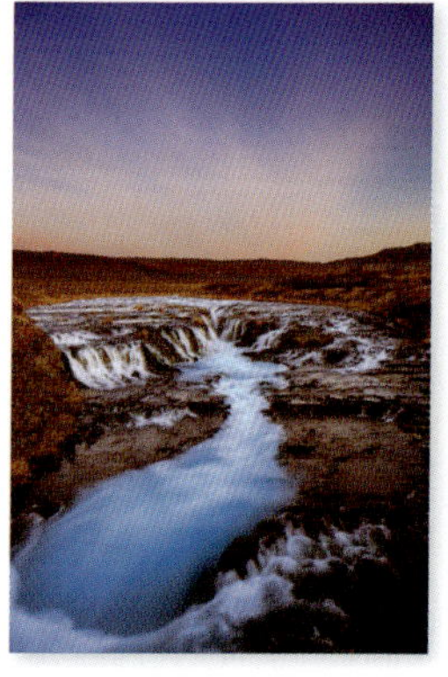 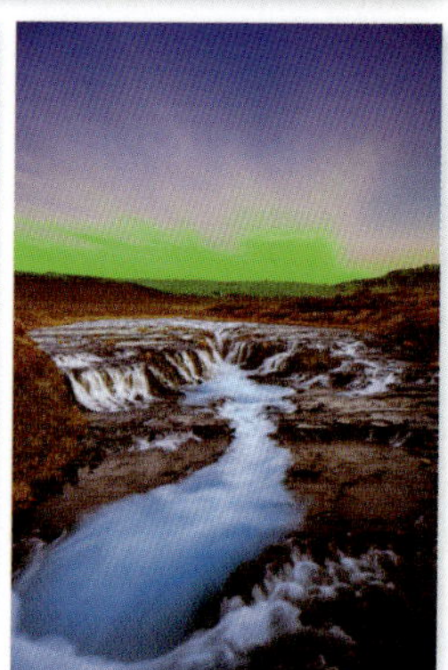

Color Range: This allows you to isolate areas based on color by clicking on the color you desire within the image. You can also click and drag to isolate all the colors found in the rectangular area you define. Holding **Shift** and clicking again will allow you to include additional colors (up to five total). You can then adjust the **Refine** setting to specify how far you'd like to deviate from the colors you clicked on.

Masks Panel Options

Creating a mask will cause the compact Masks panel to appear, where you'll find details about your newly created mask. The Masks panel will remain visible until you activate another tool that is located beneath the histogram or until you click on the mask icon again in order to close it.

Double-clicking on the name of a mask will allow you to assign a name to the mask, while a single click will collapse or expand the details of how the mask was produced. Each of the individual items listed in the details that collectively make up the mask can also be renamed within the list.

Section I: Fundamental Concepts

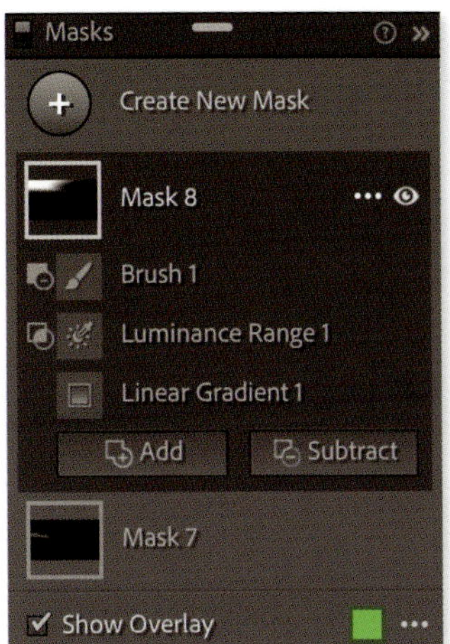

All the masks you create will appear in the Masks panel, which is only visible when the mask icon is active below the histogram. The tiny icons to the left of the mask components indicate whether they are subtracting from or intersecting the initial mask.

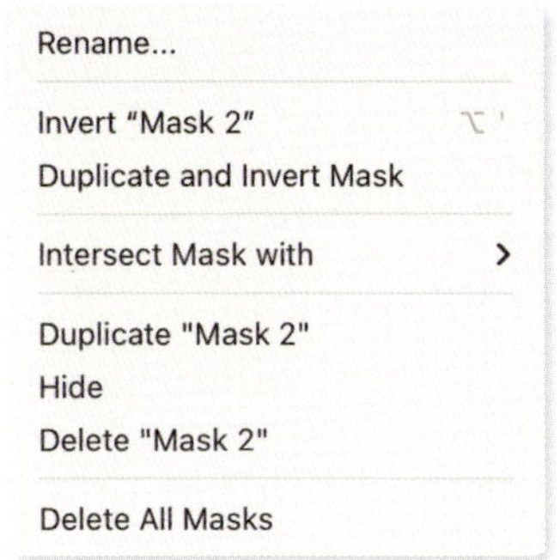

Hover over any mask within the Masks panel and click the ... menu to find additional options for refining a mask.

The **Add** and **Subtract** buttons found at the bottom of the mask details allow you to combine multiple masking options to further refine your results. Hold **Option** (Mac) or **Alt** (PC) to reveal an **Intersect** button, which effectively crops the mask so it only appears within the area of another.

The appearance of the mask overlay can be changed by clicking the three dots that appear to the right of the **Show Overlay** check box at the bottom of the Masks panel.

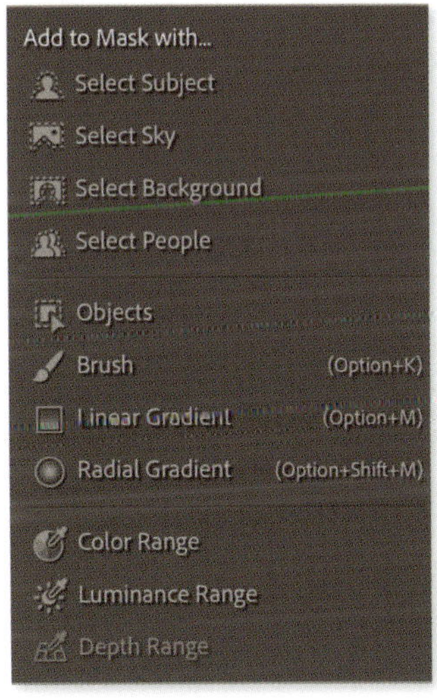

Clicking the Add, Subtract, or Intersect buttons will produce a list of available mask types that can be used to refine the active mask.

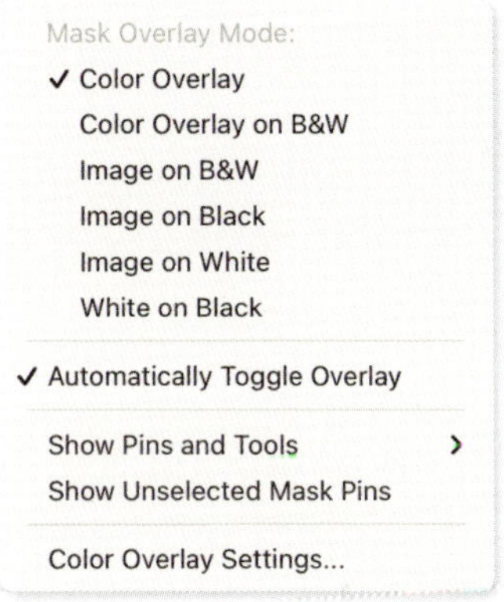

The mask display options pop-up menu is accessed via the ... menu in the bottom right of the Masks panel.

When using one of the **Color Overlay** choices, you can click on the square to the left of the menu to change the color of the overlay.

The **Automatically Toggle Overlay** setting, which is turned on by default, will automatically toggle the **Show Overlay** check box to off the moment you start to move the adjustment sliders to change the image.

Hovering over any of the mask components in the Masks panel will reveal an eyeball icon that can be used to temporarily disable a mask and an ellipsis (...) icon that can be clicked to reveal a pop-up menu of additional options. A brief click on the eyeball will cause it to toggle states, while clicking and holding will disable it for the length of your click.

*Tip: The **White on Black** overlay mode is useful for revealing undesirable artifacts that might be present in complex masks that were produced by combining multiple mask types (such as gaps between paint strokes). After all, It's better to notice such issues at an early stage when they are still changeable instead of being surprised by them after inspecting a large and expensive print.*

Complex Mask Example

Now let's take a look at a specific example of how a desired mask was produced from a combination of multiple mask types.

In the image above, I liked the look of the right side of the image, where there was a nice glow appearing between some of the mountain ranges. I wanted to extend that look into the far left side of the scene, where it was lacking that glow I desired.

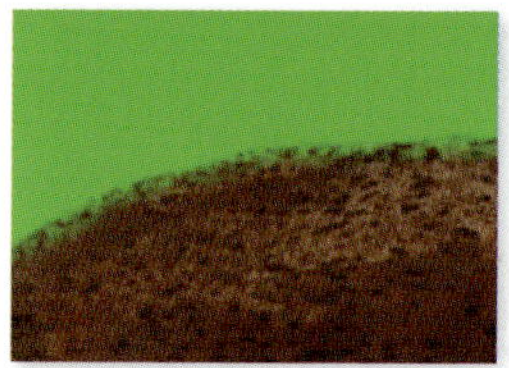

Object mask included some residue that extended into the lower mountain range.

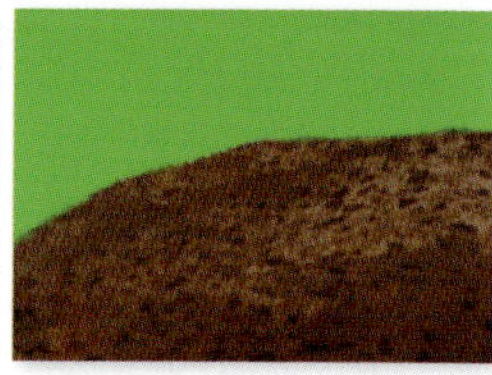

Subtracting with another Object reduced the residue.

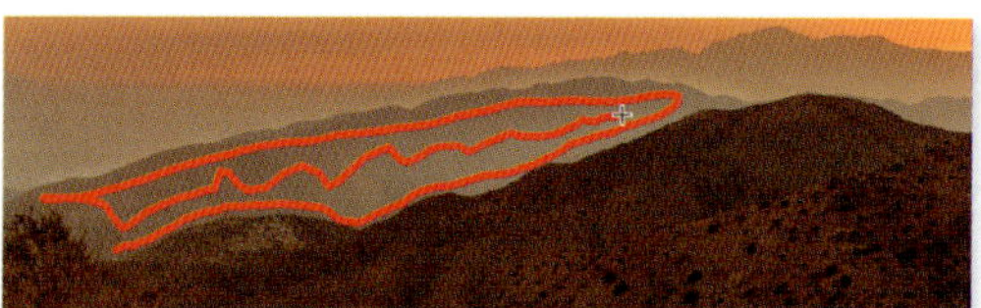

I started by creating an Object mask, painting over the mountain range I wanted to add a glow within.

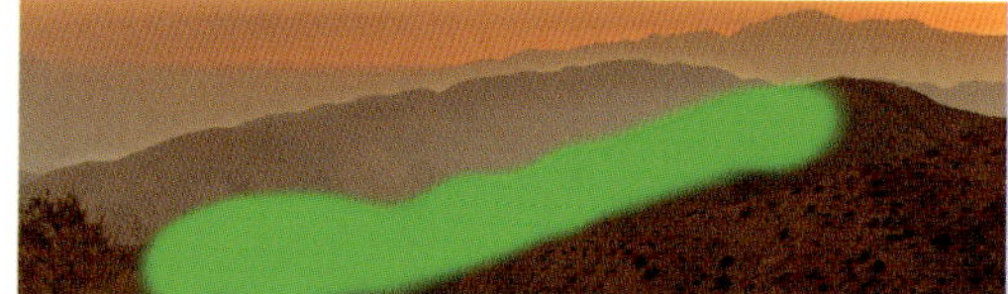

I held Option to reveal the Intersect button, chose Brush, and painted over an area that partially overlapped the first mask.

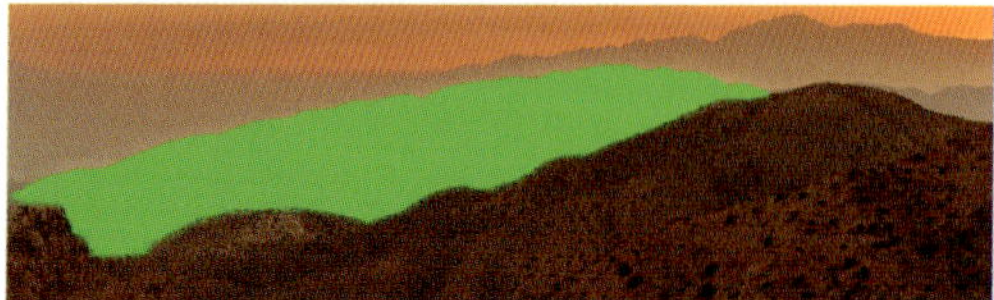

The green overlay is the result of the initial Object mask.

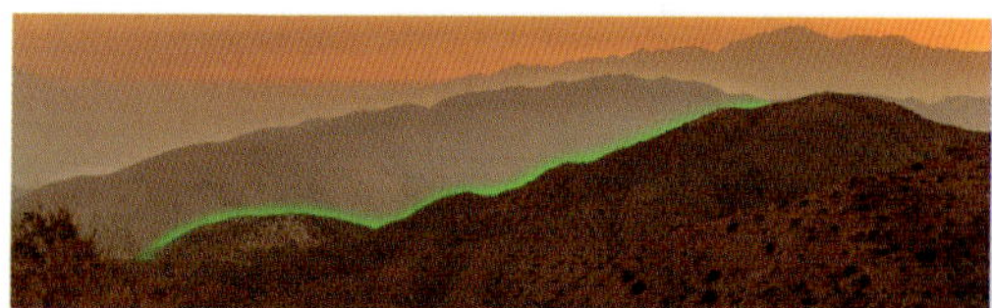

That cropped the mask so it only appeared within the brush.

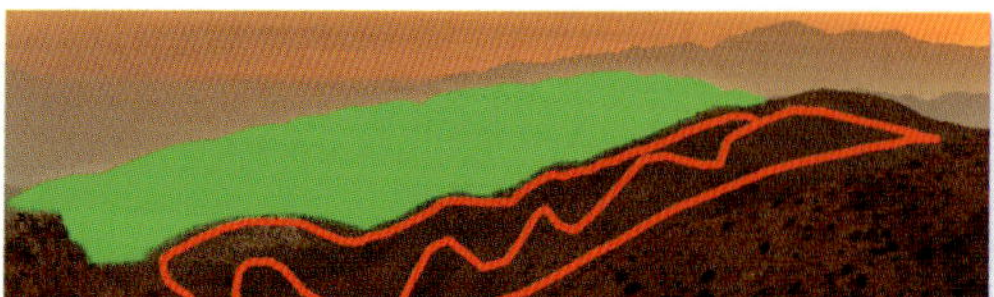

I clicked the Subtract button, chose Object, and painted the red line in an attempt to remove some residue from the previous result.

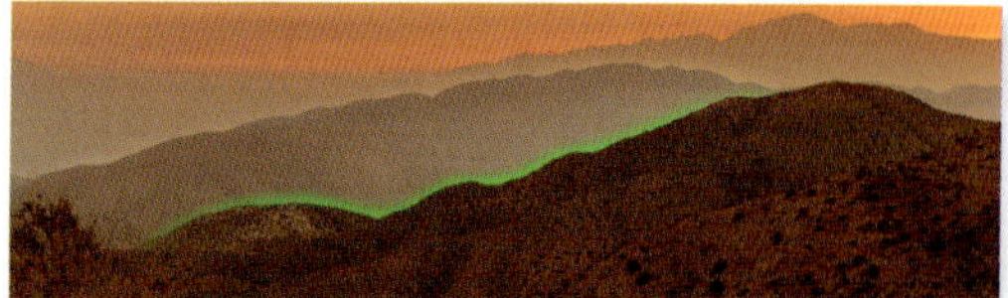

At this point, I wanted the isolated area to fade gradually on each end and subtly blend into the existing image. This is the result of subtracting from the mask using a large, soft brush and painting near the right and left ends.

Section I: Fundamental Concepts

Lightroom Classic Tips & Tricks

Double-Click to Reset Slider

Double-clicking on any adjustment slider will reset the slider to Lightroom's default settings. You can also double-click on the headings found above a group of sliders (**WB**, **Tone**, or **Presence**) to reset all the sliders within that group.

Shift-Double-Click for Auto Adjustments

Hold **Shift** when double-clicking a slider as mentioned above and you'll get the result of what Lightroom would have used for that slider if you had clicked the **Auto** button. I find this most useful when adjusting the **Blacks** slider since it will ensure you end up with a tiny area of solid black.

Update Process Version

A lightning bolt icon will appear in the area below the histogram in the Develop module if an image has been adjusted with an earlier version of Lightroom that offered different adjustment choices than are available today. Clicking the icon will update the image to use the most modern adjustment choices, but may cause the appearance of the image to change. Click that icon if you ever attempt to adjust an image and find a desired adjustment slider is missing.

Match In-Camera Appearance

Lightroom offers a set of camera-matching profiles that can be used to make your raw images match the general appearance of the in-camera processing that is used to produce JPEG images and on-screen previews. You can access them by choosing **Browse** from the **Profile** pop-up menu above the **Basic** adjustment sliders and expanding the section titled **Camera Matching**. The profiles available will be specific to the brand of camera the current raw image was captured with and should match the corresponding settings found in your camera's menu system. If you don't remember changing such a setting in your camera, then the **Standard** option was likely in use.

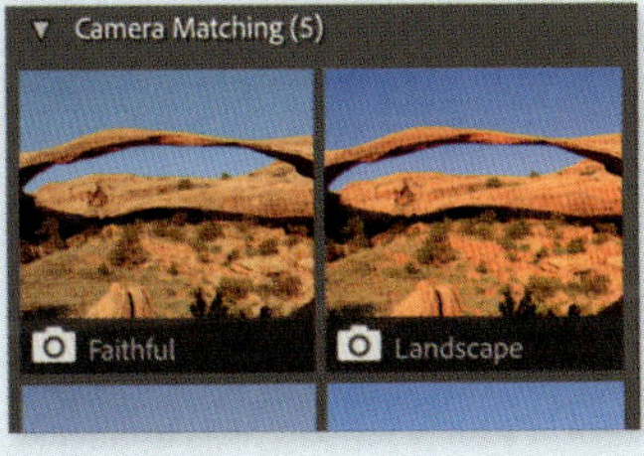

Wide Side Panels for Precision Adjustments

You can adjust the width of the side panels in any Lightroom module by dragging the inner edge of the panel. Lightroom will impose a limit on how wide the panels can become. Hold **Option** (Mac) or **Alt** (PC) while dragging to overcome the normal width limit. Having a wide panel in the Develop module allows you to have more granular control over the adjustment sliders.

Export to Specific Size

Exporting an image to a specific size such as 8.5x11" is a two-step process. Start by pressing **R** to access the **Crop** tool, then choose the **Enter Custom** option from the **Aspect** pop-up menu and enter the size you desire. In the process, notice that there is no choice for which measurement system is used. That's because you're just choosing the proportions of the rectangle that will be used to crop the image. After cropping to the desired ratio, select **File>Export**, choose the **Width & Height** option in the **Image Sizing** section, and enter the size you desire. Export is unable to change the cropping of an image, which is why this is a two-step process.

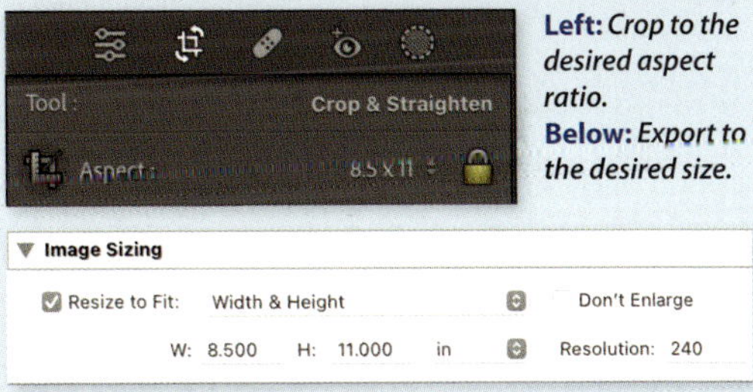

Left: *Crop to the desired aspect ratio.*
Below: *Export to the desired size.*

Swap Cropping Orientation

Press **X** when using the **Crop** tool to switch between horizontal and vertical orientations.

Learn Lightroom's Keyboard Shortcuts

Typing **Command-?** (Mac) or **Ctrl-?** (PC) will cause a window of keyboard shortcuts to appear that are specific to the module that is active.

Bypass Smart Previews in Develop Module

If an image ever displays obvious banding during adjustment, click to zoom in to 100% view, which will force Lightroom to load the actual raw image.

Retouching

Lightroom offers a single tool for performing retouching. The **Healing** tool's icon looks like a Band-Aid and appears near the upper right in the Develop module.

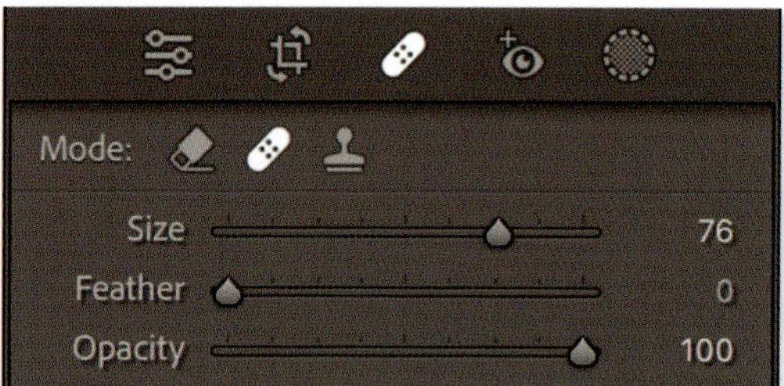

Healing tool icon and options.

Retouching Modes

When you click the **Healing** tool icon (or type **Q**), the area below will expand and present you with icons representing its three modes of operation: **Clone**, **Heal**, and **Content-Aware Remove**.

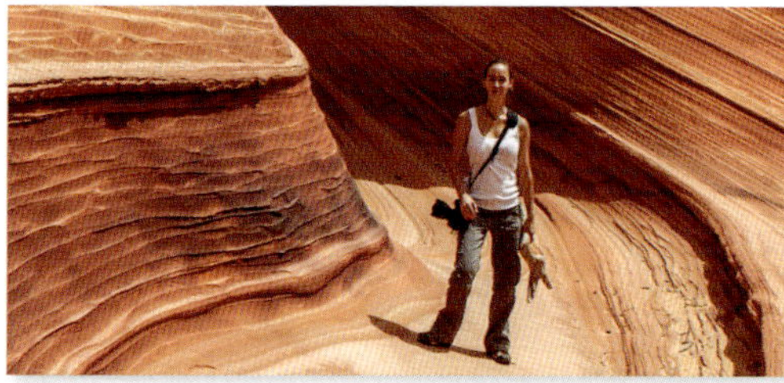

Our test subject is my amazing wife Karen at "the wave."

Clone

This is the least sophisticated of the modes and is represented by a rubber stamp icon. The mode is well named since it is limited to making an exact copy (hence clone) of one area and applying it somewhere else.

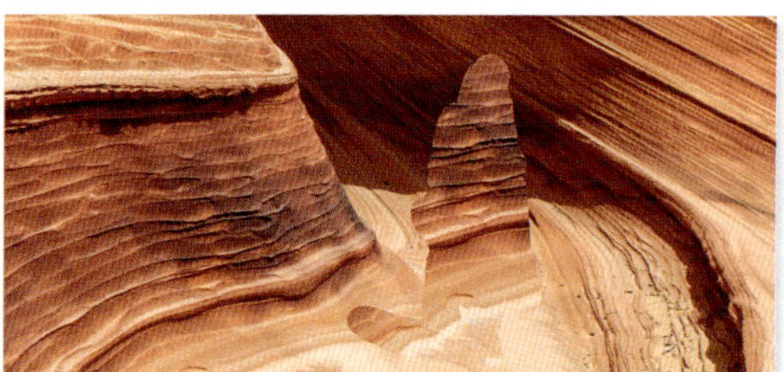

Cloning just makes a blatant copy with no adjustment at all.

This is the tool I use the least because it's up to me to make sure the area I end up copying from is the right brightness, color, and has appropriate texture to blend in with the surroundings.

Heal

Heal takes the concept of cloning to another level. It clones the detail and texture from one area and then "heals" it into the area surrounding the retouching (hence the Band-Aid icon). By heal, I mean blending to make it precisely match the brightness and color of the area immediately outside of where the tool was applied!

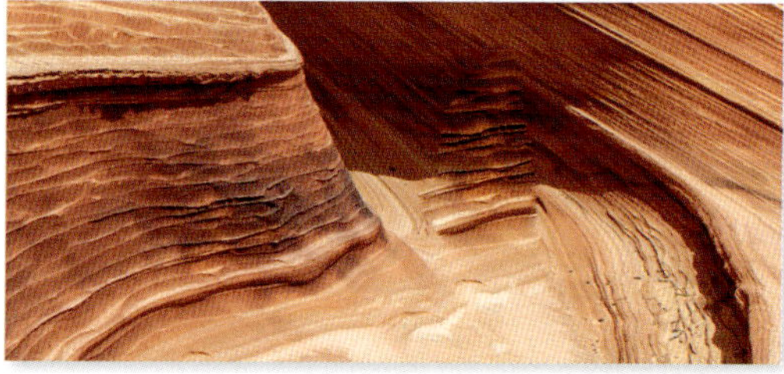

Healing attempts to match the clone to its surroundings.

This is my go-to mode for retouching in Lightroom because I don't need to worry if the area being copied from is even vaguely in the same ballpark of color or brightness. I simply don't care. I instead look for appropriate texture, detail, and brightness transitions that could potentially look appropriate for the destination.

Content-Aware Remove

Clone and **Heal** modes have been available in Lightroom for years, while **Content-Aware Remove** mode is the new kid on the block. It takes a different approach that makes it a great choice when you can't find an appropriate area to clone from. That's because it's not limited to making a blatant clone. Instead, it can construct brand-new content based on dozens of areas within the surrounding image.

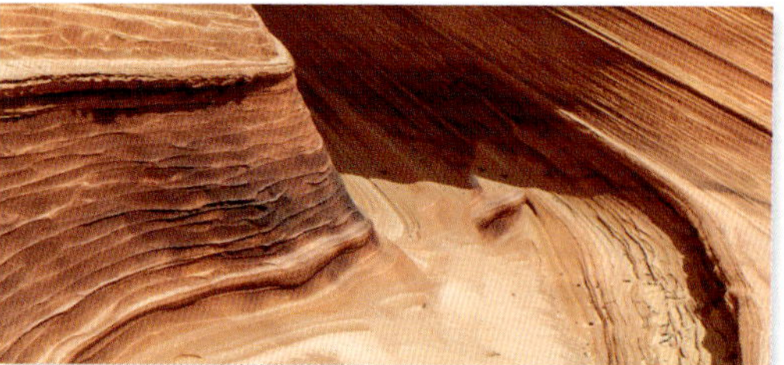

Content-Aware Remove is great on complex areas.

Section I: Fundamental Concepts

This mode is by no means a replacement for the others. Try it on something simple that **Heal** mode would do great on, and you might find it producing blotchy results that anyone would recognize as looking bad. But, at the same time, it simply shines when you feed it a difficult task that the other modes cannot handle. It's designed for complex stuff that you cannot solve with a blatant copy of part of the surrounding image.

Before you can perform difficult retouching challenges, you have to make sure you have a solid grasp of the basics, so let's take a look at the ins and outs of using these tools.

Define Retouching Area

You have just two options for how to define the area that needs to be retouched: click and release, or click and drag. If it's simple enough, get a brush big enough to cover it, then click and release. If it's a large or an unusually shaped area, then click and drag. When you're done, the retouched area will have an icon to mark the spot that matches the mode that was active. It will be surrounded by a circle of appropriate size if you clicked and released **A**. Odd-shaped areas just get the icon **B**.

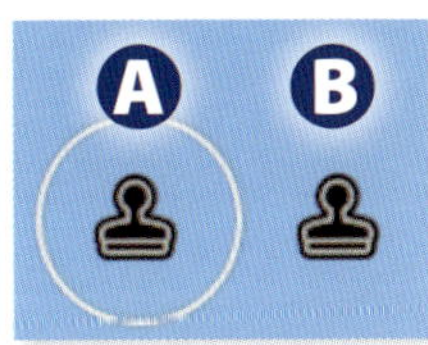

Choose Clone Source

Once you've defined the area to be retouched, Lightroom kicks in and picks what it thinks would be a good area to copy from. If you don't agree, you have two choices.

Refresh

Clicking the **Refresh** button at the bottom of the **Healing** tool options (or typing **/**) will force Lightroom to pick a new source to clone from. You can click that button as many times as you want and each time it will obediently pick another spot... but that doesn't mean it will be any better than the last.

Manual Source Selection

When using **Clone** or **Heal** mode, a second identically shaped area that represents the source **A** that was automatically chosen will appear, with an arrow pointing to the destination **B**. You can drag that source shape to another spot to force it to use that area as the source. When using **Content-Aware Remove** mode, it's a little different

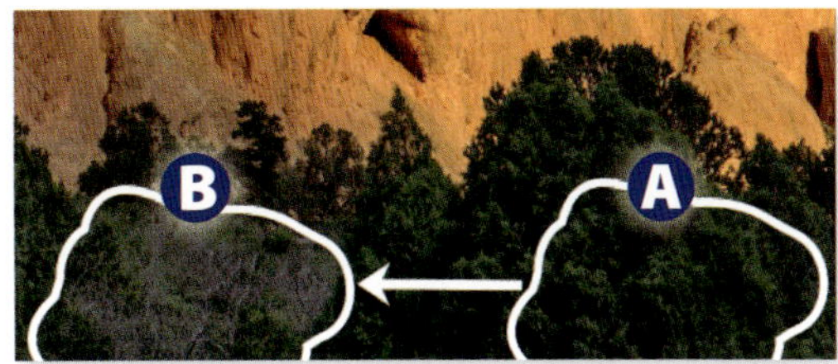

because it does not show you a source area. To force it to use content that is similar to a particular area, hold **Command** (Mac) or **Ctrl** (PC) and drag to define a rectangular area around something you think is appropriate content to use.

Tool Settings

The following settings are available when using the **Healing** tool in Lightroom:

Feather

The **Feather** setting controls the edge quality of the brush you use to define the source area. Low settings produce an abrupt transition, which is often the preferred choice when using **Heal** mode since it allows the tool to have complete control all the way to the edge of the brush. Lower settings cause brush strokes to have soft edges that help when using **Clone** mode since that mode does not attempt to match the brightness or color of the surrounding image. Feather is disabled in **Content-Aware Remove** mode because it requires a hard-edged brush.

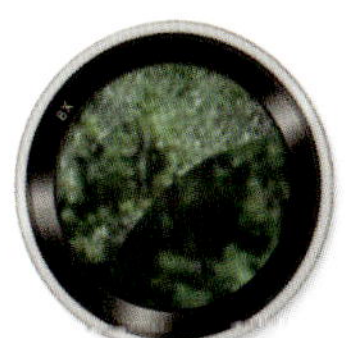

Clone mode results Feather: ↑0% ↓83%

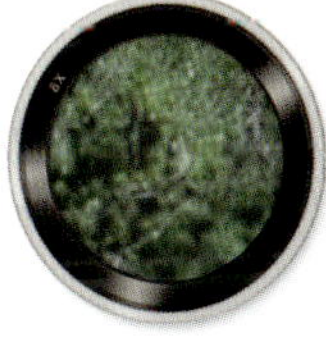

Opacity

Lowering the **Opacity** setting will cause your results to become translucent, causing the source to blend with the original image. This can be an effective way to lessen the impact of an undesirable object without completely removing it.

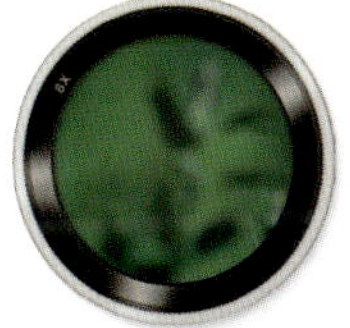

Before Cloning

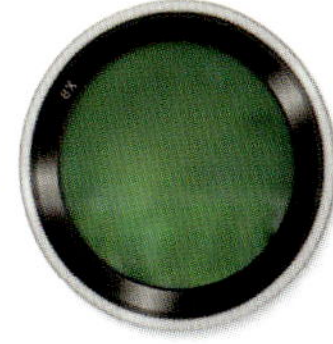

Opacity: 50%   *Opacity: 100%*

Editing Prior Retouching

You can return to any previously retouched area by clicking on the icon within the image that represents the area that was retouched, or press **Esc** to deselect all. The arrow keys can then be used to reposition (hold **Shift** to make larger moves) the source or destination area and will affect whichever of the two was clicked on last. The **Mode**, **Opacity**, and **Feather** settings will only affect the active retouching point. Pressing **Delete** (Mac) or **Backspace** (PC) will delete the active area, and holding **Option** (Mac) or **Alt** (PC) and clicking on an icon will delete it with a single click.

Type **H** to toggle the visibility of the icon overlays all together. When they are hidden, you can click right where an icon previously appeared to apply additional retouching without making the earlier retouched area active. If you find the retouching icons to be distracting, then consider setting the **Tool Overlay** pop-up menu below the lower-left corner of the image to **Auto,** which will hide the overlays any time you move your mouse outside the image.

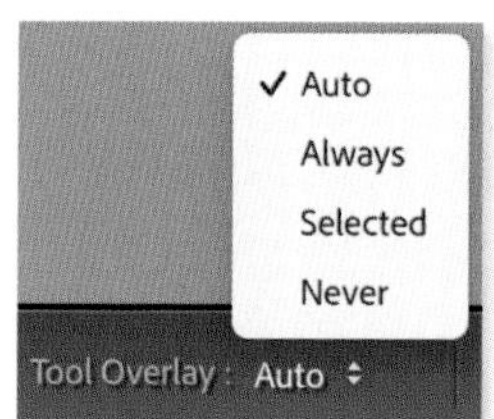

The Tool Overlay pop-up menu is found in the toolbar below your image.

Removing Sensor Dust Spots

If your images are plagued with undesirable round, shadowy spots that are most noticeable in the sky, then your camera sensor likely needs to be cleaned to remove dust. You can more easily locate these annoying spots by turning on the **Visualize Spots** check box and adjusting the slider until they are easy to spot within the unusual view the check box produces.

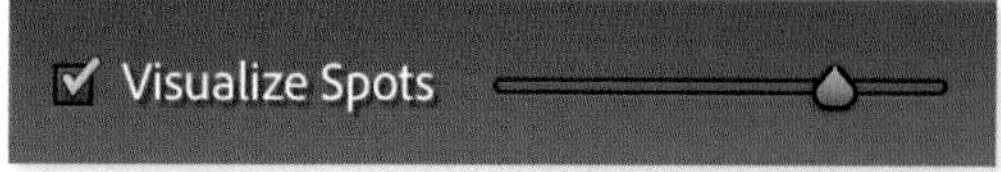

If you want to make it even easier to find them, then head over to the Basic panel and crank up the **Clarity** slider to make them more pronounced. To remove these spots, I use **Heal** mode, set **Feather** to **0**, and choose a brush just a little bit larger than the spot I want to remove. All it takes is a few clicks (or possibly hundreds if you've never cleaned your camera sensor).

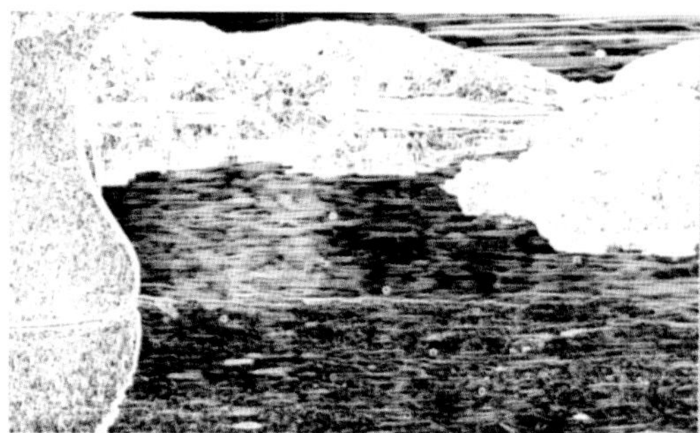

Visualize Spots causes dust spots to appear as white circles.

The dust that accumulates on a camera sensor often remains stationary until the lens is changed and wind might dislodge the dust. For that reason, you can often get away with retouching the dust spots out of dozens (or even hundreds) of images at the same time. To do so, you'll need to select a group of images that were shot on the same day, then head to the Develop module and turn on the small light-switch-like toggle to enable **Auto Sync** mode.

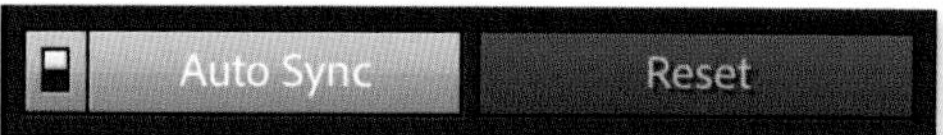

With **Auto Sync** turned on, you can retouch the dust spots from a single image and cause identical retouching to be applied to all the images that are selected.

Once you finish, you should inspect each image individually since it will not customize the position of the source that was used for each image. Therefore, you might find that where there was a sky in one image, there is a mountain in another and the initial source location would not be a good match in some of the other images. It often only requires a quick inspection to find the areas that need adjustment, and all it usually takes is to click on the spot and type **/** to force it to pick a new source location. I find that messing with the on/off toggle at the bottom of the **Heal** tool options panel can help to identify retouching that doesn't fit with its surroundings.

In the end, I do not fully trust the **Visualize Spots** feature to reveal all sensor dust spots, so I meticulously inspect every inch of any image that I plan to print large. It's much easier to spend five minutes inspecting the image than to have to make another print if you find one after printing.

Section I: Fundamental Concepts

Retouching Examples

Now that you have an idea of how the retouching features work, let's take a look at some examples of how I've successfully used these tools.

Remove Tourists

The most common tourist to get into my shots is my wife. I started with a quick application of **Content-Aware Remove** to do the heavy lifting, and then touched up the result with 8–10 quick passes in **Heal** mode with a smaller brush.

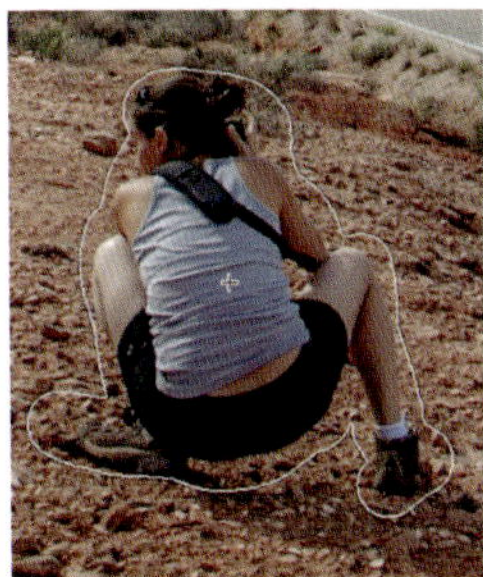
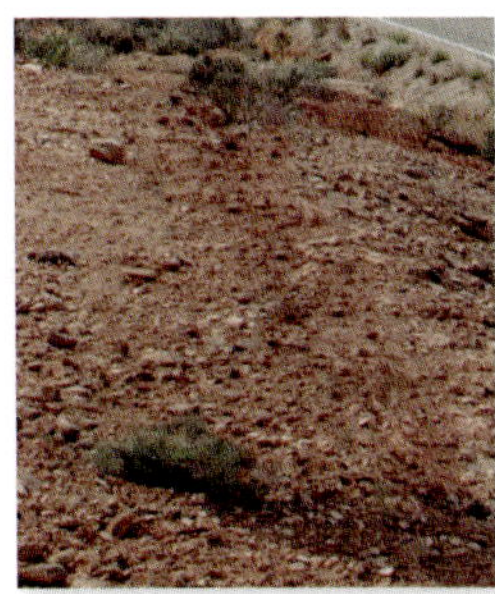

Reposition Clouds for Ideal Cropping

I wanted to crop the image below at the top, but didn't want to cut into the cloud in the upper left. I painted over the cloud while in **Heal** mode. I then dragged the source shape to almost align with the destination to effectively use the cloud as the source. I then clicked on the destination (which was only a tiny bit offset from the source) and dragged it down to effectively reposition the cloud and allow room to crop out more of the sky.

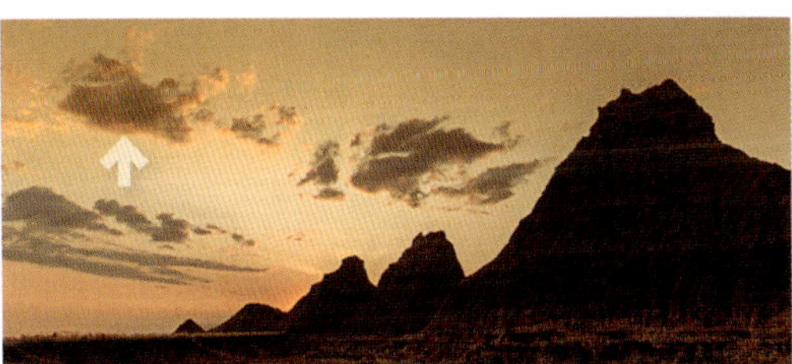

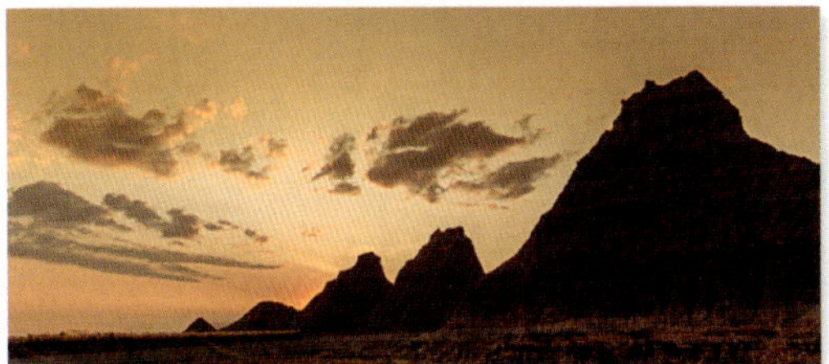

Remove Lens Flare

Shooting straight into the sun is a pretty good recipe for lens flare and I've got it here. I spent just over five minutes, starting in **Heal** mode when working on simple areas of the background and then switching to **Content-Aware Remove** for spots that required more complex source material. I pressed the / key to have it choose a new source on average 3–4 times per spot that was fixed.

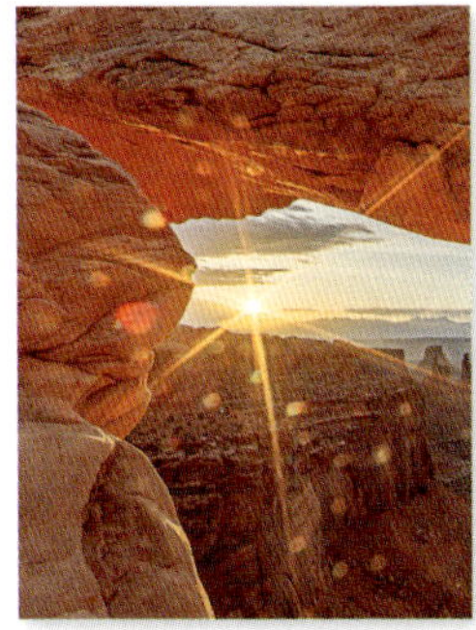
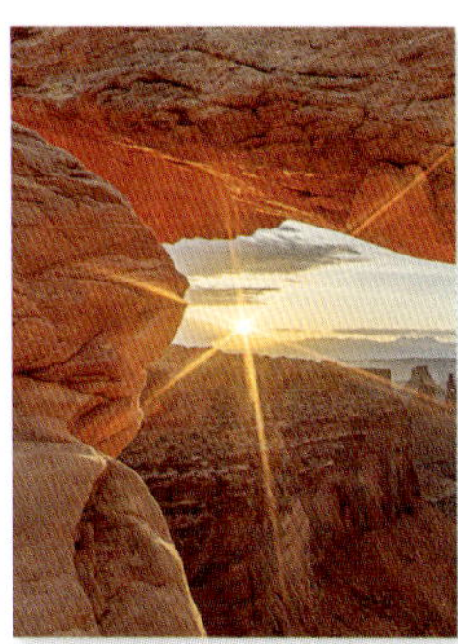

Remove Clouds

I wanted to simplify the sky by removing the clouds on the right side. I started in **Content-Aware Remove** mode and made 4–5 passes before I decided that it had contributed as much as it could, but the result was not smooth. I switched to **Heal** mode and smoothed out the results by using the opposite side of the sky as the source.

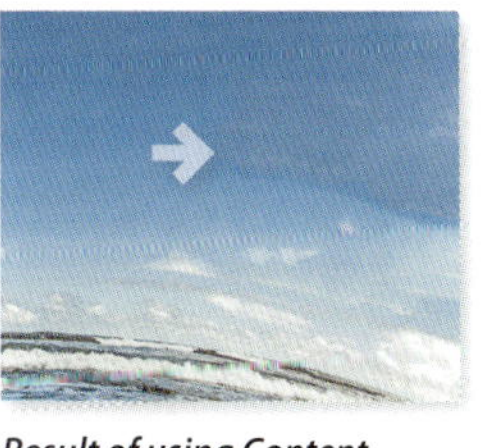

Result of using Content-Aware Remove mode.

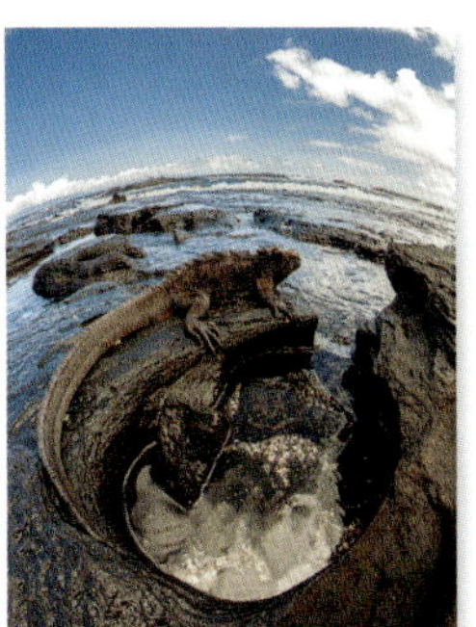
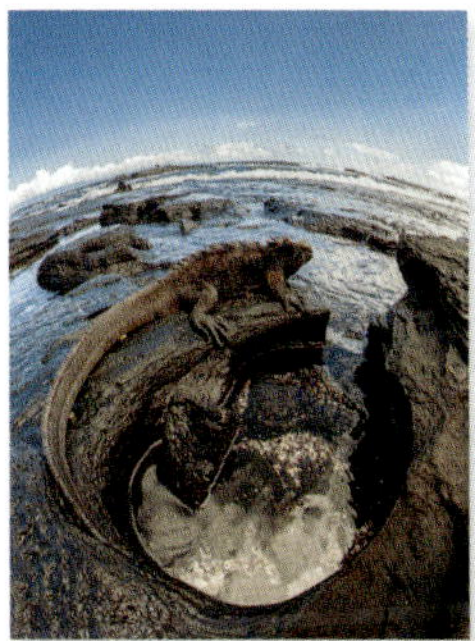

With some practice, you can go far with Lightroom's **Healing** tool. Photoshop can do a lot more.

Round-Tripping to Photoshop

When you get to the point where you feel that you're running into the limitations of Lightroom, then you'll likely want to send your image over to Photoshop. Let's look at what's involved in successfully sending an image on a round-trip journey to Photoshop and back again.

External Editing Preferences

Start by choosing **Preferences** from the **Lightroom Classic** menu (Mac) or **Edit** menu (PC), and note the settings found under the **External Editing** tab. That's where you'll determine which file format Photoshop should produce and how much information should be sent to Photoshop.

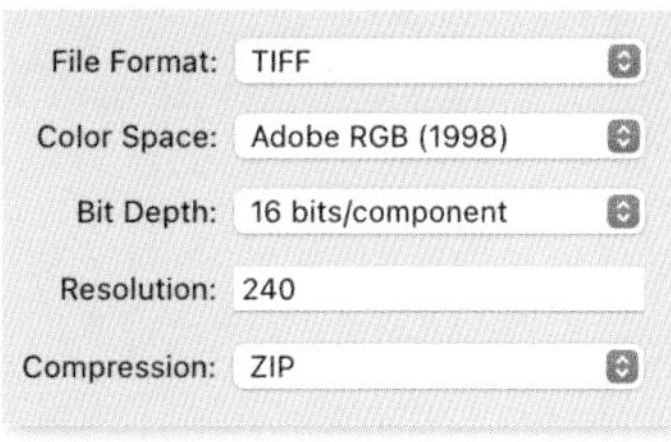

Choose what is sent to Photoshop when you open a raw file and which file format will be used to produce the resulting layered file.

File Format

You could generally flip a coin to decide on this one since there is zero quality difference between the choices. I personally use TIFF because the maximum file size it can handle is 4GB, whereas PSD can't handle anything over 2GB. You might think you'll never produce files that large, but I've done it hundreds of times when working on complex composites and panoramas.

Color Space

The **Color Space** you choose will determine just how vivid the colors in your image can become. The menu is organized with the most vivid choice at the top and the most restricted at the bottom. If you desire high-quality results, then there are really only two choices to consider.

Adobe RGB: My suggested setting for photographers who own a photo-quality inkjet printer. That's because modern printers are capable of reproducing colors that are more vivid than the choices we skipped over, and I find it to be the safest choice for people who are not mega-educated about how color works behind the scenes.

ProPhoto RGB: Some consider this to be the ultimate since it allows you to produce the most vivid colors out of all the choices available. But you should realize that it includes many colors that no monitor or printer can reproduce and some theoretical colors that are beyond the capabilities of human vision. Not only that, but you will find that adjustments you are familiar with will react a bit differently when you use **ProPhoto** because the tiniest movement of an adjustment slider will produce a more pronounced change than you may be accustomed to. I would only recommend this choice for people who feel very comfortable with managing color. I use it frequently, but would not casually suggest it to just anyone. If you use **ProPhoto**, be sure to also choose the **16-bits/component** choice below it.

Bit Depth

This setting determines whether it will deliver all the brightness levels that are available from your original raw file (**16-bit**) or if it should throw away the vast majority of the information so you can end up with a smaller file (**8-bit**). High-quality digital cameras capture a minimum of 4,096 brightness levels (known as 12-bit) and many capture even more. The choice of **8-bit** would only retain 256 brightness levels between black and white. That is barely enough to make transitions look smooth and offers no leeway for adjustments. I use **16-bit** for every single image I ever open and I suggest you do the same.

Resolution

This setting determines how large the pixels that make up your image will be when they are printed from other programs. It does not change the amount of information delivered to Photoshop. The only reason it's listed as a setting is because raw files do not have a resolution setting assigned to them and Photoshop requires one. The default setting of **240** is just fine, but feel free to change it if you have a reason to do so. I prefer to print from Lightroom, which will ignore this setting altogether. You'll be able to choose to use a different resolution setting when exporting an image, so it's not a critical setting. I leave mine at **240**.

At the bottom of the **External Editing** window is a pop-up menu where you can modify the default file naming that will be used. I use the default setting, which is to add -Edit to the end of the source file name.

Edit in Photoshop

Once you've set up your **External Editing** preferences, you can send the currently selected image to Photoshop by choosing **Edit in Photoshop** from the **Photo>Edit In** menu, or by typing the shortcut of **Command-E** (Mac) or **Ctrl-E** (PC). What happens next depends on the file format of the image that was selected.

Raw Files

Photoshop cannot handle the non-standard nature of raw files. For that reason, the settings in Lightroom's Develop module will be permanently baked into the image that is sent to Photoshop. Once you're done working in Photoshop, you can either close the file and choose **Save** when prompted, or type **Command-S** (Mac) or **Ctrl-S** (PC). This will produce a layered file using the file format that is specified in Lightroom's **External Editing** preferences that we talked about earlier.

Non-Raw Files

Photoshop has no problem handling files that don't contain raw data. But sending such files to Photoshop will cause Lightroom to present you with a list of three options to choose from.

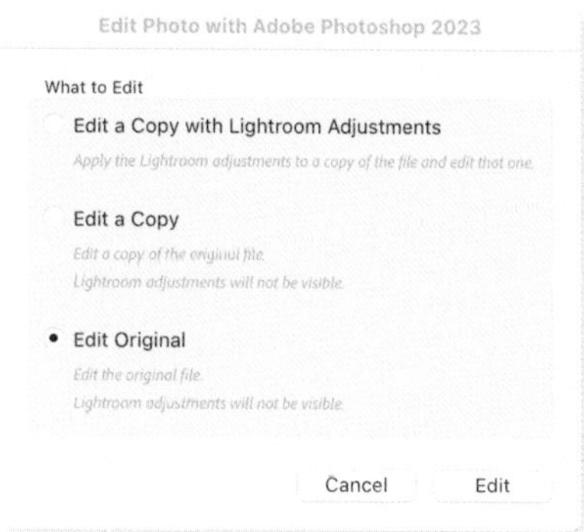

Choosing Photo>Edit in Photoshop with anything but a raw file will force you to choose between these three choices.

Edit Original: This option allows you to open the original file without any modifications as if you manually found the original using your computer's operating system and opened it directly into Photoshop without Lightroom's knowledge. This means that any adjustments that have been applied in Lightroom will be ignored. That might sound like an awful thing to do, but it's the choice that I use for 90 percent or more of all the images I ever send to Photoshop. I'll explain why after we explore the other choices.

Edit a Copy: This is the same as the **Edit Original** choice, but creates a duplicate before opening the image.

Edit a Copy with Lightroom Adjustments: This choice produces a duplicate image that has been flattened (no layers) and causes any adjustments that have been made in Lightroom's Develop module to be applied.

At first glance, you might find that none of these options are what you want. I assume you'd want to keep the layers that are inside the file and see any adjustments that were made in Lightroom. That's not possible because Lightroom does not understand what layers are. After all, Lightroom is not a pixel editor like Photoshop. It instead just has some written instructions that describe which adjustment sliders were moved. The only way it can apply them is to extract the flattened preview that is contained inside the TIFF or PSD file that you are attempting to open and apply it to that version of the image.

But you can get the best of both worlds in some cases. Let's say you have a layered TIFF file that you make some adjustments to in the Develop module, but now you want to edit the individual layers that make up the image. If you use the **Edit Original** choice when opening the image, then you'll have full access to the layers (even though you won't see the effect of Lightroom's adjustments), and when you save the image, the changes should be reflected back in Lightroom. But that's not all. Lightroom will also remember that you had applied adjustments to the image and reapply them once it notices that the base file had changed! So, if you don't mind not seeing the effect of the adjustments while you're in Photoshop, then you can have your cake and eat it too. I just wish Lightroom would explicitly indicate whether the image had adjustments or not. If there are no adjustments to worry about, then there would be no reason to use anything other than **Edit Original**. Instead, it's up to you to think of it before opening an image and looking for the little badge on the image thumbnail that indicates the image has been adjusted in Lightroom.

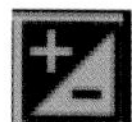

This badge indicates adjustments have been applied that are affecting the on-screen image preview, but are not reflected in the original image file.

We'll cover other methods of opening images in Photoshop in later chapters.

Exporting

In chapter 1, we learned that Lightroom adjustments don't modify the original image files. Instead, the modifications are stored as instructions in your Lightroom catalog file. A preview image, saved in the same folder, is updated and used to represent the image going forward. To share an edited version of an image, you need to export the image to produce a stand-alone file that has the changes baked in. Let's delve into some details of exporting images.

Creating Export Presets
Choosing **File>Export** will present you with an abundance of options that can be used to produce images that incorporate the changes you've made in Lightroom.

To quickly access frequently used settings, use the **Add** button in the lower left to create a preset. To use the preset, select it from the **File>Export with Preset** menu. To export with custom settings, choose **File>Export** and select the closest preset from the list on the left to get you started. Then, change only those settings that need to deviate from the preset for that particular export.

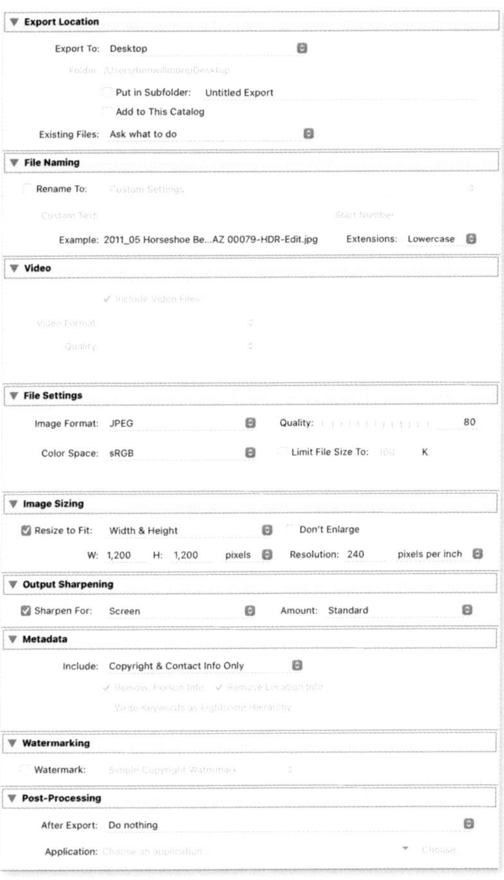

The abundance of options available when exporting images.

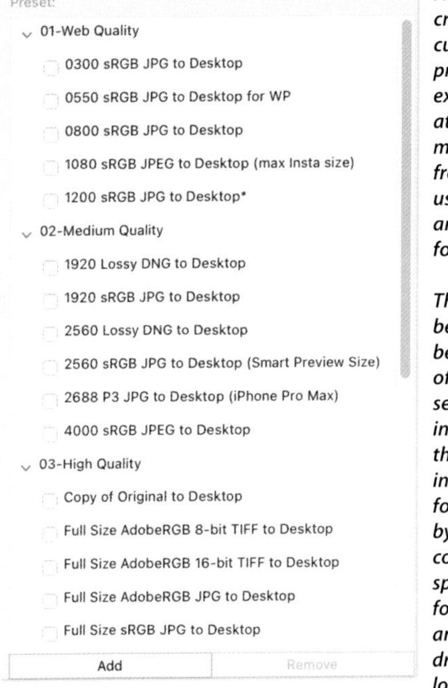

I have created custom presets for exporting at my most frequently used sizes and file formats.

The number at the beginning of the preset name indicates the width in pixels followed by the color space, file format, and hard drive location.

You can divide presets into sections by organizing them into folders. A folder can be created by right-clicking on any preset within the **Export** dialog box and choosing **New Folder**. You can then drag presets within the list to move between folders. Consider starting folder names with a number to control their order since they are sorted alphabetically, numbers first.

To modify a preset, choose **File>Export**, select the preset from the list on the left, and adjust the settings on the right. Finally, right-click on the preset and select **Update with Current Settings**.

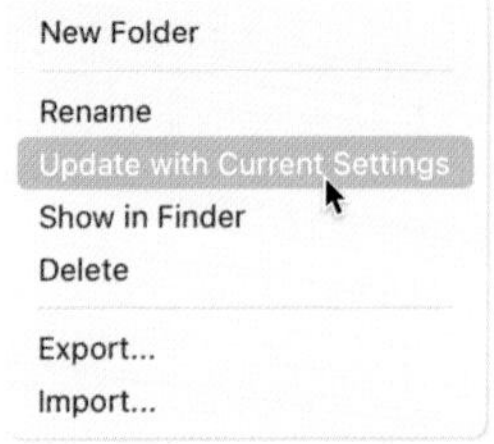

Triggering Photoshop Actions

The settings found in the **Post-Processing** section of the export options can be used to either open the resulting image in another app after it is exported, or apply an action that was created in Photoshop.

Actions in Photoshop are a subject that are beyond the scope of this book. Here, I will just show the general process for making an action available within Lightroom's export dialog box.

1) For an action to be available in Lightroom's export options, it must first be saved in a special file format by choosing **File>Automate>Create Droplet** in Photoshop.
2) To make the resulting file easy to find, click the **Choose** button, give the droplet a name, and choose your desktop as the location.

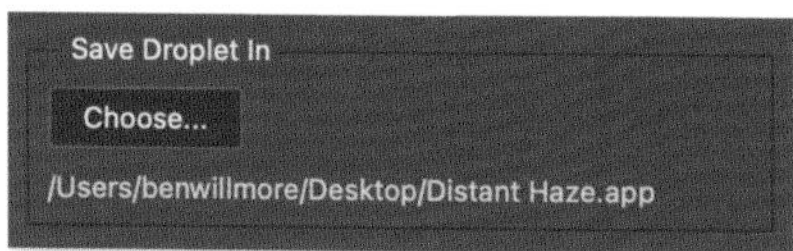

3) Choose the action you would like to trigger using the **Set** and **Action** pop-up menus.

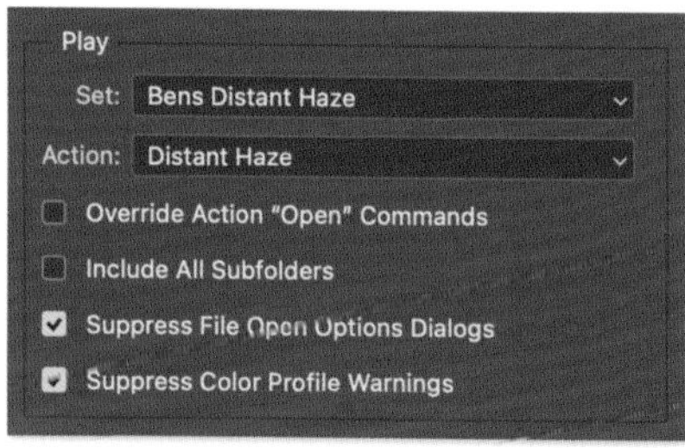

4) Set the **Destination** pop-up menu near the middle of the window to **Save and Close** and then click **OK** to save the action as a droplet file on your desktop.

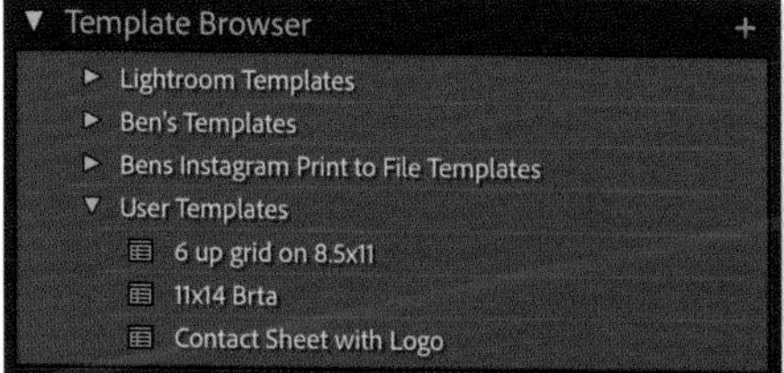

5) Back in Lightroom, choose **File>Export** and choose **Go to Export Actions Folder Now** from the **After Export** pop-up menu in the **Post-Processing** section near the bottom.
6) Drag the newly generated droplet file from your desktop to that special folder and then quit and relaunch Lightroom.
7) Choose the name of the droplet from the **After Export** pop-up menu. This will cause the action to be triggered when an image is exported using that setting.

Exporting from Smart Previews

Lightroom typically won't let you export an image if the hard drive containing the original file is not connected. Images that have Smart Previews are an exception—Lightroom will assume that the original image is 2,560 pixels at its longest, uncropped dimension, and will permit exporting based on that preview.

Export via Print Module

The Print module of Lightroom allows you to export images as JPEG files of any size. You can also combine multiple images, add text, etc. To print to a file, select **JPEG file** from the **Print to** pop-up menu in the **Print Job** panel. Then use the **Custom File Dimensions** setting to enter the desired size.

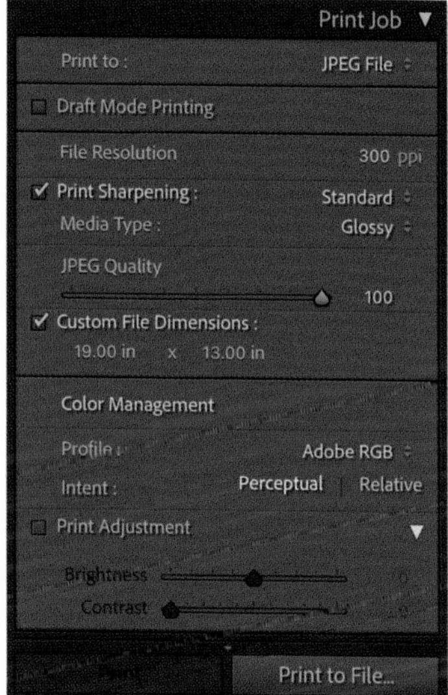

If you discover an arrangement of settings you'd like to use frequently, then click the plus symbol (**+**) in the **Template Browser** panel on the left side of the Print module to save active settings as a template for future use.

Chapter 3

Working in Photoshop

PHOTOSHOP IS A very different beast from its largely more intuitive companion Lightroom. This chapter is designed to get you up to speed with the essential concepts necessary for success. We'll start by optimizing your preference settings and establishing a versatile, non-destructive workflow. In doing so, you'll learn how to effectively combine retouching via layers, adjustment layers, and layer masks. We'll then dive into the most essential features, including selections, masks, retouching tools, layers, and adjustments. You'll also gain a fundamental understanding of Curves and Hue/Saturation, the dynamic duo that can be used to fulfill the majority of your adjustment needs.

Workflow Considerations

Before we actually start sending images from Lightroom to Photoshop, let's step back and make sure we have everything set up properly, and then develop a workflow that ensures we get the most out of Photoshop.

Optimize Photoshop Settings
Let's start by customizing Photoshop's settings to optimize the Lightroom workflow and to avoid common frustrations.

Photoshop Preferences
Below are the settings I suggest you change after choosing **Preferences** from the **Photoshop** menu (Mac) or **Edit** menu (PC). Assume the settings I don't mention are fine at their default settings.

General: Set the **HUD Color Picker** pop-up menu to **Hue Wheel**. This setting determines what will be shown when you click with the **Brush** tool while holding **Control-Option-Command** (Mac), or right-click while holding **Alt-Command** (PC). The **Hue Wheel** better aligns with the concepts that underly the two color adjustment choices we'll explore later in this chapter.

File Handling: Change the **Default File Location** to **On your computer** so any files you manually save don't end up on the cloud where Lightroom Classic can't find them. Turn on the **Use Adobe Camera Raw to Convert Documents from 32 bit to 16/8 bit** checkbox so you have familiar slider choices if you ever happen to process an HDR image with Photoshop. Turn off the **Ask Before Saving Layered TIFF Files** setting so you never accidentally exclude layers. Set **Maximize PSD and PSB File Compatibility** to **Always** so any manually saved files are compatible with Lightroom.

Performance: The **History States** setting determines how many undos will be available in Photoshop. I've increased mine from the default of **50** to **120**. Lower this setting if you start getting "scratch disks are full" errors, which is an indication that your hard drive is full and it doesn't have space to keep track of additional undos.

Image Processing: Set **Select Subject Processing** to **Cloud** since it produces higher-quality selections.

Camera Raw Preferences
Next stop is to choose **Camera Raw Preferences** from the **Photoshop** menu (Mac) or **Edit** menu (PC). Here are the settings I suggest you change:

General: Turn on the **Use Lightroom style zoom and pan** setting to make navigating images a bit more consistent between ACR and Lightroom.

Workflow: Set the **Space** and **Depth** settings so they match what is found in the **File Handling** section of Lightroom's preferences. That will ensure any raw files that you open directly into Photoshop will end up with the same settings as files opened from Lightroom. These are the same settings that you'll see as a line of text at the bottom of the Camera Raw window.

Avoid Color Issues
In later chapters, we may end up using the RGB numbers that appear in the Info panel. Let's set up the panel with the best settings so we'll be ready to use it if the need arises. Start by choosing **Window>Info** to make the panel visible. Choose **Panel Options** from the menu in the top-right corner of the panel and make sure that **Document Profile** is the only checkbox turned on.

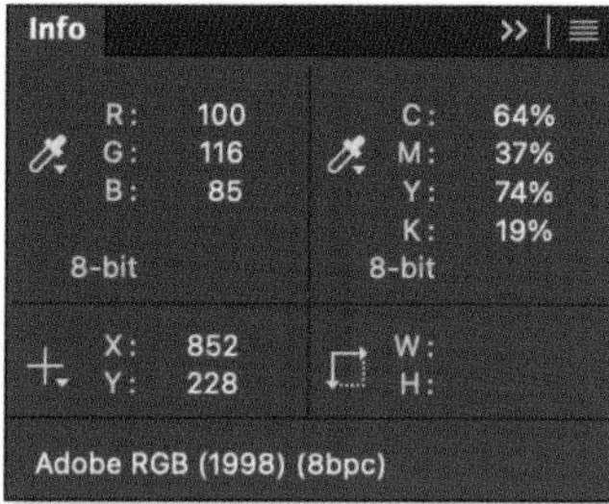

Choosing Panel Options from the menu in the upper right and turning on Document Profile will cause the color profile of the active document to be displayed at the bottom of the Info panel.

This will cause the color space of the active document to appear at the bottom of the Info panel. This is needed because the RGB numbers that appear in the panel are intended to provide a precise way of describing the colors within an image, but that is only true if they are used within a document that uses the same color space (sRGB, Adobe RGB, or ProPhoto RGB).

If you ever manually save an image via the **File>Save As** command or the choices found under **File>Export**, ALWAYS make sure that the **Embed Color Profile** option is turned on. Otherwise, the resulting image may not be displayed properly.

Section I: Fundamental Concepts

sRGB	Adobe	ProPhoto
R: 157	R: 157	R: 157
G: 112	G: 112	G: 112
B: 90	B: 90	B: 90
Adobe	**sRGB**	**ProPhoto**
R: 145	R: 145	R: 145
G: 112	G: 112	G: 112
B: 92	B: 92	B: 92
ProPhoto	**Adobe**	**sRGB**
R: 117	R: 117	R: 117
G: 98	G: 98	G: 98
B: 76	B: 76	B: 76

Left: Different RGB mixes are needed to produce visually matching colors in different color spaces.

Middle and Right: *The same RGB numbers produce different colors when used in different color spaces.*

Load Included Actions

I have created some Photoshop actions that we'll end up using in later chapters of this book. Now is a good time to get them loaded so you're set up for the later portions of this book. You can download the actions at: **www.craftingthelandscape.com/actions**

After downloading the file, you'll need to double-click on the resulting .zip file to extract its contents. You can then load the actions by choosing **Window>Actions** and then choosing **Load Actions** from the hamburger menu in the upper right corner of the Actions panel.

Working Non-Destructively

If you would like to get the most out of Photoshop, I'd suggest you adopt a non-destructive workflow. That means you will work in such a way that you avoid making changes that could not be reversed at some point in the future.

For me, the first step in working this way starts just before I tell Lightroom to edit the image in Photoshop. That's when I head to the **Crop** tool and choose the **Reset** option. I always work on the full-frame image in Photoshop so that any cropping is not permanently applied to the resulting layered file. I'll then re-crop the image after returning to Lightroom. This ensures the cropping remains an easily undoable setting that is attached to the layered version of the file.

Non-Destructive Layers

I've found that the most effective way to build an image in Photoshop is to adopt a consistent system that defines the way layers are used.

This starts with the original image being contained on the bottommost layer, preserved in the same state as it was when delivered from Lightroom. By default, this bottom layer generally starts out as a special layer called the "Background" and I never change this layer in any way. All of the changes I make are applied on layers that are stacked on top of the Background and can therefore be hidden or thrown away in order to return the image to an earlier state.

The layer that is placed directly above the bottommost layer is always used for general retouching. This occasionally ends up being multiple layers if a lot of retouching is needed, or if there are some areas I am unsure of and might want to change in the future.

> **Tip:** *You can lock the position of your retouching layer relative to the Background in order to prevent it from being repositioned and misaligned with the contents of the underlying layer. To do so, click on the Background layer to make it active, **Shift**-click on the retouching layer to make it active as well, and then click the chain icon that is found at the bottom of the Layers panel.*

Above the retouching layer, a series of adjustment layers are used to optimize the image. By keeping the retouching below the adjustments, I'm able to perform additional retouching and make changes to the adjustment layers without these two types of layers adversely affecting each other. If I were to perform retouching on a layer that is above an adjustment and later choose to discard the adjustment, the retouching would no longer match the underlying image.

When I believe I'm completely done retouching any undesirable elements out of a scene and I'm also done adjusting the image, then I'll occasionally add an additional retouching layer on top of the layer stack. This final layer is used to retouch out any artifacts that were produced by the changes I had made in the underlying layers. If any changes are later made to the underlying layers, this top layer will no longer match the rest of the image and will need to be discarded. That is why this final retouching is applied at the very end of the Photoshop workflow.

Selections and Masks

We'll need to frequently isolate areas using a selection or mask in order to limit where an adjustment is applied. Most selection needs fall into one of the following categories.

Easily Identifiable Regions and Objects

When the area you need to isolate is defined by a visually obvious boundary, then the most effective tool will usually be the **Object Selection** tool.

Object Selection Tool

This tool uses artificial intelligence to help isolate recognizable areas within an image.

When the **Object Selection** tool is active, the **Object Finder** checkbox appears in the Options Bar above the image window. Turn this setting on and the arrow icon to the right of the checkbox will start rotating as it attempts to identify the most prominent objects within the image. When it stops rotating, click the preview icon or hold **N** to see an overlay of the areas that were identified. Click on one of these regions to create a selection of that area.

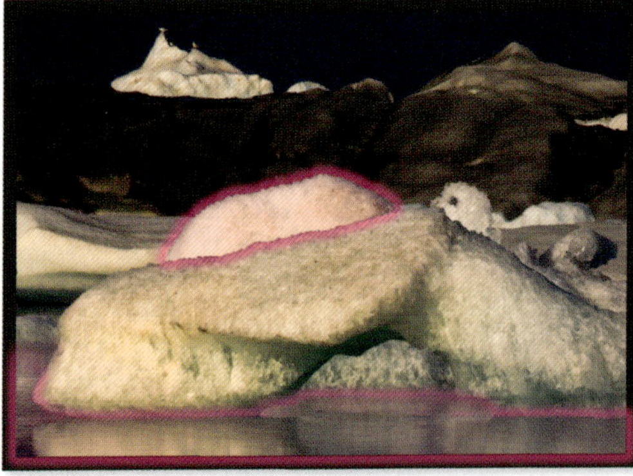

The two pink outlines represent the only areas the Object Finder was able to identify in this image.

If the area you need to select is not shown in the overlay, then click and drag within the image to designate the general boundary of the area you desire. This forces the tool to analyze that specific region and then produce a selection that clings to any well-defined edges that loosely match the area. This works best when the **Mode** pop-up menu is set to **Lasso,** as you will otherwise be limited to drawing a rectangle.

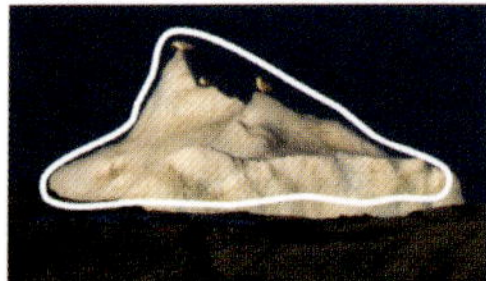
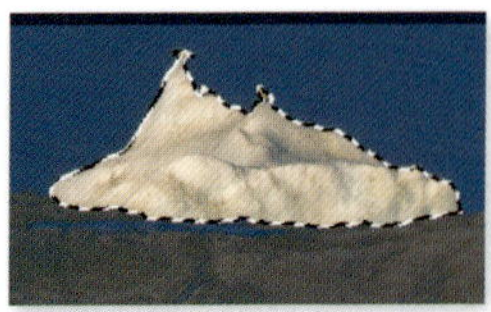

If the results are generally useful, but require some refinement, then hold **Shift** to add to or **Option** (Mac) or **Alt** (PC) to remove from the selection and simply draw around the area that demands a change.

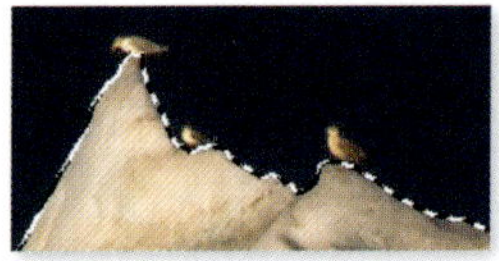
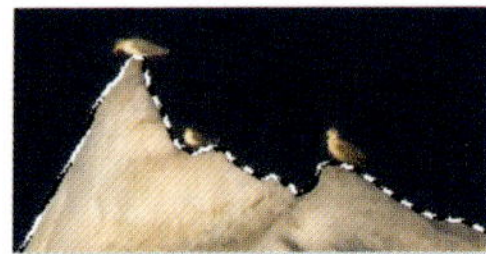

Quick Selection Tool

The **Quick Selection** tool is occasionally useful as an alternative to, or supplement to, the **Object Selection** tool. It offers a brush that can be used to paint over the area you'd like to select, and the tool will interactively produce a selection that expands until it finds an obvious boundary to the area that was painted across.

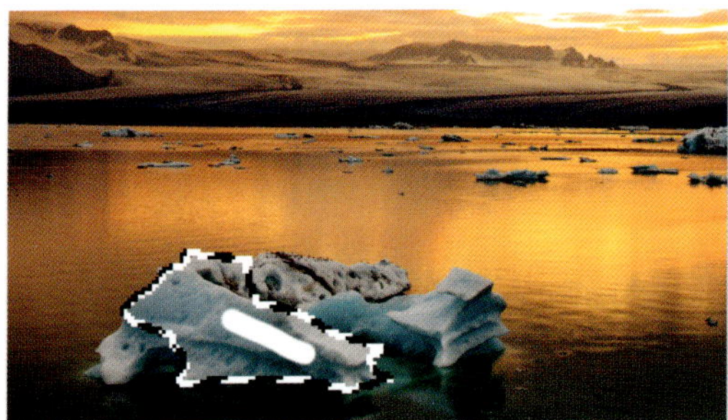

White in the image above represents the area painted across with the Quick Selection tool to produce the selection shown.

If it selects too wide of an area, then hold **Option** (Mac) or **Alt** (PC) and make a second pass, painting over the areas you'd like to remove from the selection.

Turning on the **Enhance Edge** checkbox in the Options Bar that spans the top of your screen will lower the speed at which the selection is produced, but will deliver a higher-quality result.

Section I: Fundamental Concepts

Specific Brightness Ranges

When you can describe the area you want to isolate with words such as highlights, midtones, and shadows, then **Color Range** can be used.

Color Range for Tonal Selections

To isolate a specific brightness range, choose **Select>Color Range**, start with the **Fuzziness** set to **0%**, and choose **Highlights** to select areas that include white, **Shadows** for areas that include black, or **Midtones** for areas that are not at the extreme ends of the brightness range.

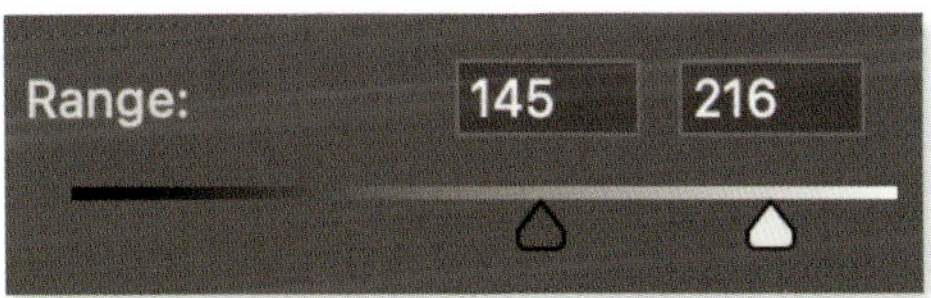

Select menu choices:

Highlights: *For areas between white and the Range slider position.*

Midtones: *For areas between the two Range sliders. The Fuzziness slider will be ineffective if either of the Range sliders touches white or black.*

Shadows: *For areas between black and the Range slider position.*

Adjust the **Range** setting to specify the brightness range you would like isolated. When using the **Highlights** or **Shadows** settings, you'll find a single slider, which indicates how far the brightness range should extend from black or white. When using the **Midtones** setting, you'll find two sliders where the brightness range between them will be selected.

Two Range sliders will appear when the Select pop-up menu is set to Midtones.

Once you have isolated the general brightness range desired, increasing the **Fuzziness** slider will cause the edge to have a gradual transition into the surrounding image.

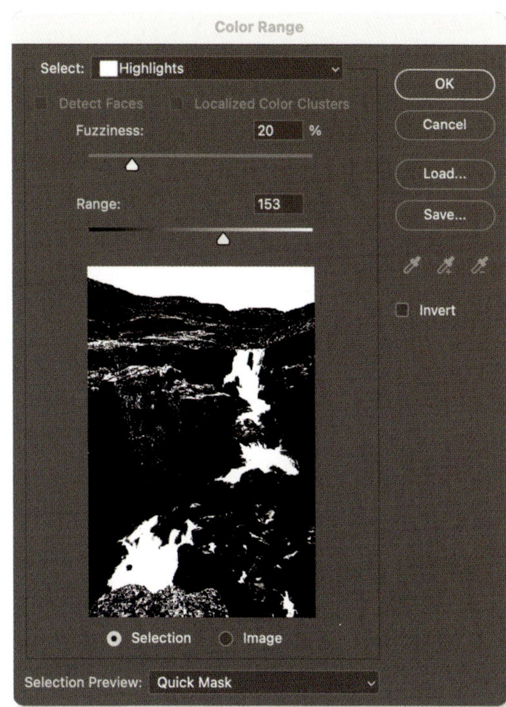

The Selection Preview pop-up menu determines which type of overlay will represent a selection within the active image.

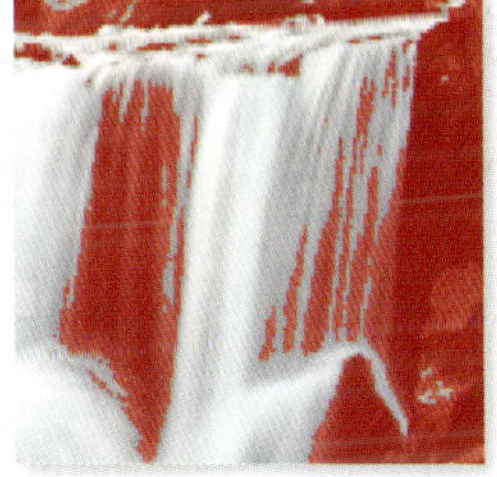

Fuzziness: 0%

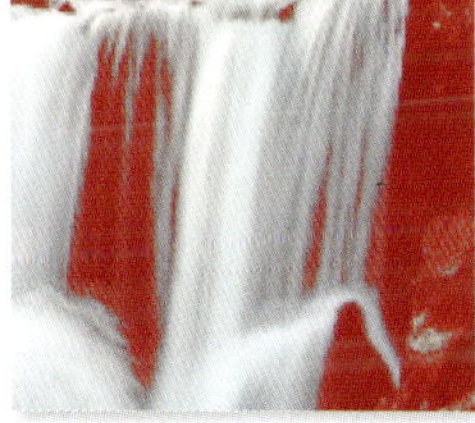

Fuzziness: 32%

With default settings, the only preview you will see is a tiny black-and-white mask preview at the bottom of the **Color Range** window. Experiment with the choices available in the **Selection Preview** pop-up menu to enable the selection to preview within the main image window.

Luminosity Masks

The luminosity mask actions that are available on this book's companion site can also be used to isolate the highlight, shadow, and midtone regions within an image. The actions produce nice soft-edged masks that can be used to limit which areas are affected by adjustments.

Specific Colors

When you're looking to make an adjustment that is limited to a particular color, you can either use one of the techniques below or make the adjustment using **Hue & Saturation**, as it offers settings that limit the range of colors affected.

Color Range for Color Selections

Start by choosing **Select>Color Range**, set **Fuzziness** to **0%**, and set the **Select** pop-up menu to **Sampled Colors**. This will cause three eyedropper icons to become available on the right side of the dialog box. You'll use a combination of those eyedroppers and the **Fuzziness** slider to produce a selection.

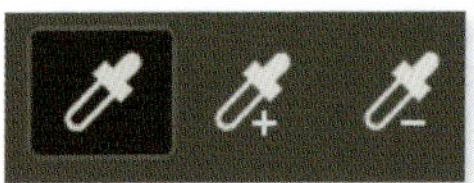

Left: *Eyedropper defines the core color being isolated.*
Middle: *Adds to color range.*
Right: *Subtracts from range.*

The eyedropper on the far left will be active by default and is used to define the basic color you desire. Click within your image on the color you'd like to select and it will likely only select a tiny area. To expand what is being isolated, hold **Shift**, which will temporarily make the middle eyedropper tool active, and click on additional areas of the color you desire that were not included in the original selection. If an undesirable color becomes selected as a result of a click, then type **Command-Z** (Mac) or **Ctrl-Z** (PC) to undo your last click. If the undesirable color was not noticed immediately, then hold **Option** (Mac) or **Alt** (PC) to access the rightmost eyedropper and click on the color you would like to exclude from the selection.

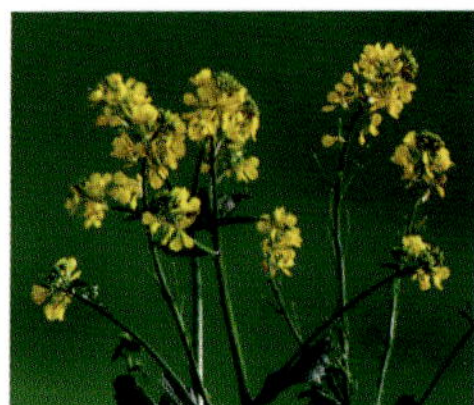 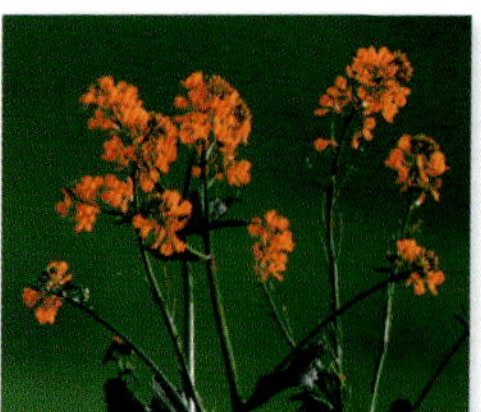

Original image.   *Inverted Quick Mask preview of resulting selection.*

The **Localized Color Clusters** option will limit the area isolated to the region close to where you clicked with the eyedropper icons, and will add a **Range** setting to determine just how far from the clicked areas it should isolate the color.

Once you have the general color isolated, adjust the **Fuzziness** setting to allow the selection to expand and produce a gradual transition into the surrounding colors.

Select>Grow and Select>Similar

Another approach to selecting a specific color is to make a crude selection using the **Lasso** tool that includes only the colors you desire. You can then choose **Select>Grow** to expand the boundary of the selection to include similar colors from the immediate surroundings. **Select>Similar** will extend a selection in a similar fashion, but it will include similar colors found anywhere within the image.

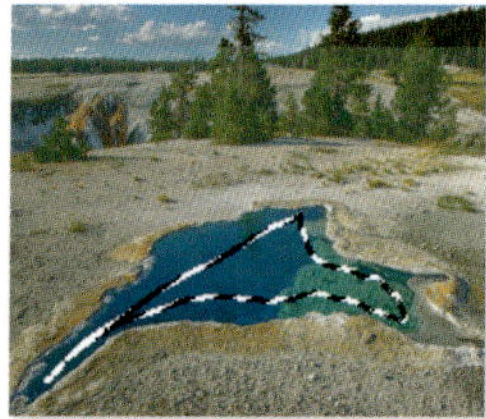 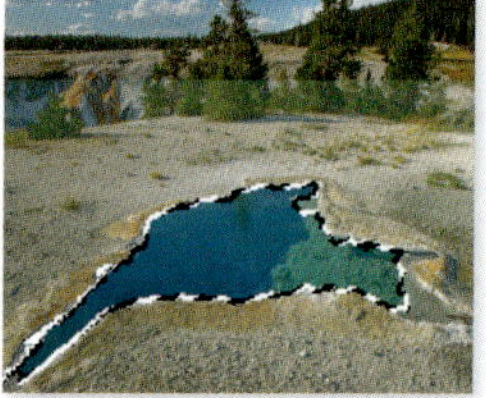

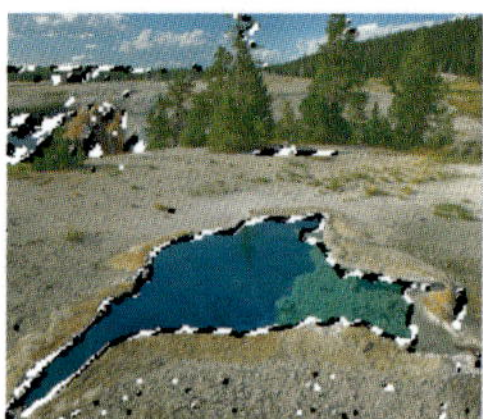

Upper Left: *A crude selection of the desired colors made with the Lasso tool.*

Upper Right: *Result of choosing Select>Grow.*

Lower Left: *Result of choosing Select>Similar.*

Both of these functions use the **Tolerance** setting associated with the **Magic Wand** tool to determine how much they will be allowed to deviate from the precise colors contained in the original selection.

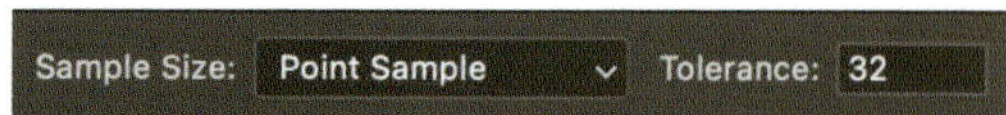

The Tolerance setting found in the Options Bar while the Magic Wand tool is active determines how much the Grow and Similar functions will deviate from the selected colors.

Free-Form Areas

When the area you want to isolate is not easy to describe, but you could paint to draw out what you desire, then **Quick Mask Mode** will usually be the best choice.

Quick Mask Mode

Start with no selection active, then type **Q** to enable **Quick Mask Mode**, type **D** to reset your foreground and background colors to black/white, and then type **B** to activate the **Brush** tool. For bonus points, type **0** (zero) and then **Shift-0** to also make sure the **Opacity** and **Flow** settings for the **Brush** tool are both set to **100%**.

You are now set up to paint to define the area you would like to isolate. This will cause a red overlay to appear over the image. If you accidentally paint too far into an area, type **X** to swap the foreground and background colors, and then paint to remove parts of the overlay. You can also lower the **Opacity** of your brush to cause an area to become partially selected.

Once you've successfully defined the area you wanted to isolate, look at the resulting overlay and know that the area covered in color will end up being what is not selected. If the overlay is showing up in the exact opposite area from what you desired (which is not uncommon), then choose **Image>Adjustments>Invert** before typing **Q** to exit **Quick Mask Mode**.

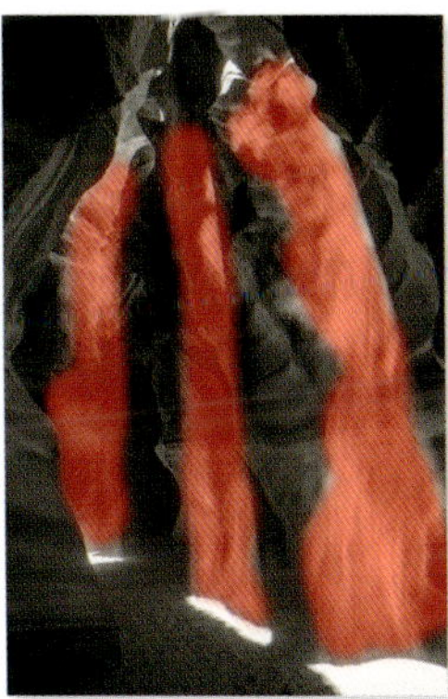
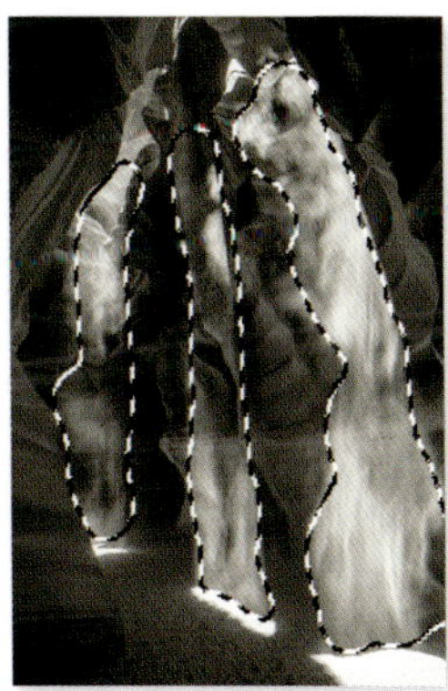

Painting with black in Quick Mask Mode produces a red overlay that represents what will be masked (meaning not selected).

Selection produced after inverting the mask to reverse where red appears and then turning off Quick Mask Mode.

I use **Quick Mask Mode** as a general preview and refinement tool for most selections I create.

I never bring the **Hardness** setting of any brush used to produce a selection above **80%**. Doing so usually produces a non-smooth edge that is undesirable.

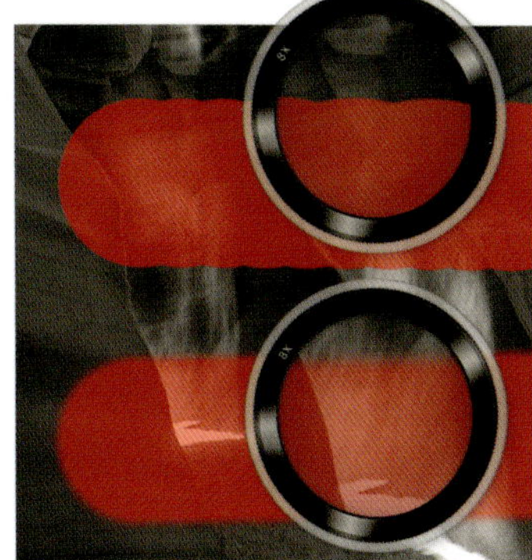

Top: 100% Hardness exposes the fact that brush-strokes are made from a series of overlapping circles.

Bottom: Reducing Hardness to 80% or below produces a semi-soft edge that disguises the circles.

If you hold **Shift** when clicking with any brush, Photoshop will produce a straight line between the last point you clicked and the current position of your brush. This can be helpful when working up against a crisp edge, such as a horizon line.

The **Hardness** setting determines what percentage of the brush will be solid before it begins to fade out. Larger brushes produce softer edges with low **Hardness** settings, so use a huge brush if you want a very soft edge.

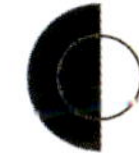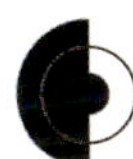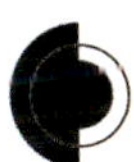

Hardness settings from left to right: 0%, 25%, 50%, 75%, 100%. The left side of each indicates how far changes will affect the image. The right side shows area receiving 100% of paint being applied. Ring indicates size of the brush on-screen.

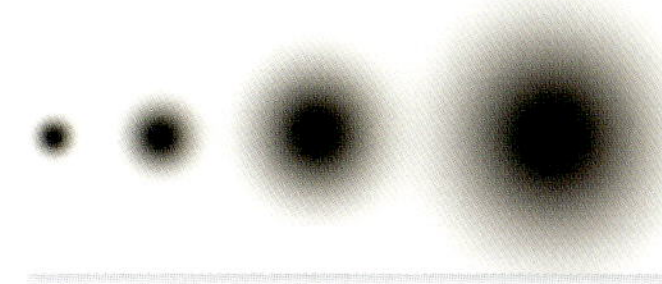

0% Hardness at various brush sizes. Larger brushes produce softer edges.

Filters can also be used when in **Quick Mask Mode**. I frequently use **Gaussian Blur** to soften my results.

Furry, Fuzzy, or Hairy Edges

If you're lucky and the furry critter you're attempting to isolate is large enough, then choosing **Select>Subject** might deliver an acceptable selection. When that's not the case, you'll need to do a bit more work.

In the case below, I started by selecting our fuzzy friend using the **Object Selection** tool, and then typed **Q** to view the results in **Quick Mask Mode**.

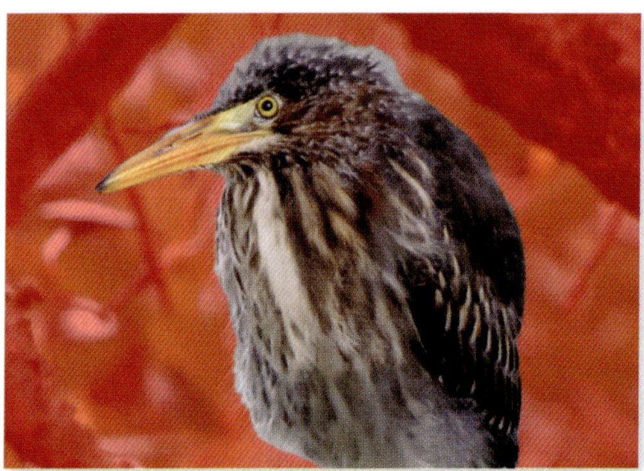

Select & Mask

Most selection tools don't seem to know how to deal with fuzzy-edged objects. When you need such a selection, choose **Select>Select & Mask** and set it up by typing **V**, **J**, **R** to change the **View** to **Overlay**, turn on the **Show Edge** checkbox, and make the **Refine Edge Brush** tool active.

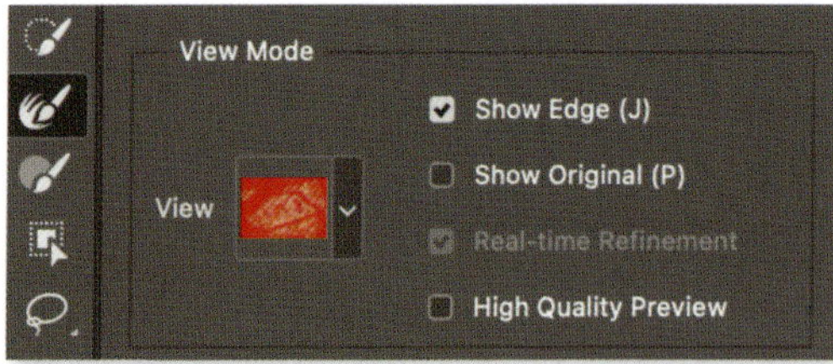

Next, set the **Radius** to **1px** to reveal a gap that will divide the image into two zones. The zone enclosed by that gap will be retained in the resulting selection (which I wish was displayed as green for clarity), while the zone outside the gap will be excluded.

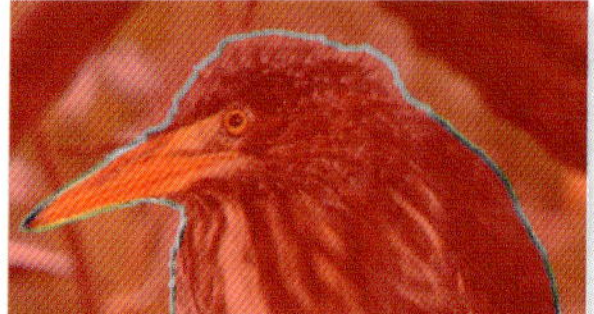

Then use the **Refine Edge Brush** tool to expand that gap and remove the outer overlay from areas that contain what should be selected (no matter how small

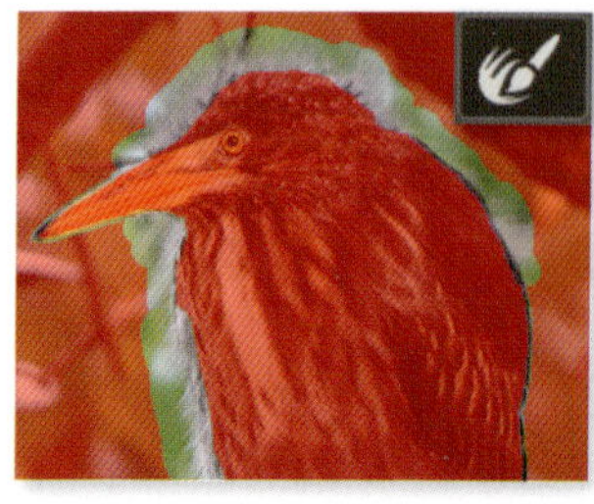

or faint). Make a second pass to remove the inner overlay from areas that contain any hint of what should be excluded from the selection. You can also hold **Option** (Mac) or **Alt** (PC) to extend either overlay and narrow the gap. The **Refine Hair** button attempts to define the gap for you, but does not always produce acceptable results.

Once the inner overlay contains only what should be kept and the outer overlay contains only what should be excluded, then turn off the **Show Edge** checkbox to reveal the results of your efforts. You can further refine the results in this view even though the gap is not visible.

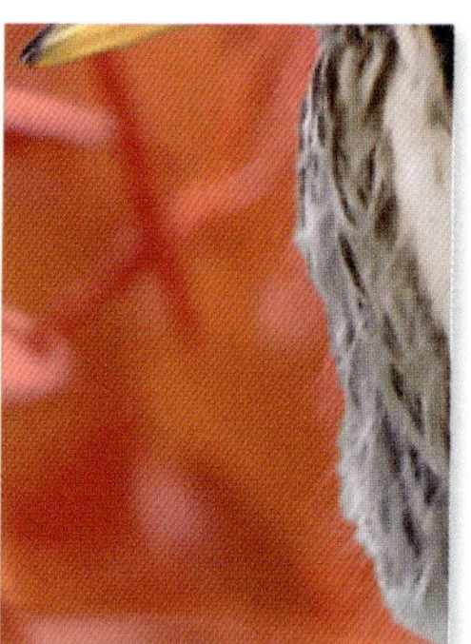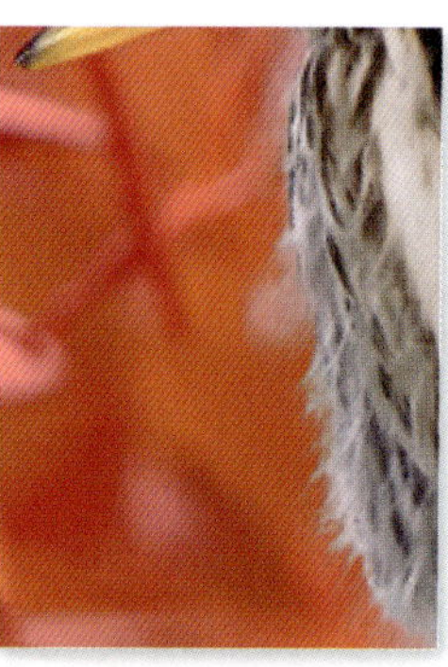

Mask created using the Object Selection tool.

Result of refining mask edge using Select>Select & Mask.

Note: *The edges of a furry object can be adjusted to make them better blend in with backgrounds that are radically different than the original by turning on the **Decontaminate Colors** checkbox and adjusting its **Amount** slider.*

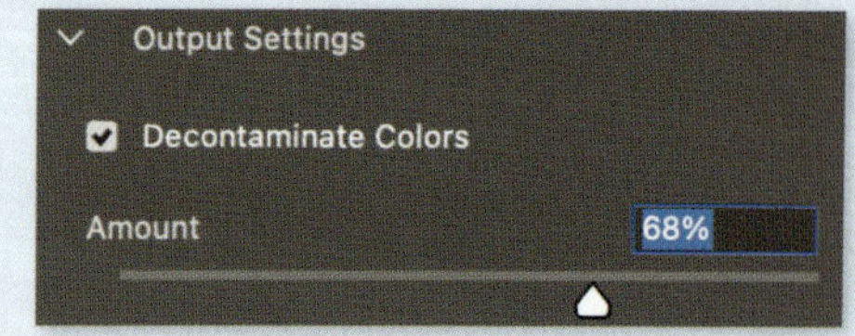

Soft-Edged Objects

The selection tools generally produce hard-edged selections and will usually need to be supplemented with one or more of the following options.

Global Refinements in Select & Mask

After creating an initial selection using one of the selection tools, choose **Select>Select & Mask** and adjust the **Feather** and **Shift Edge** sliders until the edge more closely matches the image.

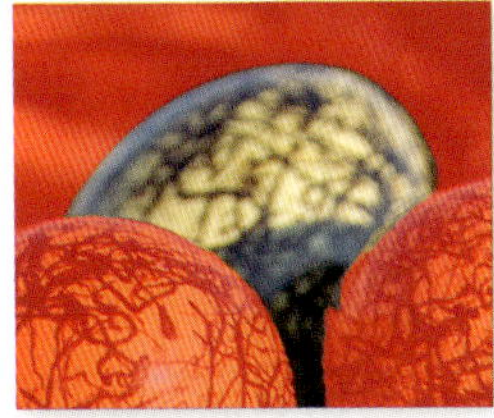

Selection produced by the Object Selection tool.

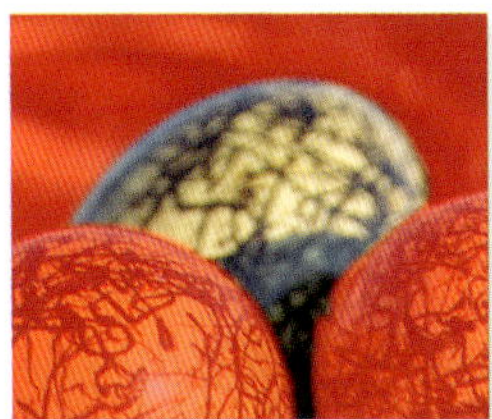

Result of adjusting the Feather and Shift Edge settings.

Soft Brushes in Quick Mask Mode

Type **Q** to enable **Quick Mask Mode** and adjust the **Hardness** setting of the **Brush** tool in an attempt to match the softness of the area to be selected. Then paint with black over an area. Paint beyond the boundary desired when the edge quality does not match the **Hardness** setting being used **A**. Switch to white and use a different **Hardness** setting to remove areas in the mask that have a different edge quality **B**. Use the **Blur** tool to apply additional blurring where needed **C**.

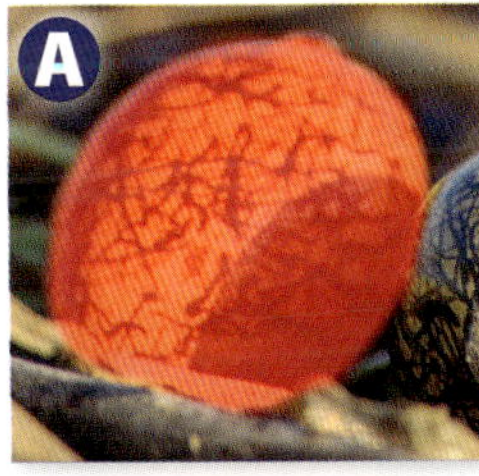

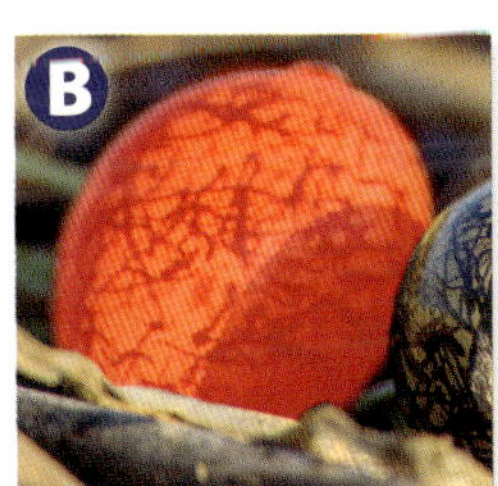

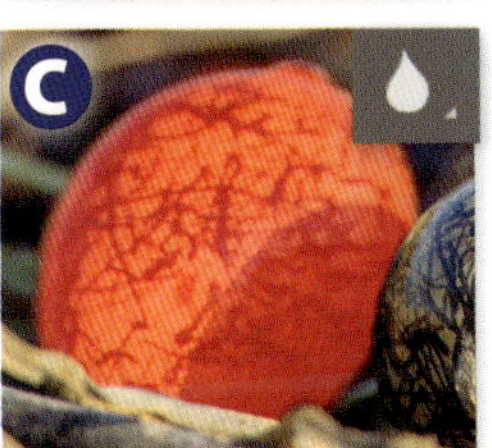

Upper Left: *Black paint applied using 50% Hardness.*

Upper Right: *White paint applied at 80% Hardness.*

Left: *Blur tool applied to soften edges.*

Edge Detection in Select & Mask

When an area visually separates from its surroundings and features a soft edge in some areas and crisper edge in others, **Select>Select & Mask** might be able to deliver an acceptable result.

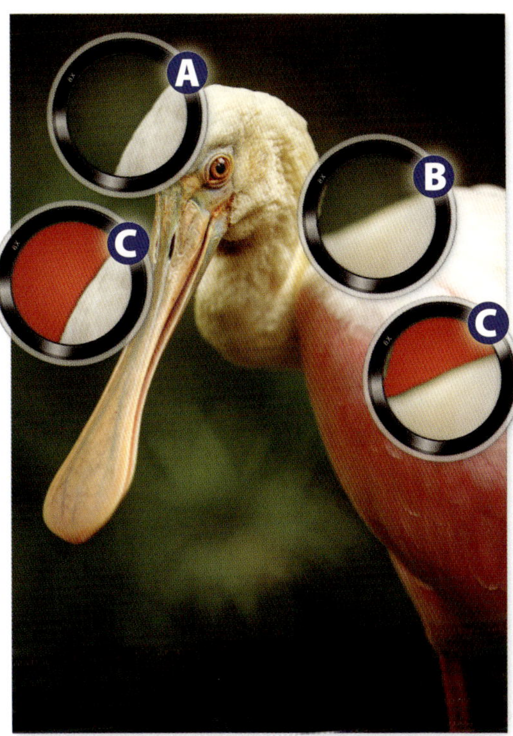

*Crisp edges **A** and soft edges **B** along with Quick Mask Mode view of selection produced by the Object Selection tool **C**.*

Set the **View** to **Overlay** and the **Opacity** to a high setting. Then adjust the **Radius** until you find a setting that causes the overlay to match the edge quality of the area.

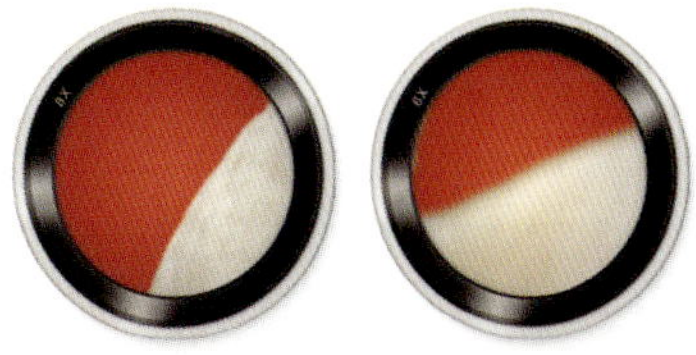

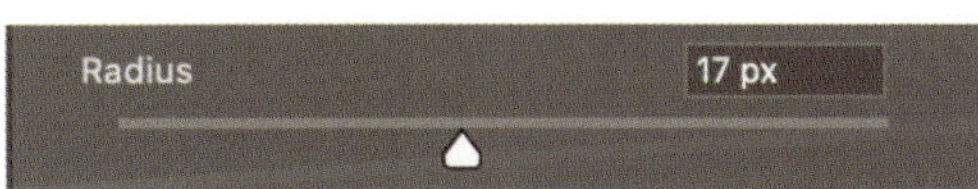

The same magnified areas as seen after increasing the Radius setting to get the selection to better match the multifaceted edge quality of the image.

Specific Depth in Scene

Photoshop can use artificial intelligence to produce a mask based on the depth at which objects are positioned relative to the camera.

Depth Mask

To create a depth mask, choose **Filter>Neural Filters**, activate the **Depth Blur** filter (click the cloud icon to download the filter if it is disabled), turn on the **Output depth map only** checkbox, and then click **OK**. You should end up with a mask where distant areas are white and near areas are dark. The result can be adjusted to isolate a specific depth within the scene.

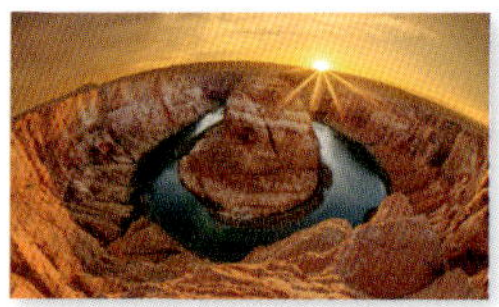

Source for depth mask.   *Resulting depth mask.*

Edge of Existing Selection or Mask

When a semi-soft selection is used to adjust an area, such as a group of trees, it's not unusual to discover what appears to be a slight glow or other problem area within the edge of the area being adjusted. That's when you can use the Edge Mask actions that are available on this book's companion site to isolate the soft fade-out region of a selection or mask.

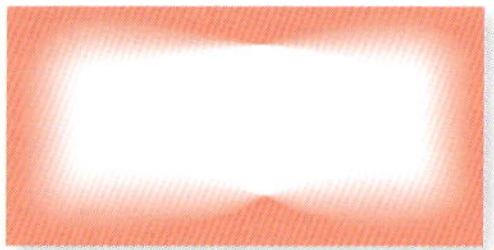
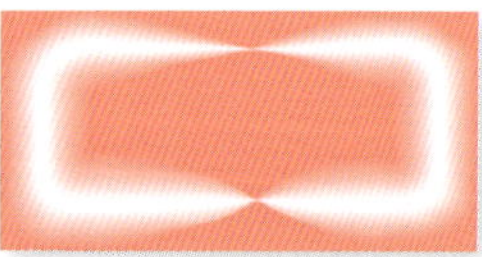

Source for depth mask.   *Resulting depth mask.*

To produce an edge mask, choose **Window>Actions**, click on the **CLP-Edge Mask from Active Selection** action if you are starting from a selection, or the **CLP-Edge Mask from Active Mask** action if a layer mask or Channel is active, and then click the play icon at the bottom of the panel.

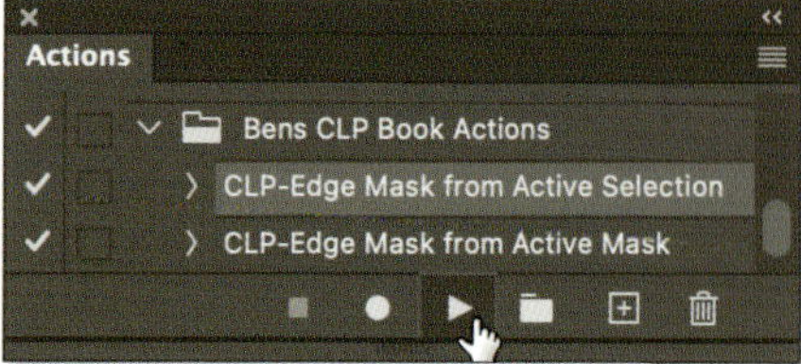

Hyper-Complex Shapes

Sometimes you have to pop the hood of an image and mess with the components it is made from behind the scenes to get an acceptable selection.

Channel-Based Masks

Choosing **Window>Channels** and clicking on the **RGB** (also known as composite), **Red**, **Green**, and **Blue** channels allows you to literally see what an image is constructed from behind the scenes. If the area you are attempting to isolate visually separates from its surroundings in one of those channels, then drag it to the new channel icon to create a duplicate.

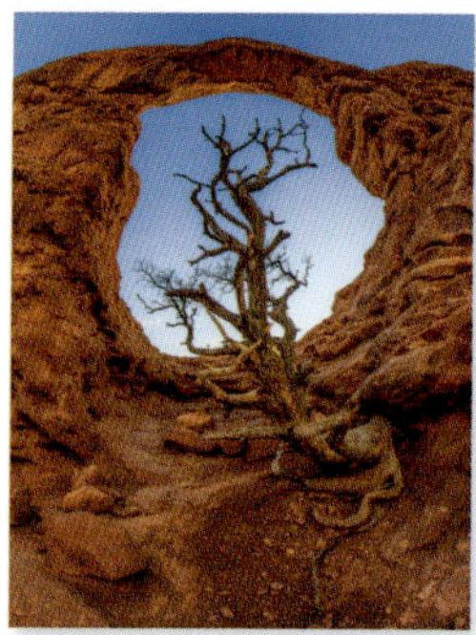

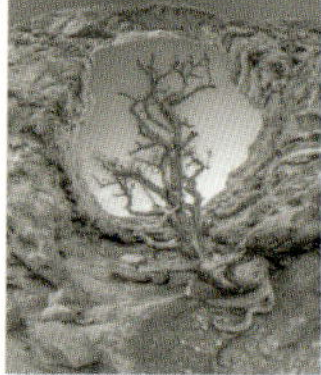
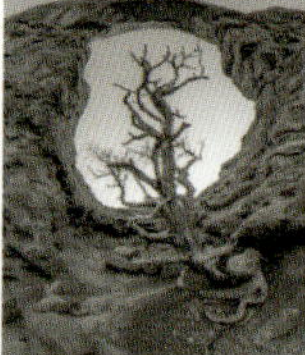
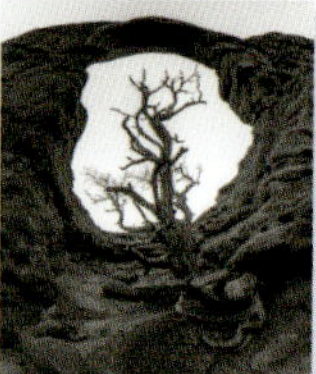

Red Channel   *Green Channel*   *Blue Channel*

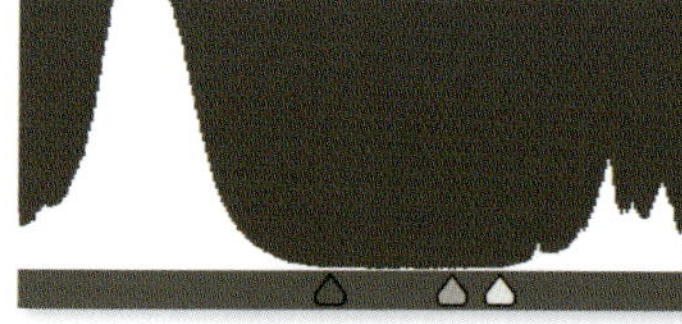

Levels adjustment used to adjust a copy of the blue channel to produce the mask shown below.

Next, choose **Image>Adjustments>Levels** and move the upper left and right sliders toward the middle until the area you wish to isolate becomes solid black or white and its surroundings become the exact opposite. Moving the middle slider will modify the transition between black and white.

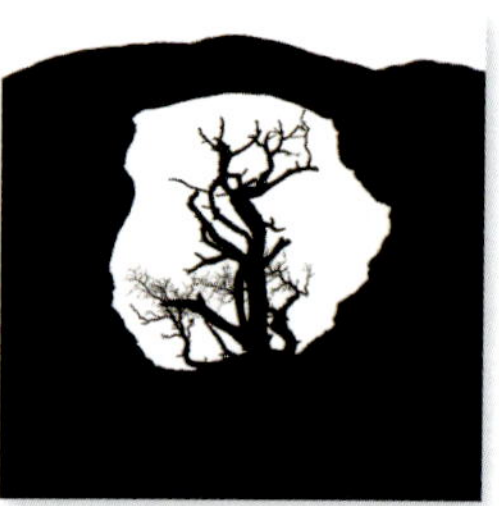

This type of mask usually requires a bit of clean-up afterward by painting with black or white to produce an artifact-free mask.

Section I: Fundamental Concepts

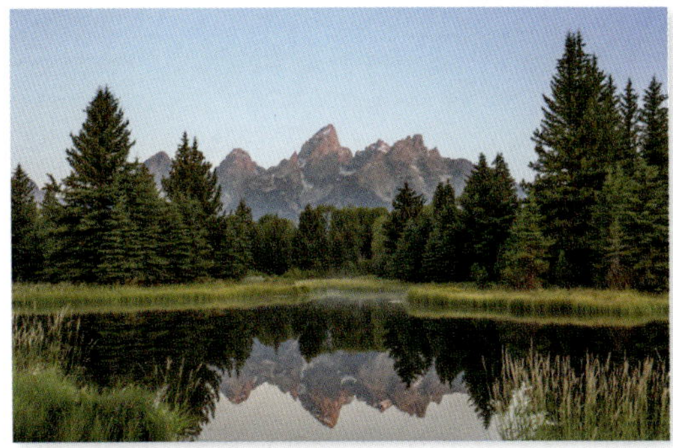

Combining Techniques

In the example above, I wanted to select the group of trees that spanned the horizontal center of the image. Here's how this was accomplished: With the **Object Selection** tool, I clicked on the sky, held **Shift**, clicked on the mountains, chose **Select>Inverse**, and then typed **Q** to turn on **Quick Mask Mode** to get an idea of what I had so far **A**.

Next, I chose the **Brush** tool and painted with white across the bottom of the photo and up to the base of the trees **B**.

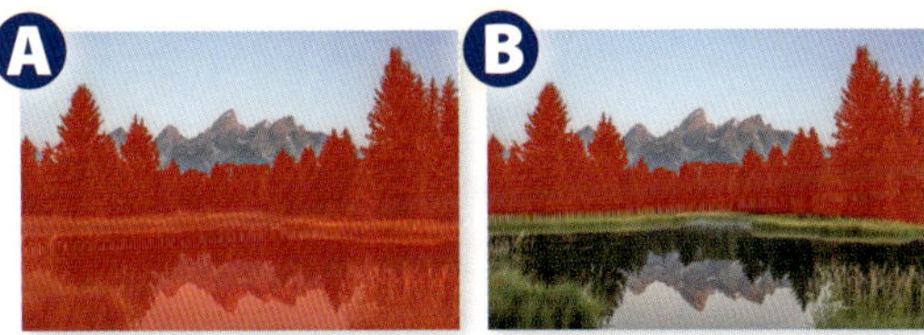

I then exited **Quick Mask Mode** by typing **Q** and saved the resulting selection into the Channels panel (as I'll describe in the next section), so I could inspect it more closely. This is when I noticed issues around the edge of the mountains and trees **C**.

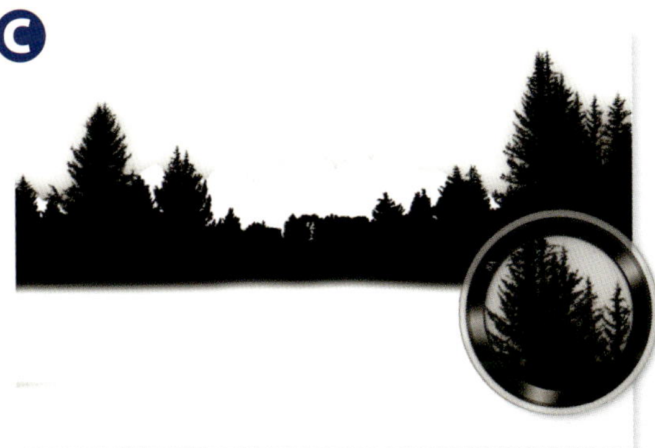

I inspected the individual red, green, and blue channels to see which one contained the most contrast between the trees and the sky, which looked to be the blue channel **D**. I duplicated that channel, chose **Image>Adjustments>Levels**, and moved the upper left and right sliders until the sky was white and most of the trees were black **E**.

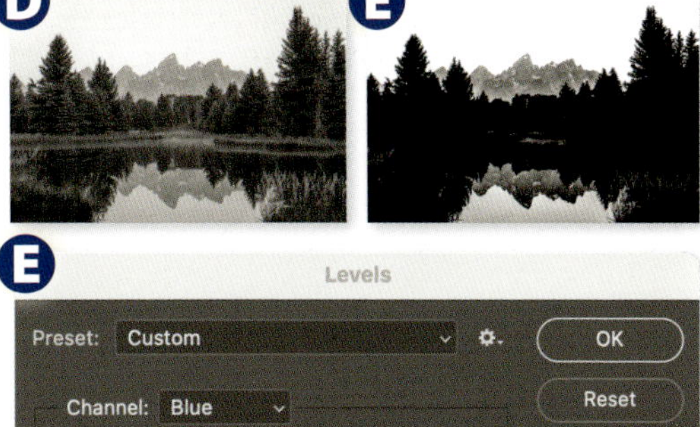

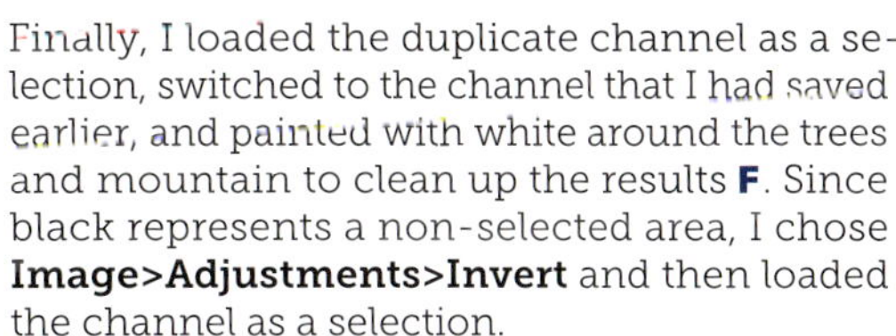

Finally, I loaded the duplicate channel as a selection, switched to the channel that I had saved earlier, and painted with white around the trees and mountain to clean up the results **F**. Since black represents a non-selected area, I chose **Image>Adjustments>Invert** and then loaded the channel as a selection.

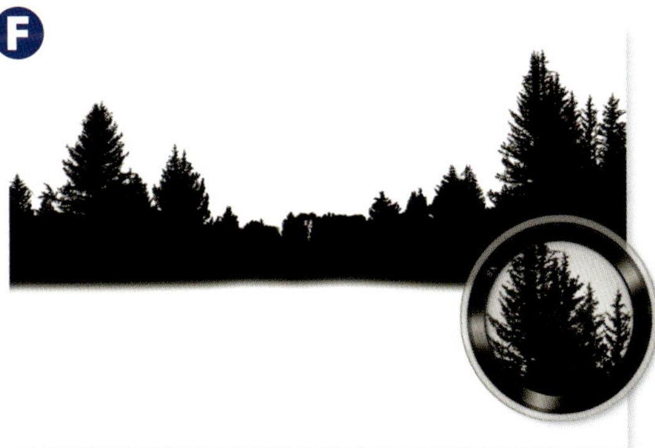

Loading and Saving Selections

Choosing **Select>Save Selection** will allow you to save the active selection for later retrieval.

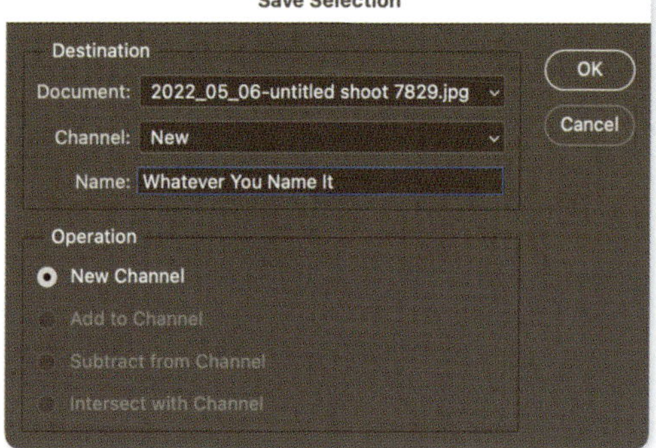

Saved selections appear in the Channels panel. You can retrieve a saved selection by doing any of the following:

1) Choose **Select>Load Selection**.
2) Drag any channel to the selection icon at the bottom of the Channels panel.
3) Hold **Command** (Mac) or **Ctrl** (PC) and click within the thumbnail-sized preview image for the channel within the Channels panel.

Refining Masks and Channels

If the contents of a channel requires refinement, then choose from the following options.

Paint in Overlay Mode: Masks often contain unwanted shades of gray that were produced by an automatic selection such as **Select>Sky**. Setting the **Brush** tool to **Overlay** mode and painting with white or black will prevent areas of solid white or black from being modified. This will allow you to concentrate on those pesky shades of gray. Painting with white will push the grays closer to white, while painting with black will darken shades of gray. Lower the **Opacity** setting on the **Brush** tool when more subtle changes are desired.

 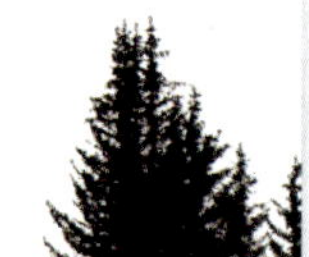 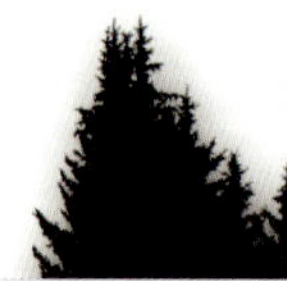

Original mask contents.   *Painting with white in Overlay.*   *Painting with black in Overlay.*

Paint in Lighten or Darken Mode: In a mask, white represents the area being selected, black represents what is not selected, and grays represent areas that are partially selected. Changing the blending mode of a brush will alter how it is able to blend with the existing contents of a mask. **Darken** mode limits a brush to being able to change only areas that are lighter than the shade of gray that is being applied. **Lighten** mode does the opposite by changing only areas that are darker than the shade being applied.

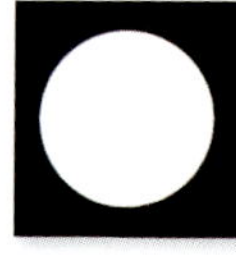  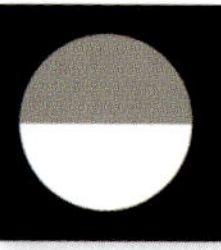 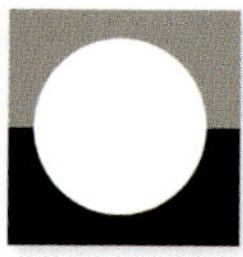

Contents of channel.   *Shade and area painted.*   *Result using Darken.*   *Result using Lighten.*

Combine Multiple Masks: Hold **Shift** to add to, or **Option** (Mac) or **Alt** (PC) to subtract from, the active selection when using any selection tool. This also works when **Command**-clicking (Mac) or **Ctrl**-clicking (PC) on any mask thumbnail image to load it as a selection.

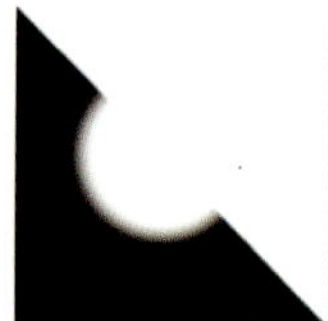  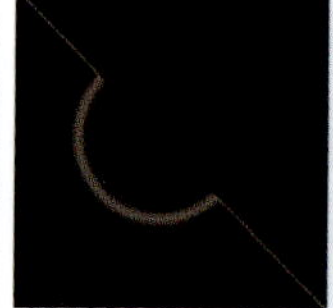

Original mask.   *Inverted mask.*   *Combined result.*

Combine with Apply Image: Combining two masks that share a common edge (such as an inverted copy) will produce edge residue. You can avoid the residue altogether by choosing **Image>Apply Image** while one of the masks is active, choosing the second mask from the **Channel** pop-up menu, and setting **Blending** to **Linear Burn** (use **Linear Dodge** to subtract).

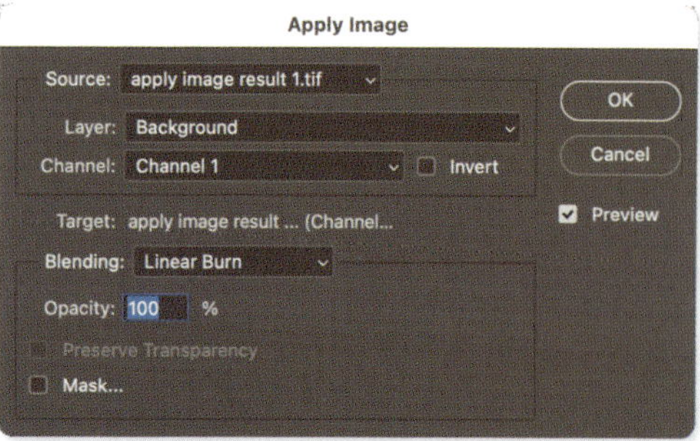

Photoshop Tips & Tricks

Alternative File Formats

After using **Edit in Photoshop** to send an image from Lightroom to Photoshop, feel free to use **File>Save As** in Photoshop and save into the same folder as the original image. If the resulting image does not show up in LR (it should), then right-click on the folder in Lightroom and choose **Synchronize folder**.

Paint with History Brush

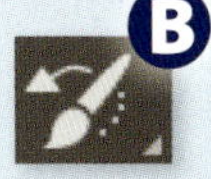

Sometimes a change you made to a layer mask (such as applying the **Gaussian Blur** filter) is useful in one area, but not another. When that's the case, choose **Window>History**, find the step that caused the undesirable change, and then click within the square that appears to the left of the history step directly above **A**. Finally, choose the **History Brush B** and paint over the area you'd like to revert to that previous stage.

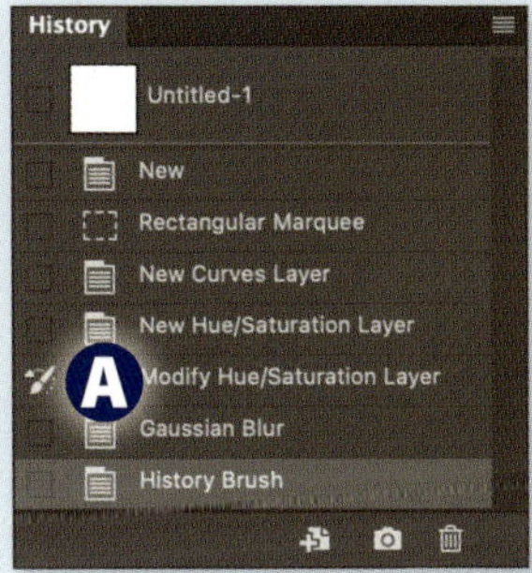

Reset Tool

If a tool consistantly produces unexpected results and you cannot figure out which setting is causing the issue, then try right-clicking on the tool's icon on the far left of the Options Bar that spans the top of your screen and choose **Reset Tool**, which will cause all the tool's settings to be reset to their default settings.

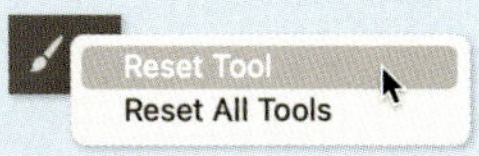

Transform Reference Point

When using the options found in the **Edit>Transform** menu, activating the checkbox on the left of the Options Bar displays a repositionable crosshair icon at the center of the layer being transformed. This crosshair serves as the pivot point for rotations. Holding **Option** (Mac) or **Alt** (PC) while scaling prevents the area under the crosshair from moving, ensuring precise alignment with underlying layers.

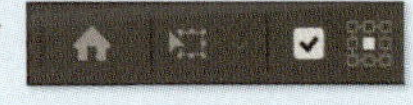

Fade after Painting

If you find a change to be too strong after painting on a mask or channel, choose **Edit>Fade Brush Tool** to adjust **Opacity** after painting (but before you do anything else).

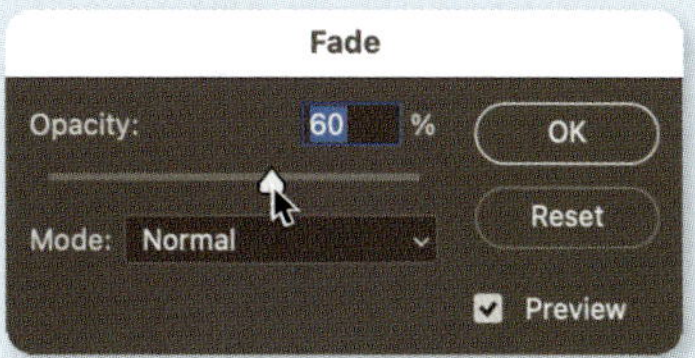

Spin Hue Bar

When applying a **Hue/Saturation** adjustment, you can hold the **Command** key (Mac) or **Ctrl** key (PC) and drag horizontally on the rainbow-filled bars to "spin the color wheel." That's useful if you ever move the color-isolation sliders and bump into the end of the color bars. They are just color wheels straightened out with matching colors on each end, which can be effectively rotated.

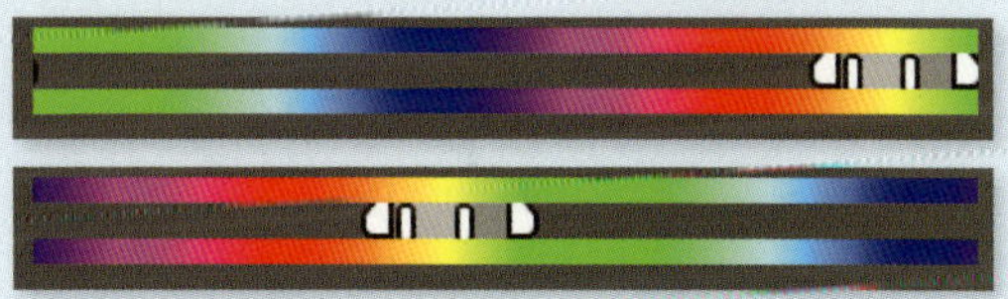

Adjust Brightness Before Color

Darkening an image will usually also cause colors to become more saturated. It is therefore advisable to adjust the overall brightness of an image before making precise saturation adjustments.

Access Eyedropper Tool While Painting

When using the **Brush** tool, hold **Option** (Mac) or **Alt** (PC) to temporarily switch to the **Eyedropper** tool. This allows you to click within the image to change the paint color.

Prevent Snapping

When using the **Move** tool or **Marquee** tool, hold **Control** (Mac or PC) to temporarily disable the snapping behavior that causes a layer or selection to precisely align with layer or document edges.

Adjustments

Your ability to transform a boring image into a brilliant one largely comes down to how well versed you are with Photoshop's adjustments.

Fundamentally Different than Lightroom

Photoshop requires a mindset adjustment for anyone who is used to Lightroom.

Lightroom's Approach

If you head to Lightroom, choose an image **A**, and crank up the **Exposure** slider to its limit of **+5**, you will cause any image to become so bright that most areas will become solid white **B**. But you can then counteract much of that change by applying a masked adjustment of **Exposure -4 C**. The result would look as if **Exposure +1** was being applied to the original contents of the raw file. As far as Lightroom is concerned, five minus four equals one.

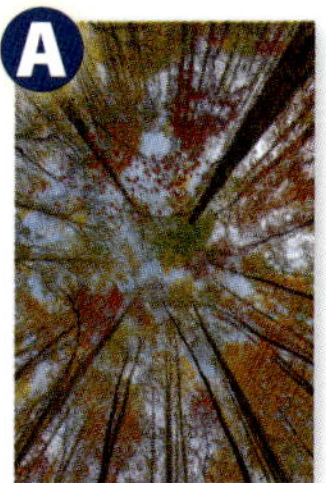 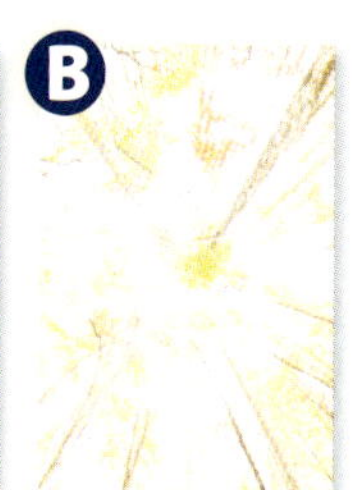 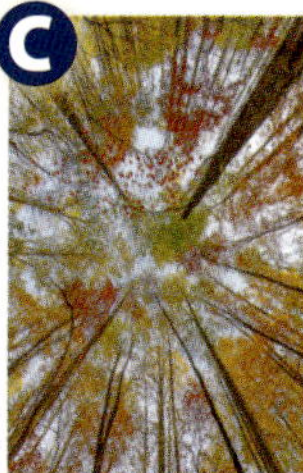

Photoshop's Approach

Open the same image in Photoshop **D** and attempt a similar initial change via an **Exposure** adjustment layer **E**, and then stack an additional **Exposure** adjustment layer on top of that, applying the same amount of a negative setting, and you'll end up with a completely different result **F**. That's because each adjustment you make in Photoshop acts on the results produced by previous adjustments. So, those white areas could only be darkened by the second adjustment.

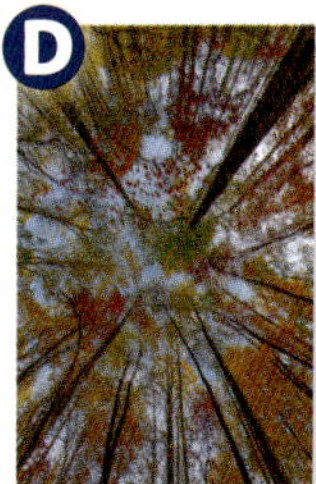 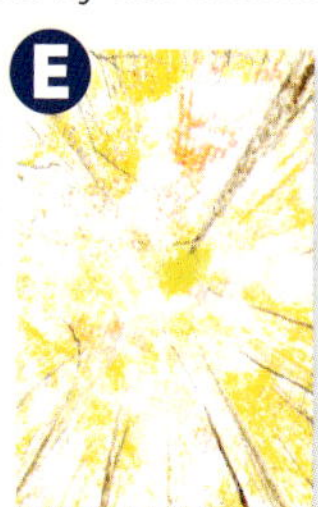 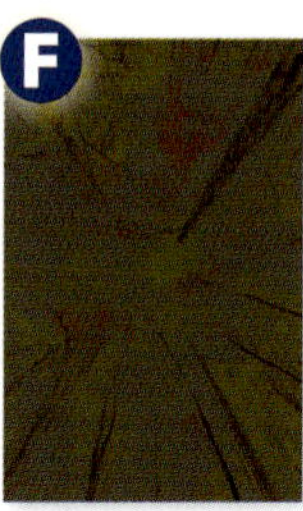

Adjustment Methods

There are four methods for applying adjustments in Photoshop.

Direct Adjustments

The **Image>Adjustments** menu contains choices that directly modify content. They are useful when editing layer masks, Channels, and Quick Mask Mode, but are less than ideal for layers.

Adjustment Layers

The choices found in the **Layer>New Adjustment Layer** menu produce a layer whose settings can be altered at any time. They are the most flexible method for applying adjustments.

Just as sunglasses alter your view of the world you see through them, adjustment layers alter your view of the layers that underlie them as if you were viewing the layer stack from above looking down.

The adjustments available are limited to those that can be updated interactively as settings are changed or the underlying layers are modified.

> **Tip:** *The blending mode option at the top of the Layers panel determines how the active layer will affect the underlying image. Choosing* **Color** *will prevent the active layer from changing the brightness, while* **Luminosity** *will do the opposite and prevent changes to color.*

Filter Adjustments

Non-traditional adjustments are found under the **Filter** menu. That's where you'll find the **Camera Raw** filter and a list of advanced adjustments known as **Neural Filters**.

Smart Filters

When a Smart Object is active (covered in another chapter), direct adjustments and filter adjustments will be applied in a non-destructive fashion and will appear just below the bottom edge of the layer. Double-clicking on the name of the adjustment will allow you to modify the settings being applied.

Section I: Fundamental Concepts

Understanding Curves

Curves is by far the most powerful and versatile single adjustment in all of Photoshop. Having said that, it is of limited value when applied to the entirety of an image. The combination of **Curves**, adjustment layers, and layer masks (all covered within this chapter) is what will make you an adjustment powerhouse.

Core Concepts

The concept behind **Curves** is simple. The bar at the bottom **A** contains all shades that can be used in a black-and-white photo. The diagonal line above **B** shows how much light your computer screen uses to display 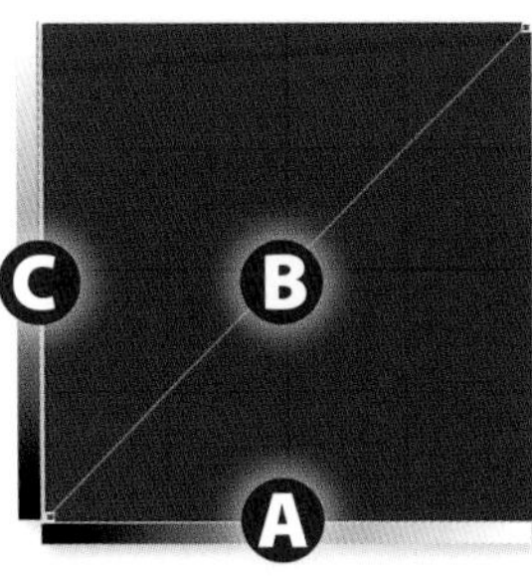 those shades. The line is at the bottom above black because no light is needed to create black. It's all the way at the top above white because it needs to use as much light as possible to make white. You could pick any shade in the bar and look straight up until you hit the line and you'd know much light was in that area.

The diagonal line can then be dragged up to add light, or down to reduce the amount of light being used. It's identical in concept to adjusting the height of physical dimmer switches that you might find in your home. The "dimmers" change the brightness of the shades found below them.

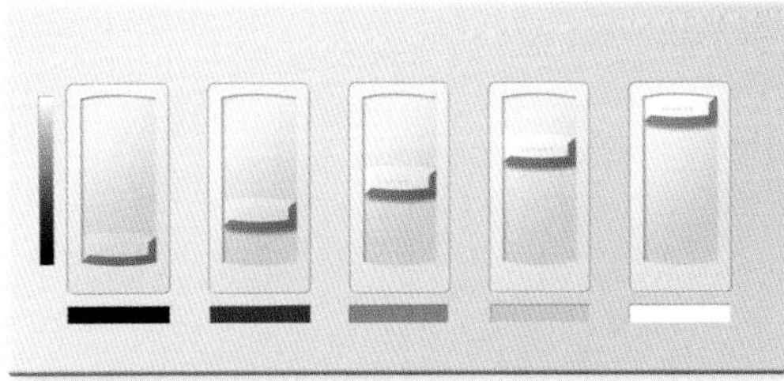

The bar found to the left of the graph **C** indicates how bright things will become if the curve is moved to a particular height. But who needs that, since most people already know how to use a dimmer switch? You simply move the switch to the top in order to max out the brightness and move it to the bottom to turn the lights off.

That diagonal line is exactly 256 pixels wide because that's how many shades of gray can be used in a typical grayscale document in Photoshop. This means that the line is like having 256 dimmer switches side-by-side on a wall. If you had that many in the real world, you'd likely use the entire palm of your hand to slide a bunch of them together instead of messing with each one individually. That's why clicking and dragging up or down on the curve causes large areas to move together.

Changing Brightness

Pushing a curve up increases the amount of light being used and therefore brightens the image.

A hint of the original diagonal line will remain visible, allowing you to see exactly how far the curve was moved over for each shade.

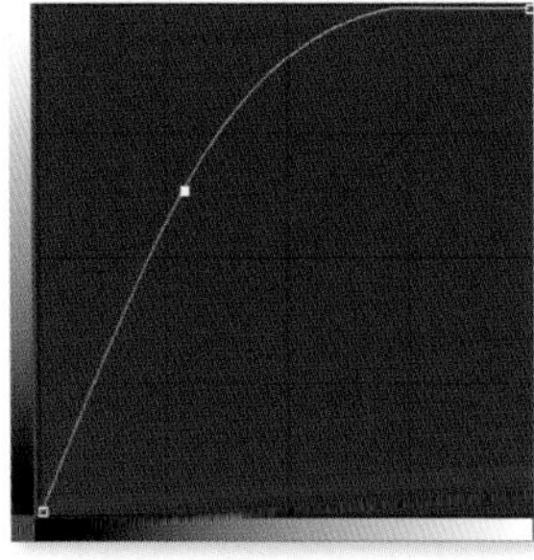

Moving the curve up brightens an image (just like moving a dimmer switch higher). The vertical distance between the curve and the diagonal line indicates how great of a change was made— In this case, less in dark areas than bright, and some areas became solid white where it hit the top.

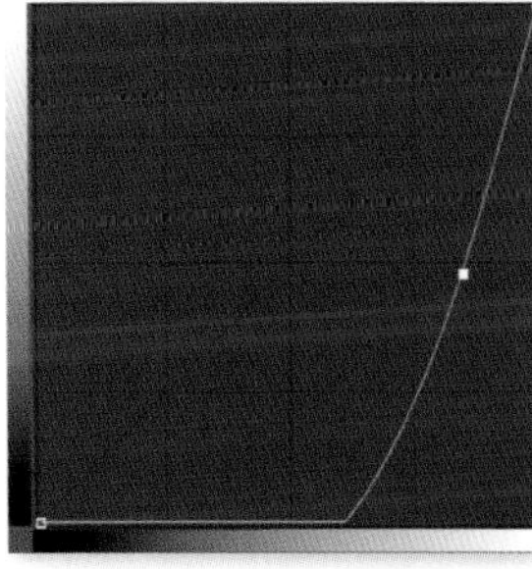

Moving the curve down darkens an image. In this case, everything darker than about 35% gray has become solid black because the curve hit bottom above those shades (just like how sliding a physical dimmer switch to the bottom of its range would effectively turn the lights off).

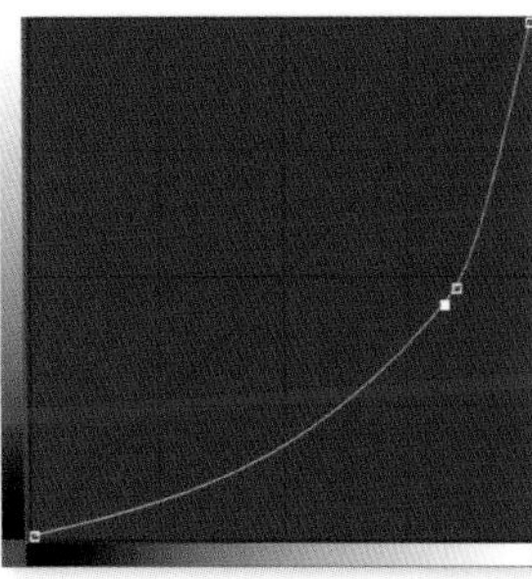

After darkening an image using the curve above, the result was refined by adding a second dot and snugging it up close to the original point. This "steers" the lower portion of the curve in an attempt to prevent the darkest areas from becoming solid black.

Histogram

A bar chart will usually be overlaid on the curve to indicate which of the shades in the bar below are found within the image. A gap on the right side indicates that nothing is anywhere near white.

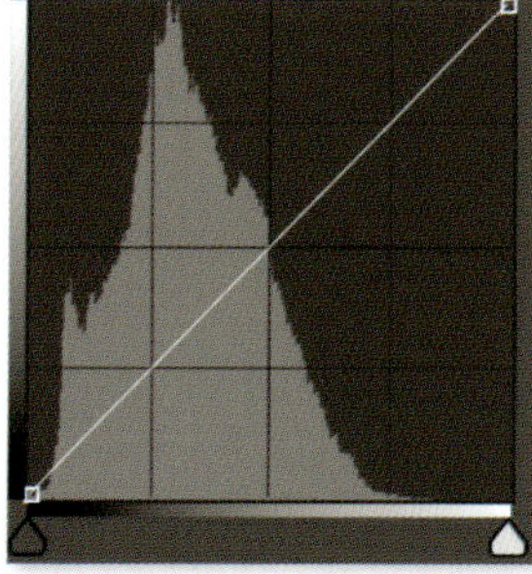

Black and White Sliders

The triangles found below the curve simply move the lower-left point or upper-right point toward the middle to force areas to solid white or black. In the curve above, the white slider could be moved until it touches the right edge of the histogram to force the brightest area of the image to white.

Targeted Adjustment Tool

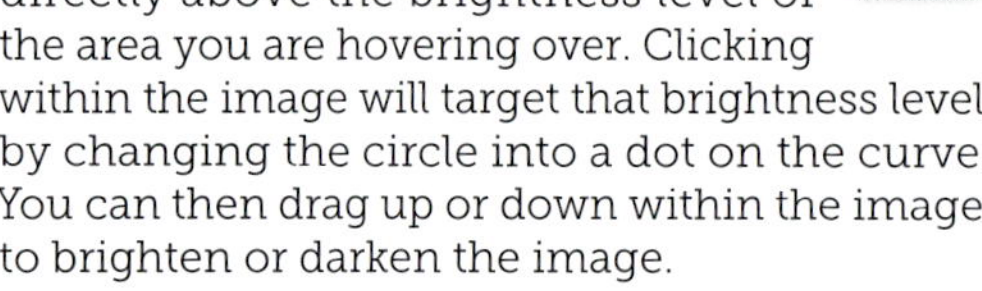

The hand icon (officially known as the **Targeted Adjustment** tool) found within **Curves** allows you to interact directly with the active image. Hovering over the image will display a circle on the curve directly above the brightness level of the area you are hovering over. Clicking within the image will target that brightness level by changing the circle into a dot on the curve. You can then drag up or down within the image to brighten or darken the image.

The **Auto-Select Targeted Adjustment** tool option in the hamburger menu of the Properties panel will cause the hand tool to be active every time you create a **Curves** adjustment layer.

Changing Contrast

The angle of the curve will reflect changes made to contrast. Increased contrast is caused by making the curve steeper, which is an indication that the difference in brightness across an area has increased. Making a curve steeper will cause detail to become more pronounced in the shades that are found below the steeper section of the curve.

Any part of a curve that becomes flatter (closer to horizontal than the original diagonal line) is an indication of decreased contrast, which causes the tones across an area to become more similar to each other and therefore makes it more difficult to discern the detail in the area.

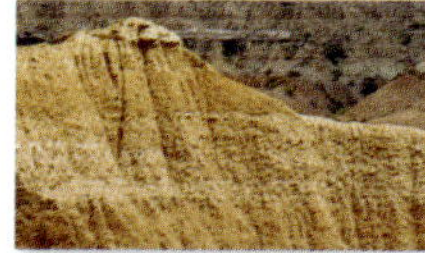
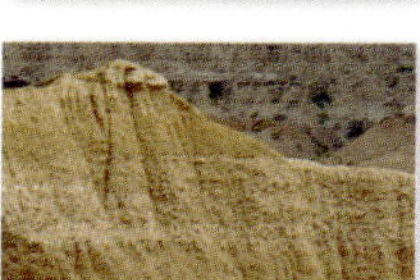
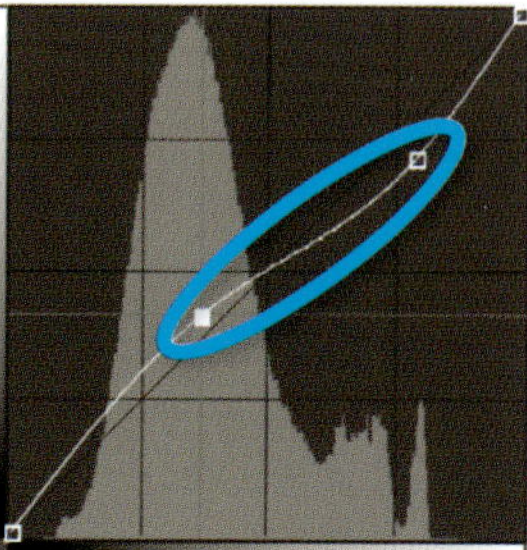

Top: *Before.* **Bottom:** *After.* **Right:** *Curve reducing contrast.*

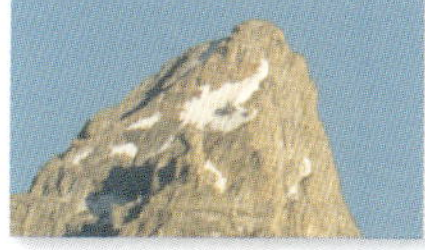
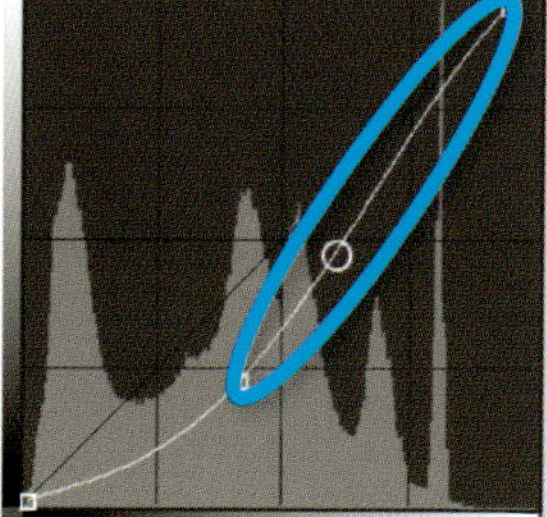
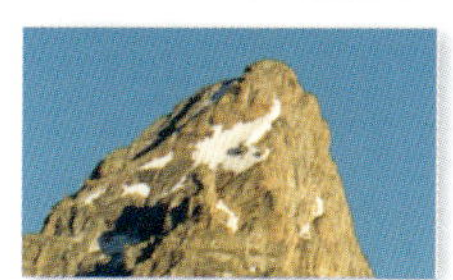

Top: *Before.* **Bottom:** *After.* **Right:** *Curve adding contrast.*

The best method for adjusting the contrast of an area is to hover over the area and drag back and forth while inspecting the range the circle covers on the curve. A dot can then be added at both ends of that range. The lower dot will control the darker area, while the upper dot will target the brighter end of the range. You can then move the lower dot down to darken the dark areas, move the upper dot higher to brighten, or do both.

Shifting Color

The pop-up menu found above the curve needs to be changed to **Red**, **Green**, or **Blue** in order to cause intentional color shifts. The **RGB** choice changes those three colors equally. This is how white light is made, so the RGB choice can therefore not be used for shifting color.

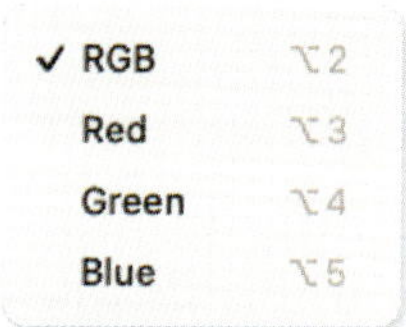
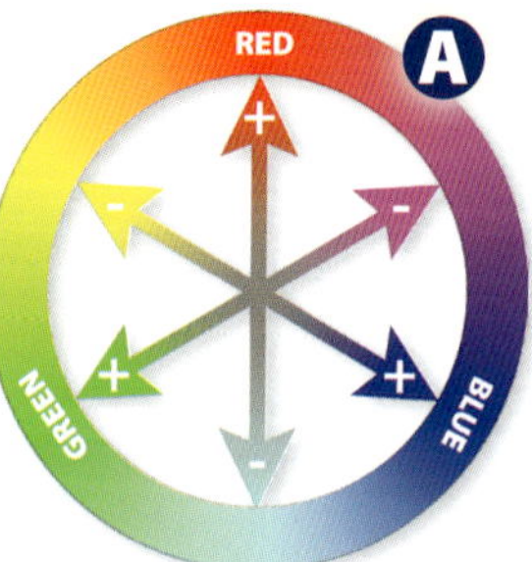

Red, green, and blue color shifts are based on the arrangement of colors found in a standard color wheel.

Section I: Fundamental Concepts

The color wheel diagram **A** indicates what color an image will be shifted toward by changing the amount of red, green, and blue contained within the image.

It's easy to grasp that adding red light will make an image look more reddish, but what happens when you decrease red? Well, take a look at the arrow that points toward red in the diagram, and then look at the opposite end of the same arrow to see what reducing red will do. If you increase both red and blue, then look at what color is found between those two colors and you'll see magenta, which is what you'll be making.

Finally, what if you have an area that is white and you want to cause it to look more reddish, green-ish, or blueish? That's not as straightforward since white would have all of those three colors maxed out and they could therefore not be increased. But looking at the color wheel diagram, the arrows pointing toward yellow and magenta provide the answer. If you shift toward those two colors, then you get what is found halfway between them, which is red! So, to shift a white area toward red, you'd need to reduce the amount of green and blue equally. This will make the already maxed-out red appear more prominent compared to the two colors that were darkened.

Matching Two Colors

The numbers found at the bottom of the curve can be used to shift the color of one area to match another. They work in concert with the RGB numbers that appear in the Info panel.

The RGB numbers that appear when hovering over a portion of an image are a precise de-scription of the brightness and color of the area under your mouse. When you want to match the appearance of two areas, write down the red, green, and blue numbers from the Info panel for both the area you want to change and the area you'd like to match. Those two sets of numbers can then be plugged into **Curves** to produce the change you desire.

In this example, I wanted to even out the blues in the sky by making the right side look more like the center. With my mouse hovering over the area I wanted to change, I saw 115 red, 152 green, and 200 blue in the Info panel. The more desirable darker-blue area of the sky that is just left of center was 64 red, 100 green, and 153 blue.

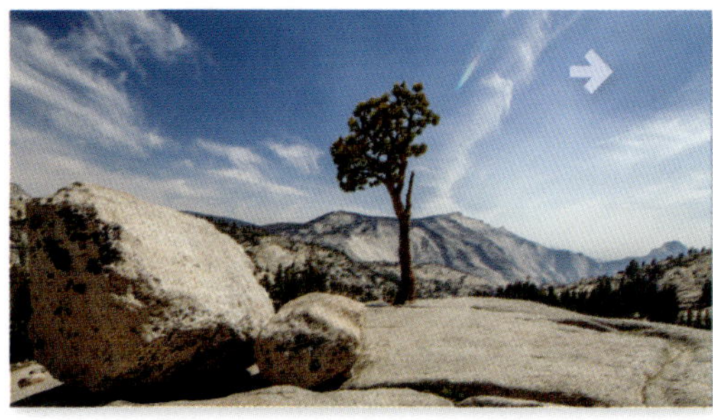

With a **Curves** adjustment layer active, I chose **Red** from the pop-up menu, clicked somewhere on the curve to add a dot, and then repositioned the dot by changing the Input number below the curve to how much red was in the area I wanted to change. I then changed the Output number to the amount of red that was found in the more desirable area of the image and ended up with Input: **115**, Output: **64**. Next, I chose **Green** from the pop-up menu, clicked on the curve to add a dot, and then entered Input: **152**, Output: **100**. Fi-nally, I chose **Blue** from the pop-up menu, clicked on the curve, and entered Input: **200**, Output **153**.

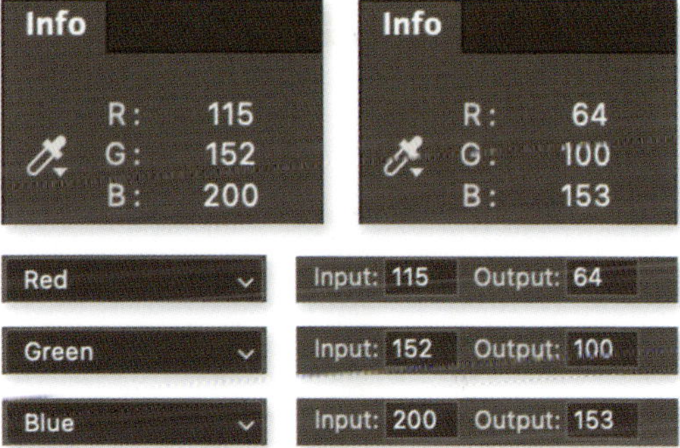

The only problem was that the change shifted the brightness and color of the entire image, so I painted within the layer mask on the **Curves** layer to limit the change to the right side of the image.

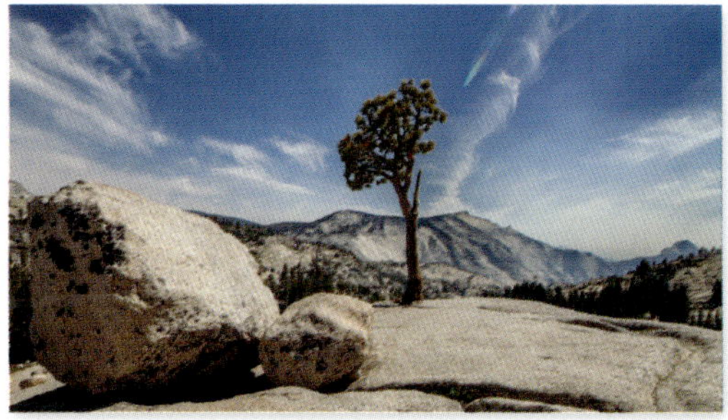

Understanding Hue/Saturation

Curves is my go-to tool when I need to adjust brightness, contrast, or to push the overall color of an image toward one side of the color wheel. I usually switch to **Hue/Saturation** when a precise range of colors needs to be isolated and adjusted.

Core Concepts

The adjustment sliders in **Hue/Saturation** are based on a color wheel, as illustrated below.

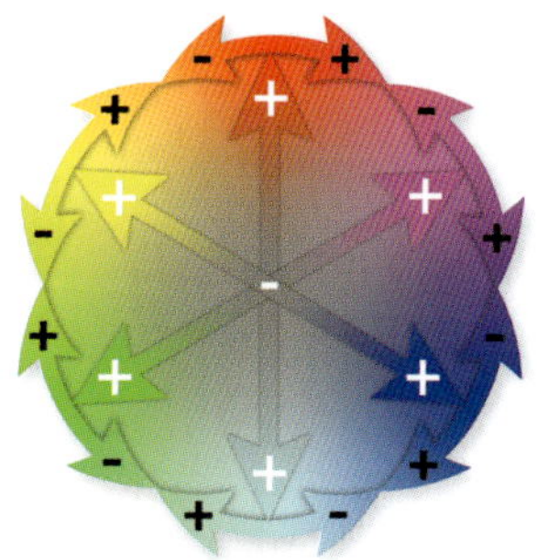

Hue: Shifts basic color by rotating colors clockwise (positive settings) or counterclockwise (negative settings) around the color wheel.

Saturation: Pushes colors toward the outer edge or center of the wheel, which makes everything more or less colorful.

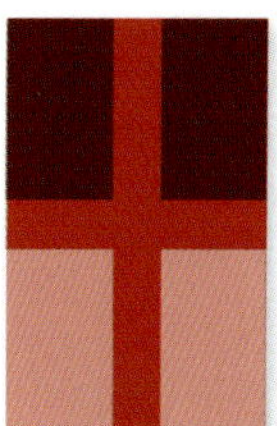

Solid-colored rectangle with corners shifted using -50% and +50% Lightness (left side) or white or black at 50% Opacity (right).

Lightness: Brightens or darkens by adding black or white.

Saturation is the only choice that is useful when applied to the entirety of an image. But when that's the case, I'd rather apply it via a **Vibrance** adjustment.

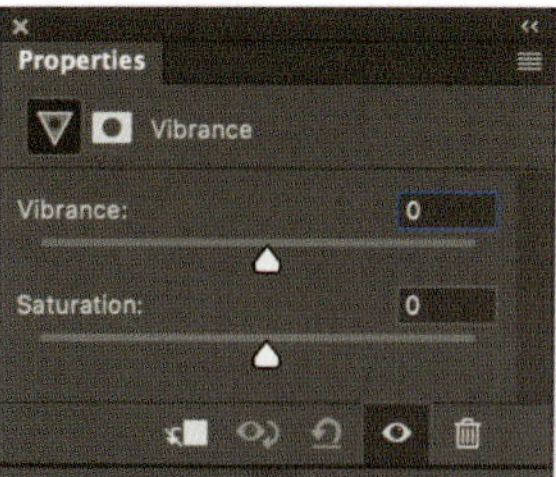

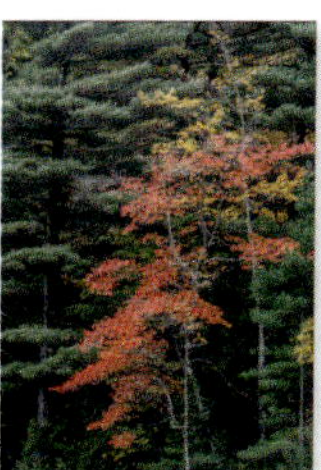
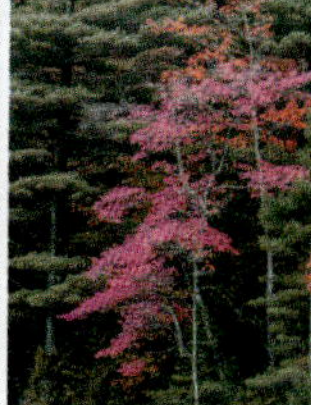
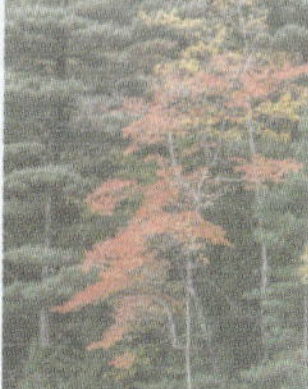

Original image. *Hue -40.* *Brightness +40.*

Isolating Colors

The pop-up menu above the adjustment sliders can be used to isolate a specific color. Choosing the **Targeted Adjustment** tool (hand icon) and clicking within the image will choose the color that most closely corresponds

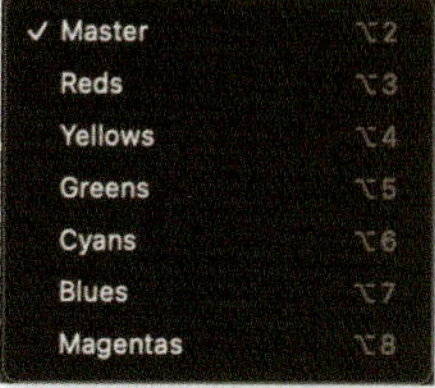

to the color you clicked on within the image. You can then drag left or right to change the **Saturation** setting, or hold **Command** (Mac) or **Ctrl** (PC) while dragging to change the **Hue** setting. Each color found within the pop-up menu can be adjusted independently of the others, allowing you to fine-tune all six colors listed if you so choose.

Choosing a color from the pop-up menu will cause a few sliders to appear between the rainbow-filled horizontal bars near the bottom of the Properties panel. The area between the two vertical sliders, which is filled by light gray, determines which basic colors within the image will receive the full force of the adjustment being applied. Looking beyond the vertical bars, you'll find dark-gray areas on each side that determine how far the adjustment will fade into the surrounding colors. The colors found beyond the outer sliders will not be affected by the adjustment. Each of those sliders can be dragged to fine-tune the range of colors being isolated.

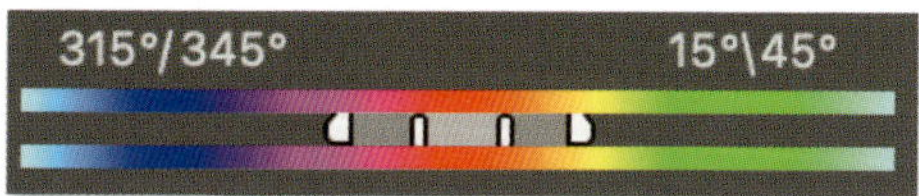

The **Hue**, **Saturation**, and **Lightness** sliders are very effective when applied to an isolated range of colors.

Precise Color Isolation

The eyedropper icons found above the rainbow-colored bars can be used to precisely isolate a specific color using the following steps:

1) Choose any color from the pop-up menu.
2) Drag one of the outer isolation sliders past the middle to effectively smash together all the sliders into a single, gapless mass.

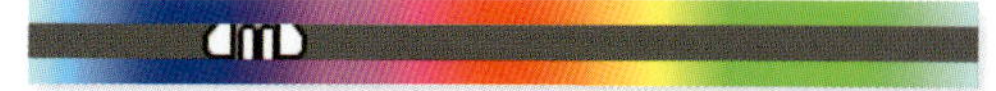

Section I: Fundamental Concepts

3) Click on the left eyedropper icon and then click within the image on the color you would like to isolate.

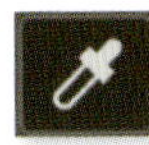

4) Move the **Saturation** slider to **-100** to remove all color from the area being isolated. This is a temporary move to make it easy to tell what has been isolated so far.

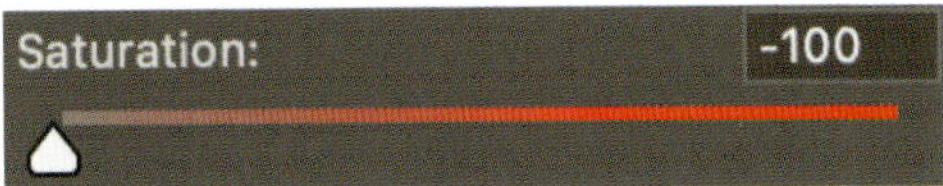

5) Hold **Shift** (which temporarily makes the middle eyedropper active) and click within the image on any areas of that color you want to isolate that are still shown in color.

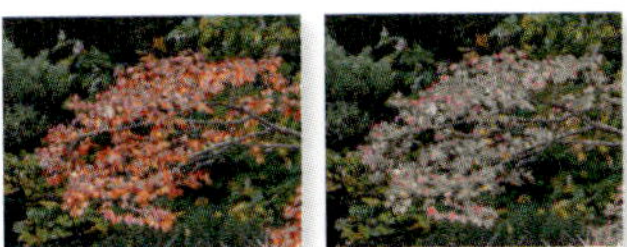

6) Once all the areas that contained the color you want to isolate appear as grayscale, then move the **Saturation** slider to **0** to return the image to an unadjusted state.

7) Adjust the **Hue**, **Saturation**, and **Lightness** sliders to produce the change you desire.

8) Move the outer isolation sliders away from the light gray bar a small amount to produce a less abrupt edge so the change looks natural.

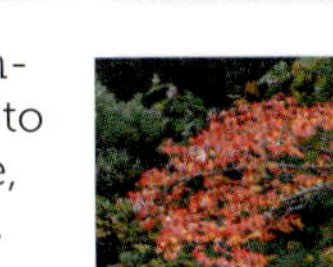

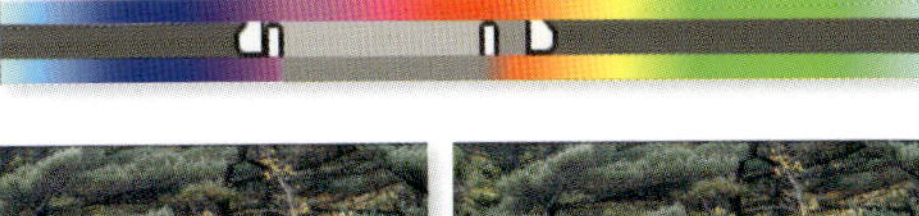

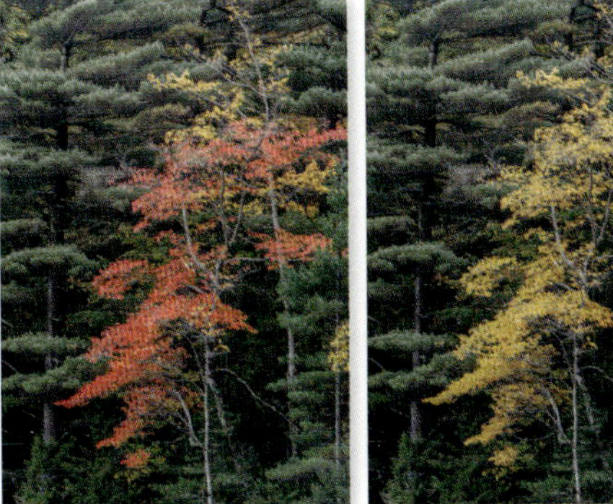

Original image.

Result of precisely isolating red and shifting color.

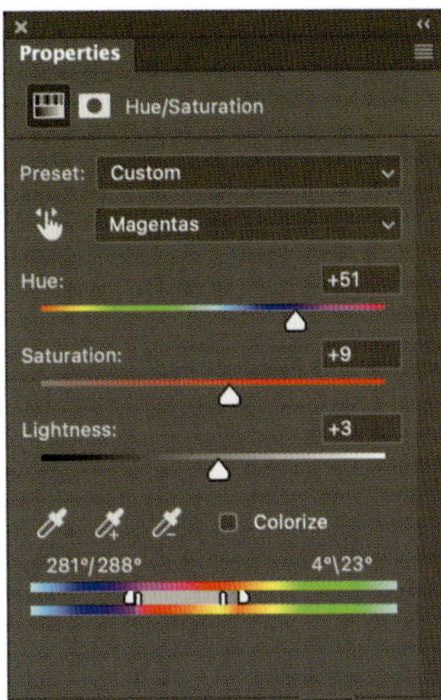

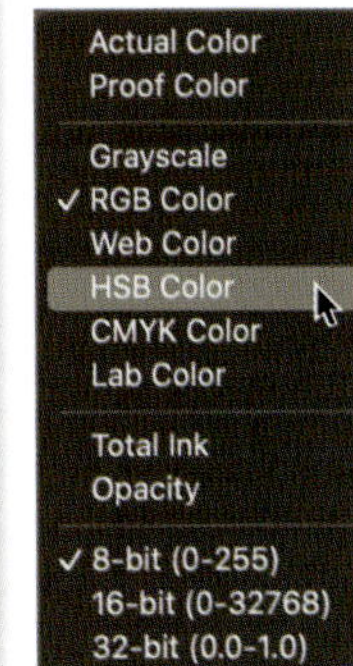

Left: Adjustment shifting red to a golden color.

Below: Info panel measurement systems available.

Precise Color Matching

The numbers that appear in the Info panel are a precise description of the color that is found under your mouse. The measurement system used can be changed by clicking the eyedropper icon to the left of the numbers. The choice of **HSB** most closely matches the sliders that are available in the **Hue/Saturation** adjustment.

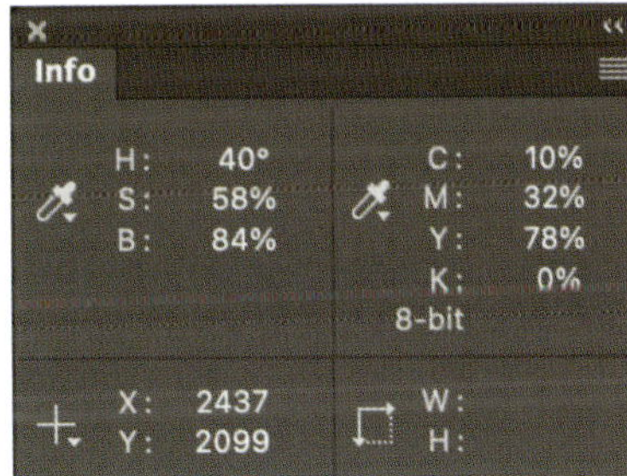

Info panel set to display HSB values. HSB is short for Hue, Saturation, and Brightness.

Comparing the HSB readings from two areas can reveal how close those areas are to matching. The difference in the H numbers indicates exactly how much the **Hue** setting would need to be shifted from its current setting. The S number can be used in a similar fashion to determine if one area is more colorful than the other. The B is a brightness reading, which does not directly correspond to the **Lightness** slider. Moving the **Lightness** slider will affect both the B and S readings, so you will likely need to go back and forth between **Lightness** and **Saturation** to get the numbers to match between the two areas.

Layers

Layers are the fundamental building blocks that most images are constructed from in Photoshop. The foundation of a layered image is almost always an image that was optimized in Lightroom and ends up as the Background layer. All changes are then made on layers stacked above to build up a desired result. Let's explore a few features that are essential to being effective using layers.

Adjustment Layers

The most versatile method for applying an adjustment is to choose it from the half-black, half-white circular Adjustment Layer icon at the bottom of the Layers panel. 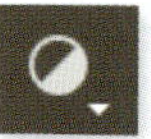

A new adjustment layers always appears directly above the layer that was active at the time it was created. Adjustment layers only affect layers that are found below them. For that reason, new adjustment layers should almost always be added to the top of the layer stack so they do not modify what existing adjustment layers are acting upon.

The adjustment settings for an adjustment layer will be will be found in the Properties panel. At the bottom of that panel are icons for deleting and temporarily hiding the layer, as well as the following icons that serve less obvious functions.

Reset Adjustment: Reverts to default settings for the adjustment. Its behavior changes if you switch to a different  layer and later return to make further changes to the adjustment. When that's the case, clicking the icon will revert to the previous state of the adjustment, and clicking it a second time will revert all the way back to the default settings.

View Previous State: Temporarily shows what the image would look like if the adjustment settings were reverted 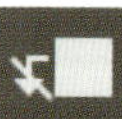 to their previous state. Holding \ will do the same. It's exactly the same as pressing the reset icon and then choosing **Edit>Undo**.

Clip to Underlying: Causes adjustment to only affect the layer directly below it (indicated by a down-pointing arrow to the left of the adjustment layer). When an adjustment layer is below, then its layer mask will also limit where this layer applies.

Layer Masks

Layer masks are used to non-destructively hide portions of a layer and can be added to the active layer by choosing an option from the **Layer>Layer Mask** menu or by clicking the **Layer Mask** icon at the bottom of the Layers panel. When working with layer masks, you can do the following: 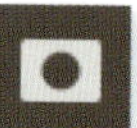

Switch Between Mask and Layer: Layers that have a layer mask attached will feature two side-by-side thumbnails in the Layers panel. L-shaped brackets will be displayed on each corner of the thumbnail that is active for editing. You can click on the thumbnails to switch between working on the actual contents of the layer and the mask. The brackets will move to indicate what's active.

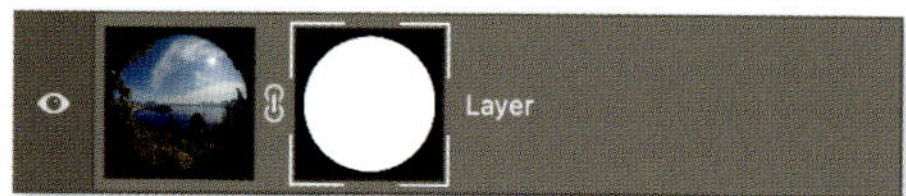

Use Black, White, or Grays: Painting with black when the mask is active will cause areas to be hidden. Areas that are white will leave the layer visible, and shades of gray will produce various levels of transparency.

Disable Mask: **Shift**-clicking on the mask thumbnail will temporarily disable the layer mask and display a red X within the mask thumbnail. Doing so a second time will re-enable the mask.

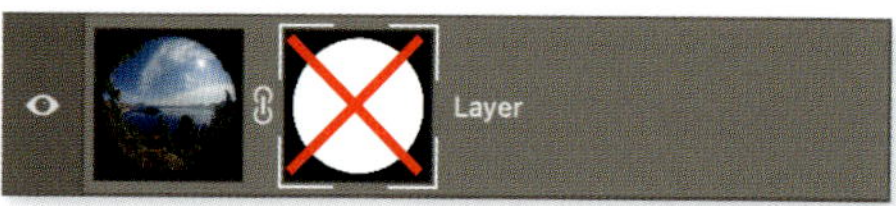

View Contents: **Option**-clicking (Mac) or **Alt**-clicking (PC) will display the contents of the layer mask within the main image window. Doing so a second time will return the mask to its previously hidden state.

View as Overlay: Pressing \ will toggle the visibility of a mask overlay within the image. This is especially useful when the mask has been disabled.

> **Tip:** *An image can be copied from, or pasted into, a layer mask while the mask is being viewed directly or overlaid onto the image.*

Section I: Fundamental Concepts

Move or Copy Between Layers: Drag any mask thumbnail to another layer to move the mask to a different layer. Hold **Option** (Mac) or **Alt** (PC) while dragging to move a copy of the mask.

Load as Selection: Hold **Command** (Mac) or **Ctrl** (PC) and click the mask thumbnail to load the white areas as a selection. Add **Shift** to add to any active selection, or **Option** (Mac) or **Alt** (PC) to subtract from the selection.

Properties: The Properties panel displays mask-specific settings when a layer mask is active.

Density causes hidden areas to become partially visible without modifying the actual mask.

Feather softens the transitions within the mask without actually changing its con tents.

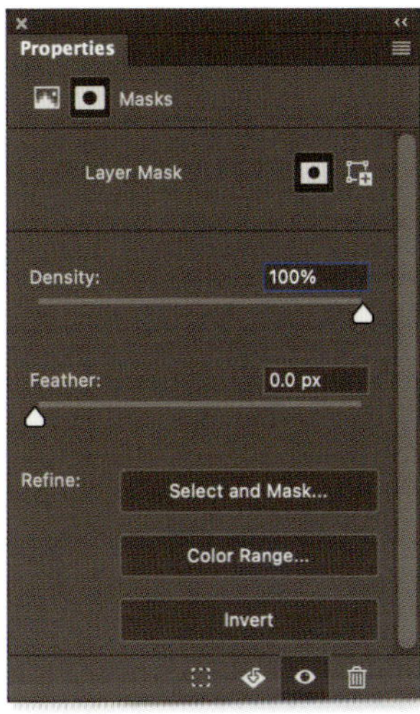

Blending Sliders

Another method of non-destructively hiding portions of a layer is to choose **Layer>Layer Style>Blending Options** and adjust the sliders near the bottom of the resulting dialog box.

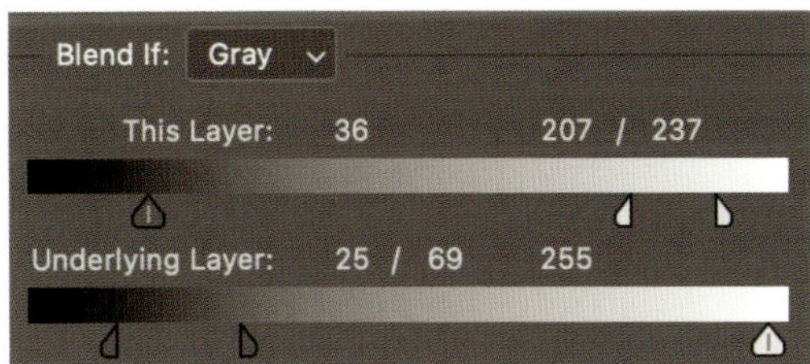

This Layer

The gradient in this section represents the brightness levels of the active layer. Moving the upper-left slider will cause any areas that contain brightness levels found to the left of the slider to be hidden. Moving the right slider will hide shades found to the right of the slider. Either

of the two sliders can be split apart by holding **Option** (Mac) or **Alt** (PC) and dragging either side away from the other to produce a gradual transition between the visible and hidden areas.

Underlying Layer

The lower gradient represents the underlying image as if you merged any layers into a single layer. The left slider will cause areas that are in the brightness range to the left of the slider to break through the active layer and become visible. The right slider will do the same for any areas found to contain shades brighter than the shade it is positioned below. These sliders can also be split in half to produce a gradual transition.

Blend If Channel

With default settings, the sliders apply as if they are working with a grayscale version of the layers. Choosing **Red**, **Green**, or **Blue** from the pop-up menu above the sliders will cause the sliders to work with the grayscale images that appear in the Channels panel.

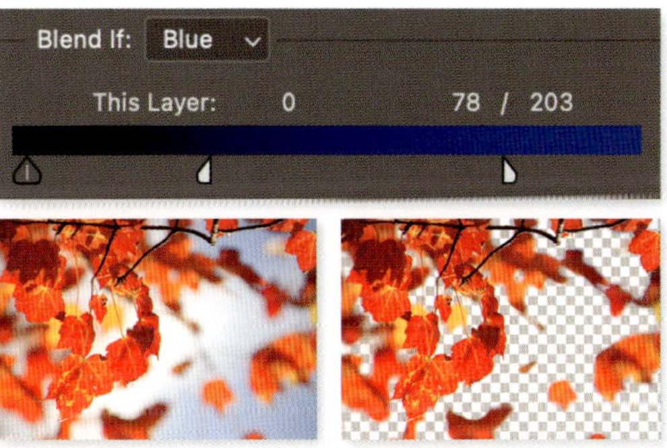

The blending slider setting shown above was used to hide the background on the leaves.

Layer Groups

Clicking the folder icon at the bottom of the Layers panel creates a Layer Group. Layers can then be dragged onto the group, and the group can be collapsed to effectively organize the layers and reduce the clutter of the Layers panel. Adding a layer mask to a group will cause it to apply to all the layers contained within.

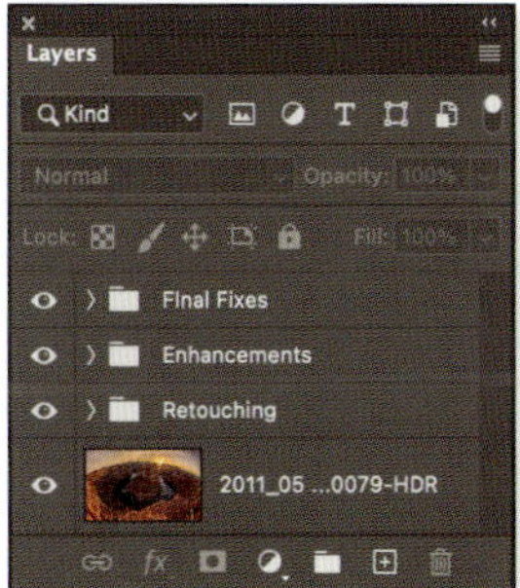

Retouching

Photoshop's retouching capabilities go way beyond what Lightroom is capable of, allowing you to clone between documents and rotate, scale, or flip content before it is used elsewhere.

Spot Healing Brush

This tool offers a brush that is used to paint over the area to be retouched, ideally making sure that its dark overlay extends just a little beyond the bounds of the object. When the mouse button is released, the covered area will be replaced with content that resembles the surrounding area.

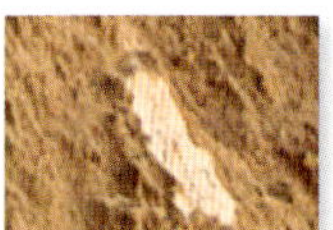 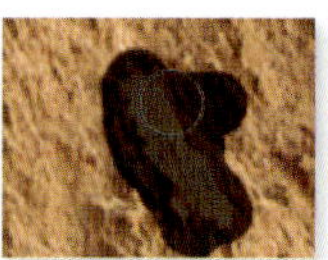 

The **Content-Aware** setting will produce the best results in most situations. Also, the **Sample All Layers** checkbox must be enabled if you plan to perform retouching on an empty layer in an effort to work non-destructively.

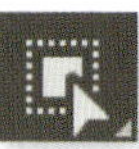

Delete and Fill Selection

One of the simplest methods for removing an undesirable object is to crudely trace around it using the **Object Selection** tool and then type **Shift-Delete** (Mac) or **Shift-Backspace** (PC).

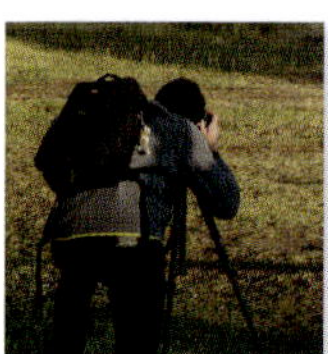 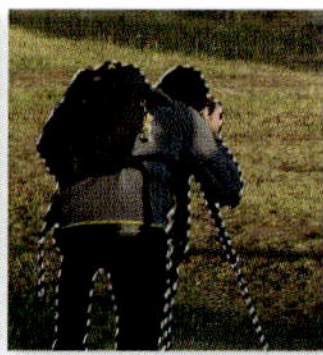 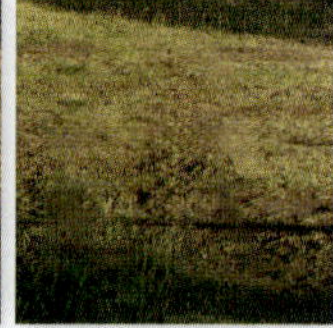

The same retouching process can be applied to a selection created with any tool by **Control**-clicking (Mac) or right-clicking (PC) and choosing **Delete and Fill Selection** while a selection tool is active.

The process mentioned above is only able to utilize the contents of the active layer and therefore cannot be applied to content made from multiple layers. To get around that limitation, click on the topmost layer to make it active, then hold the **Option** key (Mac) or **Alt** key (PC) and choose **Layer>Merge Visible** to produce a new layer that contains a copy of all the underlying layers merged together. After applying the retouching technique to that new layer, choose **Select>Inverse** and then press **Delete** (Mac) or **Backspace** (PC) to delete the areas that were not affected by the retouching.

Content-Aware Fill

The last two techniques utilized Adobe's **Content-Aware Fill** technology, which attempts to construct new unique material by combining small chunks of the surrounding image. If you want to use the same technology and have control over the process, then choose **Edit> Content-Aware Fill** while a selection is active.

This will cause your screen to be reconfigured with a series of panels and toolbars that allow you to control how **Content-Aware Fill** will construct material to fill the selected area.

Sampling Area Overlay

The left side of the screen will feature a green overlay over the image indicating what areas have been designated as potential source material. The appearance of the overlay can be changed via settings found at the top of the upper-right panel.

Preview

To the right of the overlay image is a preview of the results produced using the current settings. If you find the preview image to be too small, then drag the left edge of the panel to expand it. The slider below the preview image can be used to magnify the results for a more critical view.

Toolbar

The top tool is the **Sampling Brush** and it is used to modify the overlay, which determines the areas that can be used as source material for retouching. The icons found near the left end of the Options Bar that spans the top of the screen determines if you'll be adding or removing from the overlay. You can momentarily activate the opposite setting by holding **Option** (Mac) or **Alt** (PC) while painting.

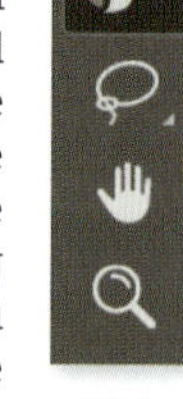
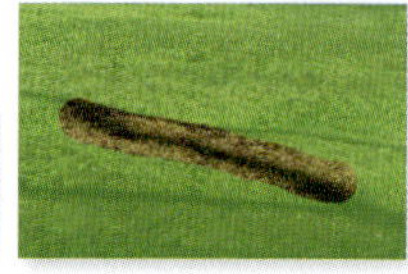
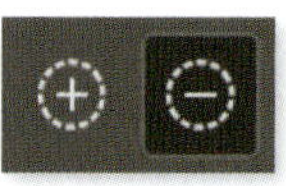

Section I: Fundamental Concepts

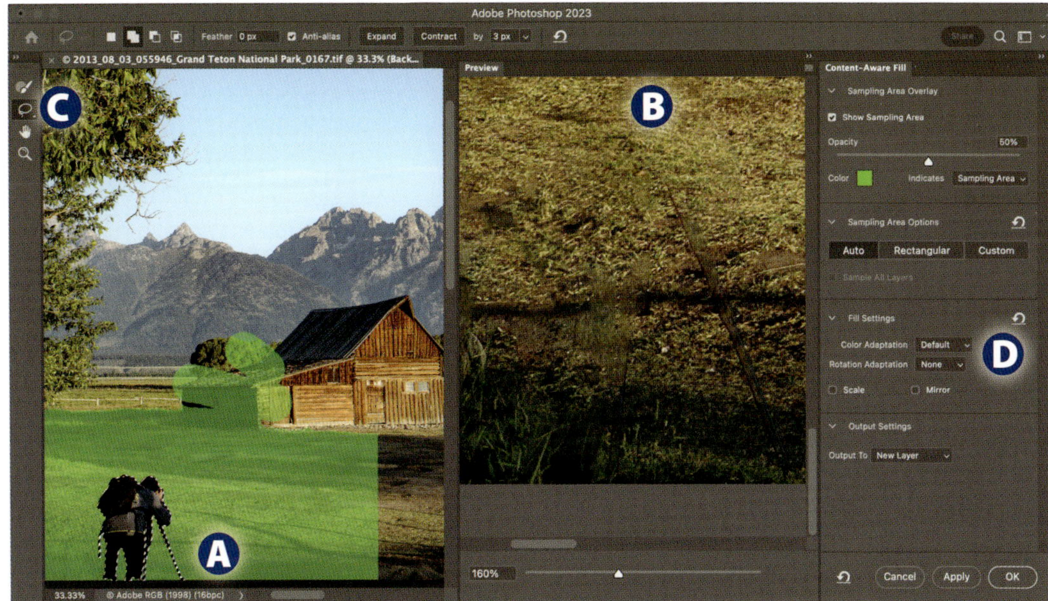

*The Content-Aware Fill workspace features a sampling area overlay **A**, a results preview **B**, Toolbar **C**, and Fill Settings panel **D**.*

The **Lasso** tool allows changes to be made to the selection to expand or further limit the area being retouched. The **Expand** and **Contract** buttons in the Options Bar will make the selection larger or smaller by the number of pixels specific to the right of the buttons. Expanding a selection is often essential to avoid edge artifacts, especially when starting from the tight-fitting selections produced by the **Object Selection** tool.

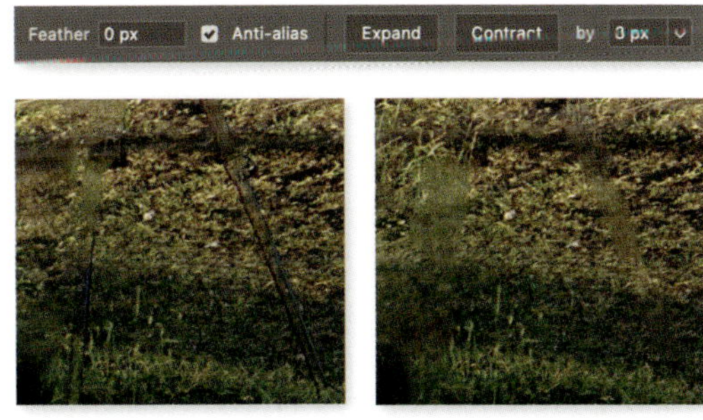

Using selection created by Object Selection tool.

Result of expanding the selection by six pixels.

Fill Settings

The settings under this heading on the right side of the screen determine how the material found within the overlay can be used within the area being retouched. **Color Adaptation** controls how much the brightness and contrast can be changed to match the surroundings. **Rotation Adaptation** controls how much source material can be rotated before being applied. **Scale** allows the source material to be resized before being applied, which makes it so areas at different depths are better utilized. **Mirror** allows the source to be flipped horizontally.

Retouch Multiple Areas

When you're finished retouching one area, you can click the **OK** button to exit the **Content-Aware Fill** workspace. Or, if you'd like to work on a different area without leaving the workspace, click the **Apply** button, which will refresh the overlay window to reflect your results. You can then use the **Lasso** tool to define another area to be retouched. This is a great way to quickly retouch multiple areas, or to further refine the area affected by your initial retouch. Once you click the **OK** button, each retouched area will appear on a separate layer.

With the tools we've discussed so far, Photoshop has done most of the work for us. Now let's switch gears and take a look at the tools that we'll need to fall back on when the more automated options fail us.

Clone Stamp

This is the tool that I hope to use the least on any given day. That's because it makes me do all the thinking to ensure that the area I copy from has the proper brightness, contrast, color, and detail to match the area being retouched. I also have to get the **Hardness** setting of the brush just right to ensure that the retouched content seamlessly blends into the surrounding areas. All this tool does is copy from one area and put an exact copy of it somewhere else.

Option-click (Mac) or **Alt**-click (PC) on the area you'd like to copy from, release the mouse, move to where you'd like the content to appear, and then click and drag. While dragging, you will see two cursors moving in sync within your image. A crosshair indicates where you're copying from and a circle shows where it is being applied.

Healing Brush

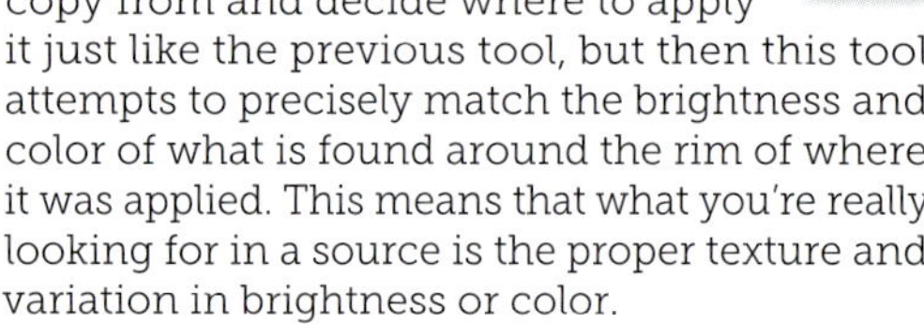

This is a high-tech version of the **Clone Stamp**. You still need to tell it where to copy from and decide where to apply it just like the previous tool, but then this tool attempts to precisely match the brightness and color of what is found around the rim of where it was applied. This means that what you're really looking for in a source is the proper texture and variation in brightness or color.

A smooth, gray, overcast sky from one image can even be used as a source to remove a bird from a smooth blue sky in another. The texture and variation in brightness from the source get applied to the colors that surround the destination area.

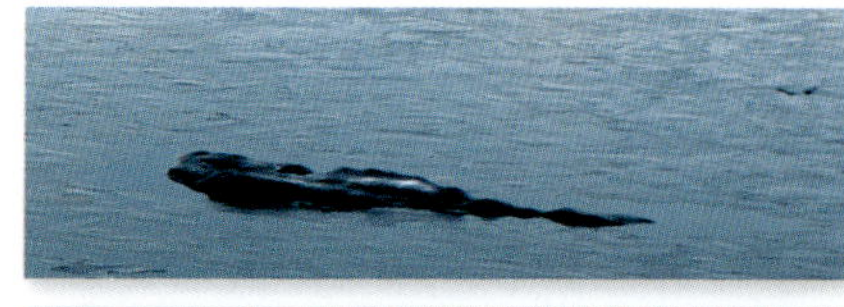

Original image.

Clone Stamp tool.

Healing Brush with Diffusion set to 7.

Healing Brush with Diffusion set to 1.

The **Diffusion** setting determines how smoothly the material will transition into the surrounding colors. Lower settings are better for areas that contain fine detail, while high settings are better for smooth areas that contain little detail, such as a sky.

> **Tip:** *Setting the **Sample** pop-up menu in the Options Bar to **Current & Below** for either tool will allow it to work on an empty layer for non-destructive retouching.*

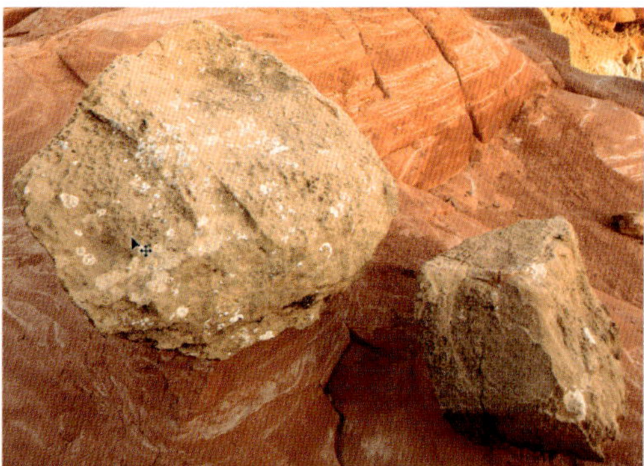

Original image before retouching.

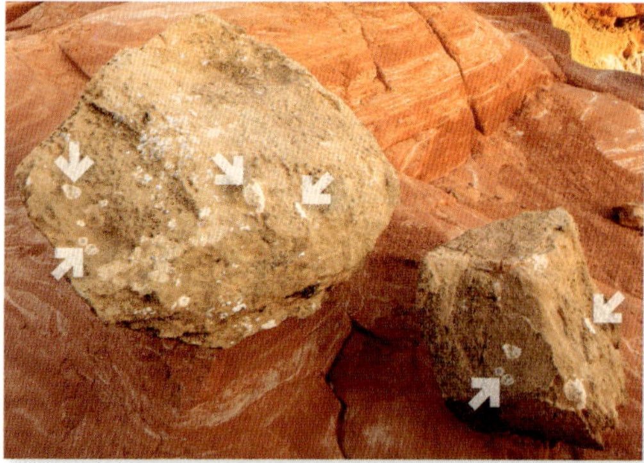

Each rock was retouched using the other as a source to remove small specks and transfer some of the large specs.

Section I: **Fundamental Concepts**

Clone Source Panel

Choosing **View>Clone Source** allows the source of the **Clone Stamp** or **Healing Brush** to be scaled, rotated, or flipped before being applied.

It is usually more useful to utilize a special set of keyboard shortcuts than to manually enter numbers, as you'll see the changes update interactively within your brush. Hold **Shift-Command** (Mac) or **Shift-Ctrl** (PC) and then type one of the following depending on the setting you want to change: < or > to rotate, [or] to scale, or the **arrow keys** to nudge the position. I often click the flip icons that are found next to the width (**W**) and height (**H**) settings **A** when copying generic texture in an attempt to make it look different from what I am copying from. When you're finished retouching and want to reset everything back to normal, click the U-turn icon **B** that's found to the right of the angle setting.

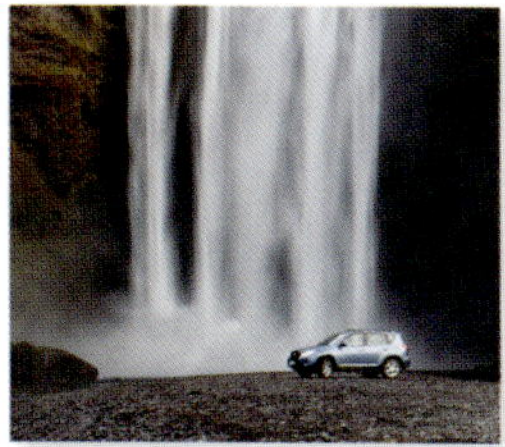

A waterfall in Iceland that someone parked their car in front of. It's not surprising a barrier has been added to the area in recent years.

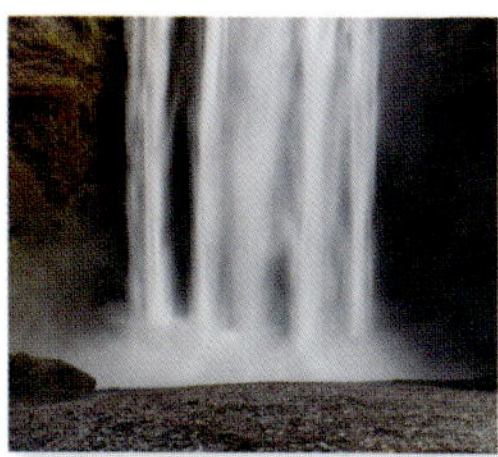

Result of healing with content from the left edge of the waterfall utilizing the flip horizontal setting.

Be sure to turn on the **Aligned** checkbox in the retouching tools and then click within the image to retouch a small area before attempting to nudge the position (known as the **Offset**) of the source material.

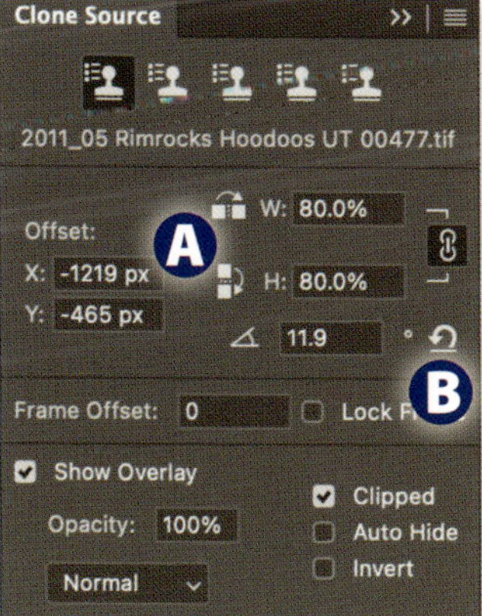

The Clone Source panel

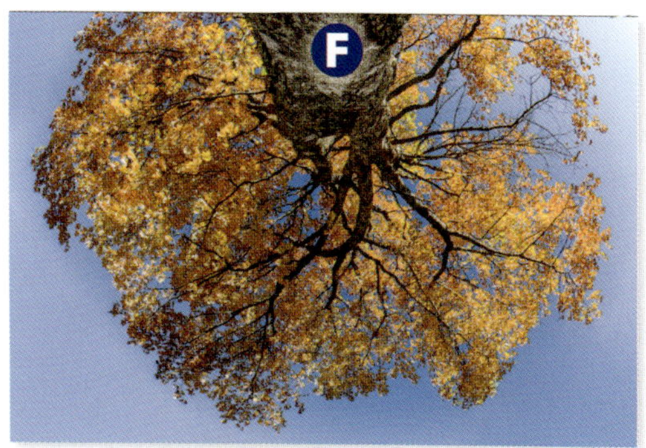

Using the Tools Together

The scene above originally contained undesirable content in the corners that I wanted to remove **C**.

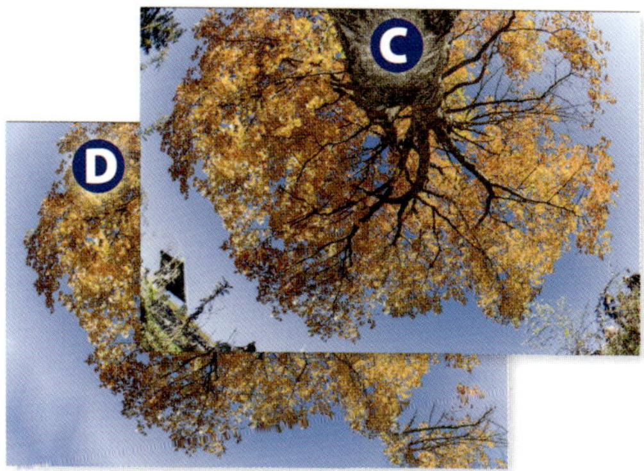

I made a crude selection of the upper-left corner and chose **Delete and Fill Selection**. I repeated the same process for the remaining corners. The lower-left area had to be done twice to get it to be relatively clean, but I was unable to get the lower right to become clear **D**. I then chose the **Clone Stamp** tool and created a gap of blue sky between the tree and remaining corner **E**.

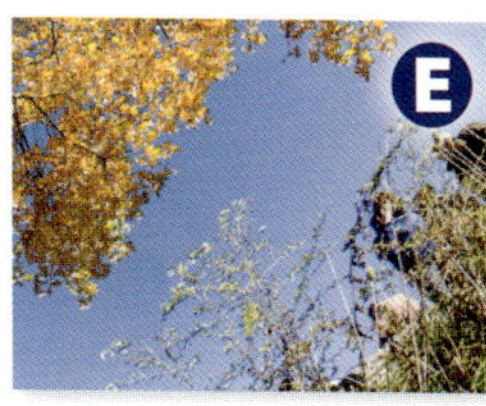

Finally, I chose the **Healing Brush** and switched to a document that contained an overcast gray sky, **Option**-clicked in the middle of it, then switched back to the tree image and used that smooth content to replace the contents of the lower-right corner and clean up the other corners **F**. That's right! You can clone or heal between documents as long as they are the same bit-depth and color mode (16-bit RGB in my case).

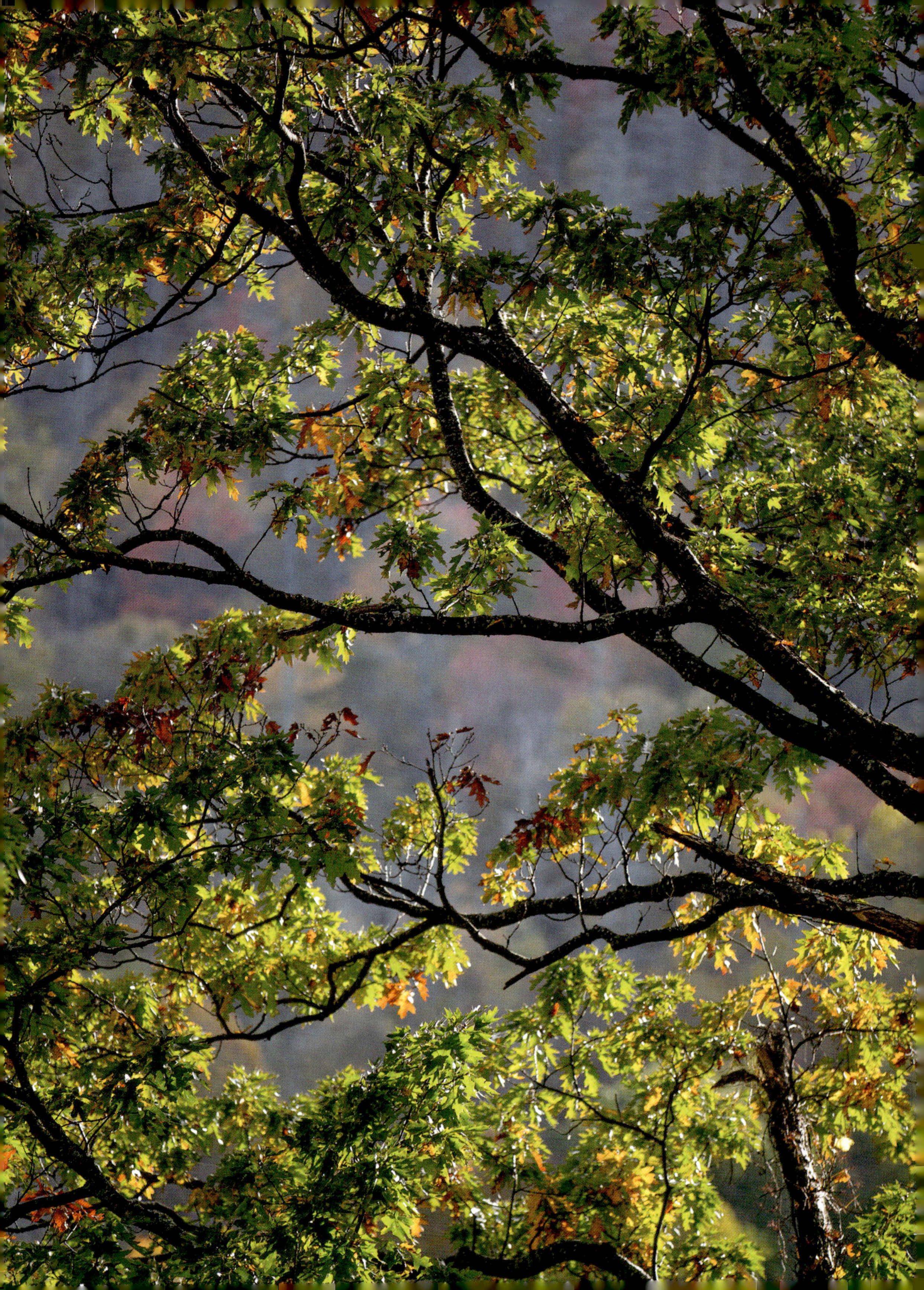

Section II

Quality Considerations

IF YOU WANT to produce results that you can be proud of even under close examination, then you'll need to ensure quality is on your mind at every step in your workflow. Our Initial quality will be achieved by reducing or eliminating artifacts that were caused by how the image was captured. We can then see if it's necessary to go beyond the technical limitations of your camera by combining multiple exposures. Then we'll make sure you're equipped to deal with any undesirable artifacts that crop up as a result of the enhancements you apply in an attempt to transform a raw capture into an image worthy of framing.

Chapter 4

Eliminate Shooting Artifacts

DECISIONS MADE BEFORE pressing the shutter have consequences that influence how an image will later be processed. For example, the simple act of underexposing a scene will produce an image that demands brightening, which will inevitably exaggerate the noise that lurks in the dark areas of the image. The gear used to capture an image can also produce a variety of undesirable artifacts such as color halos, dark corners, and distortion. The techniques on the pages that follow are designed to mitigate those artifacts and ensure that further processing does not exaggerate any issues that were introduced at the time of capture.

Underexposure

When shooting a scene, a good exposure setting is one of the largest contributors to image quality, second only to capturing a sharp, in-focus subject. An underexposed scene, as indicated by a considerable gap on the right end of the histogram, will usually force you to later brighten the image in Lightroom.

Brighten in Lightroom

It's hard to believe how much information can be extracted from areas that initially appear to be solid black in a raw file. It's as easy as nudging the **Exposure** and **Whites** sliders toward the right. If you still need further brightening, either crank up the **Shadows** slider or lower the **Highlights** slider, and pair that adjustment with an additional boost in **Exposure**. If a sky doesn't benefit from such a change, then use the masking tool to isolate the sky and apply the opposite settings to counteract what was applied to the image as a whole.

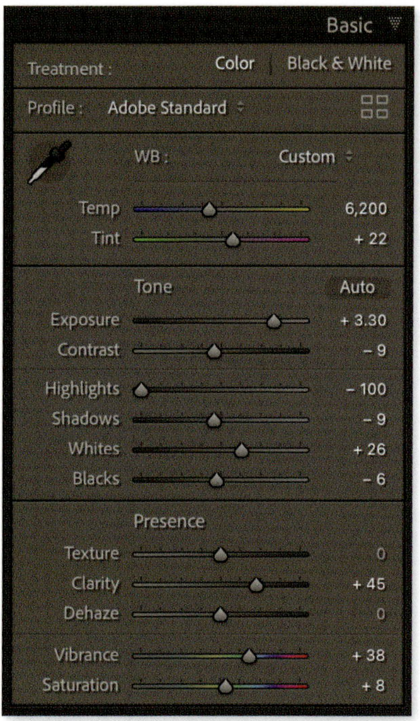

Basic adjustment settings used to transform the severely underexposed waterfall image into a potentially usable image.

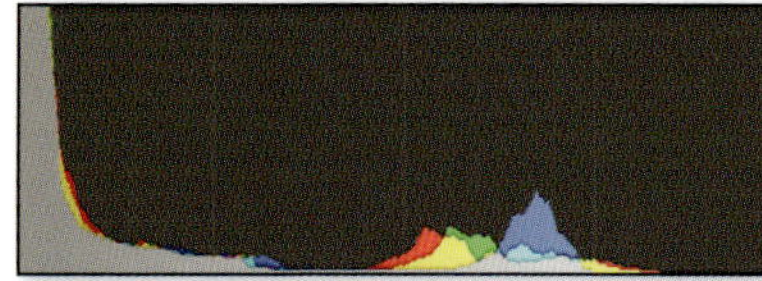

Gap on right indicates that the entire image is dark.

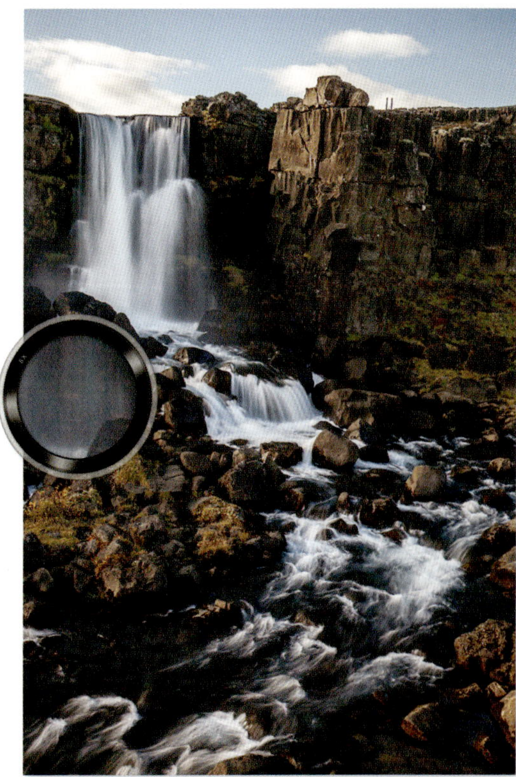

Result of being optimized using the Basic panel in Lightroom.

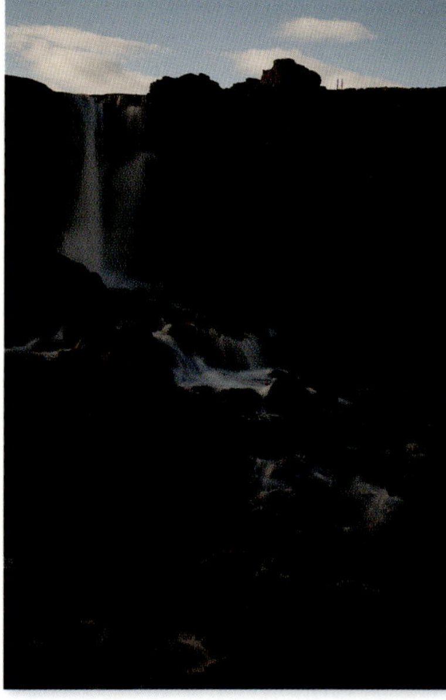

With default settings, the majority of the image had no apparent detail.

Section II: Quality Considerations

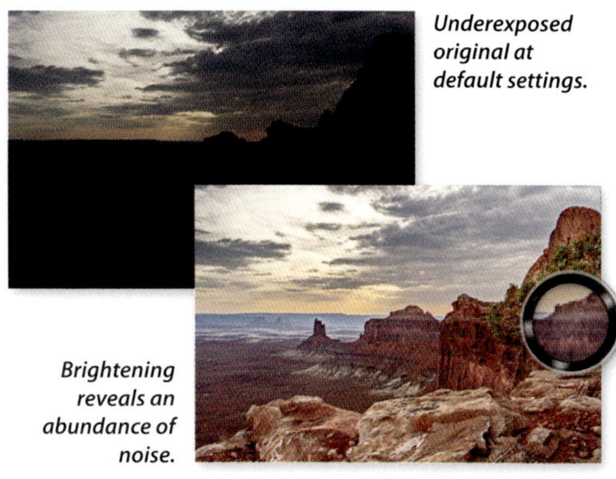

Underexposed original at default settings.

Brightening reveals an abundance of noise.

If one of the Basic panel sliders becomes maxed out and you wish it could be pushed further, switch to the Tone Curve panel, choose the left-most **Adjust** option **A**, and then fine-tune the sliders found below the curve to create a stronger adjustment.

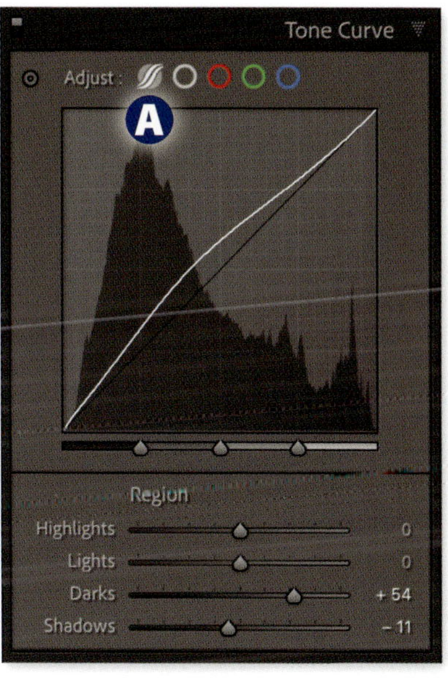

The Tone Curve can be used to supplement the Basic panel sliders.

Inverted Sky Mask

It can be useful to brighten everything except the sky. To do this, create a masked adjustment of the sky (as explained in chapter 2), choose the **Invert** option, and then increase the **Exposure** and/or **Whites** sliders.

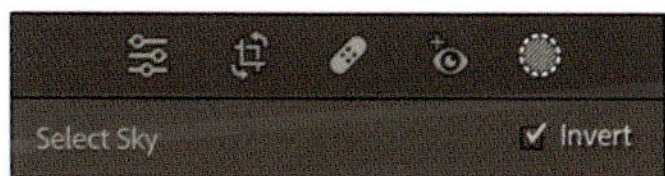

Inverted sky mask.

Noise

While it's easy to brighten an image in Lightroom, the results will be much cleaner if you instead increase the exposure at the time of capture. The difference will be the amount of noise. To understand why, let's take a brief look at just one of the causes of noise so you'll have a better idea of why it is more prominent in the dark areas of an image.

Why Are Digital Images Noisy?

Imagine setting out a grid of equally sized cardboard boxes on the ground during a hail storm and then counting how many hail stones are captured within each box over a period of time. If the storm produces an even and consistent amount of hail across the area where the boxes were laid out, would you expect to end up with an identical number of hail stones in each box? Nope. The count would be pretty consistent on average, but would fluctuate randomly by a slight amount across the boxes.

The amount of time you leave the boxes exposed to the storm would have a dramatic affect on how noticeable that variation would be. Leave them out during a heavy storm for enough time to accumulate at least 4,000 stones in each box and you might find the box with the highest count contains 4,040 stones. Leave the same boxes out for a short period of time and stop when each box contains at least 10 stones, and now any variation will be much more noticeable. A single extra stone would cause the reading to be 10% different from the average, whereas the previous test produced a variation of only 1%.

That's exactly what happens with your camera sensor, the only exception being that those boxes are awfully small and they are capturing photons of light instead of hail stones. The more light you capture, the less noticeable the tiny variation is. Another way to think about this is that the more light you capture from the scene, the higher the pure information captured rises above the noise.

It's the darkest quarter of the brightness range available that contains the most pronounced noise. Underexposing an image and later brightening it will cause the dark area to have considerable variation and exaggerate the noise that was previously in areas too dark to be noticed.

The Noise-Reduction Process

There are three stages to effective noise reduction.

Prevent Noise Exaggeration

The first step to reducing the prominence of noise is to make sure that any sharpening being applied does not exaggerate the noise. The **Masking** slider found in Lightroom's Detail panel determines which areas will be sharpened. Holding **Option** (Mac) or **Alt** (PC) when adjusting the slider will produce an alternative view of your image where areas that appear white will be sharpened and areas in black will not be sharpened. Noise will be most noticeable in areas that do not have a great amount of detail (such as a smooth blue sky), so I usually adjust the **Masking** slider until any smooth areas of sky and other areas lacking prominent detail become black.

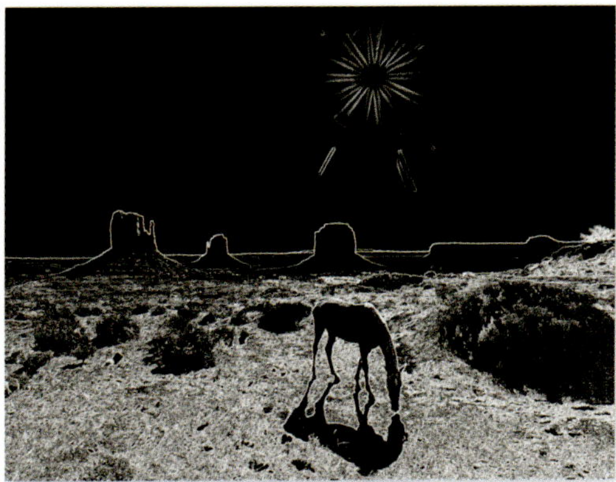

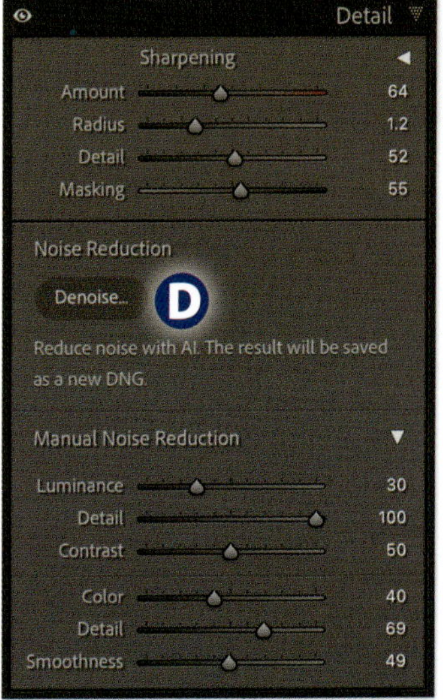

Above: *Holding Option (Mac) or Alt (PC) when adjusting the Masking slider and adjusting it until areas lacking prominent detail become black.*

Left: *Sharpening and Manual Noise Reduction settings used to reduce noise to an acceptable level on one particular image.*

Now that noise is no longer being exaggerated in the areas where it would be most obvious, we can turn our attention to reducing noise to an acceptable level.

Reduce Luminance Noise

The top three sliders found under the Manual Noise Reduction section of the Detail panel can be used to reduce random specks that vary in brightness. The sliders available include:

Luminance: Will attempt to eliminate tiny specks that vary in brightness, but will also cause fine detail to be blurred. Therefore, it's key to use the lowest setting that produces the best compromise between retaining detail and reducing noise.

Detail: This slider is somewhat like the **Masking** slider that is associated with Lightroom's Sharpening settings. It limits how much of the image will be affected by noise reduction. It will be grayed out and unavailable (along with **Contrast**) if the **Luminance** slider is lowered to zero.

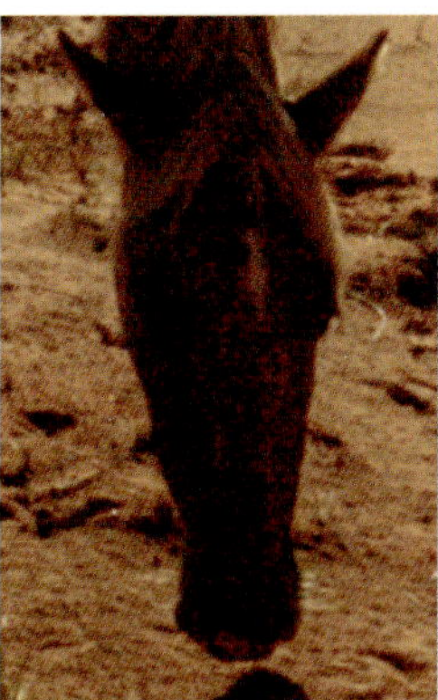

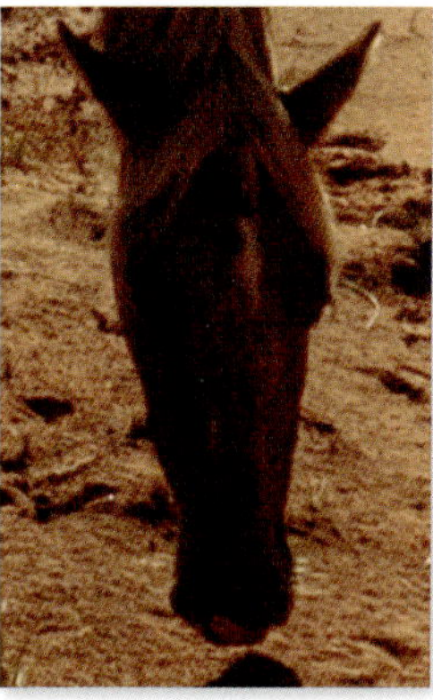

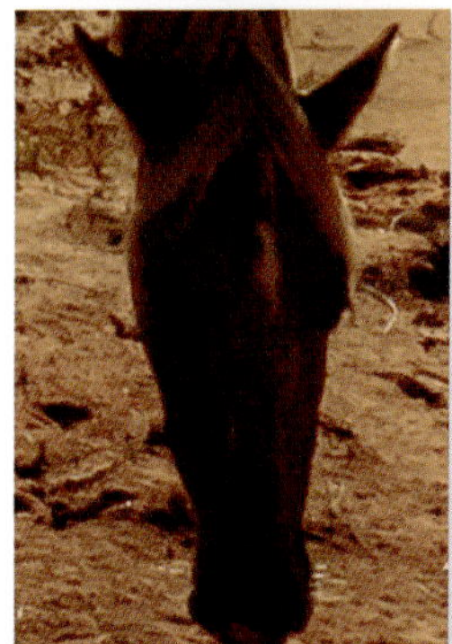

Above Left: *Noise reduction and sharpening disabled.*

Above Right: *Default noise reduction and sharpening.*

Left: *Result of optimizing sharpening and noise reduction for this specific image.*

Note: All the images above were brightened dramatically to make the effect of noise reduction obvious. (It's much easier to see on-screen than in print).

Section II: Quality Considerations

Contrast: Attempts to increase the contrast of the areas where noise reduction is applied in an attempt to make remaining detail appear more pronounced. I find that this slider is only useful on a very small percentage of images and usually does not produce a noticeable change.

Reduce Color Noise

The three sliders found at the bottom of the Noise Reduction section of the Detail panel can be used to deal with color noise. The default setting being used for these sliders was determined many years ago, back when the average camera produced a lot more noise than most modern cameras. For that reason, I find them to be a bit high for normal images. Here are the choices available:

Color: Attempts to remove tiny colored specks by shifting them to the color of the surrounding pixels. This slider is not appropriate for dealing with large, soft-edged color variations.

Detail: This slider is just like the one found below the **Luminance** slider and limits where color noise reduction will be applied.

Smoothness: Blends larger, soft-edged color variations into the surrounding image.

Manual Color Smoothing

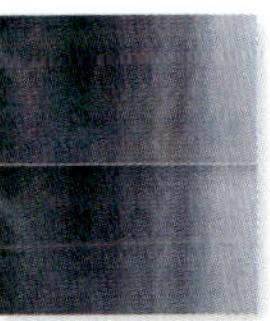

When the **Smoothness** slider is not enough to rid an image of odd color artifacts, then consider painting a positive **Moiré** setting into affected areas using the Masking tool.

Process and Mindset

With the **Luminance** slider at its default of zero, I set the **Detail** and **Smoothness** sliders to zero before adjusting the **Color** slider to find the lowest effective setting. I then crank the **Detail** slider to **100** and slowly lower it until I find the highest setting that produces effective color noise reduction. Then I bring up **Smoothness** until I find the lowest setting that rids the image of distracting soft-edged color variations. If needed, I supplement this with the **Moiré** feature I mentioned above. Once color noise has been dealt with, I adjust the **Luminance** slider to find the lowest setting that produces the best compromise between detail and noise reduction. I then adjust the **Detail** slider just like I mentioned for color.

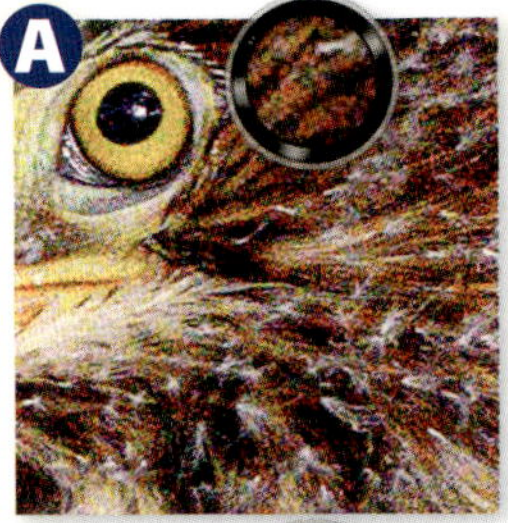

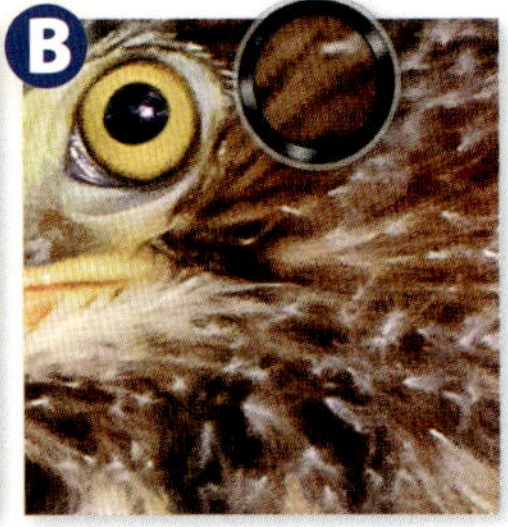

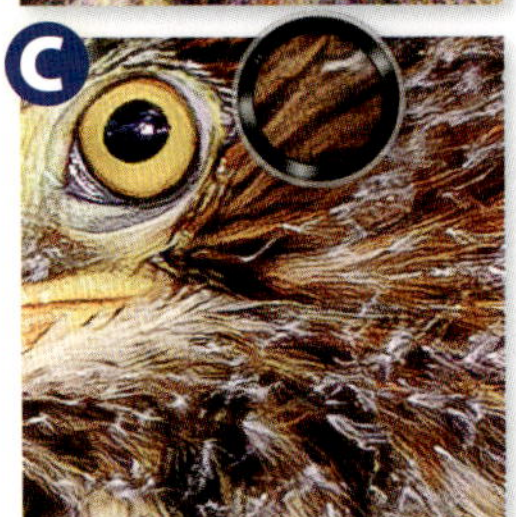

A: *Detail panel disabled.*

B: *Manual Noise Reduction applied with best compromise between noise reduction and detail retention.*

C: *Artificial Intelligence–based noise reduction applied with Amount of 69.*

Artificial Intelligence–Based Denoise

Lightroom offers an advanced noise reduction option via the **Denoise** button, which utilizes artificial intelligence to reduce noise without sacrificing detail.

This feature only works on raw files that have not been demosaiced (see chapter 1 for information on demosaicing) and will generate a .DNG file which takes up 2–3x the storage space of the raw file it was produced from, thus increasing storage needs. The function is dependent on your computer's GPU for most of its work, so it's performance will vary depending on the hardware it's applied with.

To access the feature, you can either click the **Denoise** button **D** or right-click on an image and choose **Enhance**. This will present you with a single slider to control the AI-based noise reduction.

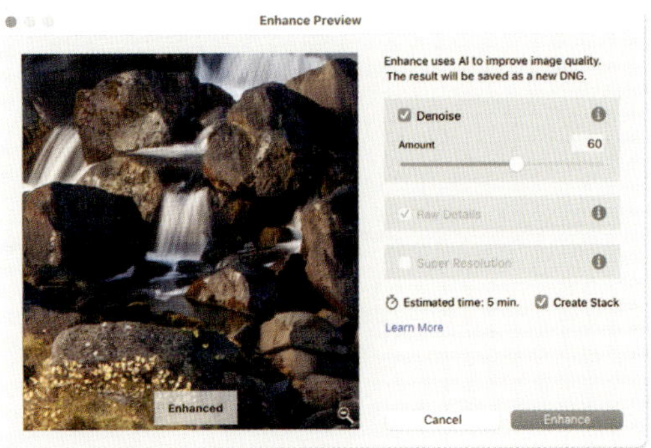

Hot Highlights

The following techniques can be utilized to bring things under control when there is an isolated area that appears unnaturally bright.

Basic Adjustments

Lowering the **Highlights** slider is the obvious choice, which may need to be supplemented by also lowering the **Exposure** slider. When the dark areas of an image could also use brightening, try cranking the **Shadows** slider as high as it goes and then adjusting the **Exposure** slider until the highlights have been sufficiently darkened.

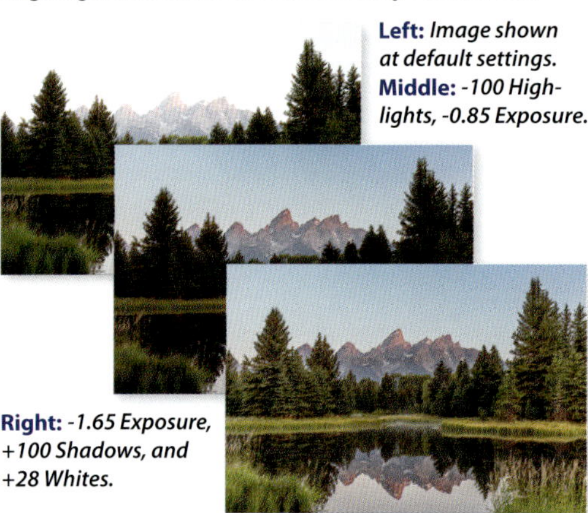

Left: *Image shown at default settings.*
Middle: *-100 Highlights, -0.85 Exposure.*

Right: *-1.65 Exposure, +100 Shadows, and +28 Whites.*

Luminance Mask

Often, bringing the **Highlights** slider down to improve one area will negatively impact other areas (such as a sky). When that's the case, I'll type **Shift-Q**, which will add a **Luminance Range** mask. I'll limit the mask to affect the absolute brightest areas and then lower the **Highlights** slider. I'll then adjust the fade-out region via the triangular sliders until the change blends smoothly with the surrounding image. To further limit where the adjustment is applied, I'll hold **Option** (Mac) or **Alt** (PC), click on the **Intersect** button, and use a **Brush** mask to paint the change into an isolated area of the image. I'll often need to fine-tune the white balance and **Saturation** settings for the area as well.

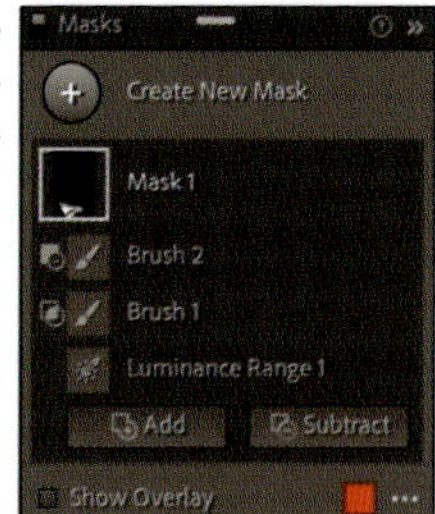

Luminance Range mask intersected with Brush mask limits area affected.

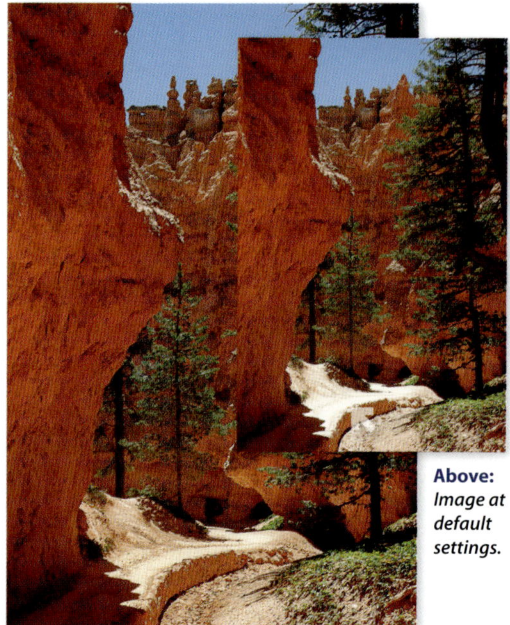

Above: *Image at default settings.*

Result of darkening highlights using a Luminance Range mask.

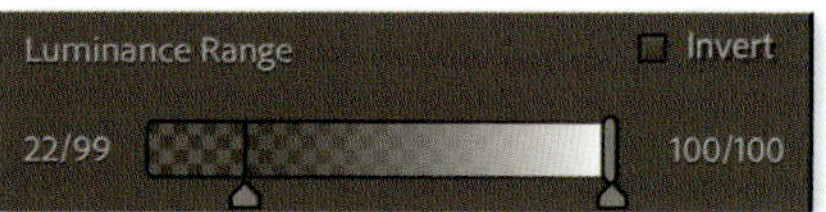

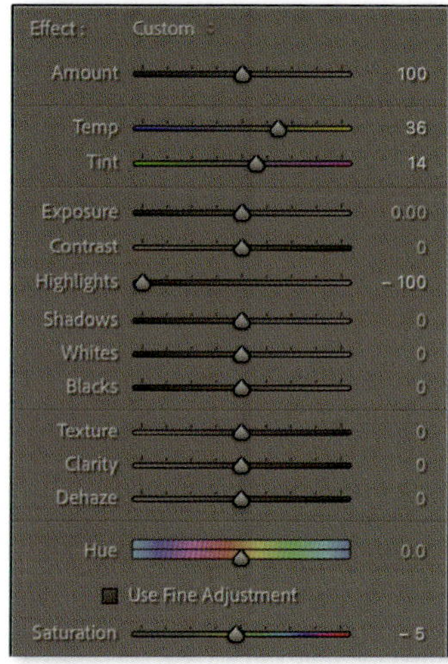

Above: *Luminance Range mask settings needed to isolate brightest areas and then smoothly blend the change into surrounding image.*

Left: *Adjustment settings applied via the mask to darken highlight areas.*

If neither of the above techniques produces a satisfactory result, it might come down to hacking Lightroom in order to prevent the contrast boost that consequently causes the brightest areas to lack contrast.

Section II: Quality Considerations

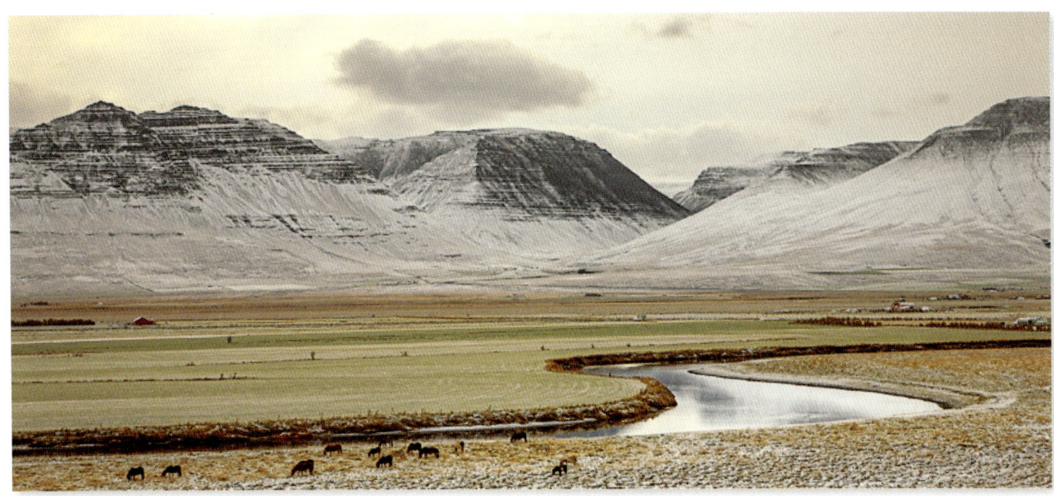

Result of optimizing image using a linear profile.

Linear Profiles

Behind the scenes, Lightroom applies a **Curves** adjustment to all raw images. This increases contrast in the shadows and midtones, at the expense of lowering contrast in the highlights. This adjustment can be disabled by installing and then applying what's known as a linear profile.

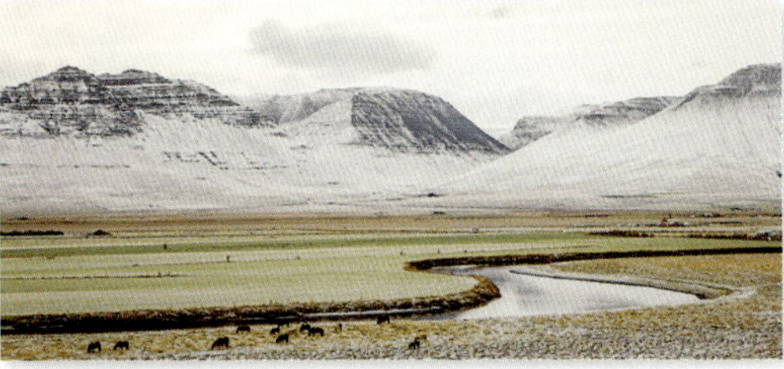

Result of optimizing image using the default profile.

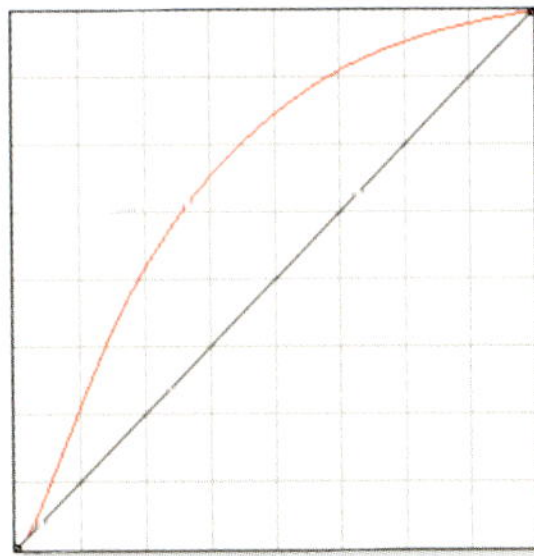

The red curve is automatically applied behind the scenes to every raw image that is processed by Lightroom or Adobe Camera Raw. The black line, which represents no adjustment, is known as a linear curve and can be applied to make it easier to see highlight detail.

Right half of histogram.
Left: *Default.*
Right: *Linear profile.*

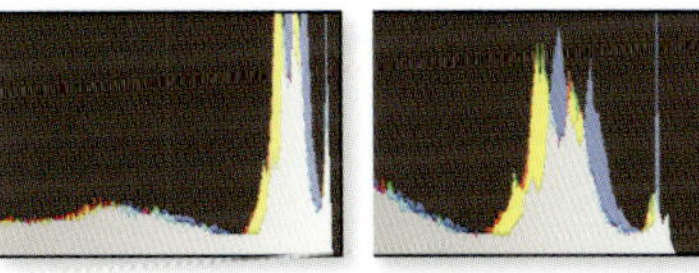

Choose Browse from the Profile pop-up menu.

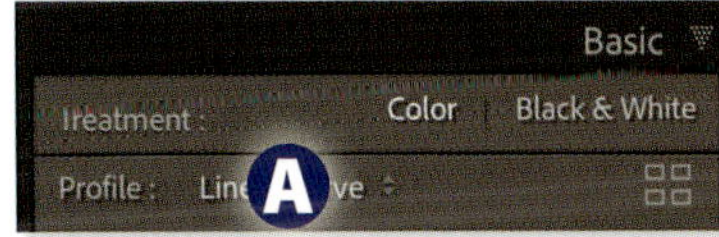

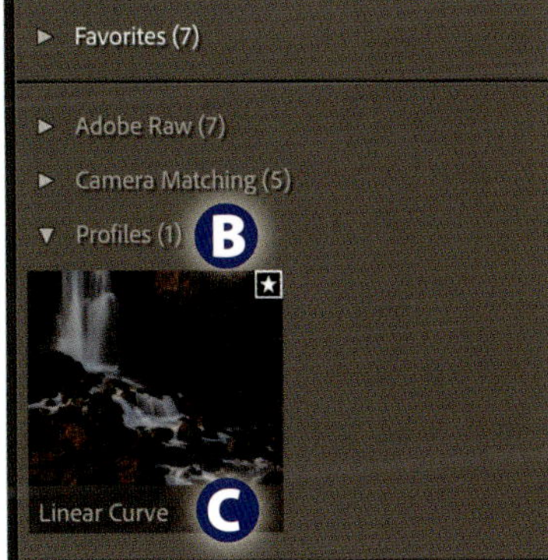

Linear profiles are usually found in the Profiles section of the profile browser. Just remember that linear profiles do not come with Lightroom and must be manually installed.

Linear profiles are unique to each camera model, so you'll need one for each type of camera you shoot with. The easiest way to obtain one is to visit the Linear Profile Repository website at **https://goodlight.us/linear-profiles.html**, where you'll also find installation instructions.

Once you've installed corresponding linear profiles for each camera you shoot with, then you can apply one by choosing **Browse** from the **Profile** pop-up menu **A** near the top of the Basic panel, navigating to the **Profiles** section **B**, and choosing the **Linear Curve** option **C**. Then you can adjust the image as you would any other, although it may look dull to begin with.

Blown-Out Skies

The sky is usually the brightest area in an image and therefore the most prone to losing detail due to overexposure. Below are some of the techniques I use when part of the sky has been blown out to solid white.

Check for Detail in Raw File
When it looks as if part of a sky is white, with no detail, start by lowering the **Exposure** slider as far as it goes to see if any detail appears. This won't help JPEG files, but raw files contain extra information in the brightest areas. This information allows for the ability to adjust white balance without losing detail. If detail presents itself, then I'll lower the **Highlights** slider to **-100** and then fine-tune the **Exposure** slider until I see sufficient detail.

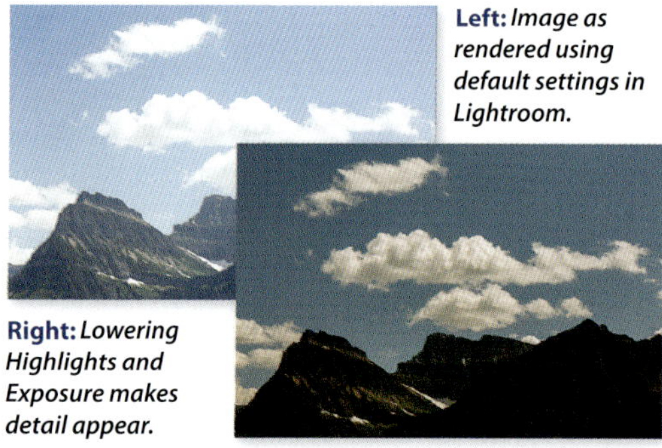

Left: *Image as rendered using default settings in Lightroom.*

Right: *Lowering Highlights and Exposure makes detail appear.*

Blue Skies Fading to Gray
When you reach the edge of the brightness range your camera is capable of capturing, lowering the **Highlights** slider will cause the brightest area to lack color. When that's the case, the area can be darkened and shifted toward blue using **Curves**.

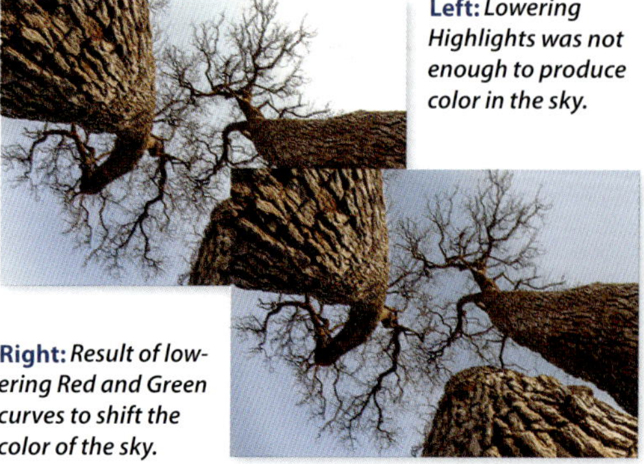

Left: *Lowering Highlights was not enough to produce color in the sky.*

Right: *Result of lowering Red and Green curves to shift the color of the sky.*

When an area of the sky is near white, the red, green, and blue light that make up the image will be near their maximum brightness. The typical way to shift an area toward blue using **Curves** is to increase the amount of blue light being used, but that won't be possible in this instance. To make blue light more prominent, the amount of red and green light need to be reduced. This will also have the effect of darkening the area.

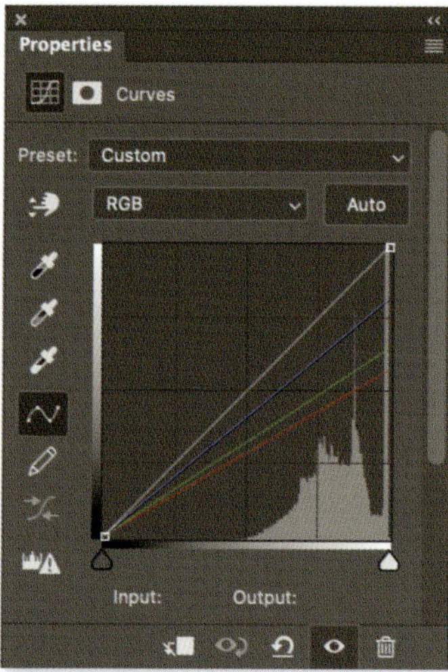

The green and red curves were moved down farther than the blue to make blue more prominent. This was done from the upper right since that is where white is represented. Blue was also lowered to further darken the sky. The layer mask attached to the adjustment layer was then edited to limit the change to the brightest areas of the image.

Sky Replacement
When none of the above tricks work, it may be necessary to use **Edit>Sky Replacement** in Photoshop, as detailed on page 108 in chapter 5.

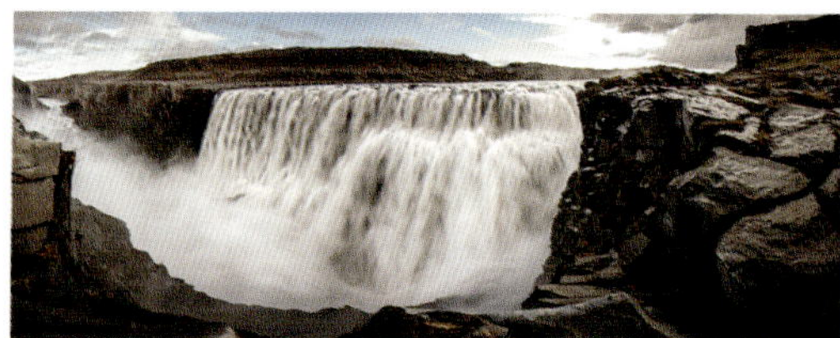

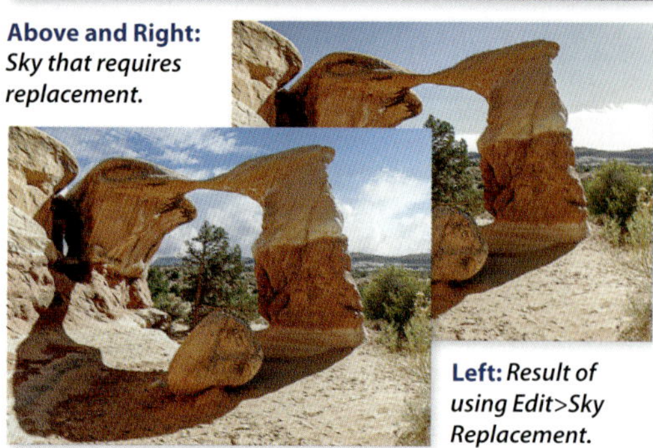

Above and Right: *Sky that requires replacement.*

Left: *Result of using Edit>Sky Replacement.*

Section II: Quality Considerations

Backlit

When the sun is behind an object, you have the choice to either expose for the object and render the sky as solid white, fill in the backlit areas with a flash, or expose for the sky and end up with a dull and lifeless subject. Below are a few ways to breath life into backlit objects.

Adjust via Inverted Sky Mask

Backlit scenes will often exhibit a split histogram that represents the sky as a tall portion in the right half and the dull-looking subject as a tall area in the left half. To get the best of both worlds, those two tall areas will effectively need to be merged so you make use of the full brightness range available.

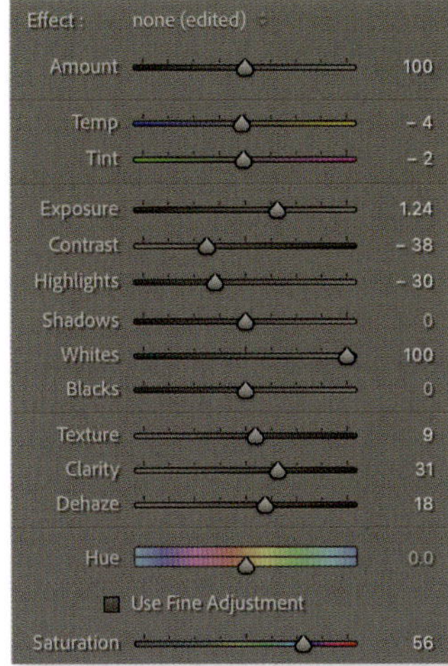

Adjustments applied via an inverted sky mask to brighten, optimize color, and exaggerate detail in dull, backlit subject.

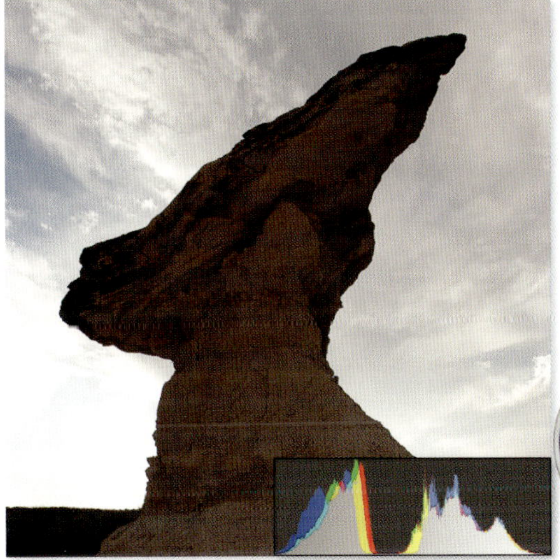

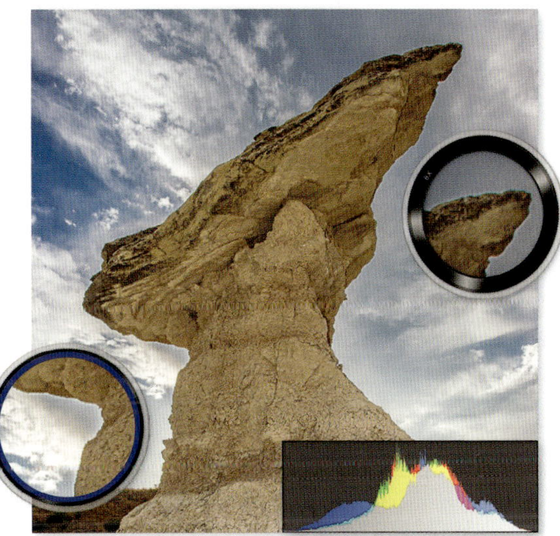

This can be done in Lightroom by isolating the sky using the masking feature, turning on the **Invert** checkbox, and then cranking up the **Whites** slider. Also, shady areas will usually look best with a custom white balance adjustment, as they will usually have a blue color cast due to being lit by the blue sky above. **Clarity** can also be useful in making the detail pop out a bit.

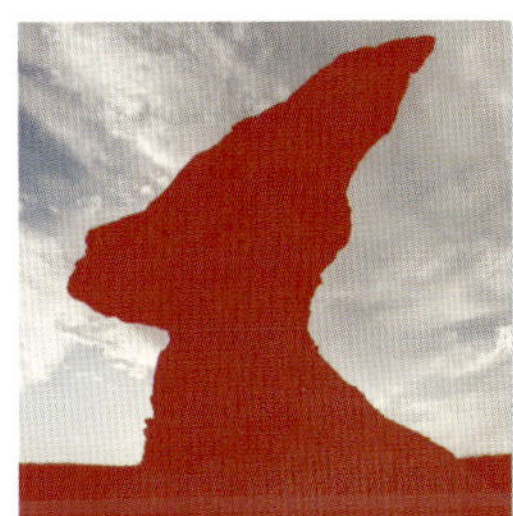

Inverted sky mask isolated the subject before Whites were boosted to brighten subject.

Use Edge Mask to Fix Transition Areas

Applying extreme adjustments will usually produce undesirable artifacts where the subject touches the sky. This can sometimes be remedied by adjusting the transition area separately with a second sky mask that subtracts the sky from the resulting mask. It sounds counterintuitive, but you'll end up with a mask that isolates just the transition between subject and sky.

Fix It in Photoshop

If that approach fails to fix the transition issues, then it may be necessary to refine the mask in Photoshop and possibly apply some halo reduction, which is covered on page 178 in chapter 9.

High-Contrast Scenes

When I encounter a high-contrast scenario, I usually view it as an opportunity to simplify the scene. This can be done by exposing for the highlights and allowing the shadows to be rendered as solid black, or exposing for the shadows to present them on a solid-white background.

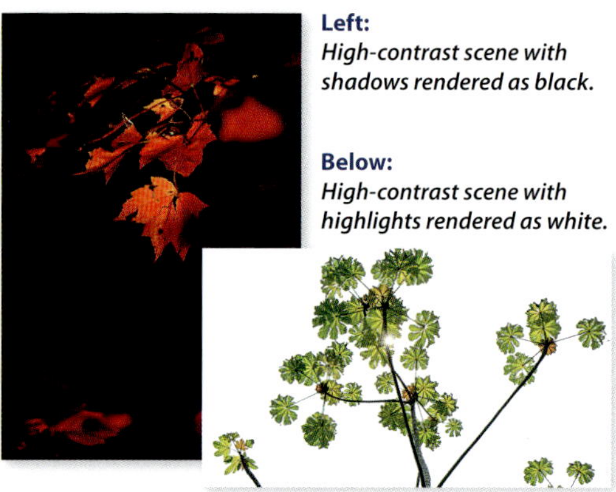

Left:
High-contrast scene with shadows rendered as black.

Below:
High-contrast scene with highlights rendered as white.

If I want to retain detail in both the highlights and shadows, then it would be best to capture multiple exposures that vary in brightness and later combine them into an HDR image as described in chapter 5.

If I didn't think to capture multiple exposures, then I'll usually end up with bright areas appearing unnaturally bright and dark areas appearing so dark that it's hard to make out the detail. In that situation, it's going to be quite a challenge to optimize the image. Let's explore what can be done with a single exposure of this sort.

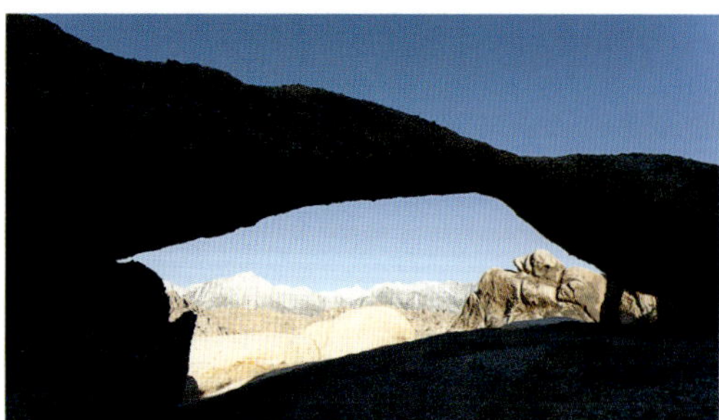

High-contrast image with default settings.

Revealing Lightroom's Limitations

Optimizing a single high-contrast exposure in Lightroom will usually require that the bright areas be isolated using the masking features, and then some rather extreme adjustments be applied. You'll quickly wish that Lightroom's masking adjustments were not limited to a small subset of adjustments offered in the rest of the Develop module.

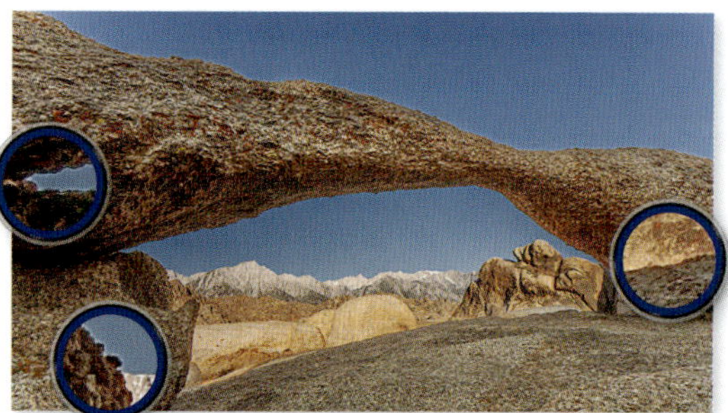

Processed using Lightroom's limited choices, which produced abrupt edge artifacts and a sky that has an unnatural look.

Multi-Processed Raw

I find it's often best to stack multiple Lightroom Develop settings as separate layers in Photoshop. Here's the process I use:

Create Snapshots in Lightroom

Start by mentally separating the image into bright and dark regions, and then process each area independently of the other. First, adjust the image until the highlights look just right, while ignoring how those changes affect the shadows. Save these settings as a snapshot by expanding the left side panel in the Develop module and clicking the **+** icon at the top of the Snapshots panel. Then, start over and process the image so the dark areas look good, while ignoring how those changes affect the highlights, and save the results as another snapshot.

Stack as Smart Objects in Photoshop

Next, stack the two versions of the image by choosing **Photo>Edit In>Open as Smart Object in Photoshop**, then choosing **Layer>Smart Objects>New Smart Object Via Copy** in Photoshop.

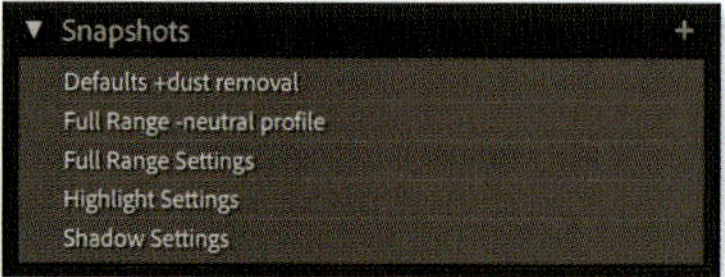

Snapshots used to store multiple raw Develop settings.

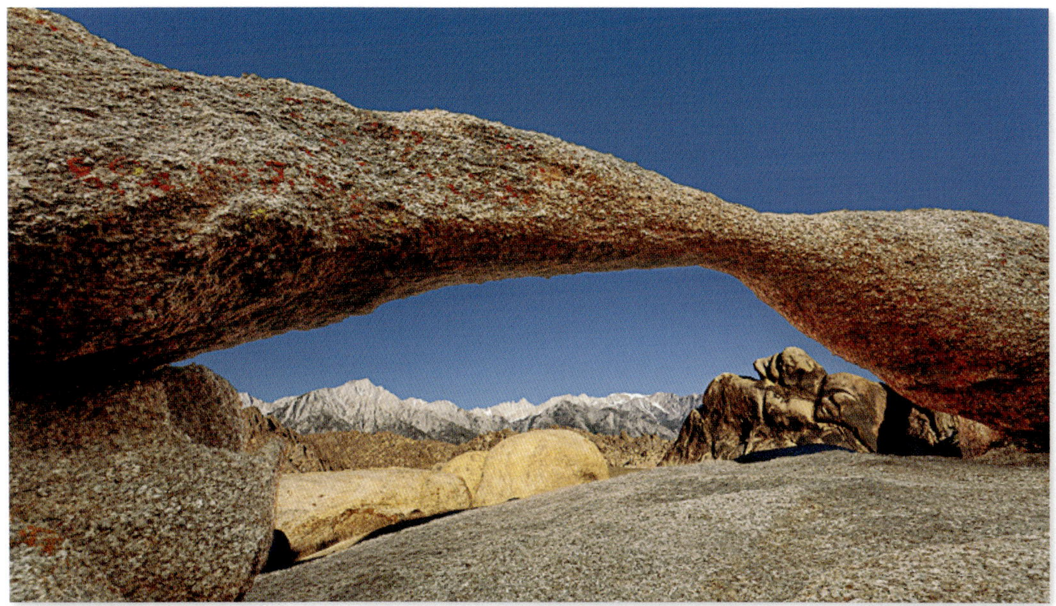

Two versions of the same image stacked on top of each other with a layer mask limiting where the top layer is visible.

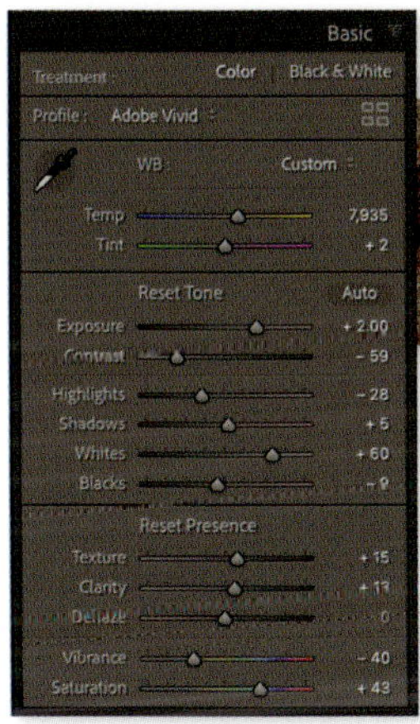

Optimized for dark areas.

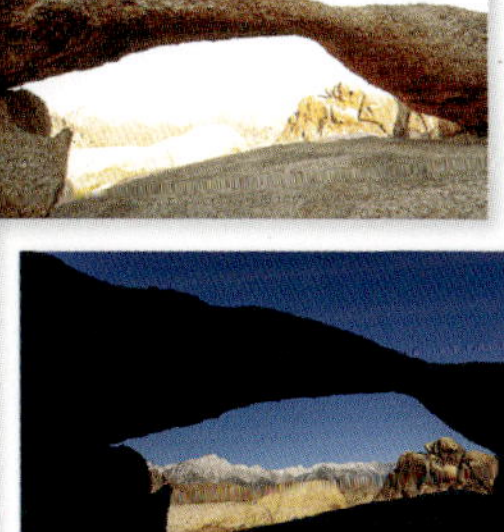

Optimized for bright areas.

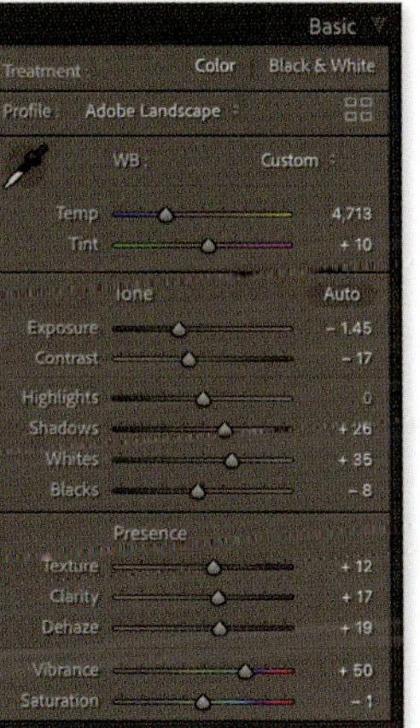

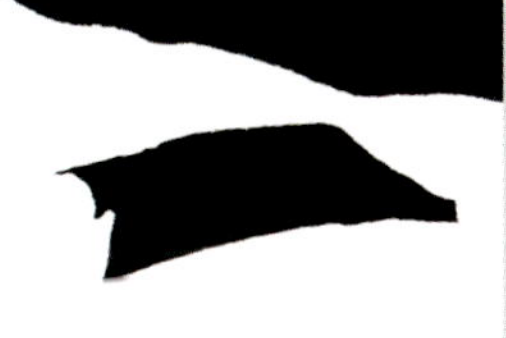

Contents of layer mask used to combine images that were optimized using two sets of raw-processing settings.

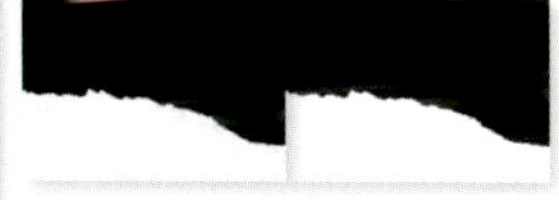

Before and after refinement.

Apply Snapshot

You can then double-click on the thumbnail image for the top layer, which will open Adobe Camera Raw. Here, you can click on the Snapshot icon near the upper right and choose which snapshot should be used for the layer.

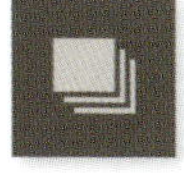

Select Optimized Areas of Top Layer

Select the optimized portion of the top layer using the selection and masking techniques covered in chapter 3. (In my case, I used a combination of **Select>Sky** and the **Object Selection** tool.)

Add Layer Mask

With the top layer active, click the Layer Mask icon at the bottom of the Layers panel. This will convert the active selection into a mask, hiding the non-selected areas to reveal the underlying layer.

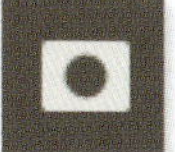

Refine Results

The result will likely need to be refined using the techniques described in chapter 3, to get the mask just right, and chapter 9, to rid the image of any undesirable processing artifacts.

Keystoning

When capturing a group of trees, I prefer to shoot from far away so I can keep my camera level and render each tree as a vertical line. Shooting from a distance also has the advantage of visually compressing the space between near and far trees.

When I'm forced to shoot from a closer distance, I'll have to tilt my camera upward in order to include the upper reaches of the trees. Tilting the camera causes the upper portion of the trees to be farther away from the camera and therefore appear smaller relative to their base.

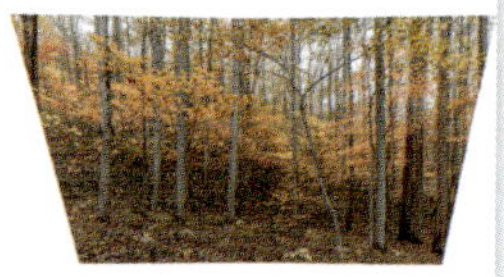
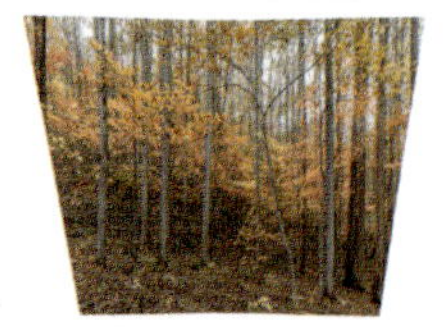
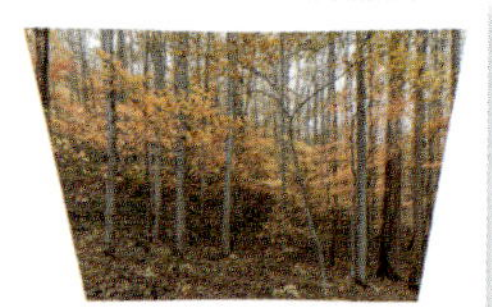

Top Left: *Aspect -100.*

Top Right: *Aspect +100.*

Bottom Left: *Aspect 0.*

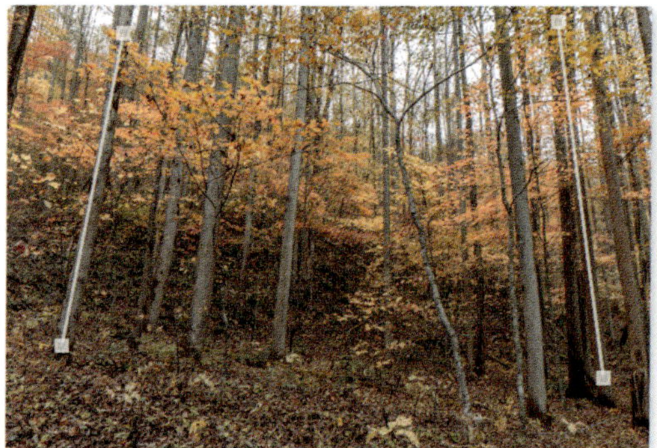

Lines parallel to trees were added on each side of the image.

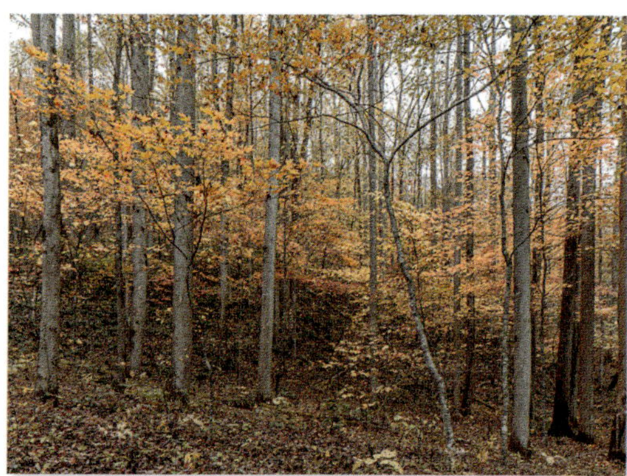

Result of using the Guided Upright tool to straighten trees.

Guided Upright
Typing **Shift-T** activates the **Guided Upright** tool in the Transform panel of Lightroom's Develop module. With that tool active, you can click near the base of a tree near the left edge of the frame and drag upward to produce a line that is parallel to the tree. Then, create a second line that is parallel to a tree on the opposite side of the image and Lightroom will transform the image to render those lines as perfectly vertical. You can also drag a third line horizontally if there is an obvious horizon that looks to be askew.

Adjust Aspect Ratio, Scale, and Position
You may find it useful to adjust the **Aspect** slider to stretch or compress the width and height of the results to make the trees feel taller or more spread apart. As a result, the newly transformed image will not likely fit within the original document's bounds. This can be remedied by enlarging or reducing the image via the **Scale** slider, and then fine-tuning its position by adjusting the **X Offset** and **Y Offset** sliders

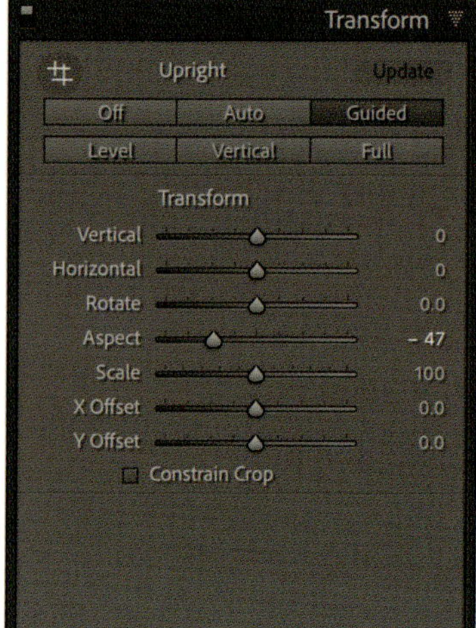

The sliders can be useful to fine-tune the results of the Guided Upright tool.

Crop to Rectangular Image
Transforming the image in this way will produce a trapezoidal image that will need to be cropped in order to produce a rectangle.

Section II: Quality Considerations

Chromatic Aberration

Light passing through the outer edges of the glass elements that make up a camera lens becomes dispersed in a similar fashion to being sent through a prism, causing the colors of light to arrive at the camera's sensor misaligned. This shows up as undesirable color fringing that clings to high-contrast edges within an image. The effect is more pronounced in inexpensive lenses, wide-angle lenses, and when shooting at a wide-open aperture. Lightroom offers three methods for dealing with this issue.

Lens Profile Corrections

Turning on the **Remove Chromatic Aberration** checkbox in the Lens Corrections panel of the Develop module will correct for the most common types of red/green and blue/yellow color fringing.

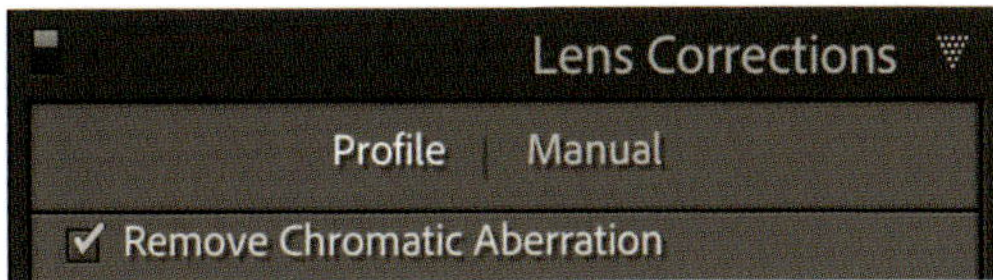

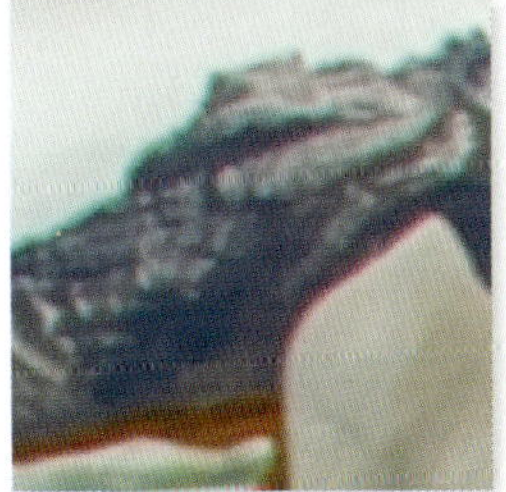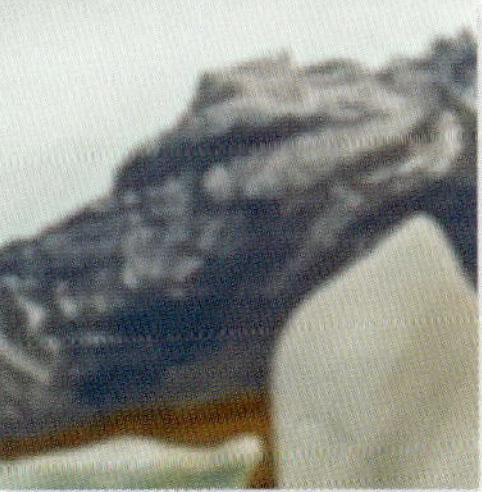

Before and after correcting for chromatic aberrations.

Manual Correction

If you find purple or green edge fringing after applying the above correction, then choose the **Manual** option at the 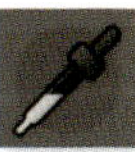 top of the Lens Corrections panel, click on the **Fringe Color Selector** icon, and click on the most intensely colored part of the undesirable color fringing. This will cause the **Amount** and **Purple Hue** or **Green Hue** sliders to be adjusted in an attempt to remove the color fringing. You may need to manually fine-tune those sliders to achieve ideal results.

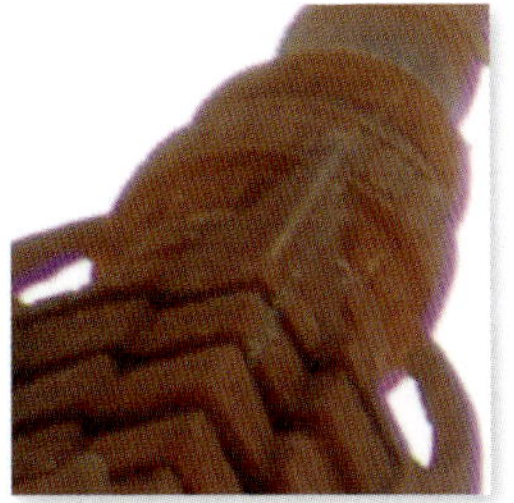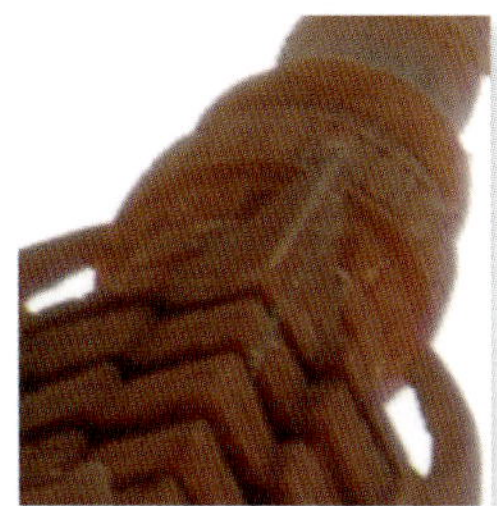

Before and after using the Fringe Color Selector tool.

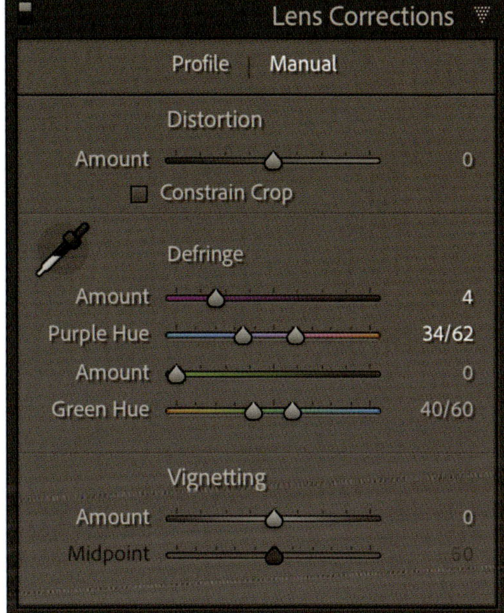

The Manual section of the Lens Corrections panel.

Defringe via Masking

Your last resort for ridding an area of undesirable color fringing on the edge of an object is to type **K** to create a new **Brush** mask, paint over the problem area, and then adjust the **Defringe** slider.

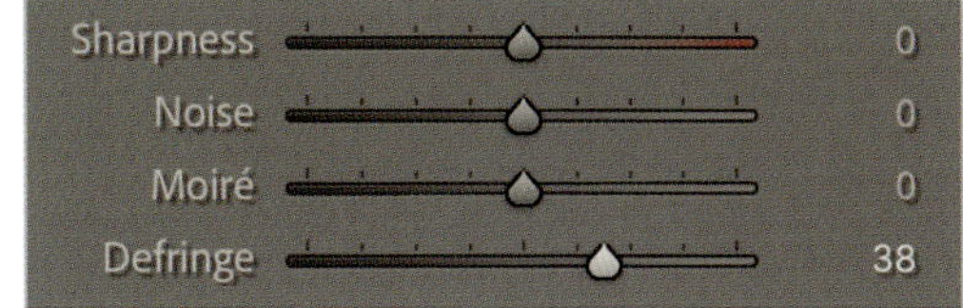

The Defringe slider is available when using Lightroom's masking features.

Crooked Horizons

The liquid in your ears acts as a bubble level that allows you to sense the angle of your head in relation to the horizon, even in pitch darkness. When the horizon in a photo is not aligned with what your brain senses as being level, then the photo can feel off, even if you're not able to point your finger at exactly what is wrong. For that reason, I try to keep my horizon level unless I have a darn good reason to deviate from it.

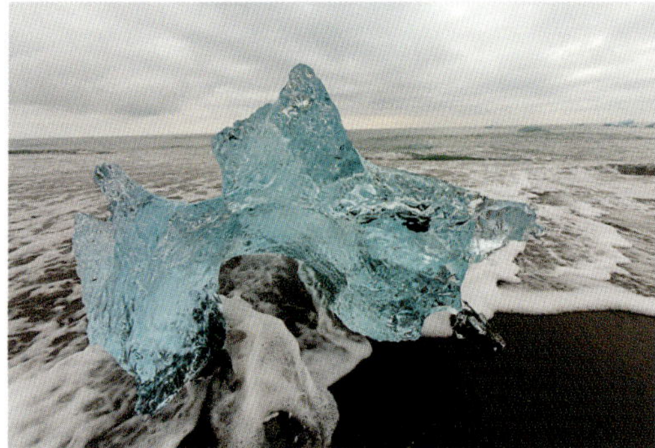

A slightly off-level horizon was the result of correcting fish-eye lens distortion in this image.

Crop and Straighten in Lightroom

Typing **R** will activate the **Crop** tool in the Develop module, where the **Auto** button can be used to quickly level images that feature a prominent horizon line. You can also opt to manually level an image by clicking on the **Straighten** tool, which looks like a bubble level, and dragging a line that is parallel to the horizon.

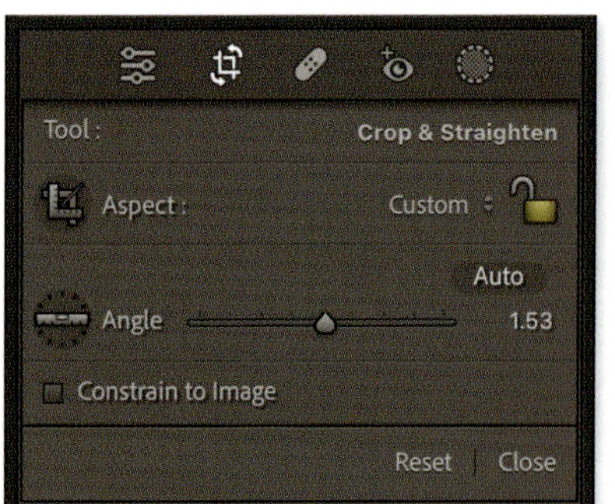

The Straighten tool is found to the left of the Angle setting when the Crop tool is active in Lightroom.

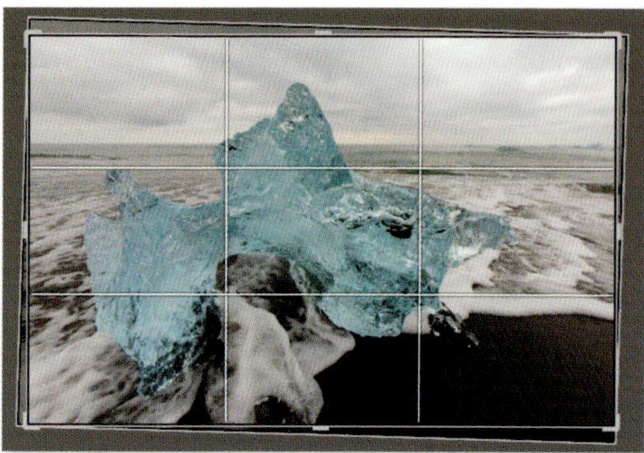

Result of straightening the horizon using the Straighten tool.

Guided Upright Tool

Typing **Shift-T** to access Lightroom's **Guided Upright** tool will allow you to straighten two independent areas instead of rotating the image as a whole. First, draw a line across the horizon to indicate that it needs to be straightened. Next, draw a second line either horizontally near the edge of the image to indicate that nothing near that edge needs to be rotated, or at an angle to also straighten a second area that appears askew. Once both lines are drawn, the image will be transformed to make both lines perfectly horizontal.

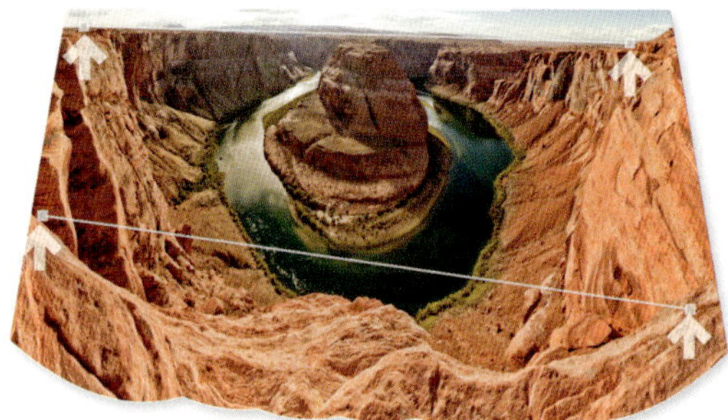

Two lines were drawn using the Guided Upright tool.

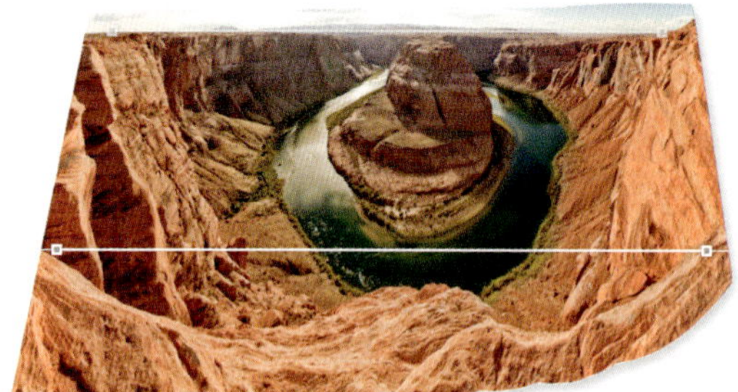

Result produced from using the Guided Upright tool.

Section II: Quality Considerations

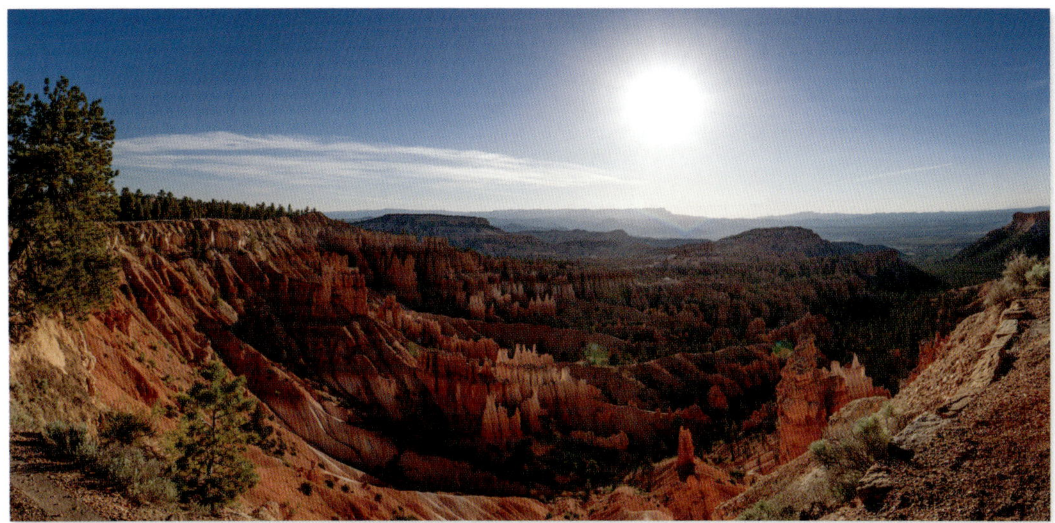

Result of straightening horizon using the Adaptive Wide Angle filter in Photoshop.

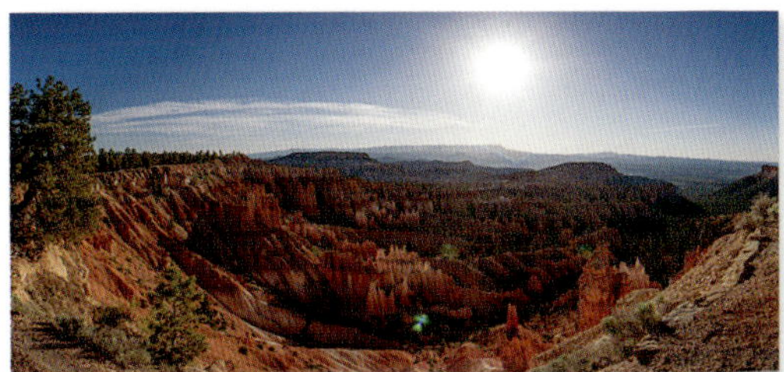

The horizon in this stitched panorama looks to droop as it makes its way toward the right edge of the image.

Adaptive Wide Angle in Photoshop

For panoramas, one option is to choose **Filter> Adaptive Wide Angle** in Photoshop, hold **Shift** (to indicate an area should become horizontal), and then drag a line across the horizon. As you drag, the line should curve in a similar fashion to the curvature of the horizon. I find that it will not always be able to match the curvature of the horizon when dragging from edge to edge. If this is the case, limit the line to three quarters of the width of the image, or instead use multiple lines.

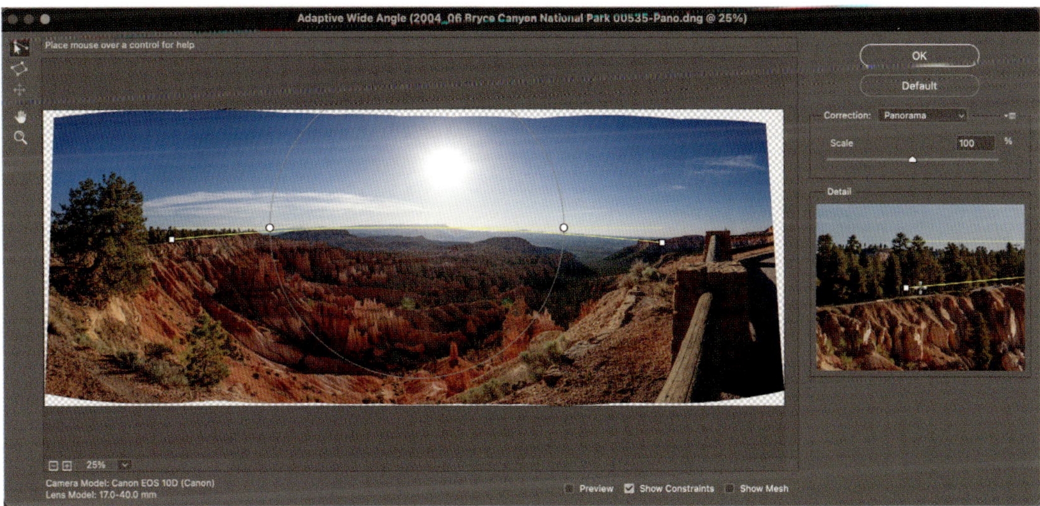

The Adaptive Wide Angle filter in Photoshop.

Lens Flare

Anytime light from the sun falls directly on the front glass element of a lens, it will create reflections that bounce between the various glass elements within the lens and produce lens flare. The anti-reflective coatings on those lens elements will cause the color of the flares to shift toward red or green and the shape of the aperture will influence their shape.

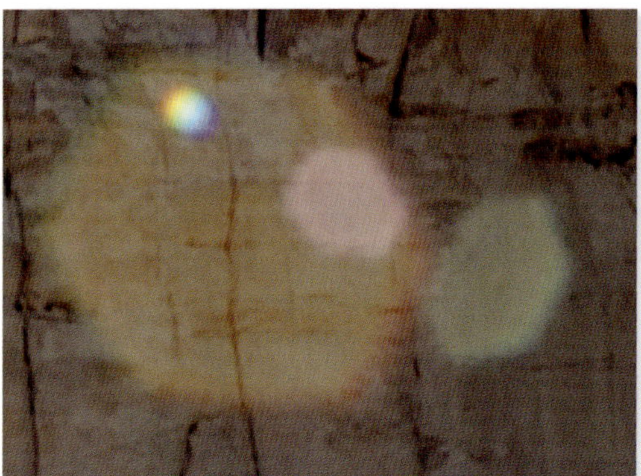

The smaller flares must be retouched out because they do not contain enough useful detail from the scene. The large flare retains detail and can be eliminated using Curves.

Lens shades help to reduce flares when the sun is not included in the photograph, but I often need to use my hand to cast a shadow onto the front element of the lens to eliminate them completely.

When the sun is included within the image, flares will be unavoidable. In that case, I often capture two shots, one with my thumb obstructing the camera's view of the sun to avoid flares and a second with the sun in view. I then mask the two images. But this chapter is about fixing shooting artifacts, so I'll assume you didn't use the above technique when capturing an image.

Some simple lens flares can be eliminated using the masking features in Lightroom, but I find that the majority of them benefit from the expanded feature set available in Photoshop.

Retouch Obscured Areas

Your only option for removing lens flares that completely obscure your view of the scene is to remove them with a retouching tool such as the **Spot Healing Brush**, as detailed in chapter 3.

Curves to Eliminate without Retouching

When the area affected by a lens flare retains a considerable amount of important detail, a **Curves** adjustment will be most effective, as it will allow you to both darken the flare and remove the color cast it caused.

Isolate Flare Using Quick Mask Mode

The first step is to create a selection to isolate the area. So, type **Q** to turn on **Quick Mask Mode**, **B** to choose the **Brush** tool, and then **D** to reset the foreground/background colors to black/white. Then paint over the area affected by the flare using a semi-soft brush.

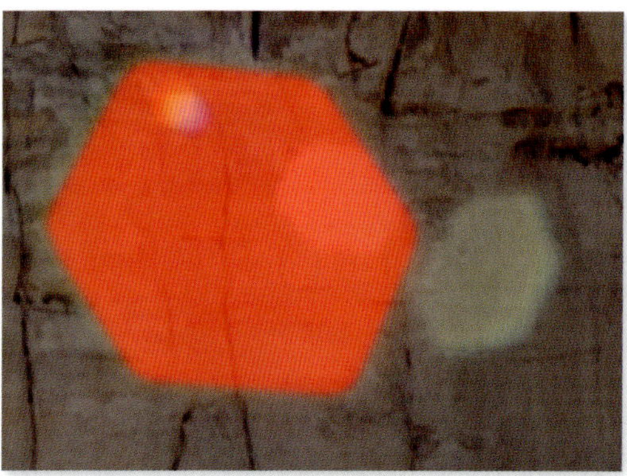

Lens flare isolated in Quick Mask Mode before being inverted.

For geometrically shaped flares, it can be useful to **Shift**-click at each corner to produce straight line segments. Since red represents areas that will not be selected, finish the selection by choosing **Image>Adjustments>Invert**, and then type **Q** to exit **Quick Mask Mode**.

Adjust Each Channel Using Curves

Next, choose **Window>Channels** and then **Layer>New Adjustment Layer>Curves**. Click on the **RGB** channel at the top of the Channels panel and then click on the **Red** channel to make it visible. If the lens flare is visible in that channel, change the pop-up menu above the curve from **RGB** to **Red**, and choose the **Targeted Adjustment** tool (that's the hand icon within **Curves**). Then, click within the flare and drag down until its brightness matches the surroundings.

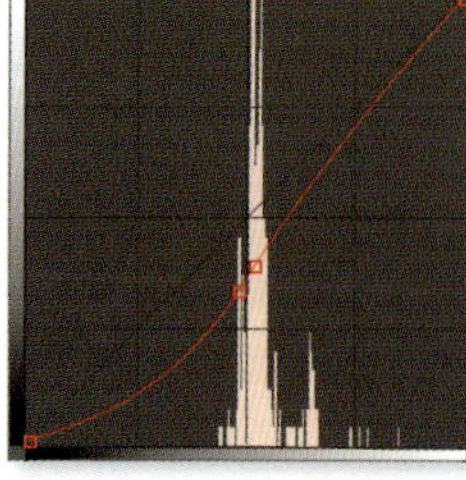

Section II: Quality Considerations

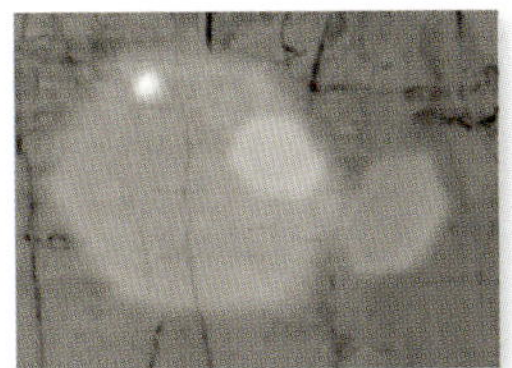 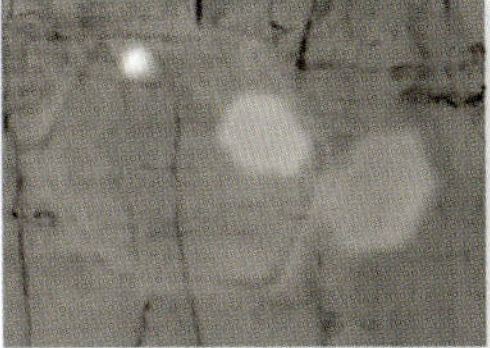

Red channel before and after adjustment with Curves.

For some images, you may need to adjust two areas within the flare, one bright and one dark, to make it match both the brightness and the contrast of the surroundings.

Now, click on the **Green** channel to make it visible, switch the menu above the curve to **Green**, and then click within the flare and drag down until it matches the brightness of the surrounding image. 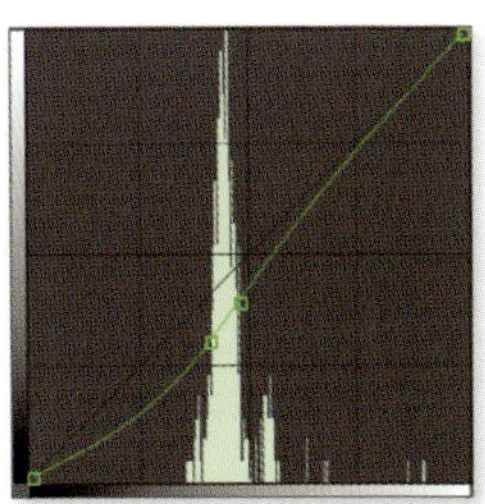

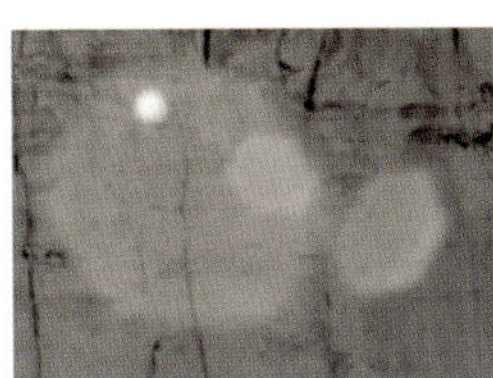 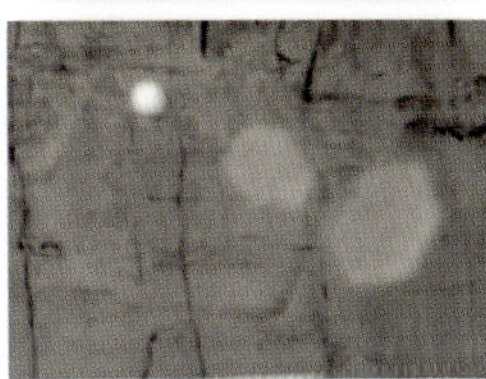

Green channel before and after adjustment with Curves.

To finish the adjustment, click on the **Blue** channel, choose **Blue** from the menu above the curve, and then click within the flare and drag down until it matches the surrounding image. 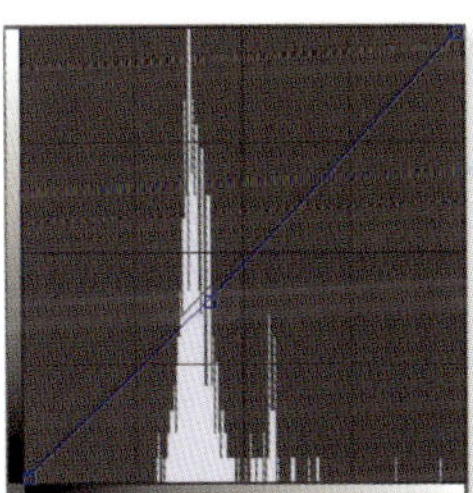

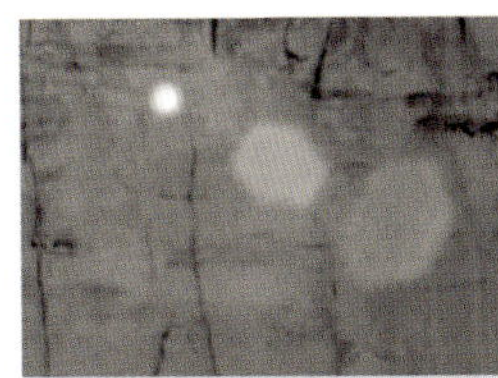 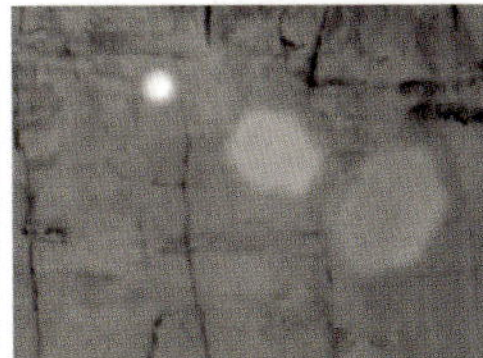

Blue channel before and after adjustment with Curves.

To see what you've done, click on the **RGB** channel to return to viewing the full-color image.

Refine Transition

At this point, you will likely have an okay adjustment, but the edges will not blend into the surrounding image. So, choose **Select>Select & Mask**, adjust the **Feather** slider to soften the edge, and then experiment with the **Shift Edge** slider to get the adjustment to blend into the surrounding image as best you can.

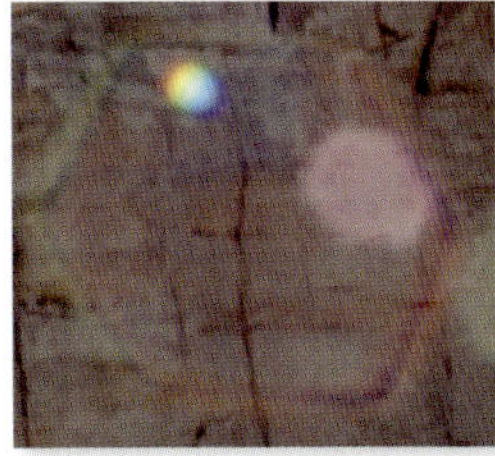 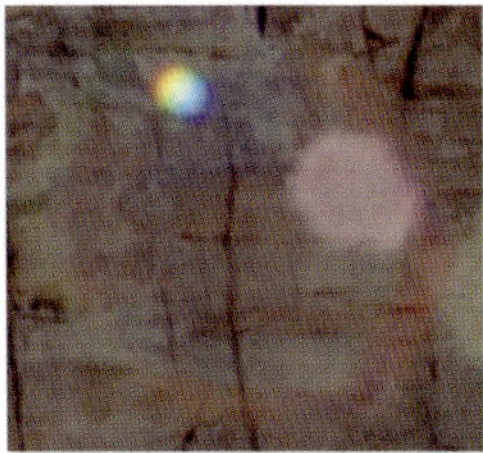

Before and after refining the transition using Select & Mask.

Eliminate Color Fringing

If the lens flare contained slightly different colors at its edge, then choose **Layer>New>Layer** and set the **Mode** pop-up menu to **Color** when prompted. Finally, type **B** to activate the **Brush** tool, choose a soft-edged brush, and **Option**-click (Mac) or **Alt**-click (PC) in an area immediately outside the flare to choose a color to paint with. Then paint over the transition area to shift its color. Repeat the process, changing colors often, and work your way around the full perimeter of the flare. 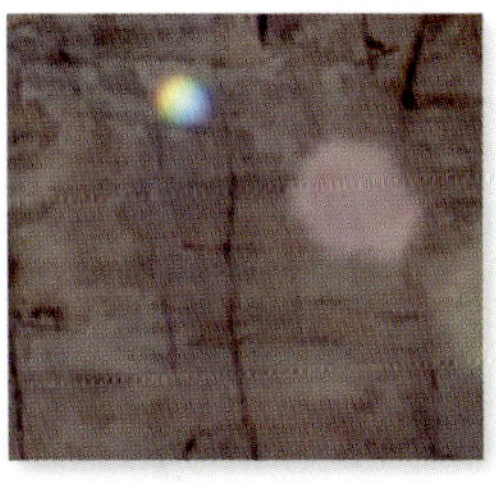

Result of painting on a layer set to Color mode.

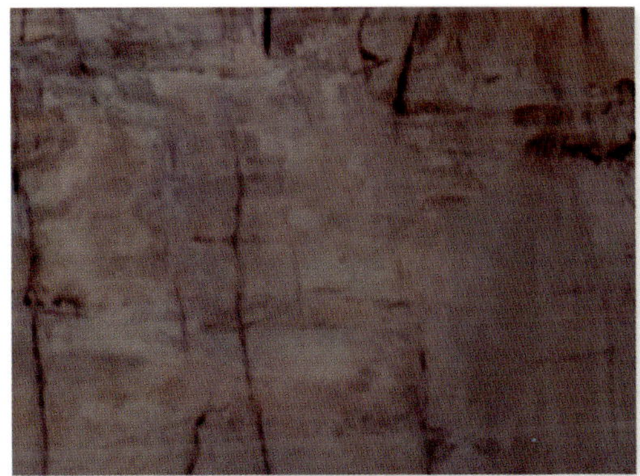

Lens flare completely eliminated.

Clone Source for Flare in Sunbursts

When including the sun within a photo and capturing it with a lens that is stopped down to f/16 or higher, it will frequently produce a sunburst that is intermixed with undesirable lens flares.

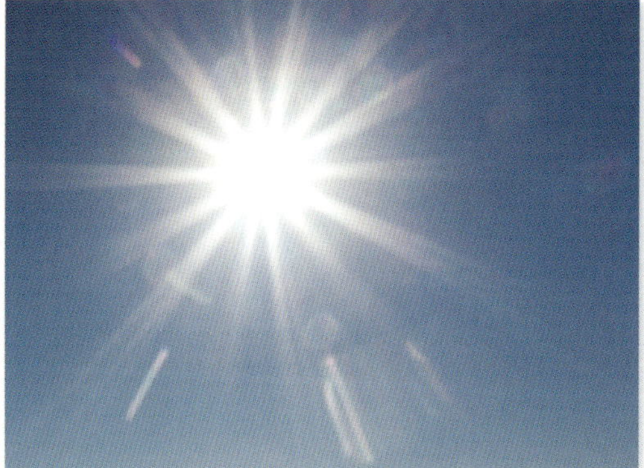

Sun captured using an aperture setting of f/22.

Create Retouching Layer

I start the process by choosing **Layer>New>Layer**, then activating the **Spot Healing Brush** and turning on the **Sample All Layers** checkbox in the Options Bar above the image.

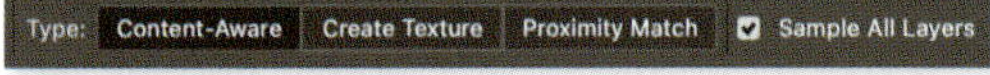

Eliminate Isolated Areas of Flare

With a hard-edged brush a little wider than an individual flare, paint over each individual flare that does not overlap the sunburst to get rid of the ones that are easy to retouch, leaving only those that are intermixed with the sunburst.

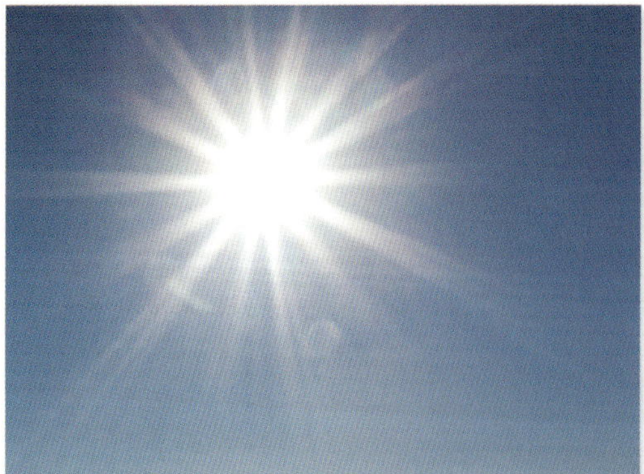

All remaining lens flares overlap the sunburst at this point.

Prepare Healing Brush

At this point, switch to the **Healing Brush** tool, set the **Sample** pop-up menu in the Options Bar to **Current & Below**, and turn on the **Aligned** checkbox.

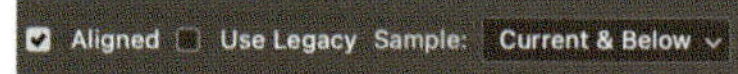

Flip, Rotate, and Scale Using Clone Source

The settings within the **Window>Clone Source** panel will allow you to scale, rotate, or flip what is being cloned by the **Healing Brush**.

It's much more convenient to utilize keyboard shortcuts to change the settings in the Clone Source panel to avoid having to move away from the area you intend to retouch. All the keyboard shortcuts involve holding **Shift-Option** (Mac) or **Shift-Alt** (PC). Add **<** or **>** to rotate, **]** or **[** to scale, or the **arrow keys** to nudge the position after clicking to establish where the retouching will be applied.

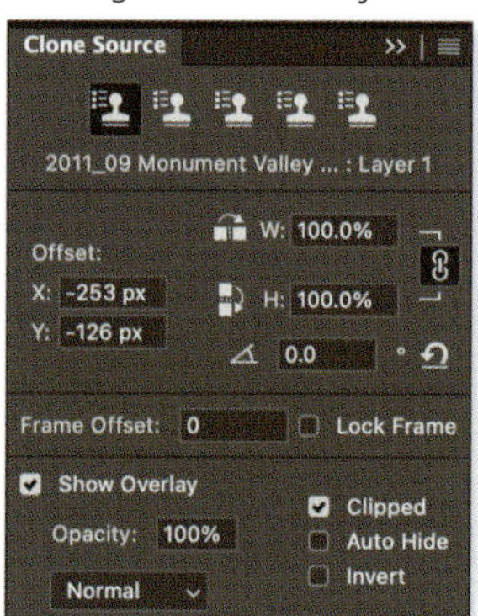

The general idea is to inspect the area surrounding a lens flare and then find a matching clean area that can be rotated and scaled to match the area requiring retouching. The retouching tools are covered in more detail in chapter 3.

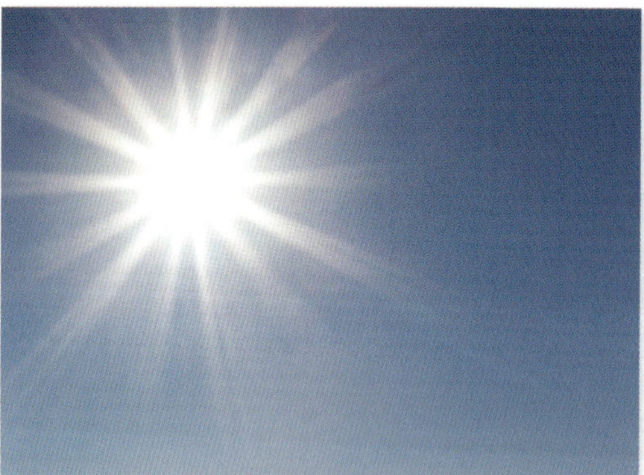

Result of using the Healing Brush to remove flare.

Vignetting and Distortion

Most lenses will produce noticeable darkening at the corners of the image. This is known as vignetting. I usually like this effect because it helps to direct the viewer's eye toward the middle of the image. However, the effect can be a bit too obvious when the image features a simple blue sky.

Lens Profile Corrections

You can attempt to correct for this darkening effect by turning on the **Enable Profile Corrections** checkbox in the **Lens Corrections** section of Lightroom's Develop module. If you find that the results do not completely deal with the issue, the **Vignetting** slider below can be used to either increase or decrease the adjustment.

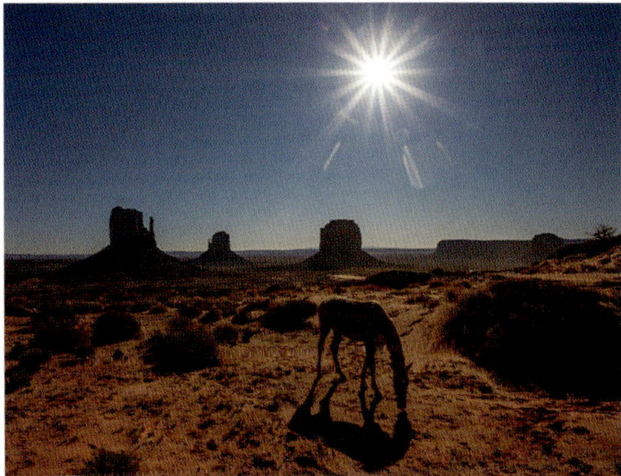

The corners of this image are darker than the center due to lens vignetting.

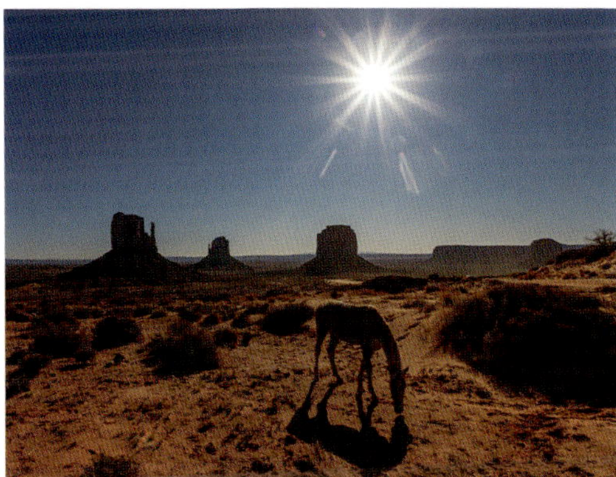

The result of turning on the Enable Profile Corrections checkbox.

Reversing Fish-Eye Lens Distortion

The same checkbox used to remove vignetting will also cause images shot with fish-eye lenses to be straightened. If you would like to remove vignetting but would prefer to maintain the fish-eye effect, then set the **Distortion** slider to zero.

Enable Profile Corrections also corrects distortion from other lenses that causes trees to bow inward or outward toward the edges of the image.

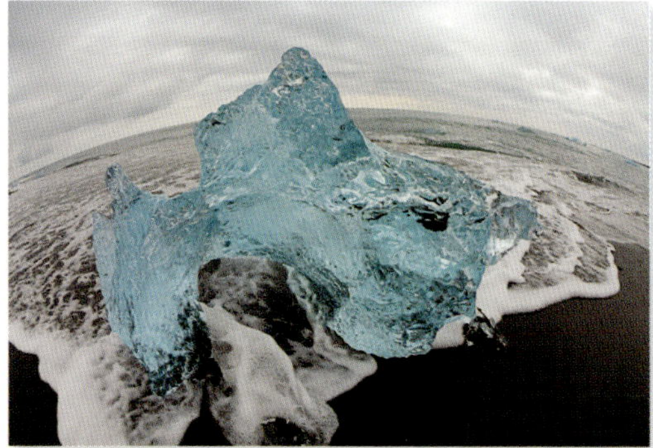

Image captured with a 15mm fish-eye lens.

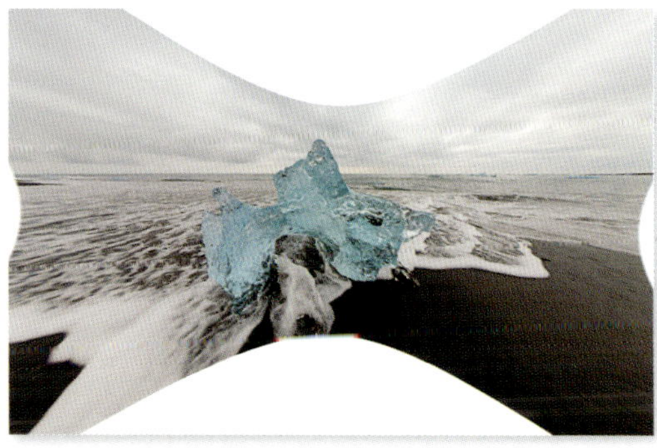

Result of applying lens profile corrections.

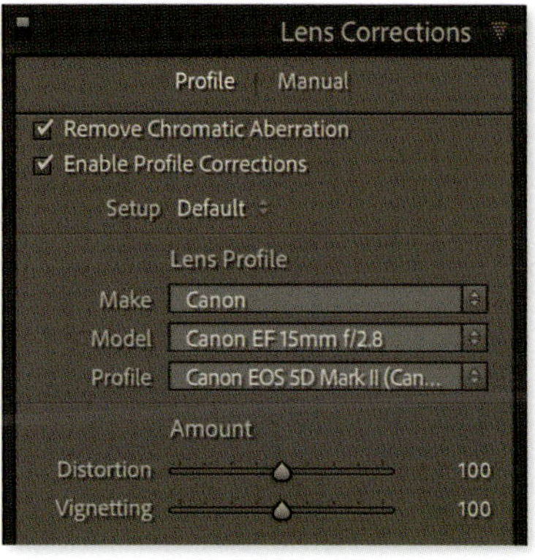

Lens Corrections settings used to straighten the fish-eye distortion in the above image.

Reducing Haze

When you point your camera in the general direction of the setting sun and allow its light to fall directly onto the front of your lens, the result is a bunch of nasty lens flares spread across the scene.

Pan your camera across the scene and the flares will shift in position, collectively forming a straight line that originates at the sun's position.

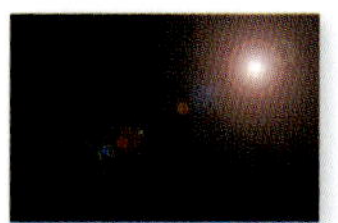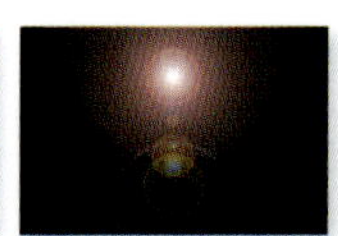

Straight line alignment of lens flares with sun position.

Pan far enough that the sun is outside the camera's view and your lens hood should block the direct sunlight and effectively prevent lens flare. If you forget to deploy that lens hood, or have one of ineffective design, then direct sunlight will rake across the front of the lens at such an extreme angle that it will bounce all over the interior of the lens and flood the sensor with light that did not come from the scene you are photographing. This causes the dark areas of the image to look as if they are obscured by a dense yellowish-white haze and pushes the histogram to the right, leaving a considerable gap on the left.

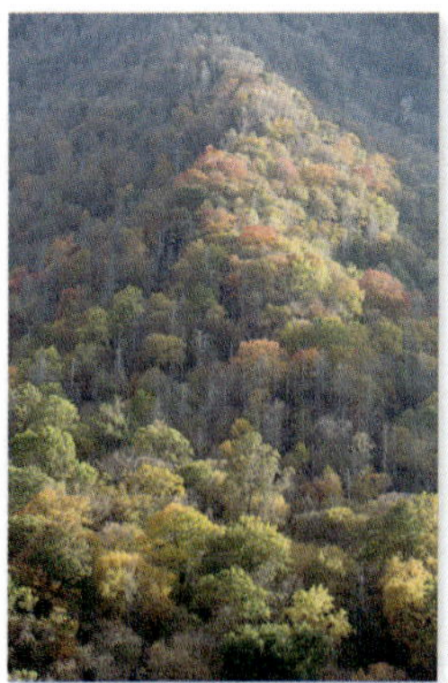

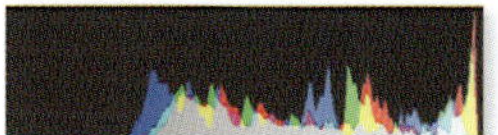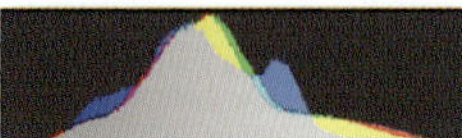

Left: *A huge gap on the left indicates the darkest area within the image is not very dark, causing the image to appear hazy.*
Right: *Gaps on both sides of the histogram indicate that no part of the image is close to black or white.*

A similar hazy appearance can occur when shooting at sunrise when the temperature has not risen enough to burn off a slight mist that hugs the ground and becomes back-lit by the rising sun.

Tone Curve for Ultimate Control

I prefer to adjust hazy images using the Tone Curve panel in Lightroom's Develop module. I use the **Point Curve** option **A** because it allows for more precise control than the parametric option that is found to its left.

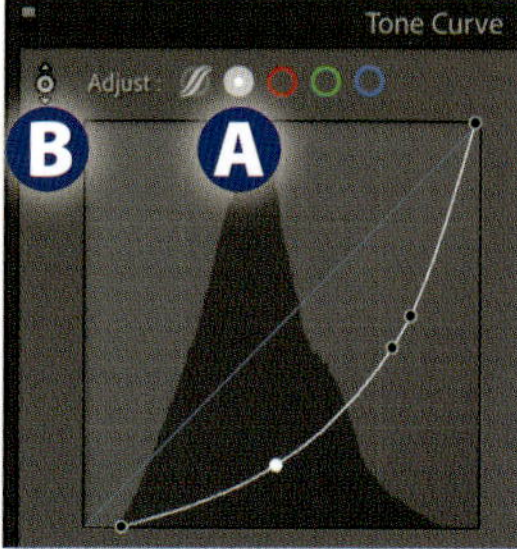

Establish Black Point

For hazy images, I usually start by clicking on the lower-left point on the curve, dragging down slightly to ensure that I don't unknowingly cause it to rise, and then slide it to the right while inspecting the darkest areas of the image. I generally want the absolutely darkest area to appear as a nice inky black. At the same time, I pay attention to its position relative to the left end of the histogram, knowing that nothing will become black until it touches the histogram. Going past the beginning of the histogram will start

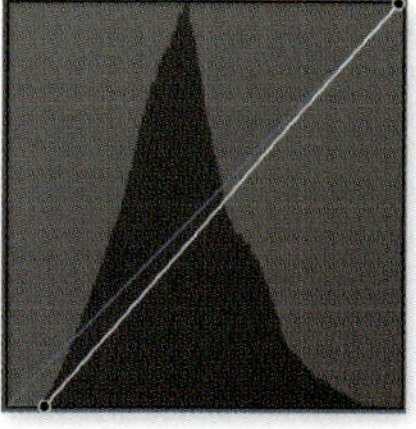

to force large areas to solid black. Most of the time, I end up with it kissed right up against that edge.

Adjust Highlight Brightness

Next, I choose the **Targeted Adjustment** tool **B**, click on what appears to be the brightest area within the image, and then drag up to brighten or down to darken the area. While doing this, I focus my attention exclusively on the brightest area and am not worried about what happens to the rest of the image. In most cases, darkening does the trick.

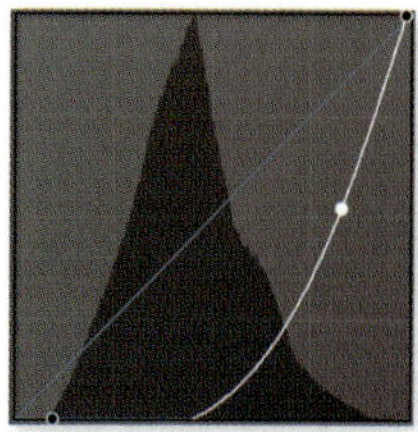

Now that the brightness of the brightest areas has been adjusted, I turn my attention to what has happened to the area between the two dots I've

Section II: Quality Considerations

adjusted so far. I look for parts of the curve that have abruptly bottomed or topped out. If that's happened, I'll click on the curve to add a point just to the left of the point that was added to adjust the brightest area. I'll then adjust its position in order to "steer" the curve so that it results in a smooth line between the existing points.

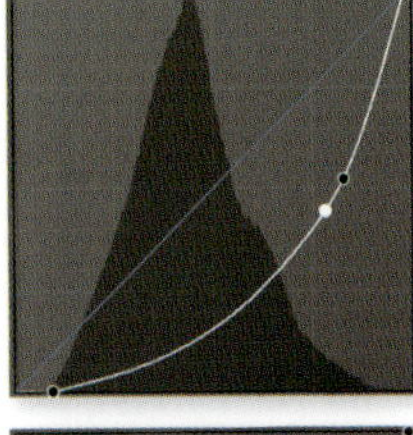

To finish the adjustment, I choose the **Targeted Adjustment** tool again, click on an area of medium brightness, and then drag up to fine-tune its brightness.

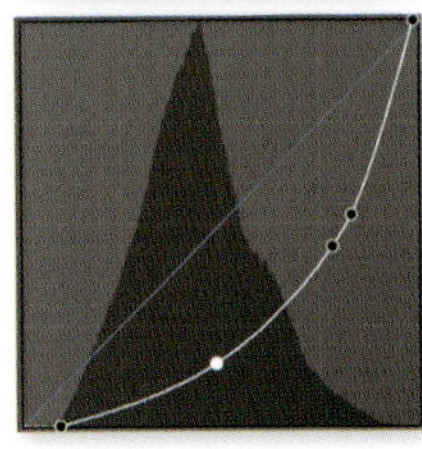

Feel free to adjust additional areas as well, but you will likely find it's difficult to produce smooth transitions as you add more points to the curve.

Fine-Tune Results with Basic Panel

Optimizing the overall brightness and contrast is only the first step, and I don't shy from heading over to the Basic panel to dial in settings such as **Texture**, **Clarity**, and white balance. I'll often supplement that with a few masked adjustments to polish off the image.

If you're not comfortable with **Curves**, you can use the **Blacks** and **Whites** sliders to establish the overall brightness range used, and then adjust **Highlights**, **Shadows**, and **Contrast** to tweak the rest of the tonal range.

The **Dehaze** slider can be especially useful with hazy images since it will concentrate on the darkest areas. When those areas get close to becoming black, it will back off and shift to darkening the medium brightness areas.

Finally, when one area seems to reach its limit, consider applying additional adjustments via a mask to limit where they affect the image.

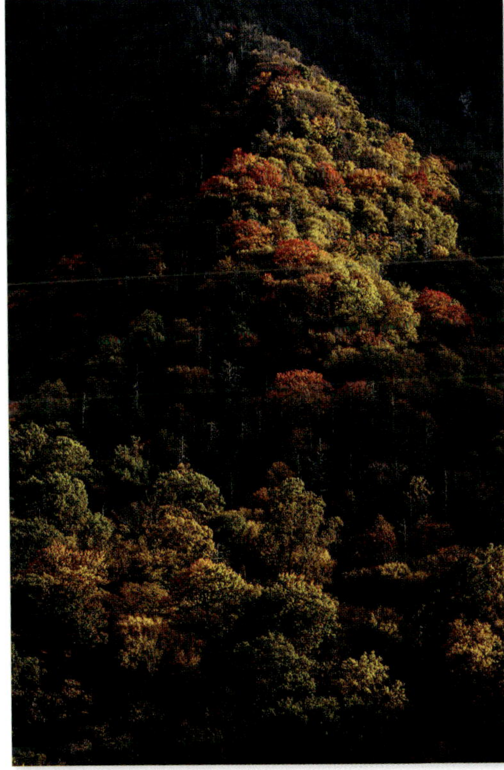

Result of optimizing appearance using the Tone Curve.

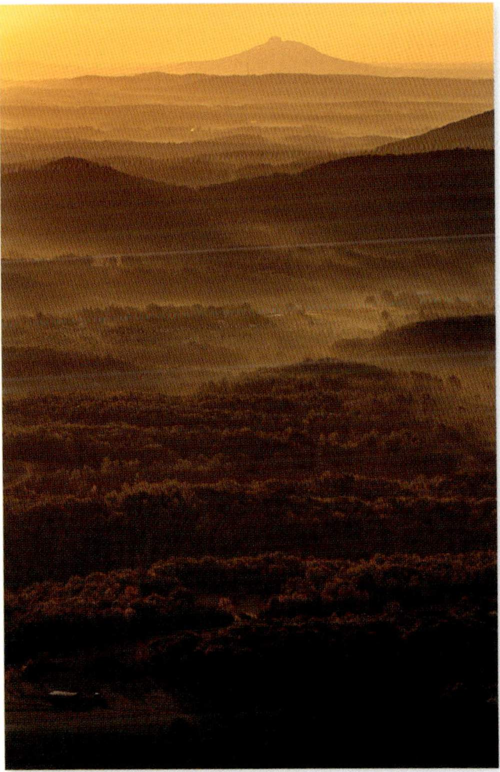

Optimized using the Basic panel and masked adjustments.

Chapter 4: Eliminate Shooting Artifacts

Chapter 5

Extend Potential with Multiple Exposures

CAPTURING MULTIPLE EXPOSURES of a scene and blending them together into a seamless composite image allows you to go well beyond the technical limitations of your camera. That includes extending the brightness range you can capture with *high dynamic range* or extending depth of field with *focus stacking*. You can even capture images at different times of day to produce an idealized image that cannot be seen by the naked eye. The key is to imagine what is possible while still in the field so you can capture the right raw material for later combining in Photoshop.

Extend Dynamic Range

Human vision is capable of perceiving detail in a crazily wide brightness range. Digital cameras, on the other hand, are capable of capturing a much more limited brightness range. That's why detail is lost when you point a camera at a scene that includes the intensely bright sun as well as areas that are in deep shadow. This causes the brightest or darkest areas to be rendered as either white or black, depending on the exposure setting used.

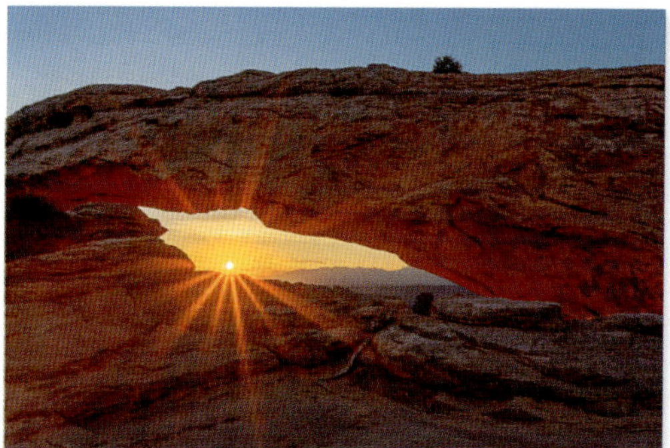

High-dynamic-rage image that produces a result that is similar to how you experienced the scene with your eyes.

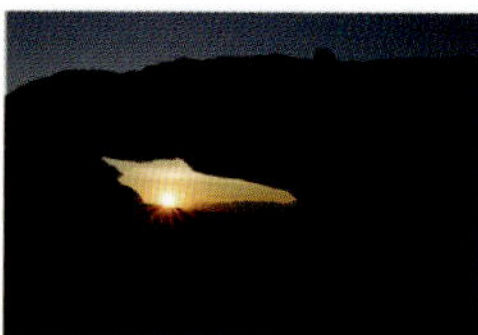
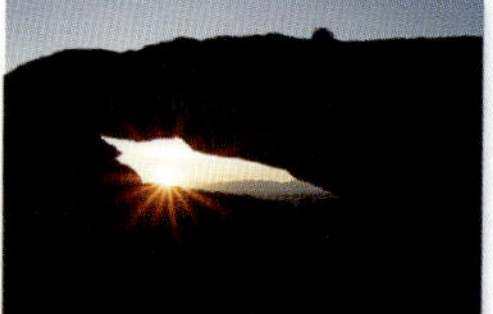
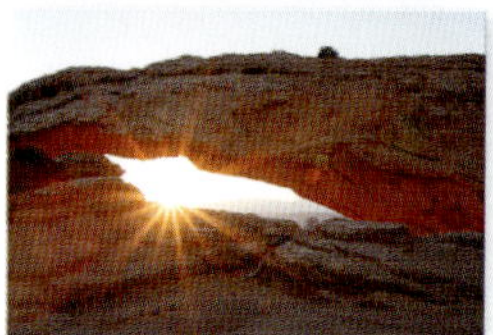

A variety of exposures captured using the limited dynamic range of a digital camera. Each image contains a large area that is lacking detail and is rendered as black or white.

The brightness range in which a camera is capable of capturing detail is known as its dynamic range and is measured in stops. A stop is defined as a doubling or halving of the amount of light. Human vision can perceive detail across up to 24 stops of range, while a digital camera is limited to 12–15 stops. When the scene you are attempting to capture contains a brightness range greater than 15 stops, your camera will be forced to either render the darkest area as solid black or the brightest area as solid white, and sometimes both.

Capture Full Brightness Range of a Scene

Histograms that are not wide enough to cover the full width available indicate that the full brightness range of the scene was captured without clipping areas to solid black or white.

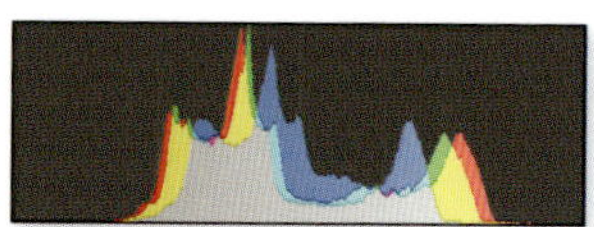
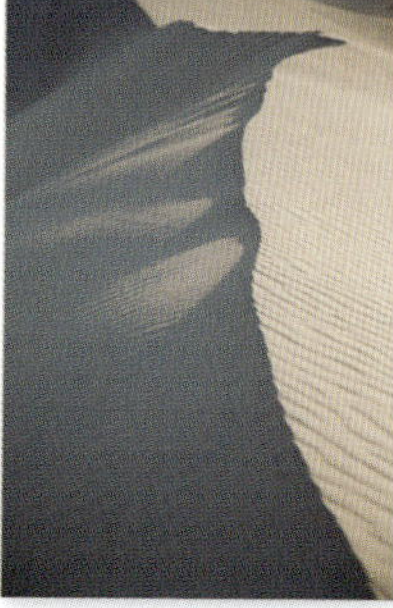

Image and histogram with a brightness range that is well within the dynamic range of the camera used.

Avoid Clipping Highlights to White

A histogram that extends all the way to the extreme right of the area available indicates that the absolute brightest area of the image is lacking detail and has been rendered as solid white. When that's the case, the height of the rightmost bar indicates how large of an area has lost detail.

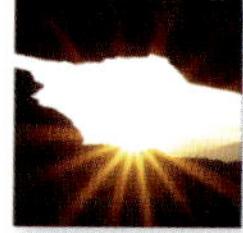
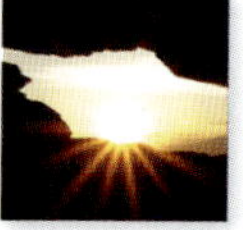
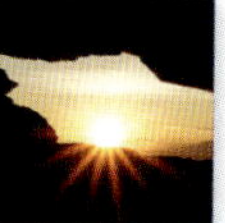
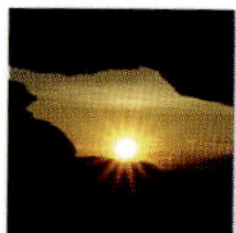

Exposures taken one stop apart and adjusted to the point where maximum highlight detail was extracted.

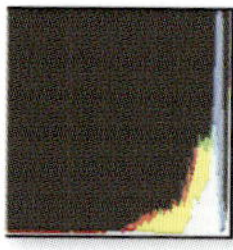
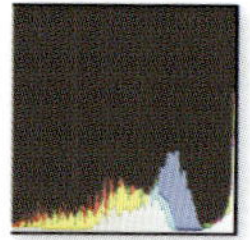
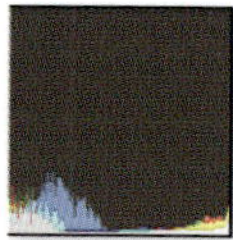
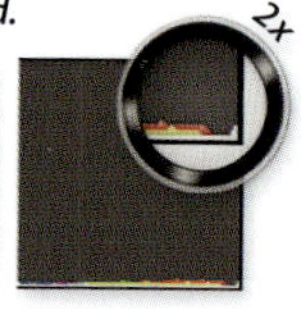

Right end of histogram for the above images, processed using settings designed to match camera-generated histograms.

To capture detail in the brightest area of a scene, an exposure should be captured that produces a gap on the right side of the histogram, indicating no areas were rendered as solid white. I'm generally okay with having the histogram hit the right side when the sun is included in a shot and it is high in the sky. I might try to maintain a gap on the right if the sun looks like a huge ball of orange to my naked eye and I want to render it that way in the image I produce. When I fail to maintain a gap, it's not the end of the world, as I can always fake it by putting an orange circle over the blown-out sun in Photoshop.

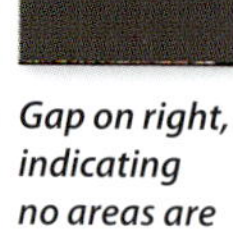

Gap on right, indicating no areas are white.

Section II: Quality Considerations

Avoid Clipping Shadows to Black

A histogram that extends all the way to the extreme left of the area available indicates that the darkest area within the image has been rendered as solid black and contains no detail. Adjusting the exposure in-camera until a gap is produced on the left end would allow shadow detail to be captured without loss of detail.

Shadows without Excessive Noise

Avoiding solid black is often times not enough to produce a satisfactory image because noise is always found in the dark areas. Brightening a dark area in Lightroom will cause the noise lurking in that area to become easier to see, and this usually produces a less than ideal result.

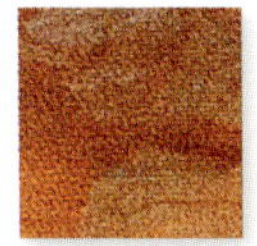 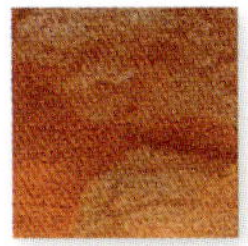 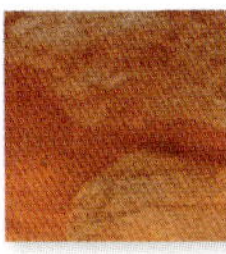 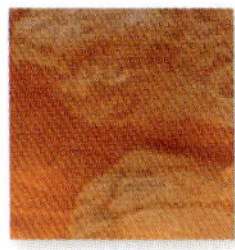

Exposures taken one stop apart and adjusted to illustrate the amount of noise in an average area of the stone arch.

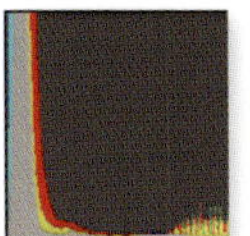 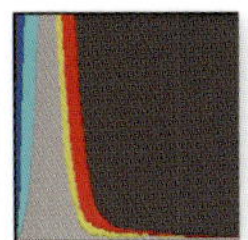 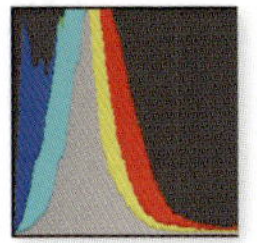 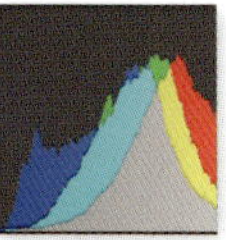

Left end of histogram for the above images, processed using settings designed to match camera-generated histograms.

Noise can generally be avoided by adjusting the in-camera exposure settings until there is a gap on the left side of the histogram and all the tall parts of the graph are pushed toward the center. Those tall areas represent brightness levels that take up a lot of space and are therefore likely to be dominant elements in the image. It's the left quarter of the histogram that contains a huge amount of noise.

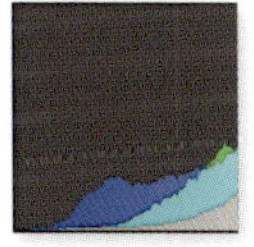

Gap on left with nothing overly tall found in the left quarter.

Bracket Exposures

Now that we know the ideal way to capture the bright and dark areas of a scene, we just need to capture those two ideals and enough shots in between to produce a smooth transition between them. This can be achieved by changing the exposure by three stops between each shot. For the majority of scenes, three exposures will be sufficient to attain a gap on the right in the darkest shot and to ensure dark areas are bright enough to avoid excessive noise in the brightest shot.

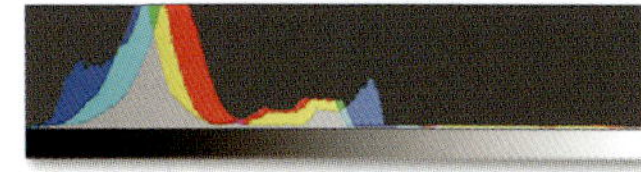

Brightness range of scene being captured.

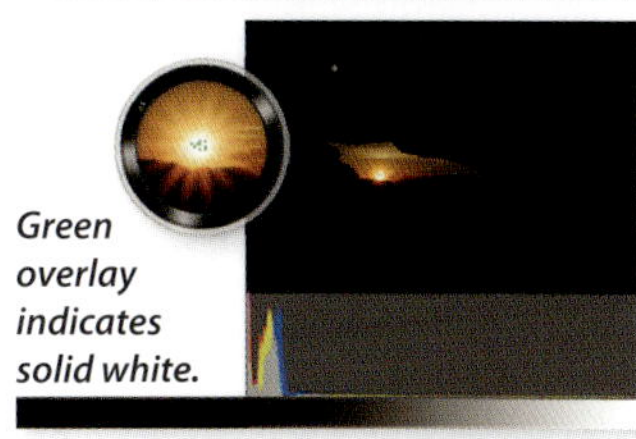

Darkest exposure contains a tiny speck of solid white, which is acceptable when found on a light source that will be rendered as white, such as the sun.

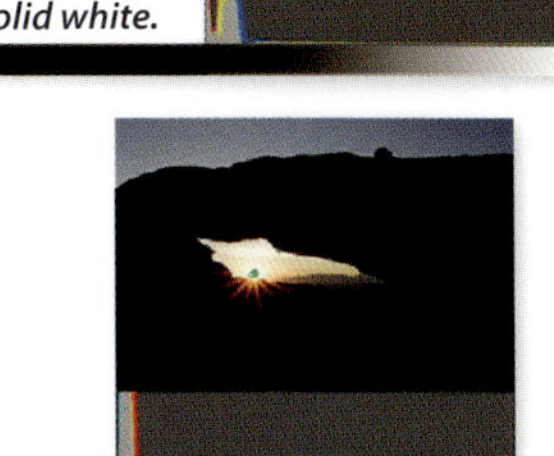

Second exposure is three stops brighter and should contain pure white. If nothing is white, then the whole set of exposures is darker than needed.

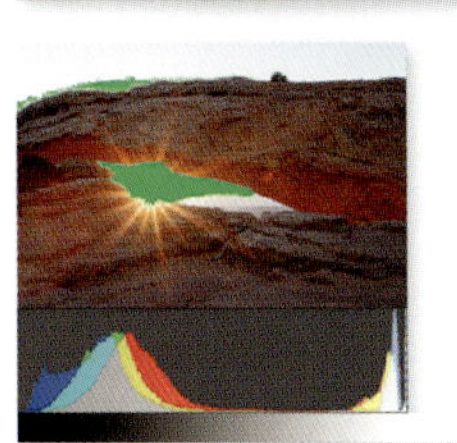

Brightest exposure should render important areas in the darkest region of the scene to be relatively bright. Otherwise, an additional exposure should be captured.

Shoot, Review, Adjust Exposure, and Re-Shoot

Most interchangeable-lens digital cameras offer a feature called auto-bracketing, which will keep the aperture setting constant to maintain consistent depth of field and vary the shutter speed to capture a range of exposures that vary in brightness.

The key is to review the results to ensure that your exposure settings and the number of shots captured were sufficient enough to capture the full brightness range of the scene and to avoid excessive noise. This can often be done by enabling a highlight warning feature that causes solid white areas to either flash or to be displayed as diagonal black-and-white lines (a.k.a. zebra stripes).

After a series of exposures is captured, review the darkest exposure to ensure that no areas are blown out to white. The only areas I don't mind being white in this exposure are the sun, when it is high in the sky, and reflections of the sun on shiny surfaces (like water). If more than one exposure is lacking white, then the darkest image is likely darker than needed and can be discarded.

All of the other exposures should contain progressively larger areas of solid white. The brightest exposure should ideally be bright enough that you can easily make out detail in the important dark areas. If the dark areas are not bright enough, then correcting the area later in Lightroom will just make noise easier to see, so it would be best to capture an additional, even brighter, exposure.

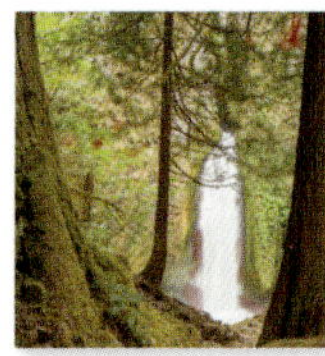
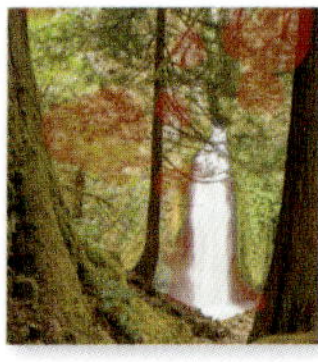
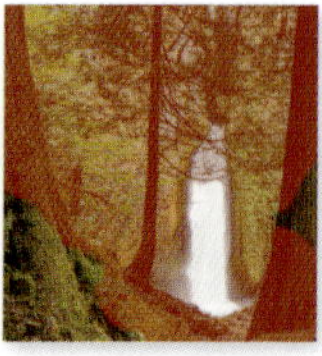

Combine Exposures into HDR Image

Combining the exposures into a high-dynamic-range (HDR) image can be accomplished by selecting the images and choosing **Photos>Photo Merge>HDR** in Lightroom Classic. Turning on the **Auto Settings** checkbox will usually make the preview image more acceptable. Otherwise, it will be shown with no adjustments applied.

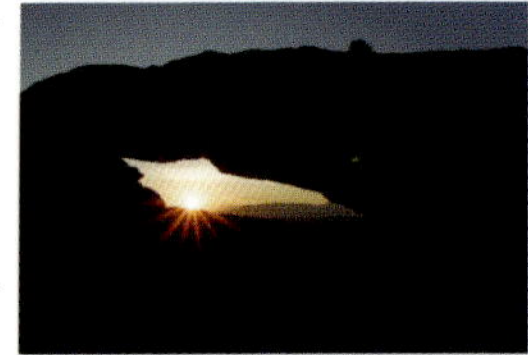

Preview with Auto Settings checkbox turned off.

The **Auto Align** option will align the exposures based on the content of each shot. It is absolutely essential when merging exposures that were shot hand-held. It usually does not noticeably degrade the quality of the results, so I even use this option for shots that were captured using a tripod.

If there is any chance that something in the scene moved between exposures (tree branches in the wind, water flowing, etc.), then set the **Deghost Amount** to **High** and turn on the **Show Deghost Overlay** checkbox. That will display a red overlay where a difference in content was detected. Experiment with the three levels to find the best compromise between reducing artifacts and producing a noise-free image.

Note: *The auto-bracketing feature on many digital cameras is limited to bracketing in 2-stop increments. When that's the case, more than three exposures may be necessary to capture the full range of some high contrast scenes.*

Tip: *Photoshop's **Merge to HDR Pro** option is limited to merging fully rendered (non-raw) images and is useful as an alternative if Lightroom produces a less than desirable result.*

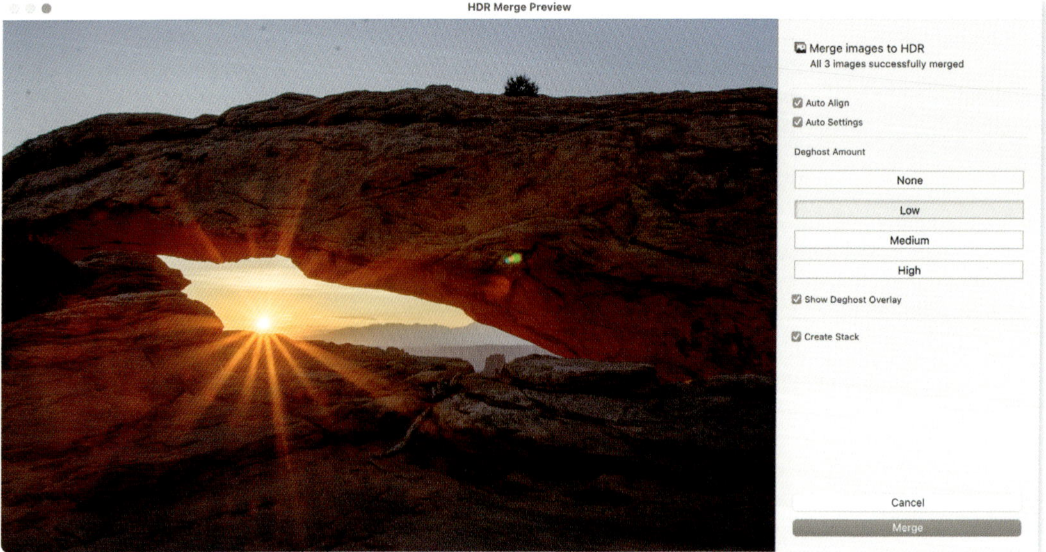

Result of selecting a series of exposures and choosing Photo>Photo Merge>HDR in Lightroom Classic.

Section II: Quality Considerations

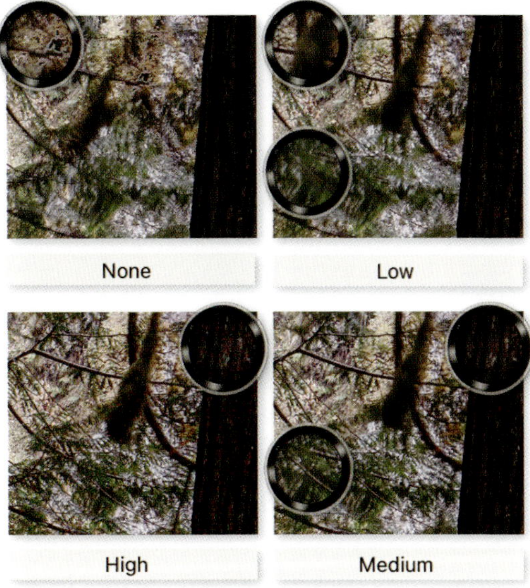

Choosing the best Deghost Amount setting is always a compromise between suppressing artifacts and avoiding noise.

Optimize Resulting HDR Image

Clicking the **Merge** button will produce a special 16-bit floating point .DNG file that retains most of the special qualities of a raw file. It can then be optimized using the same adjustment choices and mindset used to adjust any other image.

Some of the adjustment sliders may have a more pronounced effect on the resulting image because it contains a wider brightness range than a standard raw file. For instance, the **Exposure** slider's normal range is ±5 when working on raw files, but will have a range of ±10 when working on an HDR image.

> **Tip:** *Most adjustments and all retouching will be ignored when merging multiple images into an HDR image. If you had previously applied retouching to remove sensor dust spots, then right-click on one of the raw files, choose **Develop Settings>Copy Settings**, click the **Check None** button, choose only the **Healing** option, then right-click on the resulting HDR image and choose **Paste Settings** from the same menu.*

HDR in a Standard Dynamic Range System

Most software and hardware was designed to work with images that contain a brightness range, what is commonly referred to as standard-dynamic-range, or simply SDR. SDR is where all the brightness levels contained within an image are described using a range of numbers starting with zero, which represents black, to a fixed maximum number (100% in Lightroom or 255 in Photoshop) which represents white. These are the normal files that most people work with every day. Both Lightroom and Photoshop where designed with that limitation hardwired into the code.

HDR images, on the other hand, are created by combing more than one of those SDR images in an attempt to capture a wider brightness range from the scene than you could get in a single exposure. The numbers in an HDR file don't have to max out at white and therefore can describe something that is many times brighter than white. But the software and hardware most people use will max out at white and therefore an unprocessed HDR file looks no different than a single SDR exposure captured of the same scene.

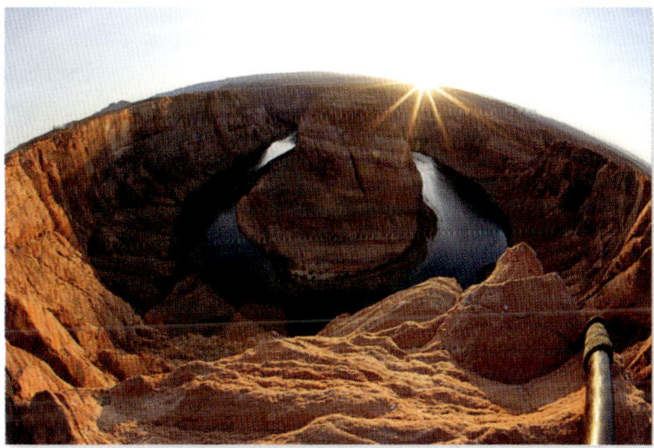

Single SDR exposure rendered using default settings.

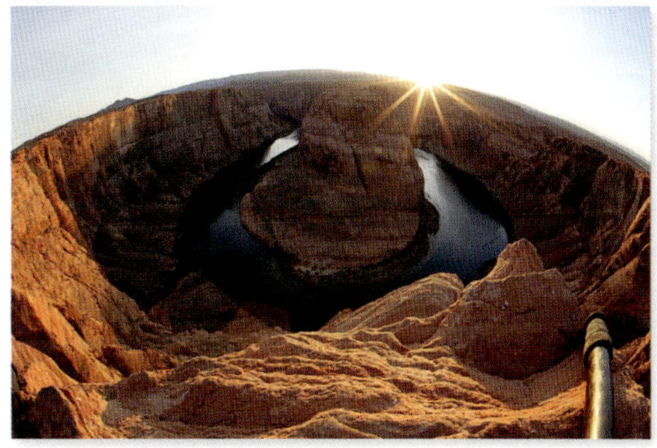

High Dynamic Range image rendered using default settings.

HDR Displays

The detail in those brighter-than-white areas will only be visible if the image is viewed on a special HDR computer display using software designed specially to deal with HDR images (unfortunately, Lightroom does not yet support HDR display output). HDR displays can interpret brightness values that are brighter than what an normal display would render as white and are capable of producing brighter highlights.

Adobe Camera Raw offers an **HDR Output** setting that can be enabled in the **Technology Previews** section of it's preferences, which can be assessed via the gear icon in the upper right of the ACR window. Enabling the feature will add an **HDR** button below the histogram which will allow ACR to send the necessary information to an HDR display and allow it to show some of the wider brightness range that is contained within an HDR image.

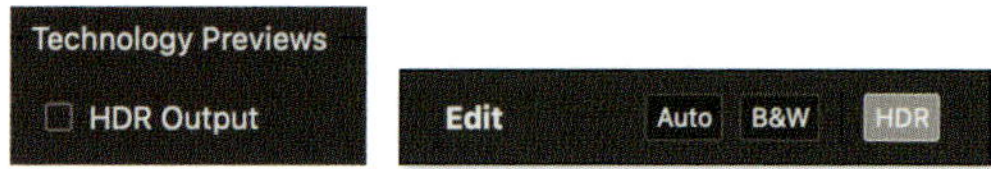

Turning on the HDR Output checkbox and restarting ACR will cause an HDR button to appear below the histogram.

When the **HDR** button is enabled, the histogram will display a vertical bar indicating the brightness level that would be rendered as white on a normal SDR display and any part of the histogram that extends to the right of that point represents areas that could be considered brighter than white.

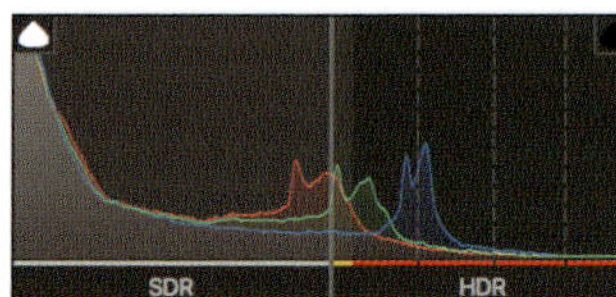

The example shown here is from an Apple MacBook Pro display, which has very limited HDR capabilities.

Note: *The **HDR Output** feature in Adobe Camera Raw requires both a display and video card that is designed to work with HDR data in order to display a wider brightness range.*

A yellow bar will extend to the right of the vertical line to indicate the additional brightness range the current HDR display is capable of displaying. A red horizontal bar beyond that indicates any areas that are beyond the capability of the HDR display being used.

Previewing on an SDR Display

When the **HDR** button in enabled, a special set of adjustment sliders will appear at the bottom of the Basic section of adjustments. Turning on the **Preview for SDR Display** checkbox within that area will cause the brightest area of the HDR image to be mapped to white, which will automatically fit the full brightness range within a standard SDR view.

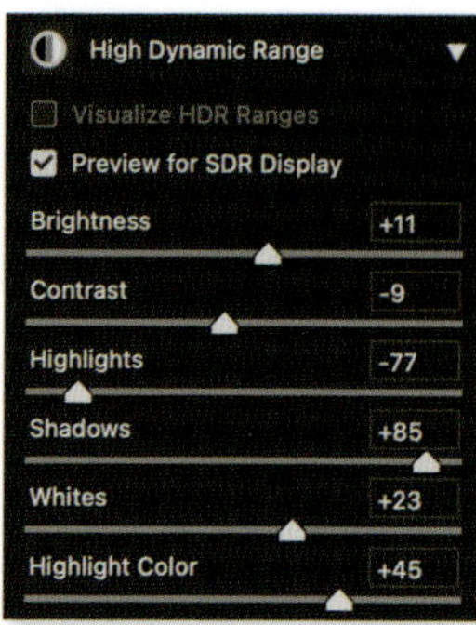

This sliders shown above are enabled when both the HDR and Preview for SDR Display features are enabled.

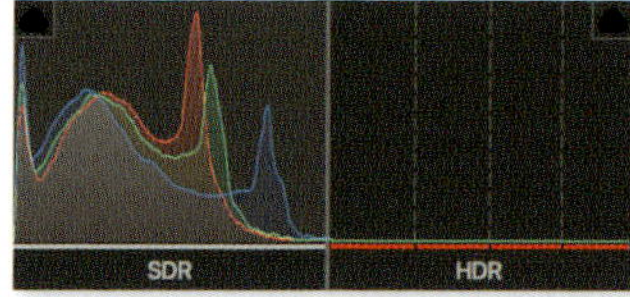

The Preview for SDR Display checkbox squishes the full brightness range of HDR into the standard SDR range.

You can then further refine this SDR rendering of the image by adjusting the sliders found below the checkbox. These sliders supplement those that are found at the top of the Basic section, but have no affect on how the image is rendered when the **Preview for SDR Display** checkbox is turned off. You can therefore optimize the image for both HDR and SDR display.

Images exported in 8 and 16 bits from within Adobe Camera Raw via the Share icon near the upper right will retain the appearance produced by the **Preview for SDR Display** checkbox. At the time of this writing, clicking the **Open** button to open an image directly into Photoshop does not respect the workflow settings that are found at the bottom of the ACR dialog box and do not reflect the preview that was shown in ACR.

Considering that the HDR Output feature and related sliders are considered a technology preview, I would expect its implementation to be refined over time and to be something that will eventually be added directly to Lightroom Classic. In the meantime, you'll likely end up performing tone mapping in the old-school method that I'll cover next and was the only way of doing it before the HDR Output features where added to ACR.

Section II: Quality Considerations

Tone Mapping HDR into the SDR Range

The process of squishing the brightness range of an HDR image into the more limited SDR range is known as "tone mapping."

Lowering the **Highlights** slider to **-100** and boosting the **Shadows** slider to **+100** and then fine-tuning the **Exposure** slider to control the overall brightness is usually all that's needed to render the full brightness range that was contained in an HDR image and make it visible on an SDR display. Making a similar adjustment to a single exposure will reveal the limits of a single exposure and will not reveal anywhere near as much detail in the brightest area of the image and will often produce very noisy shadows.

Once tone mapped, the resulting image will have a brightness range that does not exceed the standard black-to-white range of an SDR image and can be exported to any common file format. Such an image may have started out from an HDR source, but is no longer technically HDR since it would look no different on an HDR display than a standard everyday SDR display.

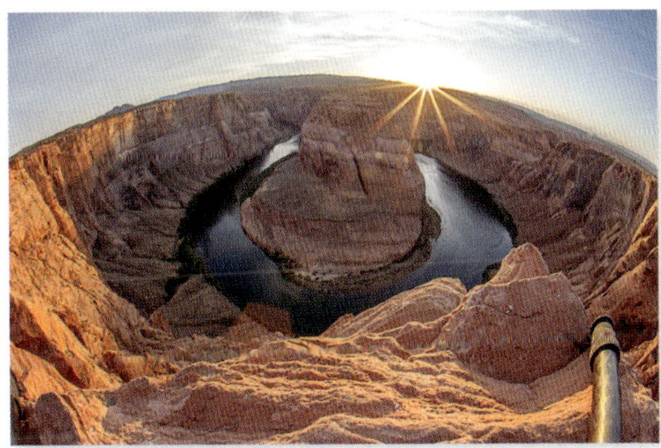

Single exposure: Highlights -100, Shadows +100, Exposure -.25.

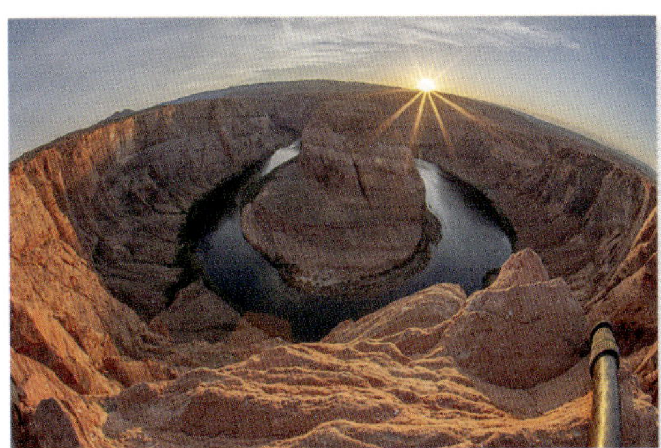

HDR adjusted to match brightness of image above.

Stitch Raw Panoramas

Stitching multiple images into a seamless panorama produces a much higher-quality result than cropping a single image into a wide format. The technique is also useful for producing results that go beyond the optical limitations of a lens.

Shooting for Success

The following concepts can help ensure your success when capturing a panorama:

1/4 Overlap: The minimum overlap between frames that Lightroom can deal with is around 15%, while anything over 40% has the potential to degrade the quality of the panorama. I suggest including about 1/4 overlap in content from one image to the next.

Expose for Highest-Contrast Area: Consider making a test exposure to ensure the area that has the greatest brightness range in the scene will be properly exposed.

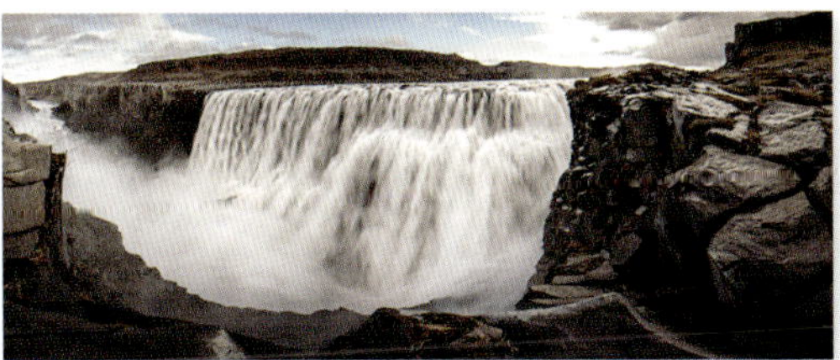

Exposure established on first shot at the left edge caused the brighter area of the sky at the right to be clipped to white.

Consistent Exposure: Setting your camera to manual exposure mode or utilizing the auto exposure lock (often a button labeled AEL) will ensure that the aperture and shutter speed settings will be consistent across all the images captured. This is essential in producing a visually seamless panorama.

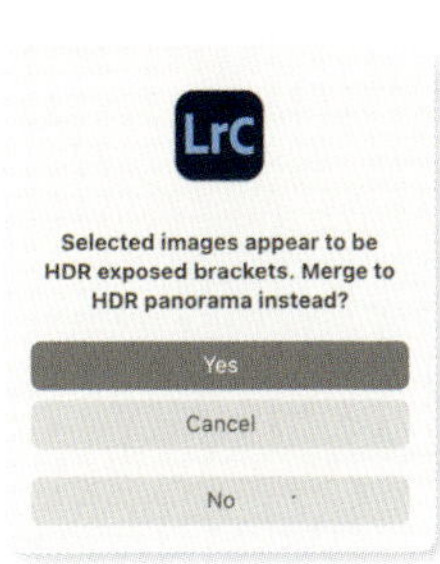

Varied exposures shown below prompted this warning message.

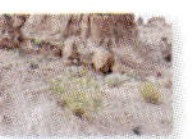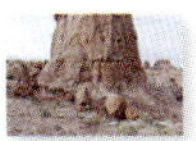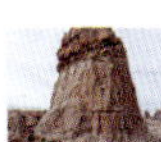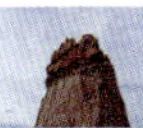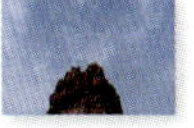

Vertical panorama shot using auto-exposure. Bright sky taking up progressively more space produced varied exposure.

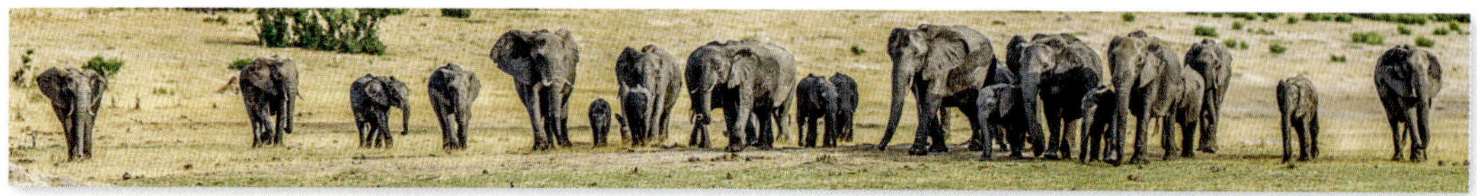

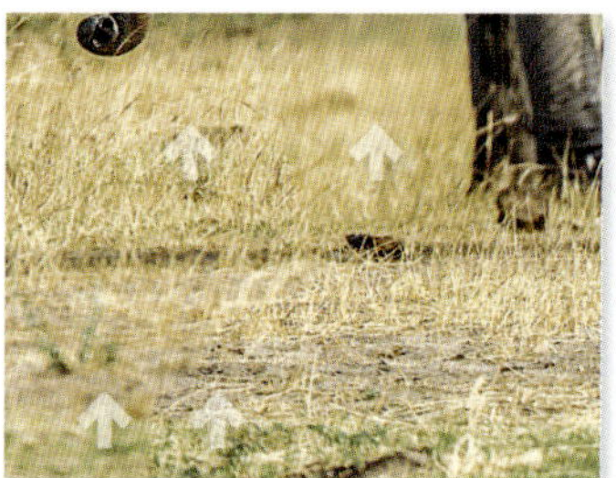

The panorama above only looks good at a tiny size because I failed to turn off autofocus, which caused the focus point to change between exposures, as seen in the enlargement at left.

Consistent Focus Point: This becomes more important when using longer lenses that capture a shallower depth of field. Some cameras feature a focus lock button for this, while others require you to flip a switch to disable autofocus.

Hand-Held Viewfinder Grid: Most mirrorless cameras offer a feature that overlays a grid on the viewfinder image. Using the grid, note the vertical distance between an object on the right edge of the frame and a grid line, then ensure the same object remains at that height when it appears on the left side of the frame after panning.

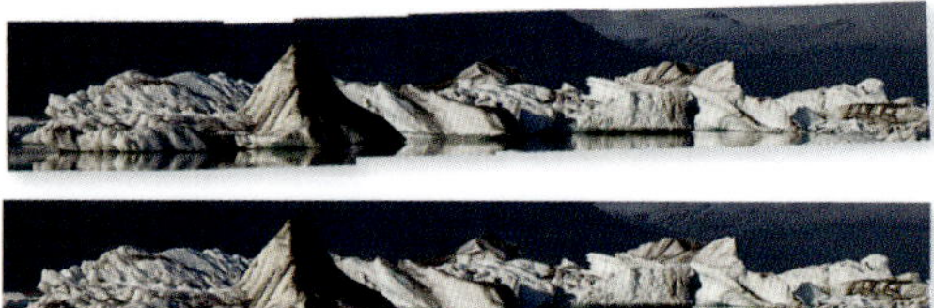

Inconsistent hand-held panning necessitated extreme cropping, which rendered this panorama useless.

Level Tripod: When shooting on a tripod, make sure that the area just below the tripod head is level. Otherwise, you may discover that your panorama is sloped, which will force you to crop into the scene in order to produce a rectangular image.

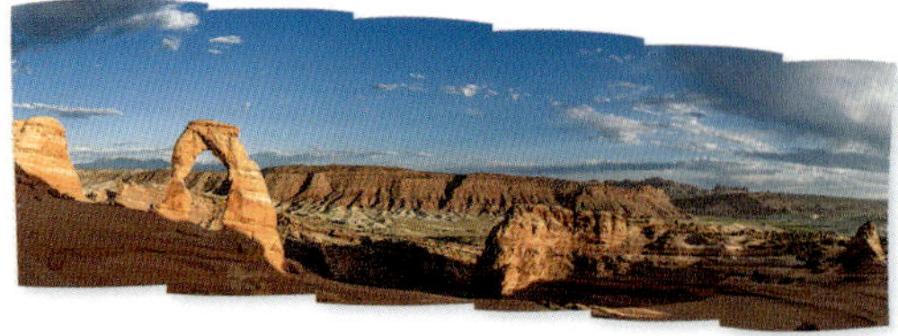

Panning across a scene using a non-level tripod head.

Level Camera: Slightly crooked images will degrade the quality of the stitched image and force you to perform more extreme cropping to produce a rectangular panorama. Most digital cameras feature an electronic level that can be used. Alternatively, a bubble level can be inserted in the flash hot shoe on the top of the camera.

Portrait Orientation for Additional Detail: More detail can be captured by rotating your camera to a vertical orientation, as the wider edge contains more pixels. This can be a welcome boost when you plan to print a panorama at a large size.

Remove Polarizer Filter: A polarizing filter will cause the brightness of the sky to change as the camera is panned across a scene. This will result in an unnaturally dark region in a panorama.

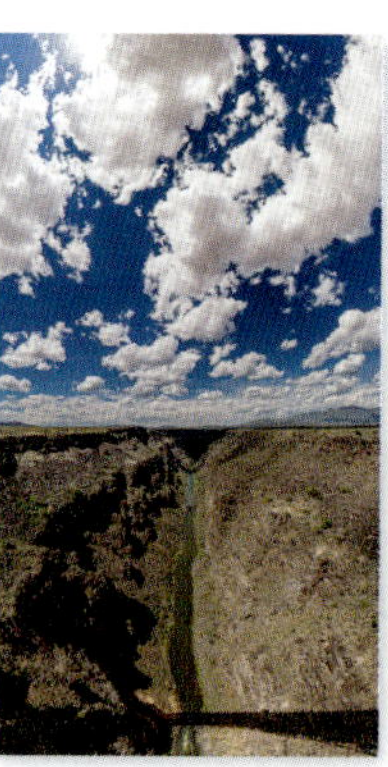

Don't Forget Verticals: Panorama stitching isn't limited to horizontal scenes. You can just as easily capture a tall expanse by stitching images together.

Pad Your Composition: Zoom out slightly from where you'd ultimately like to crop the scene. Stitching the images involves removing distortion, which will force you to crop the image slightly.

180° vertical panorama.

Avoid Close Objects: Objects close to the camera will shift in position as you pan the camera and can cause alignment problems. It's similar to what happens when you raise a finger at arms length and then switch from viewing it with one eye closed versus the other–it shifts in position relative to the background. If you need to include near objects, then Google "nodal point panorama" to find out how to accomplish it without issues.

I learned the above concepts through trial and error. Each screw-up provided a valuable lesson that helped me to be more successful over time.

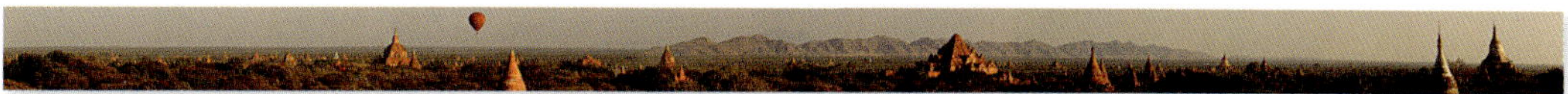

Fifteen shots stitched into a seamless panoramic image. Sensor dust spots were removed before stitching.

Prepare for Merging

There are a few steps that should be performed before you stitch images into a panorama. If you skip them, you'll make more work for yourself later and the quality of your results could suffer.

Remove Dust Before Stitching

Over time, the changing of lenses can cause dust to collect on the sensor inside the camera. Those specs of dust appear as shady circles when they become backlit and are most visible against bright backdrops, such as otherwise smooth skies. The dust spots remain in a fixed position for each shot in a panorama, so retouching them out as a group before stitching is the most efficient way to go. If you instead wait until after stitching, you'll end up retouching out the same speck multiple times as it is repeated across the length of the panorama.

The process I go through is as follows:

1) Select all of the images that you plan to combine by clicking on the first image of the sequence, holding **Shift**, and then clicking on the last image.

2) Type **Q** to activate the **Heal** tool in the Develop module.

3) Turn on the **Auto Sync** switch at the bottom of the right side panel of the Develop module. This will cause any change made to the image you are viewing to also be applied to the other images that are selected.

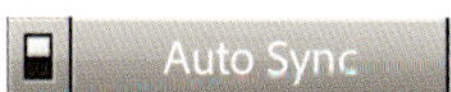

4) Choose the middle **Mode** icon (**Heal**), set the **Feather** setting to **0**, **Opacity** to **100**, and turn on the **Visualize Spots** checkbox near the bottom-left corner of the image window.

5) Choose a brush that is slightly larger than a dust spot and then click on each spot found within the image. Typing **H** will toggle the visibility of the retouching icons, which can help you locate any spots you have missed.

6) Hold the **Command** key (Mac) or **Ctrl** (PC) key and press the right arrow key to switch to the next image and retouch out any additional dust spots that are visible. Repeat until you've made it through all the images.

7) Turn off the **Auto Sync** switch so future changes will only affect a single image, then arrow through the images a second time. Your goal on this pass is to remove any retouching icons that are not located over the sky. This can be done by holding **Option** (Mac) or **Alt** (PC) and clicking on the icons. You could also click and drag to delete all icons found within the rectangle you define.

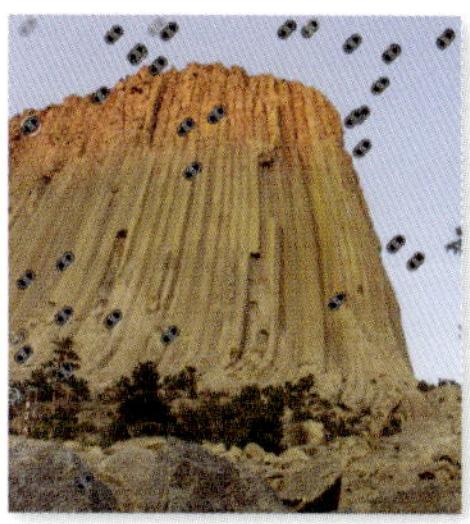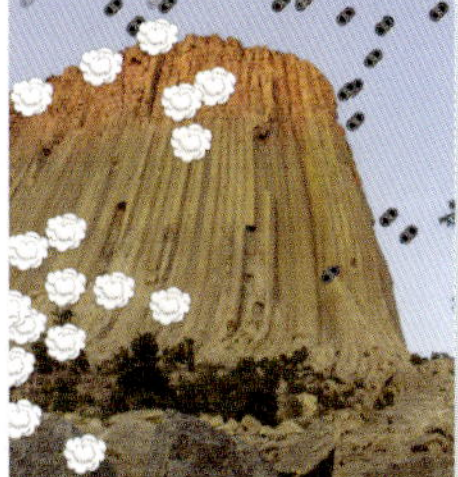

Retouching icons represent areas retouched in a previous image where the dust was located in the sky.

Drawing a rectangle over the retouching icons deleted them from this individual image.

8) Make one last quick pass through the images, this time with the retouching icons hidden by typing **H,** to make sure there are no obvious spots that were missed.

Apply Lens Profile

When merging images into a panorama, Lightroom attempts to first correct for any distortion caused by the optics of the lens used to capture the images. If you see the message below when stitching the panorama, click cancel, head to the Lens Corrections section of the Develop module, turn on **Auto Sync**, and then see if you can find a lens profile for your camera and lens.

 Unable to match a lens profile automatically. For best results, apply the appropriate lens profile to the photos before merging.

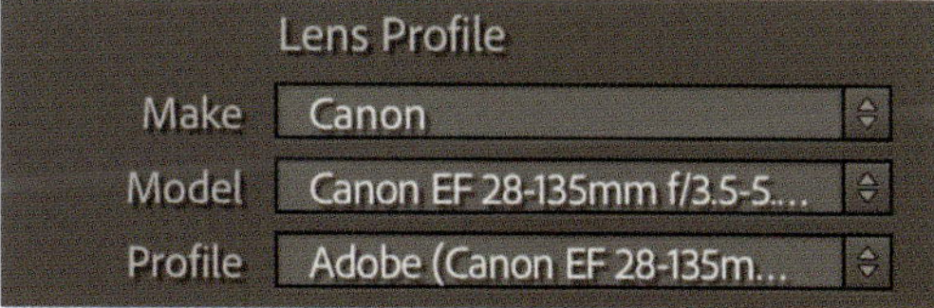

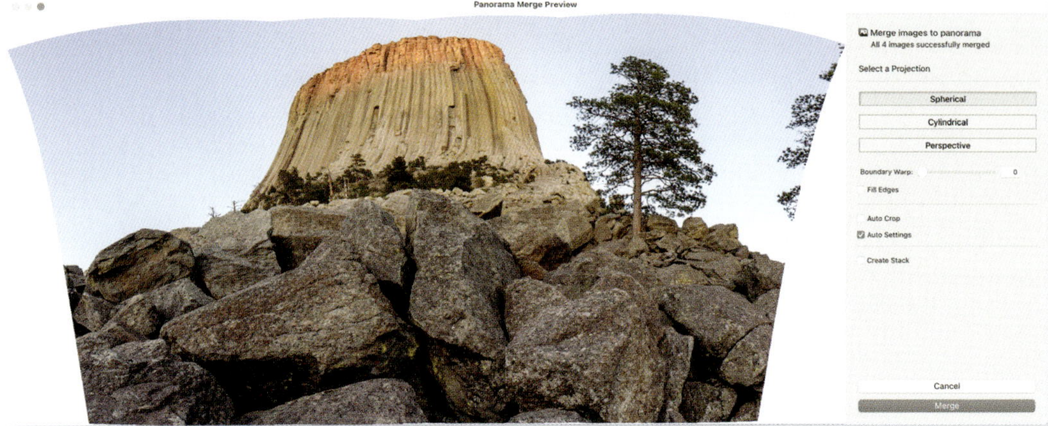

Result of selecting a series of exposures and choosing Photo>Photo Merge>Panorama in Lightroom Classic.

Stitch Panorama

With the images still selected, choose **Photo> Photo Merge>Panorama** and then fine-tune the following settings until you're happy with the overall layout of the panorama.

Projection Method

The following layout projections are available:

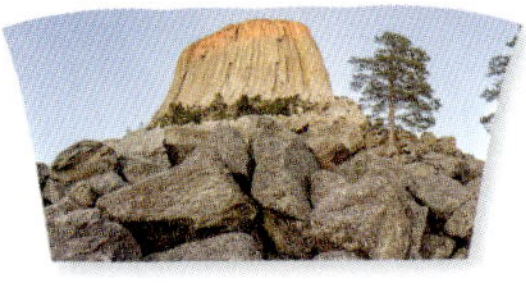

Spherical: Bends the images as if they are being laid out on the inside surface of a spherical globe.

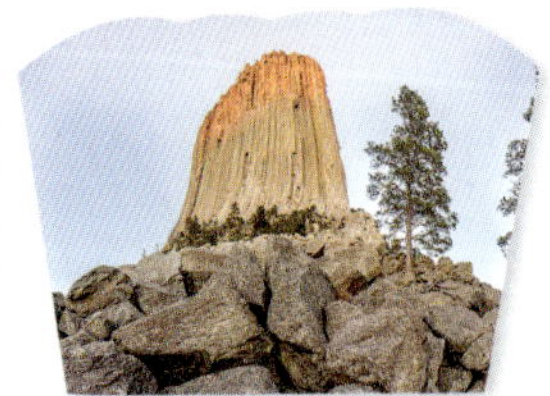

Cylindrical: Bends the images as if they are being laid out on the inside surface of a smooth, cylindrical soup can. Vertical lines remain straight with this method.

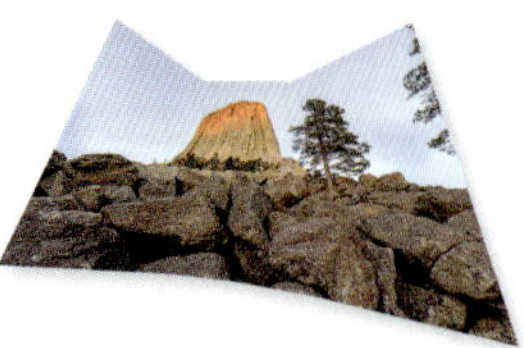

Perspective: Keeps the center image straight, then moves the corners of the remaining images to best align them with the center image. This setting is best applied to an odd number of images so the undistorted image is located in the middle of the panorama. It's not always possible to align images in this fashion.

Producing a Rectangular Result

A combination of three settings can be used to shoehorn your results into a rectangular image.

Auto-Crop: Crops the image into the largest rectangle without modifying the image content.

Boundary Warp: Stretches and warps the image until it fills a rectangle without discarding any information. I often leave **Auto-Crop** turned on when adjusting this setting so I can more easily figure out the lowest amount that produces a satisfactory rectangular image.

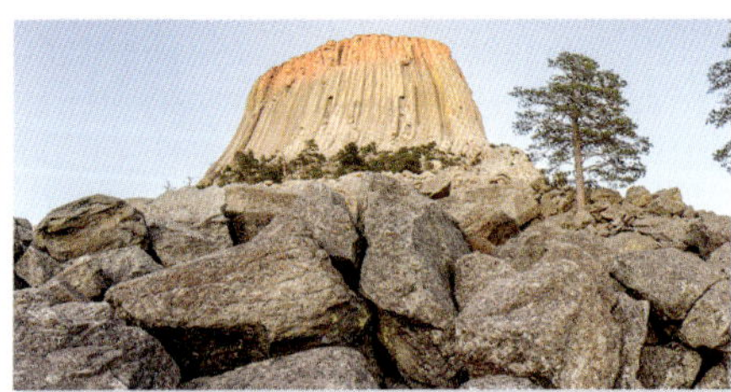

Fill Edges: Uses Adobe's Content-Aware Fill technology to fill all the white areas with new material based on the surrounding image without changing the original stitching results.

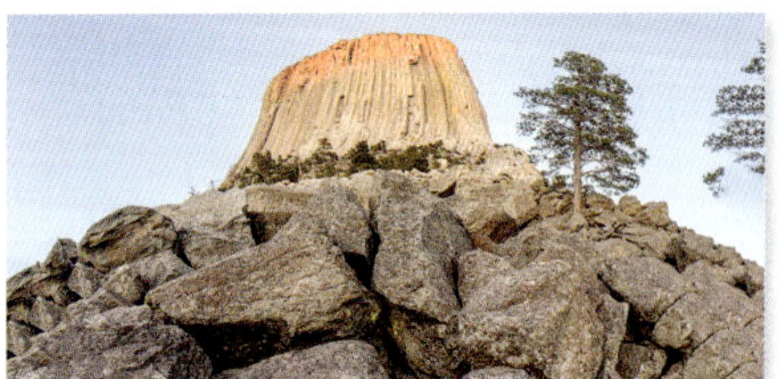

Section II: Quality Considerations

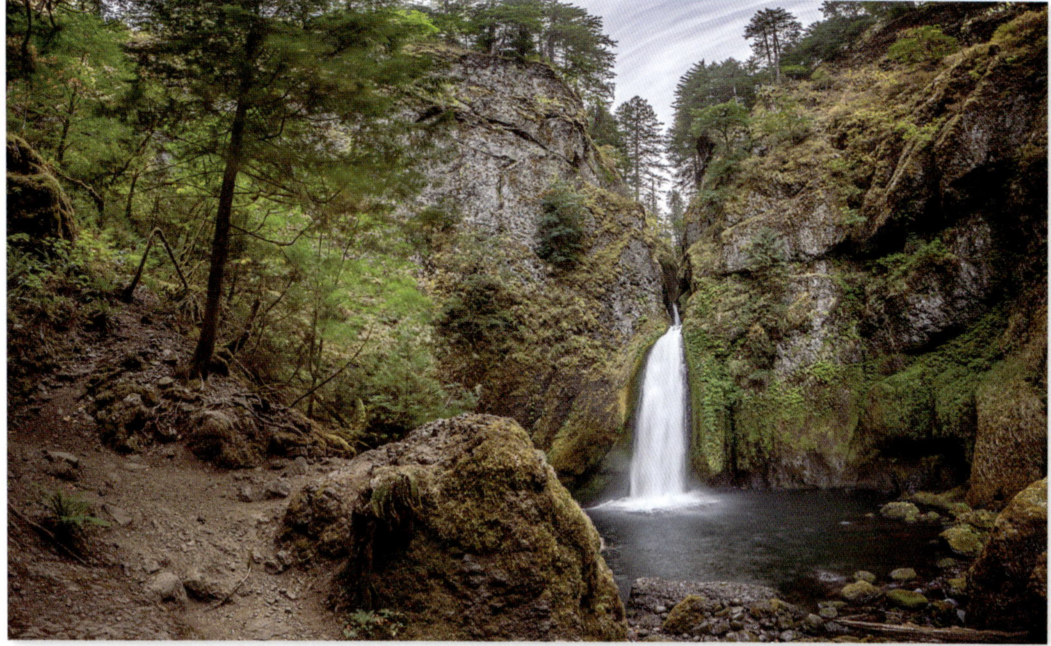

HDR panorama captured using vertical-orientation images and combined using Photo>Photo Merge>HDR Panorama.

HDR Panoramas

Lightroom Classic can also merge panoramas that were shot using a series of bracketed exposures by choosing **Photo>Photo Merge>HDR Panorama**. However, I find that you'll often achieve better results by first merging each section of the panorama into an HDR image, and then merging the resulting .DNG files into a panorama. That's because the fully automated version does not offer the ghost removal feature that is available when you produce the HDR images individually, before combining them into a panorama.

Sixteen-image, multi-row panorama captured with a 500mm lens at f/4.5. After capture, the process of creating the final image was no different than merging any other panorama.

Wide Views of Shallow Depth

Camera lenses have a limit to how far away they can be focused, as indicated by the infinity marking (∞) on the lens's distance scale. Once you hit that point, you've reached the limit and everything beyond will be rendered as sharp. Infinity on a wide-angle lens is just a few feet away, which makes it impossible to achieve a blurry background on distant objects. The infinity point on a 500mm telephoto lens, on the other hand, will be well over 100 feet away, making it much easier to achieve a blurry background, but impossible to deliver a wide view in a single shot. However, it's a different story when you stitch over a dozen of those shots into a wide view of shallow depth.

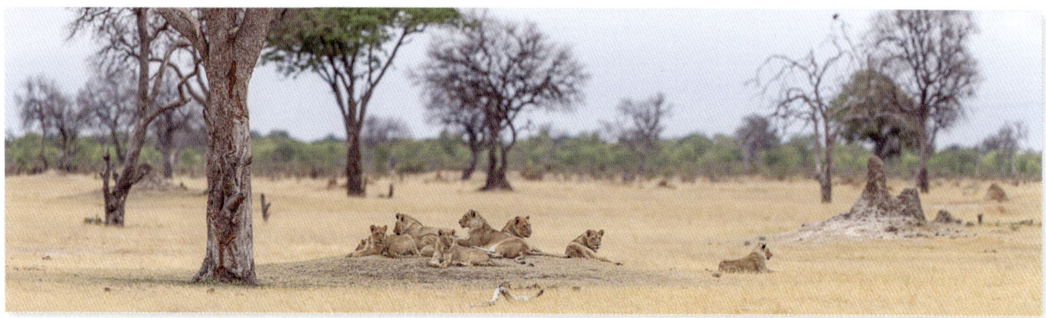

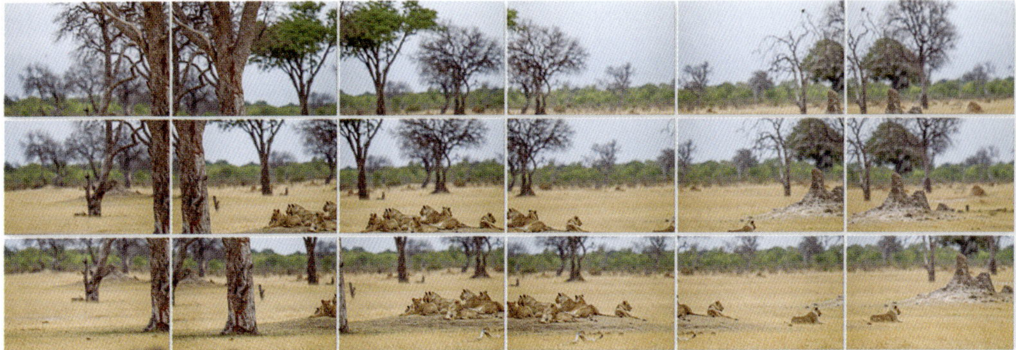

Sixteen exposures shot at 500mm at f/4.5 that were used to produce the panorama shown on the previous page.

Photoshop Panoramas

Lightroom has had the ability to stitch panoramas that retain most of the qualities of a raw file for just shy of a decade. Before that time, all stitching had to be done in Photoshop using images that had their Lightroom develop settings baked in.

You can still use the older, non-raw stitching pipeline by choosing **Photo>Edit In>Merge to Panorama in Photoshop.** The end result will no longer have the qualities of a raw file, but you'll be able to do a lot more by taking advantage of layers and other features that are not available in Lightroom.

Photoshop offers the same three layout projection methods that are found in Lightroom, along with two additional choices.

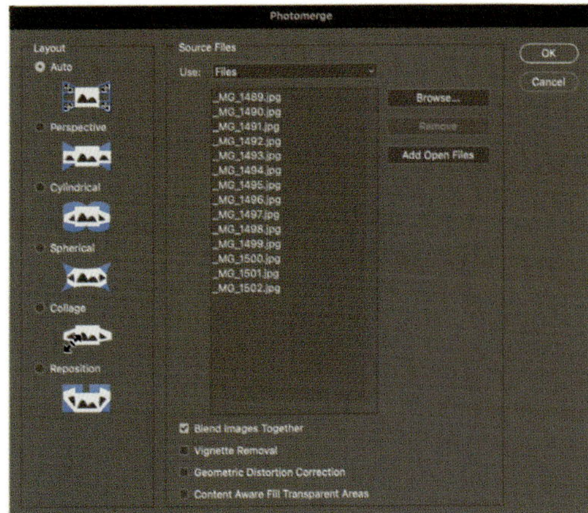

Settings found in Photoshop's Photo Merge dialog box.

Collage: Combines the images as if they were physical prints being laid out on a table, where it is only able to scale and rotate the images without distorting their shape.

Reposition: Limited to changing the position of each image and is unable to rotate or distort the images. I haven't found any great uses for this choice.

Blend Images Together
Allows you to choose between producing a seamless panorama or one that leaves the edges of each image well-defined.

The bottom three choices are optional.

Add Layer Styles for a Creative Result
When I'm looking to produce a different look, I'll turn off the **Blend Images Together** checkbox and use the **Collage** layout choice. Once the images have been aligned, I'll then click on the topmost layer to make it active, choose **Layer>Layer Style>Drop Shadow**, and fine-tune the settings so the layer feels like it is slightly elevated above the underlying image. I then add a **Stroke**, using the same menu, to produce a well-defined edge. Next, I apply the effect to the rest of the images by right-clicking on the *fx* that appears to the right of the layer name and choosing **Copy Layer Style.** I then select the rest of the layers, right-click again in the same spot, and choose **Paste Layer Style.**

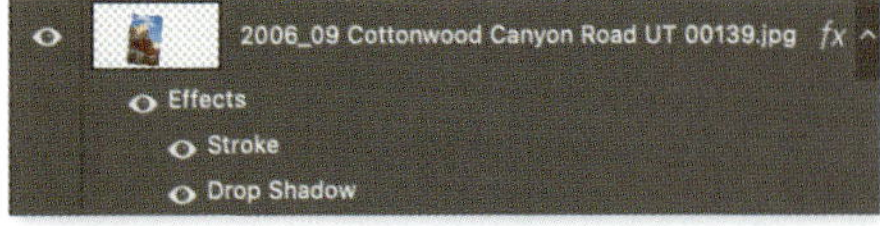

Layer Styles added to create visual separation between images.

Section II: Quality Considerations

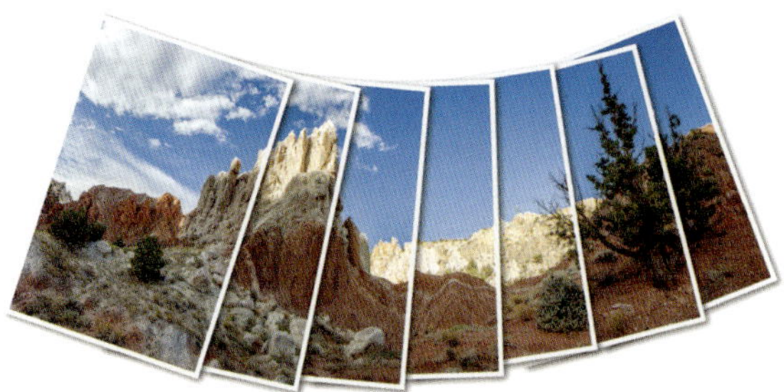

Collage layout with Blend Images Together turned off. Stroke and Drop Shadow Layer Styles were then added to each image to create visual separation between the images.

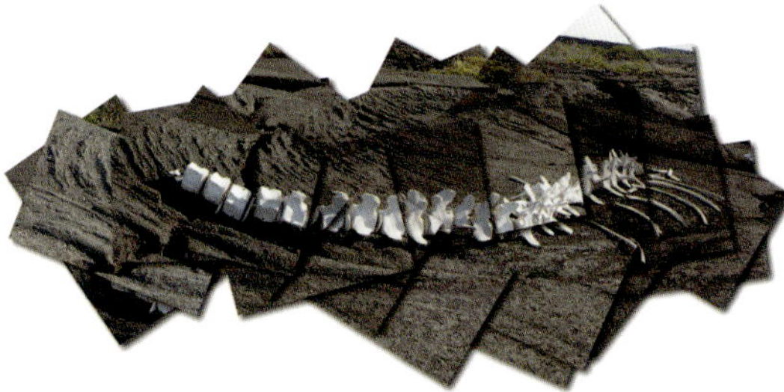

Images captured at random angles were stitched using the same method as the previous image, and a Drop Shadow Layer Style was added to increase visual separation.

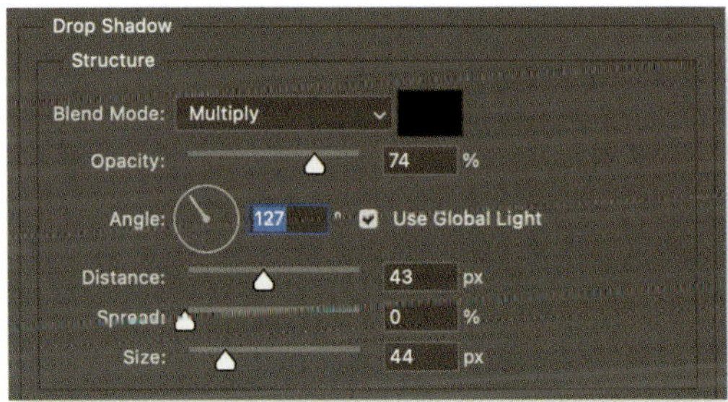

A Drop Shadow Layer Style was added to each layer.

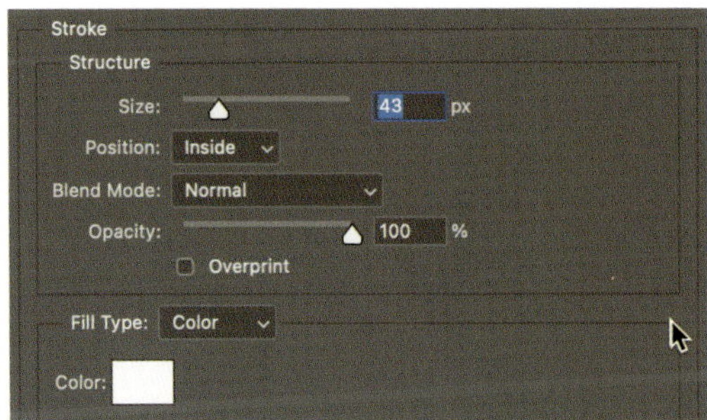

Adding a Stroke to each layer can simulate the look of traditional photographic prints that include white borders.

Breaking Down the Process

The **Photo Merge** dialog box that is used to stitch panoramas utilizes three Photoshop features behind the scenes. These features can also be useful when applied separately. They include:

Open As Layers: The process starts by stacking all of the images into individual layers. This can be accomplished by choosing **Photo>Edit In>Open As Layers** in Lightroom, or **File>Scripts>Load Files into Stack** in Photoshop.

Auto-Align: With all the layers selected from the previous stage, choosing **Edit>Auto-Align Layers** causes the layers to be repositioned, scaled, and warped in an attempt to align any content that is found in more than one of the images.

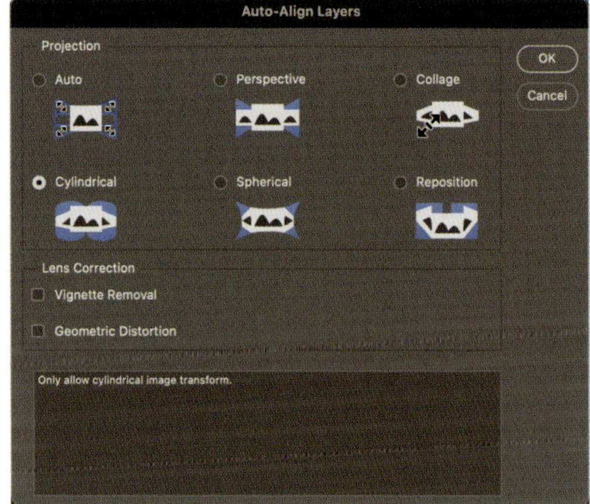

Auto-Blend: Once the layers are aligned, the seams are blended together by choosing **Edit>Auto-Blend Layers**.

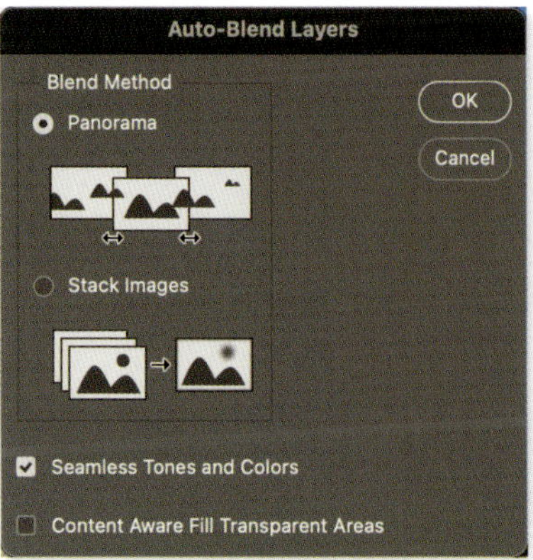

Having access to the individual steps in the process allows you to take over and manually perform any steps that did not go well when everything was done in the fully automated workflow.

Manual Alignment

Lightroom and Photoshop will occasionally be unable to merge the full length of a panorama. When that's the case, I may try to divide the images into two batches and attempt to merge those into two limited-width panoramas. I'll then manually combine the results into the full-length panorama I ultimately desired.

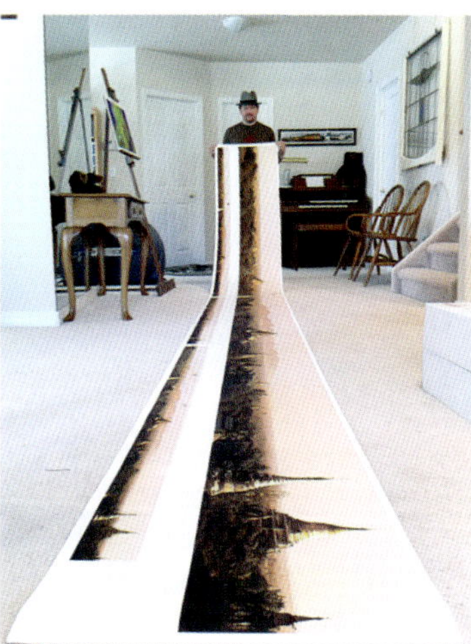

Notification that appears in Lightroom's Panorama dialog box when it is unable to align all images.

Both Lightroom and Photoshop refused to stitch the full length of this 14-image panorama. I had to manually align each image before using Auto-Blend Layers to produce a seamless image.

There are two common ways to determine if the contents of multiple layers are aligned. Lowering the **Opacity** of a layer will partially reveal the underlying layer so you can compare the contents. I prefer to change the blending mode menu to **Difference** at the top of the Layers panel. This will alter the appearance of areas that overlap, causing dissimilar areas to appear bright and similar areas to appear dark, while areas that perfectly align appear as solid black. It's not often that I achieve solid back, but I try to get the result to look as close to black as possible.

I align the layers using a combination of manual repositioning, scaling, and warping.

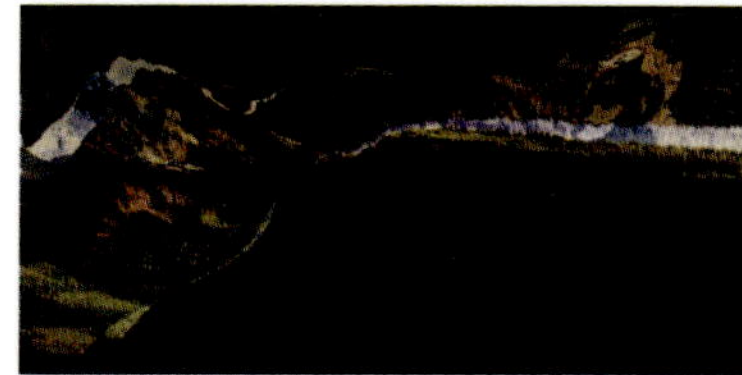

Major edges are not aligning and therefore appear bright.

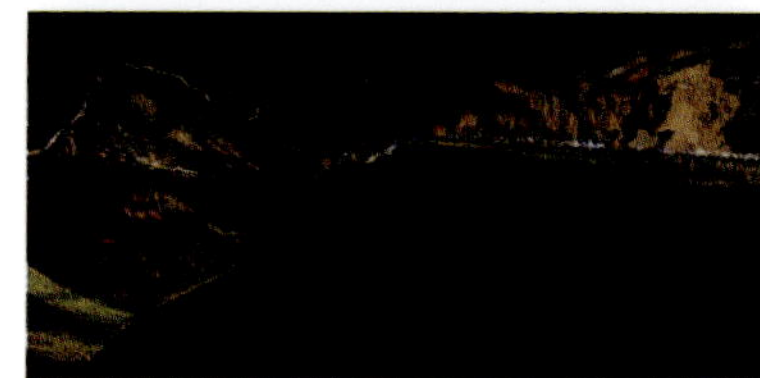

After scaling, rotating, and warping, the prominent edges are more closely aligned.

Alternative Contents

What if you shot a bunch of telephoto images to produce a wide view, had an animal move in the process, and then Lightroom used the less than desirable version when merging the panorama?

By masking out one of the heads, you can decide which one will be used before the **Auto-Blend** step is applied.

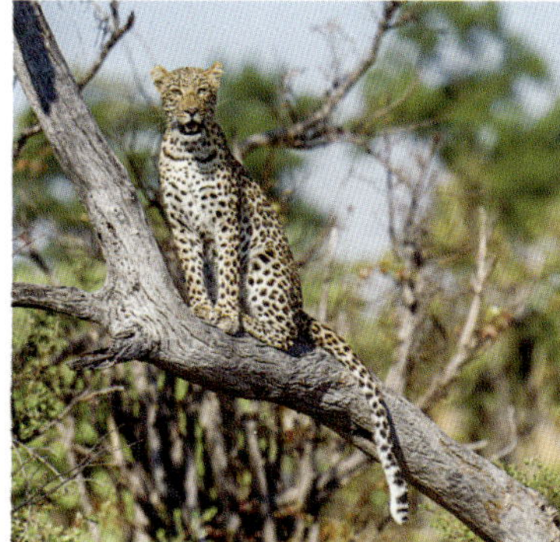

Left: *Result of combining 30 images shot at 400mm at f/5.6.*

Below: *The head moved between shots, but both versions were needed to create a seamless image.*

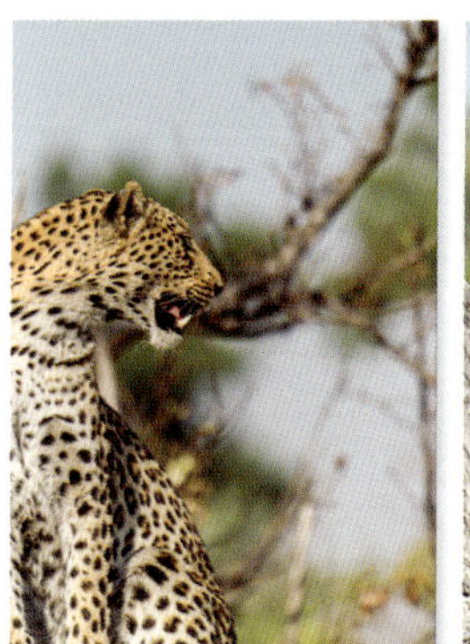

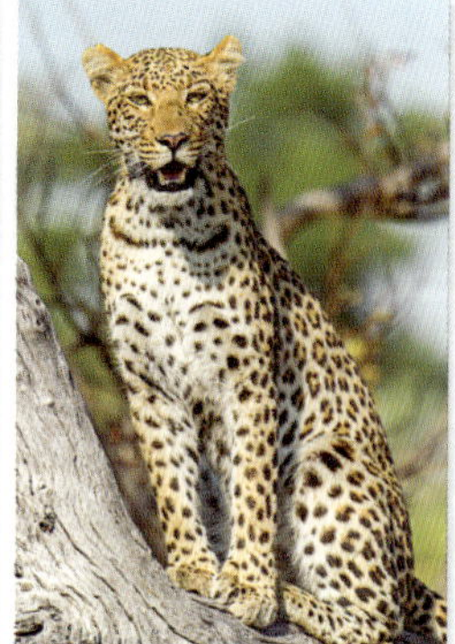

Section II: Quality Considerations

Combine Fast and Slow

It's a common practice to shoot waterfalls using long shutter speeds to produce a silky-looking motion blur within the water. But the same setup is not usually ideal for any tree branches that are being blown by the wind. You can get the best of both worlds by capturing two exposures, one with a slow shutter speed to deliver a silky waterfall and a second using a much faster shutter speed to freeze any motion in the surrounding trees. These images can then be merged in Photoshop.

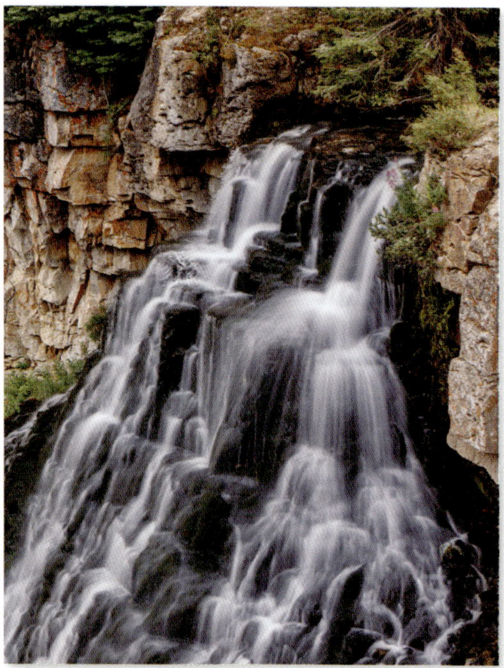
Result of masking fast and slow shutter speeds.

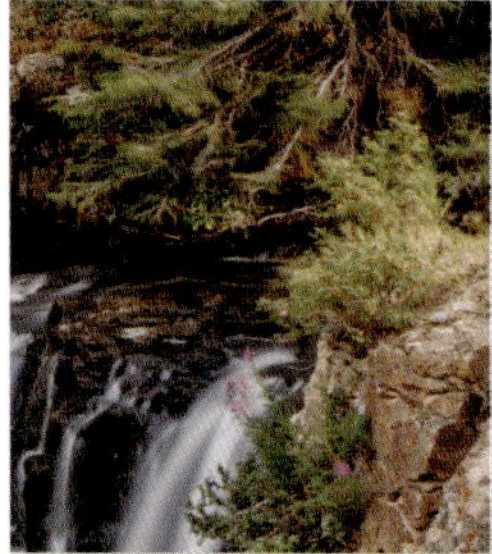
↑↓: 0.6-second exposure produced motion blur.

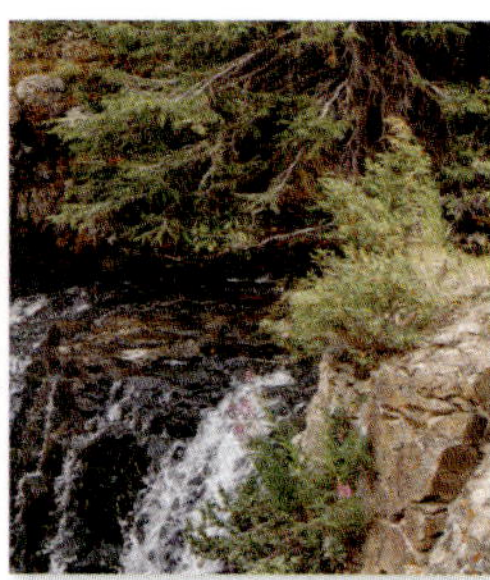
↑↓: 1/320-second exposure prevented motion blur.

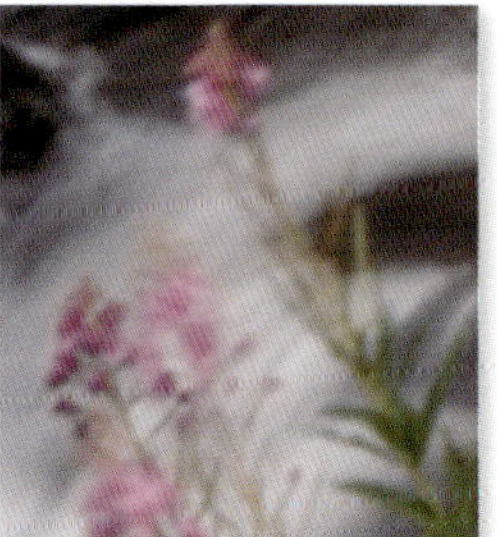

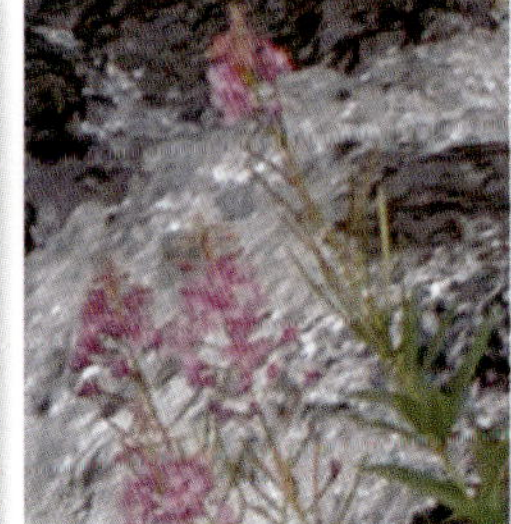

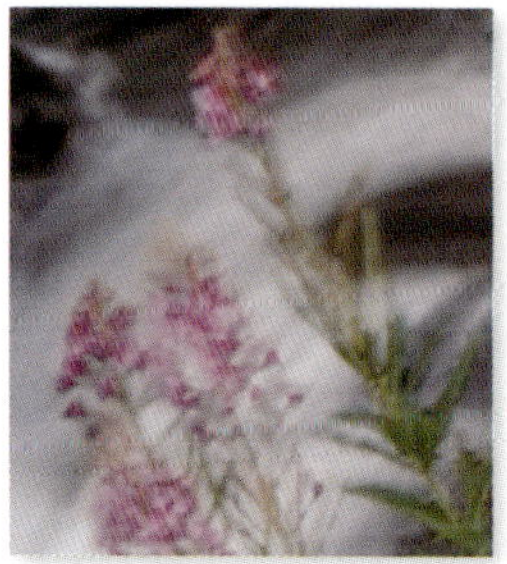
Close-up of difficult area where fast and slow overlapped in the final image.

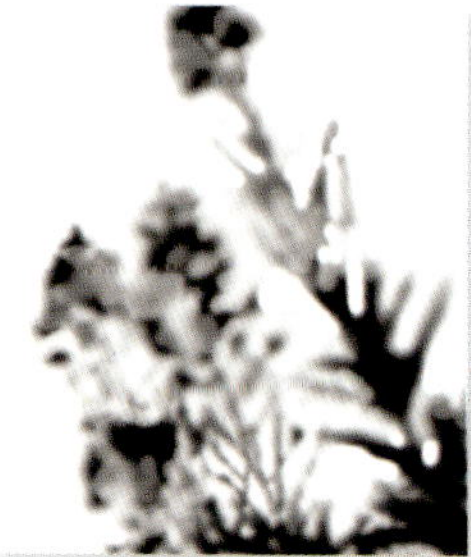
Contents of layer mask used to mix fast and slow exposures in the final image.

Prep in Lightroom Classic

Optimize the images with **Auto-Sync** turned on and both images selected. Then, choose **Photo>Edit In>Open as Layers in Photoshop**.

Align and Mask in Photoshop

Next, apply **Edit>Auto-Align Layers** to compensate for any camera movement that might cause the images to not align. Arrange your layers so whichever image you'd like to use for the majority of the frame is on the bottom of the layer stack. Then click the top layer and choose **Layer>Layer Mask>Hide All**. Finally, choose the **Brush** tool, set the foreground color to white, and paint to reveal the top layer where desired using a soft-edged brush.

Mix Motion with Stillness

The process is pretty straightforward until you encounter an area where you need crisp, motion-less foliage overlapping a silky waterfall. Those areas will require complex masking, which can usually be accomplished with a combination of **Select>Color Range** to isolate the greenery, some manual painting to clean up the results, and the **Blur** tool to soften edge transitions. The final touch usually involves painting with white or black at a low **Opacity** to produce a mix of the blurry and sharp images to end up with a hybrid that includes the best of both.

Mix Multiple Moments

The general appearance of a scene varies as time passes, and a single exposure can only capture an isolated moment in time. You can expand your possibilities by stacking multiple exposures using layers and then masking them to decide which part of the frame should depict each moment. Let's take a look at the general process for combining different times of day into a single image.

Combine

The first step is to select multiple images in Lightroom and choose **Photo>Edit In> Load as Layers in Photoshop**.

Align

Next, select all the layers in Photoshop, choose **Edit>Auto-Align Layers**, and use the **Auto** setting to compensate for any change in camera position between the exposures.

Choose Base Layer

Now, hold **Option** (Mac) or **Alt** (PC) and click on the eyeball icon for the active layer to make it the one and only layer that is visible. Before releasing that modifier key, type **]** multiple times to cycle through and view each layer individually (this only works when the active layer is the only layer that is visible). As you do this, try to determine which layer should serve as the base on which the rest of the image will be built. That will usually be the layer that either captured a critical moment or the one that has the fewest issues that need to be addressed. Drag that layer to the bottom of the layer stack to serve as the foundation of the resulting composite image.

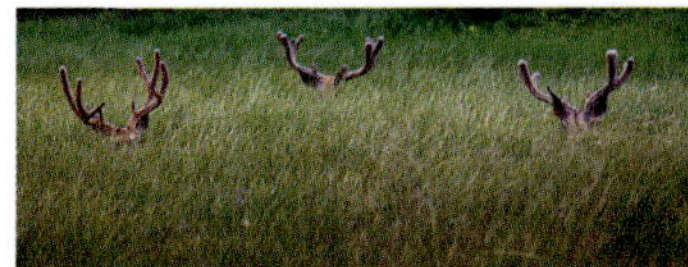

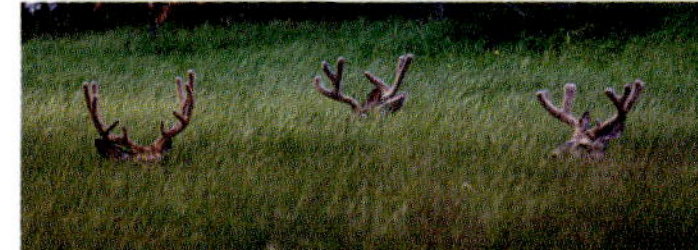

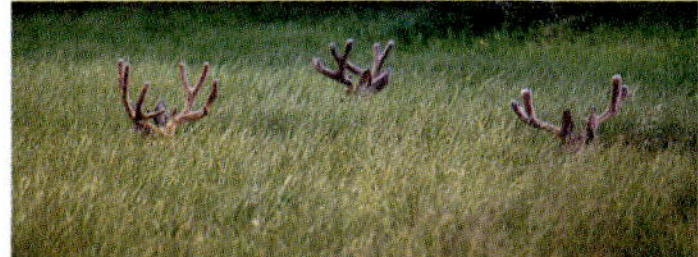

Over a five-minute period, 24 exposures were captured of three elk lounging in the tall grass of Yellowstone National Park. None of the individual images were ideal, so three were chosen to be combined to produce the idealized image shown below.

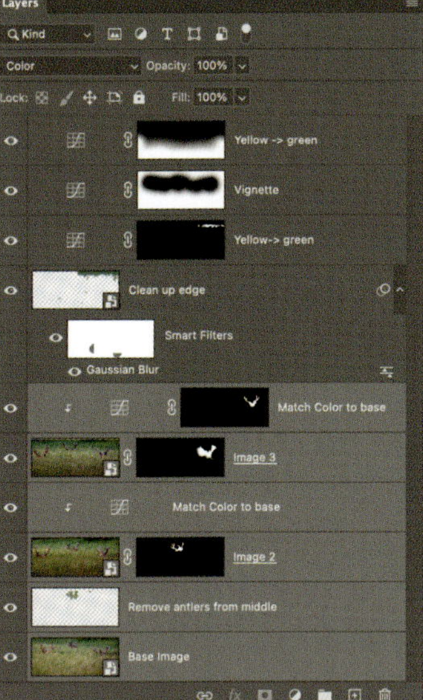

Layers from bottom up: Image used for elk at left and general background. Retouching to remove middle elk from base image. Middle elk masked. Adjustment to make color of middle elk match left elk. Right elk masked. Adjustment to make right elk match left elk. Five layers used to refine and simplify the background.

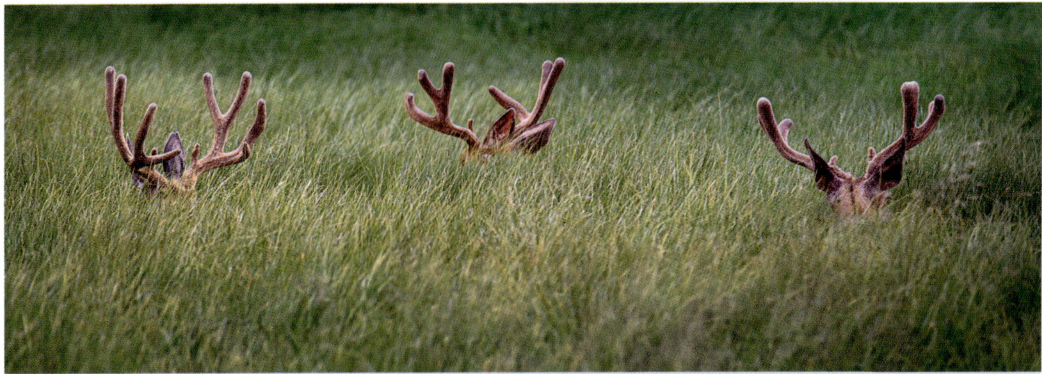

Three different moments in time were combined to produce an idealized version of the scene.

Section II: Quality Considerations

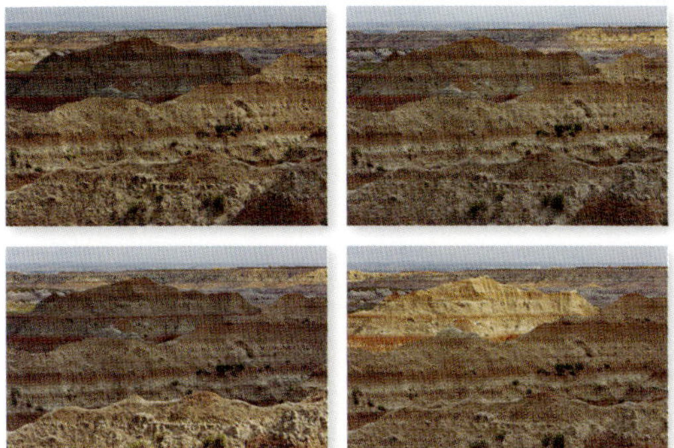

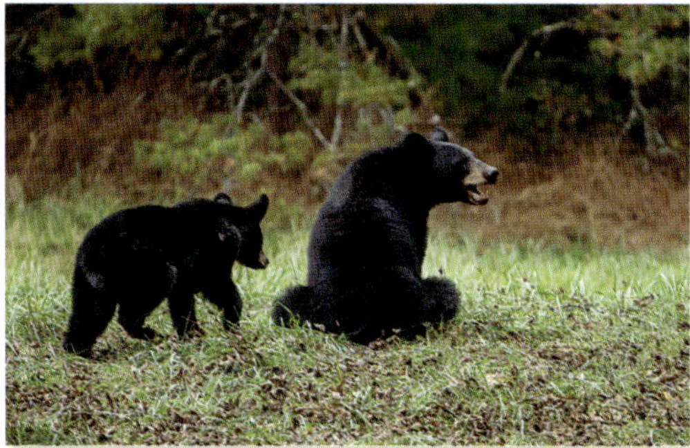

Leave your tripod in place for 5–10 minutes when clouds pass overhead, and later decide which areas you'd like to be lit.

Add Additional Layers

You can then toggle the eyeball icons next to each layer in order to compare their contents to the underlying image and decide where the active layer would best contribute to the combined image. When you find a layer worthy of contributing, choose **Layer>Layer Mask>Hide All** to hide the contents of the active layer, and then paint with a white, soft-edged brush to choose which areas should be added to the base image. Repeat until all useful layers have been utilized.

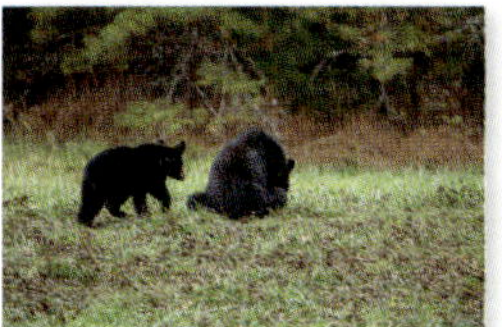

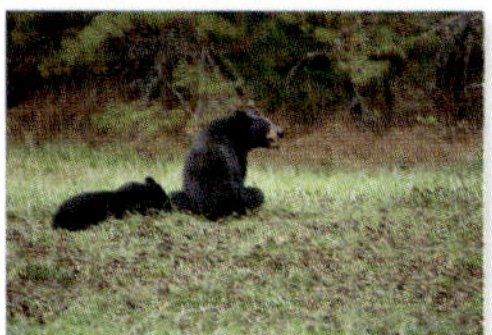

Capturing multiple exposures of groups of wildlife allows for later refinement by masking multiple images.

> **Tip:** *Paint with a vivid color on a new 50% **Opacity** layer to mark areas that need work. Then inspect only those areas when evaluating the contents of other layers for possible inclusion.*

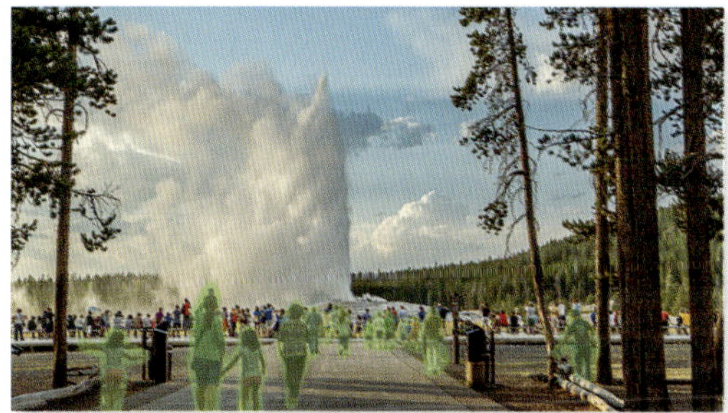

Base image with green overlay to indicate areas needing a fix.

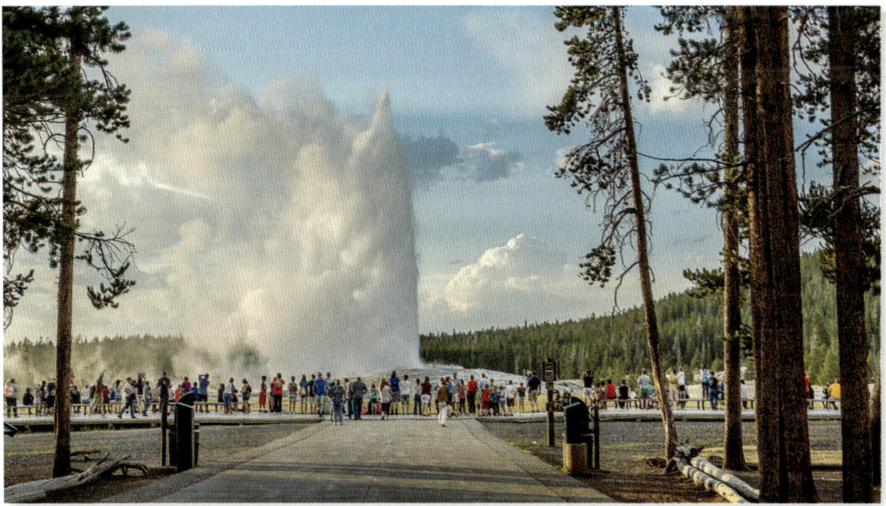

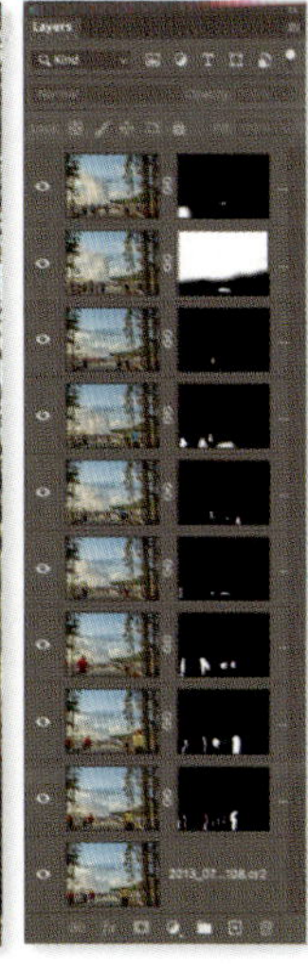

It was only by combining ten total exposures that I was able to get a relatively clean shot of Old Faithful going off.

Add or Subtract Variance

Dozens of exposures captured a few seconds apart can be combined using a unique feature known as a Stack Mode, which will mathematically analyze the difference between the images and combine them into a single image. This can be useful to eliminate noise in images captured at high ISO settings, potentially eliminate or multiply the number of tourists who are wandering around a scene, or increase or reduce smoke.

It all starts by choosing a large number of exposures taken at the same exposure settings using a tripod, selecting them in Lightroom, and choosing **Photo>Edit In> Load as Layers in Photoshop**. Then, select the resulting layers in Photoshop, choose **Layer>Smart Objects>Convert to Smart Object**, and then choose one of the options found in the **Layer>Smart Objects>Stack Mode** menu.

The examples on this page show the four modes that I find to be most useful when working with landscape images.

It can be useful to exclude one of the images captured and place it below the stack, then add a layer mask to the stack to hide portions and reveal the underlying single exposure. If you need more control, use the techniques described on the next page as an alternative.

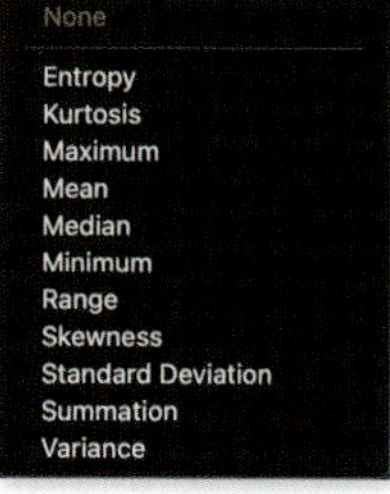

Stack Mode choices.

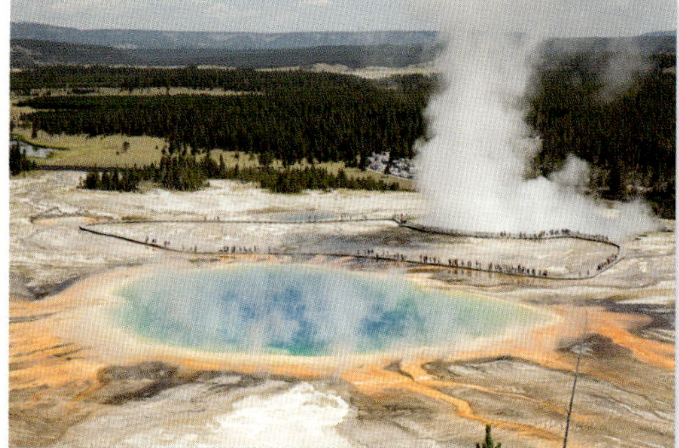

Single exposure for comparison.

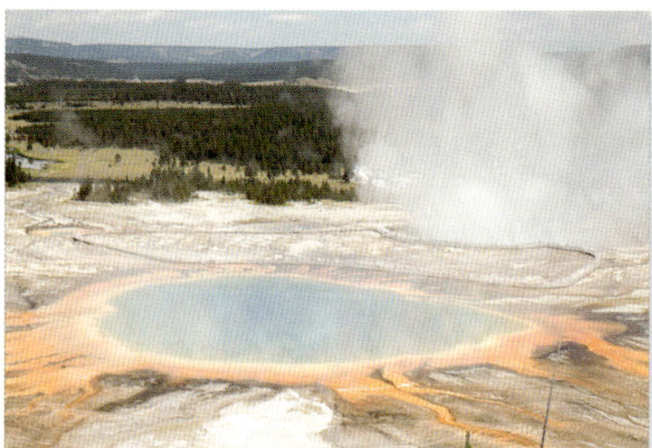

Thirty exposures in Maximum Stack Mode.

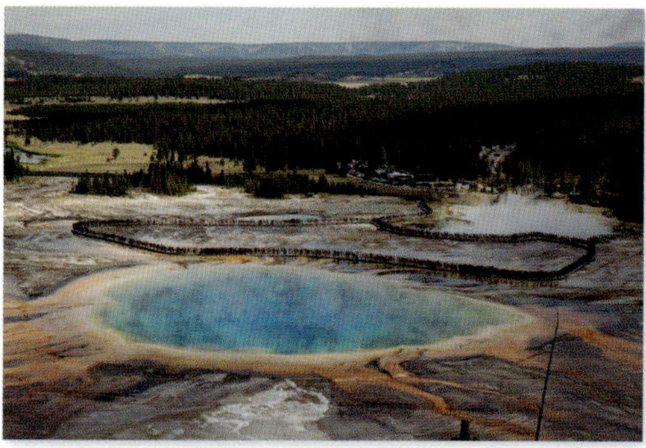

Thirty exposures in Minimum Stack Mode.

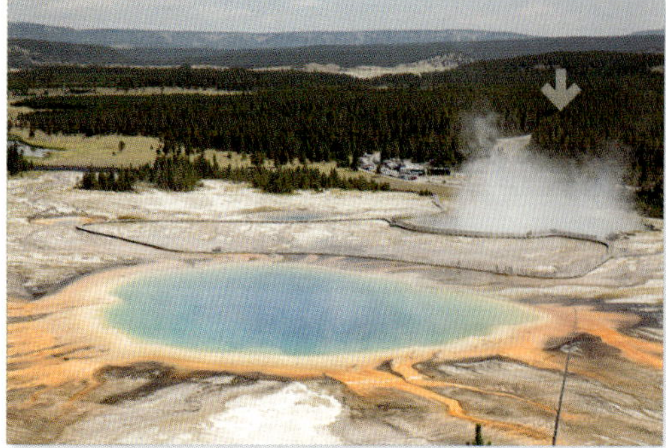

Thirty exposures in Median Stack Mode.

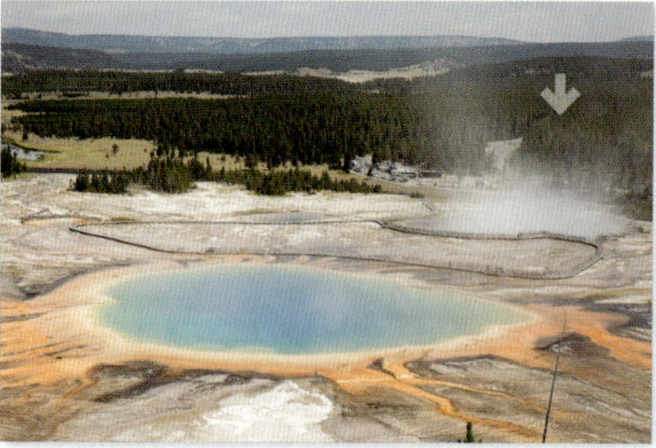

Thirty exposures in Mean Stack Mode.

Section II: Quality Considerations

Reduce Mist or Fog

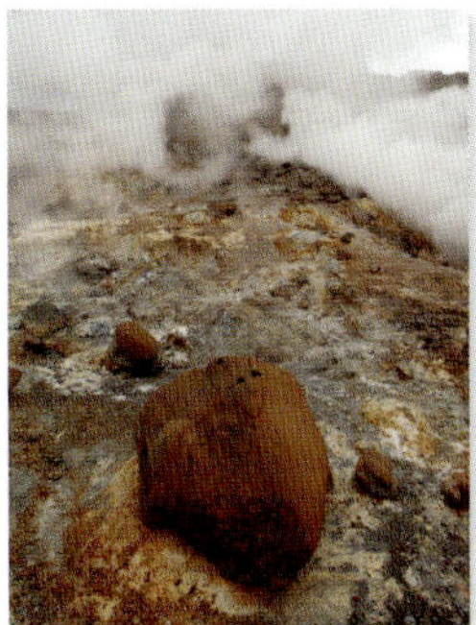

Single exposure.

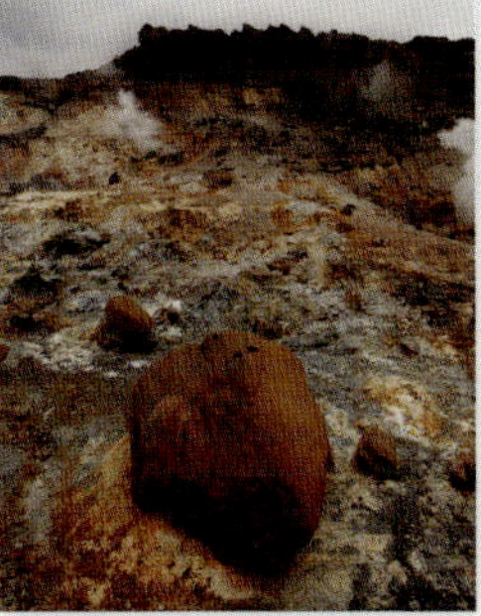

Many shots in Darken mode.

Moving fog, mist, and smoke can be reduced by capturing multiple exposures taken a few seconds apart and then stacking them as layers in Photoshop. The blending mode pop-up menu at the top of the Layers panel can then be used to control how the active layers will blend with the underlying image. **Darken** and **Darker Color** modes are useful when working with smoke.

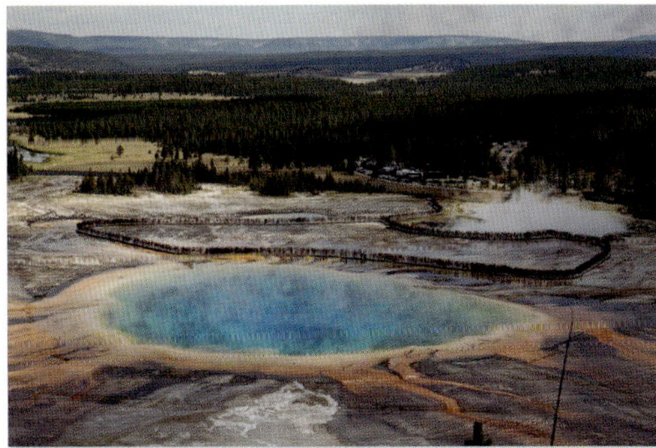

Thirty exposures in Darken blending mode.

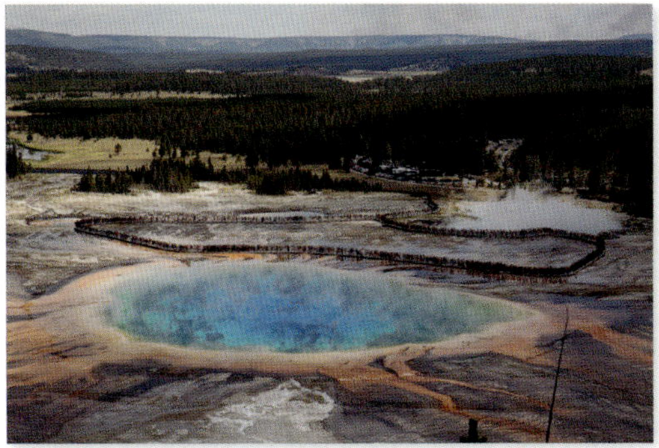

Thirty exposures in Darker Color blending mode.

Increase Haze or Water

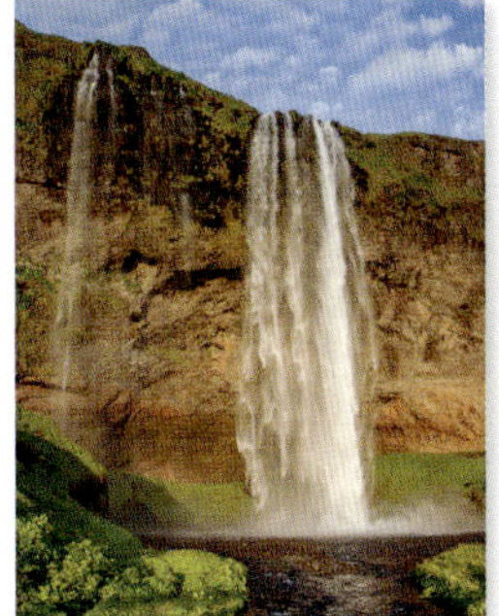

Single exposure.

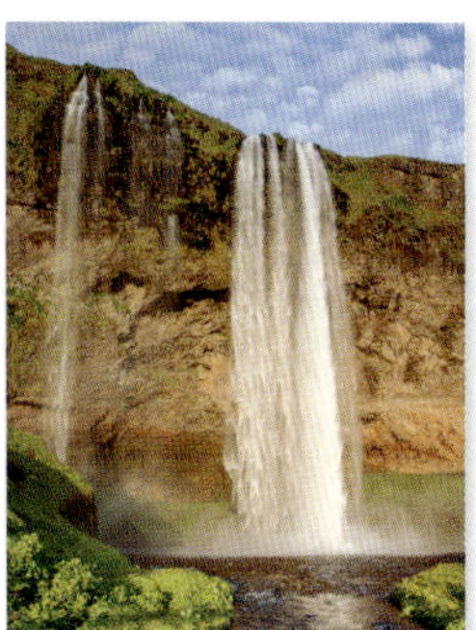

Four shots in Lighten mode.

The **Lighten** and **Lighter Color** blending modes can be used in a similar fashion to the last technique in order to increase the apparent amount of flowing water or moving smoke in a scene. It can even be used with fast shutter speeds to freeze every droplet of water in a waterfall while simultaneously increasing the apparent volume of water flowing over the waterfall.

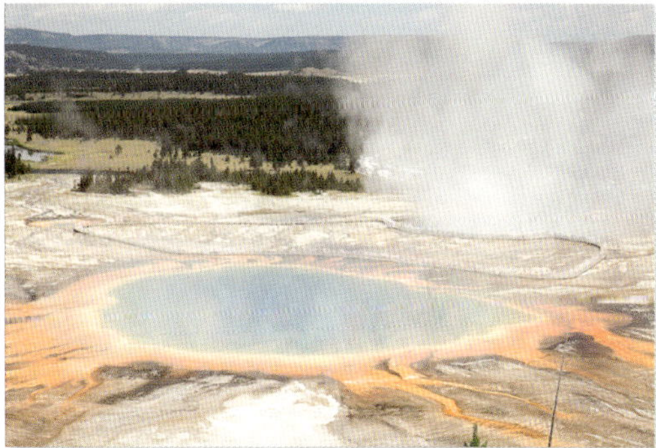

Thirty exposures in Lighten blending mode.

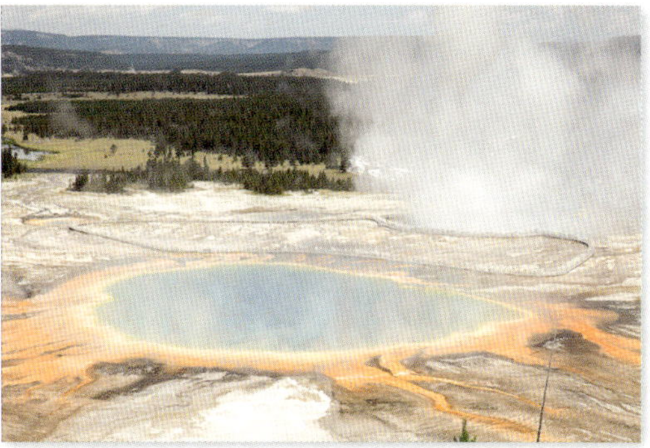

Thirty exposures in Lighter Color blending mode.

Sky Replacement

Edit>Sky Replacement is designed to streamline the process of replacing a sky and produces a sophisticated set of layers that are fully customizable so you can fine-tune the results.

Let's take a look at each control that is available and the corresponding layers that will be produced.

Sky: Click the thumbnail-sized preview image to choose which sky you desire. To load your own images, click on the gear icon in the upper right and choose **Get More Skies>Import Images**.

Scale, Move, and Flip: To precisely position the replacement sky, adjust the **Scale** slider and use the **Move** tool in the upper left. The **Flip** checkbox is useful when the sun is found on the opposite side of the replacement sky from the original image.

Shift and Fade Edge: These sliders modify the qualities of the layer mask that will be attached to the sky layer. The **Shift Edge** slider determines where the sky should end and the original image begins. Positive settings push the transition lower, while negative settings allow the original sky to appear above the horizon. Moving the **Fade Edge** slider to the right will reduce the prominence of the replacement sky within the gradual transition, while moving it left will make it more prominent.

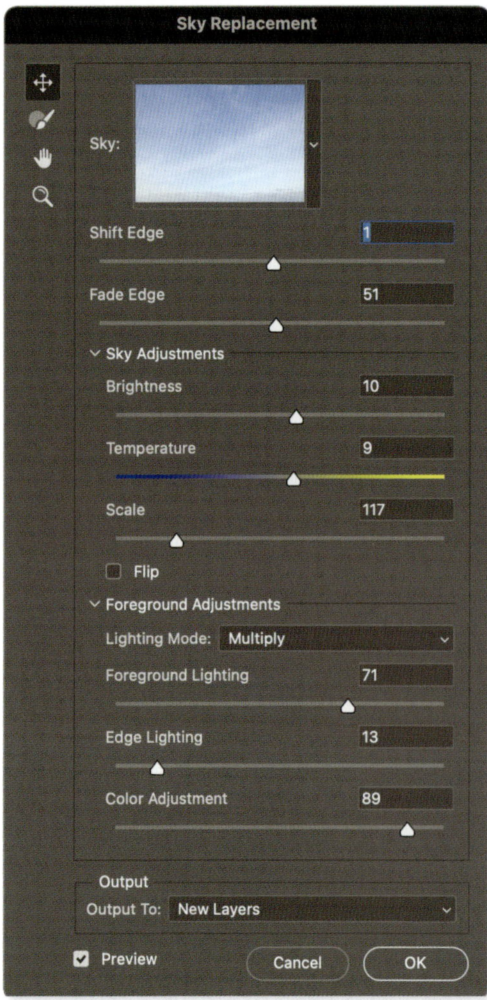

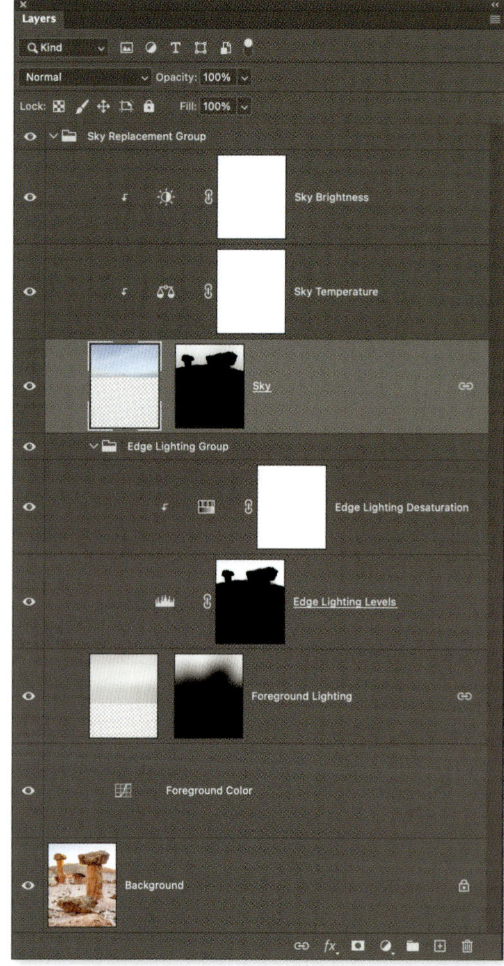

Most of the adjustment sliders produce adjustment layers.

Section II: Quality Considerations

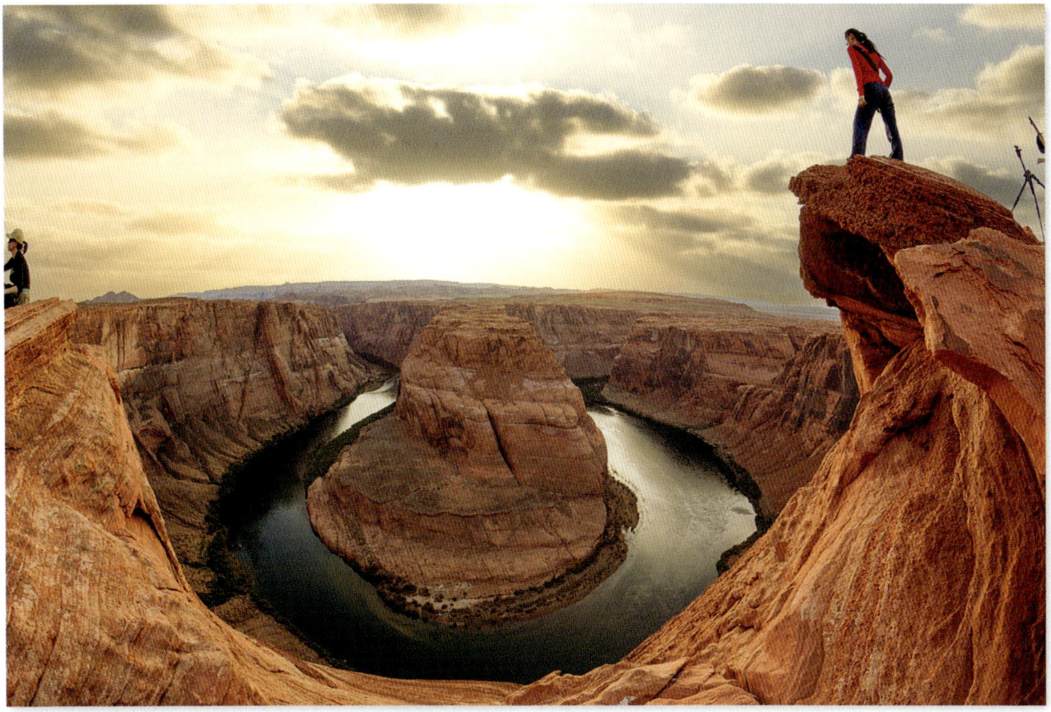

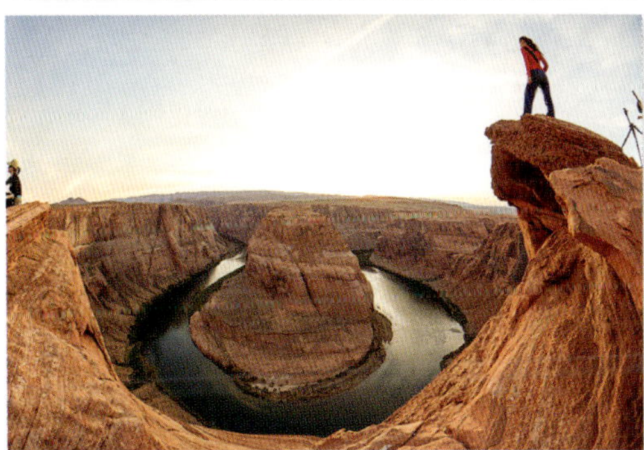

Original image before sky replacement.

Left to Right: *Shift Edge settings of Zero, -100, +100.*

Sky Adjustments: The **Brightness** and **Temperature** sliders can be used to modify the brightness of the sky or shift it toward blue or yellow in an attempt to better match the foreground. These settings can later be fine-tuned via two adjustment layers that will end up above the sky layer.

Foreground Adjustments: These adjustments modify the appearance of the foreground in an attempt to make it better match the new sky. The **Lighting Mode** setting determines whether the transition area will be darkened (using **Multiply**) or lightened (using **Screen**).

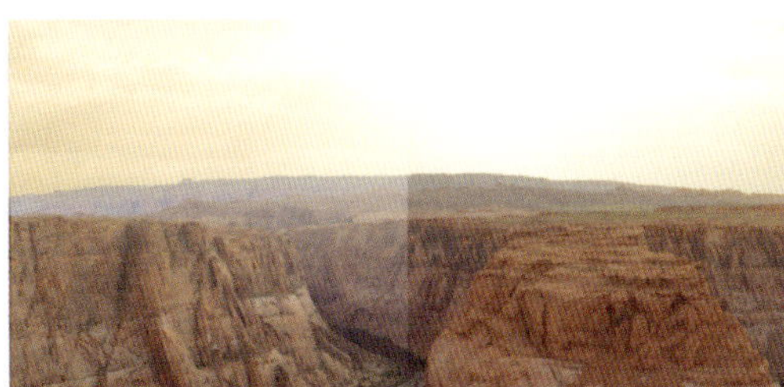

Image split in half with left side in Screen and right in Multiply.

The **Foreground Lighting** slider reduces the contrast of the original image within the transition area. The **Edge Lighting** slider changes the contrast of the sky side of the transition and can be useful to reduce or eliminate halos. The **Color Adjustment** slider determines how much the colors in the original image will be shifted toward the colors found within the replacement sky.

Expand Depth of Field

When you have both near and far areas in a scene that need to be rendered as sharp, common wisdom dictates you stop down your aperture to the highest setting of f/22. That may deliver a deep depth of field, but it's also the setting that delivers the lowest overall quality due to diffraction.

Stopping a lens down by two stops from it's lowest setting will produce a dramatically sharper result, but will also produce a much shallower depth of field.

Capture for Sharpness

To achieve the best of both worlds, capture multiple images at f/8–11 (a range that usually produces the sharpest results) and vary the focus point from near to far in order to ensure you achieve the depth desired.

This is often as simple as focusing on the farthest important area to capture one frame, and then shifting focus to a close important area to capture a second. But not all scenes can be captured in just two shots. It all depends on the focal length of the lens being used. Telephoto lenses produce a much shallower depth of field compared to wider-angle lenses and therefore may require more than two exposures in order to obtain sharpness in the full depth of the scene.

Focus Stack in Photoshop

Once you've captured enough shots to obtain sharpness in the full depth you desire, you can select the resulting images in Lightroom and choose **Photo>Edit In>Load as Layers in Photoshop** to stack the images in Photoshop. Finally, select all the layers and choose **Edit>Auto-Blend Layers**, set the Blend Method to **Stack Images**, and turn on the **Seamless Tones and Colors** checkbox.

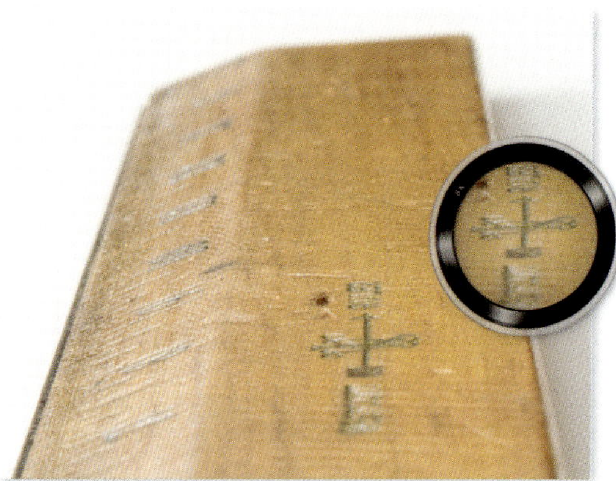

Single exposure of a ruler captured at f/22.

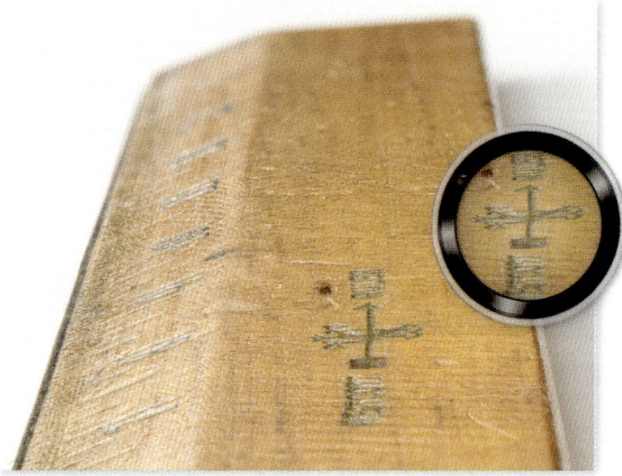

Multiple exposures captured at f/11 and merged in Photoshop.

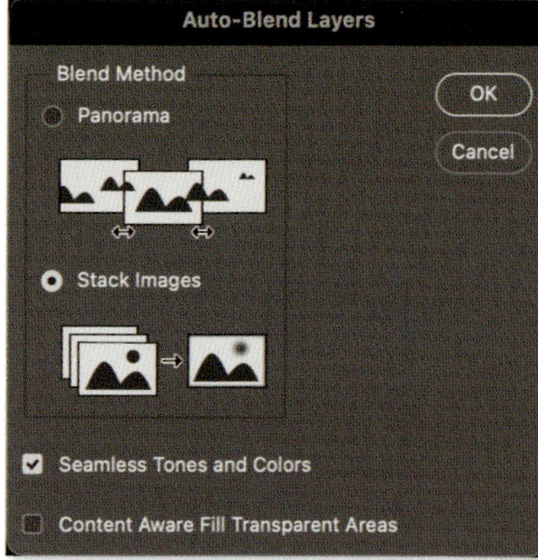

Auto-Blend Layers will compare the sharpness of each layer and mask the results so you end up with only the sharpest areas in each layer.

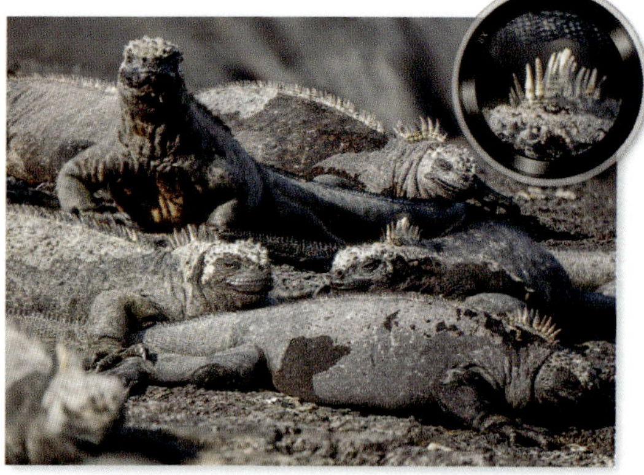

Result of having too great of a distance between focus points, which causes the image to alternate between crisp and soft.

Section II: Quality Considerations

Pull Far Objects Close

Getting up close and shooting a foreground element with a wide-angle lens can exaggerate its proportions and make it dominate the frame. But getting too close is also going to make background elements feel much smaller in comparison, in contrast to shooting from farther away, which would visually compress the space between near and far. You can achieve the best of both worlds by capturing the foreground with a wide-angle lens, and then zooming in on the background and capturing a second exposure.

The resulting images can then be stacked as layers with the zoomed image as a base layer and the wide-angle placed above with a layer mask limiting it to appearing at the bottom of the resulting image.

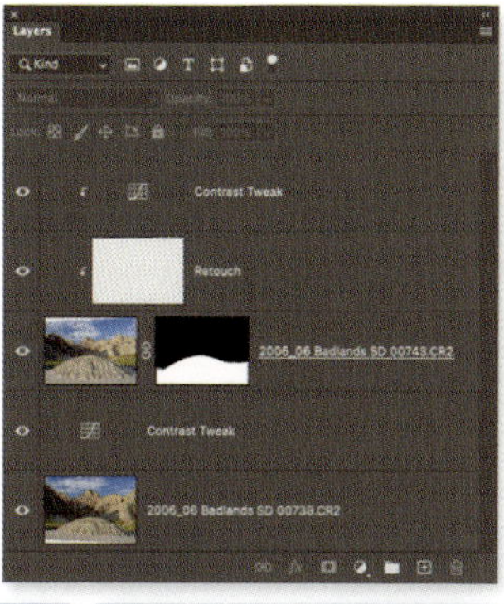

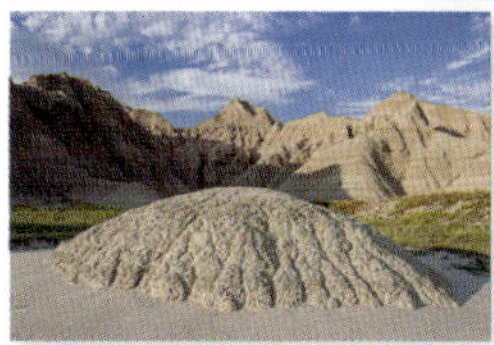

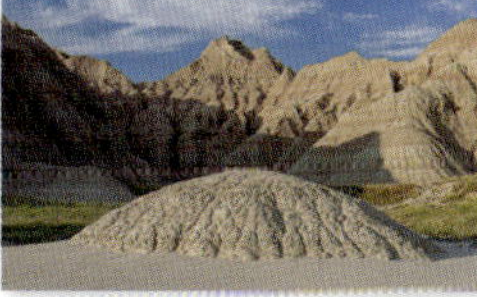

17mm lens makes the near area feel expansive, while the far area appears small.

Zooming to 27mm made the distant area feel closer and more detailed.

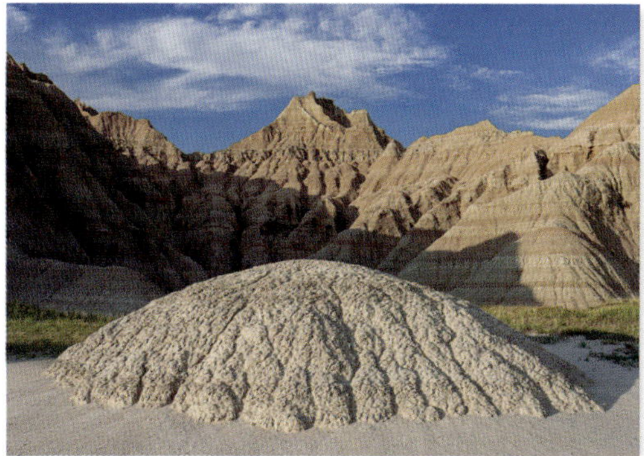

Result of combining the zoomed-in capture of the distant area with the wider-angle capture of the close object.

Smart Preview HDR and Panoramas

If you create Smart Previews via the **Library>Previews** menu before disconnecting a hard drive, you will be able to merge HDR images or panoramas, even when you're traveling and lack access to the original images. The results will utilize 2,560-pixel-wide mini raw files. While smaller than the originals, they can still be useful for posting on social media.

Alignment when Transforming

When attempting to manually align two layers, you'll commonly need to scale or rotate one layer in order to match the content found within the underlying image. This can be accomplished by turning on the checkbox that appears near the left side of the Options Bar while 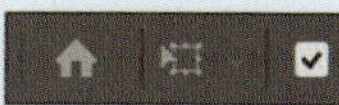 transforming. This will cause a crosshair to appear in the center of the layer. Reposition that crosshair to the spot that needs to remain in a fixed position and it will serve as the pivot point when rotating the layer. Holding **Option** (Mac) or **Alt** (PC) when dragging any of the side or corner handles will cause the crosshair to become the center point when any scaling is applied.

Batch-Merging Panoramas

Multiple panoramas can be batch-stitched if each image sequence is first stacked. Stack selected images via **Photo>Stacking>Group into Stack**. Then select the resulting stacks and choose **Photo>Photo Merge>Panorama**. Each stack will then be merged using the settings from the last panorama you stitched.

Finding Stitched Panoramas

You can quickly find panoramas in your Lightroom catalog by clicking on the **All Photographs** choice in the **Catalog** section on the left side of the Library module, then choosing **View>Sort>Aspect Ratio**. Scroll to the top or bottom of the sorted thumbnails to find vertical and horizontal panos.

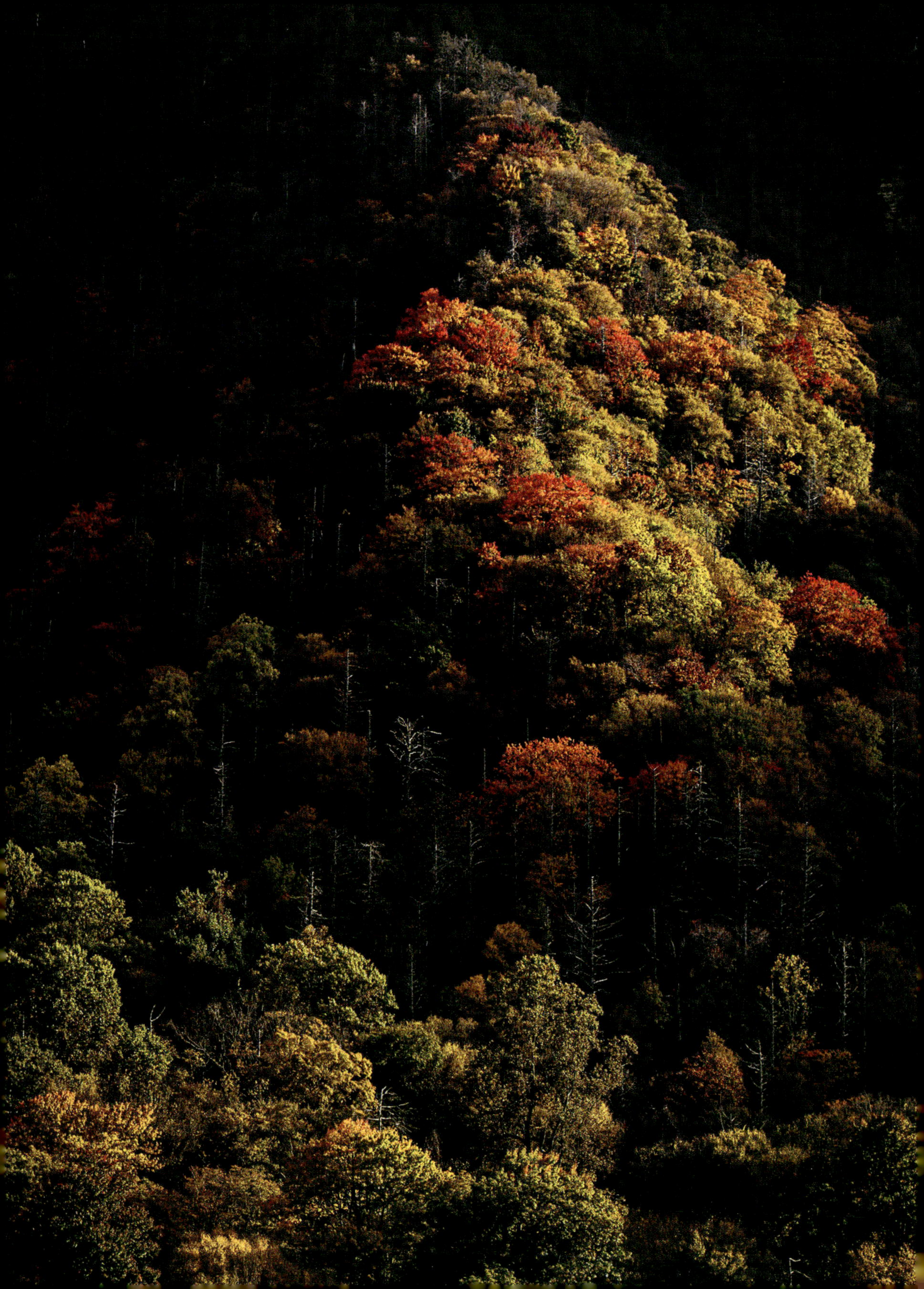

Section III

Crafting a Photograph

ALL OF THE concepts we've explored so far are absolutely necessary if you want to produce a quality image that will serve as a solid foundation worthy of building upon. But, to be honest, I wish there was a camera or software feature that would automate all of those things so that I could spend all of my time applying the techniques covered in this next section of the book. The techniques that follow will allow you to craft a unique interpretation of each image that reflects your personal style. As a result, your photographs will be distinctly different from other images that were captured at the same time and place.

Chapter 6

Lead the Eye

MY APPROACH TO leading the eye through a scene with after-capture refinement is identical to the mindset I use when I'm looking through the lens, composing an image. I take inventory of what's in front of me, dividing all elements of the scene into positive, negative, and neutral areas. I then attempt to maximize the positives (by moving closer to make them larger) and minimize the negatives (by re-framing to exclude them, or rendering them as out-of-focus or underexposed). I also prevent neutral areas, such as a boring overcast sky, from dominating the composition (by tilting down to include more landscape and less sky). I then find the vantage point that arranges those elements into a simple composition that draws the viewer into the scene and provides a path for their eye to follow through the image.

Establish a Focal Point

Most truly memorable images have a prominent focal point that draws the eye more strongly than anything else in the scene. This is the area that your eye returns to again and again, and is probably where you looked first.

For the photographer, this is usually the factor that drew you to pick up your camera and capture the moment. This star element can be supplied by nature in the form of light, color, or contrast, or instead through deliberate processing choices designed to influence the viewer's gaze.

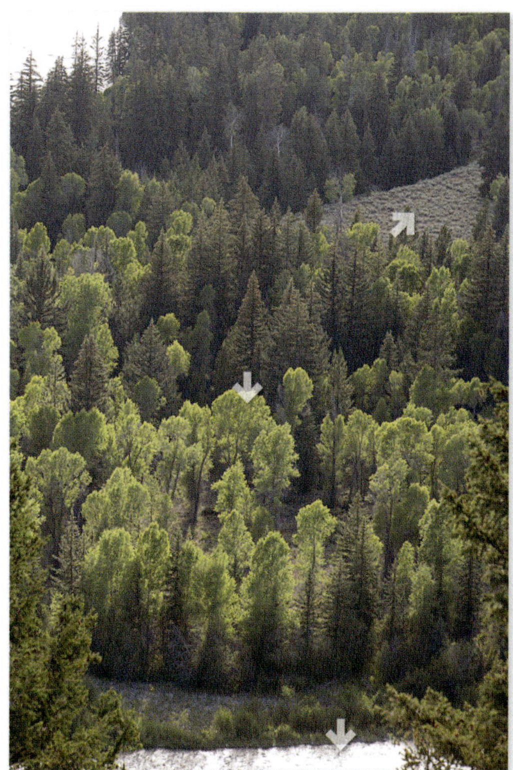

Lacking a single dominant focal point, the eye naturally wanders between areas of high contrast, brightness, color, and diagonal elements scattered throughout the scene.

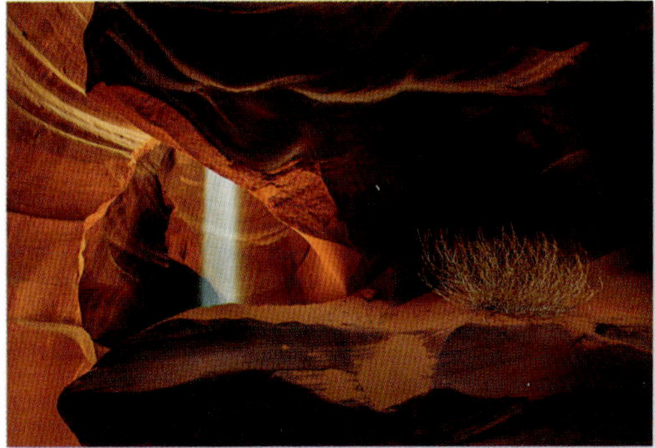

Light beam establishes the natural focal point of this image, while the light catching the canyon walls and the tumbleweed serve as supporting elements.

Therefore, the first step to leading the viewer's eye is to choose which single element or concept will serve as the focal point of the image. It could be a single physical object, a unique color that caught your eye, a few interesting shapes, or a single unusual element that stands out from a sea of sameness. Whatever it is, it's your task to make sure that anyone viewing your image will be drawn to that focal point first.

The natural brightness and contrast captured from the scene will serve as the raw material you have to start with. Lightroom and Photoshop are the tools you'll use to mold that raw material into something that matches your vision for what you'd like to present to the viewer.

Other elements within the scene should then be treated as either supporting characters or potential distractions that might pull attention away from the focal point.

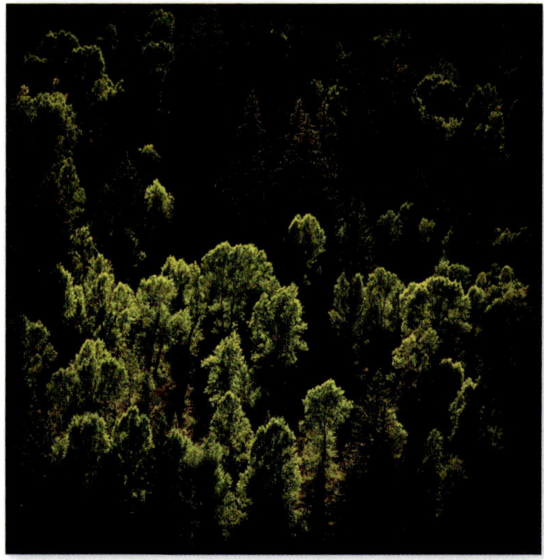

After processing to establish the highlights of trees as the focal point. Where the eyes look is no longer left to chance.

Section III: Crafting a Photograph

Take Inventory of Scene

When I walk across a landscape and feel compelled to capture a scene, my eyes are magnetically drawn to the most unique elements, and largely ignore areas that are not interesting. When I return home and view my images, I often find that what I captured pales in comparison to what I experienced. It just feels so flat and lifeless. To breathe life info the image, I take a mental inventory of what I have to work with and divide the image into the following regions:

Positive: These are areas I want to be the stars of the show and are usually the very reason I picked up the camera in the first place. This is regardless of whether they are well exposed or appear lackluster in the original capture. It is essential to be selective and use a less-is-more mindset.

Negative: Areas of potential distraction may pull my eye away from the positive elements and do not contribute to the success of the image. I'll look to see where the light is falling and decide if it is emphasizing areas that will draw my attention away from the main subject and cause my eye to bounce haphazardly around the image. I pay particular attention to complex detail found at the edges and corners of the image.

Neutral: These are areas that don't influence my gaze and do not pull my attention away from the positive elements in the scene. This would include unexciting simple skies and areas where it is difficult to see detail because the areas are dark or lacking contrast.

Assemble Your Toolbox

Your initial perception of an image does not have to be based solely on the native brightness, contrast, and color that was captured from a scene. We can influence the viewer's experience and lead their eye through an image by figuring out which qualities will attract their attention.

I find that my eyes have the tendency to flow through an image in a somewhat orderly fashion.

High Contrast to Low Contrast: My eye is initially pulled like a magnet to the area of greatest contrast between bright and dark. This could be a dark inky shadow appearing on the edge of an object that is touching a bright area in the sky. My eye then moves to slightly lower-contrast areas.

Bright to Dark: The brightest areas of an image are impossible to ignore and will be the next areas I tend to explore. Dark areas only attract my attention when they are touching bright areas, and this is the contrast that's mentioned above.

Colorful from Warm to Cool: My eye has the tendency to move from the brightest area to the most colorful areas. If there are multiple areas that are colorful, then it will usually be pulled to warmer areas (red/orange/yellow) before exploring cool areas (cyan/blue/green).

Sharp to Blurry: This circles back to the concept of contrast, as the sharpest areas will have more contrast than those that are blurry. The only difference is that we're talking about smaller areas, which some would call micro-contrast.

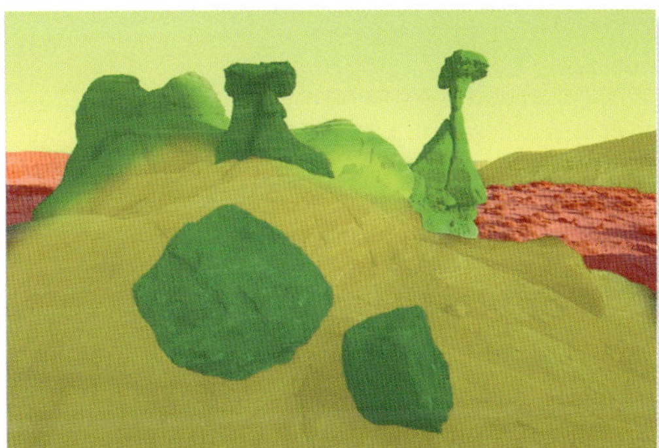

Inventory of positive elements in green, negative elements in red, and neutral elements in yellow/orange.

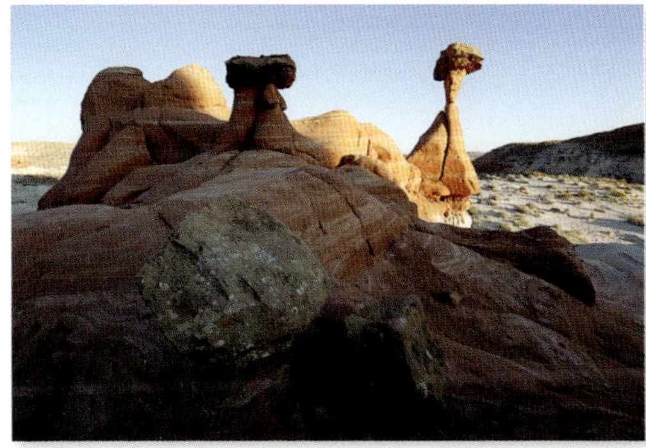

The original image with its native brightness, contrast, and color as rendered using Lightroom's default settings.

Reduce the Negative

This stage is all about toning down or removing potential distractions that might lead the eye off course and direct attention away from the positive elements within the scene. This is usually a multi-step process.

Crop to Strengthen Composition

The in-camera framing of a scene can be less than ideal due to the limited zoom range of the lens and limitations in how close you can be to the subject. Cropping can therefore be used to strengthen just about any composition.

Lightroom Cropping Is Ideal

The non-destructive nature of Lightroom's **Crop** tool makes it the ideal way to crop an image because it can be modified at any time. Add **Virtual Copies** to the mix and you can have multiple formats (vertical, horizontal, square) of the same image without the need for duplicate files.

Be careful when opening a cropped raw file into Photoshop, as any information outside of the cropping rectangle will be discarded from the resulting file. For this reason, I'll reset the crop by typing **R** to activate the **Crop** tool and clicking the **Reset** button before opening an image into Photoshop.

Photoshop Crop Overlay

Once the image is open in Photoshop, I create an overlay that represents the cropping I plan to eventually apply in Lightroom. The overlay helps me to better visualize the cropping and ensure that I don't waste time enhancing or retouching areas that will not be visible in the final image.

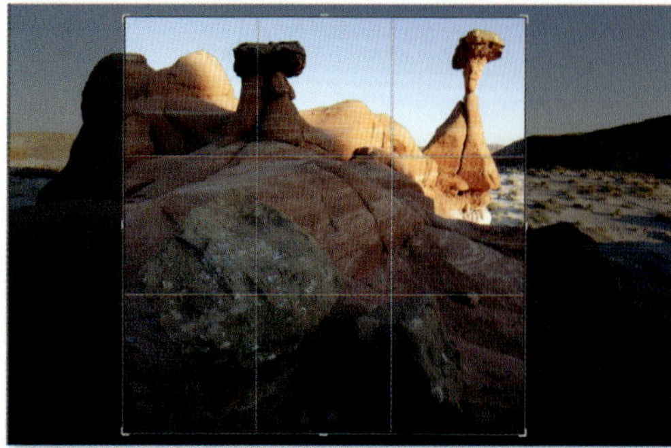

Cropping this image into a square format eliminated over 75% of the areas that were potential distractions.

To create a crop overlay, type **D** to reset the foreground/background colors to black/white, and type **U** to activate the **Shape** tool. Select the rectangular option, choose the **Shape** setting in the Options Bar above the image, and then draw a rectangle that represents the area you plan to later crop in Lightroom. Then choose the **Subtract Front Shape** setting in the Options Bar.

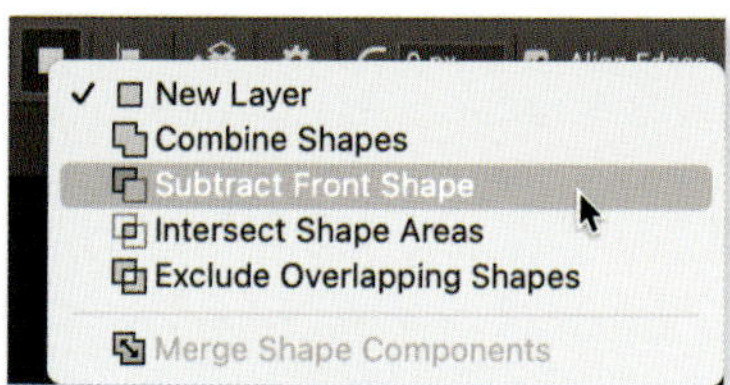

The Subtract Front Shape option will cause the shape you draw to become a hole in the overlay.

Re-Crop in Lightroom

Once a TIFF or PSD file is saved from Photoshop, the cropping that was previously removed can be reapplied in Lightroom. If you need to re-open the file in Photoshop, be sure to choose the **Edit Original** choice when prompted. This will prevent the cropping from being applied, but will reapply it as soon as the image is saved and sent back to Lightroom.

Reduce Distraction with Retouching

If your eye is going to be pulled somewhere by contrast, brightness, or color, then that area should deliver a payoff that contributes to your enjoyment of the image. If it wasn't one of the contributing elements that compelled you to capture the image and it's easy to remove, then consider doing so. I think of this step as pulling weeds from the garden that is my photograph.

In the process, pay special attention to the edges and corners of the image. Diagonal lines found in these areas will be especially distracting.

At the same time, try to restrain yourself from altering any distinctive elements that help make a scene recognizable to others. Doing this could pull attention to a simplified area where someone expects to see specific detail that is missing.

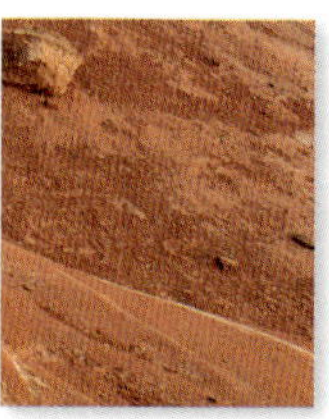
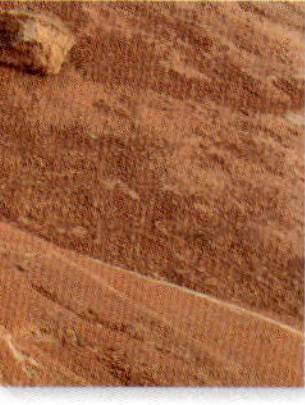

Area at right edge of frame before and after retouching was used to remove small elements and simplify the image.

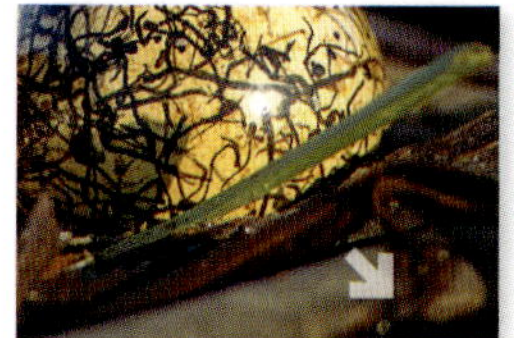 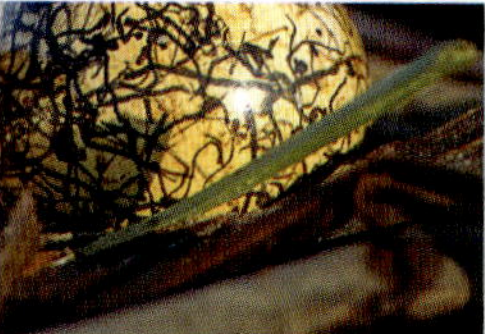

Before and after removing tiny highlights that were pulling attention away from this African egg.

Lightroom Performance

When an image has only a few areas that need attention, Lightroom will usually be up for the task. You may start to notice reduced responsiveness once you have retouched more than a few dozen areas. This is one disadvantage to Lightroom's parametric approach to image editing.

Non-Destructive Retouching in Photoshop

Photoshop is the preferred choice for extensive retouching since its performance will not degrade, even after applying a retouching tool hundreds of times across an image.

The key is to work non-destructively by applying any retouching on a new layer above the base image. Doing so will require that the **Sampling** setting for each retouching tool be set to either **Current & Below** or **Sample All Layers**. This will allow them to work with material from the underlying image. That way, the retouching can easily be altered or removed if the cropping of the image needs to be modified for use in a different aspect ratio than you had originally intended.

Reduce Contrast where Eye is Drawn

Areas that feature a great difference between bright and dark will have a tendency to attract the eye. If this causes your attention to be pulled away from the main subject, then the image may be improved by reducing contrast in those areas.

Curves for Contrast

Contrast can be reduced by choosing **Layer>New Adjustment Layer>Curves**. Activate the **Targeted Adjustment** tool (hand icon) and click on a medium-brightness tone within the area you'd like to adjust **A**. Then, either move the lower-left point up **B** to brighten dark areas, or move the upper-right point down to darken the bright areas. To limit where the change is applied, choose **Image>Adjustments>Invert** in order to start with a black mask. Then paint with white over the area where you want to apply the change **C**. Reducing saturation is an alternative option **D**.

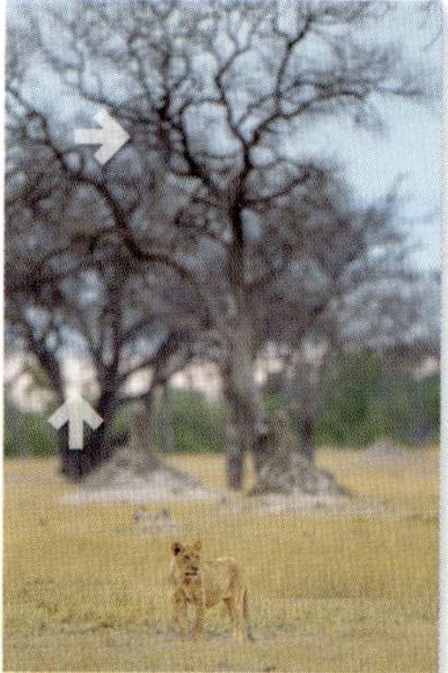 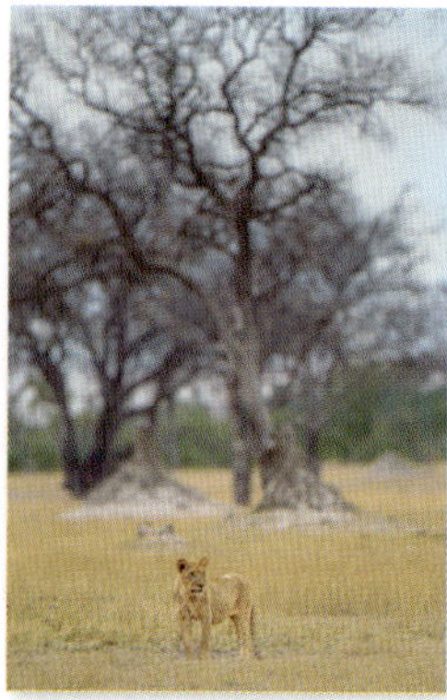

Before and after toning down areas of high contrast to prevent attention from being drawn away from the subject.

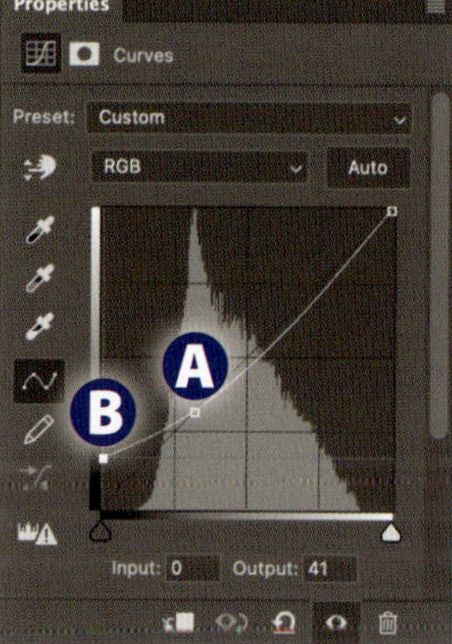

Curves adjustment used to reduce contrast in upper tree area:

A: Clicking within a medium-dark area of the trees using the Targeted Adjustment tool (hand icon) produced a point, which was not moved and therefore maintained the brightness of the area.

B: Lower-left point was raised to brighten the darkest tones.

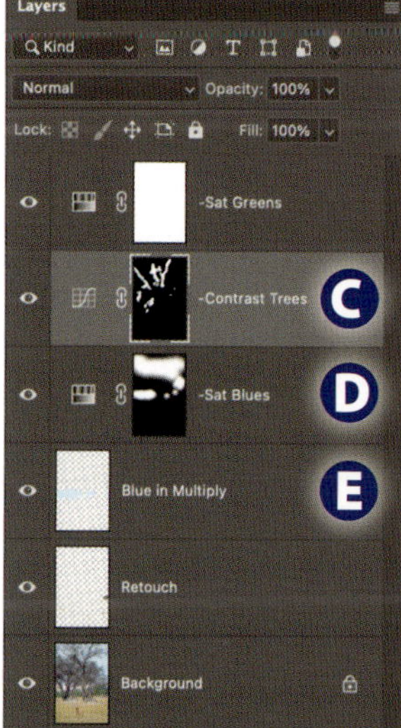

Layers for lion image:

C: Curves adjustment with mask to limit changes to desirable parts of the trees.

D: Hue and Saturation adjustment reducing saturation of blues in portions of sky.

E: Bluish-gray paint matching upper sky painted over brightest area of sky. Layer blending mode is set to Multiply to darken underlying image, then Eraser was used to remove overspray on surrounding branches.

Tone Down Distracting Highlights

The brightest area on an object or in a region of an image will tend to attract your attention. If that ends up pulling your eye away from the desirable parts of the image, then consider darkening them.

Paint in Multiply

When I need to both darken and shift the color of a bright area in order to make it more closely match another area (such as a white area of sky standing out against an otherwise bluish sky), I'll use the **Brush** tool and **Multiply** mode. To do this, create a new layer, activate the **Brush** tool, hold **Option** (Mac) or **Alt** (PC), and click within the color you desire. Then paint over the area with the color you just chose. To push the color into the bright areas, change the blending mode pop-up menu at the top of the Layers panel to **Multiply**. This will cause the layer to blend with the underlying image as if it was printed on top using ink. Then, you can either erase, mask, or experiment with the Blending Sliders (see chapter 3, page 59) to prevent the change from affecting the darker tones in the image **E** (page 119).

Curves to Mellow Highlights

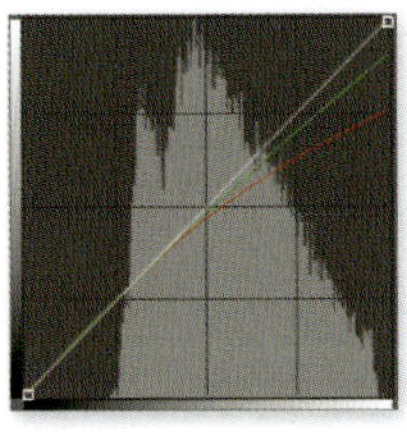

The previously mentioned technique that uses **Curves** to reduce contrast can also be used to darken highlights. If you also need to shift the color of the area, you'll need to lower the upper-right point on one or two of the **Red**, **Green**, and **Blue** curves.

Dual Raw Settings via Smart Objects

Highlight detail can often be recovered by lowering the **Highlights** or **Whites** sliders in Lightroom. When this needs to be done in an isolated area, you may find that Lightroom's masking features leave much to be desired, as it is difficult to precisely blend a change into the surrounding image. When that's the case, you may want to choose **Photo>Edit In>Open as Smart Object in Photoshop**. Then choose **Layer>Smart Objects>New Smart Object Via Copy**. This will stack two versions of the raw file on top of each other in Photoshop. You can then double-click on the thumbnail image for the top layer in the Layers panel to adjust the develop settings and darken the highlights. Then, Photoshop's more sophisticated masking features can be used to blend the result into the surrounding image.

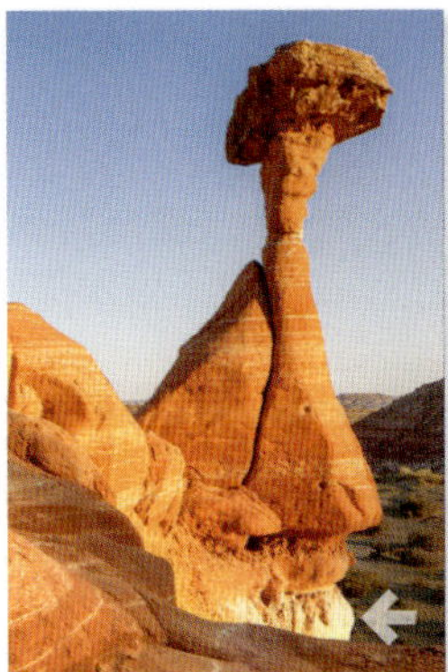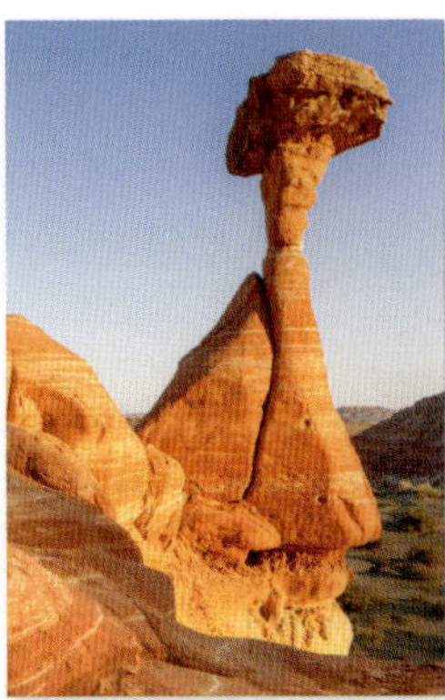

Before and after darkening a bright area using stacked Smart Objects to prevent the eye from being drawn to the area.

Soften Distracting Detail

Small specks of detail in an otherwise out-of-focus area can also send your eye on random trips around an image (especially where the sun reflects off wet objects). I usually deal with this type of issue by softening the area. This can be done by lowering **Clarity**, **Texture**, and **Sharpness** via a masked adjustment in Lightroom.

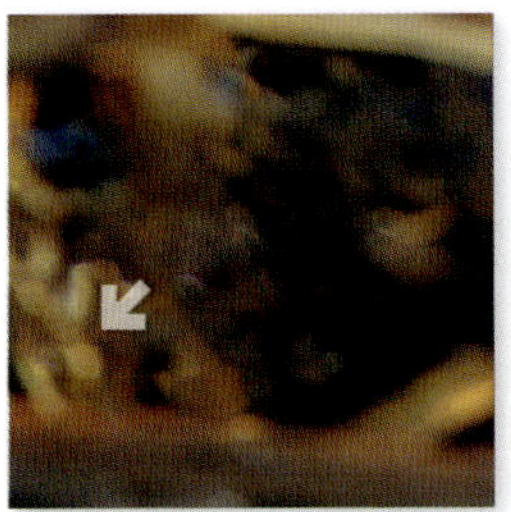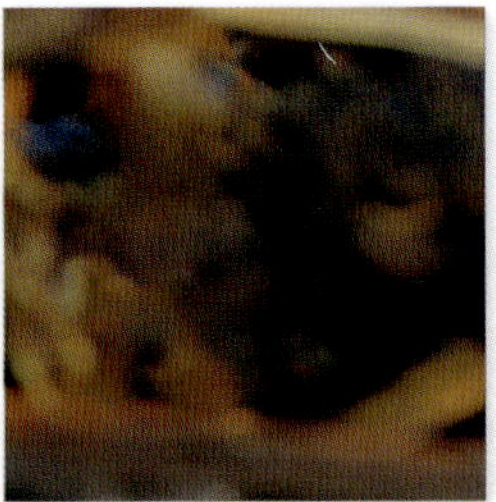

Before and after softening areas by lowering Clarity, Texture, and Sharpness via a masked adjustment in Lightroom.

Reduce Color Variability

Variation in color is another element that can draw the eye. In Photoshop, a **Hue/Saturation** adjustment layer can be used to isolate and shift a particular color to make it better blend in with its surroundings. The general technique is described in chapter 3.

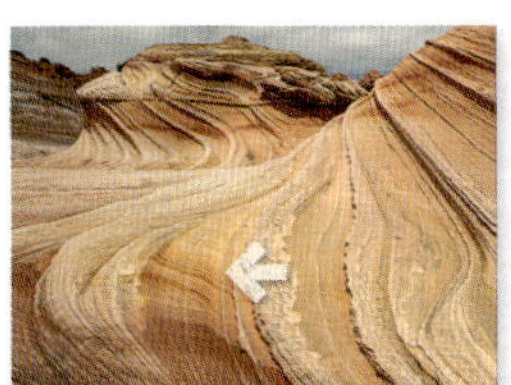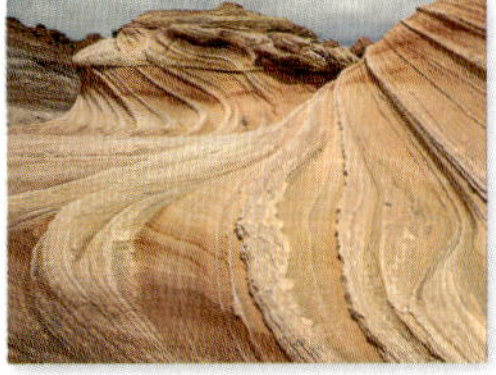

Color shifted to match surroundings using Hue/Saturation.

Emphasize the Positive

Once you've toned down the negatives, it's time to turn up the volume on the positive elements to ensure they get the attention they deserve.

Shadow into Light

The most important areas in a scene won't always be lit directly by the sun. When they are hiding in the shadows, their contrast will be dramatically lower than sunlit areas. Additionally, they will likely have a blue color cast because they're being lit by the blue sky that is overhead.

Areas in the shadows can be transformed to closely match sunlit areas by masking them and then boosting the **Exposure** and **Whites** sliders. Then, the **Temperature** slider can be moved to the right to shift the overall color away from blue.

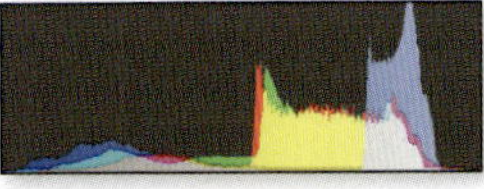

Histogram for sunlit area uses close to the full brightness range available.

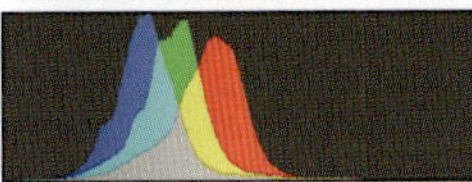

Brightness range of shadow area does not contain as bright of highlights as sunlit areas.

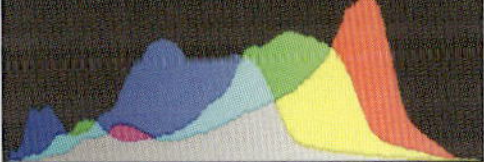

Boosting Exposure and Whites transforms shadow areas to more closely resemble sunlit areas.

Boost Contrast

Increasing the difference in brightness between the dark and bright areas of an element will help it draw more attention. That can most effectively be accomplished using **Curves**, by adding points for the brightest and darkest parts of an area and then doing one of three things.

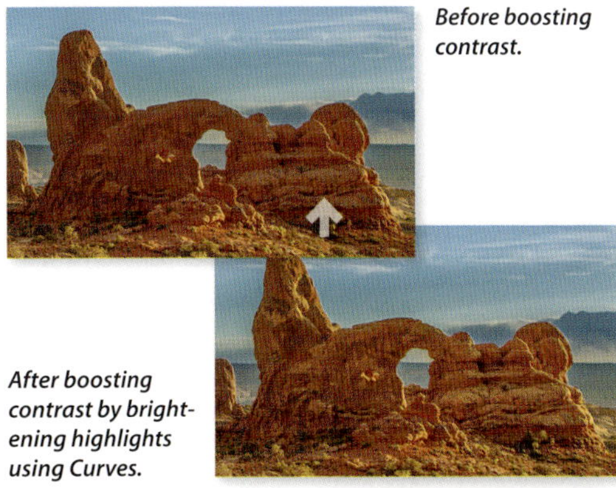

Before boosting contrast.

After boosting contrast by brightening highlights using Curves.

Increase Brightness of Highlights:

Click on a dark area with the **Targeted Adjustment** tool to lock in its brightness **A**. Then click on a bright area and drag up to brighten and increase contrast **B**.

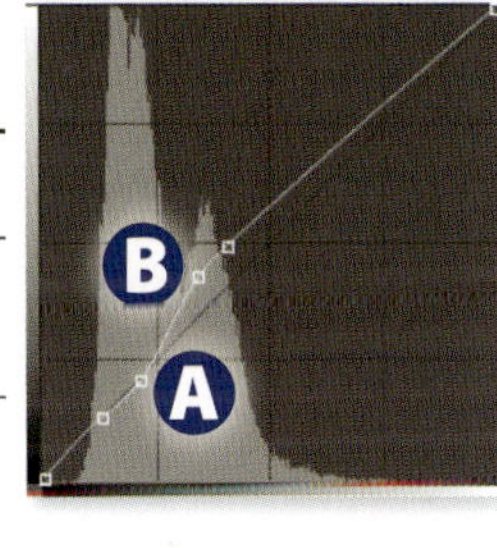

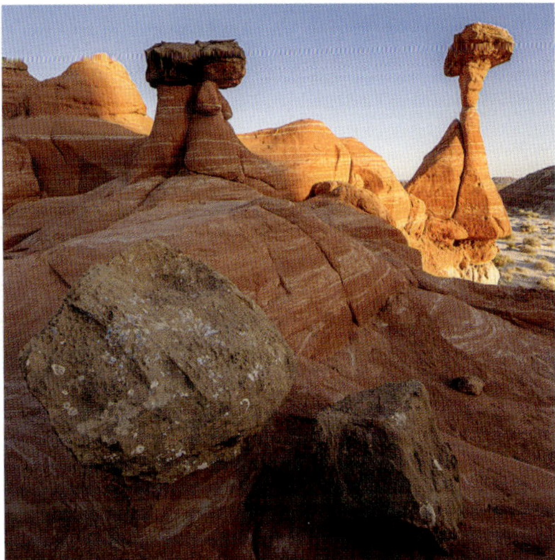

Processed to optimize natural contrast present in scene.

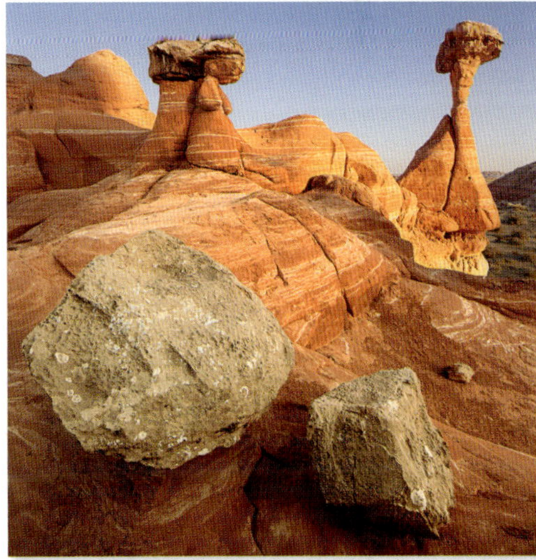

Positive elements emphasized using Lightroom and Photoshop.

Decrease Brightness of Shadows: Click on the bright area using the **Targeted Adjustment** tool to lock in its brightness **A**. Then click on a dark area and drag down to darken and increase contrast **B**.

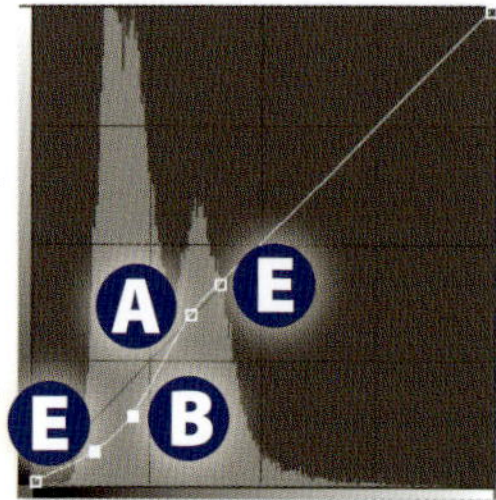

Brighten Highlights and Darken Shadows: Add a point for both the bright and dark areas using the **Targeted Adjustment** tool. Then move the highest point up **C** and lowest point down **D** in order to increase contrast.

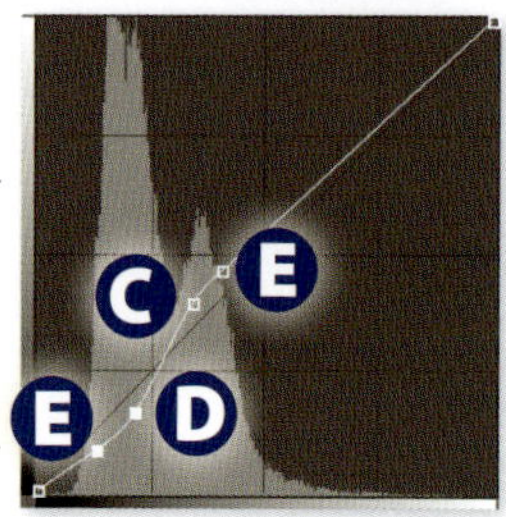

An extra point can be added just beyond the two described above in order to "steer" the curve and prevent the rest of the curve from extending too far away from its original path **E**.

Regardless of which option you choose, the color of the image will likely change. To prevent color changes, set the blending mode pop-up menu at the top of the Layers panel to **Luminosity** mode.

Separate with Color

A slight difference in color can be enough to help an object visually separate from its background. This is most commonly accomplished by masking the subject and choosing the **Invert** option. Then, either lower the **Saturation** or shift the overall color using the **Temperature** and **Tint** settings in Lightroom, or similar controls in Photoshop's **Hue/Saturation** adjustment.

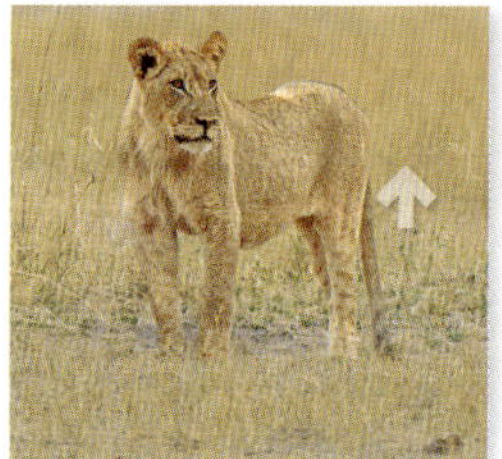 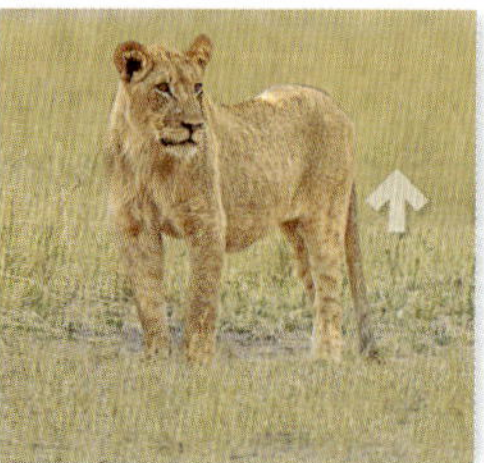

Before and after subtle shift in background color to cause lion to visually separate from background.

Optimize Lighting

Once you've toned down the negatives and emphasized the positives, it's time to look at everything in between to ensure that it supports your vision for the image. This can be done through selective brightening and darkening, a technique that is traditionally referred to as dodging and burning. This can be accomplished in a multitude of ways.

Masked Adjustments in Lightroom: Simple changes that don't require complex masking can be accomplished using a **Brush** mask. Darkening usually involves lowering the **Whites** or **Exposure** sliders, while brightening can be done with the **Exposure** or **Shadows** sliders.

Dodge & Burn Layer in Photoshop: Hold **Option** (Mac) or **Alt** (PC) when clicking on the **New Layer** icon at the bottom of the Layers panel, then set the **Mode** to **Overlay** and turn on the **Fill with Overlay-neutral color** checkbox. Then use the **Dodge** and **Burn** tools to brighten or darken.

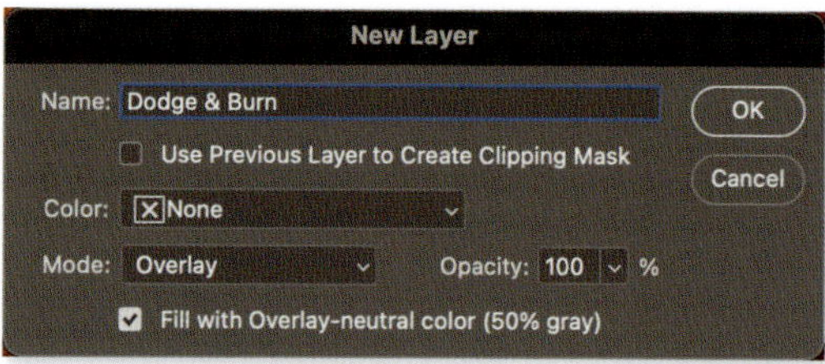

Settings used to dodge and burn using a layer in Photoshop.

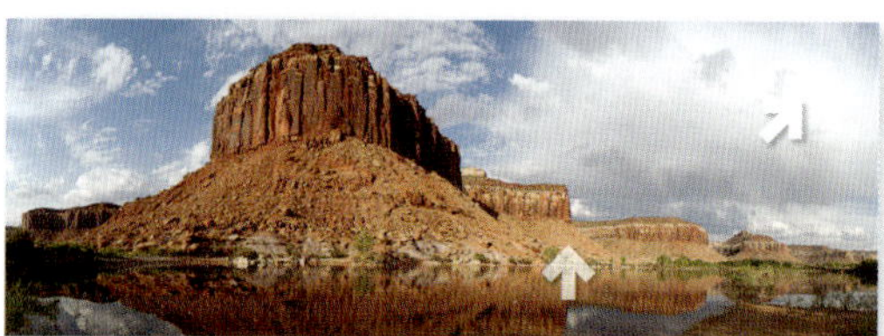

The natural brightness and contrast of the scene.

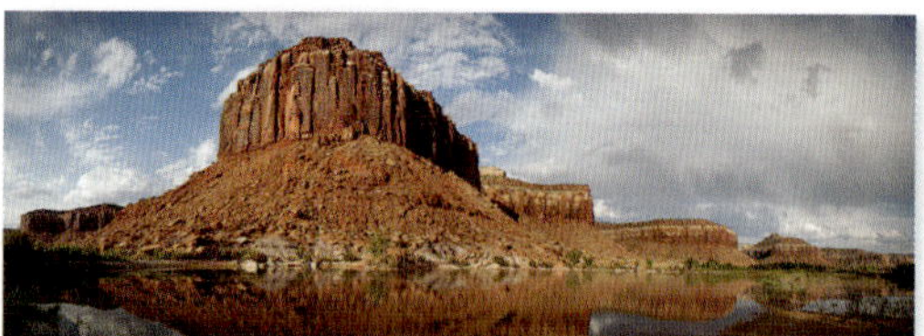

Right side darkened to keep attention closer to central portion of image.

Section III: Crafting a Photograph

Darken Edges to Keep Focus on Middle

Lenses deliver less light to the edges of an image compared to the middle, and this is known as vignetting. It can be useful to further darken the edges of an image in an attempt to keep the viewer's attention in the central portion of the image.

Post-Crop Vignetting

The **Amount** slider found under the **Effects** panel within Lightroom's Develop module can be used to darken or brighten the edges of an image. The **Midpoint**, **Roundness**, and **Feather** settings can then be used to modify the shape of the vignette. Holding **Option** (Mac) or **Alt** (PC) when dragging those sliders will temporarily max out the **Amount** slider to make it easier to see how the effect of each change is contributing to the results.

The **Highlights** slider can then be used to reduce the change, limiting its effect on bright areas.

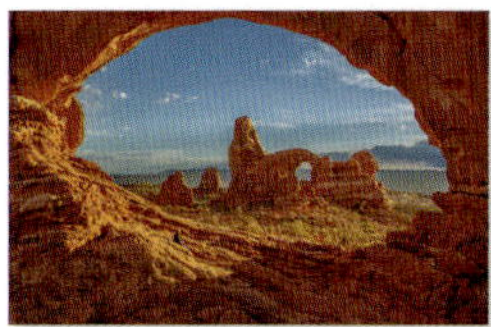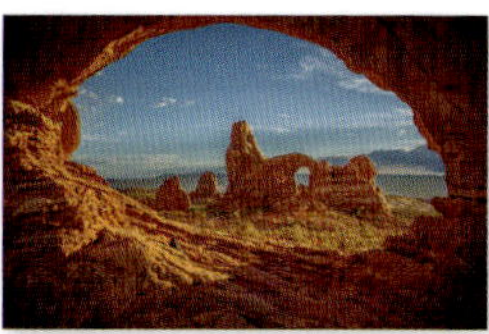

Before and after applying Post-Crop Vignetting.

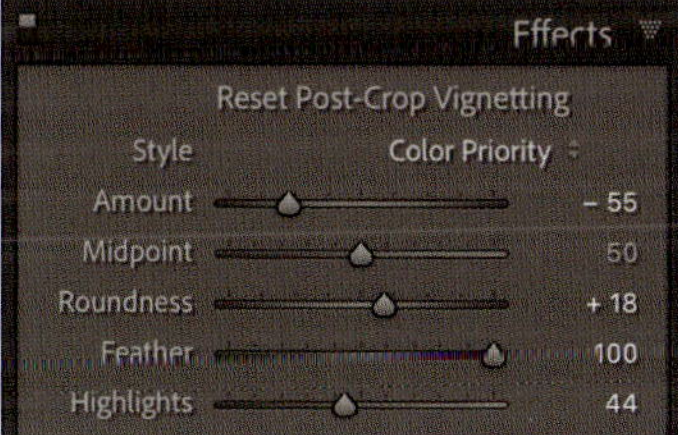

Post-Crop Vignetting settings used on the above image.

Midpoint 0   *Midpoint 50*   *Midpoint 75*

Roundness -100   *Roundness 0*   *Roundness +100*

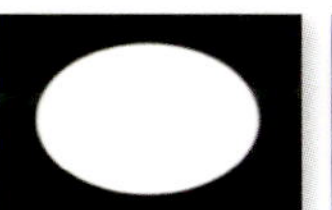

Feather 0   *Feather 50*   *Feather 100*

Masked Vignette

All too often, I find the **Post-Crop Vignetting** feature to be too limiting. In the case of the previous example, the top portion of the sky was darkened and the **Highlights** slider was not able to remove the darkening effect. When I need to have more control, I switch to creating a vignette using the **Radial Gradient** masking features in Lightroom. Here are a few tips related to its use:

Hold **Command** (Mac) or **Ctrl** (PC) and double-click within the image to create a gradient that covers the entirety of the image. **Shift**-drag any edge handle to make the gradient larger or smaller as a whole. Hold **Option** (Mac) or **Alt** (PC) to adjust a single side independently of the others. Once you have the overall shape and size you desire, turn on the **Invert** checkbox to work on the outer portion, and adjust the **Feather** setting to control the softness of the edge.

Then use the features described in chapter 2 to add to or subtract from the mask, such as using a luminance mask to prevent the highlights from changing.

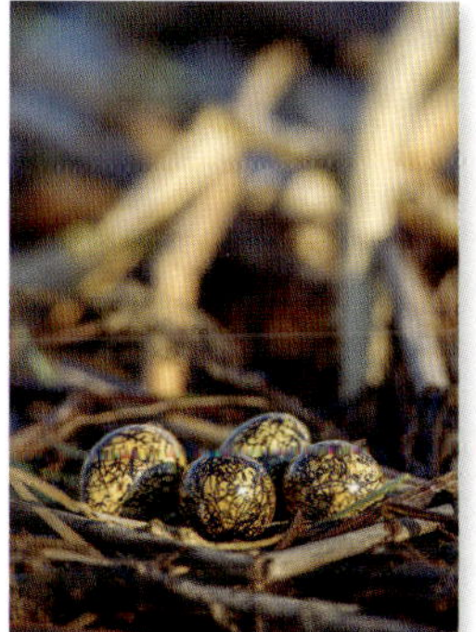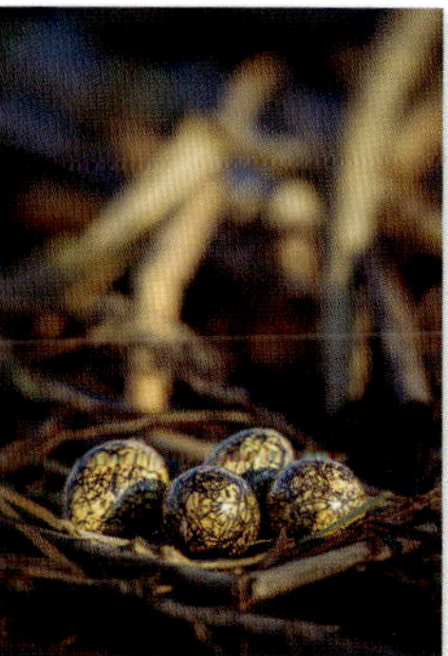

Before and after applying vignetting via a mask.

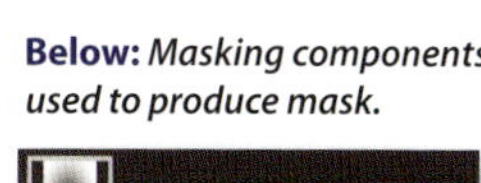

Left: *Vignette mask.*

Below: *Masking components used to produce mask.*

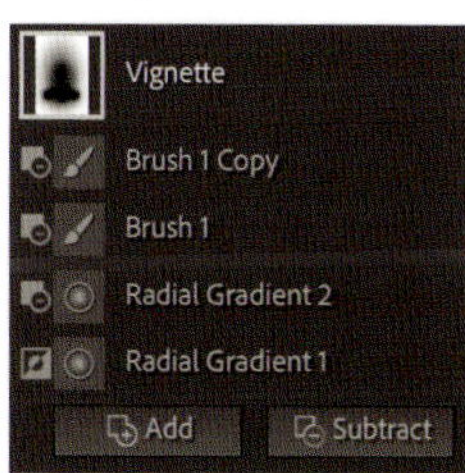

Create a Reason to Linger

The eye can't help but explore areas that contain an abundance of detail. Therefore, you can encourage someone to spend more time in a particular area by using one of the following techniques to make the detail more pronounced. Alternatively, you can do the opposite to the rest of the image to make it less interesting.

Increase Sharpness in Lightroom

Using a masked adjustment to boost the **Texture**, **Clarity**, or **Sharpness** of an area will make it stand out from its surroundings. Or, you can lower those settings in areas you don't want to stand out.

Steepen the Curve in Photoshop

You can make it easier to see the detail in an area by increasing the difference between brights and darks using a **Curves** adjustment layer. In **Curves**, activate the **Targeted Adjustment** tool (hand icon), click on the darkest part of the object, and drag down slightly to darken. Next, click on the brightest part of the object and drag up slightly to brighten. The steeper the curve between the two dots becomes, the larger the increase in contrast will be and the easier it will be to discern detail.

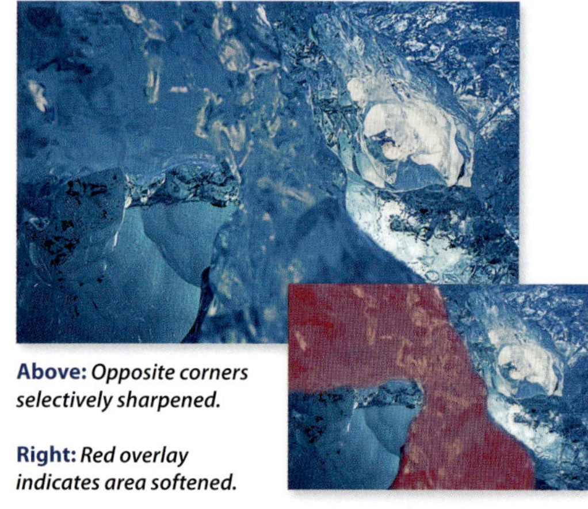

Above: *Opposite corners selectively sharpened.*

Right: *Red overlay indicates area softened.*

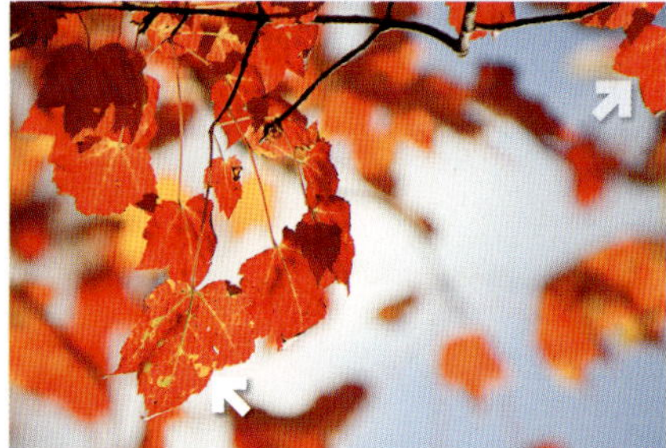

Upper-right corner softened and lower-left leaf sharpened.

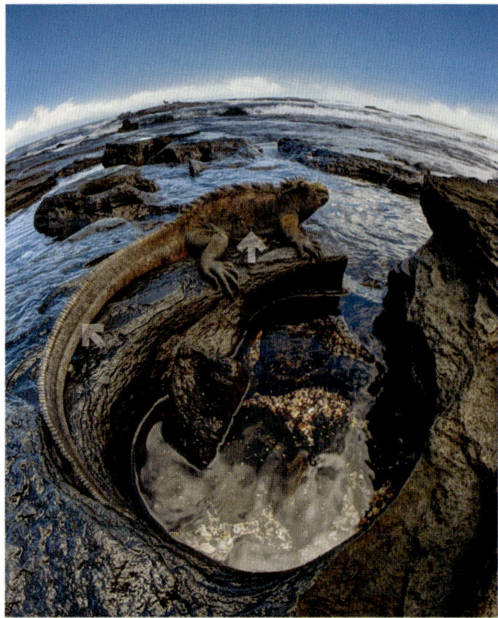

The native contrast captured from the scene makes the iguana blend into its surroundings.

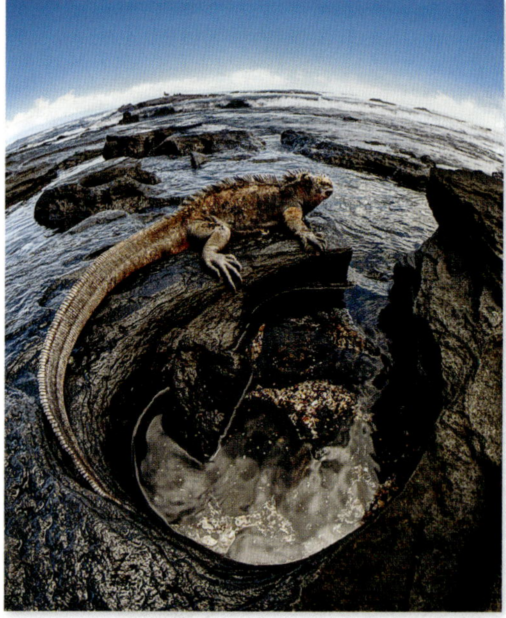

Steepening the curve on the subject caused detail to be easier to see and visually separates it from the background.

Section III: Crafting a Photograph

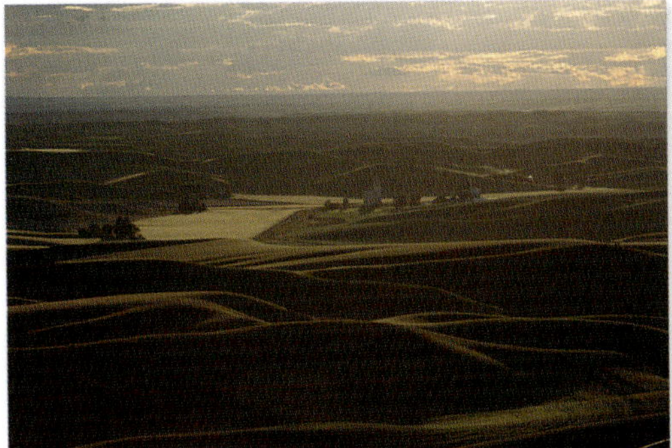

Image as rendered with default settings in Lightroom.

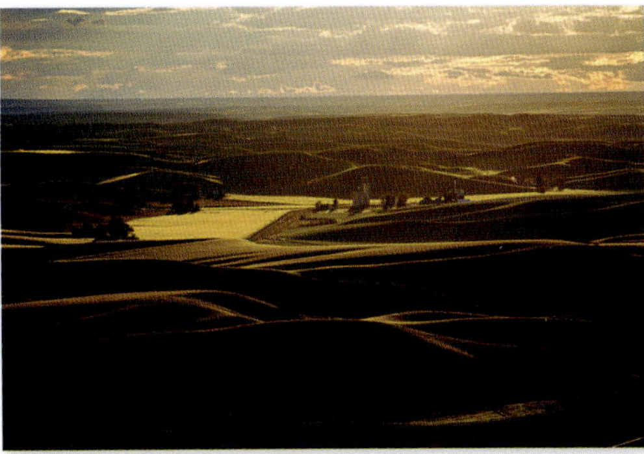

Optimized using Basic settings in Lightroom.

Optimizing an image from start to finish in a single sitting does not always produce the best results. I find it useful to make a print of the image and tape it to the wall in a place where I will see it frequently. This allows the novelty of its newness to wear off, which then allows me to take a second look at a now-familiar image. This process allows me to recognize deficiencies in the image that I can then remedy through further adjustments. Once a print can hang on my wall for a month without prompting me to think of ways to improve it, I can feel relatively confident that I've refined the image to a stage I should be happy with long-term and I can consider it done.

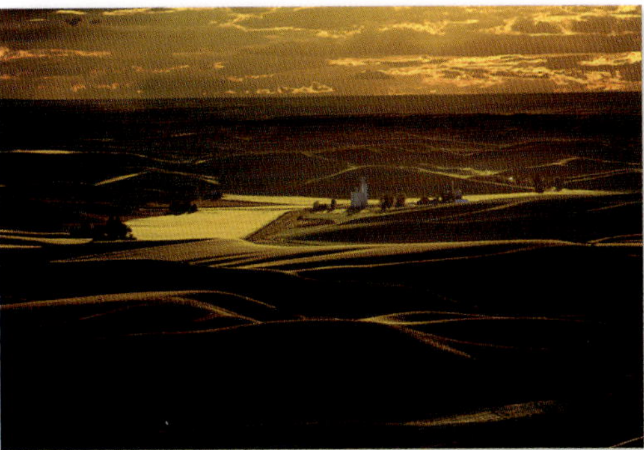

Masked adjustments applied to relight the scene.

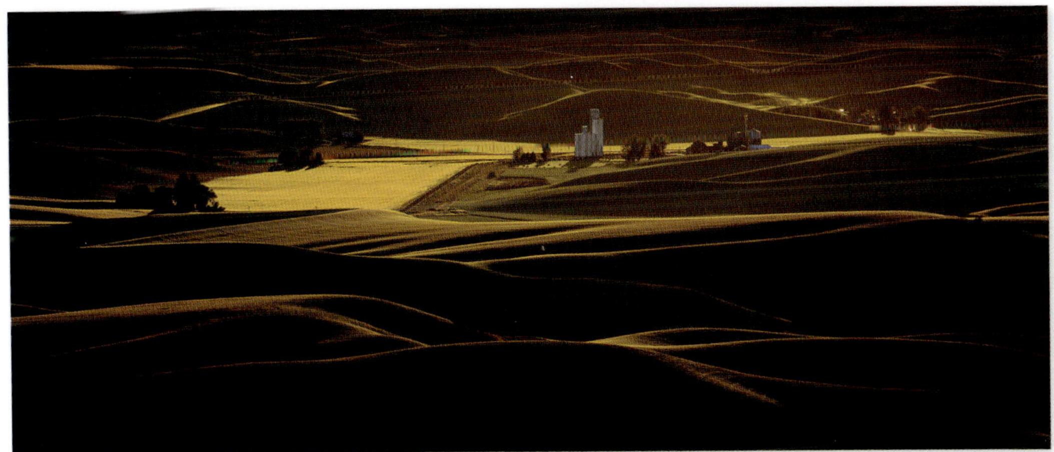

Final image after cropping to strengthen focal point of the white building and green/yellow hill highlights.

Chapter 7

Add Dimension, Atmosphere & Drama

THE TECHNIQUES THAT follow will allow you to push your images beyond optimized depictions of the scenes your camera captured. The idea is to share a world that is infused with depth, dimension, atmosphere, and drama. The colors will be so captivating that they hold the gaze of the viewer. It's about presenting something unique and different from what others have experienced, and different from what others saw at the exact same time and place. This is where we get to interpret the scene for what it could be instead of simply settling for what the camera was able to capture.

Increase Depth and Dimension

Your perception of dimension in an image is largely determined by the bright to dark shading of each object or area in a scene. Light areas usually feel as if they are closer to the camera while dark areas feel like they recede into the distance. Selectively brightening and darkening areas in Lightroom or Photoshop can increase the general feeling of depth within an image.

Lightroom Masked Adjustments

In the case of the tree example below, I started by attempting to isolate the tree using a **Subject** mask. I then used a **Brush** mask to subtract the edges of the tree trunk and the top portion of the tree. Once I had the central portion of the trunk masked, I lowered **Contrast** and moved the **Shadows** and **Whites** sliders to the right to brighten.

Then, to isolate the edges of the tree trunk, I hovered over the name of the mask, clicked the three dots icon **A**, and chose **Duplicate B**. I hovered over the **Brush** element of the duplicate mask and chose **Invert**. That produced a mask that included the top of the tree **C**, so I clicked the **Subtract** button, chose **Brush**, and painted over the top of the tree to remove it from the mask **D**.

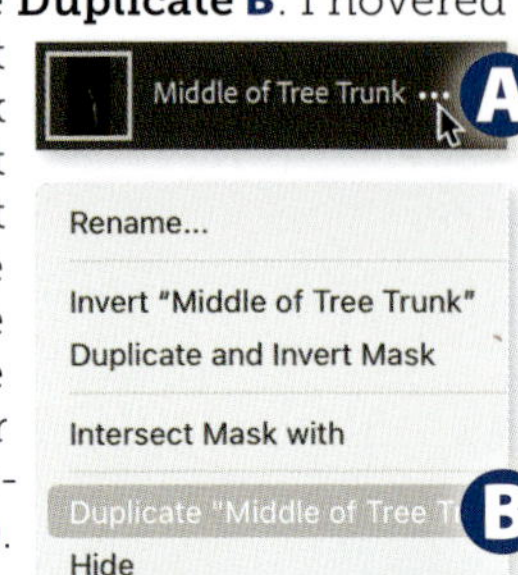

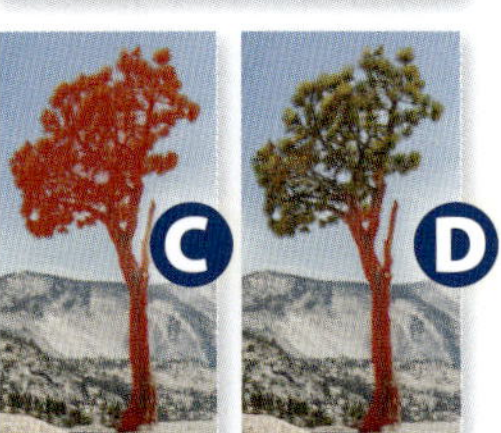

Finally, I clicked the **Reset** option above the adjustment sliders to zero them out, and then moved the **Whites** slider to the left to darken the edges of the tree trunk.

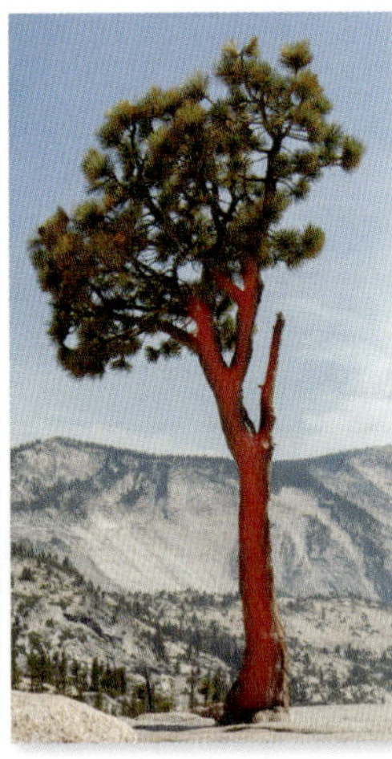

Subject masked.

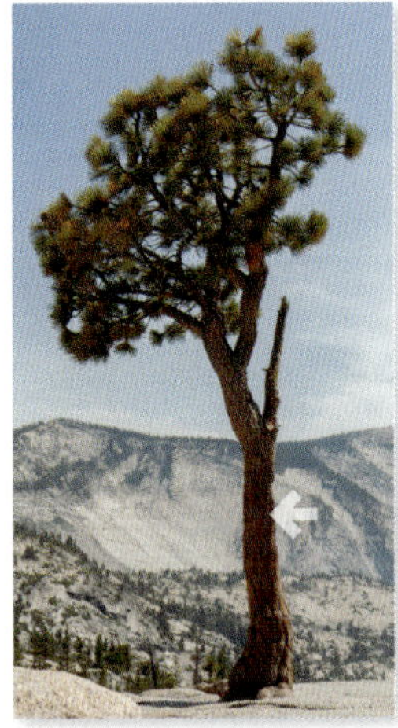

Subtracted using Brush mask.

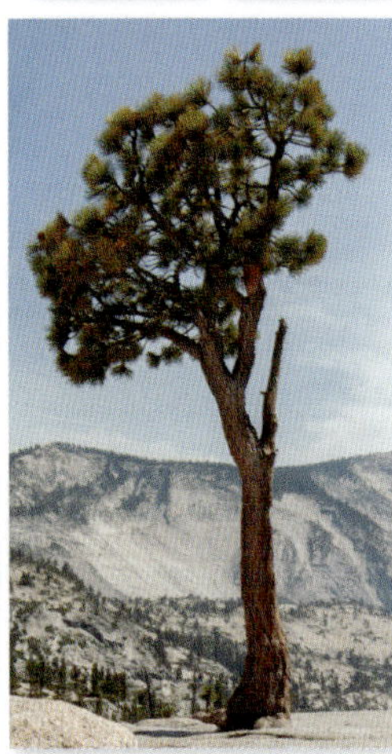

Before tree trunk adjustment.

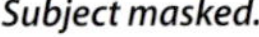

Result of increasing depth.

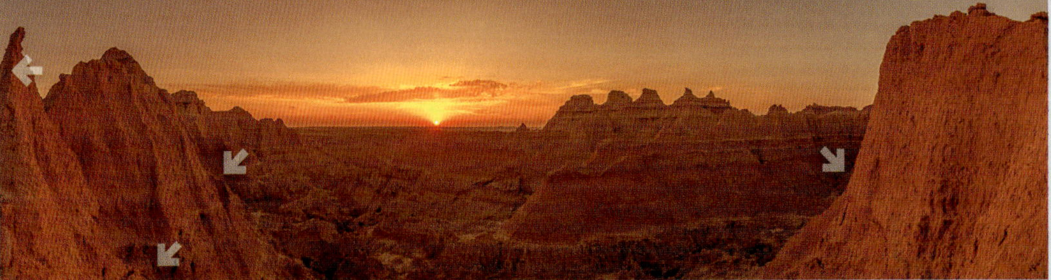

The native contrast of the scene produced a sense of depth only in select areas. Evenly lit areas lack this sense of depth.

Section III: Crafting a Photograph

Photoshop Dual Masked Adjustments

In the panoramic sunset image below, the angle of the sun helped to produce the sense of depth in the places where an area of shade touched a sun-lit area. Other areas that were not directly kissed by the sun ended up feeling more flat-looking due to their even lighting. I decided to add depth by selectively darkening the image to create more separation between near and far areas.

Increasing depth in Photoshop is a two-step process. I first isolate the object or area using a mask. Then I use a second mask to limit where an adjustment affects the area that has been isolated.

Isolate Entirety of Area or Object

Any selection tool can be used (see chapter 3) to isolate the entirety of an object or area. To use the active selection to limit the effects of one or more adjustment layers, click the **Group** icon (which looks like a folder) at the bottom of the Layers panel, and then click the **Layer Mask** icon to add a mask to the newly created group. That mask will affect all adjustments inside the group, limiting the areas where they affect the image.

Create Adjustment Layer

With the group active, choose **Layer>New Adjustment Layer>Curves** and then move the upper-right point down about a third of the way **E**.

Then add a new point near the lower left and adjust it to prevent the dark areas from becoming too dark **F**. Now that the entire area is overly dark, we can paint on the adjustment's mask to limit where the change is applied.

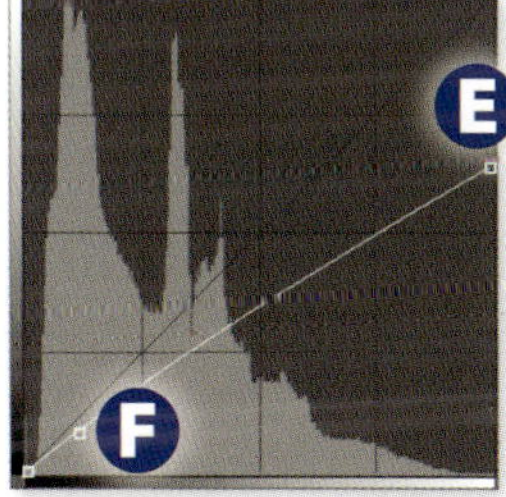

Paint on Mask to Limit Area Affected

The first masking task is to completely remove the darkening effect from one edge of the area being worked on. When the sun is prominent in the image, I always choose the edge closest to the sun. For images that were shot under the overly flat lighting of an overcast sky, I'll choose whichever edge I want to feel closer to the camera.

Once I've decided which edge should be brightest, I'll choose a small, soft-edged brush, set its **Opacity** to 100%, and set the foreground color to black. I'll center the brush on the edge and then trace the shape. I then increase the brush size so it's about eight times larger, lower the **Opacity** to around 50%, and make a second pass with the brush, indented a bit into the darkened area. I then make a third pass with a brush about twice that size and the **Opacity** set at 30%.

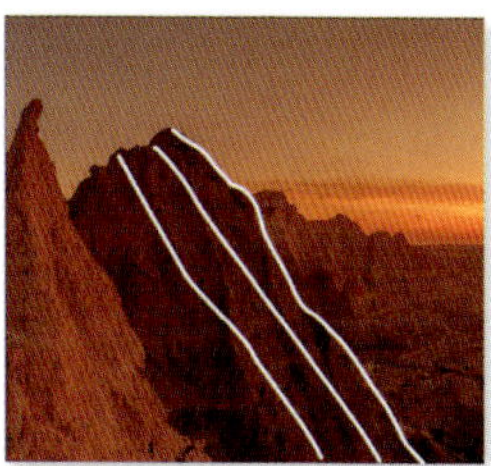

The white lines from right to left represent where the center of each brushstroke was as I painted across the image using progressively larger brushes.

Adjust Mask Transition

To fine-tune the results, I often try to produce a more pleasing transition from light to dark by choosing **Image>Adjustments>Levels** and moving the middle slider to modify the layer mask.

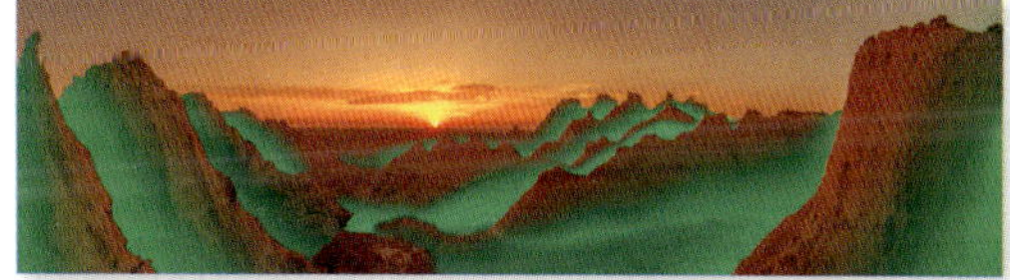

Green overlay indicates areas that were darkened.

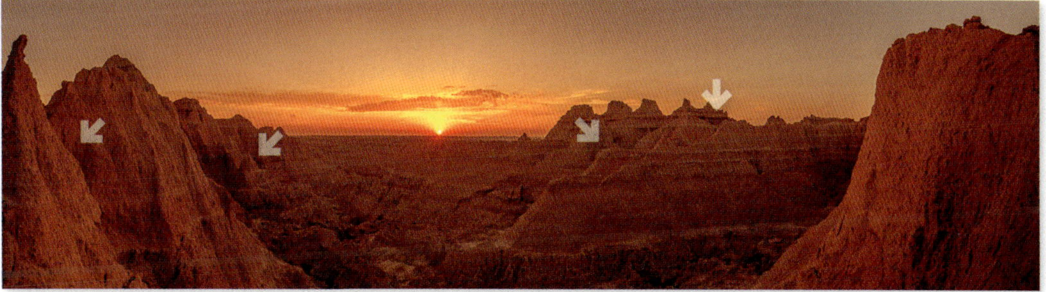

Depth and dimension enhanced by selectively darkening areas using Curves.

Add Atmospheric Depth

Distant areas often appear noticeably differ-ent than areas closer to the camera due to the haze-inducing effect of atmosphere. Tiny parti-cles of dust, smoke, pollution, and mist lingering in the air can scatter the light, causing distant areas to take on a blue haze and exhibit reduced overall clarity.

The same feeling can be simulated in Photoshop to help visually separate near and far areas.

Create Atmospheric Map
The first step to adding atmosphere is to create a grayscale image that contains black where the image should not be changed, and progressively brighter shades of gray to indicate where haze should be added. The brighter the shade of gray, the more haze will be applied.

I often create this "atmospheric map" manually by creating a new channel in the Channels panel and filling it with black. I then select various ar-eas within the image and fill each region with a different shade of gray to indicate how much haze is desired.

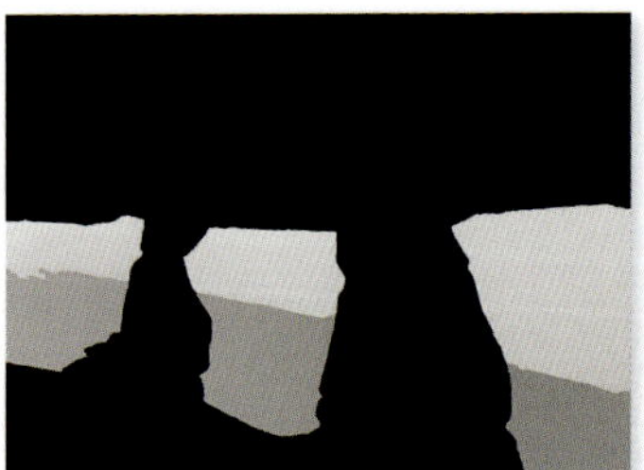

Black indicates near areas that should remain crisp and far areas that are already hazy. Shades of gray define the two regions to be adjusted.

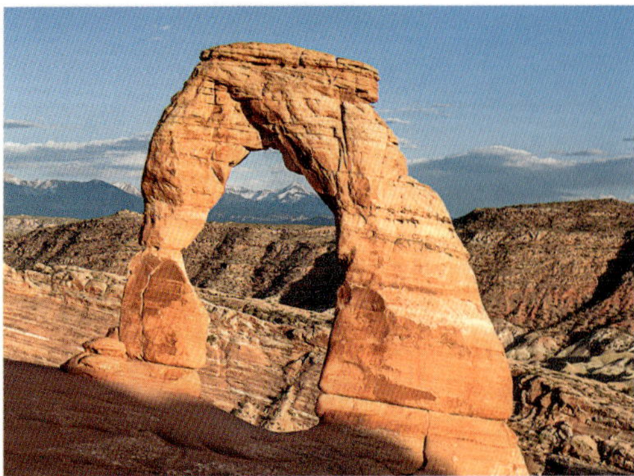

Image lacking separation between arch and background.

Artificial Intelligence–Generated Depth Map
The following technique uses artificial intel-ligence in Photoshop to produce a grayscale image that represents the apparent distance of areas within a scene: Choose **Filter>Neural Filters**, select the **Depth Blur** filter, turn on the **Output depth map only** checkbox, and click the **OK** button.

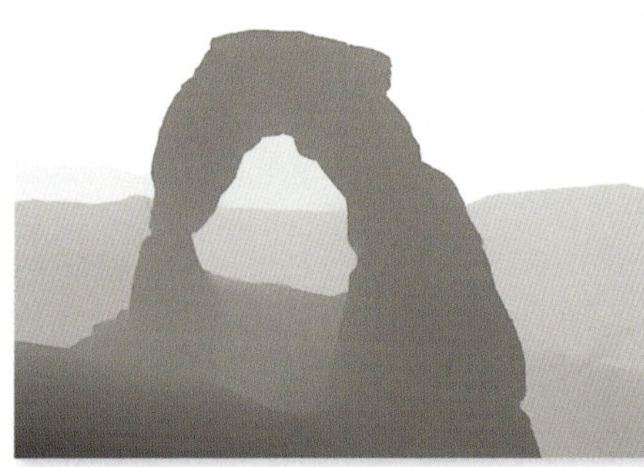

Depth map made using the Depth Blur filter.

The resulting depth map can occasionally be used "as is," but will frequently require refinement be-fore it will produce a desirable result.

Apply Atmospheric Haze
While viewing the grayscale image that indicates where atmospheric haze should be added, choose **Select>All** and then **Edit>Copy** to place it on the clipboard for later pasting. With the layer that contains the original image active, choose **Layer> New>Layer Via Copy**, choose **Filter>Convert for Smart Filters**, and then choose **Filter>Camera Raw Filter**. Any changes made using this filter will initially affect the entirety of the image. You will later use the atmospheric map created earlier to limit where the effect is applied.

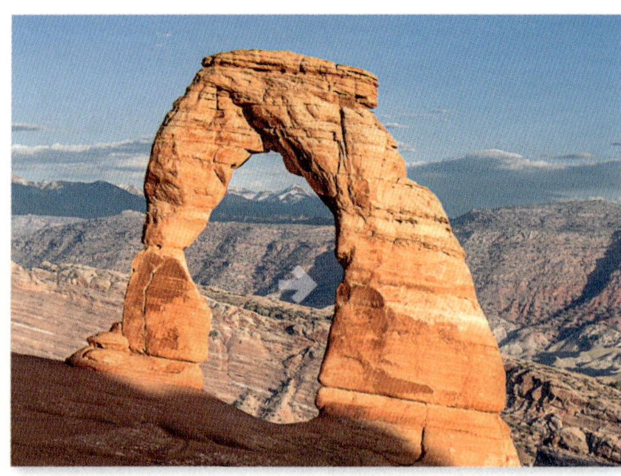

Result of adding atmosphere using negative Dehaze.

Section III: Crafting a Photograph

To produce a hazy image, move the **Dehaze** slider to the left by a large amount, the **Clarity** slider a medium amount, and the **Texture** slider a small amount. It can also be helpful to move the **Temperature** slider to the left a small amount to shift colors toward blue, and then move the **Blacks** slider to the right to brighten the darkest areas. There is no perfect formula that works for every image, so experiment until you find an appropriate adjustment for the specific image you're working on.

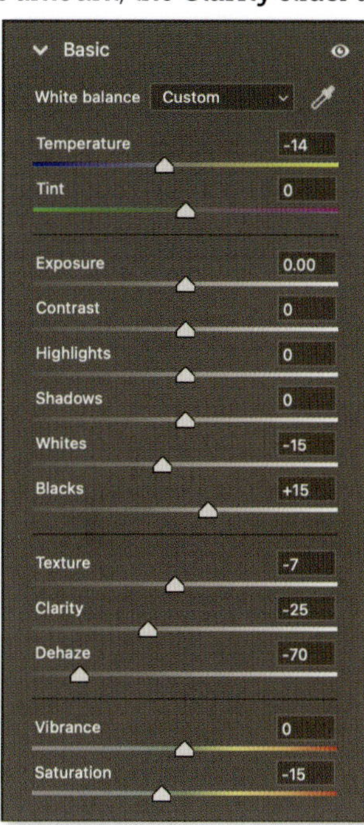

Apply Atmospheric Map

At this point, the hazy version of the image should be on a layer directly above the original image layer. All that needs to be done is to limit where the hazy layer appears. That can be accomplished by holding **Option** (Mac) or **Alt** (PC) while clicking on the mask thumbnail that appears to the left of the **Smart Filters** area in the Layers panel **A** to view the mask. Choose **Edit>Paste**, and then hold **Option** (Mac) or **Alt** (PC) and click on the same mask a second time to hide its contents.

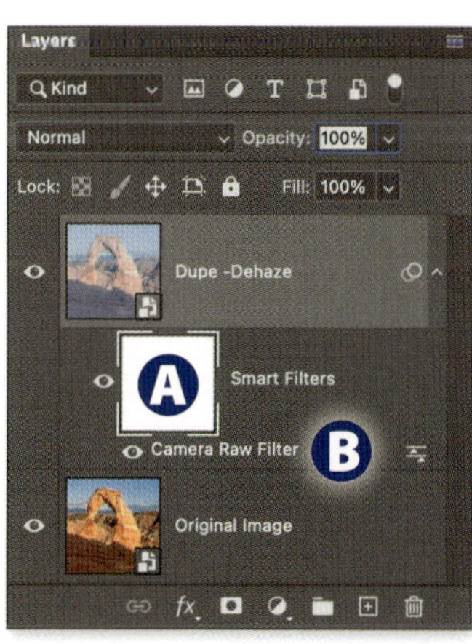

Fine-Tune Results

The initial appearance of your results may not look ideal. When that is the case, do any of the following actions to refine the elements that contribute to the effect.

Modify Camera Raw Filter Settings

Double-clicking on the **Camera Raw Filter** below the layer **B** will allow you to modify the settings used to produce the hazy effect. For instance, you may find it useful to use color grading to shift the darkest areas toward blue. The preview shown in the **Camera Raw Filter** will always show the effect applied across the entire image, and the mask will only be applied once you click the **OK** button to update the contents of the layer.

Adjust Mask with Curves

Most masks used to limit where atmospheric haze is applied only contain a few shades of gray. That makes the mask an ideal candidate for adjustment by choosing **Image>Adjustments>Curves**.

In **Curves**, activate the **Targeted Adjustment** tool (hand icon), then add points for each major shade of gray that is found in the mask. Do this by clicking within the image on each one of the regions that you isolated with a different shade of gray in the mask. Each of those points can then be moved straight up to increase the amount of haze being applied, or moved straight down to bring the region closer to its original appearance.

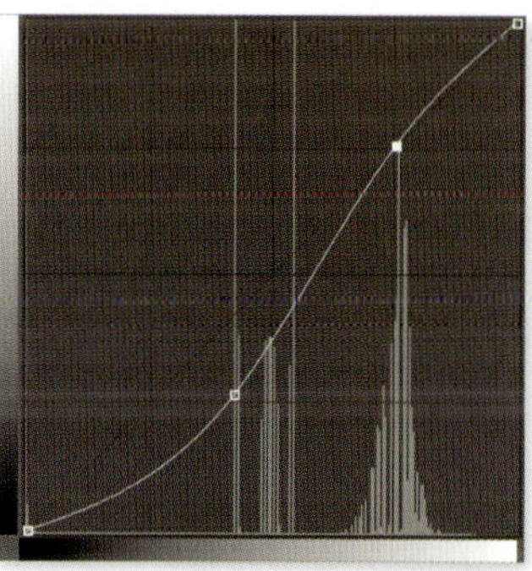

Fine-Tune Mask with Brush

When you zoom up on the image, you may notice transition areas that do not look ideal if the contents of the mask do not precisely match the contours of the original image. When that's the case, I often manually touch up an area using the **Brush** tool, or soften the transition using the **Blur** tool.

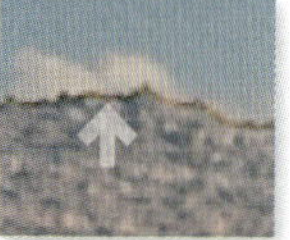

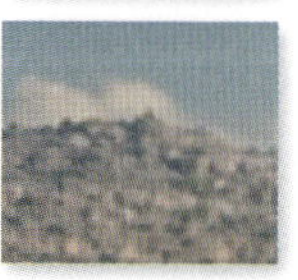

Add Ethereal Glow

When I encounter a scene where a bright element draws my eye, such as the late-day golden sun, a waterfall, or backlit fall foliage, I experience a level of emotion that is rarely evoked when viewing the resulting photograph.

Adding a light, airy type of ethereal glow adds an almost intangible element that seems to better express what it felt like to experience the moment that was captured.

The Orton Effect

Back in the 1980s, photographer Michael Orton pioneered the technique of combining a sharply focused image with a second out-of-focus shot of the same scene to produce a dreamlike glow. Let's explore a similar concept that can be applied using a single exposure and a few layers in Photoshop.

Combine Sharp and Blurry Images

Let's start off by stacking two versions of the image by choosing **Layer>New>Layer Via Copy** and naming the new layer "Orton Effect." Next, convert the duplicate layer into a Smart Object by choosing **Filter>Convert for Smart Filters**. Then, choose **Filter>Blur>Gaussian Blur** and adjust the **Radius** setting until all the fine detail has been blurred away. To simplify the appearance of the Layers panel, drag the layer mask that is next to the **Smart Filters** area to the trash **A**. Finally, set the **Opacity** setting at the top of the Layers panel to 20% in order to blend the blurry version of the image with the underlying sharp version.

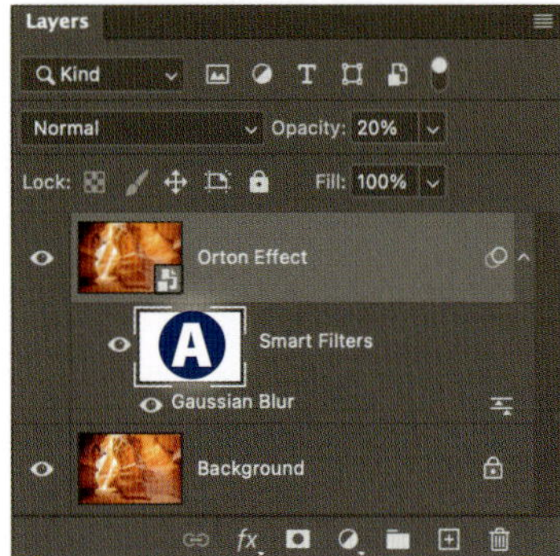

The bottom layer contains the original image, the top layer contains a duplicate that has been converted to a Smart Object and blurred. The mask for the Smart Filter will not be used and can be dragged to the trash.

Add Contrast to Blurry Image

With the blurry layer active, choose **Layer>New Adjustment Layer>Curves**, then click the **Clipping Mask** icon **B**. This will only allow the adjustment to apply to the underlying layer.

Next, move the **White Point** slider **C** to the left slightly to ensure the layer contains a small area of solid white. Then, to add contrast, click on the diagonal line about three quarters of the way up and drag the point a bit higher to brighten the bright areas of the layer **D**. Finally, to darken dark areas slightly, add one more dot about twenty percent of the way up the curve and drag it down so it ends up just a little bit lower than where that part of the curve was originally **E**.

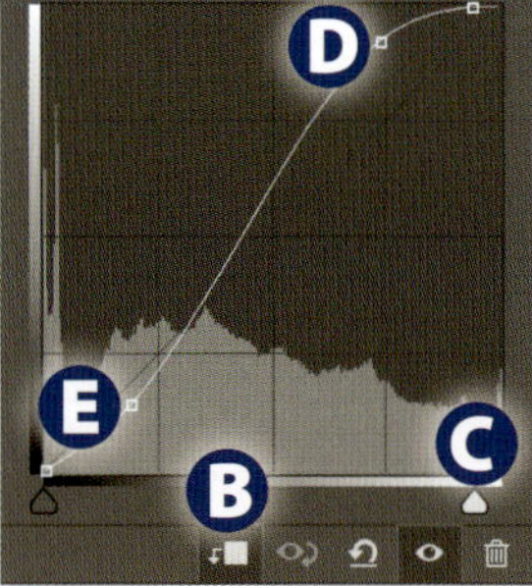

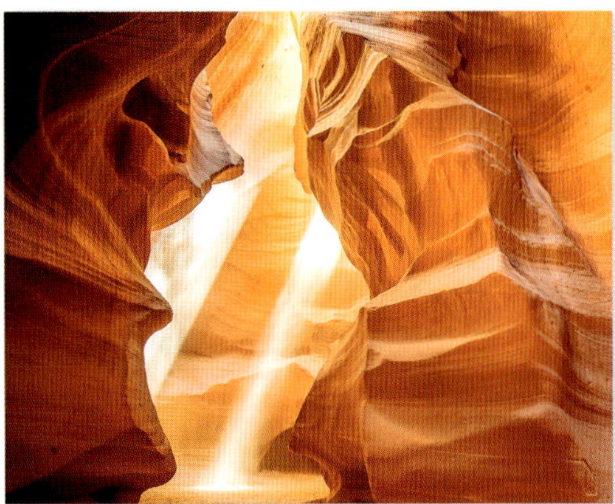

Image as it appeared before applying the Orton Effect.

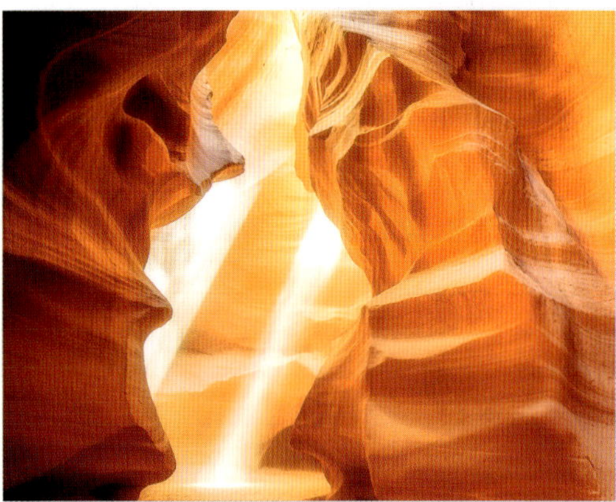

Orton Effect using Gaussian Blur Radius 35, Opacity 30%.

Section III: Crafting a Photograph

Refine Results

Once you have the general effect applied, you can do any of the following to refine your results:

Mask Blurry Layer: If you'd like to apply the effect to an isolated area, click on the layer that has been blurred to make it active. Then choose **Layer> Layer Mask>Reveal All** and paint with a black, soft-edged brush in areas where you'd like to bring back the full sharpness of the original image.

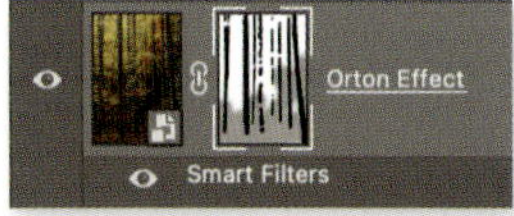

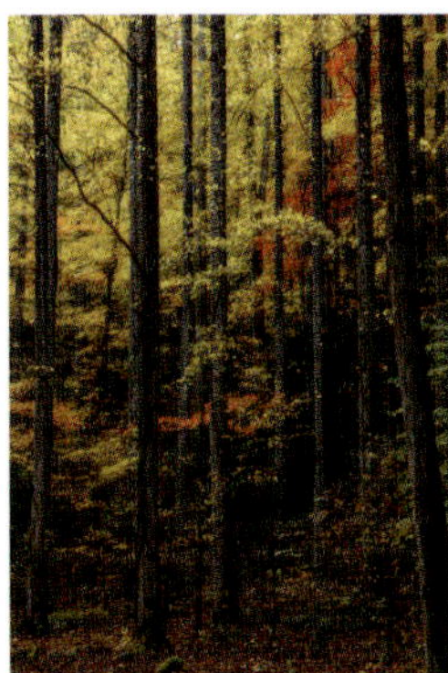
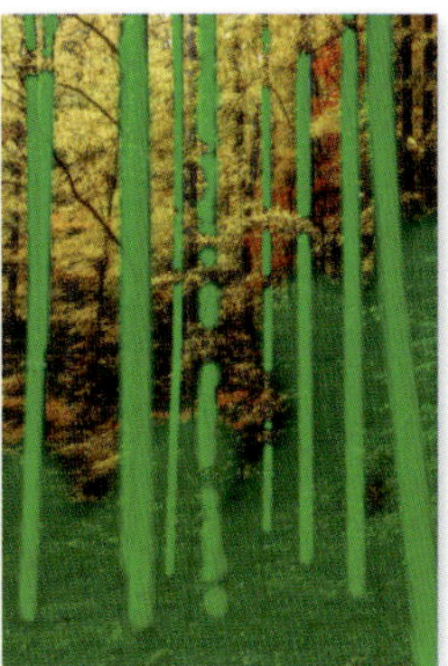

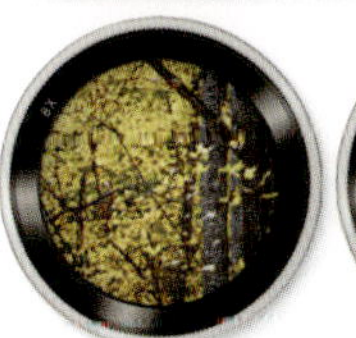
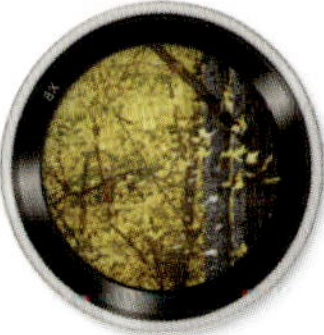

Upper Left: Image with Orton Effect applied. Upper Right: Mask overlaid on image. Left: Close-up of before and after.

Adjust Opacity of Blurred Layer: When the blurry layer is active, the **Opacity** setting at the top of the Layers panel will control the overall strength of the glow effect.

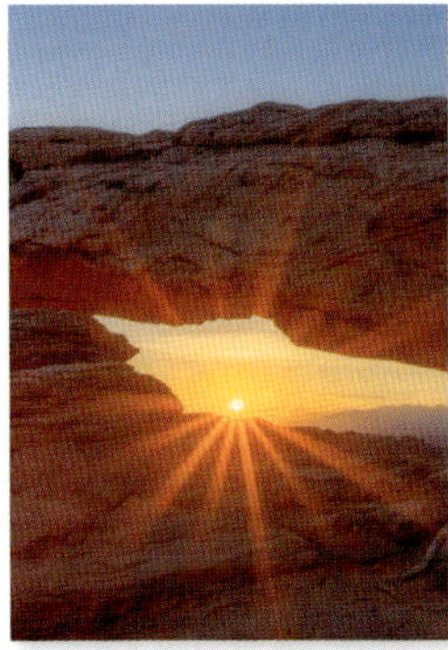
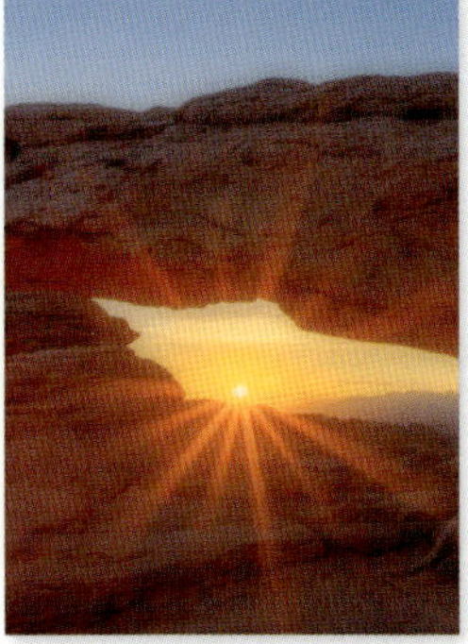

Orton Effect at 20% Opacity.   *Orton Effect at 40% Opacity.*

Adjust Blur Amount: Double-click on the **Gaussian Blur** item that appears below the blurry layer to change the strength of the blur being applied.

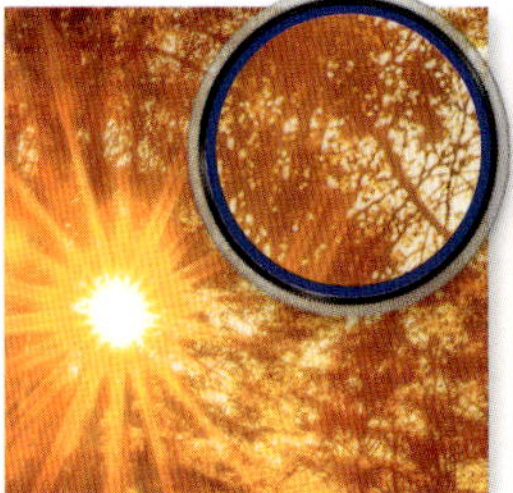
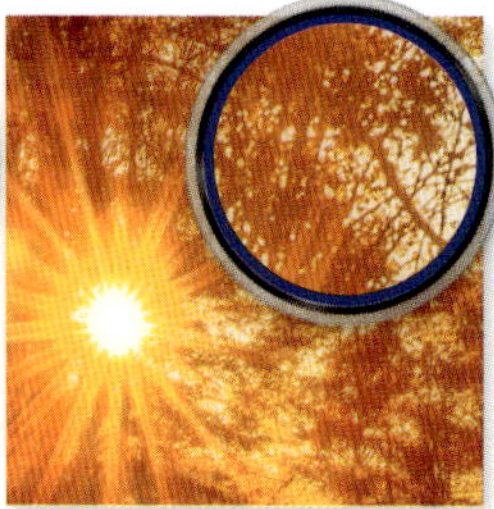

Gaussian Blur Radius 10.   *Gaussian Blur Radius 20.*

Adjust Contrast: Double-click on the **Curves** icon found on the left side of the **Curves** adjustment layer to modify the amount of contrast being added (a single click is sufficient if the Properties panel is already visible). It's commonly the point that is near the lower left **E** that needs to be fine-tuned. If this point is too low, the dark areas of the image can lose too much detail.

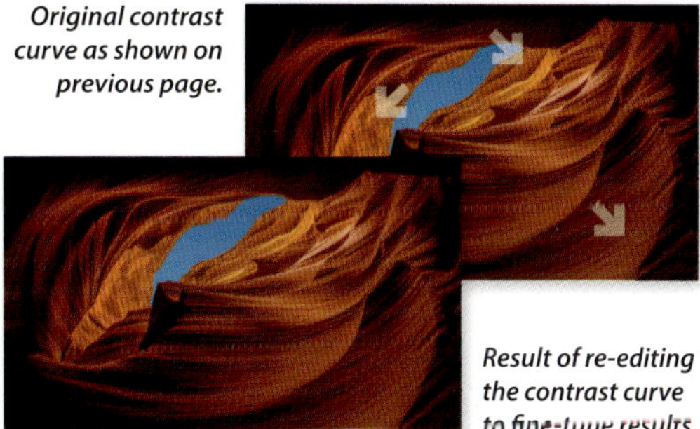

Original contrast curve as shown on previous page.

Result of re-editing the contrast curve to fine-tune results.

Change Blending Mode: If you notice any undesirable color shifts, change the blending mode pop-up menu at the top of the Layers panel to **Luminosity** while the blurry layer is active. You can also try other modes, such as **Overlay**, which might produce a more pronounced contrast and color change.

I try to use this effect sparingly since its initial novelty can quickly wear off and later make me wish that I had used it on fewer images or at a lower strength. I therefore try to restrain myself and use settings that are a bit lower than I initially think the image deserves. Many of the examples shown here are using settings higher than I would usually apply because I didn't want the effect to be so subtle that you wouldn't be able to notice it.

Suspend Reality with Black and White

Converting an image to black and white suspends the brain's expectation that what you're viewing depicts reality. That makes black and white a perfect choice when the colors in an image start to look unnatural or distract from the focal point of the scene. Issues such as blown-out highlights or unnatural contrast will also be better accepted when presented in a black-and-white image.

Let's explore various techniques for producing high-quality black-and-white images in Lightroom.

Lightroom B&W Techniques

Removing all color from an image in Lightroom is as simple as clicking the **Black & White** option in the **Basic** section of the Develop module **A**.

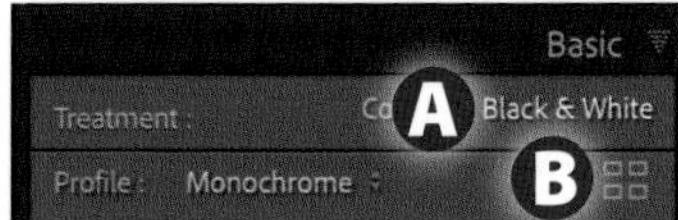

The Black & White option is at the top of the Basic section of the Develop module.

B&W Profiles

The profile indicated directly below the **Black & White** option determines how the colors within the image will be converted into different shades of gray. You can click the **Profile Browser** icon **B** to see the 17 profiles available.

Hovering over the profile preview thumbnails will cause the main image display to temporarily change to reflect how it would be rendered if you were to click to apply the profile.

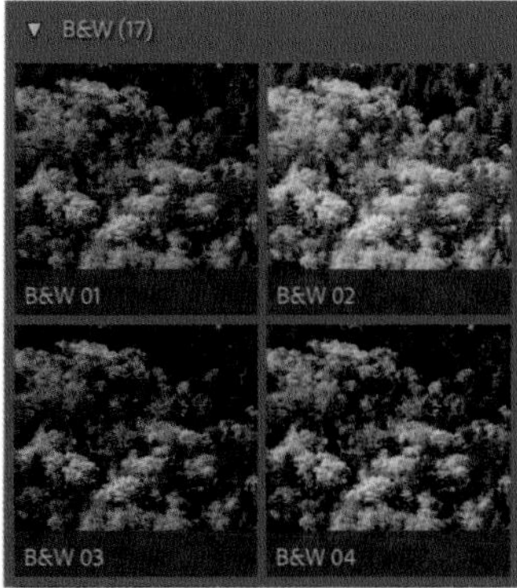

B&W Mix

Turning on the **Black & White** option will cause the **HSL/Color** section of the Develop module to be renamed **B&W** and will present sliders that

allow you to change the brightness of eight individual colors. Click the **Auto** button **C** and Lightroom will analyze the colors found within the image and adjust the color sliders in an attempt to create a reasonable amount of visual contrast.

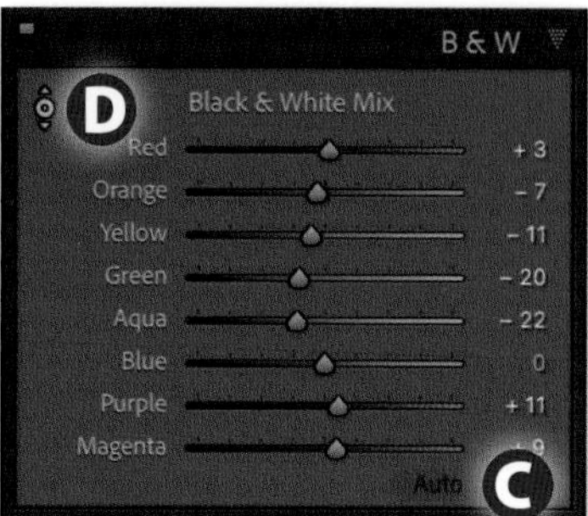

You can also choose the **Targeted Adjustment** tool **D** to click and drag within the image to fine-tune the brightness of the color that used to be found in the area where you clicked. Multiple sliders will be moved if you click on an area that contained a color that was a mix of more than one of the colors within the **B&W** panel.

White Balance

Adjusting the **Temperature** and **Tint** sliders can have a dramatic affect on how the colors from the original image are converted into shades of gray.

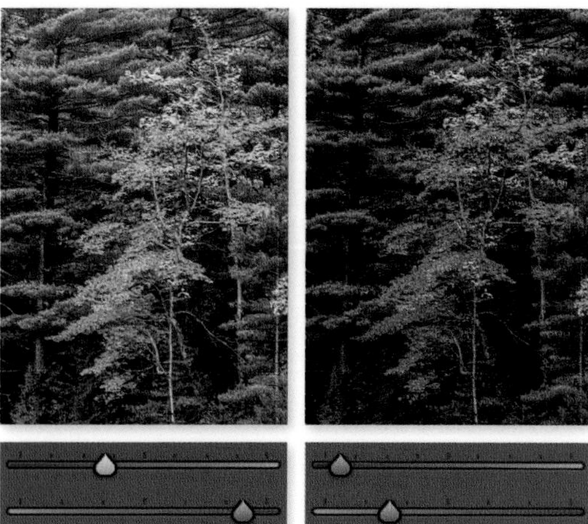

Color Tinting with Color Grading

Adding a hint of color to an otherwise black-and-white photo can add a unique personality to the image. You can do this using the settings in the **Color Grading** panel. These allow you to add a color to the entire image via the **Global** settings **A**, or separately tint the **Highlights B**, **Shadows C**, or **Midtones D**. Those last three choices can also be viewed together in a compact layout **E**.

In each of those areas, you'll find a color wheel with a small circle in the middle. When the small circle is centered, no color is being applied. You can then drag the circle toward one of the colors on the outer edge of the color wheel. The distance you move determines how strong the effect will become.

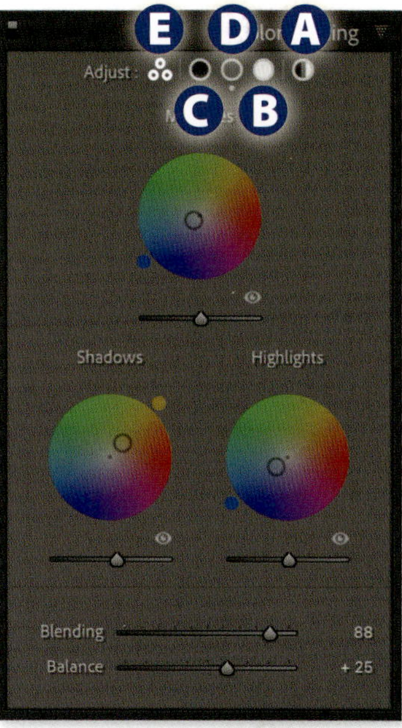

Compact view shows the Highlights, Shadows, and Midtones settings together.

I start by pulling the circle to the outer edge of the color wheel to make the color strong. I then hold the **Command** key (Mac) or **Ctrl** key (PC) to lock in the strength so I can spin the circle around to find the

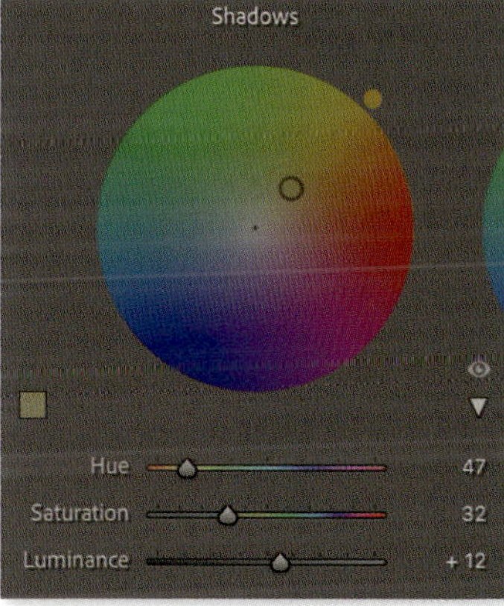

general color I desire. I then add the **Option** (Mac) or **Alt** (PC) key to produce a smaller change and dial in an exact color. I then switch to holding **Shift**, which locks in the color and only allows me to move in a straight line toward the center of the circle, so I can dial in the exact strength without shifting the color being applied.

When using the non-compact view, the circle can also be adjusted via the **Hue** slider (to rotate around the color wheel) or **Saturation** slider (to move toward the center or outer edge).

The **Luminance** slider below each color wheel can be used to brighten or darken each region being tinted. This is essential when an image contains solid black or solid white. These tones cannot be tinted without first being adjusted to make them a shade of gray.

Once the colors have been chosen, the **Balance** slider can be used to determine the balance between what is considered a highlight and a shadow. Moving the slider toward the dark end of its range will cause the color being applied to the dark areas to extend across a wider brightness range. Moving it toward the bright end will do that to the color in the bright areas instead.

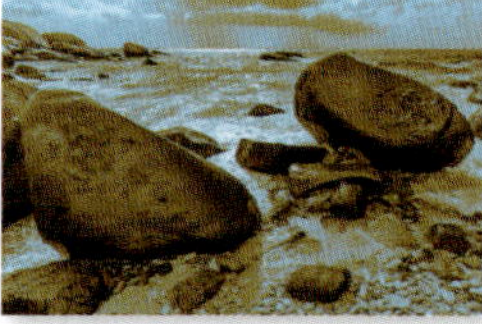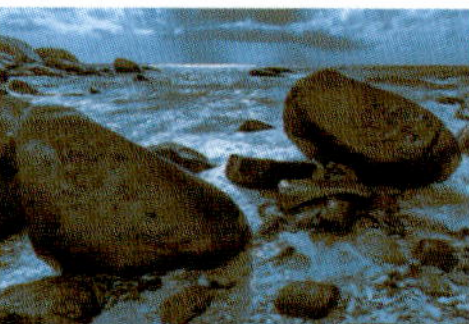
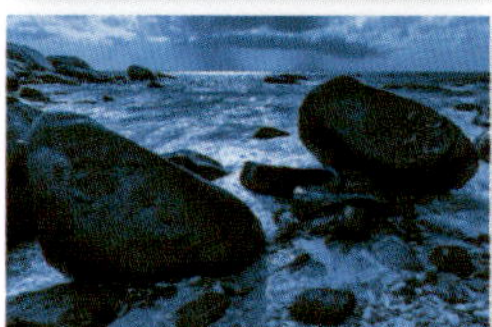

Holding Option to preview yellow shadows and blue highlights at different Blending settings at full strength:
Top Left: *Blending -50.*
Top Right: *Blending 0.*
Left: *Blending +50.*

The **Blending** slider can then be used to determine whether the colors being applied should appear distinct from one another, or if they should be allowed to mix together to produce intermediate colors. High **Blending** settings will make it harder to discern what color is being applied to the midtones because it will have the colors from both the highlights and shadows mixed in. Holding the **Option** key (Mac) or **Alt** key (PC) when moving these sliders will preview the colors at their maximum strength in an attempt to make it easier to visualize exactly how the slider is affecting the color blending.

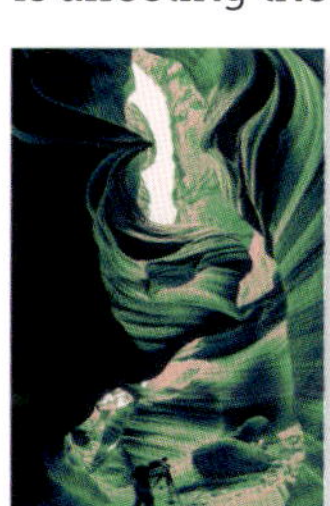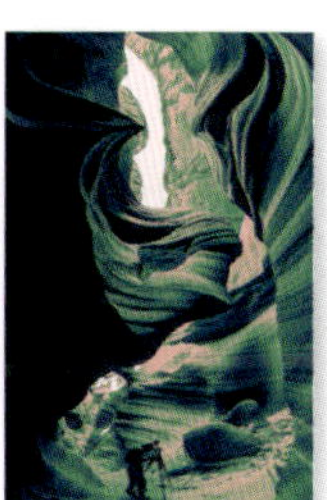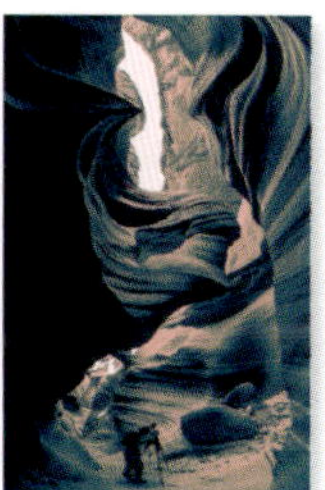

Left to Right: Three colors applied with Blending of 0, 50, 100.

Color Grade Based on Example

If you find it difficult to figure out which colors to choose when adding a hint of color to a black-and-white image, then consider using the following trick:

1) Find an example image on the web where you like the color that has been applied to a black-and-white image.
2) Resize the Lightroom window so you can see the image in your web browser at the same time as you work in the Develop module.
3) Choose the **Highlight** setting at the top of the **Color Grading** panel to view its settings separately from the other colors being applied.
4) Click the square color swatch that is found below and to the left of the color wheel **A** (which will not be shown when viewing the compact view that shows highlights, midtones, and shadows grouped together).

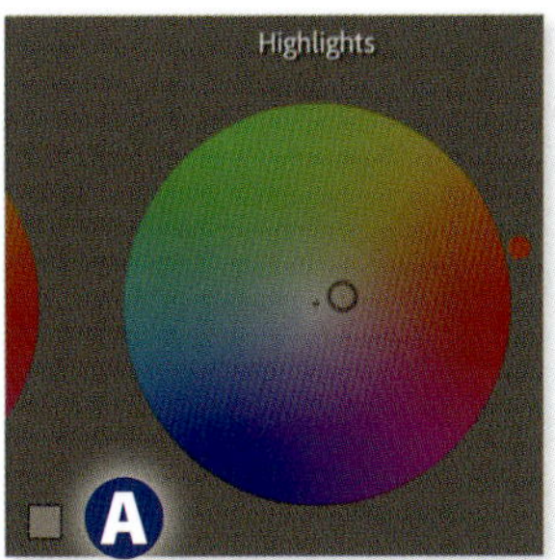

5) Click and hold on the eyedropper icon **B**, drag over the brightest area of the example image, and release the mouse button to sample that color.

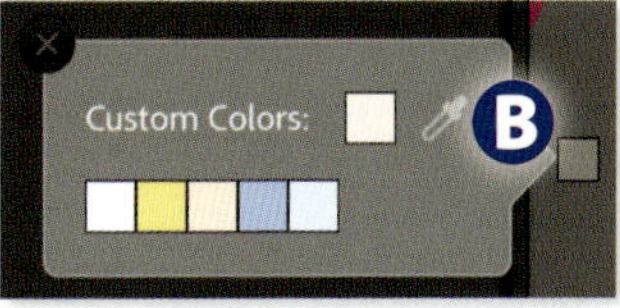

6) Choose the **Shadow** setting at the top of the **Color Grading** panel, click on the color swatch, activate the eyedropper, and drag over to the dark area of the example image.
7) Adjust the **Balance** and **Blending** sliders until your image matches the overall color of the example image.

Tint via Masking

The **Color Grading** feature used in the previous example applies color based solely on the brightness of the image. Sometimes, I want to add color to specific regions of an image regardless of their brightness level. When that's the case, I turn to Lightroom's masked adjustments.

After masking an area as described in chapter 2 (page 24), click on the small rectangular box that is labeled **Color** to bring up a color picker. Dragging horizontally will change the color being applied, while dragging vertically will change the strength of the color. You can also click within the color field where you usually choose a color, and then drag to any area of your screen to sample a color from any image that is visible on your display.

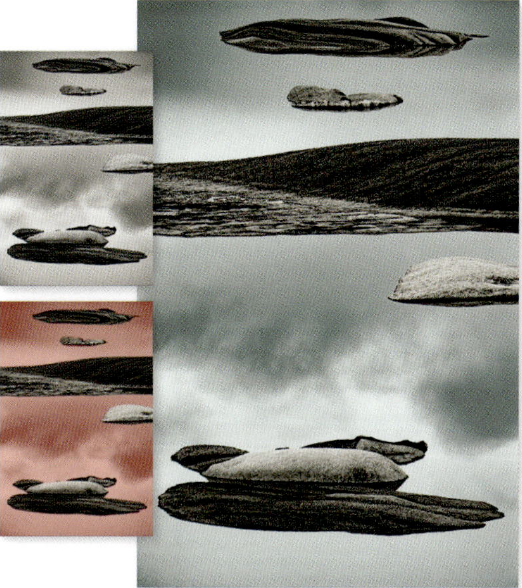

Upper Left: *Image before tinting.* **Lower Left:** *Mask overlay.* **Right:** *Result of tinting with blue where masked and adding a hint of yellow to the rest of the image.*

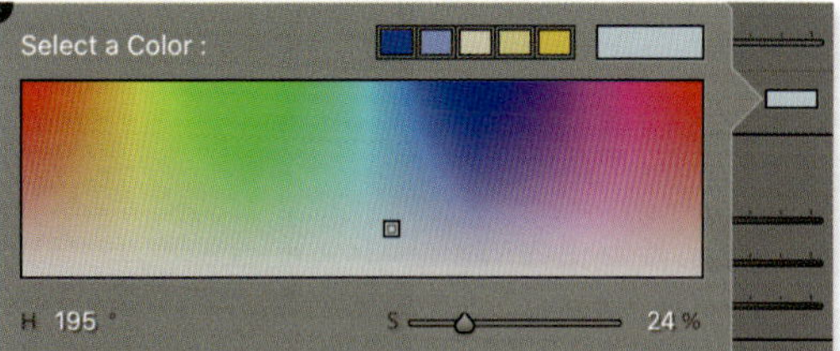

Click on the rectangle labeled Color to access a color picker that can be used to add color to a B&W image.

Photoshop B&W Techniques

Photoshop offers so many ways to manipulate color and I will not pretend to present you with a full list here. But I would like to add one technique that is useful when you want to match the overall look of an existing tinted black-and-white image.

Color Transfer Neural Filter

Open both the image you'd like to adjust and the image you'd like to match. Click on the layer that contains the original image, choose **Filter>Neural Filters**, and then choose the **Color Transfer** filter. Near the top, choose the **Custom** option and then select the image you'd like to match from the pop-up menu below. The menu may not display any image upon your first click, so you may need to pause and click again to get it to list all the documents that are currently open.

Change the **Color space** pop-up menu from **Lab** to **RGB** and back again until you find which option produces the most desirable result.

When using **Lab**, the **Preserve luminance** checkbox will attempt to maintain the original brightness of the image (but can produce odd color casts).

Once you've determined which mode produced the best result, adjust the underlying sliders to fine-tune the results.

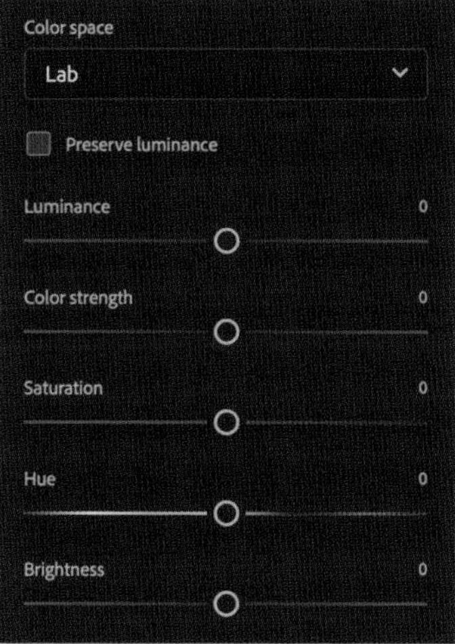
The Lab Color space option.

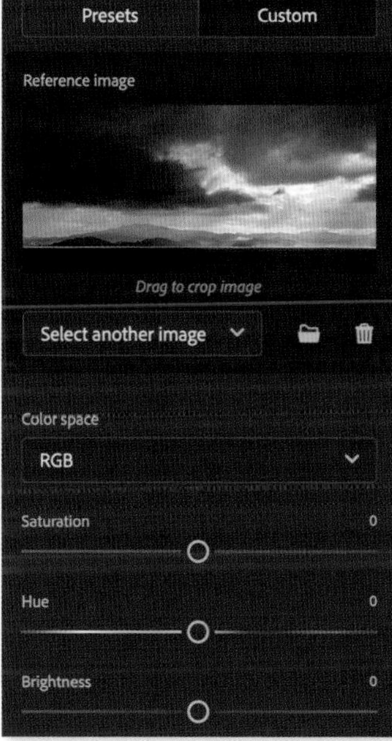

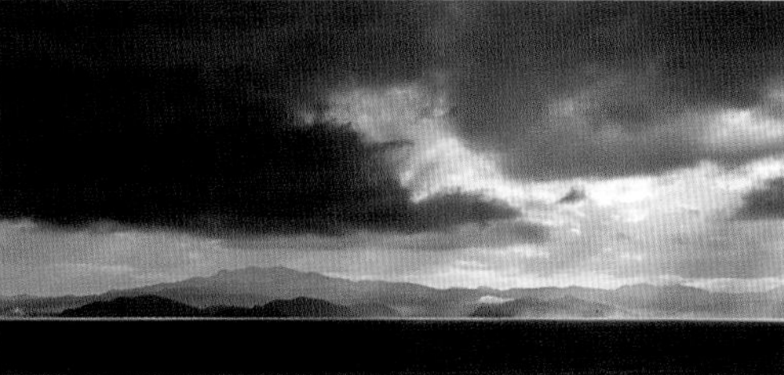
Reference image used as source for color adjustment.

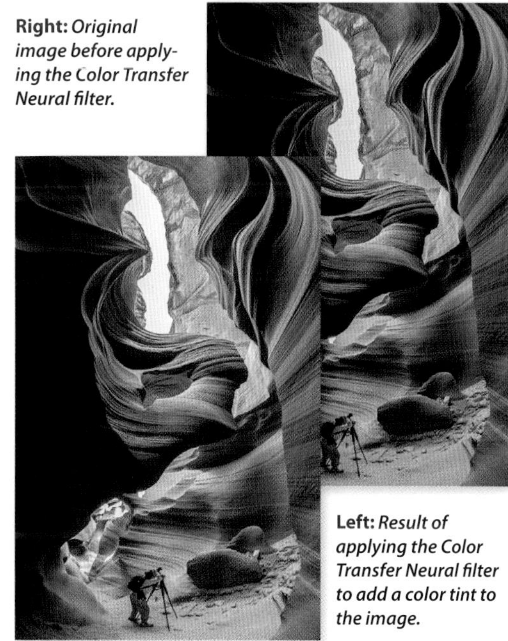
Right: *Original image before applying the Color Transfer Neural filter.*

Left: *Result of applying the Color Transfer Neural filter to add a color tint to the image.*

Dramatic Contrast with Dehaze

The **Dehaze** slider can be used to increase the amount of contrast in a black-and-white image in a way that would usually require the use of more than a dozen adjustment sliders.

Dehaze is generally designed to cut through thick fog and haze by darkening the darkest parts of the image. But once the darkest area nears solid black, it begins to concentrate its darkening effect on the midtones in an attempt to prevent large areas from becoming solid black. This has the effect of delivering dramatic contrast on images that do not contain haze. Here's how I apply it to black-and-white images:

1) Crank up **Dehaze** in the range of 70–100, depending on how dramatic of an effect you're looking to generate.
2) Hold the **Option** key (Mac) or **Alt** key (PC) and click on the **Dehaze** slider without changing its position to see how large of an area has become solid black. If it's limited to just a few tiny areas, then continue process-ing the image as you would any other. If you'd like to prevent numerous areas from becoming black or would like to see more details in the dark portions of the image, then continue with the next step, which should increase shadow detail.

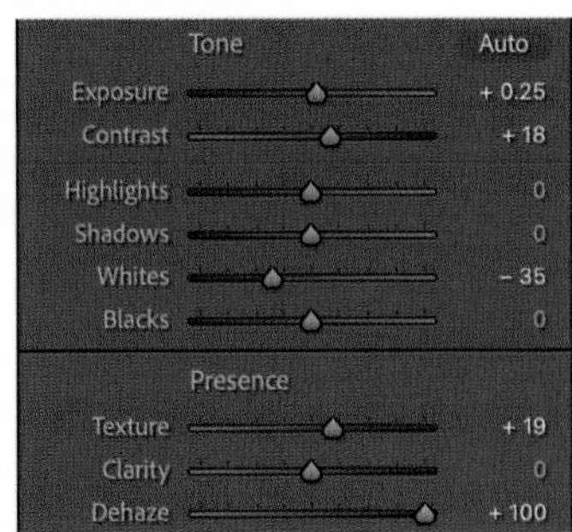

3) Create a new masked adjustment using the **Luminance Range** option, click within the image on the darkest area, and then adjust the range settings to resemble what is shown below.

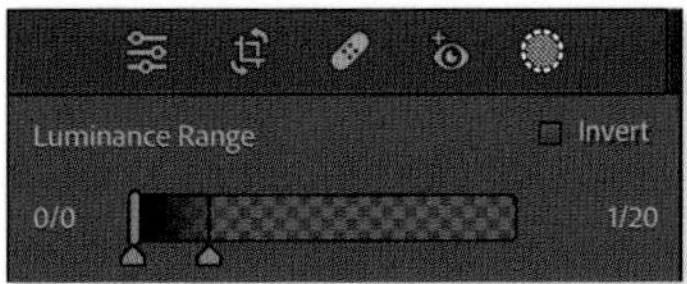

4) Lower the **Dehaze** setting and bring up the **Shadows** slider until you are happy with the amount of shadow detail. It can be useful to watch the histogram and note when any spike on the left edge is eliminated, as this indicates there are no large areas of solid black.

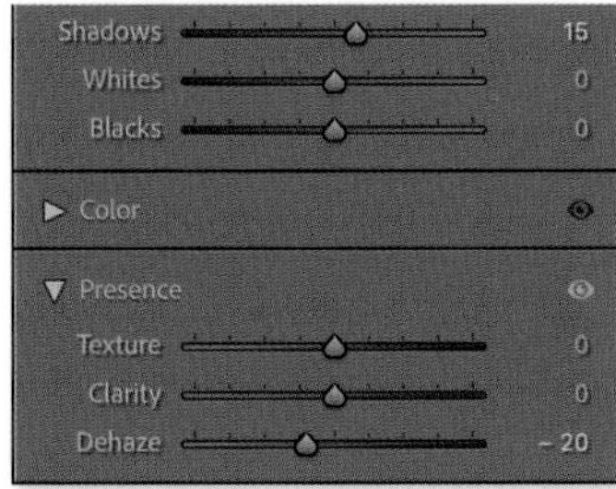

5) If some areas need less of a change than others, then consider subtracting us-ing a **Brush** mask and painting with a low **Opacity** setting to lessen the change where needed.

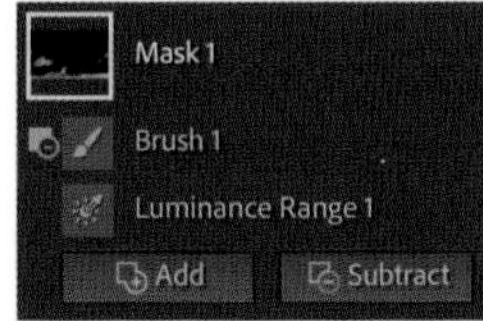

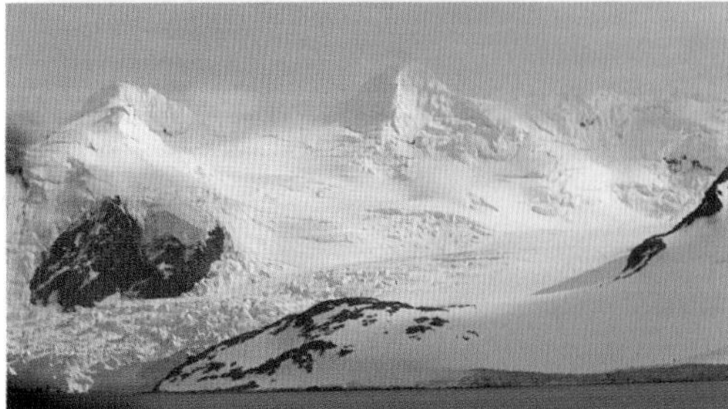

Image rendered as black and white using default settings.

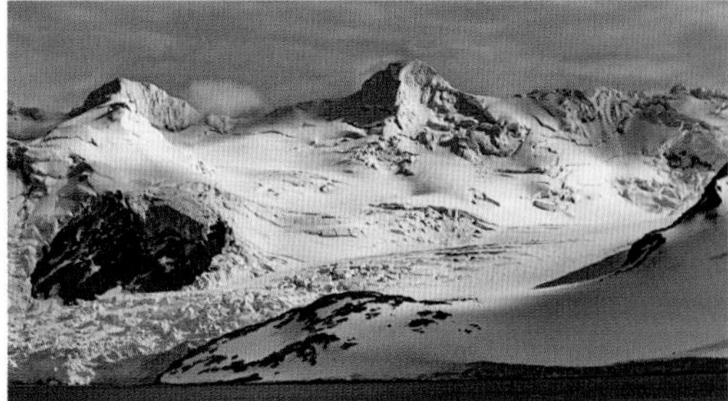

Image rendered with Dehaze set to 100.

Section III: Crafting a Photograph

Selective Focus

The eye is usually drawn to sharpness, so soften-ing areas can help to control where someone's mental focus will be directed in an image.

Apply Depth Blur Filter

This can sometimes be accomplished by choos-ing **Filter>Neural Filters**, selecting the **Depth Blur** option, and clicking within the small preview image to define the point that should be rendered as sharp (also known as the **Focal Distance**). The **Focal Range** slider can then be adjusted to control how much of the image will be sharp before the softening effect is applied.

This is possible because the filter utilizes artificial intel-ligence to generate a depth map that shows the per-ceived distance of each area in the image. It then uses that to determine where blurring should be applied.

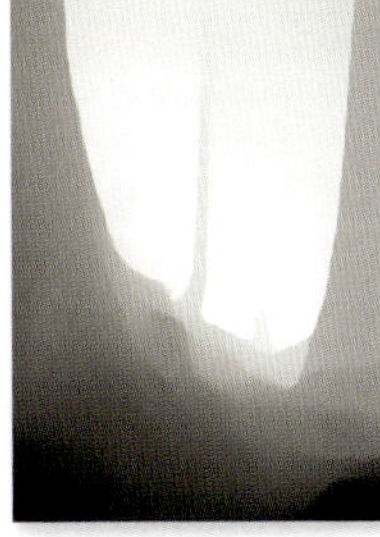

Example depth map.

After adjusting the **Blur strength** to soften the im-age, bring up the **Grain** slider a bit so that the blurred areas have a similar amount of grain as the rest of the image.

The filter will not produce a natural-looking result if there are any small tree branches that overlap the area that should remain sharp.

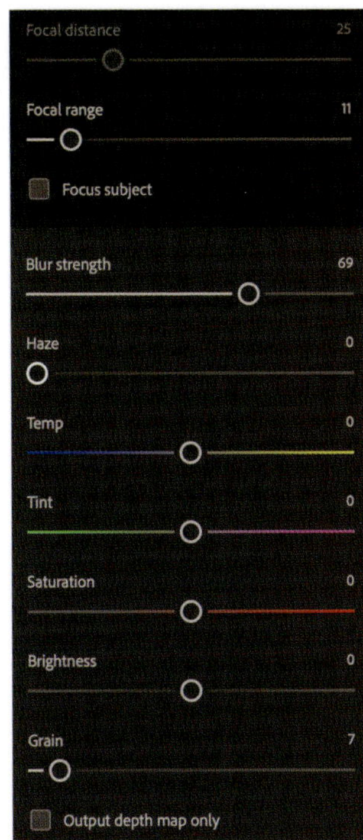

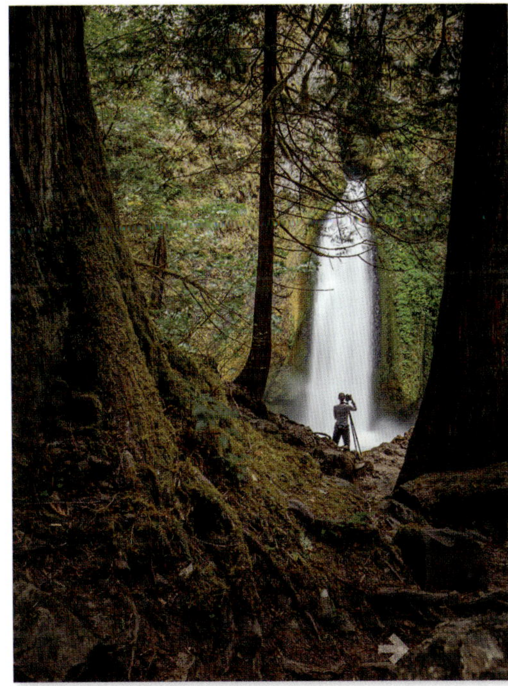

Original image before blurring.

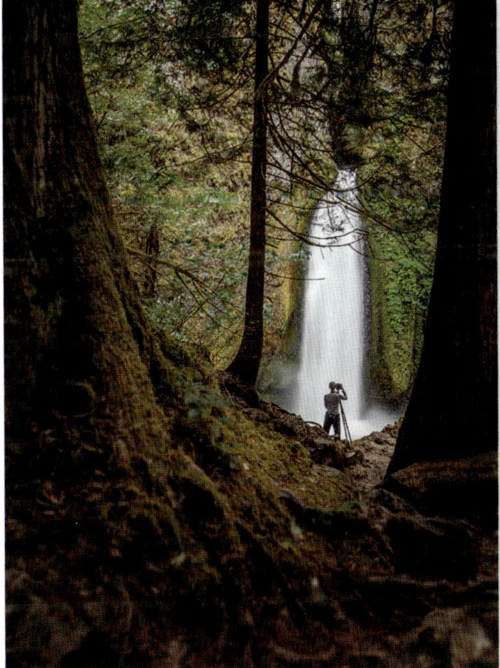

Result of applying the Depth Blur Neural Filter.

Simulate Long Exposure

The dreamlike look of a sky captured during a long exposure is something that cannot be seen by the naked eye. Capturing such images usually requires patience and the use of a dark neutral-density filter. A similar look can be achieved in Photoshop using the following technique.

Retouch Sky Boundary

Applying a directional blur to the sky will cause objects that intersect or border the sky to spread undesirably.

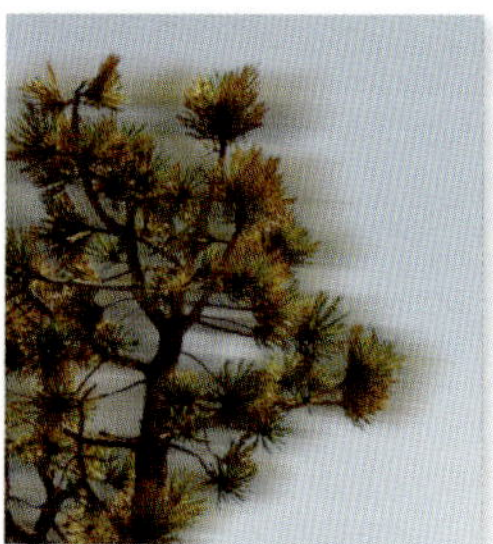

Blurred without retouching.

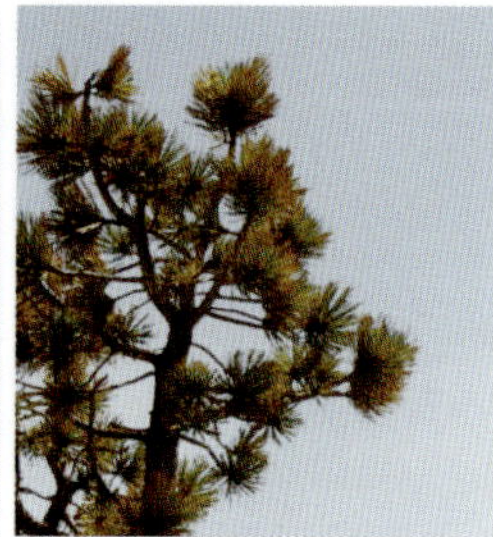

Blur applied with retouching.

To prevent this issue, I usually duplicate the original image layer and retouch out any objects that extend into the sky, and extend the sky into any areas that immediately border the sky. This is usually accomplished with the **Clone Stamp** tool.

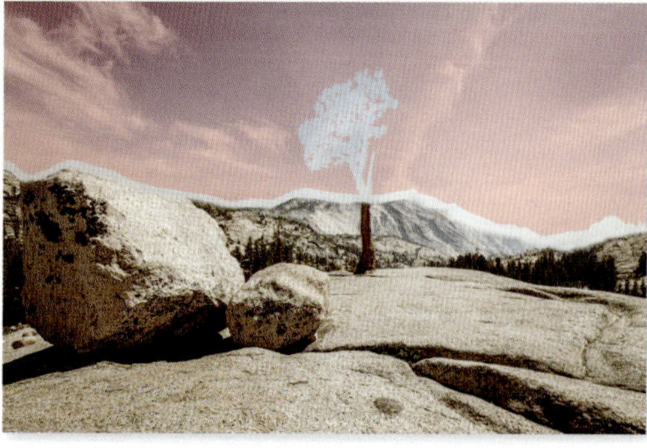

Mask Sky

Once the sky has been extended beyond its usual bounds, the next step is to switch to the layer that contains the original image and choose **Select>Sky**, or use a more sophisticated technique, such as a luminosity mask and the **Quick Selection** tool, as I did in this example image. Then, to hide all but the sky, choose **Layer>Layer**

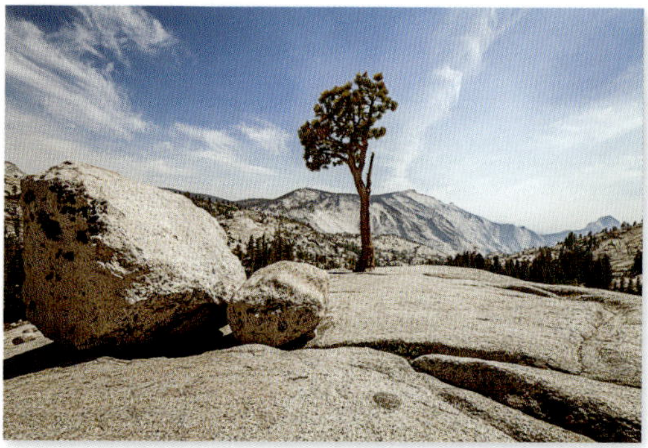

Image with original sky before applying Path Blur filter.

Mask>Hide Selection. Finally, drag the newly masked layer to the top of the layer stack.

Apply Path Blur

Switch to the layer that was previously retouched, which should be found at the bottom of the Layers panel. Choose **Filter> Convert for Smart Filters**, then **Filter>Blur Gallery>Path Blur**, and adjust the **Speed** setting to control the amount of blurring being applied.

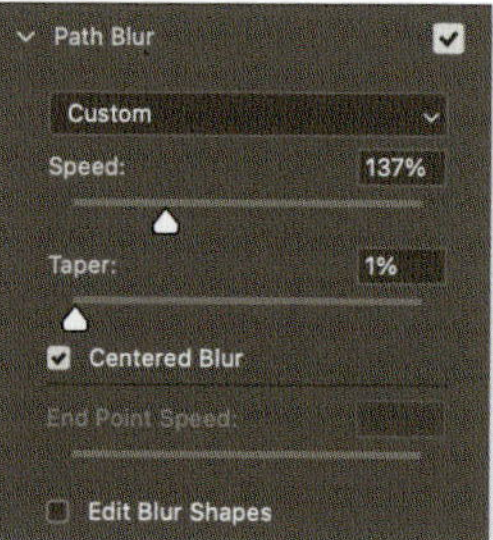

I like to apply the blur in three different amounts: a low setting for areas in the distance, a medium amount for slightly closer areas, and a high amount for areas that are almost immediately overhead. When you first open the **Path Blur** dialog, you should find a single horizontal line that can be manipulated by dragging its end and middle points. Position this line at the area that needs the greatest amount of blurring **A**.

Areas that are almost directly overhead travel a longer distance than those that are far away over the same time period. For that reason, additional directional lines will need to be added. Click where you'd like a new line to begin, drag to where you'd like it to end, and then click the point midway between the two newly added points to modify the curvature of the resulting line. If you find that additional clicks extend the line even further, then press the **Esc** key to prevent additional points from being added to the line.

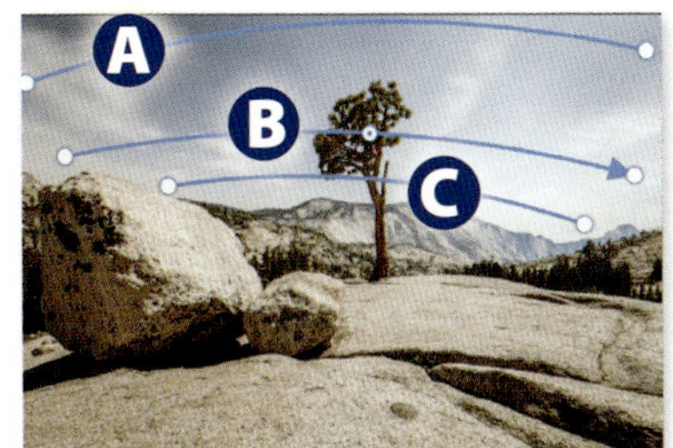

Paths used to apply progressively less blurring, top to bottom, using the Path Blur filter.

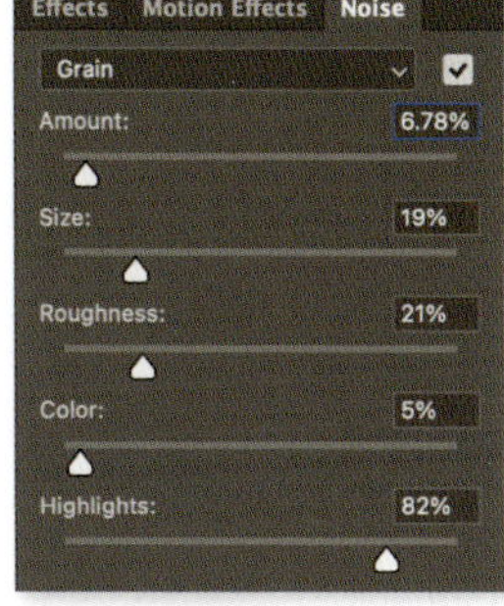

Once a second line has been added **B**, click on one of its end points and then lower the **End Point Speed** setting to lessen the amount of blurring being applied. You'll need to do the same for the point on the opposite end of the line to get a consistent amount of blur across its full length. Finally, add a third line and adjust its end points to apply even less blurring near the horizon on the image **C**.

Add Noise

Blurring the sky will cause it to look much smoother and more noise-free than the rest of the image. The **Noise** tab that is found below the **Path Blur** settings can be used to add noise/grain in an attempt to match the overall look of the rest of the image. I like to start with a large **Amount** to make it easier to see the effect of the other settings. Then, once I have the **Size**, **Roughness**, and **Color** settings dialed in, I'll fine-tune the **Amount**.

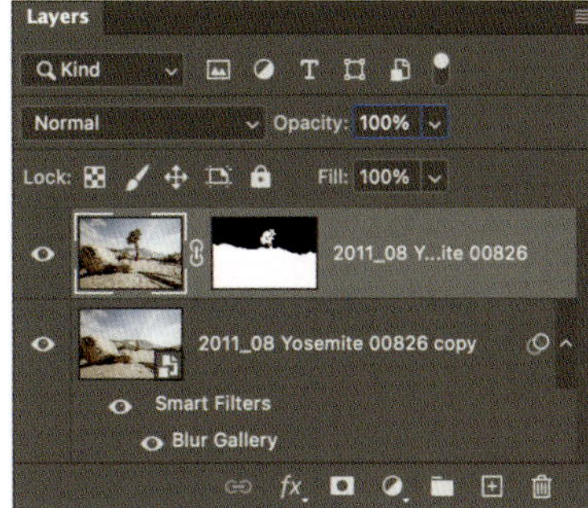

The original image is the top layer with a layer mask to hide sky. The bottom layer is a copy of the top, converted to a Smart Object, with the Path Blur filter applied.

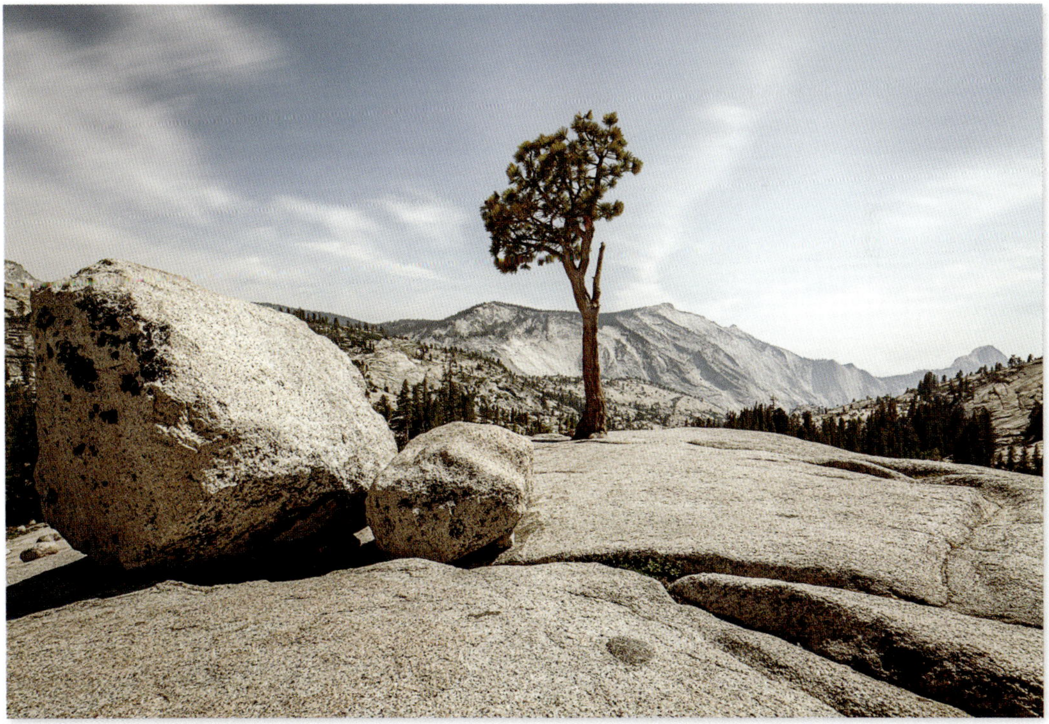

Result of applying Path Blur filter to the sky with progressively higher directional blur added as you move higher in the image.

Enhanced God Rays

When the sun is low in the sky and its light is interrupted by clouds, it sometimes puts on a show that is commonly referred to as "god rays." When the rays of light are a bit too subtle to feel "center stage," I'll use the following technique to make them stand out.

Inspect Color Channels

It all starts by choosing **View>Channels**, and clicking through the **Red**, **Green**, and **Blue** color channel thumbnails to see which one has the best depiction of the rays. They don't have to be very prominent to be useful. You're looking for which has the best-defined rays that look different in brightness from their surroundings. In this example image, it was the **Green** channel that I thought had the cleanest depiction of the rays without any other obvious issues.

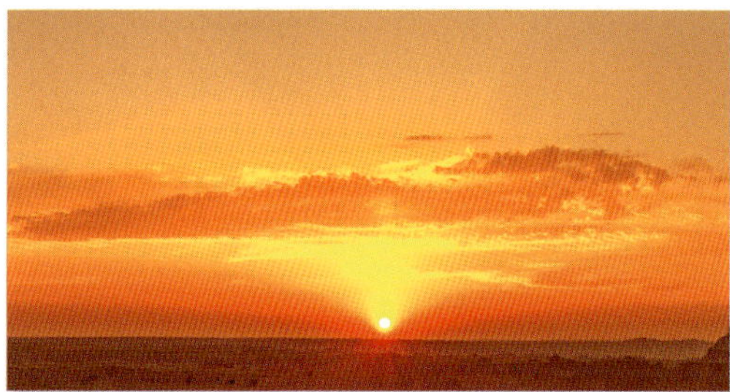

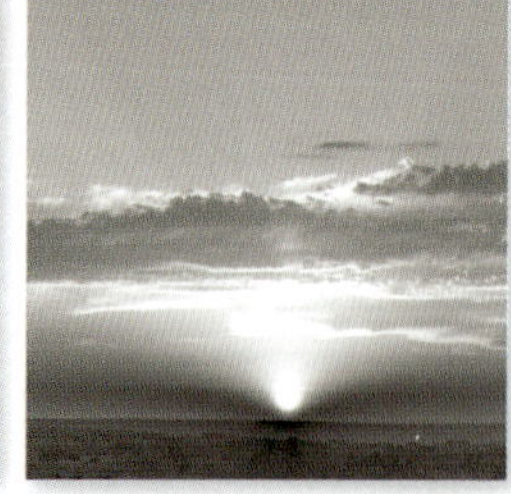

Top:
Full-color original image.

Clockwise from Upper Left:
Red channel
(no hint of upper rays).

Green channel
(faint hint of rays).

Blue channel
(hint of rays, but too similar
to surrounding image).

Duplicate and Adjust Best Channel

Now that the best channel has been selected, we'll make a duplicate and use it to produce a mask in an attempt to isolate the rays from their surroundings. I dragged the **Green** channel to the new channel icon at the bottom of the Channels panel and then chose **Image>Adjustments>Curves**.

In **Curves**, I chose the black eyedropper icon and clicked in the dark area between the rays to force the area to solid black. This moved the lower-left slider over **A**. I then chose the white eyedropper icon and clicked on the brightest area in one of the rays to force the area to white. This caused the right slider to move over **B**. I then activated the **Targeted Adjustment** tool (hand

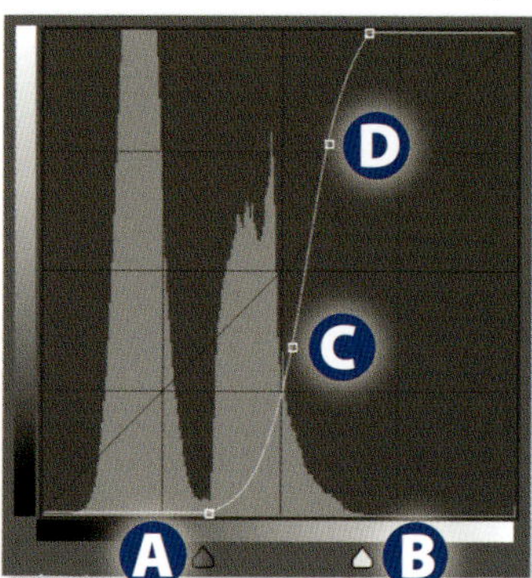

icon), clicked on a dark area (that was not black) between the rays, and dragged down to darken. This produced an additional point on the curve **C**. Finally, I clicked on a bright part of a ray that was not white and dragged up to brighten. This produced yet another point on the curve **D**.

Adding so much contrast to the channel revealed a few defects, such as sensor dust specks and a few edges that needed some cleanup.

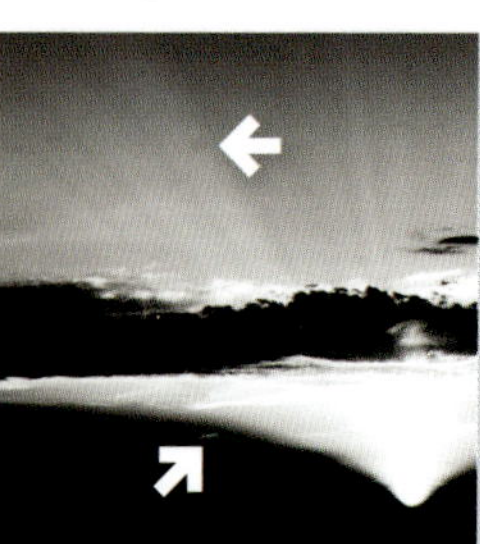

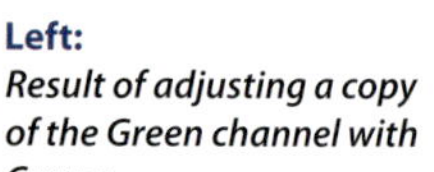

Left:
Result of adjusting a copy of the Green channel with Curves.

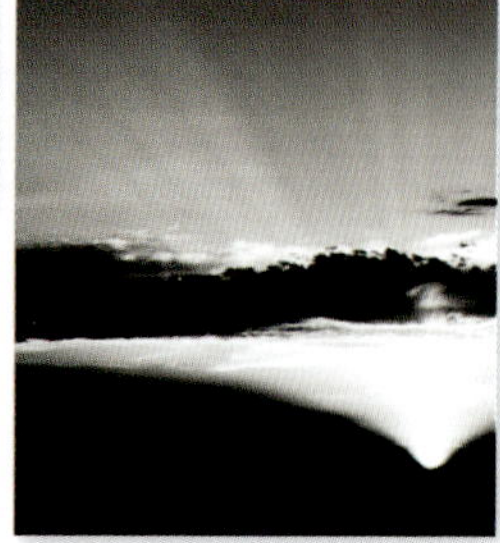

Right:
Result of retouching and cleanup of mask.

Section III: Crafting a Photograph

Use Mask to Limit Sky Adjustment

To make the rays stand out more from their background, I then dragged the channel that was just edited to the **Selection** icon at the bottom of the Channels panel to load it as a selection. This can then be used to limit where an adjustment will be applied. To make the adjustment, I chose **Layer>New Adjustment Layer>Curves** and activated the **Targed Adjustment** tool (hand icon).

I then clicked on the brightest part of a ray and dragged up to brighten **E**. I clicked on the dark area between the rays to add another point and dragged down to darken **F**. To finish the adjustment, I adjusted the position of the two sliders below the curve until I liked the look of the results.

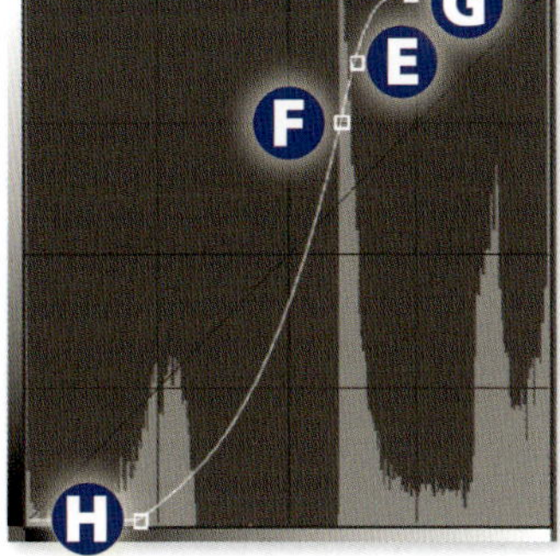

The adjustment caused the rays to become more prominent and stand out from the background, but it had the side effect of blowing out the detail in the area that was just above the sun.

> **Tip:** *If the resulting rays appear a bit grainy, then consider blurring the mask slightly.*

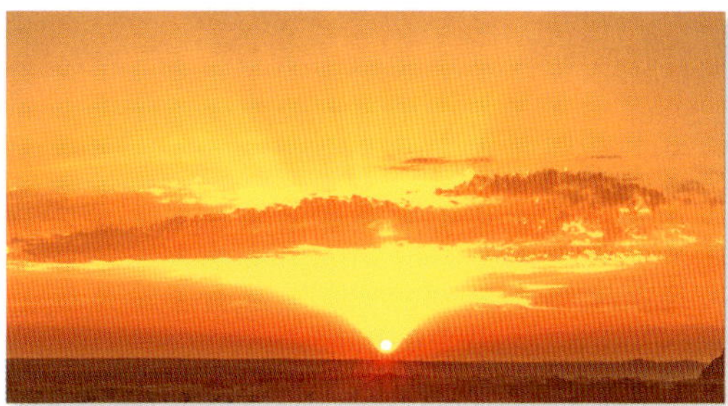

The adjustment caused undesirable changes near the sun.

Dual-Mask to Limit Area Changed

Holding **Shift** and clicking on the **Group** icon (folder icon) at the bottom of the Layers panel caused the **Curves** adjustment layer to be placed within a new group. I then clicked the **Layer Mask** icon at the bottom of the Layers panel and then painted with black in the areas where I did not like the look that the adjustment produced.

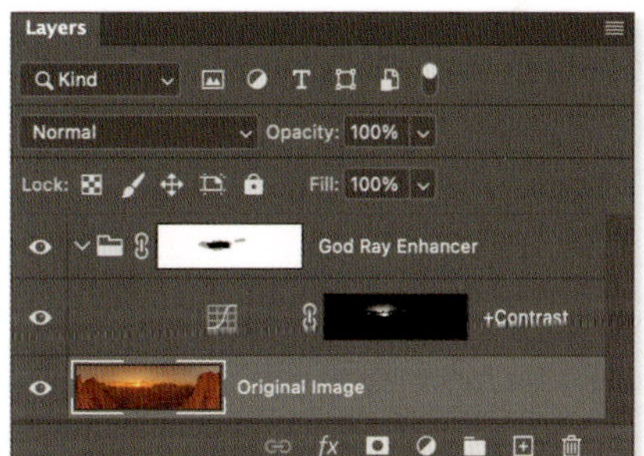

Layers panel view of image.

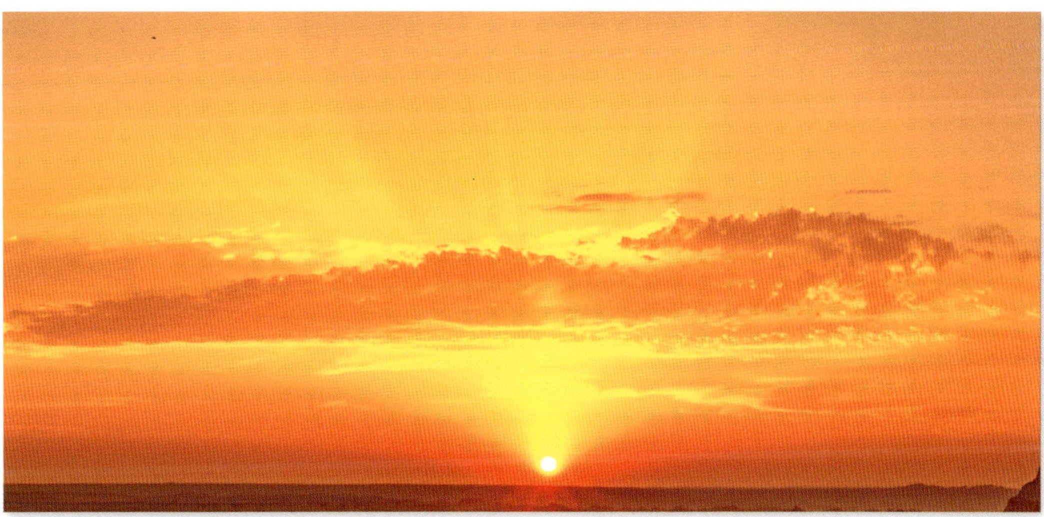

Result of enhancing "god rays" with a channel-based mask and Curves.

Color Contrast of Area

When the light falling on an area is consistent in color, as it is when an area is fully contained in either sun or shade and not a mix of the two, the area will have the tendency to appear very consistent in color. The following technique can be used to produce a larger difference in color across an area, which will usually make it appear more enticing.

Lock in Color of Dark Area in Red Channel

Start by choosing **Layer>New Adjustment Layer>Curves** and changing the pop-up menu above the curve to **Red**. Activate the **Targeted Adjustment** tool (hand icon) next to the curve. Next, click on a darkish area within the image that contains color (not one that looks black) to add a point to the curve. The resulting point on the curve **A** will be left in its original position to prevent the amount of red light found in the dark area from changing in subsequent steps.

Shift Color of Bright Area in Red Channel

Now, move to the brightest area that contains color (not one that looks white), click and drag up slightly to add a point to the curve, and increase the amount of red light in that area **B**. This will cause the bright area to become even brighter and shift slightly in color.

Prevent Change Outside Desired Range

The change in the last step likely caused the curve to shift considerably in the area above and below the two dots that were added. Click on the curve above and below the points added earlier to add two more points. Then fine-tune their positions to minimize that excessive adjustment **C**.

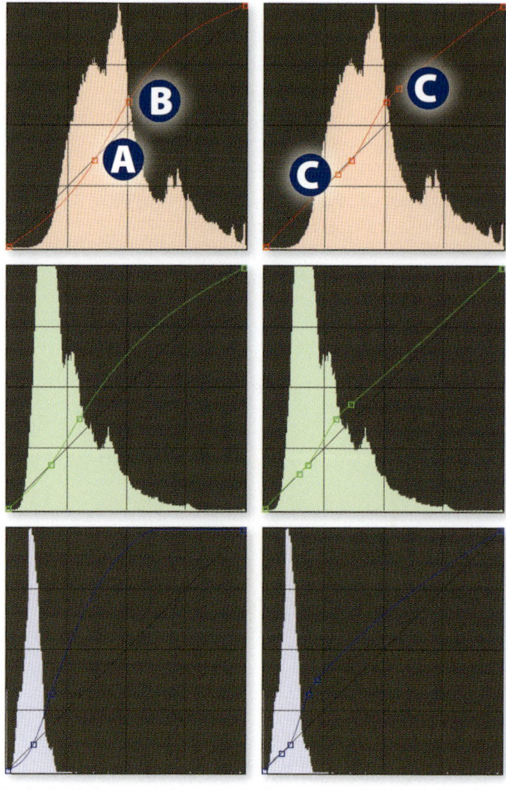

Left: *Initial contrast boost in Red, Green, and Blue channels.*
Right: *Points added on each side to prevent excessive change outside of the desired brightness range.*

Boost Contrast in Green and Blue

Change the pop-up menu above the curve to **Green** and then repeat the process to add contrast. When finished, do the same with **Blue**. To finish things off, paint with black on the layer mask to limit where the change is applied in the image.

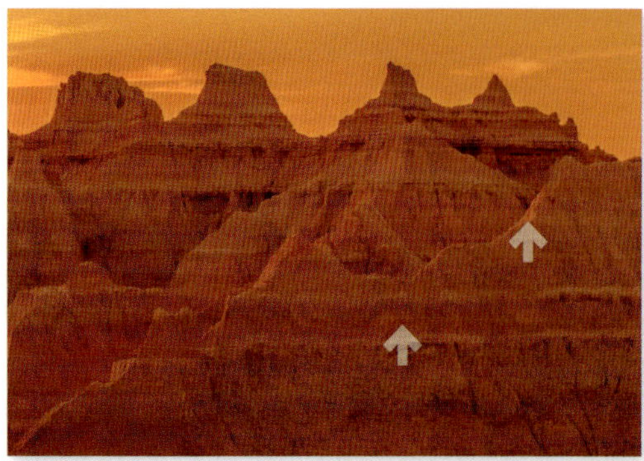

Area where color of highlights and shadows are similar.

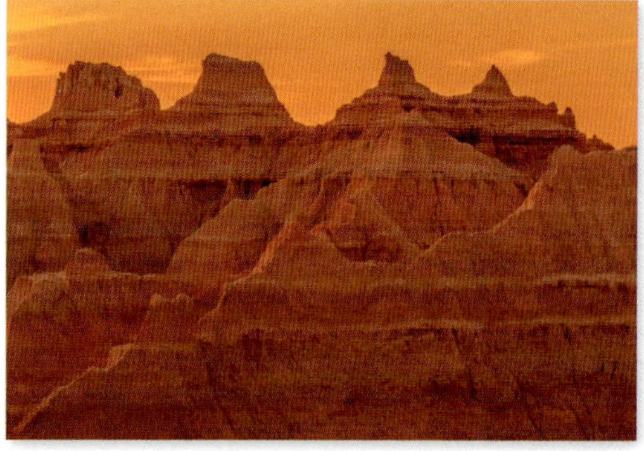

Result of increasing color contrast for better color separation.

Section III: Crafting a Photograph

Color Contrast of Objects

The previous technique increased the difference in brightness and color across an area. The key to the color change was that the individual **Red**, **Green**, and **Blue** curves were brightened by different amounts. Had they all been identical, then it would have only changed the brightness. Let's expand on that technique to increase the difference between objects and their surroundings.

Isolate Area

Use any of the selection and masking techniques that are found in chapter 3 to isolate an object from its surroundings.

Target Color of Isolated Area

With an object selected, choose **Layer>New Adjustment Layer>Curves** and activate the **Targeted Adjustment** tool (hand icon) next to the curve. Hold **Shift** and **Command** (Mac) or **Shift** and **Ctrl** (PC) and click on the most prominent color found within the object to add points to the individual **Red**, **Green**, and **Blue** curves. Those points reflect the exact amounts of those colors found in the area upon which you clicked.

Shift Color

Change the blending mode pop-up menu at the top of the Layers panel to **Color** to prevent the adjustment layer from being able to change the brightness of the area. Then switch between the **Red**, **Green**, and **Blue** curves and adjust the heights of the points that were added in the previous step to shift the color of the object.

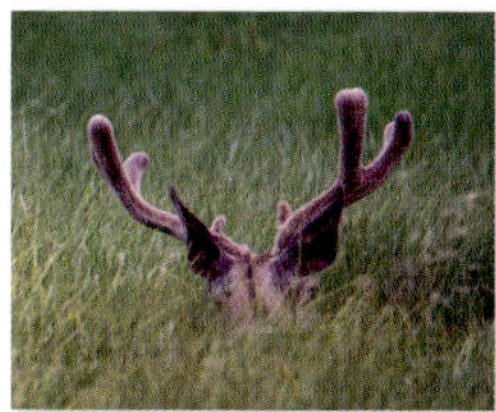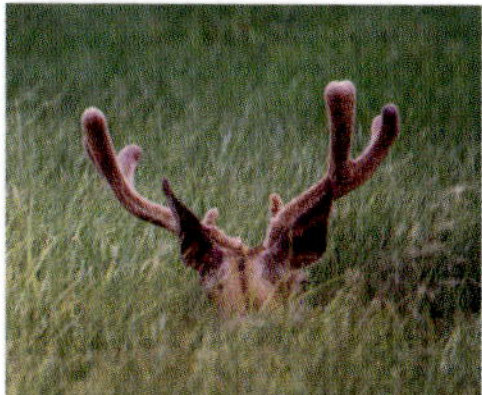

There are many options for how to make the color shift and I'm using **Curves** here, as it provides the most versatility because I can add multiple points, if needed, to adjust the bright and dark areas separately.

Reduce Color Contrast Elsewhere

I often selectively reduce the color contrast of areas in the surrounding image by creating a new layer, setting its blending mode to **Color**, lowering its **Opacity**, and then painting with a color from the surrounding image.

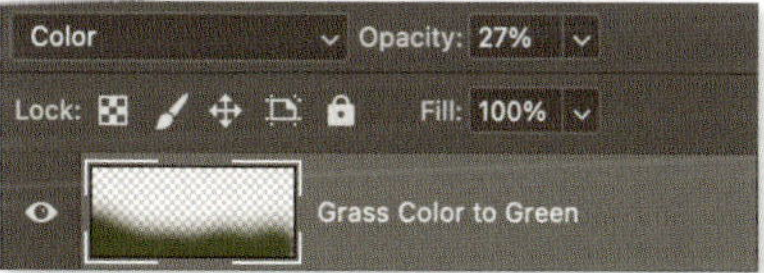

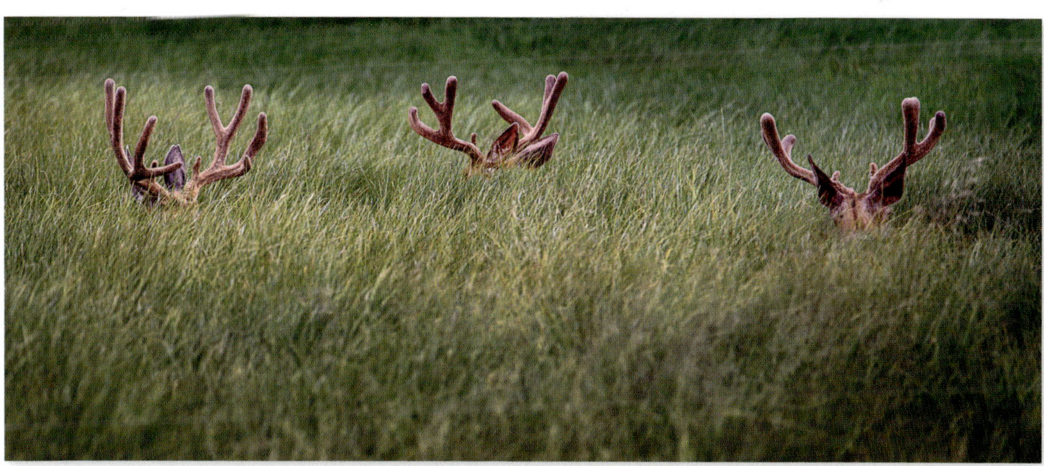

Changing the color of objects prevents them from blending into their surroundings.

Add Flare or Sunburst

Scenes that have no obvious focal point will often leave your eye wandering aimlessly with no real sense of direction. Adding a light flare above the horizon can serve as an obvious entry point for the eye to find and eventually return to as it explores the image, providing a more gratifying experience that helps directs the gaze.

Capture Light Flare

I prefer to capture real light flares instead of relying on Photoshop's **Filter>Render>Lens Flare** filter, which produces more sterile and artificial-looking flares.

Light flare produced using Photoshop's Lens Flare filter.

Capture Real Optical Light Flares

Pointing a flashlight directly into the lens of your camera in an otherwise dark environment should produce a light flare. Your shooting distance, focal length of the lens, and aperture setting will have a dramatic effect on the shape of the flare. Smaller, colorful flares can be avoided if you center the light source in the frame. Just make sure to use manual focus and a low ISO setting.

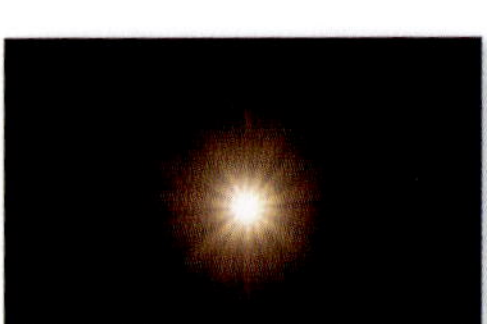
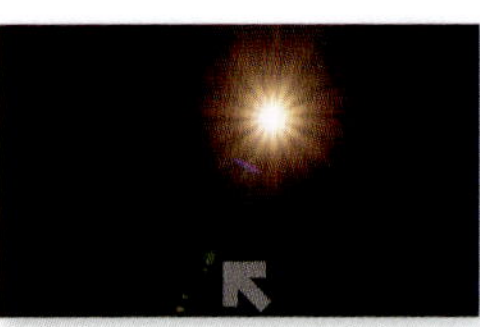

Lens flares can be avoided by centering the light source.

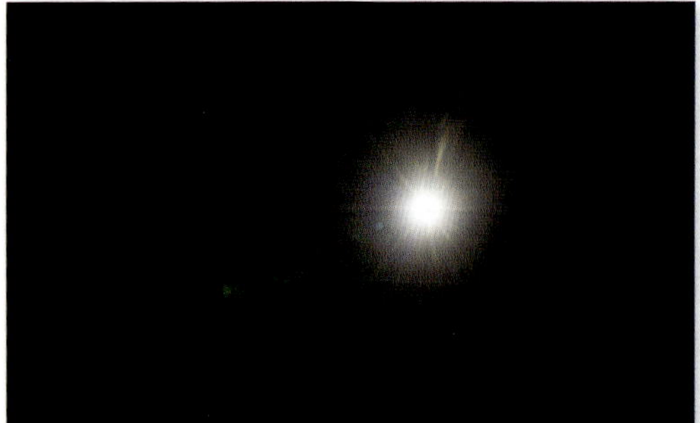

Image rendered using default settings in Lightroom.

Optimize Flare Images

Pushing the **Temp** and **Tint** sliders to the right is usually necessary in order to produce a flare that resembles the color that would be produced when the sun is low in the sky.

Flares that are surrounded on all sides by solid black can be positioned anywhere within an image. Holding **Option** (Mac) or **Alt** (PC) while moving the **Blacks** slider to the left will display an alternative view that displays colors where the image contains areas that are not solid black, making it easier to find the setting that surrounds the flare with black.

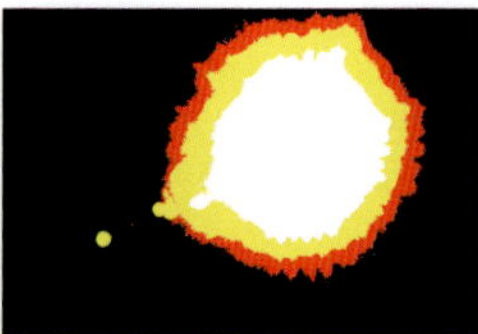

The **Dehaze** and **Clarity** sliders can be used to further enhance the haziness of the image, and the **Texture** slider can be useful in controlling the appearance of any fine rays.

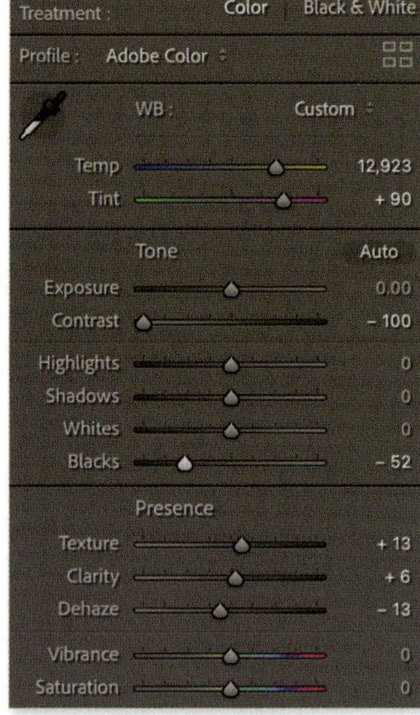

You might also want to consider fine-tuning the sharpening and noise reduction settings found in the Detail panel.

Image after optimization to shift color and enhance flare.

Apply Light Flare

Once you've captured and adjusted a light flare, it can be applied to an image in order to provide an obvious visual entry point into the photograph.

Apply Using Screen Mode

Placing the light flare on the layer above an image and setting that layer's blending mode to **Screen** will cause all of the solid-black areas to disappear, and any brighter areas will brighten the underlying image.

Control Color of Flare

If you'd like to infuse the flare with additional color, choose **Layer>New Fill Layer>Solid Color** and choose the color you desire. Then change the blending mode pop-up menu at the top of the Layers panel to **Overlay**. Finally, choose **Layer> Create Clipping Mask** to limit the change being made so it only affects the contents of the underlying layer containing the light flare.

Obscure Detail at Source

If the area within the central portion of the flare contains distracting detail, then you may want to consider painting over it with a soft-edged brush and then lowering the **Opacity** of the layer.

Fine-Tune Flare

The overall appearance of the layer that contains the flare can be fine-tuned by choosing **Image>Adjustments>Levels** and doing any of the following:

- Limit extent of flare by moving the upper-left slider to force more areas to solid black.
- Control transition by moving the middle slider in **Levels**.
- Lessen the brightness of the central area by moving the lower-right **Levels** slider toward the middle.

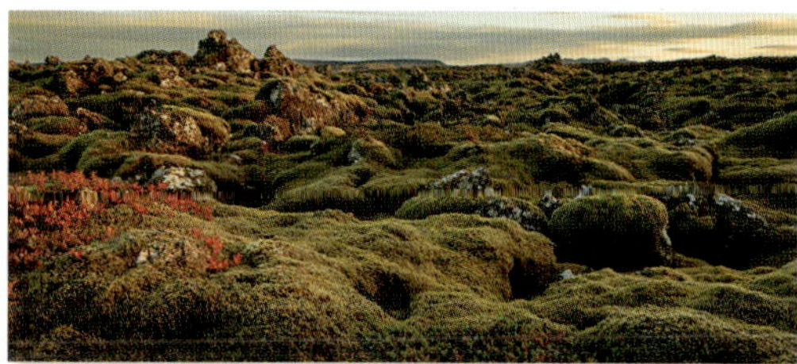

Image before addition of light flare.

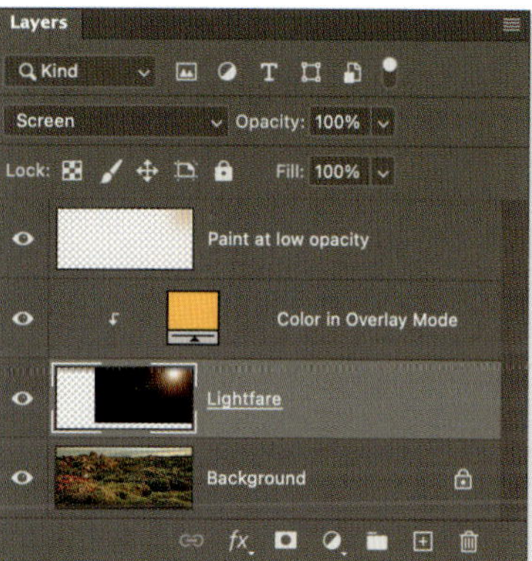

Layers panel view of light flare, including layers used to shift color and partially obscure the flare.

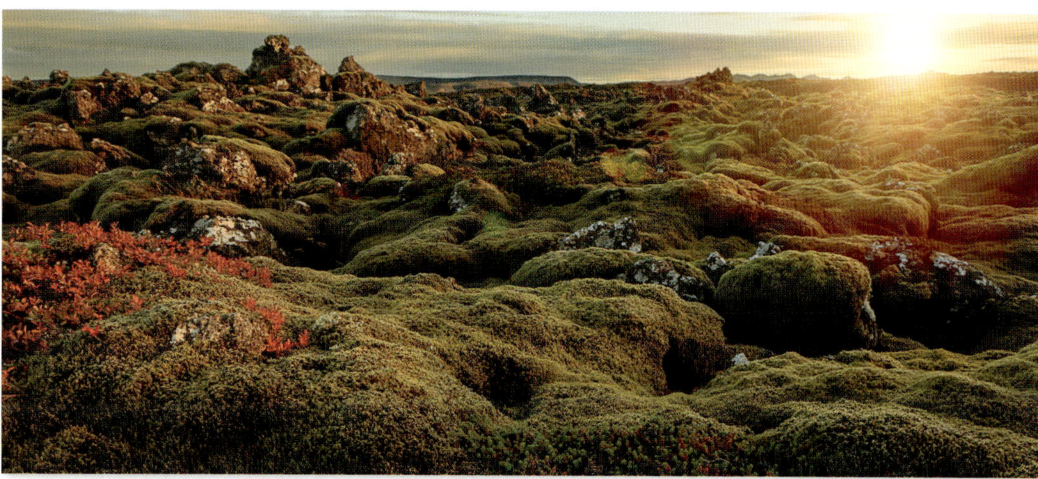

Result of adding flare to add drama to an otherwise evenly lit scene.

High Contrast

I often find I can produce a more compelling image by thinking of the original capture as raw material that is just waiting to be reinterpreted and possibly pushed into being less photographic and more purely graphical.

This can involve rendering large areas as solid black in order to simplify the image, and pumping up the saturation beyond what might initially feel like a reasonable level. It also means treating white balance as more of a creative tool, knowing that any color cast left in the image will likely be noticed by the viewer and therefore can be used to influence their reaction to the image.

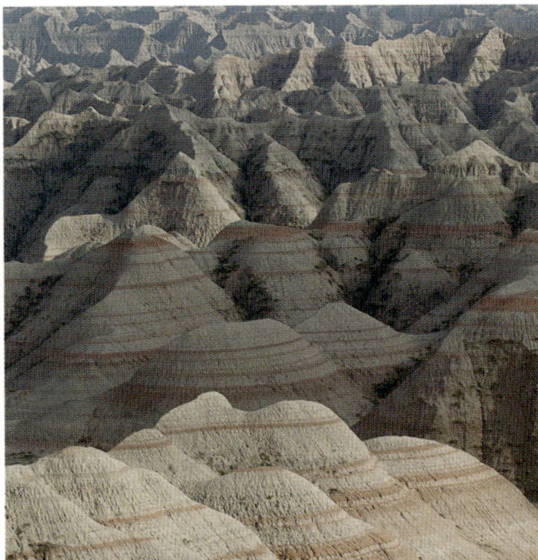

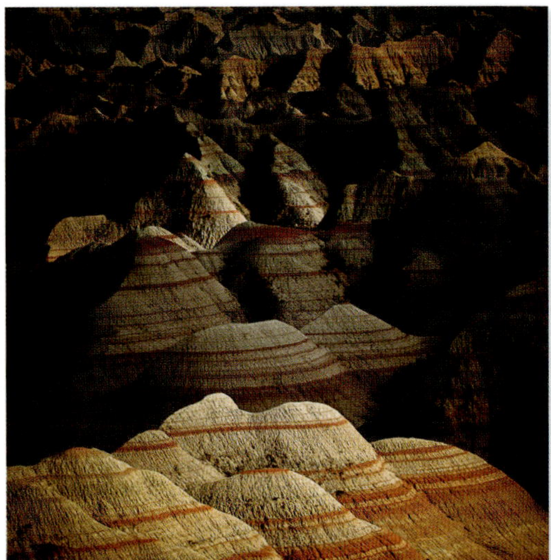

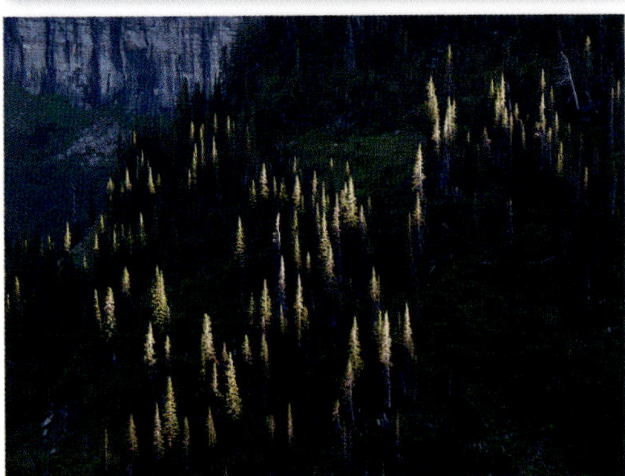

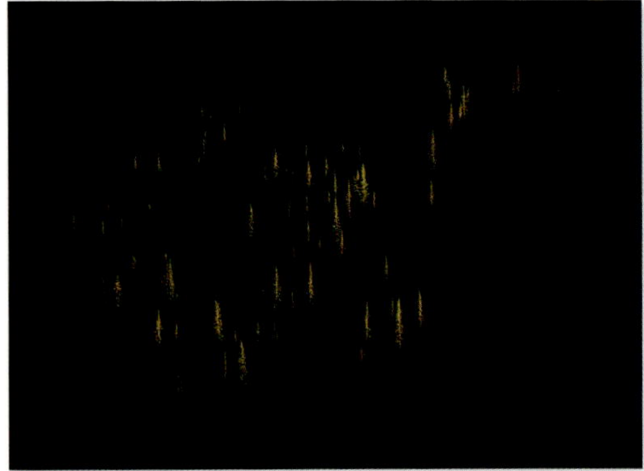

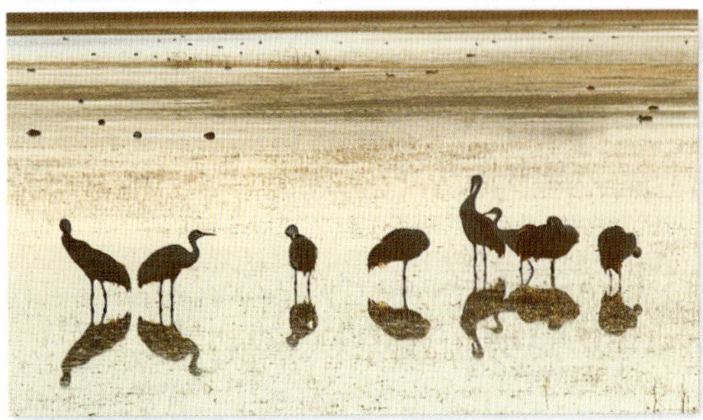

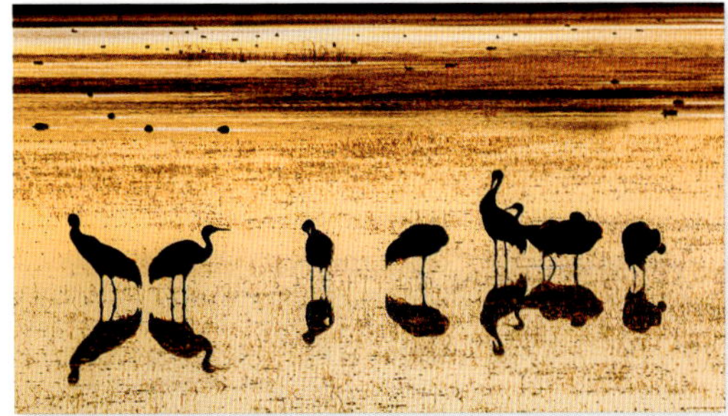

Section III: Crafting a Photograph

The images shown on this two-page spread show the original image as rendered with default settings beside the final high-contrast, graphical interpretation of the image.

These examples serve to show how radically different the end results are from the original image. It's often more about your mindset than the specific techniques you choose to employ.

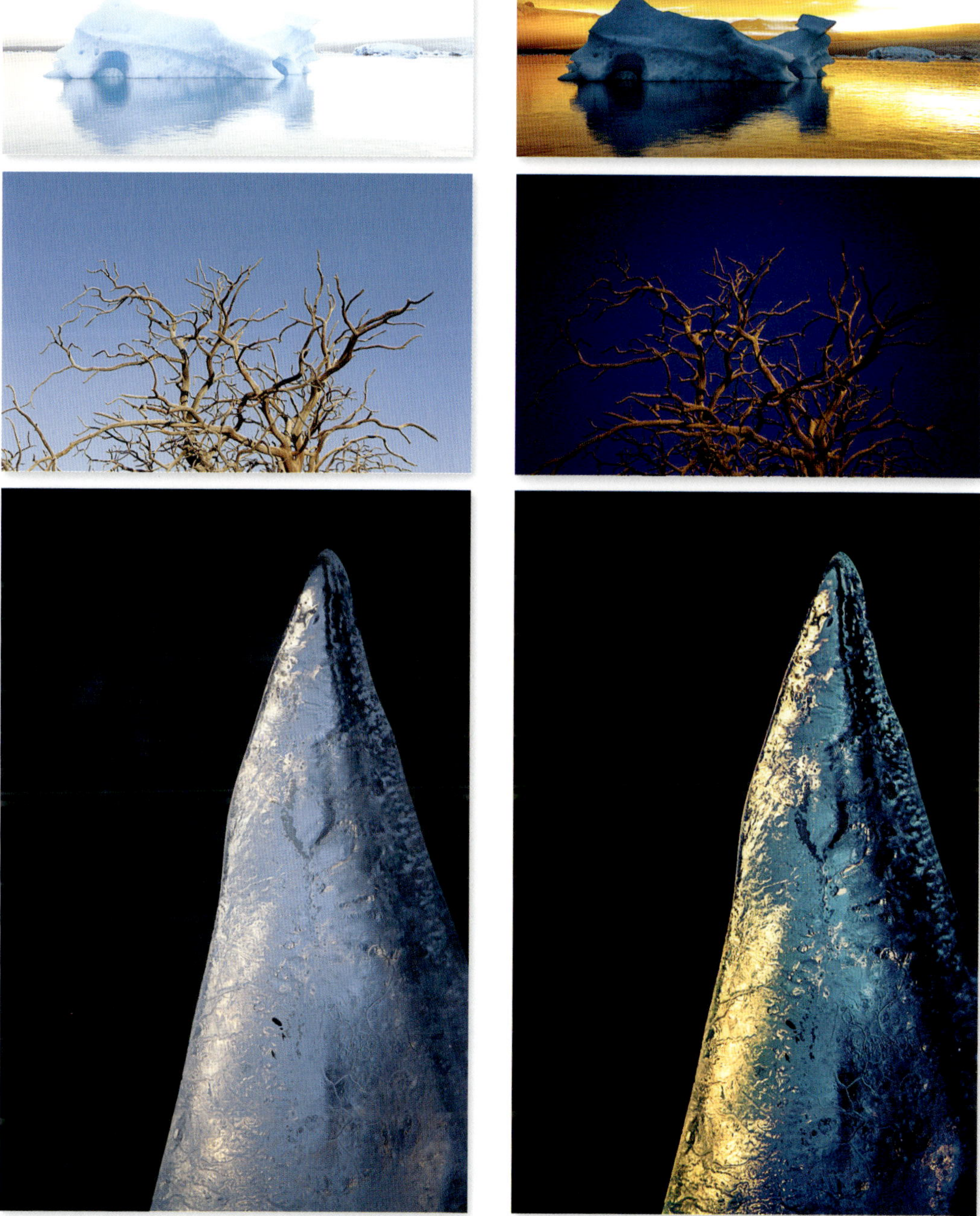

Chapter 8

Produce Engaging Color

HAVE YOU EVER found yourself drawn to a particular image without being able to describe exactly why it's holding your gaze? Chances are, it had something to do with the color. This chapter is all about making the colors pop in order to lure viewers into your image and then hold their attention. Color is a complex topic with literally hundreds of enhancement possibilities. In this chapter, we'll look at what Lightroom has to offer, starting with global adjustments that apply to the entire image. Then we'll explore a few selective adjustments that will apply to isolated areas. Finally, we'll jump over to Photoshop to hone in on more specialized techniques that are beyond Lightroom's capabilities.

Global Adjustments

Engaging color starts with the most basic of adjustments, which are applied within the Develop module of Lightroom Classic. Let's take a brief look at the color-related adjustments that are available and dive deeper into some of the topics that were covered earlier in the book.

White Balance

The first step to producing engaging color is to find the optimal white balance setting in order to render the scene such that it appears natural to the viewer. This is more complex than you might think, so let's explore what's involved.

Perception versus Reality

The color of light you experience throughout the day varies more than you might realize. The simple act of stepping out of a sunlit area and into the shade causes the color of light entering your eyes to shift rather dramatically. After all, the noonday sun produces white light, but the shady area under a tree will likely be lit by the blue sky. This causes the light in these two areas to be quite different in color.

Your brain compensates for such differences so your perception of the colors in your surroundings remains consistent, regardless of the varying lighting conditions experienced throughout the day. It's only when you encounter extremes, such as the yellow-orange light of sunset, that your brain stops compensating for the color of light and allows you to see the true effect it has on the scene.

Your Perception of Photographs is Different

Your brain does not usually compensate for the color of the light depicted in a photograph. That's because it's busy compensating for the environment in which the photo is being presented, making it appear as if the room is being lit with white light. For that reason, most photos (other than those shot during the golden hour of sunrise or sunset) will only be perceived as looking natural if they appear to be lit with white light.

Auto White Balance

The auto white balance setting in your digital camera attempts to compensate, much like your brain, in order to render the colors of a scene consistently under varying lighting conditions.

JPEG Images Are White Balanced In-Camera

JPEG images have a white balance correction permanently applied before the file is generated. That's why Lightroom's **Temp** and **Tint** sliders, which are collectively known as white balance, 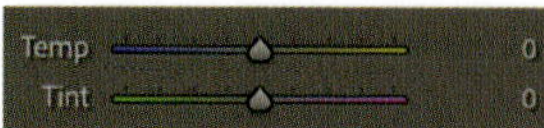 default to zero on JPEG files. No attempt to correct color issues with those sliders will be as successful as changing the white balance setting in-camera and recapturing the scene.

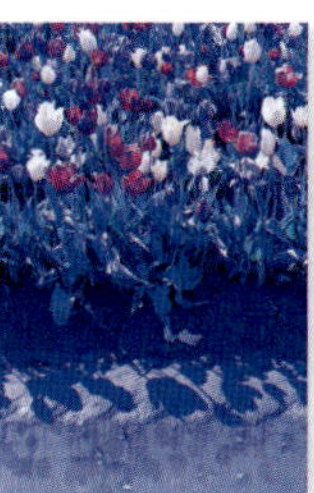 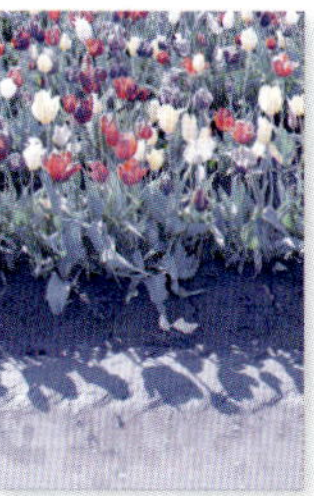 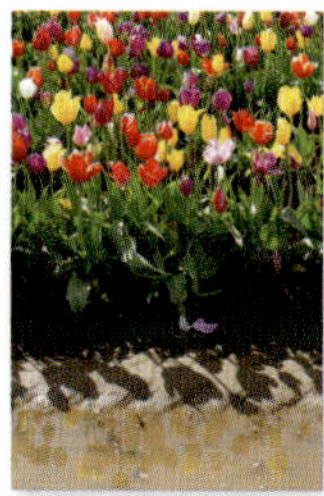

Left: *Image captured using in-camera white balance setting that does not reflect the color of light illuminating the scene.*
Middle: *Result of opening the first file (which was captured as a JPEG file) in Lightroom and attempting to correct the color issues with white balance settings.*
Right: *Result of changing white balance in-camera and capturing a new photograph of the same scene.*

Raw Files Are Unprocessed

Raw files, on the other hand, have little or no processing applied and the camera's white balance setting does not change the contents of the saved image. Therefore, changes in the color of light falling on the scene will cause noticeable changes in the raw data captured, as no white balance correction has been applied. The in-camera white balance setting is only used to generate the in-camera preview image that you might review after capture. It's then added to the file as two numbers that are recorded in the same way as the shutter speed and aperture settings.

White Balance in Lightroom

When a raw file is loaded into Lightroom, the in-camera white balance settings are read. These become the initial settings dialed into the **Temp** and **Tint** sliders that perform white balance correction in the De- 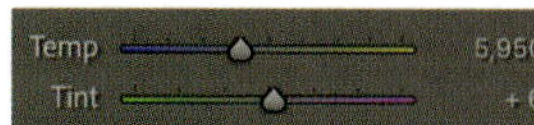 velop module. Correcting color issues on a raw file by adjusting Lightroom's white balance settings will produce the same quality result as changing the white balance setting in-camera before capturing the scene. When the **Temp** and **Tint** settings accurately reflect the color of light under which an image was captured, the white balance correction should compensate, just like your brain would if it was viewing the scene first-hand. That is, it will look as if the scene was lit with white light.

When the **WB** (short for white balance) pop-up menu above the sliders is set to **As Shot**, it's an indication that you have not yet deviated from the camera-supplied white balance settings. Once you move the sliders, it will change to **Custom**.

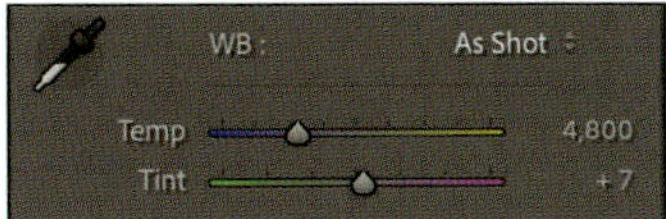

"As Shot" indicates the Temp and Tint settings reflect the in-camera white balance settings.

Red, Green, and Blue Numbers

When you're in Lightroom's Develop module, you can hover over the image and look at the red, green, and blue percentages that appear directly below the histogram. Those values reflect how each color is being made behind the scenes in Lightroom. If those numbers ever become perfectly balanced, it means you are hovering over an area that is a shade of gray and contains no color whatsoever. That's what I'll refer to as being neutral gray. All the brightness levels that can be displayed on a B&W TV would be considered neutral shades of gray.

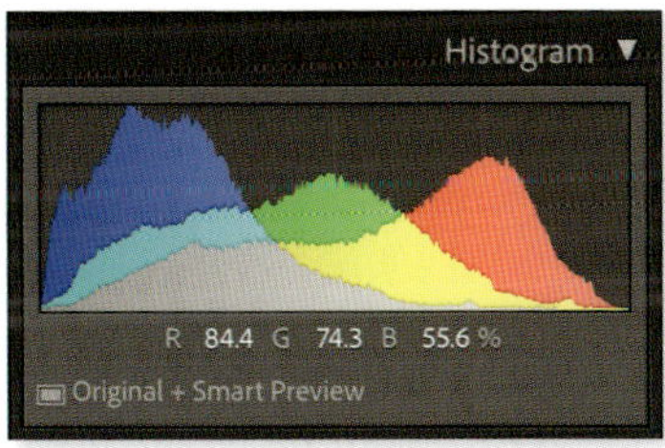

The RGB numbers below the histogram indicate the blend of light used to create the color being hovered over. Balanced RGB indicates a shade of gray.

White Balance Selector Tool

Clicking within an image using this eye-dropper-shaped tool will automatically move the **Temp** and **Tint** sliders to the settings that would balance the RGB numbers under the histogram. As a result, the color that you clicked on will shift to be rendered as a neutral shade of gray. Clicking on a cloud or the blurry white water of a waterfall might create a good starting point. Then you can fine-tune the **Temp** and **Tint** sliders to find the setting that produces a pleasing rendition of the scene.

Use a White Balance Card for Natural Color

I try to include a neutral gray object in each scene I photograph so there is always something to click on with the **White Balance Selector Tool**. I use a WhiBal card, which is a chunk of plastic that is a neutral shade of gray. (WhiBal is a specific brand, and there are several other brands to choose from.) Just as a red light bulb hung above a white sheet of paper will cause a photograph of the paper to look reddish, this little gray card will shift to take on the color of light under which it is photographed. The key is to ensure that the light falling on the card is of the same color as the light illuminating the scene you are capturing. The only time I don't use this card is during the golden hour, when I want my images to have a severe yellow-orange color cast.

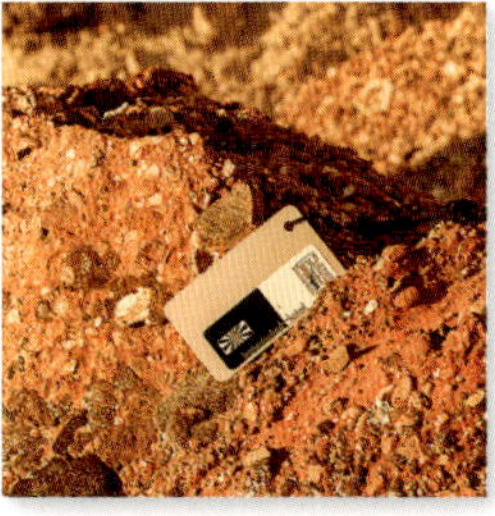
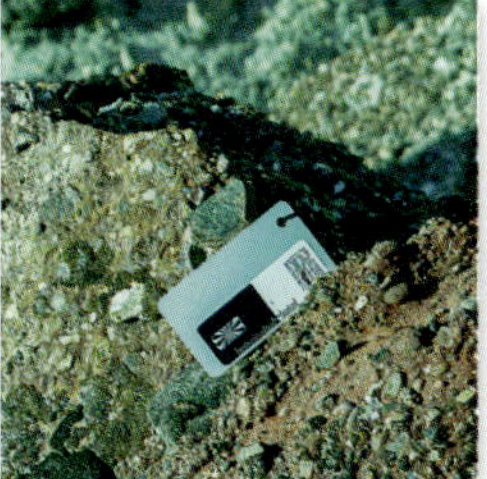
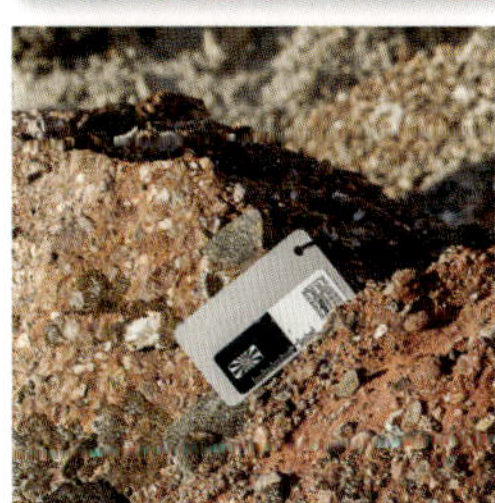

Top Left: *White balance setting set too warm.*

Top Right: *White balance setting set too cool.*

Left: *Ideal white balance determined by clicking on the WhiBal card with the White Balance Selector Tool.*

Using that gray card to set white balance affects the entirety of the image. We're just using the card to figure out which direction the sliders need to move and exactly how extreme of an adjustment is needed.

You can include that card in one of your photographs and then continue shooting in that same lighting condition without it. You should again include the card in a photo when you move from one lighting condition to another, like the shady light under a tree to the open sun. Then you can adjust a whole series of images at once. Just make sure all the images are selected and the **Auto Sync** option is turned on before clicking on the card.

Render with Warm or Cool Color Bias

White balance may have been designed to correct for unwanted color casts, but that doesn't mean you'll want every image to be rendered as if it was lit by perfectly neutral, white light.

I often fine-tune the overall color rendering by manually adjusting the **Temp** and **Tint** sliders. In doing so, I may decide to purposefully create a color bias, causing the image to look slightly warm or cool, in order to influence the perception of the viewer. The viewer's brain will not compensate for the color in a photograph because it will instead compensate for the viewing environment in which the photo is presented.

When it comes to the golden hour, white balance can be used to control whether the overall color should be rendered to look more yellowish-orange or maybe even include a hint of purple. It's your choice, depending on which white balance setting you decide to use.

Mixed White Balance

Many images are lit by mixed lighting and may benefit from more than one white balance setting. This can be accomplished by utilizing Lightroom's masked adjustments, which offer **Temp** and **Tint** sliders of their own.

In the example below, the white balance was initially set by clicking on the waterfall with the **White Balance Selector Tool**. This caused the surrounding image to look undesirable. Three separate masked adjustments were then used to change the white balance being applied to the surrounding image.

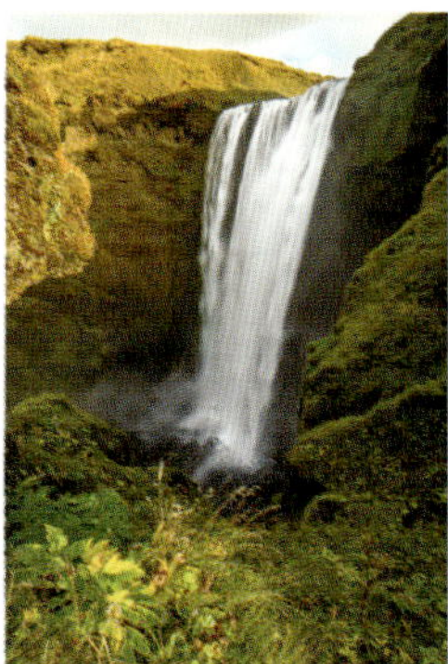

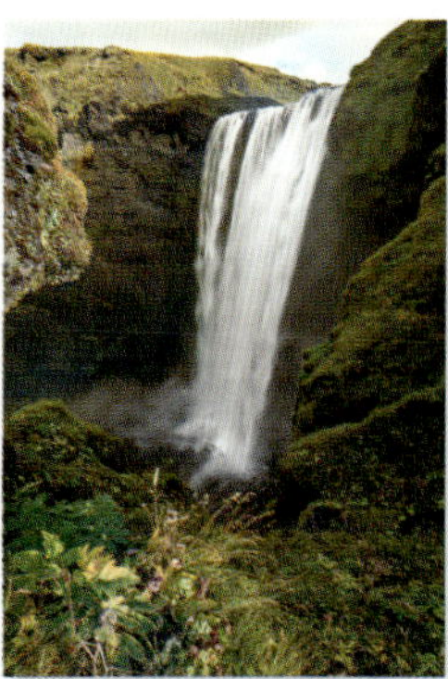

White balance set to render white of waterfall as neutral.

Result of applying multiple white balance settings.

Color Rendering and Creative Profiles

Every image that is captured with a digital camera has a color-rendering profile applied. This profile determines how the overall color and contrast of the image will be interpreted before any of the adjustment sliders are moved in Lightroom's Develop module.

Profile Browser

To change the color-rendering profile on a raw file, choose **Browse** from the **Profile** pop-up menu (or click the icon to its right), which is found near the top of the Basic panel in Lightroom's Develop module. That will send you to what's known as the profile browser, which can later be dismissed via the **Close** button found near the top.

Camera Matching

The **Camera Matching** choices mimic how your camera would perform initial processing in-camera when generating on-screen previews and creating JPEG images. These choices match the options available within the in-camera menu system and are useful when you want the initial view of an image in Lightroom to match how images appear in-camera.

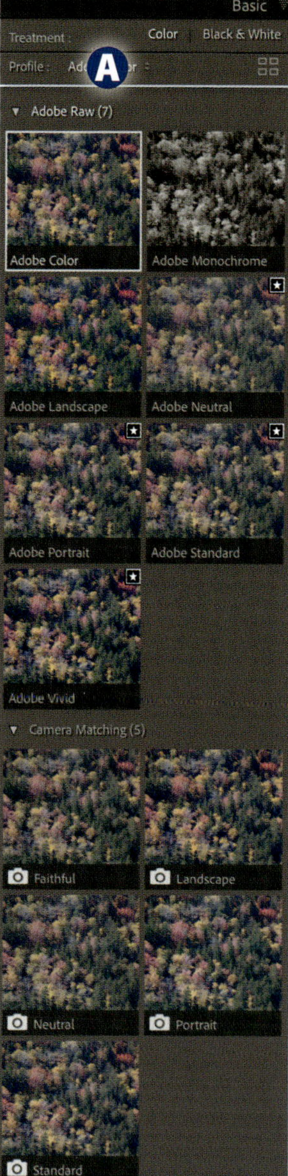

Adobe Raw

The **Adobe Raw** choices are designed to deliver consistent results regardless of which brand of camera an image is captured with. These are unlike the **Camera Matching** profiles, which deliver the unique look that each camera manufacturer is known for.

The choices available vary from mild (with **Adobe Neutral**) to wild (with **Adobe Vivid**), with **Adobe Color** in between. Then there are more specialized choices such as **Adobe Portrait**, which is especially careful with rendering skin tones, and **Adobe Landscape**, which attempts to amp up the colors most commonly found in landscape images (but can wreak havoc on skin tones). Finally, **Adobe Standard** is a legacy choice that was previously applied to every image before the other choices were added to Lightroom. **Adobe Color** is an updated version that usually produces generally superior results.

JPEG Embedded Profiles

The two types of profiles we've covered thus far are only available when working with raw files. When shooting in JPEG format, the profile that's applied is chosen within your camera's menu system and is permanently applied before the file is generated. Therefore, it cannot be changed after an image is captured. As a result, the profile in Lightroom will be called "Embedded" for such pre-

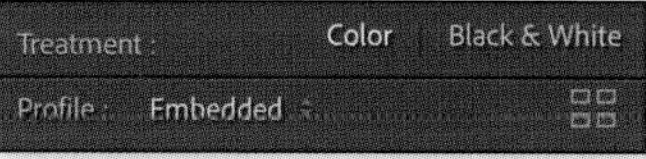

processed files. When shooting in raw format, the setting in your camera's menu system is only used for the in-camera preview images and does not affect the raw data itself.

Creative Profiles

The profiles found in the **Artistic**, **Modern**, and **Vintage** sections all apply the Adobe Standard color rendering profile, and then infuse that basic color rendering with creative processing to ef-

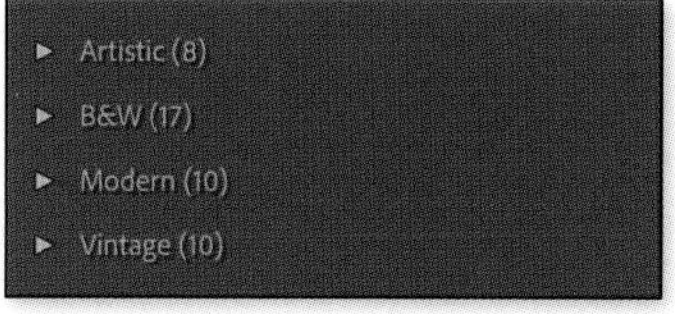

fectively style the image. Most of these profiles will cause an **Amount** slider **B** to appear at the top of the profile browser, just below the **Profile** pop-up menu. This setting can be used to dial in the strength of the effect.

These creative profiles can be applied to raw and jpeg files alike. I use these when I'm

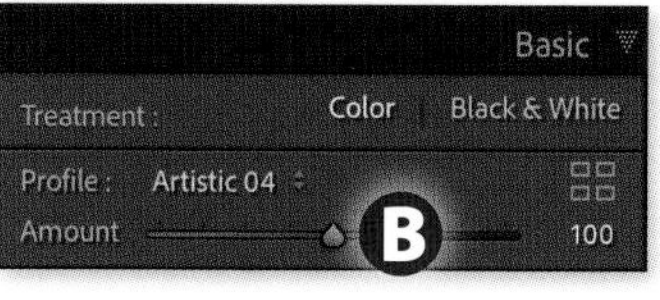

being lazy and don't feel like crafting an image from scratch, or when I run into a situation where I'm simply not happy with the results I'm getting. In this case, a profile can provide a creative foundation on which I can build a finished image.

Define Default

Once you've experimented with color-rendering profiles on dozens of images, you'll likely discover that one most closely reflects your personal preference for how you like colors to be initially rendered. Once you've discovered your personal favorite, then you can use the following technique to make it the default setting that will be applied to all future images:

1) With a raw file open in the Develop module, click the **Reset** button near the bottom right of the screen to ensure the image is processed using the current default settings.

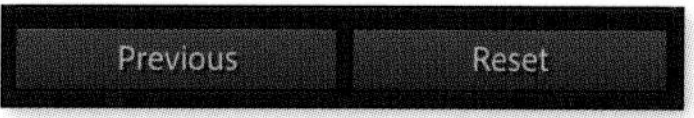

2) Choose **Browse** from the **Profile** pop-up menu and apply the profile you would like to use as your default.

3) Click the **+** icon to the right of the **Presets** heading on the left side of the Develop module and choose **Create Preset**. Click the **Check None** button, turn on the **Treatment & Profile** checkbox, and enter something memorable in the **Preset Name** field, such as "Ben's Default Settings." Set the **Group** to **User Presets** (or an alternative that you prefer) and click the **Create** button.

4) Choose **Preferences** from the **Lightroom Classic** menu (Mac) or **Edit** menu (PC), click on the **Presets** tab, and select the preset you created earlier from the **Global** menu.

As an alternative, the **Camera Settings** option in the **Global** menu can be used if you'd like to have Lightroom automatically apply the **Camera Matching** profile that matches the in-camera setting that was in use when an image was captured.

Calibration

The sliders found within the **Calibration** panel were originally intended to customize the color rendering of various camera models in order to achieve consistent color between brands. That has largely been replaced by the **Adobe Raw** profiles, discussed earlier in this chapter, and the **DNG Profile** editor, which allows you to create your own custom camera profiles. This feature remains in Lightroom for legacy purposes and can be used for creative color effects.

Reinterpret Color Rendering

If you hover over various parts of an image and inspect the RGB numbers that appear under the histogram, you'll see that every single color that makes up the image is made from a mix of red, green, and blue light. The sliders found in the **Calibration** panel allow you to modify the exact shades of red, green, and blue the image will be built from. This means any change to these sliders will affect every single color that is found within the image.

This is where some common color effects are applied, such as the teal and orange look that was popular a while back. That one is made by moving the **Red Primary Hue** slider to the right and the **Blue Primary Hue** slider to the left.

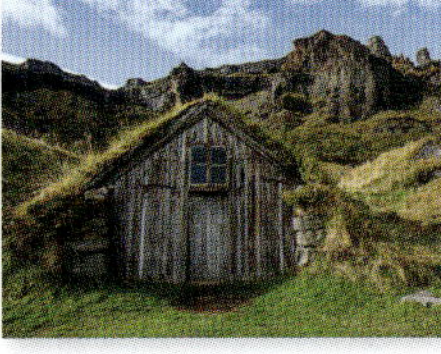

Original Image.

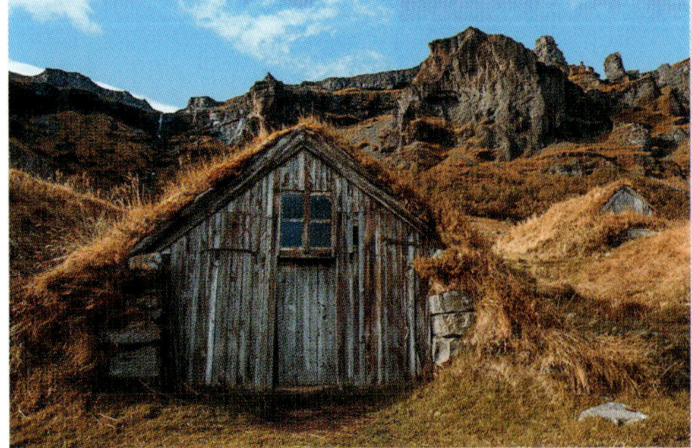

Teal and orange color effect created using Calibration.

Calibration can be effective any time you encounter an image where you do not like the overall color rendering and find that none of the profiles discussed earlier produce an acceptable result. The process I use starts with wildly swinging each **Hue** slider to figure out which direction produces a more pleasing image. I'll then move it in smaller increments to find an amount that is effective. Next, I'll move on to adjusting each of the **Saturation** sliders.

The **Tint** slider is designed to compensate for odd color casts that appear in the dark areas of some camera models and will only be effective on raw images.

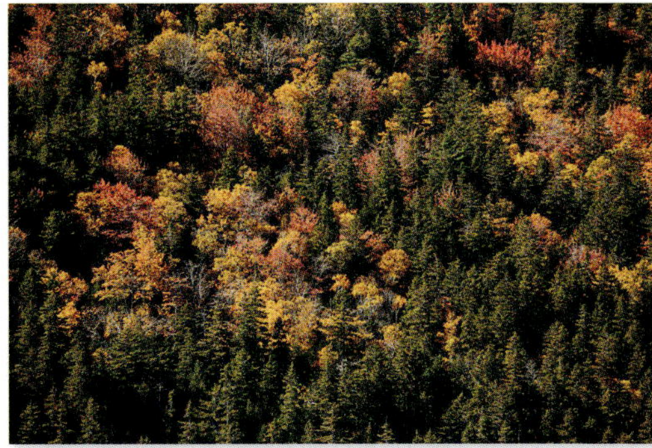

Image rendered with Calibration sliders zeroed out.

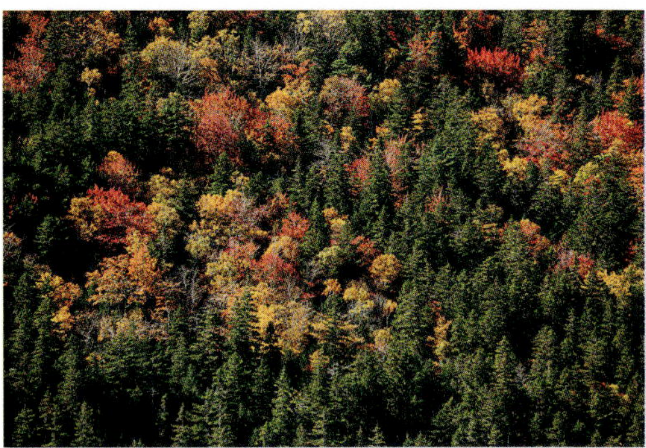

Image rendered with custom Calibration settings.

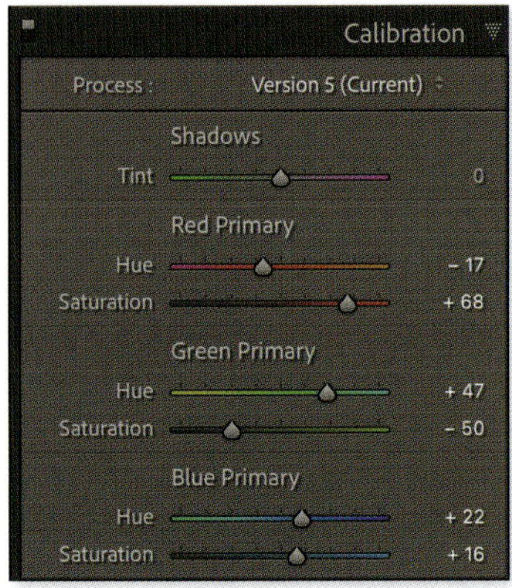

Calibration settings used to transform the image above and produce a more pleasing color rendering.

Section III: **Crafting a Photograph**

Selective Adjustments

Now that we've explored the adjustments that affect the entirety of an image, let's shift gears and look at the ones that work on isolated areas.

HSL/Color

This section of the Develop module offers sliders to isolate and adjust eight individual colors. The **Targeted Adjustment** tool **A** allows you to click and then drag vertically within the image to automatically target the color upon which you click. If the area where you click is somewhere between the colors available, the tool will adjust multiple sliders.

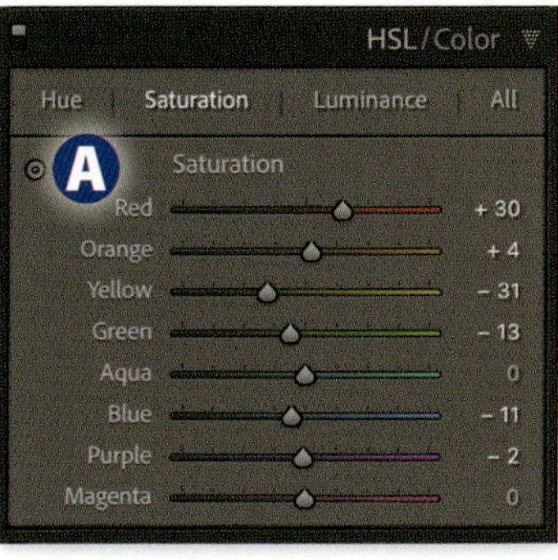

The sliders found in the **Hue** section control the basic color. The **Saturation** section controls how vivid the color will become and the **Luminance** section allows you to fine-tune the brightness. The **All** option will show the three other sections combined. This is especially useful when reviewing images to see if the HSL settings have been changed.

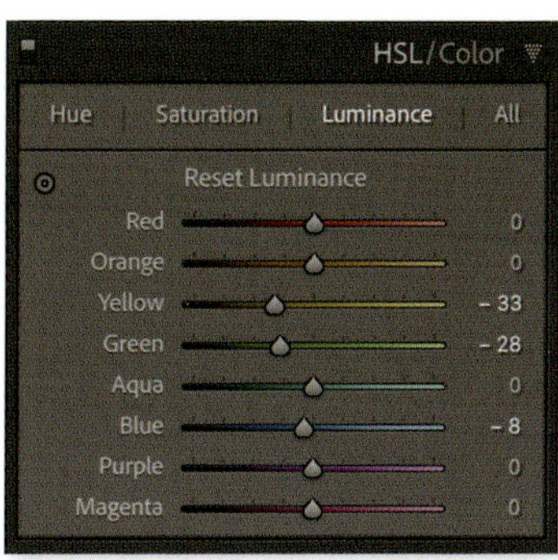

Be warned that indiscriminately swinging these sliders to their extremes without moving the surrounding colors a similar amount can easily produce abrupt and undesirable changes.

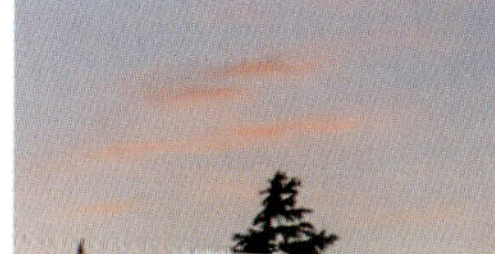
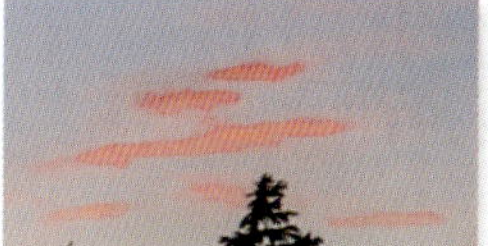

Before HSL/Color Adjustment.   *Red Saturation +100.*

Color Grading to Absorb Color

The **Color Grading** panel, which is covered in chapter 7, can be used in a somewhat counter-intuitive manner to lessen the amount of color in the highlight, midtone, or shadow areas of an image. All you have to do is find the color you'd like to absorb from within the appropriate color wheel and figure out which direction you'd need to move to end up at the center of the wheel **B**. Then take the circle that appears in the center of the color wheel and drag it in the same direction, toward the outer edge of the wheel **C**. For example, when you add yellow, blue will end up being lessoned in the process.

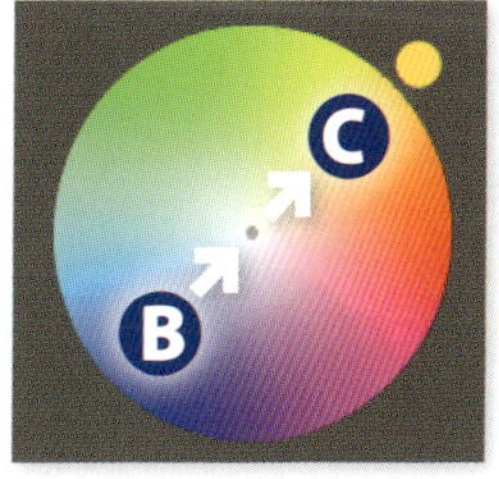

Now let's switch gears again and take a look at some specialty adjustments that can only be accomplished in Photoshop.

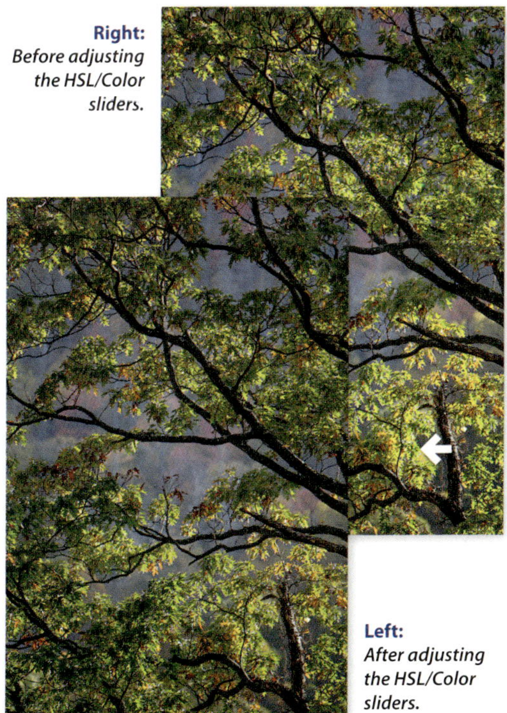

Right:
Before adjusting the HSL/Color sliders.

Left:
After adjusting the HSL/Color sliders.

Increase Color Variation

Monochrome areas (containing a single color) are easy to pass over because there's not much mental processing needed to understand what you're looking at. One method for attracting more attention is to introduce more varied color to the area. This will likely stop a viewer's eye, as it needs to linger in order to process the more complex color that's being experienced.

The following technique can be useful when you can see an almost imperceivable variation in color that you would like to become more pronounced. I'm not talking about a variation in brightness or color intensity. I'm talking about an area where some parts are more reddish, yellowish, greenish, or blueish than other parts. Any tiny variation in color can be exaggerated using Lab mode.

Convert to Lab Mode

Choosing **Image>Mode>Lab Color** in Photoshop will send your image into a special mode where color is separated from brightness behind the scenes. This will allow for certain specialized adjustments that are not possible when working in **RGB Color** mode.

Select Region

Make a selection of the area where you'd like to increase the color variation. This can be done with any selection tool and it does not have to be a precise selection. It just should not contain any hint of colors that are radically different from those you'd like to adjust. For example, make sure no hint of the sky is included when attempting to adjust a mountain.

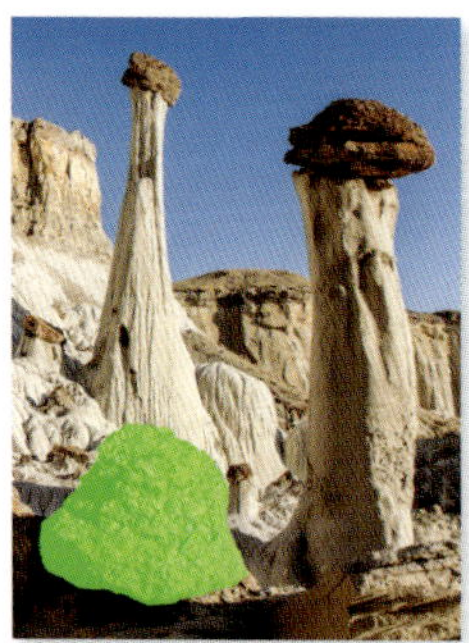

Green overlay represents the area that was selected in this example image.

Define Range in a and b Channels

Choose **Layer>New Adjustment Layer>Curves**, and choose **a** from the channel pop-up menu **A**. In order to adjust the area that was selected earlier, we need to add two points to the curve that precisely line up with the left and right edges of the histogram.

We'll go about that in a slightly odd way, by doing the following:

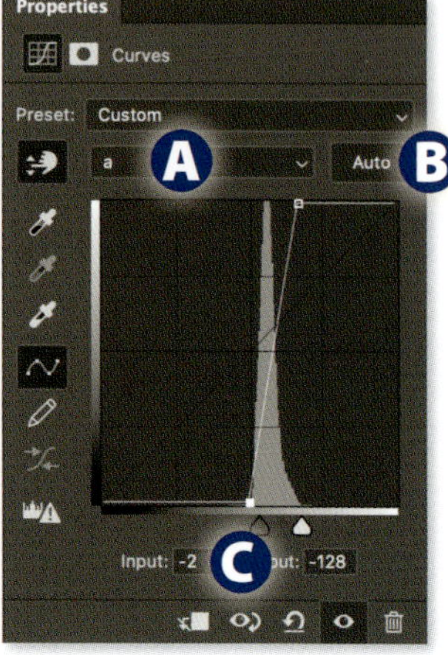

1) Click the **Auto** button **B**, which will cause the sliders below to snap to the edges of the histogram.
2) Press **+** on your keyboard to cause one of the two points on the curve to become active (solid white indicates active). Then note what number appears in the **Input** field below the curve **C**. Repeat this for the second point by pressing **+** again and noting the **Input** number.
3) Drag the two sliders that are found below the curve to their default locations, where the dark one ends up in the lower-left corner of the curve and the bright one is at the far right.
4) Click in the middle of the curve to add a point. Then enter the lower of the two numbers that you noted earlier into both the **Input** and **Output** fields below the curve.
5) Click in any area above the previously added point to add a second new point to the curve. Then enter the higher number you noted earlier to both the **Input** and **Output** fields below the curve.
6) Change the channel pop-up menu above the curve from **a** to **b** and then repeat the process detailed above to end up with a point aligned with the left and right edges of the histogram.

At this point, you should have added two new points on both the **a** and **b** curves that flank the width of the histogram and therefore target the precise color range that was found in the area you selected earlier.

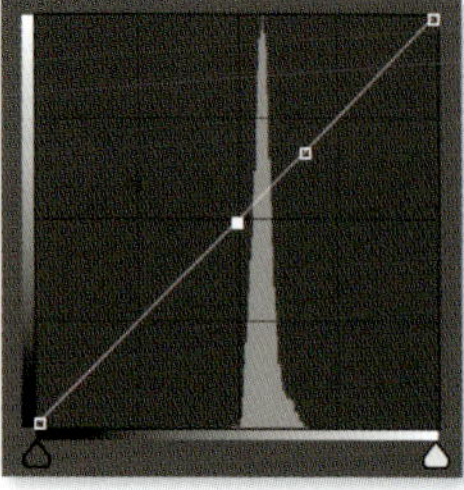

Section III: Crafting a Photograph

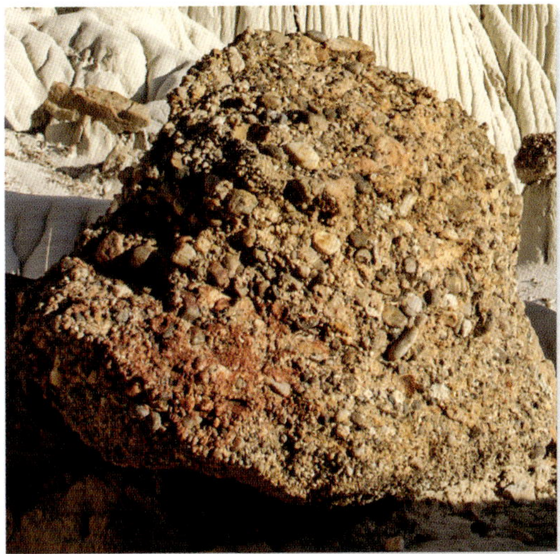

Largely monochromatic area before adjustment.

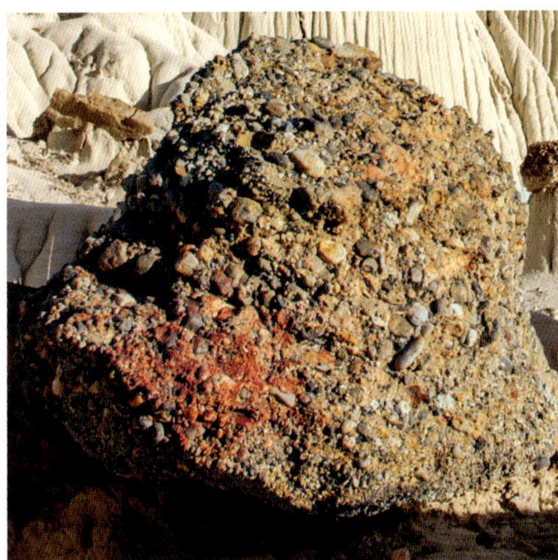

Result of applying Curves to a and b channels in Lab mode.

Increase Color Variation with Curves

Increasing the vertical separation between the two dots that were added earlier will cause the variation in color to increase. The **a** curve controls the variation of colors between green and magenta, while the **b** curve controls colors between blue and yellow.

I usually just glance at the area that was selected and ask myself which color should become more prominent, green or magenta. If the answer is green, then I move the lower point down; if it's magenta, then I'll instead move the upper point higher on the **a** curve.

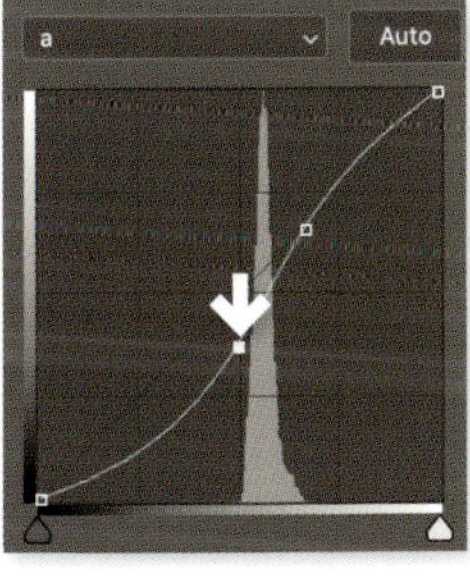

I then switch to the **b** curve and ask myself the same about blue and yellow. If the answer is blue, I move the lower point down. If it's yellow, then I'll instead move the upper point higher on the **b** curve. In the end, I almost always adjust both the **a** and **b** curves.

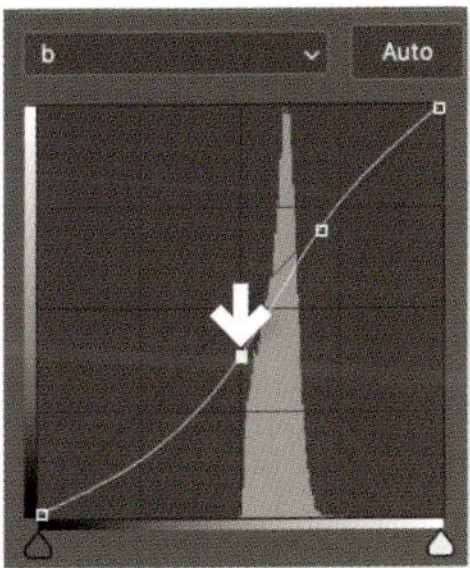

Fine-Tune Overall Color with Curves

I next select both points by holding **Shift** and clicking on whichever of the two points is not selected (it appears hollow instead of solid). Then I use the **up** and **down arrow** keys to change the position of both points. Doing so will shift the overall color of the area toward green and magenta or blue and yellow, depending on which of the two curves is active.

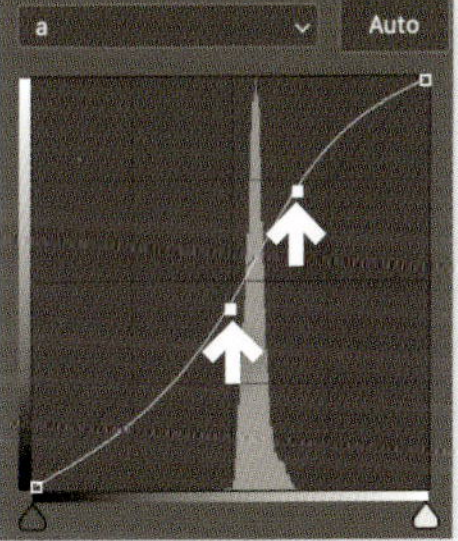

After finishing my adjustment of both curves, I re-evaluate the results and decide whether the change I made was dramatic enough, or if I need to tweak the curves to make the effect more or less radical.

Convert Back to RGB Mode

Once you're finished adjusting an image in **Lab** mode, choose **Image>Mode>RGB Color** to get it back into a more standard color mode where filters and adjustments will work in a more predictable fashion.

Becoming comfortable working in **Lab** mode comes only after working with dozens of images, and demands a lot a practice. There have been entire books written on just this subject, so don't feel bad if you're not comfortable right away.

Contrast of Color Intensity

It can be useful to isolate the not-so-colorful areas in a scene from those that contain vibrant color so you can then fine-tune the color, contrast, and brightness of those regions separately. This can be accomplished by installing an optional plug-in from Adobe that has been available for over twenty-five years.

Install HSL/HSB Plug-In

If you visit **https://tinyurl.com/HSLHSBplugin** you will find the Optional Plug-ins page on Adobe's website. That's where you'll find a special plugin, along with installation instructions, that is designed to add support for old and unusual file formats. It just happens to include the HSL/HSB plug-in, which can be used to isolate areas based on saturation.

Create Saturation Mask

With the plug-in installed, choose **Layer>New>Layer Via Copy**, then **Filter>Other>HSB/HSL**, and set the **Input Mode** to **RGB** and the **Row Order** to **HSB**. Applying this filter always produces a crazy-looking image that, at first glance, does not appear to be useful.

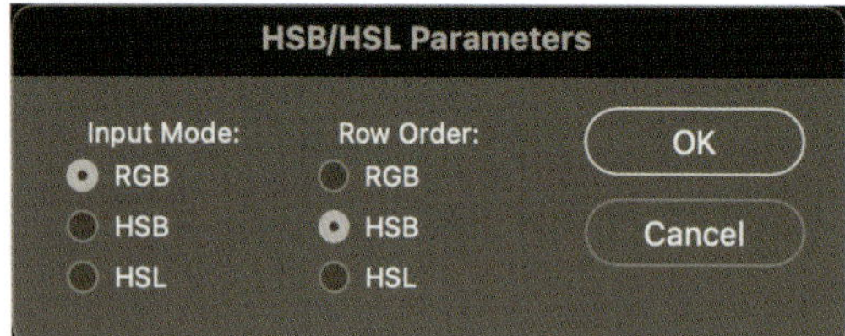
The HSB/HSL filter from the downloadable Optional Plug-ins.

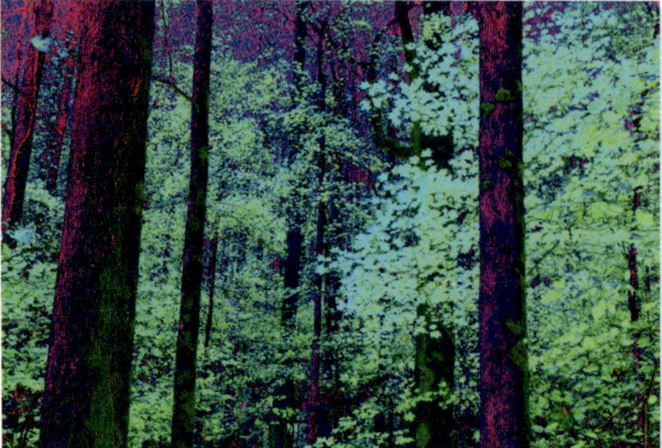
Result of applying HSB/HSL filter going from RGB to HSB.

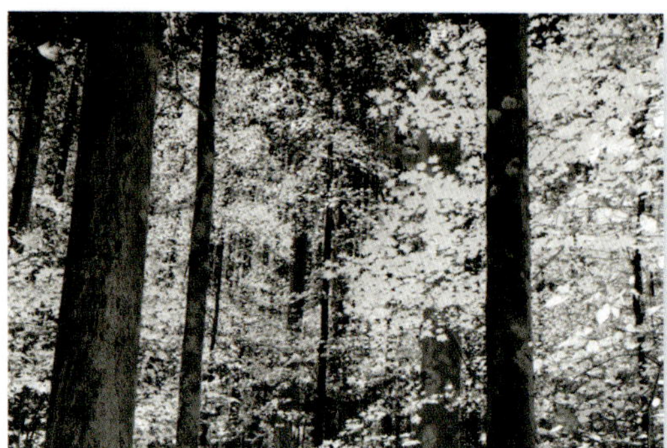
The Green channel contains a saturation mask.

However, inspect the contents of the **Green** channel in the Channels panel and you will see that the filter produced a channel that contains shades of gray. These shades represent how colorful areas were in the original image. White represents 100% saturation, black represents a neutral shade of gray, and everything in between reflects the saturation of each pixel in the image.

Adjust Mask

The most colorful areas can be fully isolated from the less colorful areas by choosing **Image>Adjustments>Levels** and setting the **Channel** pop-up menu to **Green A**. Then, move the upper-left slider until it is positioned at the end of the hump that appears on the left end of the histogram **B**. Move the upper-right slider to align with the center or left edge (depending on the level of isolation desired) of the hump that appears near the right edge of the histogram **C**.

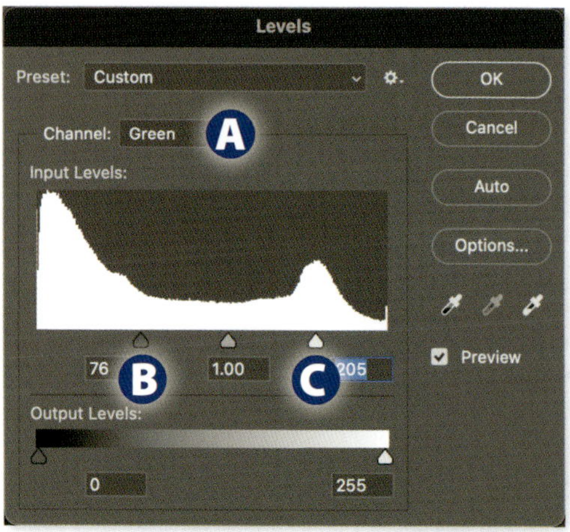
Levels settings used to isolate the most colorful areas.

Section III: Crafting a Photograph

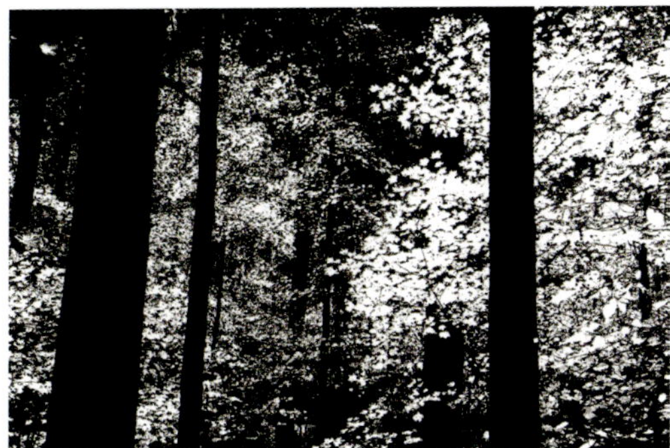

Result of applying Levels to the Green channel.

The histogram will look different for each and every image you work with, but you should find two prominent humps when working with an image that contains large areas of vivid colors combined with large areas that are not very colorful.

After applying **Levels**, the contents of the **Green** channel will display the vividly colored parts of the image as white, and this is what will be isolated if the result is used as a selection or mask. If you'd rather isolate the non-colorful areas in the image, then activate the **Green** channel and choose **Image>Adjustments>Invert**.

Adjust Using Green Channel as Mask

At this point, the layer that the filter was applied to has served its purpose. You can either drag the **Green** channel to the **New Channel** icon at the bottom of the Channels panel to duplicate it for later use, or drag it to the **Selection** icon to load it as a selection. Once you've done that, you can drag the layer to the trash. With the channel-generated selection active, you can then apply whatever changes you desire.

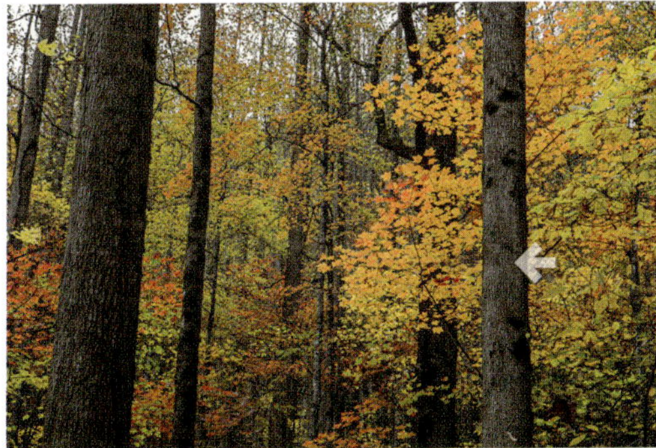

Original image before adjustment.

Example Adjustment

For the example image on this page, the non-colorful areas were isolated, and then a **Curves** adjustment layer was applied to increase contrast. That adjustment layer was then put inside of a group 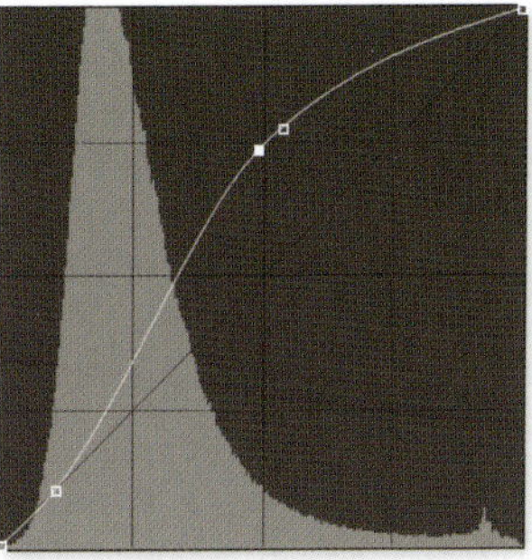and a second mask was used to limit the adjustment so that it only affected a few of the trees. The initial mask prevented the adjustment from applying to the vividly colored areas.

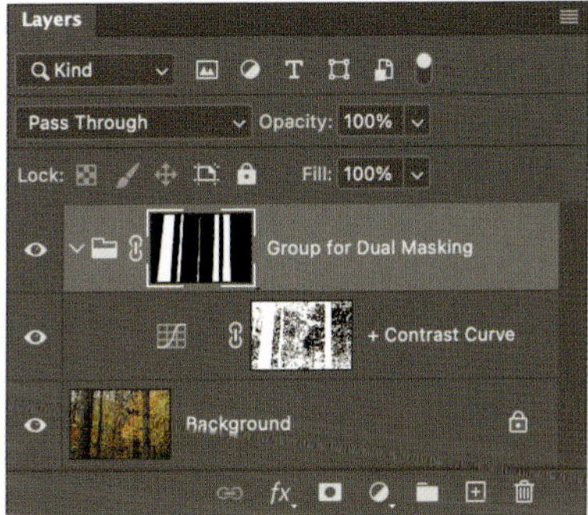

Mask attached to adjustment layer prevents adjustment from affecting colorful areas. Mask on group further limits adjustment to five trees.

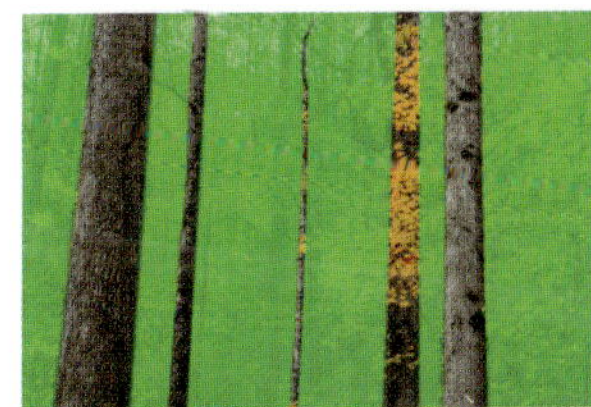

Mask overlaid to show the five trees being adjusted. Areas not covered in green include vividly colored areas that will not be affected since they are black in the initial mask.

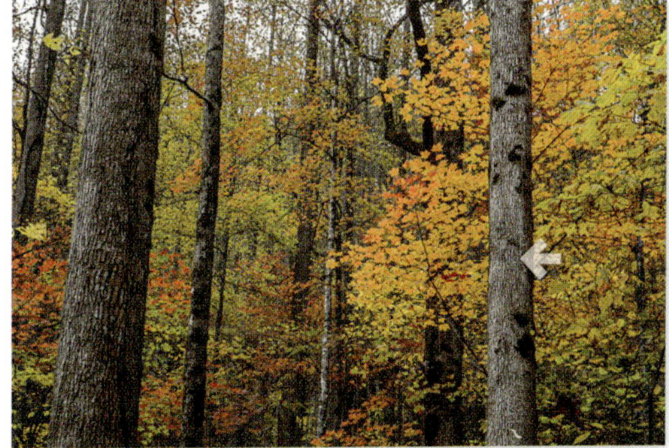

Result of isolating and adjusting the non-colorful areas.

Enhance Monochromatic Sunrises and Sunsets

During the golden hour, as the sun nears the horizon, the sky and the surroundings usually become awash with a show of color. When the sky is filled with primarily yellows and oranges, the following technique will allow you to fine-tune how those colors are rendered in the image.

Isolate Sky

Start by choosing **Select>Sky**, then hold the **Option** key (Mac) or **Alt** key (PC) and click the **Group** icon (folder icon) at the bottom of the Layers panel. Name the layer "Sky Adjustment," then choose **Layer>Layer Mask>Reveal Selection**. Now that layer mask will prevent any adjustment layers that end up inside the group from affecting anything other than the sky.

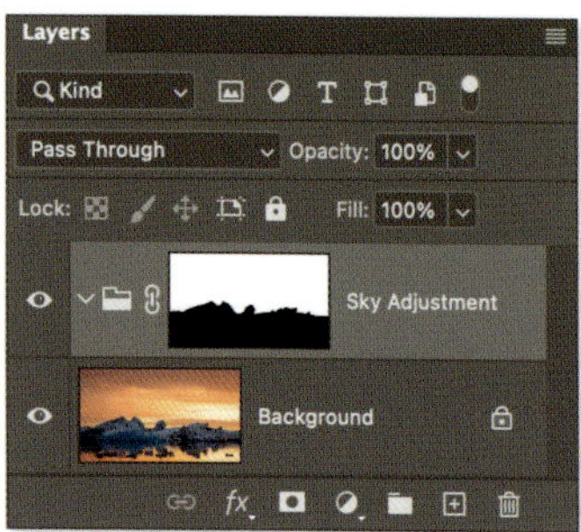

All adjustments to the sky will reside inside the group. This will cause the layer mask attached to it to limit where the adjustments can affect the image.

Adjust Midtone Color

To effectively adjust the sky, we'll need to think of it as being made out of three colors: the highlight color (which is most commonly yellow), the midtone color (which often is more orange), and the shadow color (which is often less colorful and sometimes contains a hint of purple).

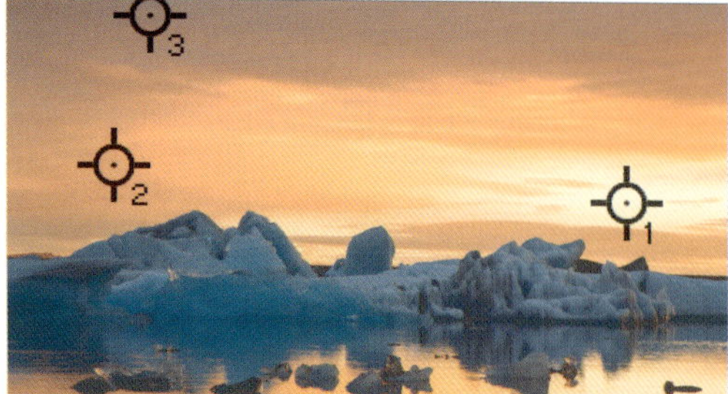

The sky can be divided up into three regions:
1) Highlights, 2) Midtones, and 3) Shadows.

We'll start with adjusting the color found in the midtone area by choosing **Layer>New Adjustment Layer>Color Balance** and leaving the **Tone** pop-up menu set to **Midtones**. Move the three sliders back and forth to find the setting that produces the most desirable color in the midtone area while ignoring any changes that happen in the shadows and highlights.

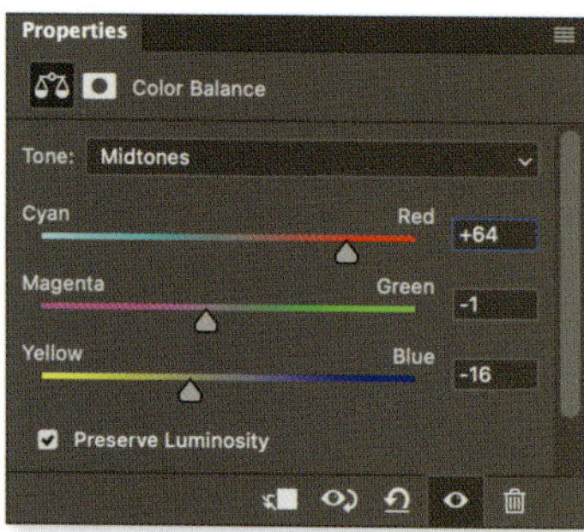

Color Balance was used to make the midtone color more saturated and orange in appearance.

Isolate and Adjust Shadow Area

To isolate the shadow area, choose **Layer>New Adjustment Layer>Hue/Saturation**, turn on the **Colorize** checkbox, and move the **Hue** slider to produce a color that is radically different than what was found in the sky. Now, let's get the bright areas of that layer to become hidden. Choose **Layer>Layer Style>Blending Options** and move the lower-right slider until the color only appears in the darkest areas **A**. Then hold **Option** (Mac) or **Alt** (PC), click on the right edge of the same slider, and drag to the right to split it into two halves. Fine-tune the position of the two halves until the result of the adjustment only affects the darkest areas and smoothly fades into the surrounding image **B**. Once that's been achieved, turn off the **Colorize** checkbox and then adjust the **Hue** and **Saturation** sliders until you like the appearance of the dark area.

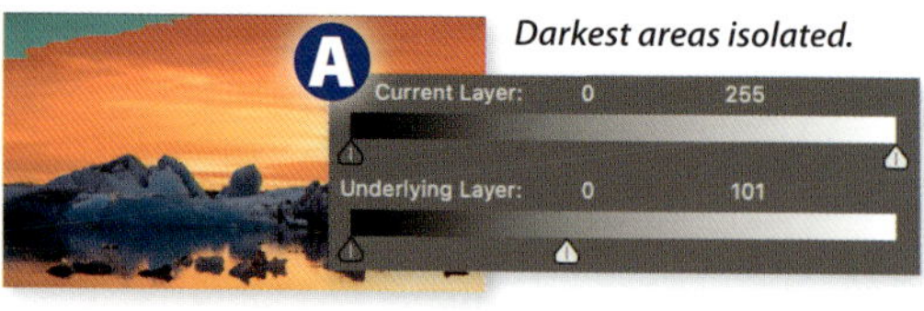

Darkest areas isolated.

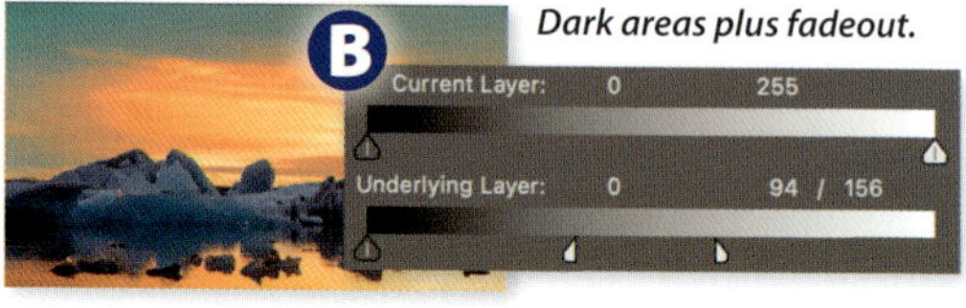

Dark areas plus fadeout.

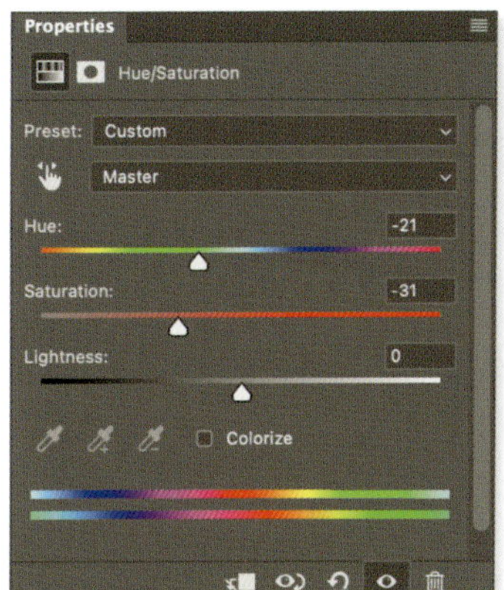

Hue/Saturation settings that were used to shift the dark area of the sky toward purple/magenta.

Once the bright areas have been isolated, turn off the **Colorize** checkbox and then adjust the **Hue** and **Saturation** sliders until you like the appearance of the bright areas. The **Lightness** slider can be also used on the highlights as long as the changes are tiny (±5 maximum).

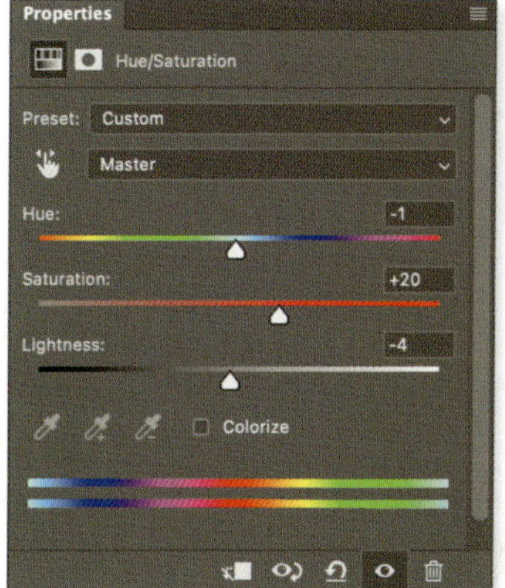

Hue/Saturation settings that were used to shift the bright area of the sky toward yellow/orange.

Isolate and Adjust Highlight Area

Repeat the last step, which involved creating a new **Hue/Saturation** adjustment layer, using **Colorize** to radically shift the colors in the image and then adjusting the blending options to limit where the adjustment can affect the image. But this time, isolate the bright areas **C**.

Bright areas plus fadeout.

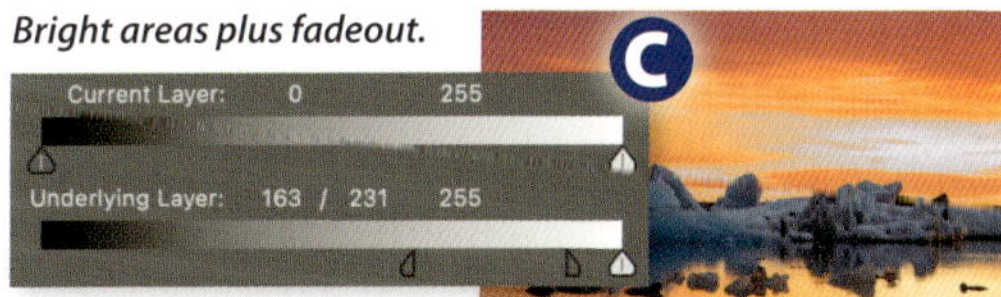

Include Reflections in Water

If the image contains water that is displaying a mirror image of the sky, then consider using **Select>Color Range** to select those colors, and paint with white on the mask that is attached to the group to shift those areas.

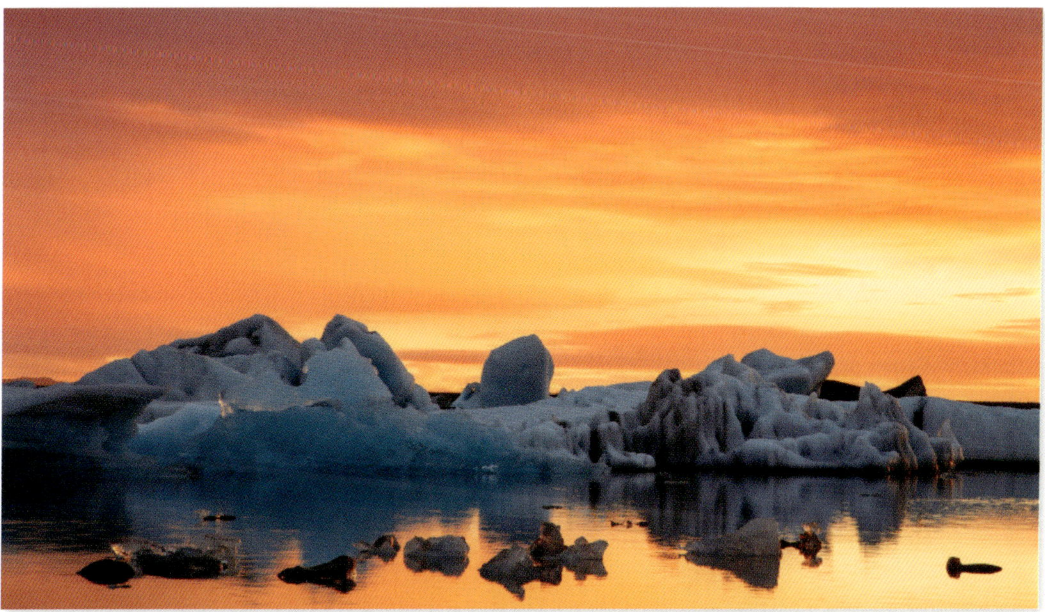

Result of adjusting all three areas of the sky to transform a previously monochromatic sky into one that has more color variation.

Learn to Visualize Color

What's going on with the color in an image is not always blatantly obvious. The following three visualization tools can be used to better educate yourself about the colors found in a photograph.

Saturation Map

A saturation map transforms an image into shades of gray where black represents an area that contains no color whatsoever (like the grays in a B&W photo). Progressively brighter shades of gray reflect the intensity of color in the rest of the image, with white representing fully saturated colors. But, mind you, there is no indication of how bright an area is or what specific colors would be found in the image.

1) Choose **Selective Color** from the **Layer> New Adjustment Layer** menu and then drag the layer mask attached to the resulting layer **A** to the trash icon at the bottom of the Layers panel.

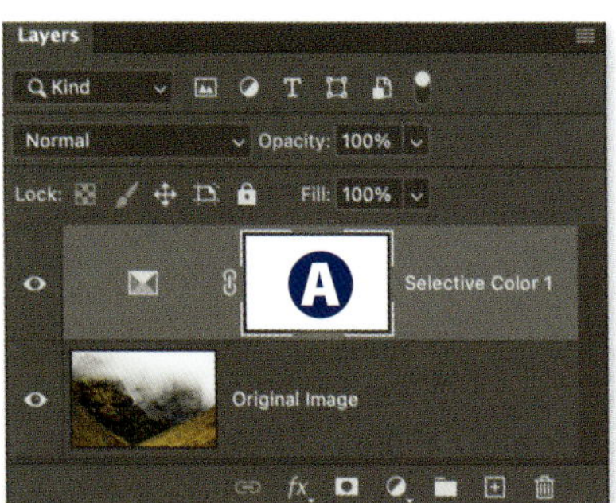

2) Choose the **Absolute** setting **B**, then move the **Black** slider to **-100** to brighten any areas that contain reds within the image.

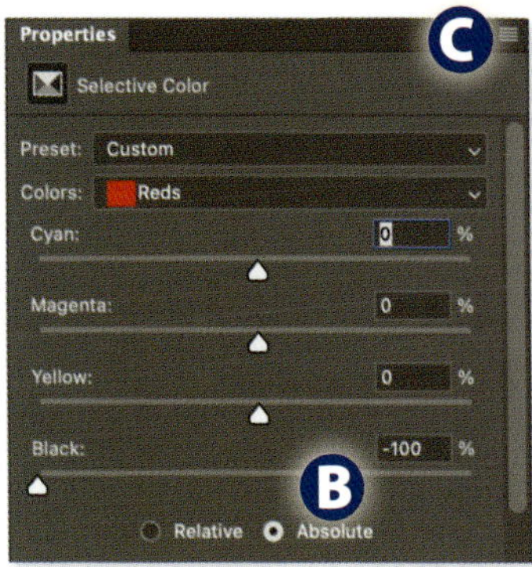

3) Change the **Colors** pop-up menu to the second color found in the list and then move the **Black** slider to **-100**. Repeat this process for all the vivid colors found within the **Colors** pop-up menu.

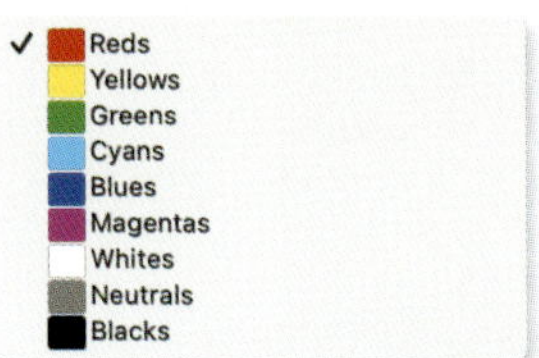

4) Cycle through the **Whites**, **Neutrals**, and **Blacks** choices in the **Colors** pop-up menu and set **Black** to **+100** for each of them.

The resulting grayscale image reveals all areas that contain color. You will often be surprised to find the presence of color in an area you previously believed to contain a neutral shade of gray, such as a snow-capped mountain.

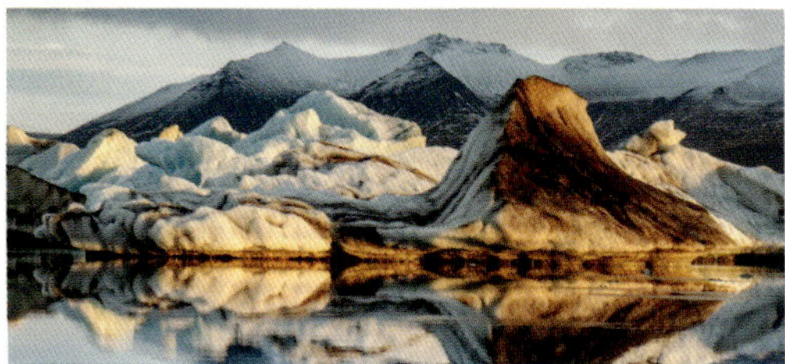

Source image for saturation map.

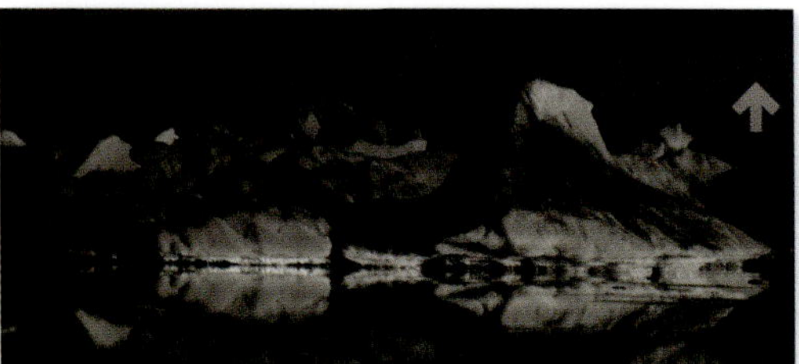

Resulting saturation map.

> **Tip:** *To make it easy to create saturation maps in the future, click on the hamburger menu **C** in the upper right of the Properties panel and choose **Save Selective Color Preset**. Name the preset "Saturation Map" and save it in the default folder that Photoshop brings you to so it will appear in the **Preset** pop-up menu the next time you create a **Selective Color** adjustment layer.*

Hue Map

A hue map will reveal which hues (the pure form of a color, ignoring brightness and saturation) are found throughout an image.

1) Choose **Layer>New Fill Layer>Solid Color** and name it "For Hue and Color Maps." When the color picker appears, set the **Hue** to **0°**, **Saturation** to **50%**, and **Brightness** to **50%**.

2) Drag the layer mask attached to the newly created layer to the trash icon at the bottom of the Layers panel and then drag the layer below the original image. If the original is on a layer called Background, then click the lock symbol on the right edge of that layer before attempting to change the layer stacking order.

3) Click on the original image layer and change the blending mode pop-up menu at the top of the Layers panel to **Hue**.

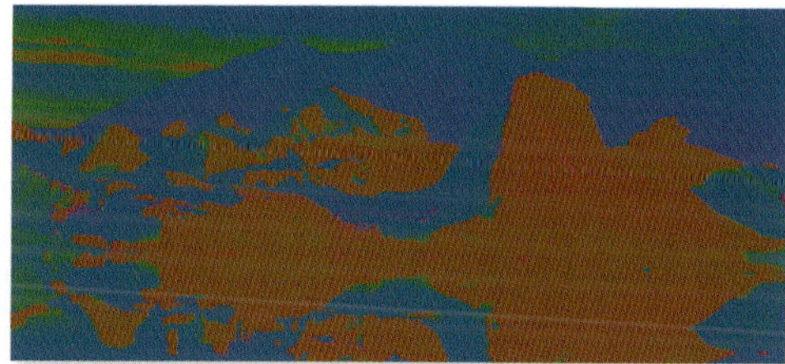

Hue map of the same image used in the previous example.

A hue map transforms the colors in an image to display them all at the same color intensity and brightness level. This makes it easier to determine the basic color of each area within the image. The only areas that will not appear in color are those that contain shades of gray, and therefore contain no hint of color whatsoever.

A hue map can be especially useful after a saturation map informs you that color is present in an area you previously thought to be neutral, as the hue map can be used to reveal which color is found in the area.

Just be aware that a hue map can be very misleading if you don't understand that it causes all colors to appear rather colorful and does not reflect how colorful the areas are in the actual photo.

Color Map

A color map is very similar to a hue map, in that it reveals which basic colors are found throughout the image, but it also reflects the saturation of the colors from the original image and displays them at a 50% brightness level.

The hue-map technique mentioned above can be transformed into a color map simply by changing the blending mode of the original image layer to **Color**.

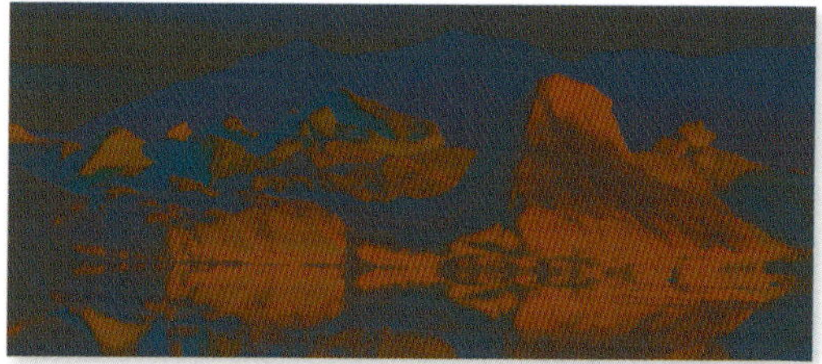

Hue map of the same image used in the previous example.

Real-World Examples

With the image used on a previous page, I was initially unaware that the white-capped mountains in the distance contained color. A saturation map made me aware of the color, so I switched to viewing a color map to learn which color was in the snow and just how colorful it was.

I then made an adjustment to lower the saturation of the blues in that area because I wanted the mountains to be relatively neutral.

A hue map revealed green in a few areas, but the saturation map made me decide against adjusting the areas, as there was so little saturation that I didn't think it would be noticed.

I don't use hue, saturation, and color maps on every image I work with, but I find them to be extremely useful when I want to be overly critical of the colors in an image, in preparation for making a large print that would be expensive to replace if I found an issue and wanted to do a reprint.

> **Note:** *The saturation map described on the previous page is very similar to the results achieved by the HSB/HSL filter that is covered earlier in this chapter. The difference is that the map will update interactively as you make changes to the original image layer.*

Chapter 9

Eliminate Processing Artifacts

THERE ARE HUNDREDS of adjustment, masking, and retouching techniques that have the potential to radically transform an image. Though they are generally useful, many of these choices tend to produce undesirable side effects that may not become apparent until you zoom in to closely inspect an image. If the presentation of your photographs is limited to social media, where images are presented at a small size, then many of the techniques in this chapter may not be needed. If, on the other hand, you plan to make large prints that may be inspected closely, then you'll likely want to study the techniques that follow and incorporate them into your daily workflow.

Over-Editing

Many of the adjustment sliders in Lightroom have a practical limit on how far they can be pushed before the quality of the resulting image starts to be compromised. Let's explore the most common issues you may encounter from over-editing an image and why it can occasionally be desirable.

Blown-Out Highlights

Moving the **Exposure**, **Highlights**, or **Whites** sliders to the right can potentially cause the brightest area of an image to be rendered as solid white. This is often referred to as "blowing out the highlights" because it causes areas that originally contained detail to be rendered with no detail whatsoever.

Blown-Out Light Sources

Light sources look great when rendered as solid white since it makes them appear radically brighter than anything else in the scene.

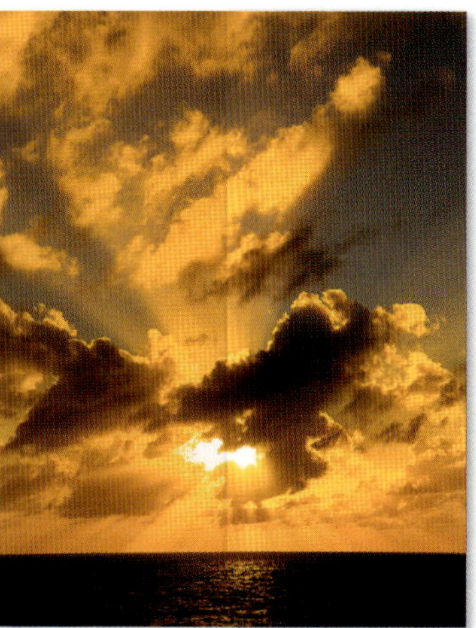

The left half of this image has been adjusted to retain detail in the highlights.

The right half has been adjusted to ensure that the brightest area is rendered as solid white, which helps make the light source appear extremely bright.

Water and other shiny surfaces may reflect light sources to produce what is commonly referred to as specular highlights, which also looks great as small areas of solid white. That's why waterfalls can benefit from pushing the **Whites** slider high enough to cause tiny areas to be rendered as solid white—it makes the water appear to be shiny.

> **Note:** *The term* specular *refers to a perfect mirror-like reflection of a light source.*

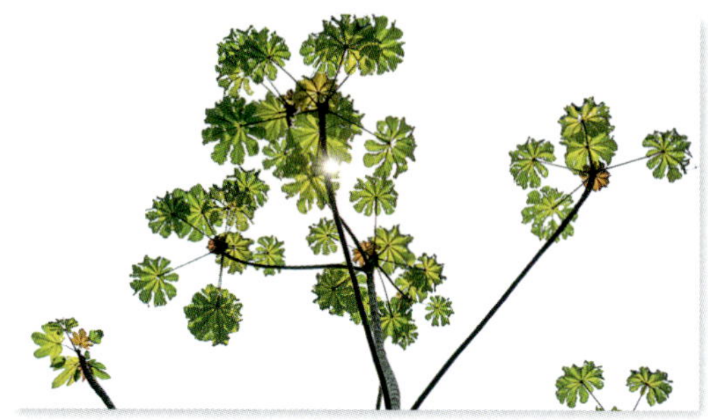

Blowing out the sky to solid white simplified this image.

Blow-Out to Simplify

I often blow out the highlights to render a sky as solid white in an effort to simplify an image. That way, I can present darker areas on a solid-white backdrop instead of showing detail across the entire image.

Unintentionally Blown Highlights

I always try to make it a conscious choice to blow out the highlights or render them with detail. If you're not careful, you can easily blow out the highlights unintentionally any time you boost the **Exposure**, **Highlights**, or **Whites** sliders. I use the following concepts when I want to ensure that the brightest area of an image retains detail.

Monitor the Histogram: The rightmost bar on the histogram represents the brightest area contained within an image. The position of that bar relative to the right edge of the histogram panel indicates how close it is to becoming solid white.

When the histogram does not extend all the way to the right, then the size of the gap to the right of the histogram indicates how much the highlights could be brightened before they would start to blow out and lose detail. The larger the gap, the more leeway you have to further brighten the image without losing detail.

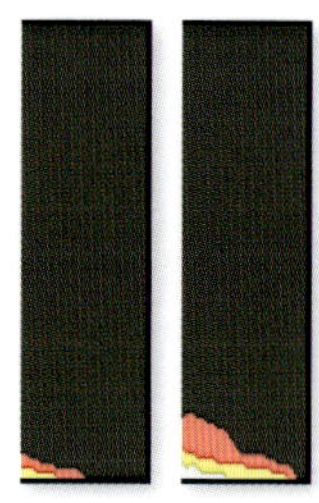

When the histogram extends all the way to the right of the area available, then the brightest area in the image is reaching its maximum brightness and detail is being lost in the highlights.

Section III: Crafting a Photograph

Behind the scenes, all images are made from varying amounts of red, green, and blue light. Because of this, there are three levels of potential detail loss depending on how many of those colors have reached their maximum brightness. The color of the rightmost bar indicates the extent of detail loss. A red, green, or blue bar indicates that only one of the three colors that make up the image is becoming blown out, while the other two colors still contain some hint of detail. A cyan, magenta, or yellow bar indicates that two out of the three colors are maxed out and therefore only one color contains any hint of detail. A white bar indicates that all three of the colors that make up the image are maxed out. Therefore, the brightest area has become solid white and contains no hint of detail whatsoever.

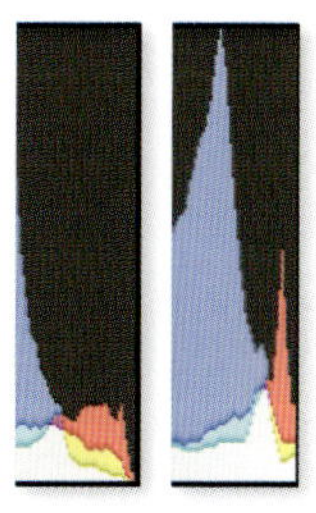

Left:
Red has reach its maximum.

Right:
All three colors reached maximum.

The height of the bar on the right edge of the histogram indicates how large of an area within the image is becoming blown out. That bar will usually be multi-colored with the white portion representing areas that are becoming solid white and the color representing other areas that are losing partial detail.

The histogram is a rather crude way to monitor what's going on in an image. After all, any camera that is capable of producing a raw file will capture over 4,000 brightness levels from a scene, which are then represented in a bar chart that contains only 256 bars. High-resolution camera sensors capture many millions of pixels, which are then represented using bars that max out at around 100 pixels tall. That's almost as bad as reproducing an image out of a few thousand LEGO® bricks that have a very limited palette of available colors. A histogram may represent your image, but it is not a very precise way of seeing what's truly happening.

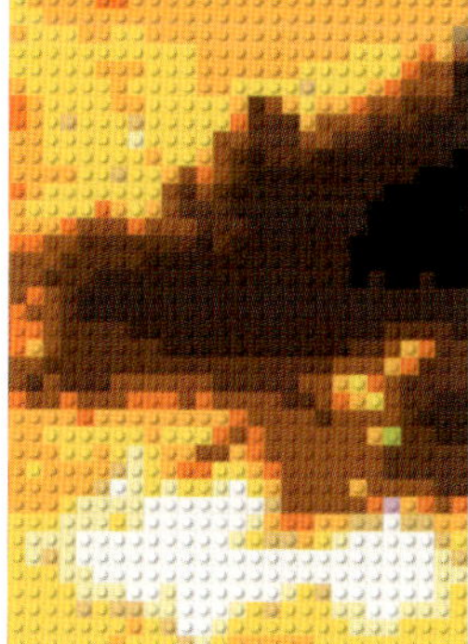

Portion of image shown on the previous page reproduced with LEGO® bricks.

Clipping Indicators: Clicking on the triangular icon found in the upper right of the histogram **A** will enable a feature known as the Clipping Indicators, which will cause a red overlay to appear anywhere within the image where solid white is found. This can be a good way to figure out if an adjustment is causing detail to be lost in the highlights of an image.

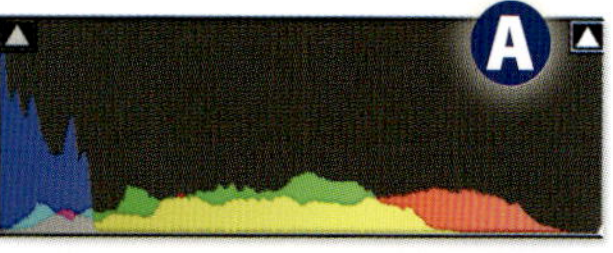

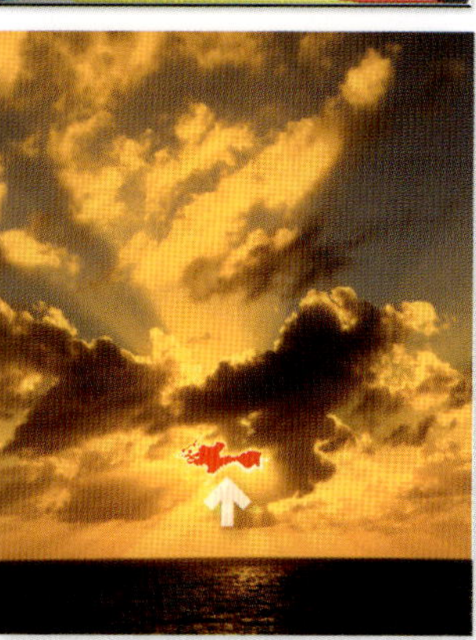

Clipping Display: The most precise, and therefore my personal favorite, method of determining if the **Exposure**, **Highlights**, or **Whites** sliders are causing detail loss in the brightness areas is to hold the **Option** key (Mac) or **Alt** key (PC) while moving any one of those sliders. This will change the appearance of the entire image to display black where there is detail in all three colors that make up the image behind the scenes. Color will be displayed where detail is being lost in one or two of the three colors that make up the image (the colors mean the same thing as they do in the histogram). White will be displayed where all three colors are being blown out and you therefore have solid white with no detail whatsoever.

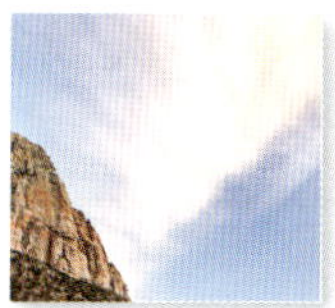

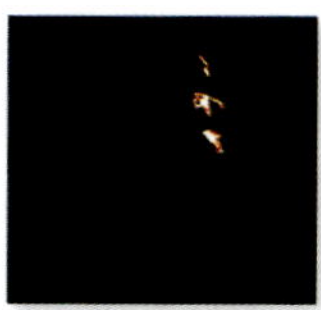

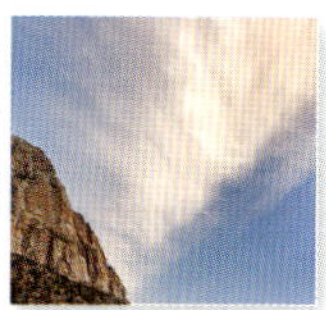

Image with small area of highlights blown out to solid white.

Clipping Display view showed precisely where detail was being lost.

Result of reducing Whites to prevent blown-out highlights.

The options we've covered so far are specific to Lightroom. When working in Photoshop, you can substitute any of the following techniques.

Histogram Panel: You can view a histogram in Photoshop by choosing **Window>Histogram**. To set it up in a similar fashion to the one found in Lightroom, choose **Expanded View** from the hamburger menu in the upper right and turn off the **Show Statistics** 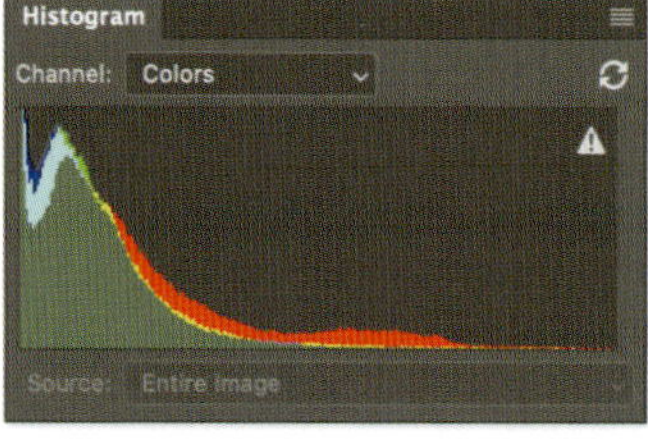 choice in the same menu. Finally, set the **Channel** pop-up menu above the histogram to **Colors**.

Levels Clipping Display: To produce a clipping display similar to what's found in Lightroom, click on the topmost layer, choose **Layer>New Adjustment Layer>Levels**, hold **Option** (Mac) or **Alt** (PC), and click the upper-right slider.

Interactive Clipping Display: If you like the clipping indicator available in **Levels** and want it to become interactive so you can make changes on the underlying layers and see it update in real time, then try the following: With the top-most layer 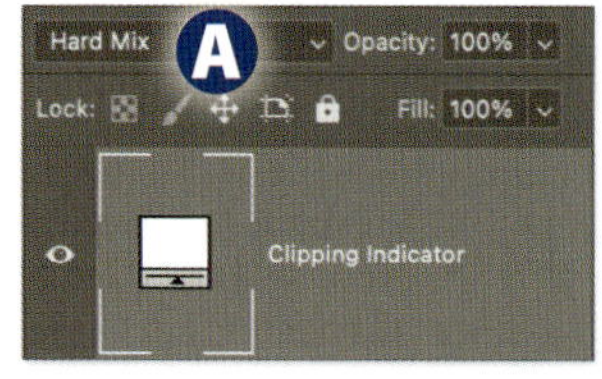 active, choose **Layer>New Fill Layer>Solid Color**, choose white when prompted, and then change the **Blending Mode** pop-up menu to **Hard Mix A**.

Threshold Layer: If the colors shown in the previous options are distracting, then choose **Layer>New Adjustment Layer>Threshold** and move the slider all the way to the right. This will display black where there is full detail and white where areas are blown out to solid white. 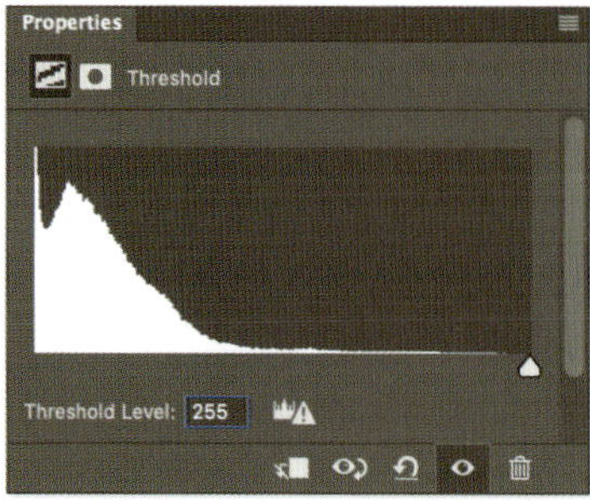

Clipped Shadows

Moving the **Exposure**, **Shadows**, or **Blacks** sliders to the left can potentially cause the darkest area of an image to be rendered as solid black. This is often referred to as "clipping" because the brightness levels in an image are recorded in a file as numbers that represent how much light is present. Once you hit zero (black) in one spot, any further darkening of the image "clips" off any variation in brightness to zero as areas get pushed to the minimum value and are not allowed to become any darker. The same is true on the bright end of the range where "blowing out the highlights" can also be described as "clipping the highlights" since they've reached their maximum value and can't be pushed any further.

Silhouetted Objects

One way to simplify an image is to render the dark areas as solid black in an effort to produce a recognizable solid-black shape (such as a tree or animal) known as a silhouette. This is primarily useful when the subject that will become black is backlit by the sun. When that's the case, it's as easy as lowering the **Blacks** slider until you can no longer see detail in the area. 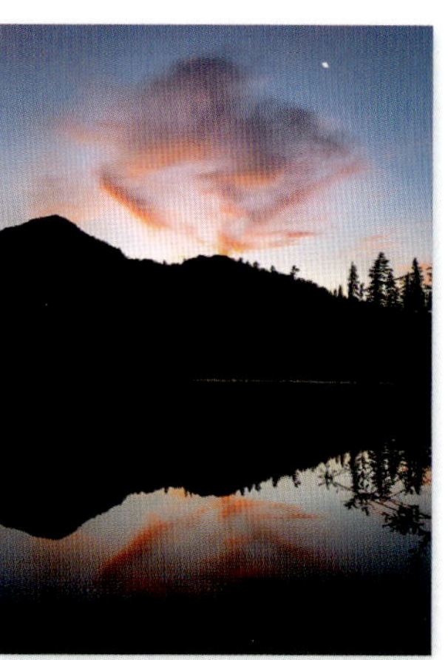

Consistent Shadow Density

If the absolute darkest area in a normal high-contrast image (as apposed to hazy, foggy, or highlight-heavy image) is not solid black, then the image will likely appear dull if viewed next to another image that does contain black. For this reason, I always try to ensure that a tiny area of most images is adjusted to become solid black. This can usually be accomplished by holding **Shift** and double-clicking on the **Blacks** slider. Doing so will cause Lightroom to automatically adjust the **Blacks** slider to ensure a tiny area becomes solid black.

Section III: Crafting a Photograph

Unintentionally Clipped Shadows

If you're not careful, you can unintentionally clip the dark areas any time you lower the **Exposure**, **Shadows**, or **Blacks** sliders. The same controls that I covered earlier when discussing highlight detail in this chapter are also available to monitor clipping of the dark areas in an image. Here are a few differences between monitoring the status of the highlights and shadows:

- When monitoring the histogram, inspect the far-left end, which represents the darkest area of the image. A histogram that does not extend all the way to the left edge of the histogram panel indicates that the image does not contain black.
- Clicking the triangular icon in the upper left of the histogram will cause its outline to change from dark to bright, indicating the shadow Clipping Indicator has been enabled. This will cause a blue overlay to appear within the image where the shadows are clipped to zero. The triangular icon will also change in appearance. It will be dark gray when full detail is present in the darkest area. It will change to a color when one or two of the three colors that make up the image behind the scenes gets clipped. It will become a light shade of gray when all three colors are clipped and therefore the darkest area is solid black.
- Holding **Option** (Mac) or **Alt** (PC) while moving the **Shadows** or **Blacks** sliders will invoke the Clipping Display. This will change the appearance of the entire image to display white where there is detail in all three colors that make up the image. Color will be displayed where detail is being lost in one or two of the three colors that make up the image (the colors mean the same thing as they do in the histogram). Black will be displayed where all three colors are being clipped and you therefore have solid black and no detail whatsoever.
- In Photoshop, make the following changes to monitor clipping of the shadows instead of the highlights: In **Levels**, **Option-click** (Mac) or **Alt-click** (PC) the upper-left slider instead of the upper-right slider. In **Threshold**, move the slider all the way to the left instead of the right. For the interactive clipping display, choose white instead of black.

You don't need to remember every single option for determining whether your highlights or shadows are being clipped. It's just good to know the available options, try them out, and then pick a favorite method to rely on long-term.

Limited Adjustments

More often than not, the clipping indicators are simply a signal that prompts me to start using masked adjustments to prevent further brightness adjustments from causing the extremely bright or dark areas to lose detail. That way, the risk of highlight or shadow clipping will not limit the extent to which the image can be brightened or darkened.

> **Note:** *The clipping display that is available by holding **Option** (Mac) or **Alt** (PC) when clicking some of the adjustment sliders does not work when applying the same sliders via a masked adjustment. For that reason, I keep an eye on the histogram or use the triangular Clipping Indicator icons in the corners of the histogram to figure out when a masked adjustment might cause highlight or shadow detail to be clipped.*

Unrealized Contrast

When I think I'm done with an image and am about to stop working on it, I double check the **Blacks** and **Whites** sliders and the clipping indicators as a finishing technique.

To check the dark area, hold **Option** (Mac) or **Alt** (PC) and adjust the **Blacks** slider to ensure a tiny area is solid black, or just hold **Shift** and double-click the slider for an automated adjustment if you're in a hurry.

Anytime I see a sizable gap on the right end of the histogram, I move the **Whites** slider while inspecting the histogram, and stop once the gap is gone. I then evaluate the image, thinking of that as the maximum setting I should use, and then lower it to see which setting makes the image look its best. This process often results in a better-looking image for me. I usually reserve solid white for light sources and their reflections on shiny surfaces.

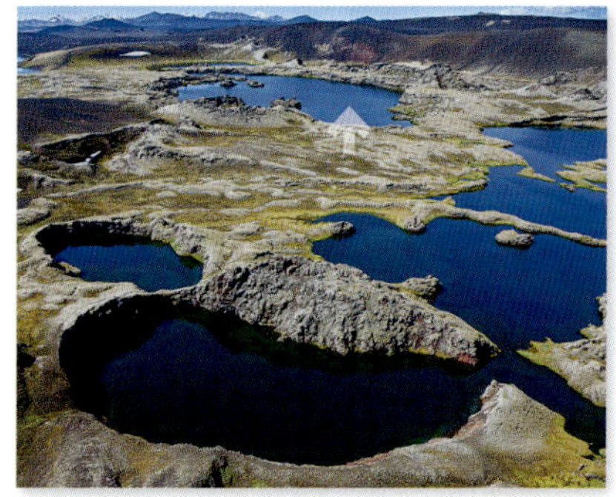

Setting Vibrance to +58 caused the water to become too colorful.

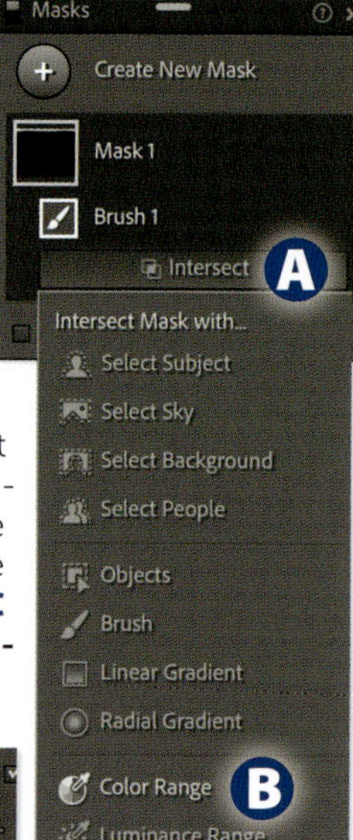

Result of moving the Blue slider to -40 in the Saturation section of the HSL/Color panel.

Excessive Vibrance

The **Vibrance** slider was designed to not only make the colors in your image more vivid, but to also improve the look of skies. That's accomplished by darkening and more aggressively boosting the color of anything that is blue. You'll need to be cautious when blue appears anywhere other than the sky. Use one of the following methods any time the blues in your image look to be unnatural due to excessive **Vibrance**.

HSL/Color Panel: Open the **HSL/Color** panel in Lightroom's Develop module. In the **Saturation** category, move the **Blue** slider to the left in order to cause just the blues to become less colorful. You may also need to move the **Blue** slider under the **Luminance** category to the right in order to compensate for the darkening caused by **Vibrance**.

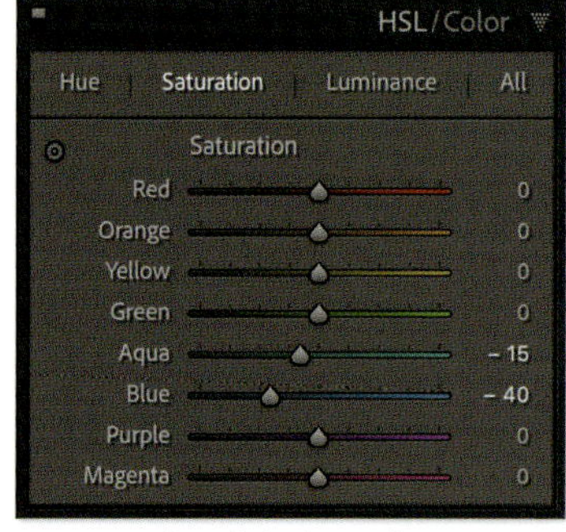

Masked Adjustment: When the special treatment of blue is beneficial in one area but undesirable in another, then consider masking the undesirable area and moving the **Saturation** slider to the left to make the area less colorful.

If you want the adjustment to affect only the blues within the masked area, hold **Option** (Mac) or **Alt** (PC), click the **Intersect** button below the active mask in the **Masks** panel **A**, and choose **Color Range** **B**. Click on an area within the masked part of the image that contains blue and fine-tune the **Refine** setting above the adjustment sliders **C** before adjusting the **Saturation** slider.

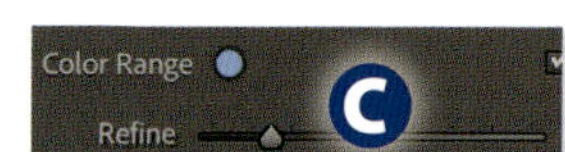

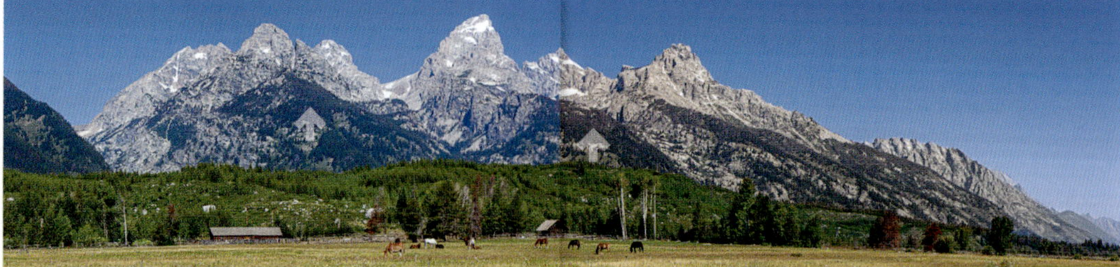

Left Half: *Setting Vibrance to +41 caused the atmospheric haze in the mountains to become unnaturally colorful.*
Right Half: *Result of using a masked adjustment to lower saturation and shift the white balance of the mountains.*

Section III: Crafting a Photograph

Excessive Saturation

This is an issue that only rears its head once you want to use an image outside of Lightroom's Develop module. It can be as simple as opening an image in Photoshop, printing from within Lightroom, exporting to a standard file format such as JPEG or TIFF, or even viewing an image in Lightroom's own Library module. In those cases, pushing the **Saturation** (or even **Vibrance**) slider too far can cause the colorful areas within an image to lack detail.

Lightroom's Develop Module Color Space

The reason for potential detail loss comes down to a few technical concepts related to how color is reproduced in Lightroom and other programs. As I've mentioned many times before, behind the scenes, all your images are constructed from a mix of red, green, and blue light. You can see this first hand by visiting the Develop module, hovering over a color within your image, and looking just below the histogram, where the exact amount of red, green, and blue being used is displayed.

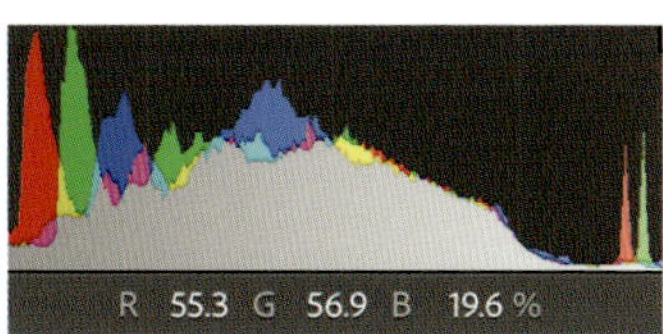

Red, Green, and Blue color mix.

But those numbers are not quite enough to precisely describe a color. We also need to know the precise color of red, green, and blue that is being used. Just as you can measure distance in miles, meters, or microns, you can describe color using different versions of red, green, and blue. The particular set of red, green, and blue colors used to construct an image is known as the image's color space, which is referred to by a name such as ProPhoto RGB, Adobe RGB, or sRGB.

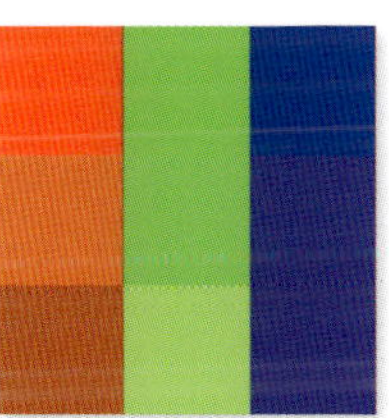

The relative difference between the most common RGB color spaces (top to bottom): ProPhoto RGB, Adobe RGB, sRGB.

Lightroom's Develop module uses very vivid versions of red, green, and blue, collectively known as ProPhoto RGB. This not only allows it to reproduce all the colors that your camera is capable of capturing, but it also allows you some leeway for adjusting your images to make the colors even more vivid.

Converting to Different Color Spaces

When you send an image outside of Lightroom, it may end up being converted to a different color space, as ProPhoto RGB is not commonly used by the general public. Converting to a different color space means that the image will be constructed from less vivid versions of red, green, and blue. But that doesn't necessarily mean that its appearance will change in the process.

You can think of it like converting between different sweeteners in a cooking recipe. Imagine professional chefs have access to a special sweetener that is not commonly available to the general public and is ten times as sweet as sugar. When they share a recipe with the public that calls for one cup of the special sweetener, they have to convert that to ten cups of sugar so the general public can use the recipe and get the same results.

Saturation Clipping

But unlike sweetener, which can be used in unlimited quantities, the RGB numbers that describe the colors within our images max out at 100% and can go no higher.

The color space used in Lightroom's Develop module is made from versions of red, green, and blue that are much more vivid than the most popular color space, which is sRGB (see the relative difference between ProPhoto and sRGB at left). That difference can result in undesirable consequences when an image is exported to a JPEG file in the sRGB color space (the most common setup for files used on the internet).

Imagine a photo of a red rose where moving across the most vivid areas displays numbers for red between 92% and 99% below the histogram. Then consider that sRGB uses a red that is only 85% as saturated as the red found in ProPhoto RGB. That means you'd need to use 108–116% red in sRGB to reproduce that rose without changing its appearance (after all, 85% of 108 is 92, and 85% of 116 is 99). But the numbers can't go that high and therefore the amount of red across the rose would end up being clipped to the maximum value of 100%. This would cause detail to be lost (red would be clipped, but there would potentially still be detail found in the green and blue that makes up the image). The rose would also become less colorful since 100% red in sRGB is less colorful than 92% red in ProPhoto RGB.

Hopefully this gives you the sense that changing from one color space to another can potentially cause issues for some technical reason that you really don't want to think about.

But don't get too worried about it, as this is usually only an issue for images that contain overly vivid colors. As you boost the saturation, the amount of red, green, or blue is increased to make one or more of those colors more prominent, and it's only when you push them beyond what can be reproduced in a smaller color space that you might see the colors shift when you export. More detail about color spaces, sending an image to Photoshop, and exporting are found in chapter 2 of this book.

Previewing a Destination Color Space

If you know an image will need to be saved in a color space other than ProPhoto, then you may want to use a feature called Soft Proofing in order to preview what the result will look like and fine-tune the image to optimize it for the destination color space.

To preview the result of a conversion to another color space, head to the Develop module, choose **View>Soft Proofing> Show Proof**. Set the **Profile** pop-up menu to the desired color space, and set the **Intent** to **Perceptual** in the area below the histogram.

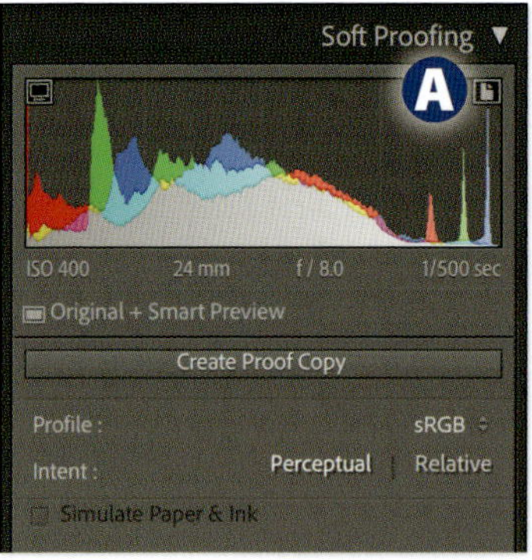

Enabling Soft Proofing will cause the histogram to reflect the result of a conversion to the destination color space. A histogram that extends all the way to the end of the area available and displays a tall color spike on the end is an indication of potential saturation clipping. You can then see where within the image such clipping occurred

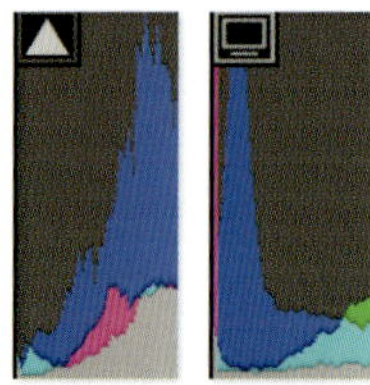

Histogram before and after enabling Soft Proofing. A tall spike indicates potential saturation clipping.

by choosing **View>Soft Proofing>Destination Gamut Warning** or clicking the icon that appears in the upper right of the histogram **A**.

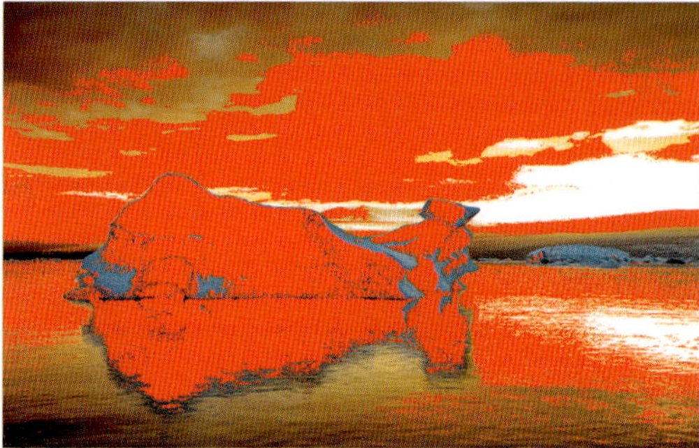

Result of enabling the Destination Gamut Warning.

The red overlay represents areas where colors were more colorful than what can be represented in the color space that is being previewed. I suggest typing **Shift-S** to toggle the visibility of the overlay, and typing **S** a few times to toggle the Soft Proofing feature off and back on again so you can evaluate how a conversion to the destination color space will affect the colors within the image. Just keep in mind that nobody else will be able to see this overlay and it does not mean that the color shift being made will even be noticeable. Those are just the areas you should evaluate with a critical eye as you toggle Soft Proofing on and off to see if they need to be further optimized in order to have them be satisfactorily rendered in the destination color space.

Optimizing for Destination Color Space

If you move any of the adjustment sliders while Soft Proofing is enabled, Lightroom will prompt you to choose between the following options.

Undo: Reverts the image to the state it was in when you first enabled Soft Proofing.

Make This a Proof: Allows you to continue adjusting the image; records the **Profile** and **Intent** settings in the **Copy Name** field, which can be seen in the Library module's **Metadata** panel; and automatically reloads those settings any time you view the image while Soft Proofing is enabled.

Create Proof Copy: Creates a Virtual Copy in order to preserve the appearance of the image and produce a dedicated copy that can be optimized for the color space being previewed. As with the

Section III: Crafting a Photograph

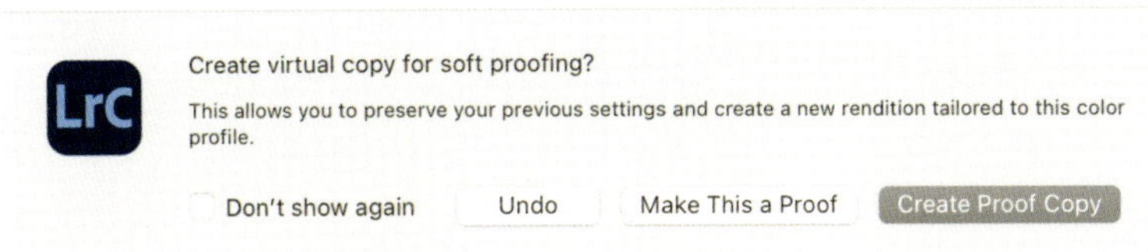

Moving any of the adjustment sliders while Soft Proofing is enabled will prompt Lightroom to ask if you'd like to create a virtual copy to contain the color space–specific adjustments, or if you'd like to directly adjust the original by choosing Make This a Proof.

previous option, this will save the Soft Proofing settings and reload them any time the feature is enabled in the future.

If you would rather not have to make this choice every time you attempt to adjust an image while Soft Proofing is enabled, turn on the **Don't show again** checkbox, and then click either **Make This a Proof** or **Create Proof Copy** to define it as the default setting.

I often use the sliders found in the **HSL/Color** panel to fine-tune any colors that shifted in an undesirable way. The goal is not to get the red overlay to completely disappear, but to simply make sure the colors are acceptable while Soft Proofing is enabled.

Saturation Clipping in Photoshop

There are two general methods for determining where colors are being clipped due to excessive saturation when working in Photoshop.

Existing Color Space: Images that have been sent from Lightroom to Photoshop will end up in whatever color space is specified in Lightroom's **External Editing** preference. To see if any areas are clipped in the current color space, choose **Layer>New Fill Layer>Solid Color**, choose white for highlight clipping or black for the shadows, and then change the blending mode pop-up menu at the top of the Layers panel to **Hard Mix**. Clipped areas will appear as colors surrounded by solid black or white.

Preview Alternative Color Space: If you plan to convert to a different color space, then you can preview the results using a feature that is equivalent to Lightroom's Soft Proofing by choosing **View>Proof Setup>Custom**. To toggle the preview on and off, choose **View>Proof Colors**, or type **Command-Y** (Mac) or **Ctrl-Y** (PC). Then choose **View>Gamut Warning**, or type **Shift-Command-Y** (Mac) or **Shift-Ctrl-Y** (PC) to see where the colors have shifted as a gray overlay (just like the red overlay available in Lightroom).

Unnatural Reflections

If you ever isolate the lower portion of an image and increase its brightness, pay attention to how such a change affects areas that contain water. Water will look unrealistic if it appears to be able to magically amplify the amount of light falling on its surface.

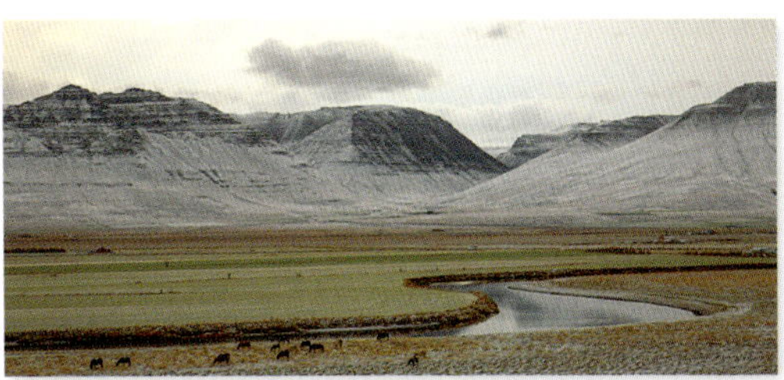

Originally, the sky was brighter than the reflection it produced in the stream that appears in the lower portion of this image.

So, if you're going to brighten the lower part of an image and it includes a reflection on water, consider either brightening the sky (if it's what's being reflected) to at least match the brightness of the reflection, or limit how much the reflection is brightened. This can also become an issue when a sky is darkened dramatically and reflections are not adjusted in a similar fashion.

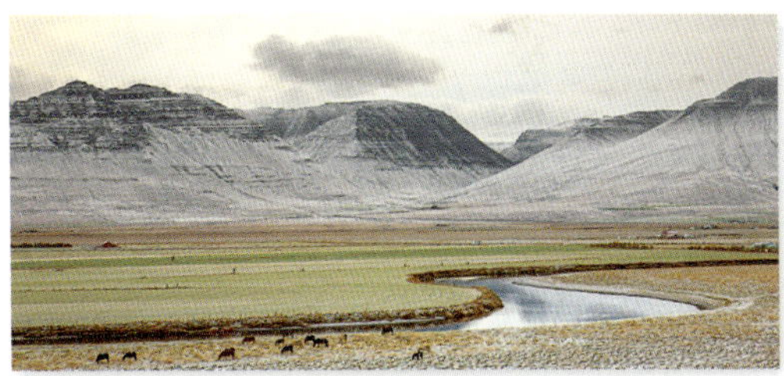

The lower portion of this image has a masked adjustment applied that brightened the reflection and rendered it brighter than the source of the reflection.

This particular idea might be a pet peeve of mine since many people would never notice. But when I see an image with unnatural-looking reflections, my brain automatically switches gears and starts to analyze how the image was processed, as opposed to simply enjoying the image as a whole.

Unevenly Lit Skies

If you find yourself moving the **Highlights**, **Shadows**, **Clarity**, or **Dehaze** sliders up quite a bit, then be sure press the \ key multiple times to toggle between the before and after versions of the image (or press and hold the \ key for a temporary preview) to see if the sky ended up with any unnaturally dark areas. Those particular adjustments can tend to make the central portion of the sky unnaturally dark, especially on images that feature objects extending into the sky, such as trees or mountain peaks. There are two general methods for fixing such issues.

Adjust Sky with Opposite Adjustment Values

All of the adjustments mentioned above can be counteracted by applying opposite values via a sky mask. For instance, let's say you applied **Highlights -60** to the image as a whole in Lightroom's Basic panel. You can then isolate the sky via a mask and apply **Highlights +60** in order to cancel out that global change to effectively end up with a setting of **Highlights 0** in the sky. Doing this with all of the potentially problematic sliders mentioned above should smooth out most unnatural-looking skies.

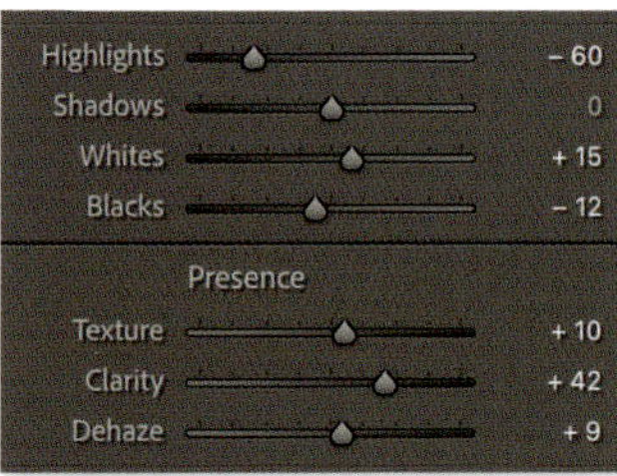

Settings applied in the Basic panel of Lightroom's Develop module.

Highlights, Shadows, Clarity, and Dehaze have the potential to produce an uneven sky.

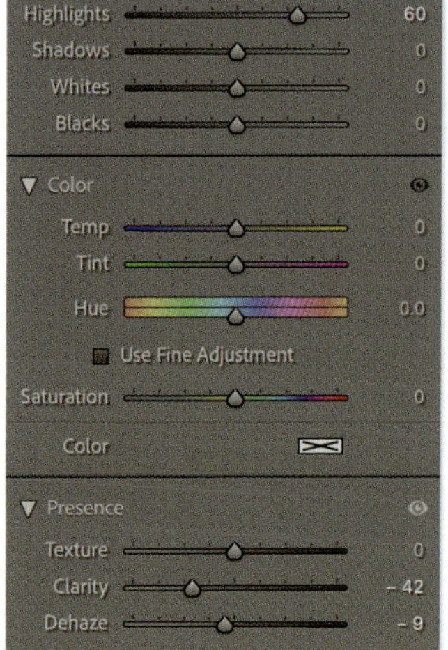

The adjustments applied to the image as a whole via the Basic panel can be canceled out by applying opposite values of the same sliders in a masked adjustment.

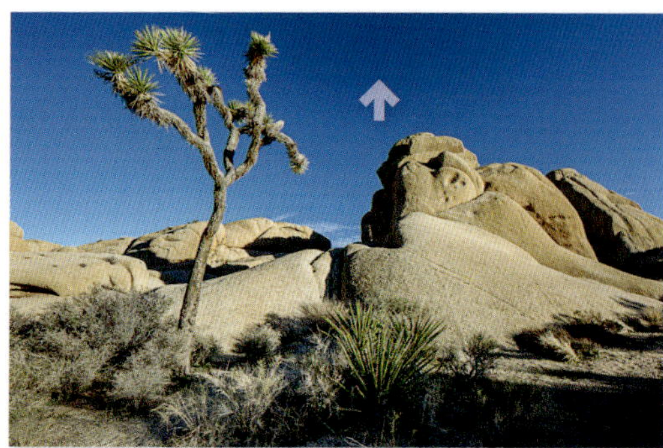

The unnaturally dark area in the middle of this sky was caused by the settings that were applied in the Basic panel.

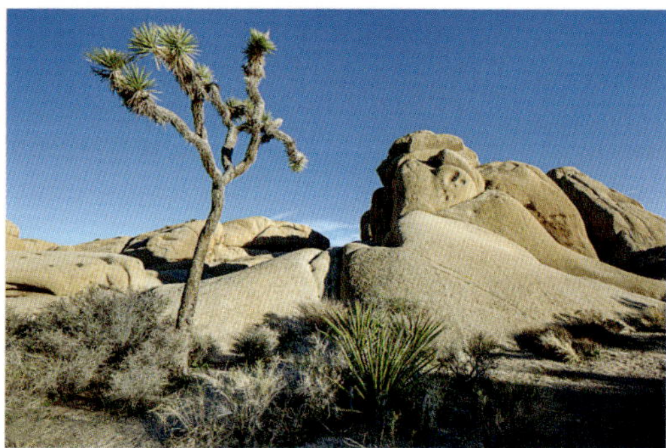

Applying opposite values of the Highlights, Shadows, Clarity, and Dehaze sliders via a mask smoothed out the sky.

Selective Brightening

You may find that you like the overall look produced by the sliders mentioned above and only find a limited area to look unnatural. When that's the case, try creating a sky mask, then holding the **Option** key (Mac) or **Alt** key (PC) to reveal the **Intersect** button below the mask. Click the button and choose **Brush** from the resulting pop-up menu, set the **Feather** setting to **100**, the **Flow** setting to around **30**, and the **Whites** slider to **70**.

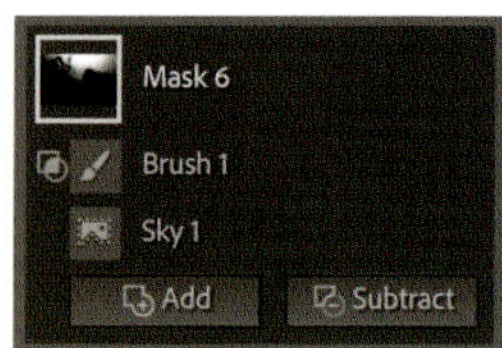

Mask created by first masking the sky, then intersecting the result with a brush mask at a low Flow to build up the brightening effect.

With that setup, you should be able to effectively paint light into the areas that appear too dark. Painting over the same area multiple times while the **Flow** setting is below **100** will build up the effect and often produce a smoother result.

Section III: Crafting a Photograph

Odd-Looking Suns

The same sliders that can cause skies to become uneven (discussed on the last page) can also cause the sun to lose its natural smooth glow and be rendered with an unnatural halo around its edge.

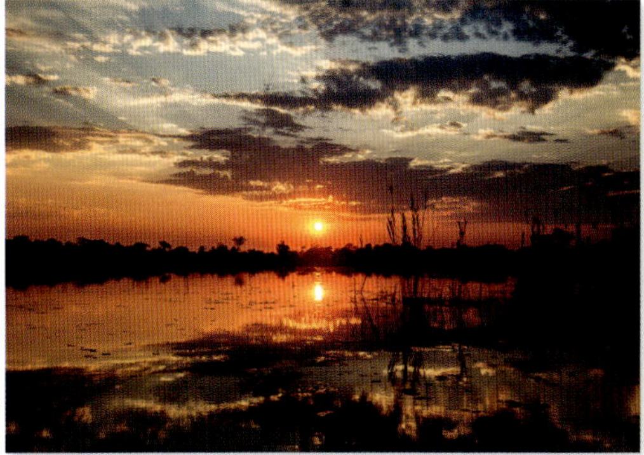

This image may be fine for social media where nobody can zoom in and inspect the details.

As with skies, applying a masked adjustment using opposite settings can make the sun look more natural. The only difference is that a soft-edge brush mask or radial gradient mask should be used in order to limit the adjustment to the sun and its immediate surroundings.

Adding a little negative **Texture** to the masked area is often the finishing touch needed to produce a smooth, radiant-looking sun.

Left: The Highlights, Shadows, and Clarity settings applied to the image as a whole produced an abrupt edge on the sun.

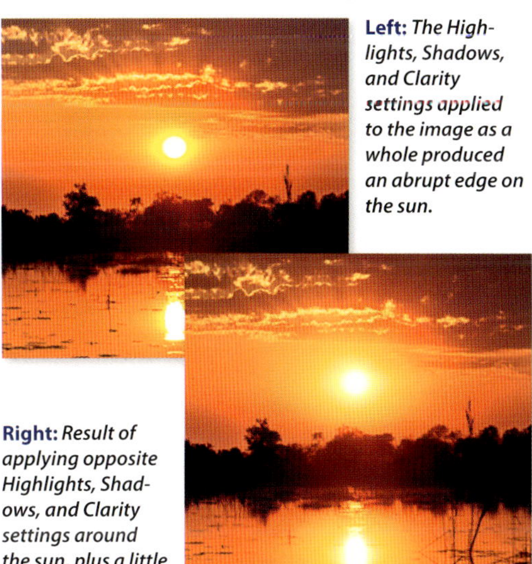

Right: Result of applying opposite Highlights, Shadows, and Clarity settings around the sun, plus a little negative Texture.

Overly Colorful Shadows

It's very common to boost both the **Shadows** and **Vibrance** sliders when optimizing an image. Doing this can cause the dark areas to appear unnaturally colorful since shady areas are rarely colorful in nature.

Lower Saturation in Dark Areas

When the darker areas in an image appear to be unnaturally colorful, isolate those areas by typing **Shift-Q** to create a Luminance Range mask. Then, to make the image less colorful, lower the **Saturation** setting of the mask to around **-30**. To limit the change to the darkest areas, drag the right end of the range tab **A** all the way to the left **B**.

Then, to cause the adjustment to seamlessly blend into the surrounding image, move the upper fall-off slider **C** to the middle or beyond.

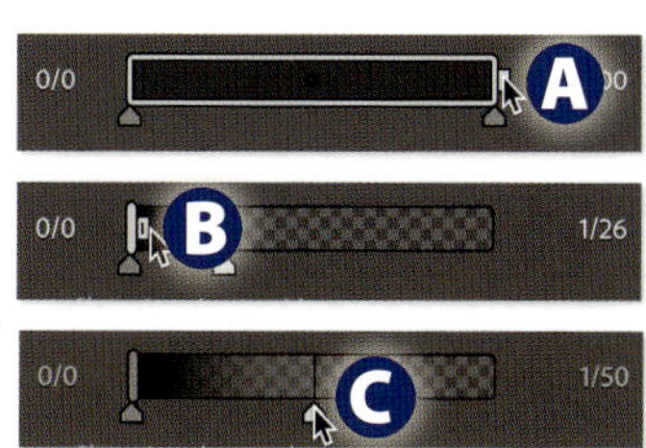

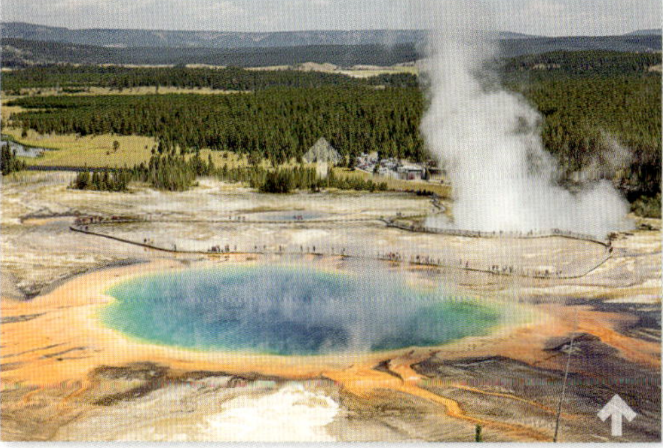

Image with Shadows and Vibrance boosted.

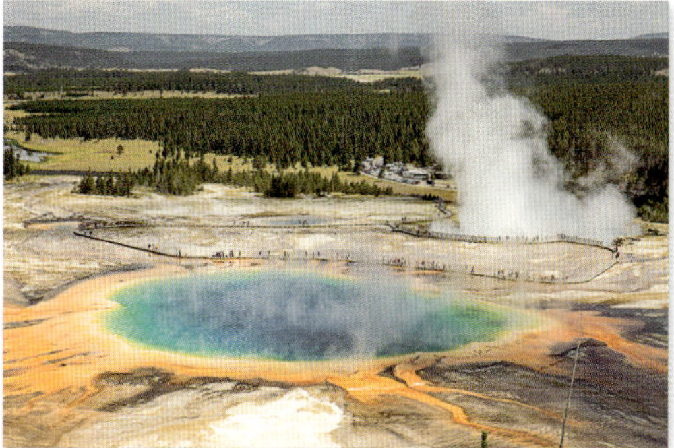

Result of lowering Saturation through a Luminance mask.

Object Halos

Few objects in nature glow, except for the sun, yet it's not uncommon to encounter glowing objects in photographs that have been "optimized" digitally. The **Highlights**, **Shadows**, **Clarity**, and **Dehaze** adjustments can potentially produce bright or dark halos around the edges of areas where abrupt changes in brightness are found.

Substitute Masked Adjustment

The most common area to find an unnatural halo is where a dark object touches the sky, causing the sky to become brighter around the edge of the object.

It's usually easy to fix such issues by choosing **Tools>Create New Mask>Select Sky** in the Develop module, and then applying the opposite setting to the slider that is causing the halo. Then, substitute an alternative adjustment that does not commonly cause halos.

In this example, applying **Highlights -100** caused a halo to appear around the perimeter of the sky. To fix the issue, a sky mask was used to apply **Highlights +100** to remove the halo, and then **Exposure -1.18** was substituted as an alternative method for darkening the sky.

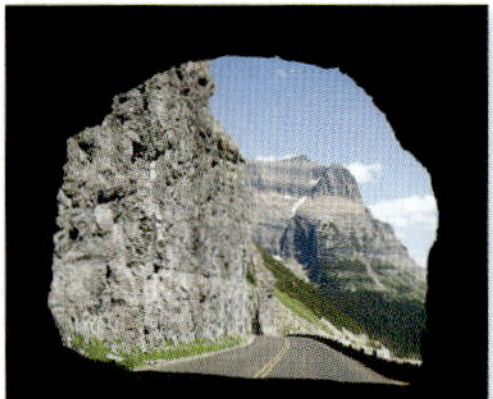

Before lowering Highlights.

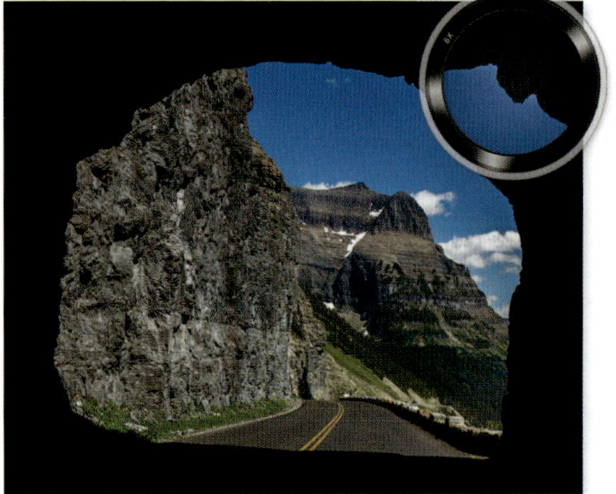

Applying -100 Highlights caused the edge of a tunnel to glow and the sky to have unnaturally dark areas near the clouds.

When the above technique is inappropriate for the situation, you'll have to head into Photoshop and apply a more sophisticated solution.

Selective Sharpening

Sharpening is performed by adding tiny halos around the edges of detailed areas. Wherever distinct differences in brightness are found, the bright side of the edge is brightened slightly and the dark side is darkened to increase contrast and make the transition more obvious. This increases the apparent sharpness of the image.

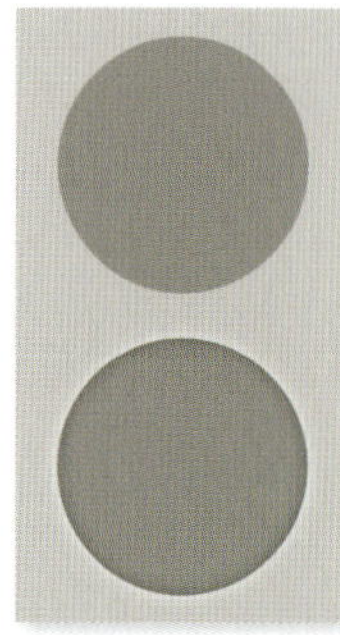

The tiny halos that result are usually small and subtle enough that they go unnoticed. But every so often, the bright halos get noticed. This is most common where a crisp-edged dark object touches a detail-lacking blue sky. It is more noticeable in images that are displayed on-screen, where every pixel is on display, than when an image is printed. That's because inkjet printers utilize hundreds of tiny dots of solid cyan, magenta, yellow, and black ink to reproduce each pixel that makes up an image. This has the effect of concealing the tiny halos that sharpening produces.

When halos produced by sharpening are distractingly obvious, the following technique can be useful to selectively eliminate the bright halos while keeping the dark ones at full strength:

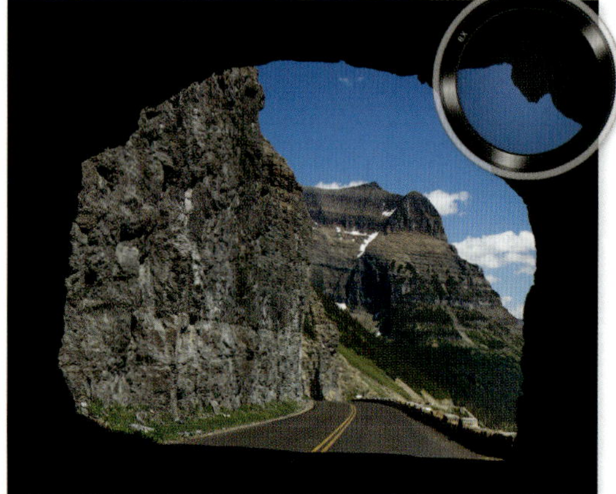

Result of applying a sky mask with +100 Highlights to counteract the global one, and -1.18 Exposure to darken the sky.

Section III: Crafting a Photograph

1) Turn off Lightroom's default sharpening by visiting the **Detail** panel of the Develop module and changing the **Amount** setting under the **Sharpening** heading to **0**.

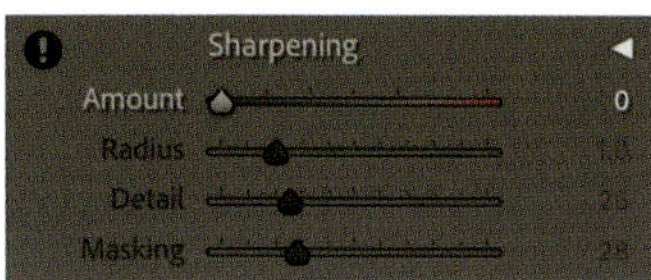

2) Open the image in Photoshop by choosing **Photo>Edit In>Edit In Photoshop**. It is important to use this method instead of **File>Export**, since additional sharpening would usually be applied when exporting.

3) Create a copy of the original image layer, so you can sharpen it separately from the original, by choosing **Layer>New>Layer Via Copy**, or type its keyboard shortcut **Command-J** (Mac) or **Ctrl-J** (PC).

4) Now it's time to sharpen that duplicate layer by choosing **Filter>Sharpen>Unsharp Mask** (or **Smart Sharpen**, which is a more feature-rich alternative). Fine-tune the settings to your liking while ignoring any distracting bright halos.

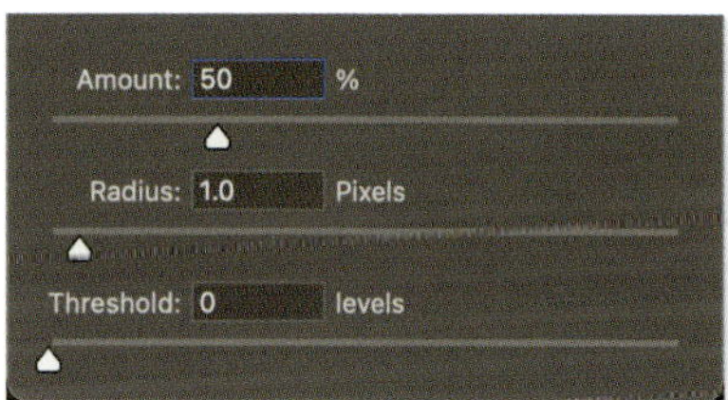

> **Note:** *Lightroom's default setting uses **Amount 40**, **Radius 1**, and **Masking 0** (Masking is similar to Threshold in Photoshop's Unsharp Mask filter). But keep in mind that exporting an image for screen use would have caused a second round of sharpening to be applied on top of that, making it impossible to precisely reproduce the same result using a single application of this filter in Photoshop. The goal is not to reproduce Lightroom's results, but to make the image look nice and sharp while knowing that any obvious bright halos can be eliminated using the steps that follow.*

5) To limit the sharpened layer so that it can only darken the image, change the blending mode pop-up menu at the top of the Layers panel to **Darken A**. Then double-click on the name of the layer and change it to something like "Sharpening-Darken" so its purpose is obvious.

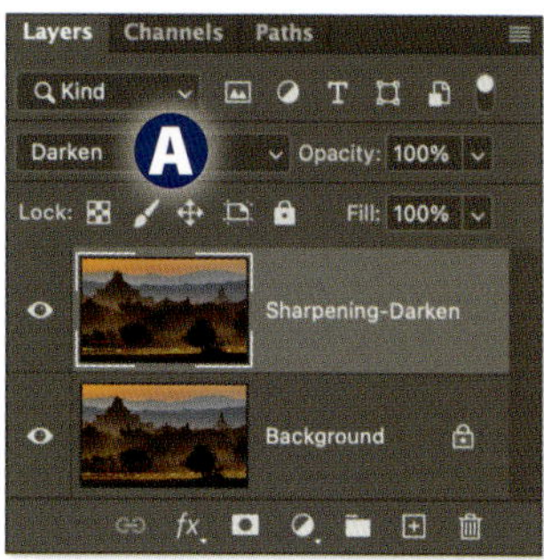

6) Now let's bring back the missing bright halos by choosing **Layer>New>Layer Via Copy** once again, and then changing the blending mode pop-up menu at the top of the Layers panel to **Lighten**. Then, double-click on the name of the layer and name it something like "Sharpening-Lighten."

7) Now it's time to eliminate any of the bright halos that are distracting. With the layer that is set to **Lighten** still active, choose **Layer>Layer Mask>Reveal All**. Activate the **Brush** tool, type **D** to set your foreground color to black, and then paint over the image wherever you find the bright halos to be distractingly noticeable.

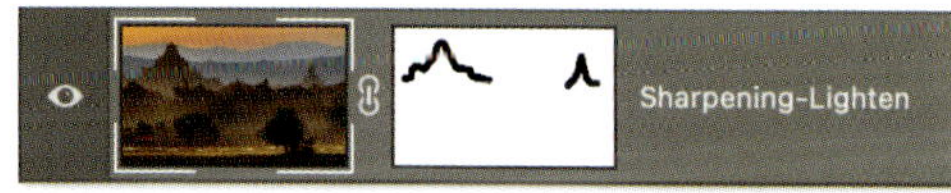

8) Export without additional sharpening: Once you've finished, save and close the image and return to Lightroom. Then, when you need to produce a file in a common file format, choose **File>Export** and choose the preset that is closest to your desired results from the list on the left. Then fine-tune any appropriate settings on the right and be sure to turn off the **Sharpen For** checkbox that's found in the **Output Sharpening** section.

Clone in Darken Mode

When an undesirable halo is only a few pixels wide, a combination of retouching and blending modes will usually be enough to eliminate the halo using the following technique:

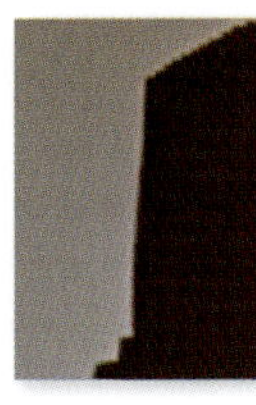

1) In Lightroom, choose **Photo>Edit In>Edit In Photoshop**.
2) In Photoshop, select the **Clone Stamp** tool. Then, in the Options Bar that spans the top of the screen, turn on the **Aligned** checkbox and set the **Sample** pop-up menu to **Current & Below**.

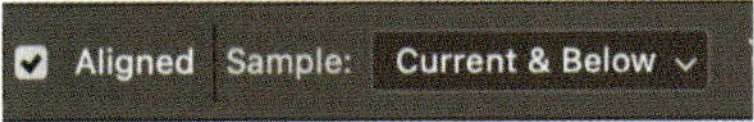

3) Next, create a new empty layer by choosing **Layer>New>Layer**, or by holding **Option** (Mac) or **Alt** (PC) while clicking on the **New Layer** icon at the bottom of the Layers panel. In the **New Layer** dialog, name the layer something like "Halo Removal," set the **Mode** pop-up menu to **Darken** and then click **OK**.

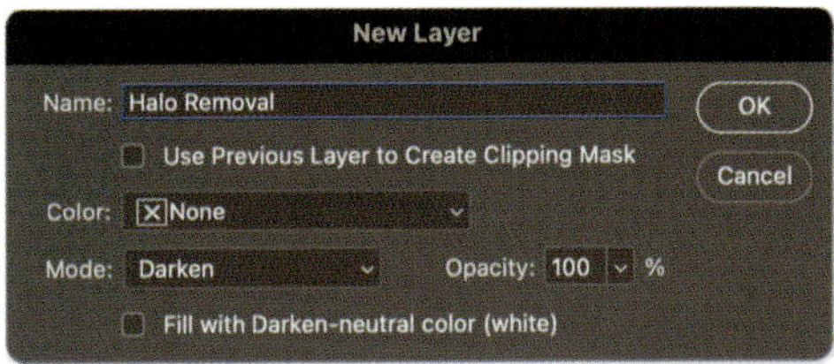

4) Hold **Option** (Mac) or **Alt** (PC) and click just outside one of the undesirable bright halos to set the area as the source for the **Clone Stamp** tool. Be sure the area would be a good replacement for the halo.

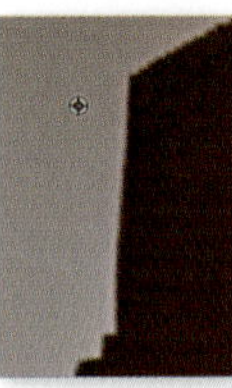

5) Using a small, soft-edged brush, paint over the nearby bright halo to replace it with the area you defined in the previous step. Since the layer is in **Darken** mode, your retouching will not be able to brighten the image. Therefore, overspray onto darker areas will not affect the image.

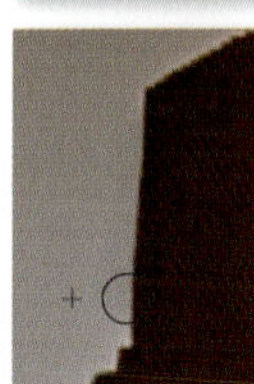

Masked Curves Adjustment

When a halo is so large that it could be described as a glow, then you may need to use an adjustment layer to change the brightness of the affected area, and then use a mask to limit where the adjustment can affect the image. Let's tackle this in two parts. First, we'll perform the appropriate adjustment. Second, we'll limit the adjustment to affect only the area that contains the glow. To correct for a glow, do the following:

1) Starting in Photoshop, choose **Layer>New Adjustment Layer>Curves**.
2) Activate the **Targeted Adjustment** tool (hand icon) in **Curves**. Then make sure the **Sample Size** pop-up menu found in the Options Bar that spans the top of the screen is using a setting no higher than **3 by 3 Average**.

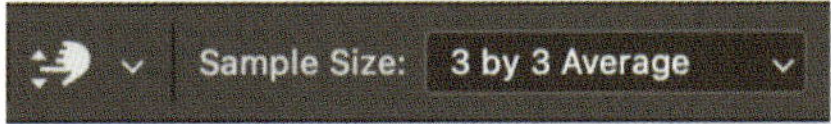

3) Click on either the brightest part of the bright glow or darkest part of a dark glow, while ensuring that you are at least one pixel away from the edge of the object that appears to be glowing. This will add a point to the curve, and the **Input** number below the curve will indicate the exact amount of light contained in the area where you clicked.

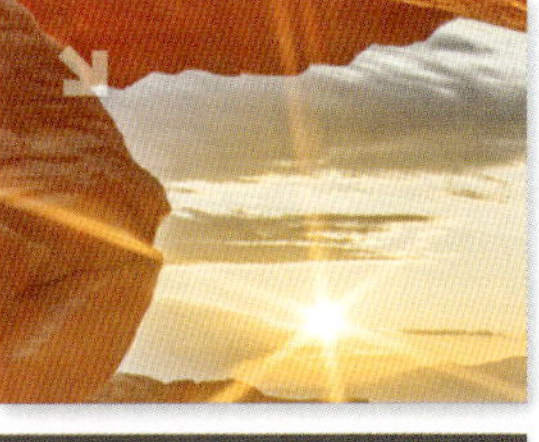

4) Now, find a reference spot in the image that is immediately outside the glow and represents the brightness you want to end up with when replacing the glow. Once you've found an appropriate spot, hover over it (but don't click) and note the number that appears in the **Input** field below the curve. That tells you the exact amount of light that's currently in the reference spot.

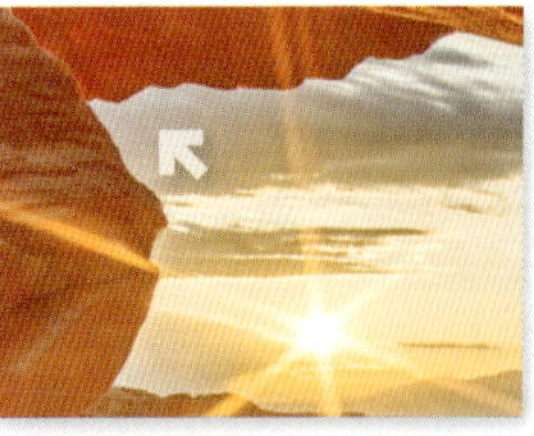

5) Finally, click within the **Output** field below the curve and enter the number you noted in the previous step. This will cause the area

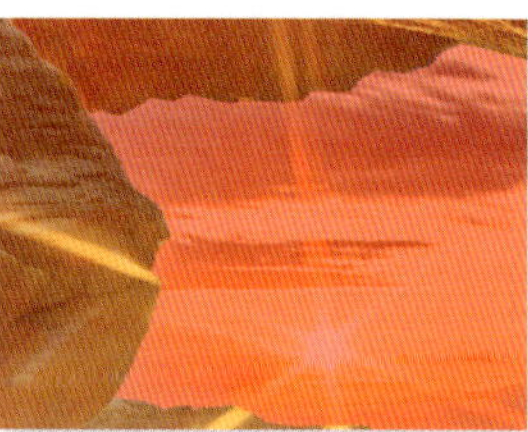

you clicked on within the glow to match the brightness of the reference spot.

> **Tip:** *If you need to match both the brightness AND the color of the glow to that of its surroundings, then replace the last three steps in the technique above with the technique described on page 55. It can be found in the section that describes curves and demonstrates how to match the brightness and color between two areas.*

At this point, the glow will have been adjusted so that it matches the brightness that was originally found immediately outside its bounds. Now the adjustment needs to be masked in order to limit its effect to a specific area in the image. This can be accomplished by doing the following:

1) Start by isolating the area that contains the glow from the rest of the image. You can do this by making a selection using the techniques covered in chapter 2.

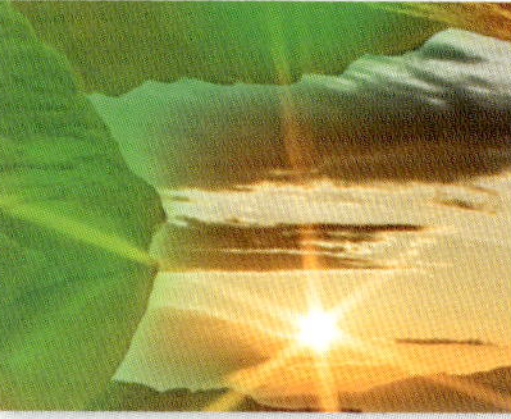

Red indicates area selected.

2) With the **Curves** adjustment layer active, hold **Shift** and click on the **Group** icon **A** at the bottom of the Layers panel. Then click on the **Layer Mask** icon **B** in order to transform the selection into a mask. That group **C** will prevent the **Curves** adjustment from affecting areas that are outside the selection that was created in the previous step.

3) Click on the layer mask that is attached to the **Curves** adjustment layer **D** to make it active. Then choose **Image>Adjustments> Invert** to fill the mask with black. This will prevent the adjustment from affecting the image.

4) Activate the **Brush** tool and choose a large, soft-edged brush. Type **D** to ensure the foreground color is white, and type **3** to change the **Opacity** of the **Brush** tool to **30%**.

5) Finally, paint over the object that appears to be glowing and extend into the glow using multiple paint strokes and varying brush sizes to gradually build up the adjustment until the glow has been effectively eliminated.

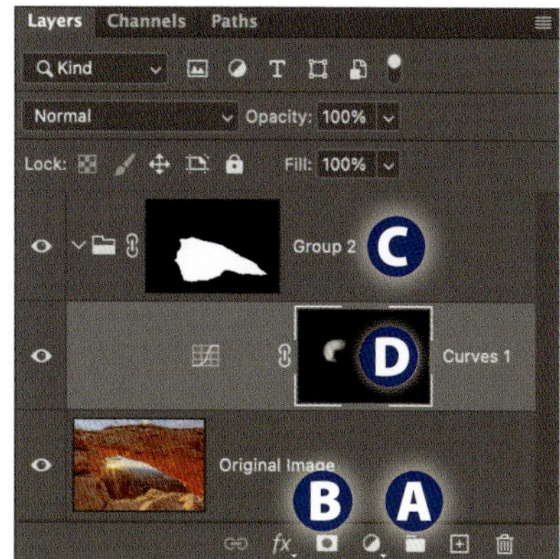

Green indicates area painted.

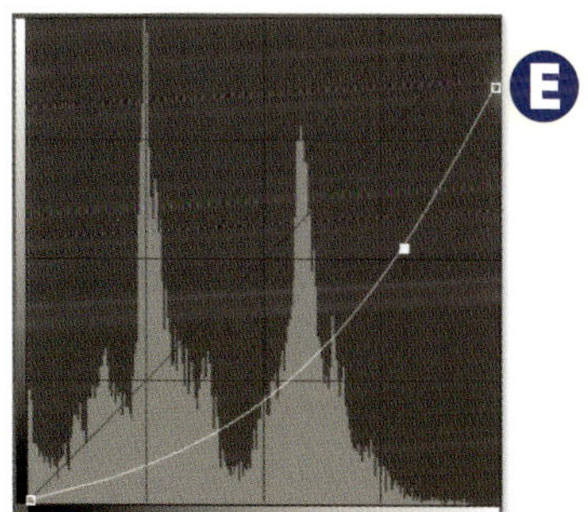

6) If the brightest part of the adjusted area remains too bright, then drag the upper-right point on the curve downward **E**.

E

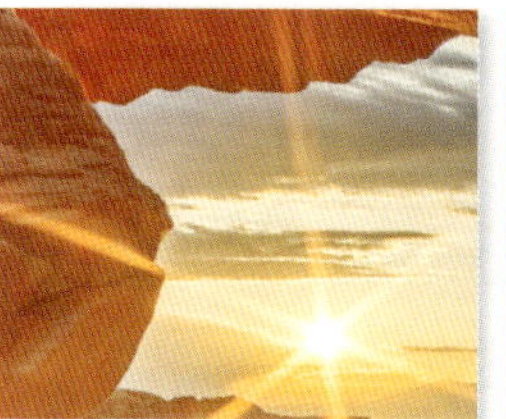

Before: Glowing edge.

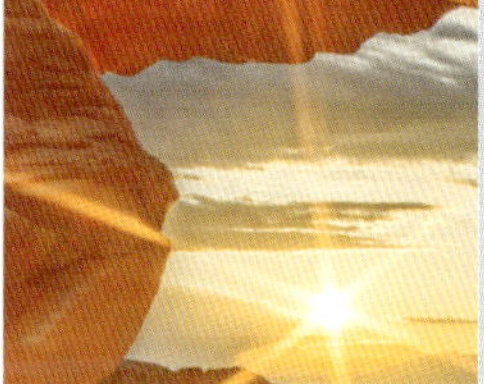

After: Glow eliminated.

Masking Artifacts

When a mask is used to either combine multiple exposures or limit where an adjustment affects an image, problems contained within the mask itself have the potential to create visual artifacts in the resulting image.

Masking Issues in Lightroom Classic

Lightroom Classic presents a unique set of challenges due to its catalog-based, parametric approach to working with images. To learn more about how Lightroom differs from Photoshop, see chapter 1.

Smart Object–Based Previews

If a masked adjustment ever produces transitions that don't look smooth, or generates a generally chunky-looking result, it may not be a true problem. It could instead be a sign that Lightroom is utilizing a Smart Preview as a substitute for the original image in an attempt to improve the program's processing speed.

A Smart Preview is a scaled-down copy of the original image that contains only a small fraction of the brightness levels that were originally captured and has had significant lossy compression applied in an attempt to minimize its file size. Those special previews can be created by turning on the **Build Smart Previews** checkbox that is available when importing images, or by choosing **Library>Previews>Build Smart Previews**.

Lightroom will utilize those previews, when they are available, to improve the responsiveness of the Develop module if the **Use Smart Previews instead of Originals for image editing** checkbox is enabled in the **Performance** section of Lightroom's **Preferences**. This setting only affects the on-screen display of the image and does not affect what is exported, printed, or opened into Photoshop. Zooming into the image by choosing **View>Zoom to 100%** will cause Lightroom to load the original image and refresh the display to reflect the true quality of the adjustment result.

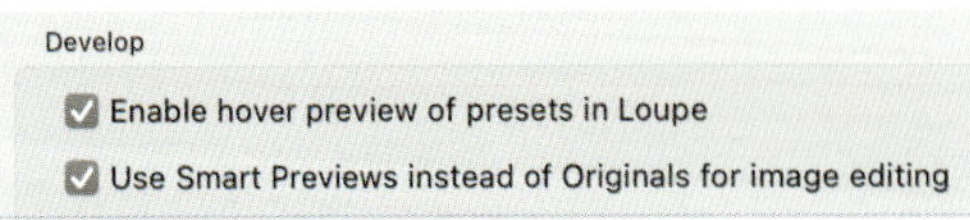

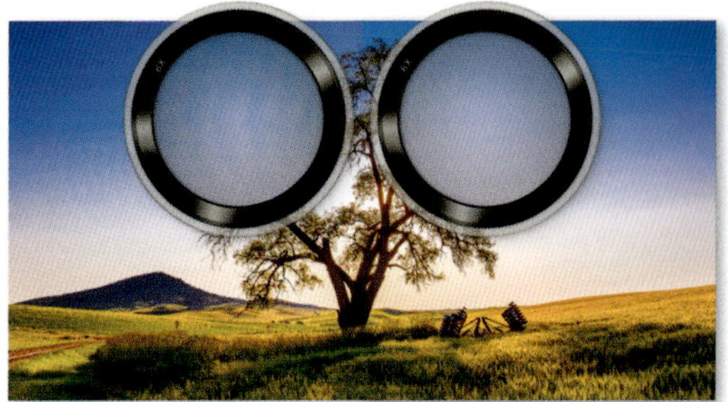

The left half of this image shows the on-screen Smart Preview–based view shown in the Develop module. The right half shows the result of zooming in to load the original image.

Using Zoom Levels Not Divisible by 100

Any time an image is viewed at a zoom level below 100% (as shown in the Toolbar at the bottom of the Develop module **A**), Lightroom will be incapable of showing the full detail contained within the image. That's because it is attempting to display the pixels that make up the image at a size that is smaller than the fixed size of the squares that make up the computer screen being used to display the image. That's like trying to fit five cars into a garage that only has space for one.

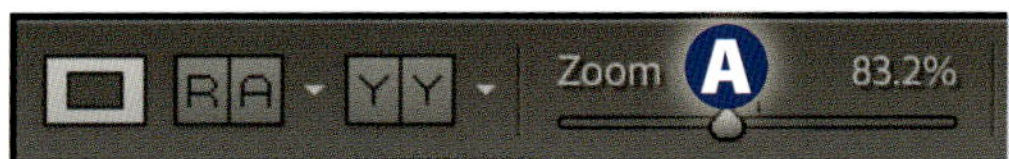

A 100% zoom level is where each pixel contained within an image is displayed using a single pixel of the computer display. Above that, only zoom levels that are evenly divisible by 100 will accurately reflect the contents of the image. A 200% zoom does it by using a square 2x2 grouping of screen pixels to display each pixel contained in an image, 300% uses a 3x3 square of pixels, and so on. Any zoom level that's not a multiple of 100 is asking to display an even number of image pixels using an odd number of screen pixels. That's like trying to evenly distribute 10 coins into nine boxes.

I would not advise that you make critical evaluations of image quality at zoom levels such as 95%, 205%, 280%, etc., because the image will not be accurately displayed. All it takes is a zoom level of 100%, 200%, or 300% to accurately display every pixel that makes up the image.

This issue is not unique to Lightroom. It affects all programs that can display pixel-based digital images.

Trusting the Color Overlay View of a Mask

Lightroom's default method of representing the area that is being isolated by a mask as a color overlay can be deceiving. It can be difficult to tell the difference between areas that are fully masked compared to areas that don't have the mask at full strength. Also, tiny subtle artifacts can be difficult to discern. This can become critically important when making large prints because some artifacts may become apparent when the image is printed large enough.

When I think I'm finished with an image, I like to choose **White on Black** from the mask overlay pop-up menu **B** and then hover over the thumbnail image for each mask **C** so I can inspect the contents of each, looking for the following:

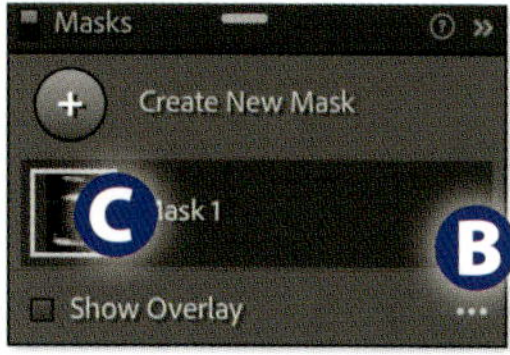

Gaps Between Brushstrokes: After painting back and forth using a soft-edged brush to cover a large area, it is not uncommon to discover areas that are unevenly masked. This happens when the soft portions of the brush only partially overlap in multiple paint strokes to produce only partial coverage.

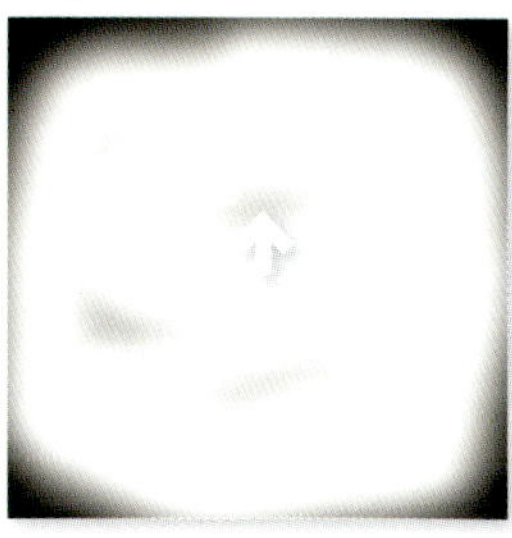

Inaccurate AI-Generated Masks: Just because Lightroom may be able to quickly select the sky or subject of a photo does not ensure that the resulting mask will be of high enough quality to be usable without further refinement. More often than not, I find the mask can be improved by adding or subtracting areas using a **Brush** mask.

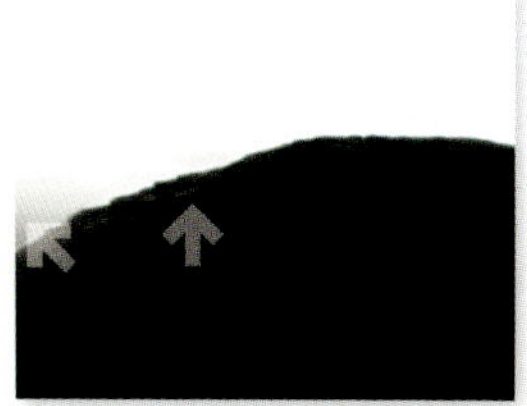

Gaps at Document Bounds: This happens when a masked area that was meant to extend to the edge of the image has a small gap where a brushstroke did not extend all the way to the edge of the image.

AI Masks and Subsequent Retouching

The following mask types utilize artificial intelligence (AI) to analyze the contents of an image to produce the mask: **Subject**, **Sky**, **Background** & **Objects**. Such masks do not automatically update when retouching is subsequently applied to change the contents of the image.

Combine that with fact that Lightroom always applies its features in a predefined order behind the scenes, where retouching is always applied before masked adjustments, regardless of the order in which they were applied by the user, and you end up with a formula that will occasionally produce unexpected results.

For example, such a result would occur after using an AI-based **Sky** mask to darken a sky and then applying retouching to remove a bird.

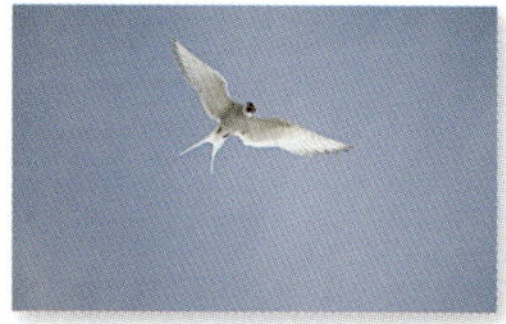 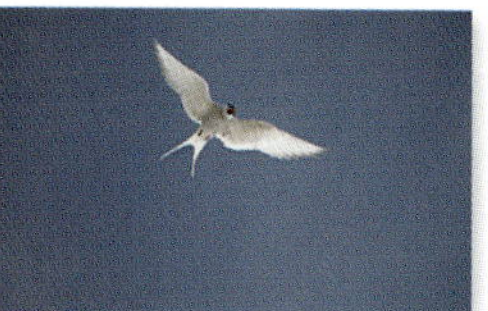

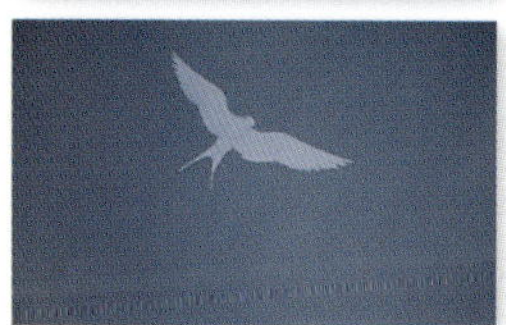

Top Left: *Original image.*

Top Right: *AI-generated Sky mask used to darken the sky.*

Bottom Left: *Retouching applied to remove bird.*

For that reason, it's a good practice to revisit the **Masks** panel after performing retouching to see if any AI-generated masks were previously used to adjust the image. Clicking on such a mask from within the **Masks** panel will reveal an **Update** button that can be used to recalculate the mask based on the retouched version of the image.

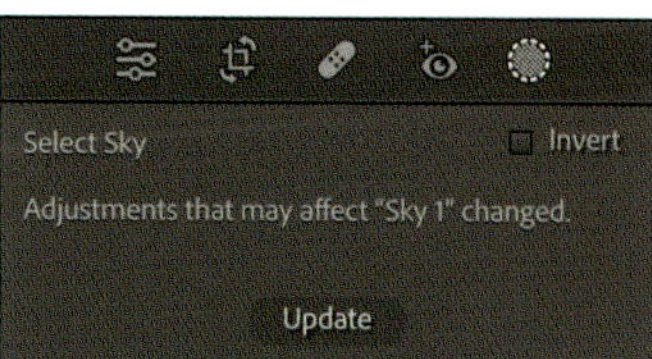

Clicking the Update button after performing retouching will cause the active AI-generated mask to be recalculated.

Result of clicking the Update button on the AI-generated Sky mask to produce an updated mask that reflected the retouched version of the image.

Upgrade Masks Created with Older Versions

I occasionally run into an old image that was optimized using a previous version of Lightroom that did not offer the AI-based **Sky** mask and wish I could update it to improve the quality of the original results. Here's how that can be accomplished:

1) With the image selected, type **Shift-W** to access the **Masks** panel in Lightroom's Develop module. Then click on the mask to make the individual mask components visible.

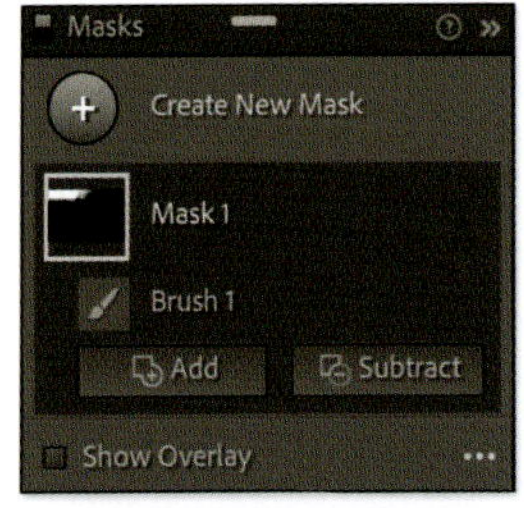

2) Click the **Add** button below the mask and choose **Select Sky** from the resulting pop-up menu. This will add a **Sky** mask component to the existing mask **A**.

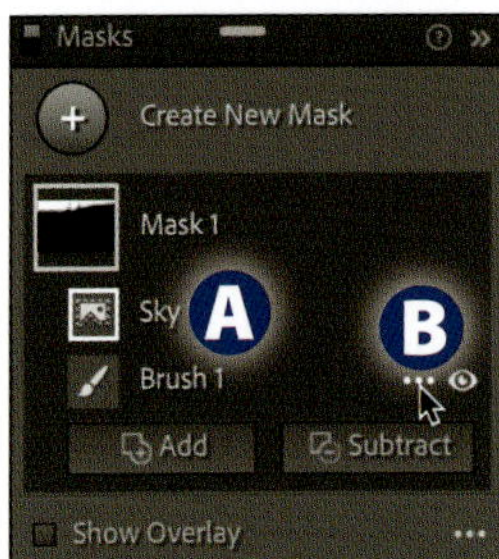

3) Hover over the bottommost mask component in the list to reveal its options menu **B**, then click and choose the delete option that corresponds to the name of the mask component your are attempting to replace (**Delete "Brush 1"** in this example).

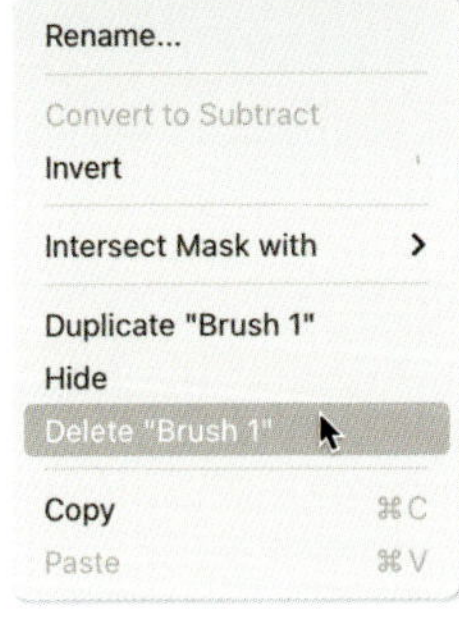

In the example above, Mask 1 was originally created using a **Brush** mask. An AI-generated **Sky** mask component was later added to that mask. Then, the original **Brush** mask component was deleted, allowing for the **Sky** mask to take its place as the base component of the updated mask.

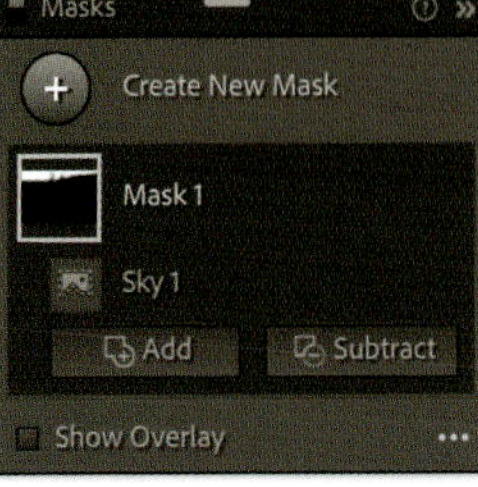

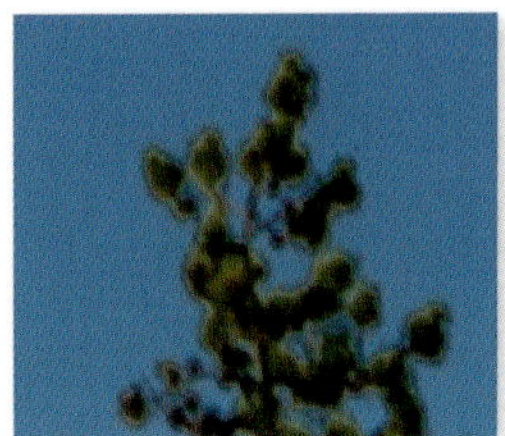

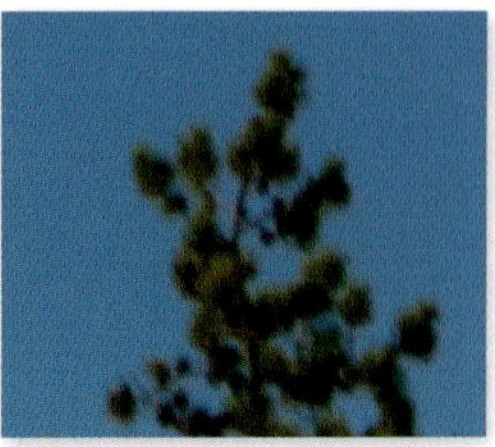

Image as processed using an older version of Lightroom.

Result of replacing the old Brush mask with a Sky mask.

*Note: The masks produced in Lightroom's **Masks** panel are not based on the current state of the image you are viewing. Masks are instead based on a minimally processed version of the image. That way, a mask produced before an image has been optimized will be identical to one produced using the same method after the image has had extensive changes applied.*

*The following adjustments are then applied to the mask contents in a non-destructive fashion, so the settings can be changed at any time to update the mask: **Noise Reduction**, and **Chromatic Aberration Removal**. None of the other adjustment sliders have any affect on the contents of a mask.*

*Of course, any change that would affect the overall shape of the image relative to the document bounds, such as those found in the **Transform** panel, affect the entirety of the document, including masks.*

With that setup, it is generally unimportant at which stage a masked adjustment is created.

*But this setup also limits what masked adjustments are capable of being used for. For instance, a **Luminance Range** mask will be incapable of isolating a bright halo that was produced by cranking the **Highlights**, **Shadows**, and **Clarity** sliders because the mask is based on a version of the image that does not have those sliders applied. Such an area could only be isolated by manually painting in a **Brush** mask. The **Auto** mask checkbox could not be used to mask the halo because it would not react to changes made by the adjustment sliders. However, a **Subject** mask or **Object** mask could be utilized to eliminate overspray onto the object around which the halo appears.*

Section III: Crafting a Photograph

Masking Issues in Photoshop

Now let's transition to masking artifacts that are produced when working in Photoshop. Before we get into actual techniques for preventing or eliminating artifacts, let's take a look at the options Photoshop offers for working with existing layer masks.

Disable: Holding **Shift** and clicking within the layer mask thumbnail image in the Layers panel will toggle between disabling (which causes a large red X to appear on the thumbnail) and re-enabling the mask. This can be a good way to determine how the mask is effecting the image.

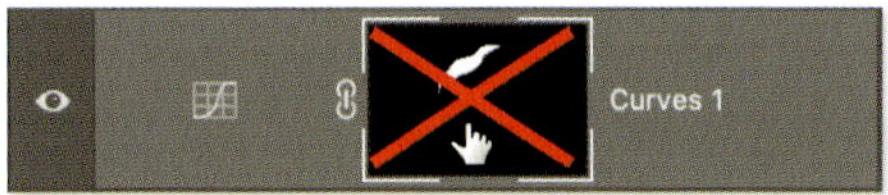

Overlay: Pressing \ will display the mask attached to the active layer as a color overlay within the image window. I've heard that this functionality is not available on some international keyboards. In that case, the overlay can be turned on and off by clicking to the left of the layer mask from within the Channels panel **C**.

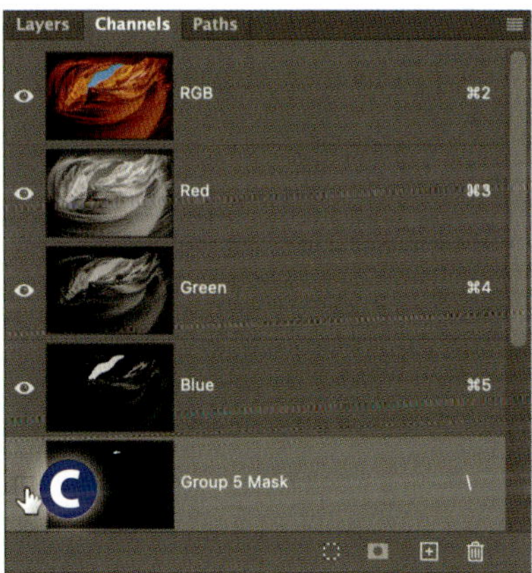

Direct View: To directly view the full contents of a layer mask, hold **Option** (Mac) or **Alt** (PC) and click on its thumbnail image in the Layers panel. Doing so a second time will return you to viewing the image instead of the mask.

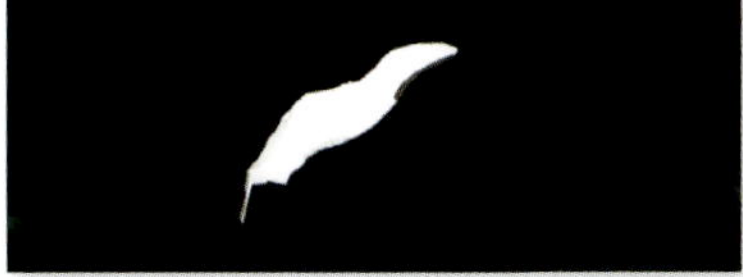

Now let's turn our attention to methods for preventing or eliminating artifacts in Photoshop.

Halo-Inducing Masks

Most images that have their initial processing done in Lightroom have had some level of sharpening applied (even at default settings), which produces tiny halos around the edges of objects that help to make the image appear sharp. When a sharpened image is opened into Photoshop and its contents are used to produce a mask, the bright halos found within the image will cause adjustments applied using the mask to be more pronounced where the halos appear.

In the rare case that the bright halos become distracting, the following technique can be used to generate a mask that has not been sharpened:

1) Switch to Lightroom, locate the raw file the image is based on, and then view the image in the Develop module.
2) In the **Detail** panel, set the **Sharpen** slider to **0** to disable sharpening.
3) Choose **Photo>Edit in Photoshop** so you can work with this non-sharpened version of the image in Photoshop.
4) Choose **Select>Select All** and then **Edit> Copy** to place a copy of the image onto the clipboard so it's ready to be pasted elsewhere.
5) Choose **File>Close** and when prompted, choose the **Don't Save** option, which should also cause the document you were working on previously to become active once again.

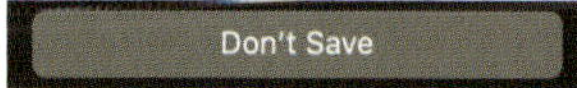

6) Click on the channel, or hold **Option** (Mac) or **Alt** (PC) and click on the layer mask thumbnail image in the Layers panel for the mask you'd like to replace to make it visible.
7) Choose **Edit>Paste** to replace the contents of the mask with the non-sharpened version of the image that you copied earlier.
8) Finally, return to Lightroom and expand the **History** panel on the left side of the Develop module. Click on the history step that appears second from the top in order to restore the sharpening settings that were applied prior to starting this technique.

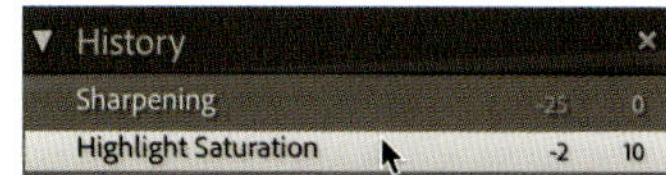

Noisy Masks

Images captured in a dark environment or at a high ISO setting usually contain a prominent amount of noise. When a mask is produced based on the contents of such an image, it will also contain noise. Adjustments applied using such masks will commonly cause the overall noise to become more pronounced in the resulting image.

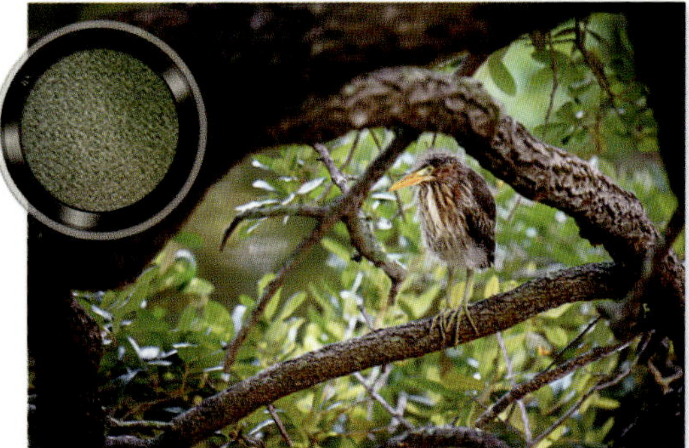

The image above is very noisy because it was captured with a camera that was set to ISO 12,800.

It is essential to apply the noise-reduction techniques that are covered in chapter 4 before working with an overly noisy image in Photoshop. This is critical, as Lightroom's default sharpening settings will exaggerate the noise, making it impossible to reduce noise in masks that are based on such images. At minimum, hold **Option** (Mac) or **Alt** (PC) while adjusting the **Masking** slider that is found in the **Detail** panel of Lightroom's Develop module until areas that contain excessive noise become solid black. In that view, black areas will not have sharpening applied.

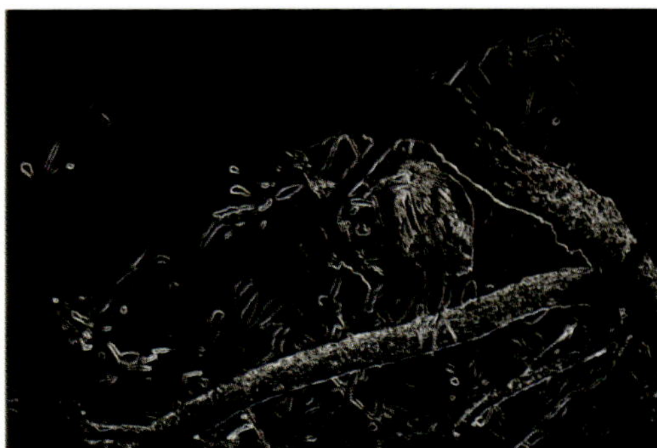

Holding Option (Mac) or Alt (PC) while adjusting the Masking slider will display an alternative view of the image.

Choosing **Filter>Noise>Median** in Photoshop, with a **Radius** setting no higher than **2**, can be an effective way to reduce noise in masks.

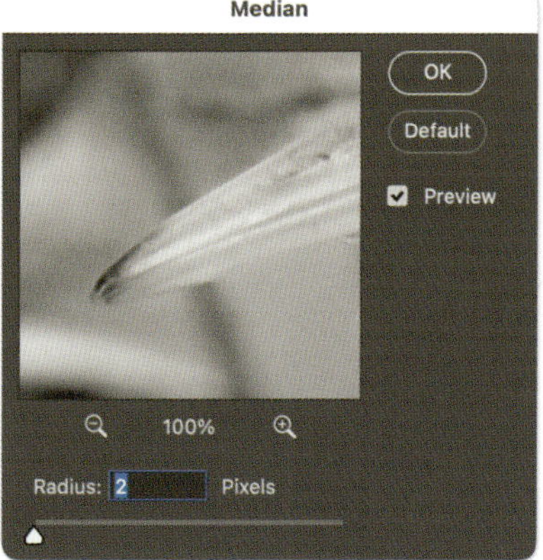

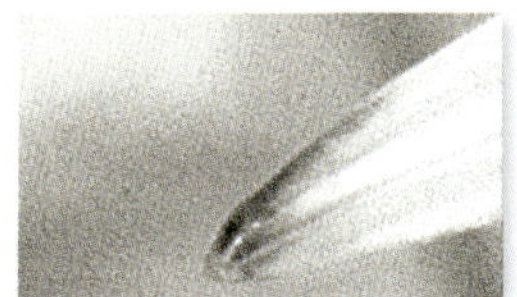

Close-up with Lightroom's default sharpening and noise-reduction settings applied.

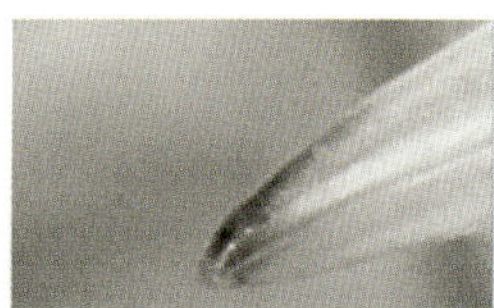

Result of increasing the Masking setting until the noisy areas become black.

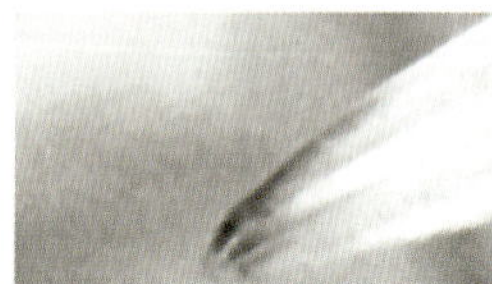

Median filter applied with Radius of 2 is ineffective when the noise has been sharpened in Lightroom.

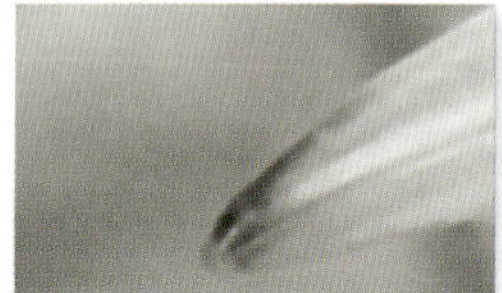

Median filter applied with Radius of 2 is much more effective when applied to areas that are not sharpened.

Section III: Crafting a Photograph

Masks Created Prior To Retouching

The order in which you perform adjustments, apply retouching, and create masks in Photoshop has consequences that you might not realize until you discover an undesirable artifact. Let's look at a step-by-step example of how such an artifact could be caused. Then I'll share how such issues can be remedied.

In the image shown below, **Select>Sky** was used to isolate the sky, then **Layer>New Adjustment Layer>Levels** was chosen and the middle slider was adjusted to darken the sky.

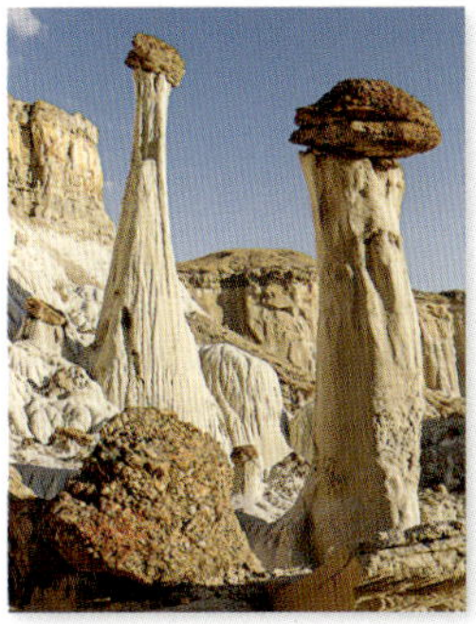

Original image.

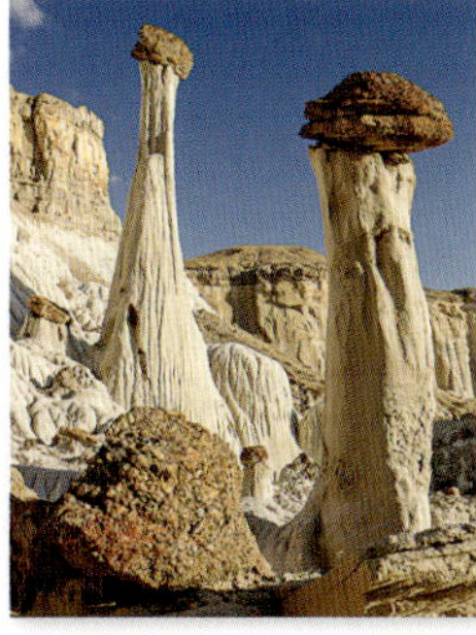

Sky darkened.

Next, a new empty layer named "Retouching" was created and positioned between the adjustment layer and the original image in the Layers panel. The **Spot Healing Brush** was used, with the **Sample All Layers** option enabled, to remove the cloud from the upper-left corner. Then a selection was made of the sky and the **Clone Stamp** tool, with its **Sample** pop-up menu set to **Current & Below**, was utilized to remove a much smaller cloud from a lower area within the sky.

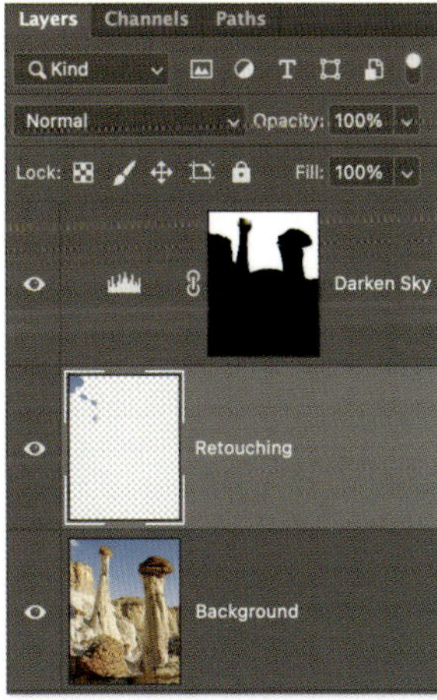

At that point, a problem was discovered. The smaller cloud simply refused to go away regardless of how many times the area was retouched!

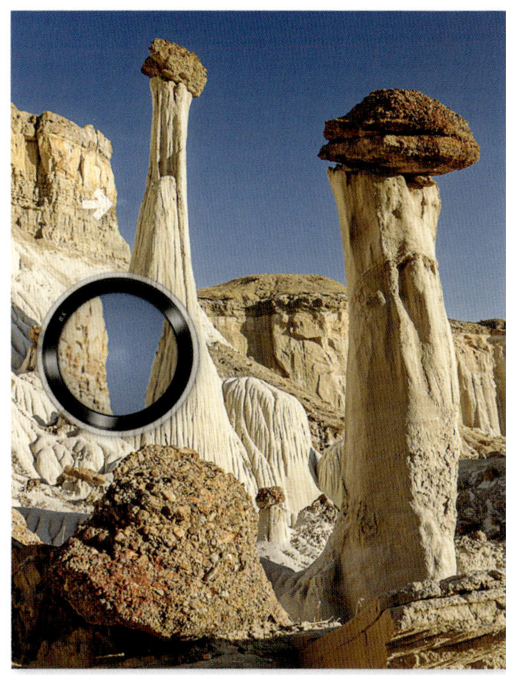

Result of attempting to remove clouds via retouching.

The source of the problem was only revealed when the contents of the layer mask attached to the adjustment layer was inspected. Choosing **Select>Sky** had isolated the majority of the sky, but had neglected to include the smaller cloud. Had the retouching been performed first, this would not have been an issue, as the cloud would have been gone before the sky was selected.

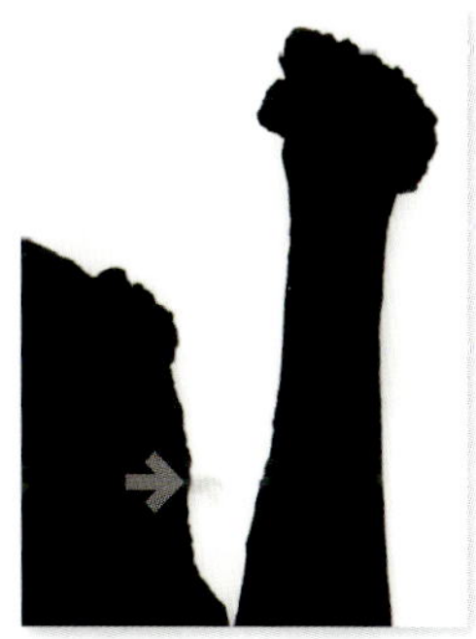

Attempts to remove the cloud from within the mask were initially unsuccessful. Each time it was attempted, the **Clone Stamp** tool deposited the contents of the image itself, even though the mask was being viewed directly and the image was not visible.

Changing the **Sample** setting for the **Clone Stamp** tool to **Current Layer** was necessary in order to make it copy from the mask and successfully remove the cloud from the mask.

Edge Fringing on Combined Masks

Combining multiple masks that share a common edge will usually produce undesirable artifacts due to the semi-soft-edged nature of most masks. An example would be a mask of the moon and a mask of the black sky that surrounds the moon.

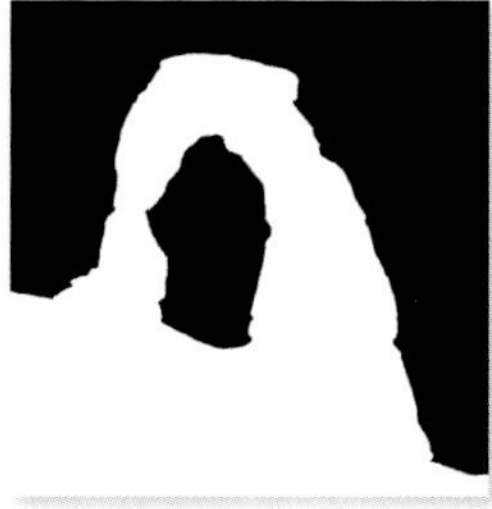

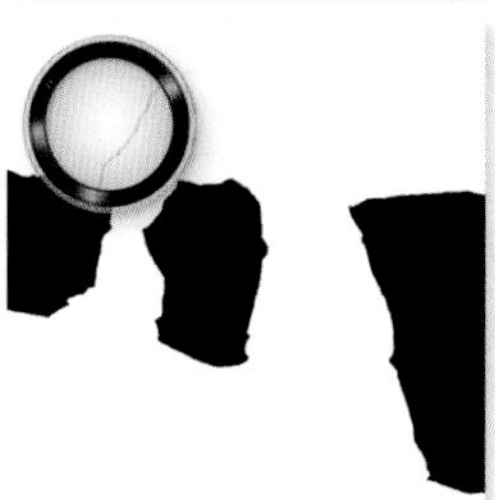

The two masks shown above were combined to produce the mask at left.

The area where the masks shared a common edge produced an undesirable artifact.

The contents of any mask can be loaded as a selection by holding **Command** (Mac) or **Ctrl** (PC) and clicking within the mask's thumbnail image in the Layers panel or Channels panel. Doing so when a selection is already active will cause it to be replaced with one based on the contents of the mask. Adding **Shift** when loading a mask as a selection will add to a selection that is already active. **Option** (Mac) or **Alt** (PC) can also be used to subtract from an active selection, or both keys can be held to intersect (crop one using the other).

After combining two selections or masks and using the result as a layer mask or channel, be sure to closely inspect the result and look for edge artifacts where two selections shared an edge. Cleaning up the results can be as simple as painting with black or white with the **Brush** tool. An alternative is to choose **Filter>Noise>Median** and adjust the **Radius** setting until the artifact disappears. Then use the **History Brush** technique that is detailed in "Photoshop Tips & Tricks" on page 51 in order to limit which areas are affected by the filter. The issue can often be avoided altogether by using the ideas described in the "Refining Masks and Channels" on page 50.

Low-Quality Luminosity Masks

Masks that isolate a specific brightness range within an image are commonly referred to as luminosity masks. Techniques for creating such masks are covered in "Selections and Masks" on page 42. There are two situations that can cause a luminosity mask to be of low quality.

8-bit Images from Lightroom: Raw files produced by digital cameras contain a minimum of 4,096 brightness levels (also known as 12 bits). A single setting in Lightroom can cause the vast majority of the information the camera captured to be needlessly discarded, delivering only 256 brightness levels to Photoshop (known as 8 bits). The same is true if the camera was set to save images in the JPEG file format, which is incapable of saving more than 256 brightness levels.

To ensure that nothing is discarded when an image is sent to Photoshop, choose **Settings** from the **Light-room Classic** menu (Mac) or **Edit** menu (PC) and set the **Bit Depth** pop-up menu to **16 bits/component**.

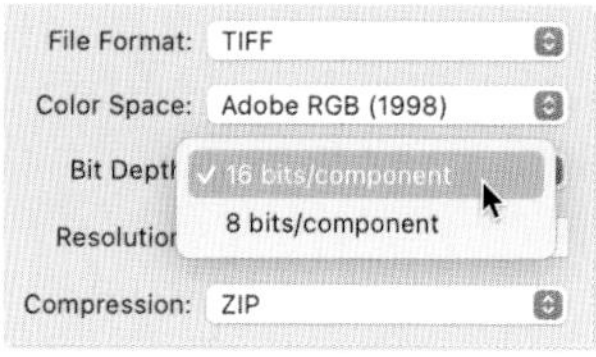

Using Selections instead of Masks: Using the **16 bits/component** setting mentioned above will allow all the masks contained within the resulting file to potentially contain up to 16,384 brightness levels. Selections, on the other hand, can contain no more than 256 brightness levels, even if they are used within a 16-bit file.

Since luminosity masks are created by manipulating the brightness levels that make up an image, they can benefit from having access to all the information that is contained in the original raw file. It is therefore best to avoid loading a mask as a selection, and to instead copy and paste or use **Image>Apply Image** to move information between masks if it will subsequently be used to produce a luminosity mask.

This concept is mainly important when working with luminosity masks. Most other masks, such as those displayed elsewhere on this page, rarely contain more than 256 brightness levels. Therefore, converting to a selection would not cause anything to be lost in the process.

Section III: Crafting a Photograph

Refining Masks with Levels

Image>Adjustments>Levels is one of the most useful tools for refining the contents of a mask. Below, you'll find descriptions of the **Levels** settings and how each relates to the horizontal bar **A** that is found near the bottom of the **Levels** dialog. This bar represents the brightness range that might be found within a mask.

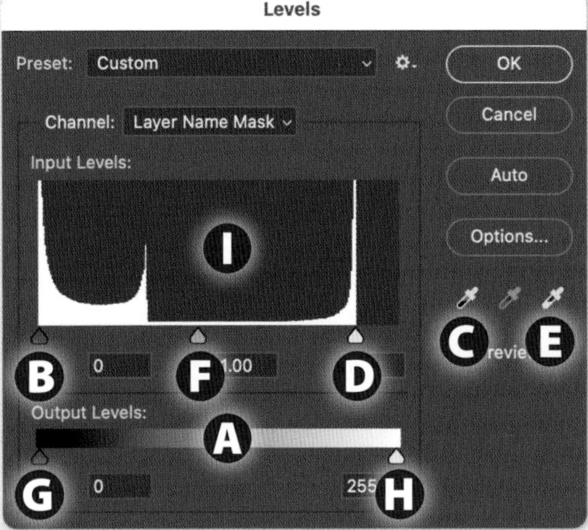

Black Input Level: The upper-left slider **B** forces everything to the left of it in the bar below to become black. In a mask, black represents an area that would not be selected or visible and therefore would not impact the image.

Black Point Tool: Clicking within a mask with the black-filled eyedropper **C** will cause the Black Input Level slider to position itself directly above the brightness level upon which you clicked. That will effectively cause the area where you clicked to become black.

The **Sample Size** setting (in the Options Bar) determines how large of an area will be averaged to determine which brightness level is measured.

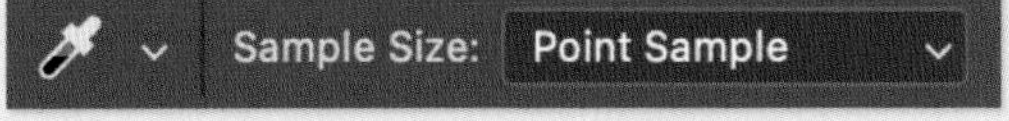

White Input Level: The upper-right slider **D** forces all tones to the right of it in the bar below to become white. White in a mask represents an area that is fully selected or visible and therefore will have the greatest impact on the image.

White Point Tool: Clicking within a mask with the white-filled eyedropper **E** will cause the White Input Level slider to move so it is positioned directly above the brightness level upon which you clicked. That will effectively cause the area you clicked upon to become white.

Midtone Input Level: The middle slider **F** forces the shade directly below it to become 50% gray. This causes the gradual transitions between black and white to become weighted more heavily toward the bright or dark tones. Moving the slider to the left causes selected or masked areas to visually extend further across a transition, while moving it to the right shrinks the transition.

Black Output Level: The lower-left slider **G** causes black to become the shade found in the bar above the slider and lightens the darker tones to maintain a smooth transition to white. Since black in a mask represents an area that would not be selected or visible, moving this slider causes areas that previously did not have any impact to start to influence the appearance of the image.

White Output Level: The lower-right slider **H** causes white to become the shade found in the bar above and darkens the lighter tones to maintain a smooth transition to black. This causes the overall effect of a mask to be reduced. It is similar to lowering the **Opacity** of a layer.

Histogram: The bar chart in **Levels I** indicates which of the shades found in the bar below are found within the image and how much space each takes up relative to the other shades. The shade found in the bar below the leftmost bar is the darkest shade in the mask and the shade below the rightmost bar is the brightest.

Posterization

Banding, stair-stepping, and posterization are all terms frequently used to describe an area that should contain a smooth, seamless transition but is instead broken up into a series of large, visually distinct bands of color. Posterization is the official term for this artifact, which reproduces an image using a smaller number of tones. It's analogous to anticipating a smooth, gradual ramp on which to roll your luggage, but instead encountering a series of abrupt raises in elevation (a.k.a. stairs). Below are some of the causes of posterization and methods for eliminating it.

Smart Previews in Lightroom: When viewing or adjusting an image in Lightroom, it is not uncommon to see posterization appear that will not be present if the image is exported or opened into Photoshop. This is due to Lightroom's preference for utilizing lower-quality Smart Previews in order to improve its responsiveness. This is discussed in more detail in the "Masking Artifacts" section earlier in this chapter. Choosing **View>Zoom to 100%** will cause Lightroom to load the original image and update its on-screen appearance, which will usually remedy this type of faux posterization.

Manipulating 8-bit Images: Working with JPEG files or setting Lightroom's **External Editing** preference to deliver 8 bits of information to Photoshop (see page 188 for more on that setting) will produce an image that is made from only 256 brightness levels. That's enough information to make an image look great on-screen and is the setting used for nearly all images seen on the internet. But manipulating that small amount of information by radically brightening, adding contrast, or boosting the colors can quickly cause posterization to appear. The solution is to capture images in the raw format (which delivers at least 4,096 brightness levels) and to make sure Lightroom is set to generate 16-bit files when images are opened into Photoshop. Use the JPEG file format only when saving finished images that will not require additional adjustments.

Low-Quality Luminosity Masks: Isolating and adjusting a limited brightness range is apt to produce posterization if the techniques described on the previous page are not utilized.

Exaggerating JPEG Compression Artifacts: The JPEG file format utilizes a type of compression that is easily capable of producing an image that is one-tenth the size of the original with little perceptible loss in quality. However, if the image is subsequently brightened or the contrast is increased, the loss in quality produced by such compression can become not only noticeable, but also distracting. True detail can tend to look as if it's been replaced by popcorn! This is most commonly an issue when an image has been downloaded from the internet and has to be repurposed with the original raw file being unavailable.

These compression artifacts can be reduced in Photoshop by choosing **Filter>Neural Filters**, choosing the **JPEG Artifacts Removal** option from the list in the left column, and then experimenting to see which **Strength** setting is most effective.

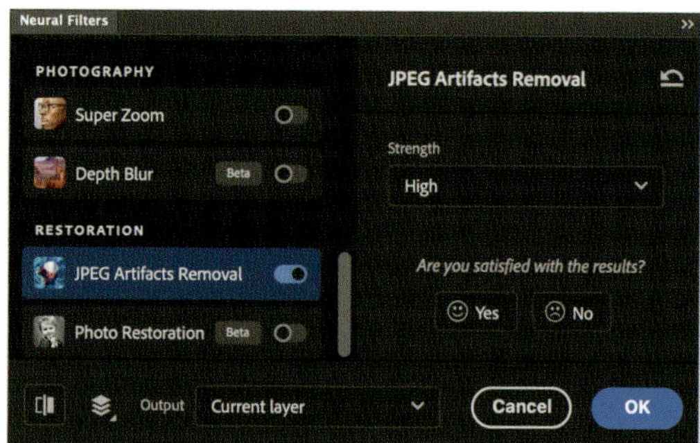

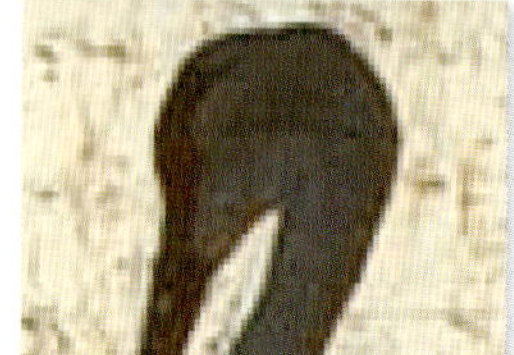

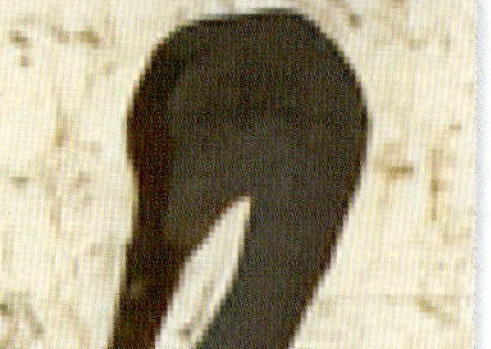

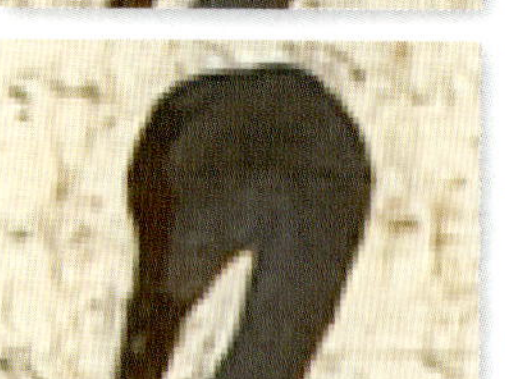

Top Left: *Prominent JPEG compression artifacts.*

Top Right: *JPEG Artifacts Removal applied using High.*

Bottom Left: *JPEG Artifacts Removal applied using Low.*

Artificial Highlight Colors: With raw files, areas that are rendered as solid white at default settings do not represent the point at which a camera reached its limit and stopped picking up detail from the scene. Additional detail can be revealed by lowering the **Highlights** or **Whites** sliders in Lightroom.

There is, of course, a limit to how much information can be recovered. For example, you won't have the ability to reveal sunspots in images that include the noonday sun. When you start to approach the limits of the information contained in the brightest area of a raw file, odd colors that did not originate from the camera will start to appear. Eventually, areas will appear that contain no color whatsoever.

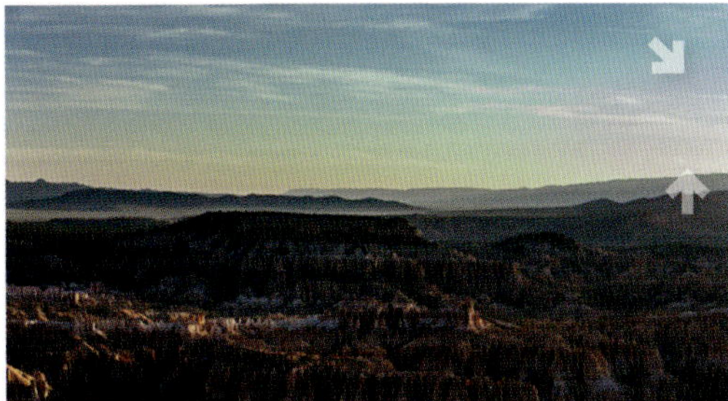

A large portion of the sky looked white before the adjustment.

Odd colors will appear when Lightroom attempts to darken and extract detail from an area that was so bright that the amount light falling on the lens was beyond the maximum amount the sensor was capable of measuring and was therefore recorded as 100%. Cameras capture red, green, and blue information for each pixel. As you get into the brightest area, one of those three colors reaches its maximum first. When this happens, Lightroom substitutes the information from one of the other two colors, which is what causes the colors to shift. When two of the three colors are clipped to their maximum, the one remaining color that contains detail is used as a substitute for all three colors. The result is an area that contains no detail whatsoever because a balanced amount of red, green, and blue is the formula for producing a shade of gray.

There is no universal remedy for artificial highlight colors other than adjusting the in-camera exposure. This more commonly happens in skies, which makes a sky replacement the common solution to this issue.

Smoothing Posterization: Unnatural and abrupt transitions can often be smoothed using the following technique:

1) In Photoshop, choose **File>New** and create a brand-new RGB mode document that is filled with white. Make sure it is of a similar size and has an identical bit depth (8- or 16-bit) to the image that requires retouching.
2) Choose the **Healing Brush** and set the **Sample** setting in the Options Bar to **Current & Below**. **Option**-click (Mac) or **Alt**-click (PC) in the center of the newly created document to set it as the source for retouching.
3) Switch to the document that is posterized, create a new layer, and then paint over all the areas that have abrupt transitions and need to be smoothed, using short brush-strokes until they have all been smoothed.
4) Choose **Filter>Camera Raw Filter** and adjust the settings within the **Effects** section in order to add grain to the retouched areas. The goal is to match the grain that is found in the original image.

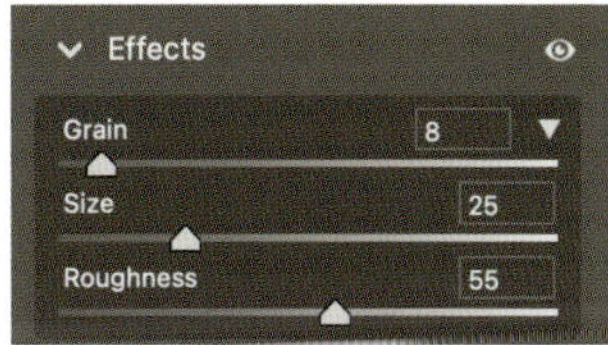

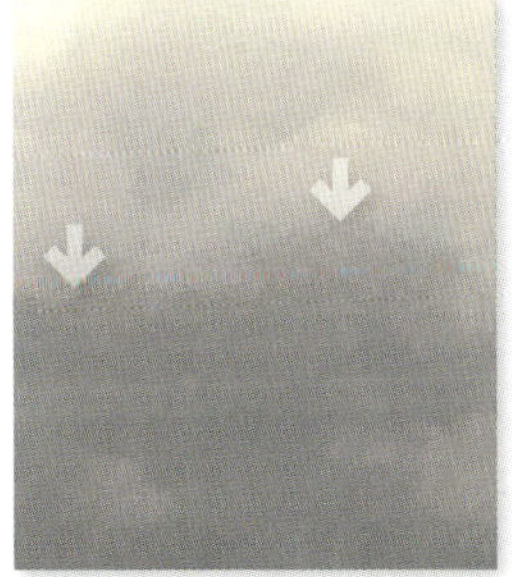

Top Left:
Original image.

Top right:
Result of smoothing transitions using the Healing Brush.

Bottom Left:
Result of adding noise to the retouched area that is similar to the surrounding image.

Panorama Artifacts

The general process for capturing a series of images and stitching them into a seamless panorama is covered in chapter 5. This section focuses on issues that might be discovered after a panorama is stitched.

Motion Blur Due to Camera Movement

I used to think that the best camera ISO setting for capturing panoramas was ISO 100. Being the default ISO for most cameras, it tends to produce images that contain little or no noise. That's ideal when shooting on a tripod, using the three-second self-timer setting in order to avoid camera movement. However, it is not ideal for handheld shooting. These days, I set my camera to use its Auto ISO setting so it dynamically adjusts the ISO setting to ensure I never end up with a shutter speed that is too low for handheld shooting. I'd rather have a noisy panorama than one that is unusable due to motion blur. The images shown below were captured before I developed that mindset.

ISO 100 produced a 1/60th sec. exposure, which was slow enough to generate one soft image due to camera shake. I generated a usable result by simply excluding the soft image. This created a tiny V-shaped gap in one spot, which was easily filled by turning on the **Fill Edges** checkbox when the panorama was stitched.

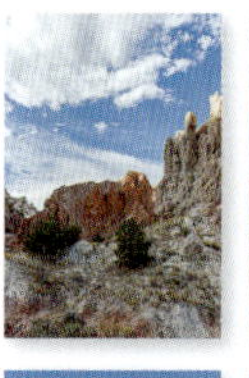
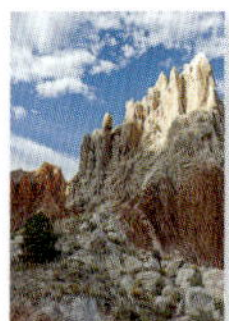
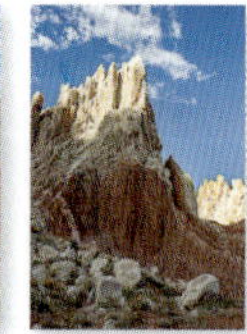
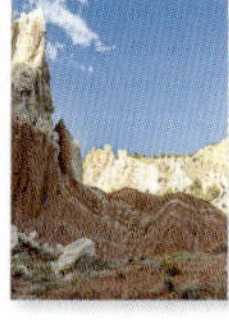
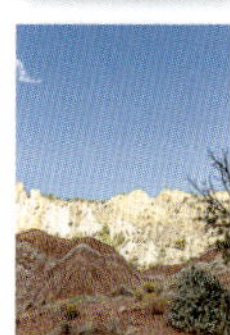
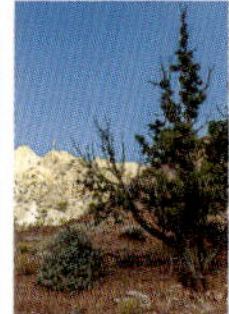
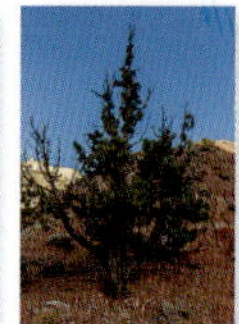

One of these seven images was excluded when stitching to avoid a soft area in the panorama.

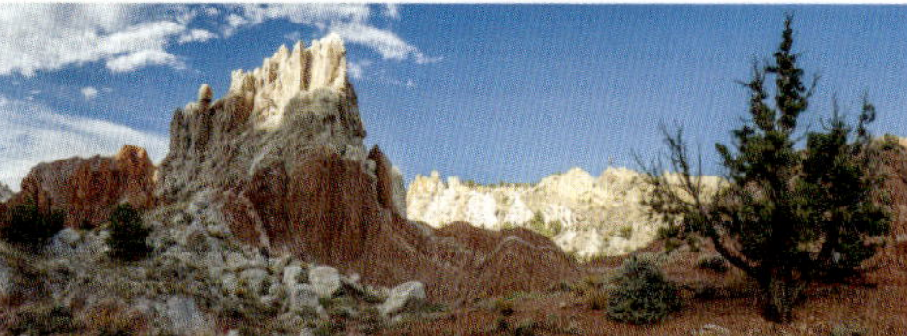

Clipped Fisheye Panoramas

When stitching multiple fisheye images in Lightroom, too much of the image is commonly discarded. Better results can usually be achieved by choosing **Photo>Edit In>Merge to Panorama in Photoshop**. Then use the **Auto** layout setting and turn on the top three options that are found under the file list.

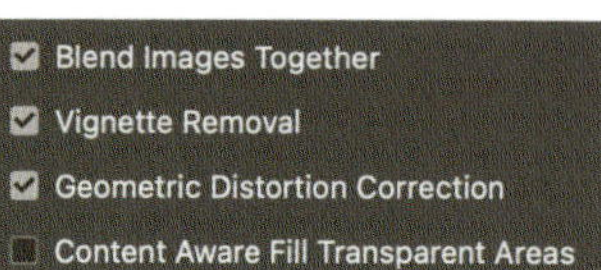

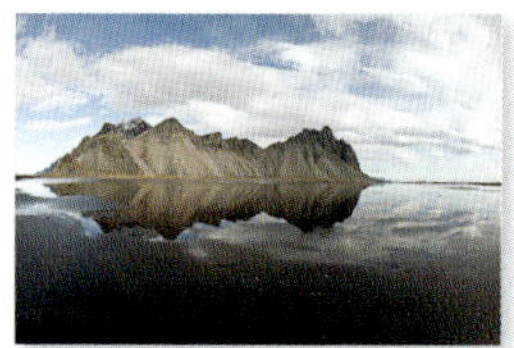
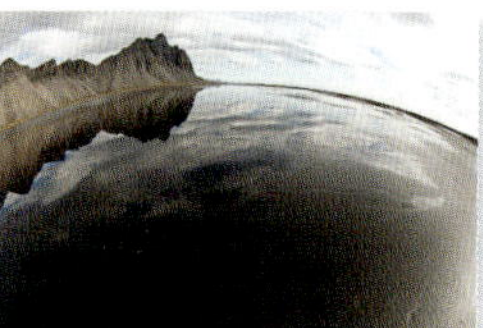
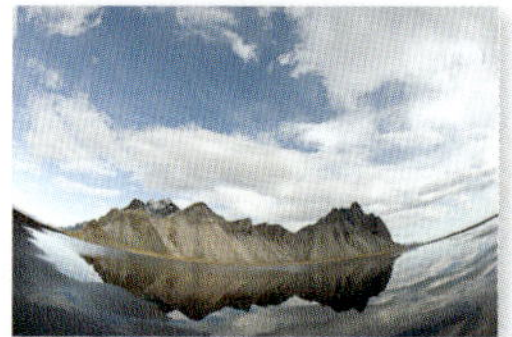
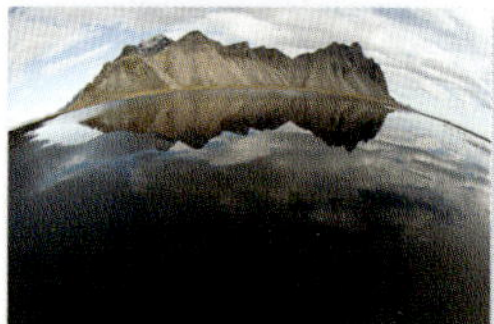

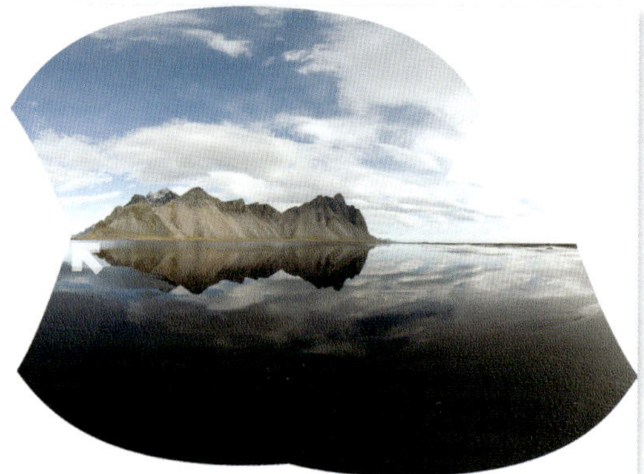

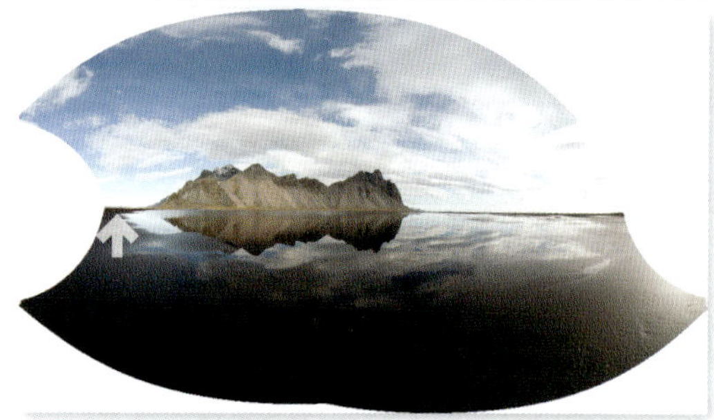

Top: *Stitched in Lightroom.* **Bottom:** *Stitched in Photoshop.*

Angled Horizons and Trees

When the horizon in a panorama is not level, it can be straightened using the rotation feature in the **Crop** tool. However, this will commonly force you to crop too far into the edge of the image, creating an unusable result. In the image below, the tree that is closest to the camera appeared to be tilted even after straightening the horizon.

An alternative to the **Crop** tool is the **Guided Upright** feature that is found in the **Transform** section of Lightroom's Develop module.

Start by choosing the **Guided Upright** tool from the **Transform** panel and then click and drag within the image to produce lines that are parallel with at least two areas that should be perfectly horizontal or vertical. In this example, lines were added that aligned with the horizon and trees on both ends of the image **A**.

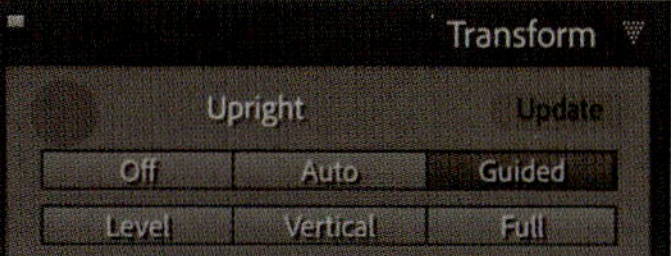

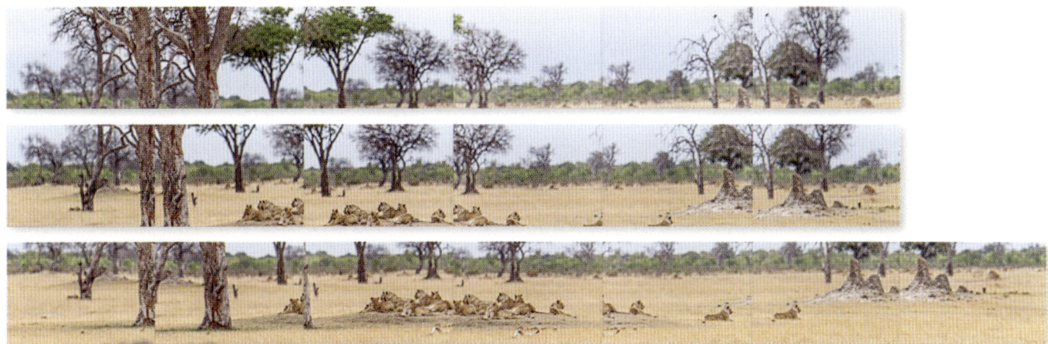

These images were captured starting with the bottom row. In the top row, the camera moved downward in each successive shot.

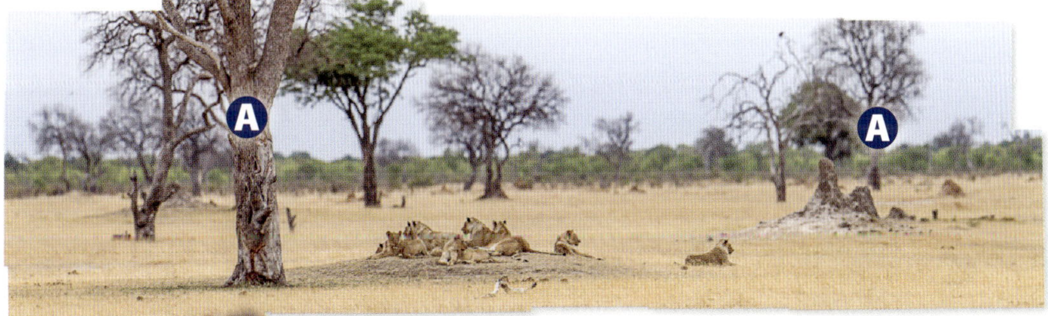

*Stitching the nineteen exposures shown above, with a 500mm f/4 lens, produced an angled horizon and tilted tree **A**.*

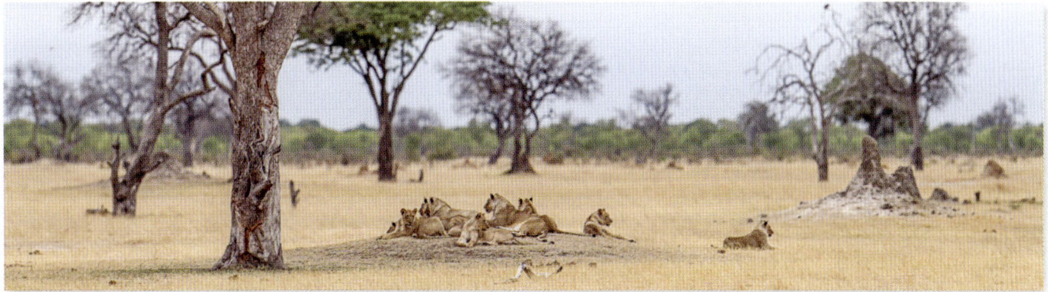

Result of adding a horizontal line parallel with the angled horizon and vertical lines parallel with two trees in Upright.

Chapter 9: Eliminate Processing Artifacts

Lens Flares Multiplied

When stitching a panorama from images that were captured while the camera was pointed at the sun, it's common to end up with multiple lens flares. This contrasts with the single lens flare you'd get if you had captured the same scene as a single exposure. When lens flares are present, they form a series of straight lines that originate from the sun's position. Panning the camera between exposures causes the sun's position to change, resulting in the flares appearing at different locations in each shot. The easy way to eliminate excessive lens flare is to avoid them in the first place. This can be done by shading the lens with your hand to prevent direct sunlight from entering the lens. But that's only possible when the sun is not visible in the composition.

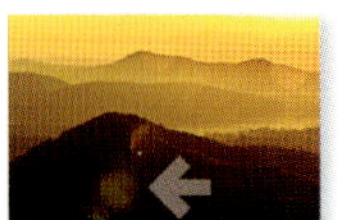
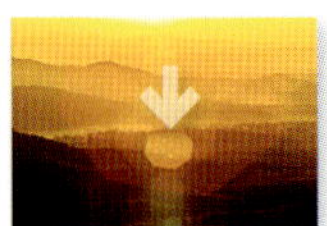
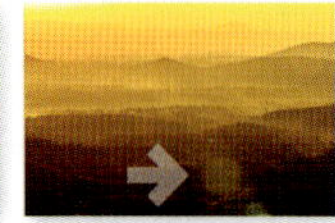

Lightroom Stitching Multiplies Lens Flares

Lightroom Classic offers no control over which parts of each frame are used to produce a panorama. As a result, the flares from multiple images are often combined, leaving you with an unusable image. To gain control over the stitching process, we'll need to utilize Photoshop.

Raw versus Processed Panoramas

Panoramas created in Lightroom contain unprocessed data, just like the raw files they were generated from. Therefore, there is no quality difference between making adjustments to the individual images before merging and adjusting the resulting panorama.

The same is not true of Photoshop, which can only work with images that have been processed in such a way that any further adjustments will not be of the same quality as those applied to raw files in Lightroom. To obtain the highest quality, the individual images will need to be optimized in Lightroom before being stitched in Photoshop.

Utilizing a Sacrificial Raw Panorama

For a panorama to be truly seamless in nature, all adjustments must be applied to the images as a group. But figuring out the optimal settings for the entire width of a panorama while viewing a single image is darn near impossible. Therefore, I like to stitch a panorama in Lightroom and use it to determine the most ideal processing settings. Once that image has been optimized in the Develop module, its settings can then be transferred to the individual images. Once that panorama has served its purpose, it can be discarded.

Transferring settings is as easy as right-clicking (or **Control**-clicking when using a single-button mouse) on the optimized panorama in the Library module and choosing **Copy Settings**, then selecting the individual exposures that image was created from and choosing **Paste Settings** from the same menu.

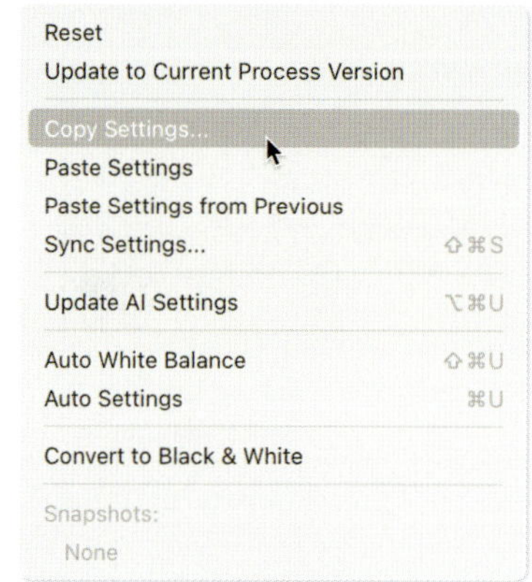

When copying settings, the dialog box that appears will allow you to determine exactly which settings will be copied. I use the settings shown on the next page because they are the ones that contribute to the overall appearance of the panorama and would be applicable to the individual images it was produced from. Some of the settings may produce a slightly different result when applied to an image that is not as wide as the panorama, but I find this method to be the best way to figure out what settings would be appropriate for the individual images.

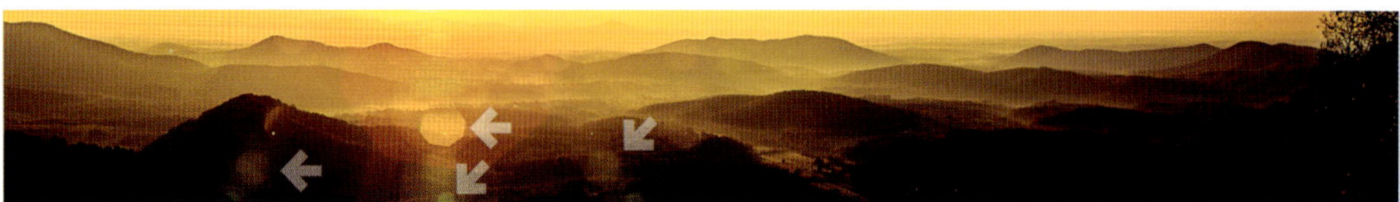

Panorama stitched in Lightroom Classic from nine images, seven of which contained lens flares.

Section III: Crafting a Photograph

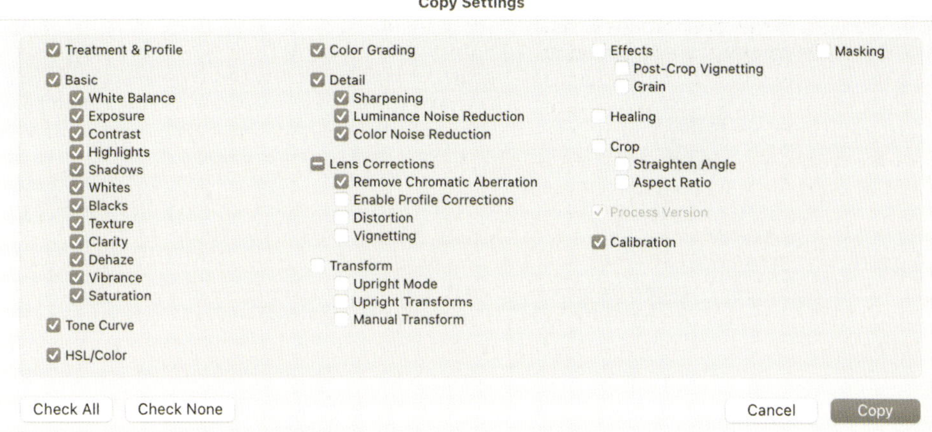

The options that are turned off would only be appropriate if pasted to an already stitched panorama.

Stack and Align Using Photoshop

Now, with all the individual images still selected, choose **Photo>Edit In>Merge to Panorama in Photoshop**. When prompted for options, be sure to turn off the **Blend Images Together** checkbox. This will align the images but will skip the blending process so it can be performed later.

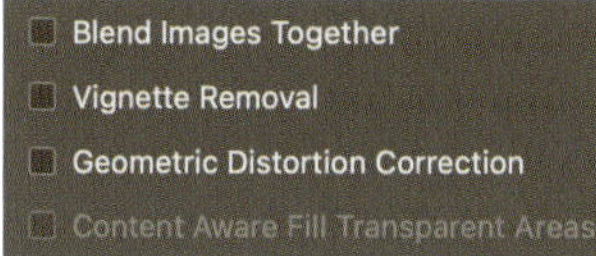

Mask Problem Areas

At this point, areas that contain lens flares can be hidden to prevent them from appearing in the final panorama. This can be accomplished by doing the following:

1) Hide all the other layers by holding **Option** (Mac) or **Alt** (PC) and clicking on the eyeball icon for the topmost layer in the Layers panel.

2) If a lens flare is visible, make a crude selection around its bounds using the **Lasso** tool.

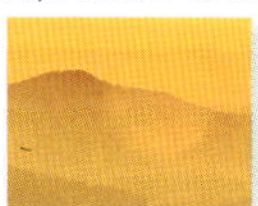
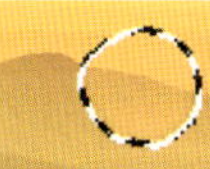

3) If more than one flare is visible, hold **Shift** before clicking to produce selections of the additional flares.

4) Once all the lens flares are selected, they can be hidden by choosing **Layer>Layer Mask>Hide Selection**.

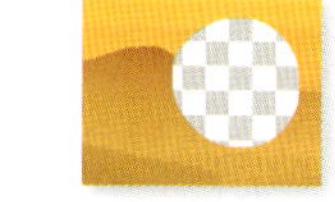

5) Repeat the preceding steps for all the remaining layers so that none of the images contain any visible lens flares.

6) Make all the layers visible by holding **Option** (Mac) or **Alt** (PC) and clicking on the eyeball icon for the layer that was last masked.

7) Inspect the image as a whole, looking for gaps where an area was hidden on multiple layers. Those gaps need to be filled by painting with white in one of the associated masks.

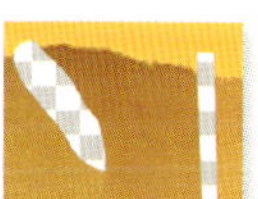

Blending Images into a Seamless Panorama

Now that the lens flares have been hidden from each layer, the seams in the panorama can be removed by choosing **Select>All Layers**, then **Edit>Auto-Blend Layers**, and using the default settings of **Panorama** with **Seamless Tones and Colors** enabled.

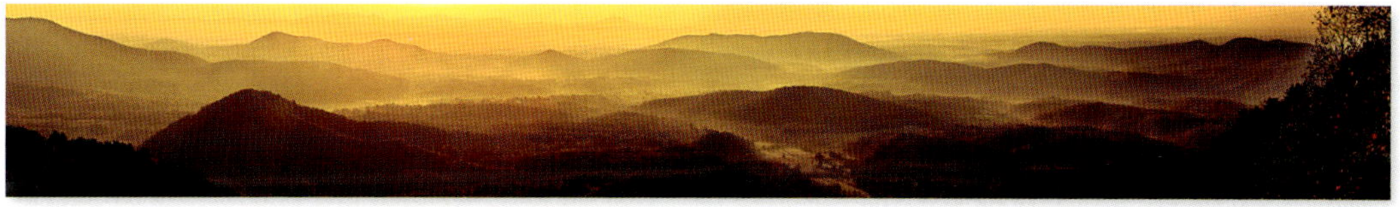

Panorama crafted in Photoshop by hiding the areas that contained lens flares before seamlessly blending the images.

Low-Resolution Panoramas

Lightroom allows panoramas to be generated based on low-resolution Smart Previews when the original images are not available. This can be useful when you're traveling without the hard drive that contains the original image files. I often create low-reso

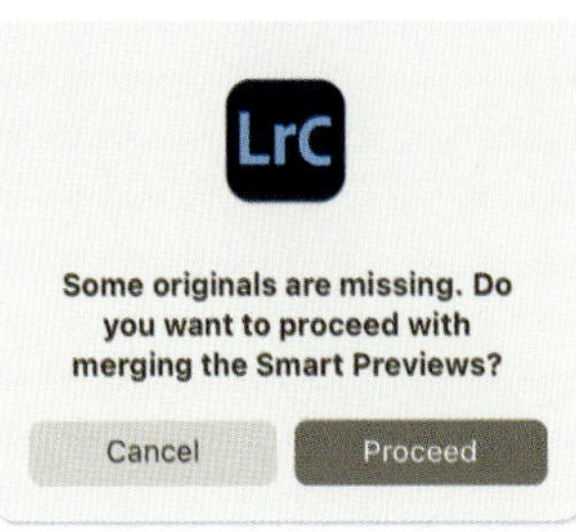

lution panoramas when I'm traveling, and then use the following technique to upgrade to full-sized panoramas once I return and have access to the original full-resolution images.

Locate Smart Preview Panoramas

Start by locating the low-resolution panoramas. Choose **All Photographs** from the **Catalog** panel on the left sidebar of the Library module. Then type **Command-F** (Mac) or **Ctrl-F** (PC), set the **Text** pop-up menu to **Filename**, and enter "**smartpreview-pano**" into the search field in the filter bar that appears near the top of the screen.

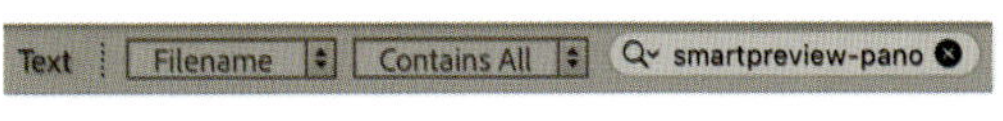

Locate Original Source Images

Right-click on the panorama you would like to upgrade to full size and choose **Go to Folder in Library** from the resulting contextual menu. This will navigate to the folder that likely contains the original high-resolution images.

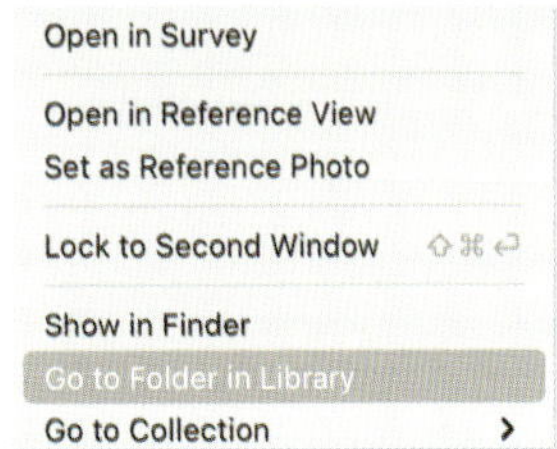

Restitch from High Resolution Originals

Select the original photos the panorama was made from and choose **Photo>Photo Merge> Panorama**.

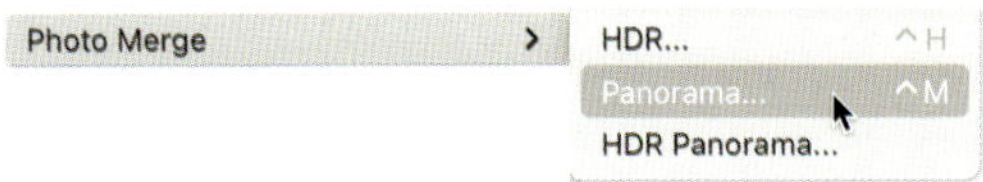

Transfer Settings from Low-Resolution Version

Once the high-resolution panorama has been generated, settings from the older file can be copied by right-clicking on the version that was created using Smart Previews and choosing **Develop Settings>Copy Settings**. Click the **Check All** button and then the **Copy** button. Then right-click on the version that was produced using the original high-resolution images and choose **Develop Settings>Paste Settings**.

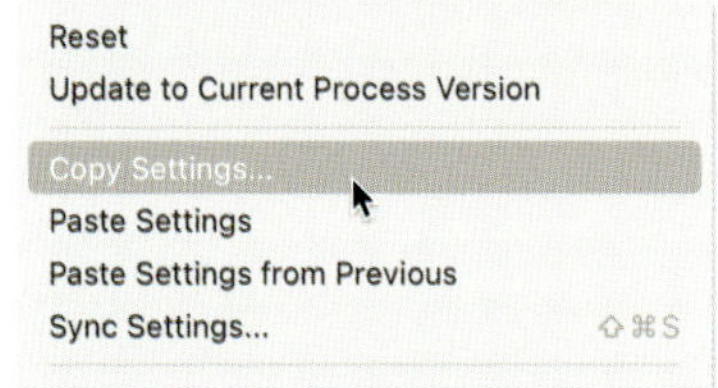

Fine-Tune Develop Settings

The sharpening and noise-reduction settings found in the Detail panel will produce different results when applied to a high-resolution image, so they may need to be readjusted to achieve the desired results on the high-resolution panorama. The same is true for the **Clarity** and **Texture** sliders found in the **Basic** panel.

Transfer Photoshop Layers

Adjustments and retouching that were applied to a Smart Preview–based panorama in Photoshop can often be transferred to a higher-resolution version of the same panorama if they were stitched using identical settings. The process is as follows and only works if no cropping has been applied in Photoshop:

1) Select both the newly stitched high-resolution panorama and the layered lower-resolution panorama that was produced using Smart Previews in Lightroom. Then choose **Photo>Edit In>Edit in Photoshop**.

2) In Photoshop, switch to the layered lower-resolution panorama. Scale it up to match the size of the larger file by choosing **Image>Image Size**, choosing the name of the high-resolution panorama from the bottom of the **Window** menu, and clicking **OK**.

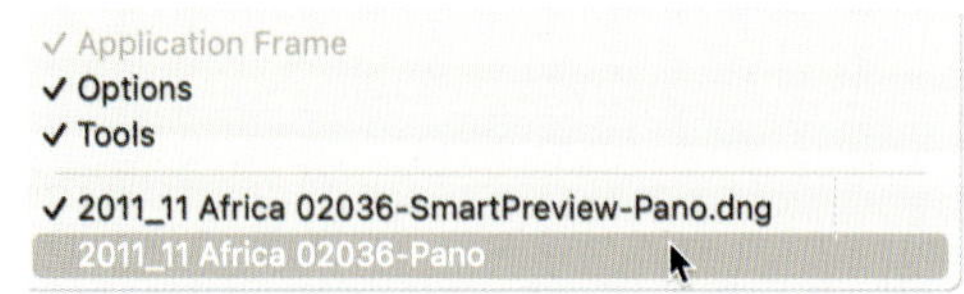

3) Then, select all but the bottommost layer (which will usually contain the untouched panorama) by choosing **Select>All Layers**. If the bottommost layer is not called "Background," then you'll also need to **Command**-click (Mac) or **Ctrl**-click (PC) on the bottom layer within the Layers panel to exclude it from the active layers.

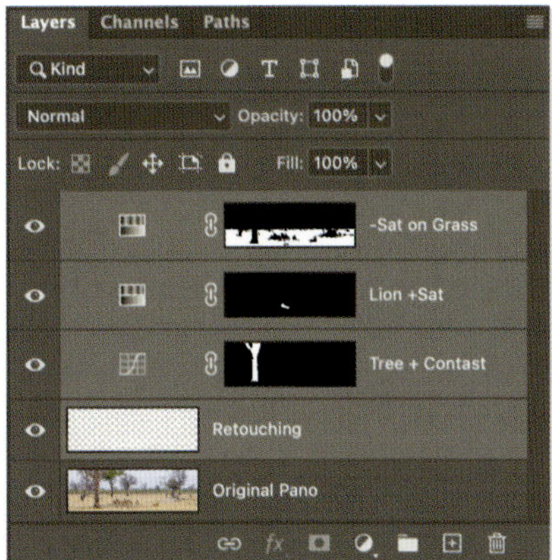

4) Now, to move a copy of the active layers to the high-resolution image, choose **Layer> Duplicate layers**, set the **Document** pop-up menu to the name of the high-resolution file, and then click **OK**.

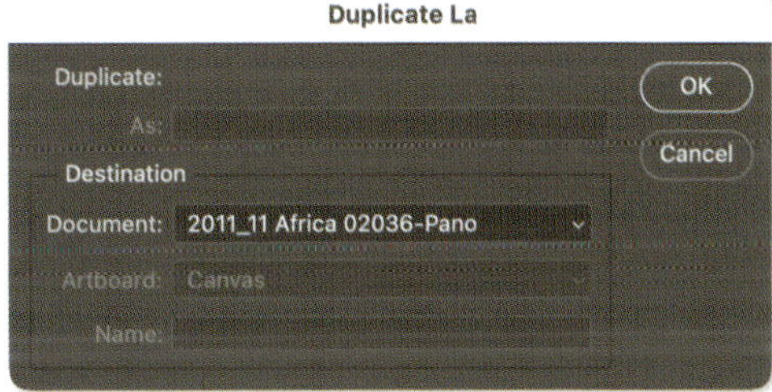

5) Now that the layers from the low-resolution version of the file have been transferred, close that file and do not save any changes.

6) If a retouching layer is present, its contents will appear soft due to the scaling that was applied earlier. Its contents can usually be upgraded so that it is based on the high-resolution information. That can be done by holding the **Command** key (Mac) or **Ctrl** key (PC) and clicking on the thumbnail image for the retouching layer in order to produce a selection. Then choose **Edit>Fill** and use the **Content-Aware** setting.

General Panorama Issues to Look Out For

The following problems are common when working with panoramas in Lightroom and Photoshop.

Older Images Appearing Tiny: The previews in Lightroom's Library module don't always reflect the true size of a panorama. If a panorama ever appears to become dramatically smaller when switching from the **Fit** view to **100%** zoom level, then head to the Develop module and zoom to **100%** or higher. This will usually cause the preview to update. If that does not work and the image is a TIFF or PSD file, choose **Photo>Edit In> Edit in Photoshop**, and that should do the trick.

Opening a Can of Worms: When a panorama is stitched using Photoshop, you may see a series of squiggly lines, resembling tiny worms, at the junctions between photos. These lines are artifacts that are only visible when you attempt to view a huge image at a zoom level of less than 100%. They're not actually part of the image. Zooming in by choosing **View>100%** or combining the layers by choosing **Layer>Merge Visible** will cause the lines to disappear.

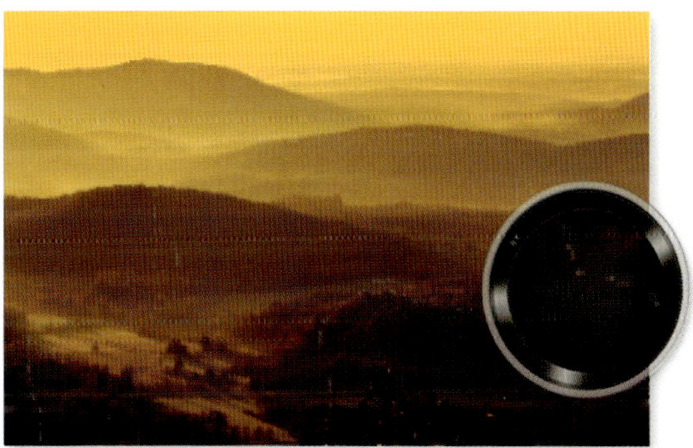

Trusting Auto Fill: When stitching a panorama, Lightroom's **Fill Edges** and Photoshop's **Content-Aware Fill Transparent Areas** options will fill the empty areas of a non-rectangular result as an alternative to cropping. It is essential to critically inspect the areas that have been filled afterward and perform additional retouching wherever there are repeated elements or the content does not look appropriate.

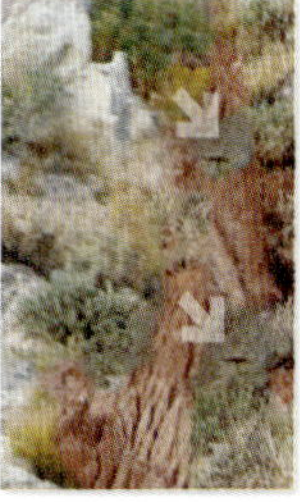

HDR Artifacts

Images that were produced by merging multiple exposures into an HDR image (as detailed in chapter 5) commonly contain visual artifacts that can cause the image to look unnatural when viewed up close. Therefore, be sure to choose **View>100%** (or **200%** if you're working on a high-resolution retina display) and scroll around to look for the following issues before you decide that the image is done and ready to show the public.

Uneven Brightness

It's common practice to crank the **Highlights** and **Shadows** sliders to opposite extremes in an attempt to squish the huge brightness range of an HDR image into a range that can be viewed on a normal monitor. Unfortunately, this causes intermediate areas to become uneven in brightness.

In the example below, the mountains directly to the right of the sun appear dark and become brighter as you move away from the light source. Inspecting one of the individual exposures used to produce the HDR image reveals how the brightness would fall off naturally as you move farther from the sun.

Process for Midtones

I started by inspecting the **Highlights** and **Shadows** settings that were applied to the image as a whole in the **Basic** panel in Lightroom, knowing

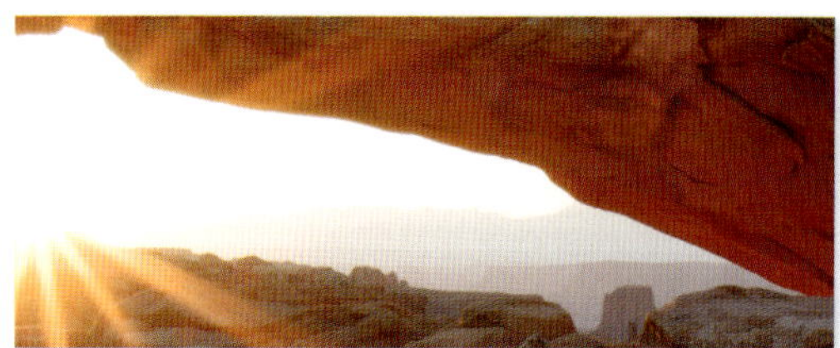

A single exposure reveals the natural light falloff of the scene.

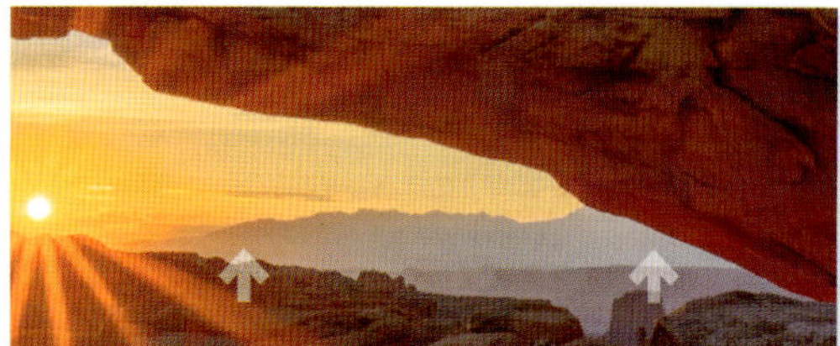

Moving the Highlights slider to -100 caused the light falloff to look unnatural in the mountains to the right of the sun.

that those settings were likely causing the uneven appearance within the mountains. I then isolated the mountains using a combination of **Luminance** and **Object** masks. I set the **Highlights** and **Shadows** on the mask to the exact same settings that were applied to the image as a whole, but swapped the + and - symbols that appeared at the beginning of each setting.

For example, if **Highlights -80** is being applied to the image as a whole, then I'd set the masked **Highlights** setting to **+80**. This way, the mask cancels out what is applied to the entire image.

Convert to Photoshop Layers

Upon close inspection, I found that Lightroom's masking features were not able to precisely isolate the mountains. That's when I decided it was time to head to Photoshop so I could incorporate the masking ideas that are covered in chapter 3 in order to produce a more accurate mask.

I used the following steps to convert the masked adjustment made in Lightroom into multiple layers in Photoshop:

1) I started by clicking the eyeball icon **A** to the right of the mask. This temporarily disabled the mask, giving me an acceptable base image for the layered Photoshop file.

2) I then sent the image to Photoshop in a special way by choosing **Photo>Edit In>Open as Smart Object in Photoshop**. Using a Smart Object embedded a copy of the raw file into the resulting layer and will therefore allow access to the masked adjustment that was made in Lightroom.

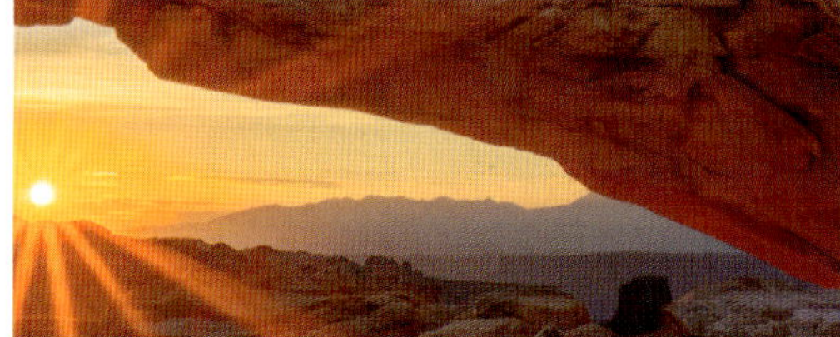

Result of effectively zeroing out the Highlights and Shadows settings to make the mountains look more natural.

3) Next, I needed to duplicate the layer so I could mask two versions of the image. A normal duplicate would not do the trick because any subsequent change made to the raw settings of one layer would also affect the duplicate. To produce a layer that is independent from the existing one, I chose **Layer>Smart Objects>New Smart Object via Copy**.

4) Then, to apply different settings to that newly created layer, I double-clicked on its thumbnail image within the Layers panel. This caused the Camera Raw window to appear.

5) Within Camera Raw, I clicked on the mask icon on the right edge of the window. This revealed the mask that I had disabled back when I was in Lightroom. I then hovered over the mask and clicked the eyeball icon to the right of the mask in order to turn it back on.

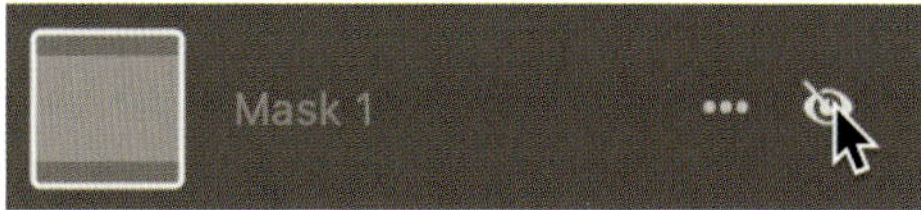

6) I then needed to get the masked adjustment to apply to the entire image instead of just the mountains. This was accomplished by clicking on the name of the mask to reveal the list of components it was made from. I clicked the **Add** button below the mask, chose **Brush**, and painted across the entirety of the image before clicking the **OK** button to exit Camera Raw.

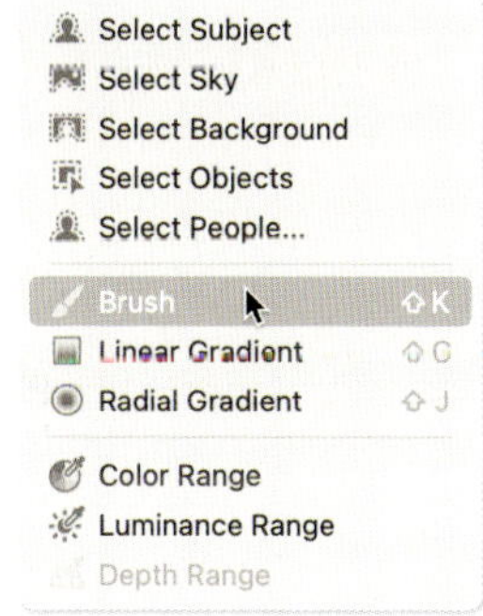

At this point, the image had been successfully converted into a stack of layers in Photoshop. This allowed me to use all the techniques mentioned in chapter 3 to more precisely mask the mountains.

Unnatural Light Sources

When something as bright as the sun is visible within an HDR image, be sure to inspect it closely to see if there are any unnaturally abrupt transitions that might benefit from smoothing.

Selective Clarity

Sometimes the problem is caused by something as simple as the **Clarity** slider being boosted so high that the transition area surrounding the sun has too much contrast. When that's the case, there is no need to lower the **Clarity** setting that's being applied to the image as a whole, since it may be improving the look of everything but the sun.

To selectively reduce **Clarity**, apply a masked adjustment to the area around the sun, and then move the **Clarity** slider to the left, applying a negative amount. Negative settings can be used to counteract the amount being applied to the image as a whole. For example, having **+40** applied globally and **-30** applied through a mask will cause **+10** to remain in the masked area. The same concept can be used to selectively reduce any other setting that can be applied both globally and as a masked adjustment.

Selective Smoothing

One or more of the following adjustments can be useful when applied as a masked adjustment to smooth the area surrounding the sun:

Texture: Moving this slider to the left will cause fine details to be softened and will produce a soft glow that is similar in appearance to the Orton effect that is covered in chapter 7.

Clarity: Negative **Clarity** will reduce contrast by brightening the dark areas that surround the sun.

Sharpness: Applying negative **Sharpness** will blur the image overall.

Defringe: Positive settings will soften the transition between bright and dark areas.

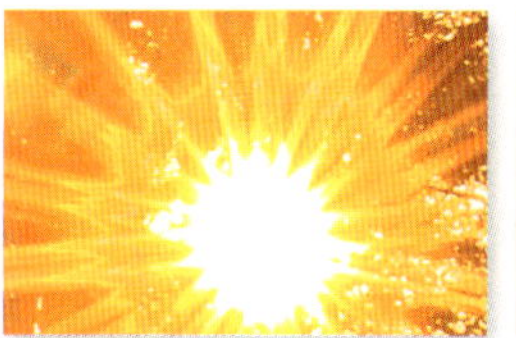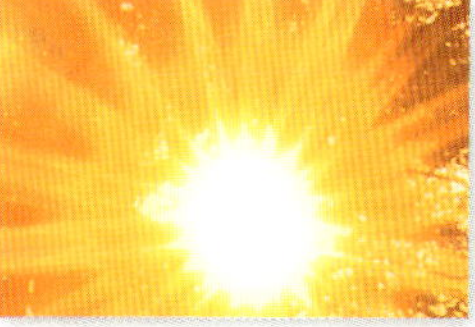

Before and after selectively smoothing unnatural transitions.

Motion Artifacts

Objects that change position between exposures can produce undesirable artifacts if they are located in an area that contains a wide brightness range. An example would be dark tree branches moving in the wind surrounded by a bright sky. When the **Deghost** settings that are available when merging multiple exposures into an HDR image are not effective, try one of the following techniques for dealing with motion artifacts.

Substitute Single Exposure for HDR

The only real options for dealing with motion artifacts in Lightroom Classic are to either start over again, using different deghosting settings when merging the exposures, or to abandon the idea of HDR altogether and process a single exposure as an alternative.

When choosing a single exposure out of a bracket of exposures that were originally intended to be a merged HDR image, choose the brightest exposure that retains a hint of detail in the brightest area so it is not blown out to solid white. If it was a true HDR-worthy scene, then you will likely end up with excessive noise in the dark area of the image after processing. That's when you'll have to apply dubious amounts of noise reduction to produce a usable image.

More advanced solutions will require the use of the more sophisticated features offered in Photoshop.

Retouch HDR from Single Exposure Source

Photoshop's **Healing Brush** can be used to blend a single exposure into areas that contain motion artifacts. Let's start in Lightroom by prepping two images for later blending in Photoshop:

1) Browse the individual exposures that were used to produce the HDR image. Inspect the area where the motion artifacts were an issue and find the brightest single exposure that still has a hint of detail in the highlights.
2) Type **D** to enter the Develop module, type **Shift-R** to enable **Reference View**, then drag the HDR version of the image from within the filmstrip at the bottom of the screen **A** to the reference area on the left side of your screen **B** to view the two side-by-side.

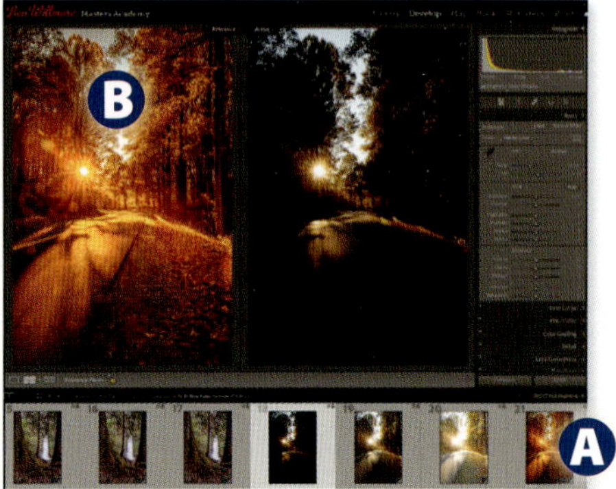

3) Adjust the single exposure, which is on the right side of the screen, and attempt to match the overall brightness and contrast of the HDR image on the left side of the screen. Don't be concerned with the brightness of the image as a whole. Instead, only try to match the brightness of the specific area that contained undesirable motion artifacts.

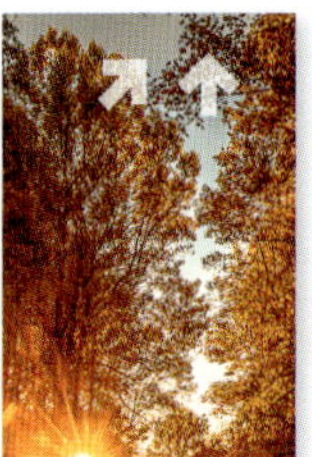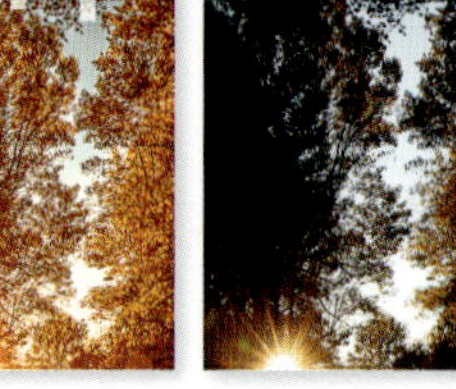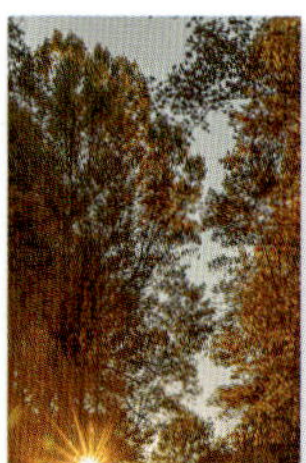

HDR that contains undesirable motion artifacts. *Single exposure at default settings.* *Single exposure processed to match HDR.*

4) Once the brightness and contrast of the area matches, adjust the noise-reduction settings found in the **Detail** panel to ensure the single image does not contain excessive noise.

Now let's see how the HDR image can be retouched using the single exposure as a source.

1) With the single exposure still active, choose **Photo>Edit In>Edit in Adobe Photoshop** to open it in Photoshop.
2) In Photoshop, choose the **Healing Brush** tool, hold **Option** (Mac) or **Alt** (PC), and click anywhere within the image to define it as the source for retouching.
3) Return to Lightroom, select the HDR image that contains undesirable motion artifacts and choose **Photo>Edit In>Edit in Adobe Photoshop**.

Section III: Crafting a Photograph

4) Using the **Healing Brush** in Photoshop, click anywhere within the HDR version of the image to establish it as the destination for retouching.

5) Choose **Edit>Undo** to remove the result of the retouching you just performed. Even though you just told Photoshop to undo your last action, it is only the result of the retouching that was undone. Establishing the HDR image as the destination for retouching and recording where you clicked within each document will still affect future steps.

6) Choose **Window>Clone Source** and then change the **X** and **Y** settings in the **Offset** section of the Clone Source panel to zero to indicate you'd like to use the source information from the single exposure and the HDR image to align instead of being offset.

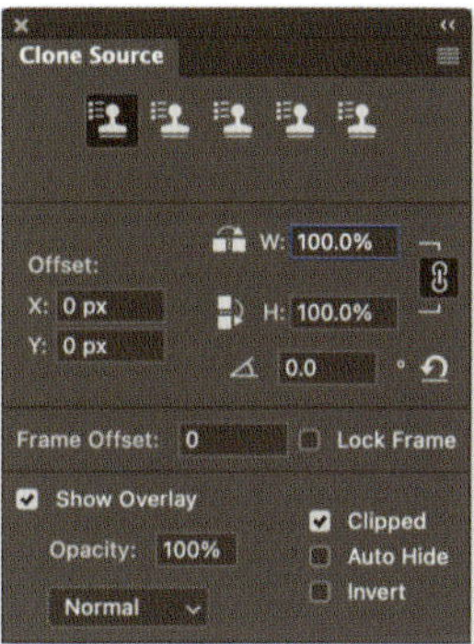

7) Paint over the area that contains the motion artifacts with the **Healing Brush**, ensuring that you cover the entire area and overlap a tiny portion of the surrounding image that does not contain artifacts.

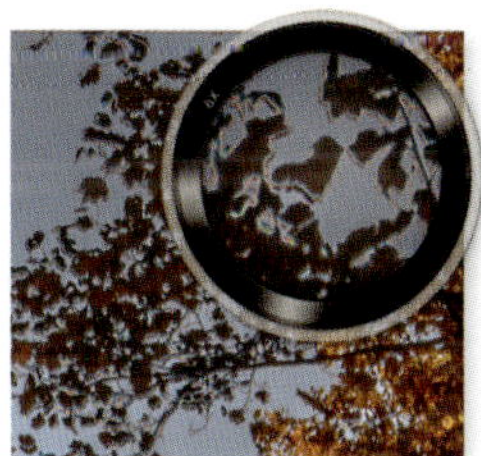
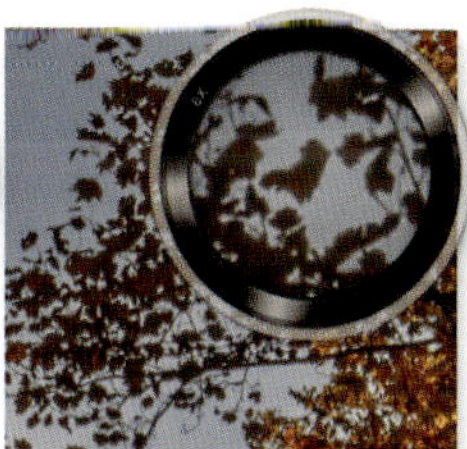

Leaves moving in the breeze caused artifacts where two exposures needed to be blended.

Result of healing from a single exposure processed to resemble brightness and color of HDR image.

If the above technique does not produce acceptable results, then intricate manual retouching may be required.

Sharpness Issues

HDR images usually produce softer-looking results when compared to a single exposure of the same scene. It is therefore advisable to compare the HDR version of an image to a single exposure to see which produces the best result.

Brightest Exposure with Highlight Detail

It's best to start with the brightest exposure that contains detail in the brightest areas. Lowering the **Exposure** slider to **-100** is an effective way to determine if detail has been captured in the brightest areas.

Compare Single Exposure to HDR Image

Once the most ideal single exposure has been found, head to the Develop module and choose **View>Open in Reference View**. In that view, the HDR version of the image can be dragged from the filmstrip at the bottom of the screen to the empty area beside the single-exposure version to view the two images side-by-side.

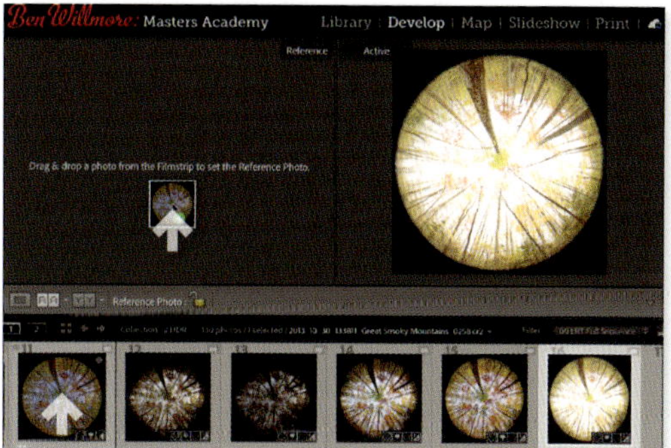

Optimize Single Exposure

To make the single exposure look similar to the HDR version, set **Highlights** to **-100**, **Shadows** to **+100**, and adjust **Exposure** to get overall brightness to look similar. Then adjust **Contrast** and **Clarity** until the image does not look dull. If the sky is visible, use an inverted sky mask to isolate the darker areas and then boost the **Whites** slider to brighten. Brightening an image to this extent will usually require judicial amounts of noise reduction.

Zoom and Compare

Switch to the Library module, select both the HDR and optimized single exposure, choose **View>Compare** and then **View>Zoom to 100%**, and critically evaluate the images to determine which produced the more ideal result.

Conclusion

WE'VE COVERED A lot of ground over the last nine chapters. Now let's discover how the techniques we've covered can be put into practice by looking at how they were used to craft some specific examples. We'll then look at how to create a cohesive body of work by ensuring the images collected share common qualities that make them look like they belong together. This is a crucial topic that is often overlooked but can make all the difference in how your work is perceived. Lastly, I'll provide insights on how you can continue to grow as an image maker with the hopes that this book has made a contribution to your evolution as a photographer.

Real-World Examples

Let's look at how the techniques covered earlier in this book were used to craft a few specific images.

Simple Everyday Optimization

The image that appears on the cover of this book was captured in Upper Antelope Canyon on a Navajo reservation near Page, Arizona. When capturing the image, I used the in-camera histogram and changed the exposure settings until I was sure that the bright area at the top retained detail. I then optimized the image from start to finish using just Lightroom.

Optimizing Brightness and Contrast

Basic optimizations included boosting **Shadows** to make it easier to see the detail in the dark areas, reducing **Highlights** to make it easier to see detail in the brightest areas, and then boosting **Contrast** and **Clarity** to make the image "pop."

Once the overall brightness was looking good, I double-clicked on the **Blacks** slider to make sure the image contained a small area of black.

At that point, I noticed a gap on the right of the histogram, which indicated I could brighten the overall image by adjusting the **Whites** slider.

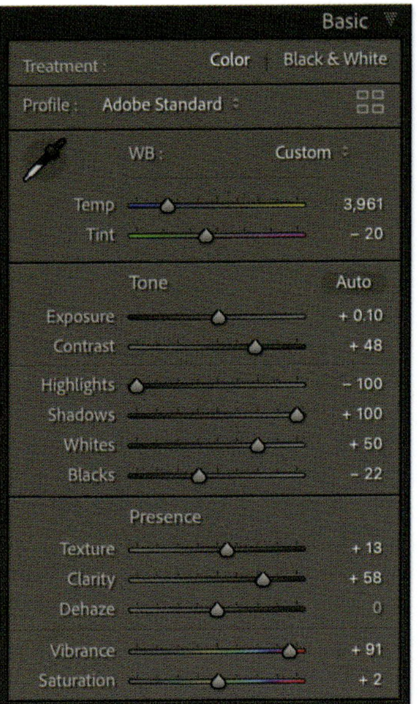

Basic panel adjustments.

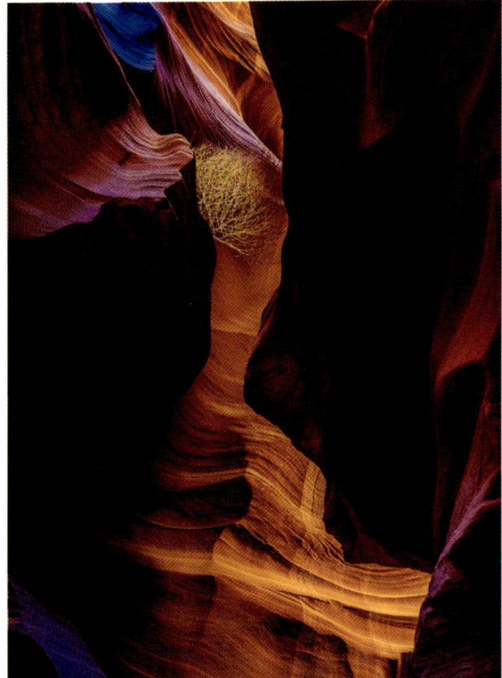

Finished image processed using only Lightroom Classic.

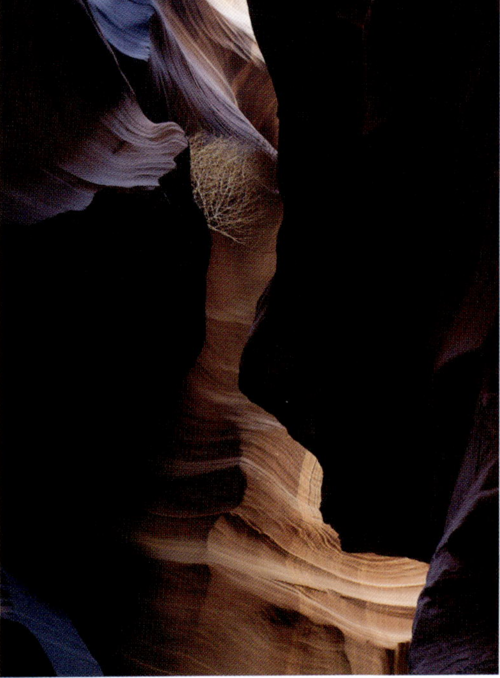

Raw capture shown using default settings.

Section III: Crafting a Photograph

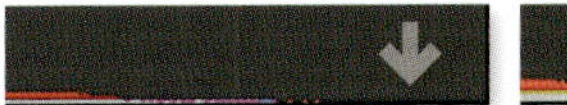 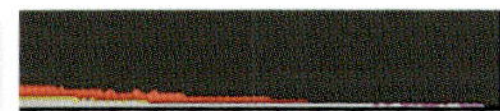

*Right half of histogram before (**left**) and after (**right**) adjusting the Whites slider to brighten the image as a whole.*

Making Color the Focus of the Image

What initially caught my eye when I first inspected this image was the variation in color found in the sandstone walls of the slot canyon. To make the colors more prominent, I cranked up the **Vibrance** setting. After that, I adjusted the **Temp** and **Tint** sliders and experimented until I discovered the setting that caused the colors to look distinctly different from each other.

Next, I utilized the various color sliders found in the **Saturation** section of the **HSL** panel to make the hint of blue in the upper left more prominent and to bring out the purples and reds that were only faintly visible.

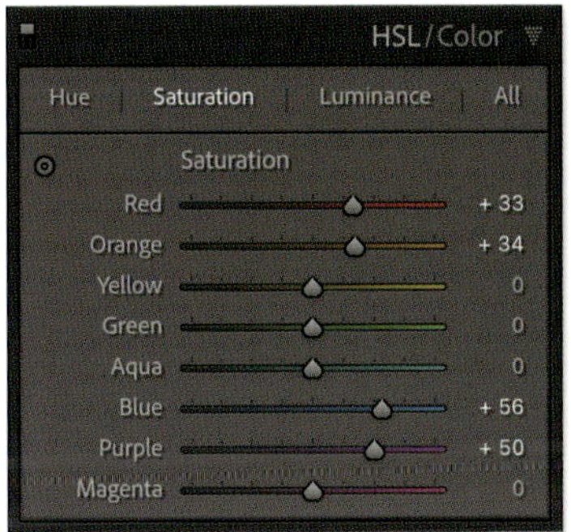

HSL/Color panel adjustments.

Looking back at this image, which was optimized a while ago, I'm amazed I neglected to utilize the **Calibration** panel sliders to fine-tune the colors.

Masked Adjustments

Once the image was starting to take shape, I transitioned to applying masked adjustments to the following areas:

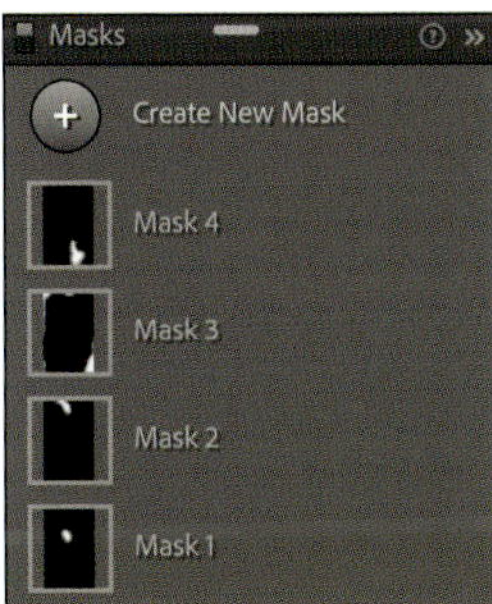

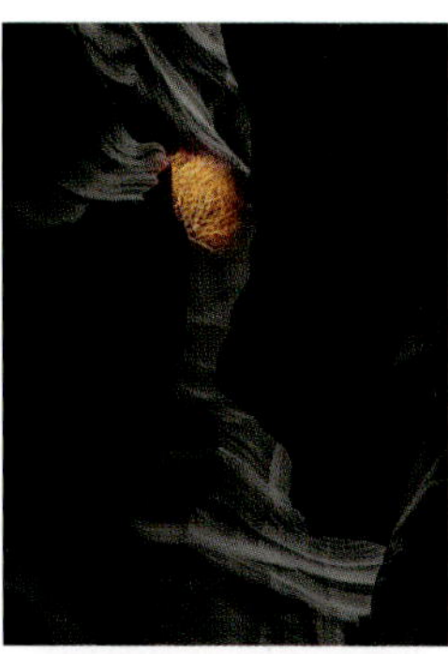

Mask 1: After choosing the tumbleweed as the focal point for the image, I masked the area and boosted the **Highlights** slider to make it appear as if more light was falling on the area.

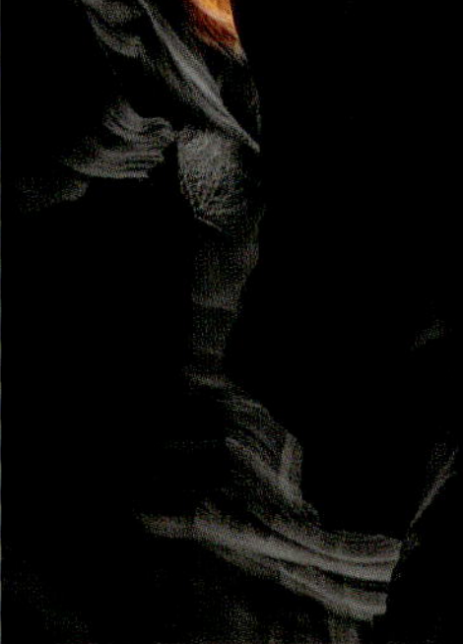

Mask 2: A small bright area at the top edge of the image was drawing the eye due to its excessive brightness. To remedy the situation, I applied a masked adjustment with the **Highlights** slider moved to the left to darken the area.

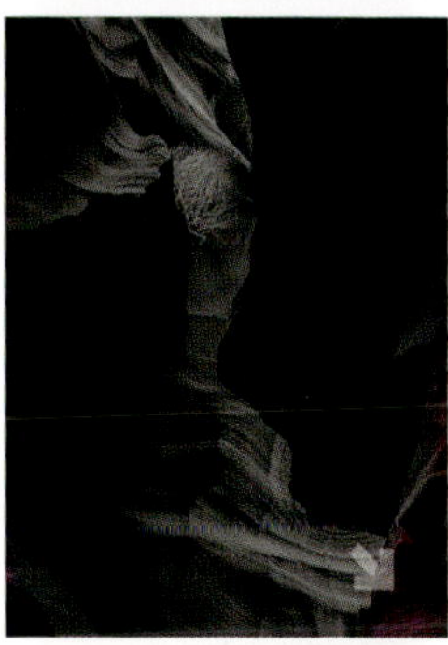

Mask 3: There were a few areas around the edges of the image that were pulling my attention away from the central portion of the image. I used a **Brush** mask to darken those areas with the **Exposure** slider.

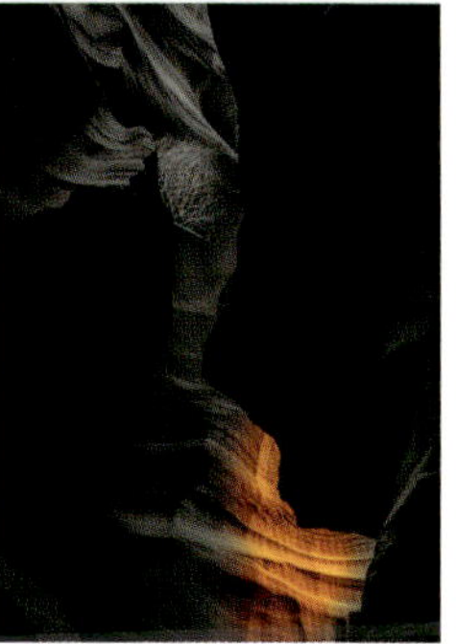

Mask 4: Then, to draw the viewer's attention to the detail in the lower right of the image, I increased the **Texture** setting.

This is an example of an image that did not require any advanced techniques and could be finished using just Lightroom. That's true of over half of the images I produce.

Pushing What's Possible with Photoshop

The panorama below was captured in the Badlands of South Dakota way back in 2006. At the time, I was shooting with my trusty Canon 20D, which produced 8.2 megapixel images. Stitching eight such images into a panorama produced a result that contained over 30 megapixels, which allowed me to produce large detailed prints.

Merge and Develop in Lightroom

I initially thought this image was just going to need a quick trip through Lightroom since I remember the colors being so amazingly vivid at the time I captured the image. After merging eight exposures into a panorama (as detailed in chapter 5), I was amazed to discover just how bland of an image I had produced.

In the **Basic** panel, I cranked the **Vibrance** slider to get the color to become more prominent, and then pushed the **Temp** and **Tint** sliders to the right to warm up the image. I then lowered the **Highlights** slider to darken the sky and boosted the **Shadows** slider to reveal more detail in the dark areas before fine-tuning the **Contrast** setting. The image was then feeling a bit flat, so I boosted **Clarity** to make the image pop. At that point, I could tell the image was going to need some work in Photoshop, as the central portion of the image felt flat and lacked dimension.

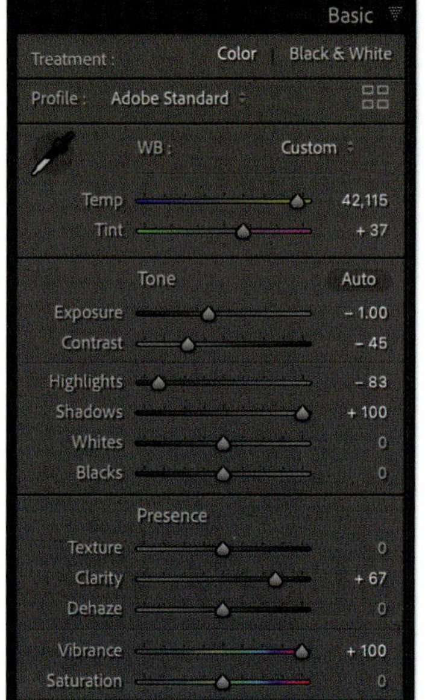

Basic panel adjustments.

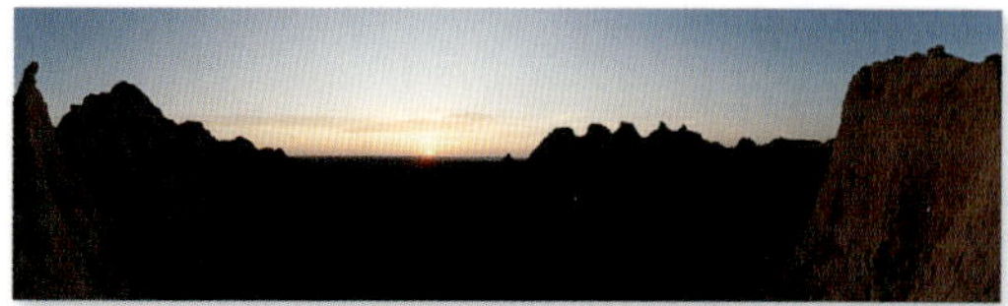

Stitched panorama shown with default develop settings.

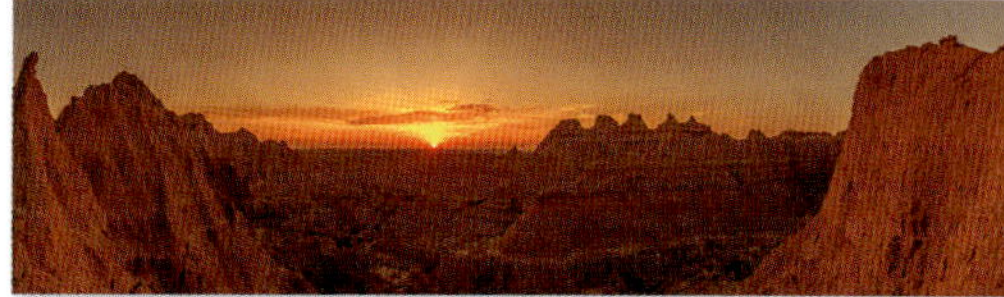

After initial optimizations using the sliders in the Basic panel.

Fixing the Sun Transition

The first thing I noticed when zooming in on the sun was a semi-abrupt edge that looked unnatural. I decided to use the curves technique that is detailed in chapter 3 to create an adjustment layer that would allow me to extend the color of the sun slightly and soften its transition.

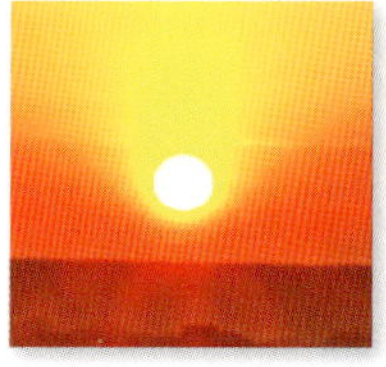
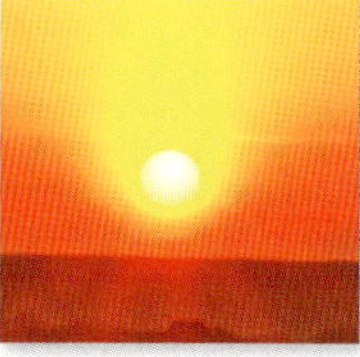

Increase Sense of Depth and Dimension

I attempted to breath some life into the central portion of the image by applying the ideas found in chapter 7. That allowed me to increase the sense of visual separation between elements that originally looked like a single mass.

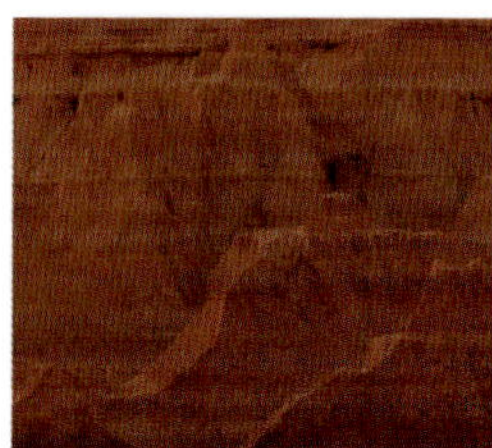
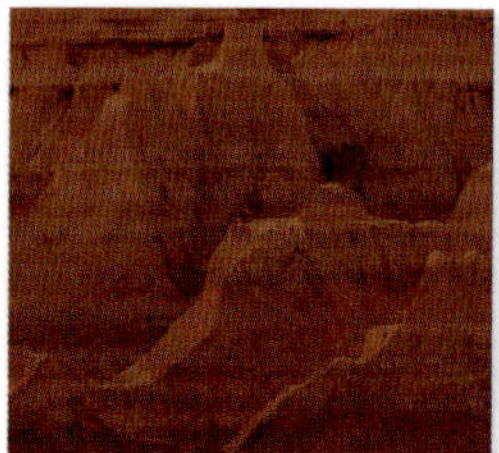

Increase Contrast in Lower Image

At that point, I realized that the lower portion of the image could use more contrast, so I chose **Select>Sky** and then **Select>Inverse** to isolate that lower part of the image. I then created a group and added a layer mask so that I could subsequently apply a few **Curves** adjustment layers to tweak the contrast without affecting the sky.

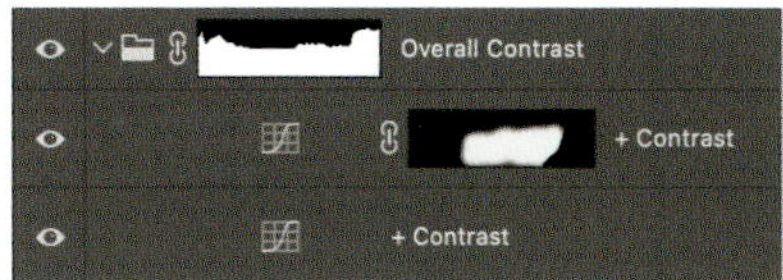

I used a masked group to prevent the sky from changing.

Craft Appearance of the Sky

Having refined the lower portion of the image, I then turned my attention to the sky. I created a new group, which I named "Sky Tweaks." I chose **Select>Sky** and then added a layer mask. That way, the subsequent **Curves** adjustments, which resided inside the group, would not affect anything outside of the sky:

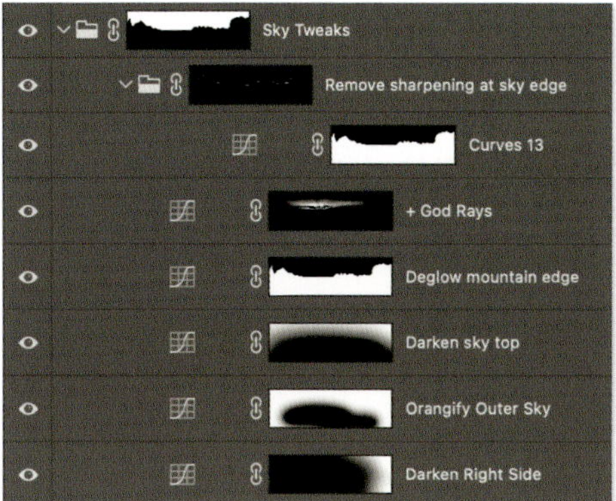

Darken Right Side: The upper-right part of the sky looked brighter than the top and left side, so I darkened that area and used a soft-edged brush to limit the effect to the right side of the image.

Increase Orange in Outer Sky: The outer reaches of the sky appeared to be less colorful and almost gray compared to the area close to the sun. To remedy the situation, I noted the RGB numbers for a colorful area near the sun and used the color-matching technique from chapter 7 to push that color into the outer area.

Darken Outer Sky: The area at the top of the image, directly above the sky, was brighter than the areas found beside it, so I used **Curves** to darken the area. I ultimately extended that adjustment further than I had originally planned and it ended up forming a vignette effect to keep the viewer's attention from deviating too far from the sun.

Remove Glow from Edge of Mountain: Cranking up the **Highlights**, **Shadows**, and **Clarity** sliders in Lightroom had caused top edge of the land to have a hint of a dark halo right at the horizon. I used a **Curves** adjustment to shift the brightness of that halo so it matched the brightness of the area below.

Enhance God Rays: There was just a hint of some light rays radiating out from the sun, so I used a technique from chapter 7 to make the rays more prominent.

Remove Sharpening Halos: The sharpening setting used in Lightroom helped the general appearance of the image, but the effect was visually obvious where the sky made contact with the mountains near the left and right sides of the image. I used a fancy combination of an additional group and two additional masks to tone down that issue.

The final tweak was to apply a funky **Curves** adjustment to the entire image, fine-tuning the color of both the shadow and highlight areas to make the colors separate a bit more.

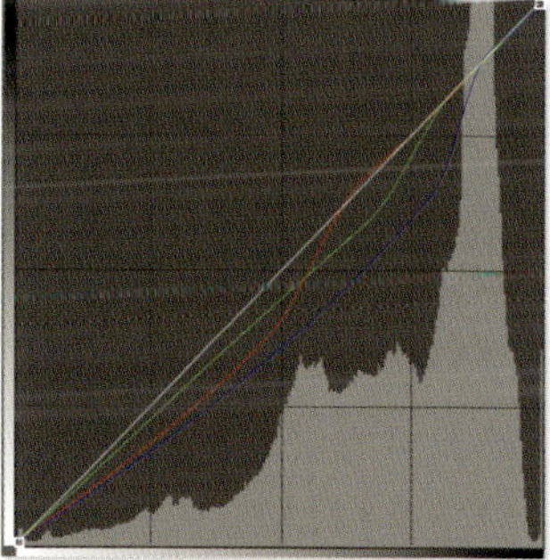

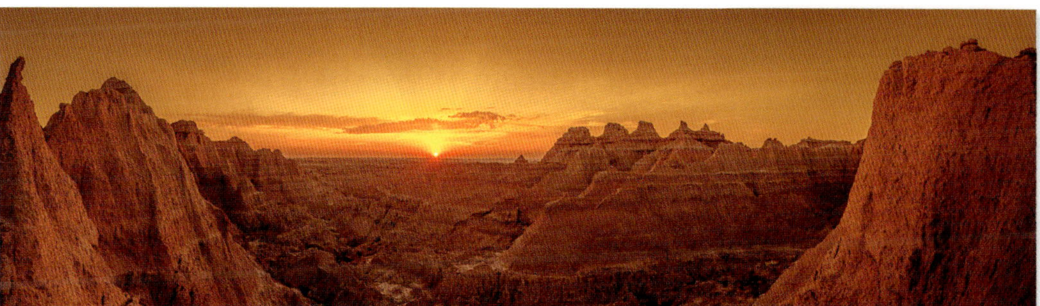

Salvaging a Difficult Capture

I captured the image below at Horseshoe Bend near Page, Arizona. With the sun pointing straight into the camera and the river below in deep shadow, a single exposure was not enough to deliver detail in both the river and the sky **A**.

I underexposed a second exposure by two stops in an attempt to retain detail in the area of the sky that surrounds the sun **B**. I took two additional exposures, one two-stops **C** and a second four-stops overexposed **D**, to ensure detail was captured in the river.

Merging all four exposures into an HDR image and then optimizing the result in the Develop module (as outlined in chapter 5) produced detail across the entire dynamic range **E**.

Multi-Processed Raw in Photoshop

That's as far as I took this in Lightroom. Next, I used **Photo>Edit In>Open as Smart Object in Photoshop** and then created an independent duplicate layer by choosing **Layer>Smart Objects>New Smart Object Via Copy**. I double-clicked on the thumbnail for that layer to access ACR, where the settings dialed in were idealized for the sky **F**. I repeated the process to produce a third version that was optimized for the river area **G**.

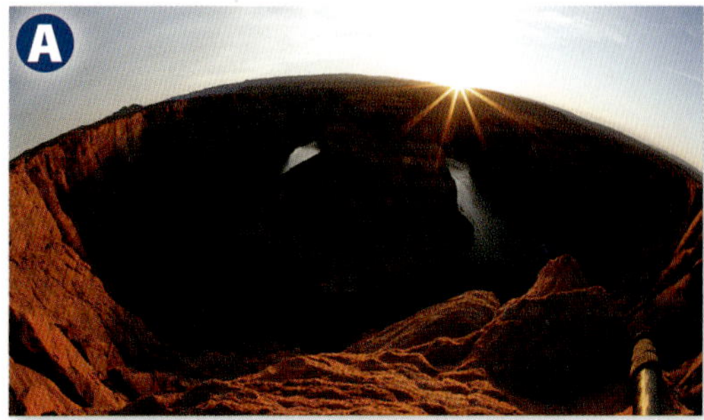

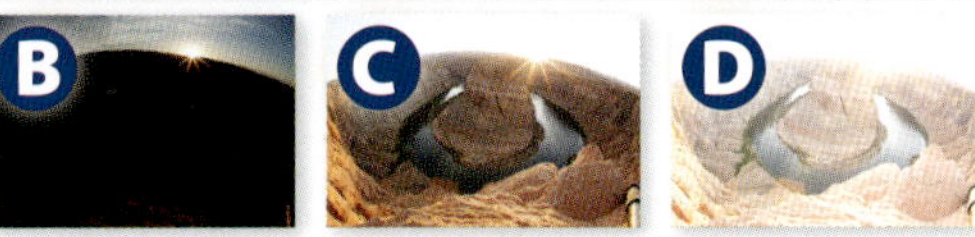

Four exposures as they appeared with default settings, which were used to produce a high dynamic range (HDR) image.

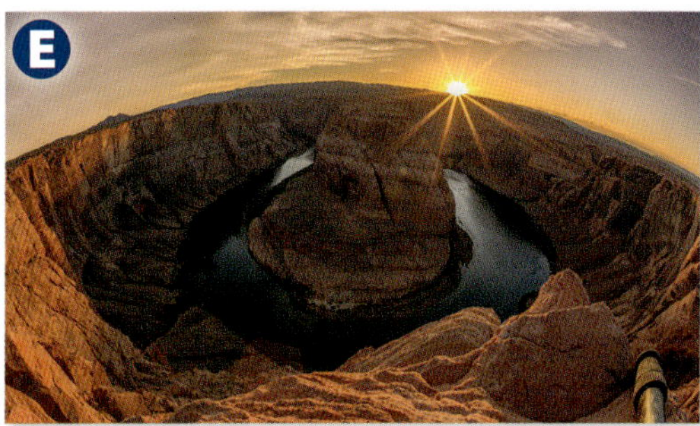

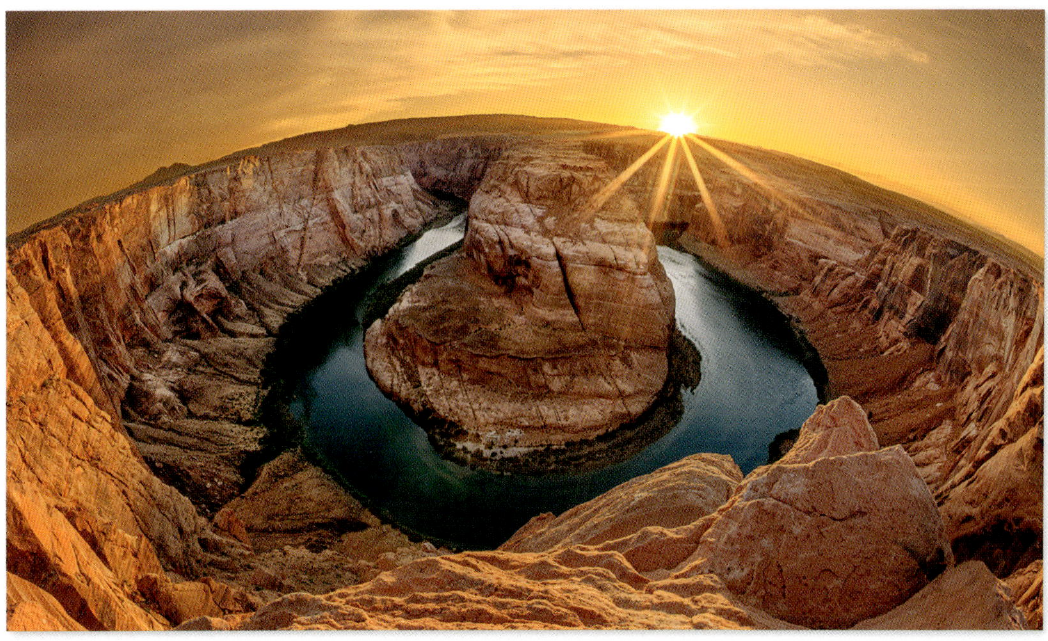

Section III: Crafting a Photograph

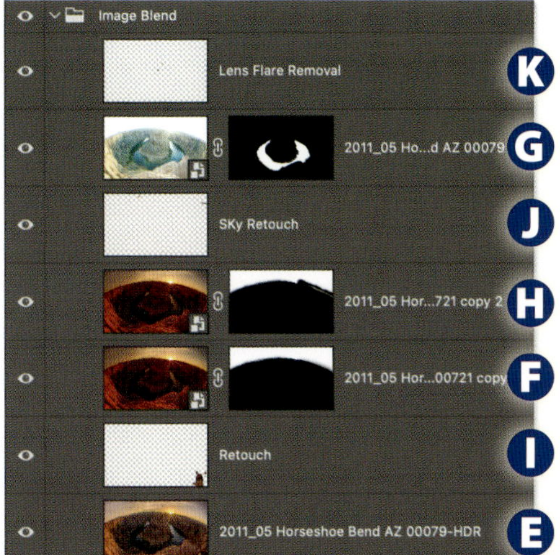

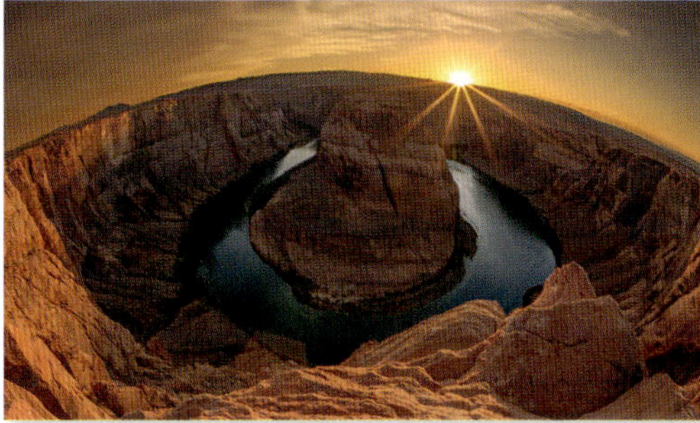

Image separately optimized for sky, river, and overall.

Fix Luminous Horizon

I then duplicated the layer optimized for the sky, set its blending mode to **Luminosity** to prevent color shifts, and added white to the mask in areas where the ground was too bright near the horizon **H**.

Retouching

I used three different layers to retouch undesirable areas, such as the tripod leg that appeared in the lower-right corner **I**, a few undesirable clouds **J**, and lens flares **K**.

Crafting the Landscape

The real transformation of this image was made through just shy of sixty **Curves** and **Hue/Saturation** adjustment layers that I used to selectively fine-tune the image.

This is an example of how mastering your craft will allow you to transform just about any image.

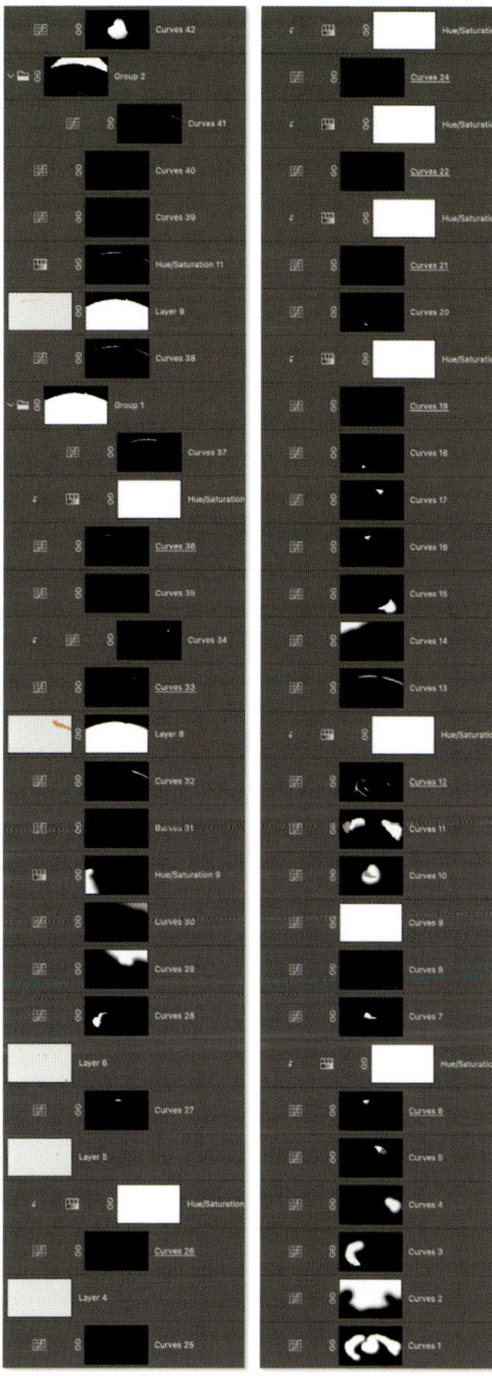

A group called "Enhancements" contained almost sixty adjustment layers that I used to craft this image.

Creating a Body of Work

When displaying a collection of images that share a common theme, the following ideas can help to ensure that each image feels like it belongs with the others and forms a cohesive body of work:

Similar Scale, Complexity, and Contrast: Choosing images that share similar qualities can help to avoid abrupt transitions as your viewer moves from one image to the next.

Matching Cropping Aspect Ratio: When images are displayed side by side, slight variations in aspect ratio can become distracting. To apply a consistent ratio (all square, or 16:9, etc.), right-click on an image that has been cropped with the ratio you desire, choose **Develop>Copy Settings**, click the **Check None** button, and turn on the **Aspect Ratio** checkbox before clicking the **Copy** button. Then, select all the images that should share that cropping ratio, right-click on any one of the images, and choose **Develop>Paste Settings**. If the cropping needs to be fine-tuned, then be sure to click the lock icon when using the **Crop** tool to ensure the crop aspect ratio remains unchanged.

Consistent Color Treatment: If the images share similar content, such as blue skies, a setting sun, or mountains, then consider using the techniques from chapter 8 to fine-tune the overall color rendering of each image while viewing a reference from the group. This will create consistency between the images.

To view two images side by side in the Develop module, choose **View>Open in Reference View**, then drag an image from the Filmstrip at the bottom edge of the window to the reference area on the left side of the window. If you'd like to use the same reference image when switching back and forth between the Library and Develop modules, then click the lock icon in the toolbar below.

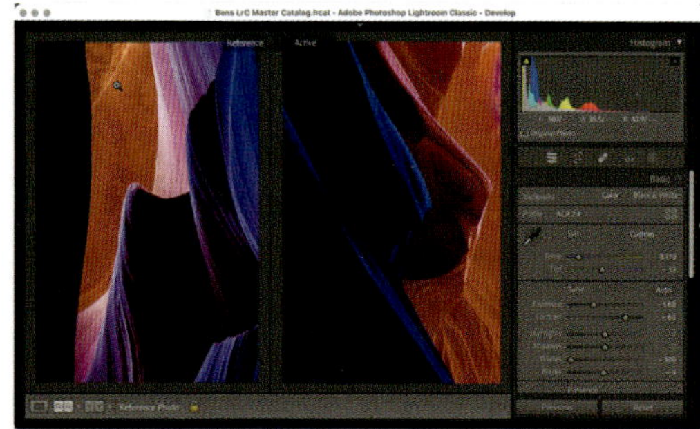

Two images viewed side by side in Reference View.

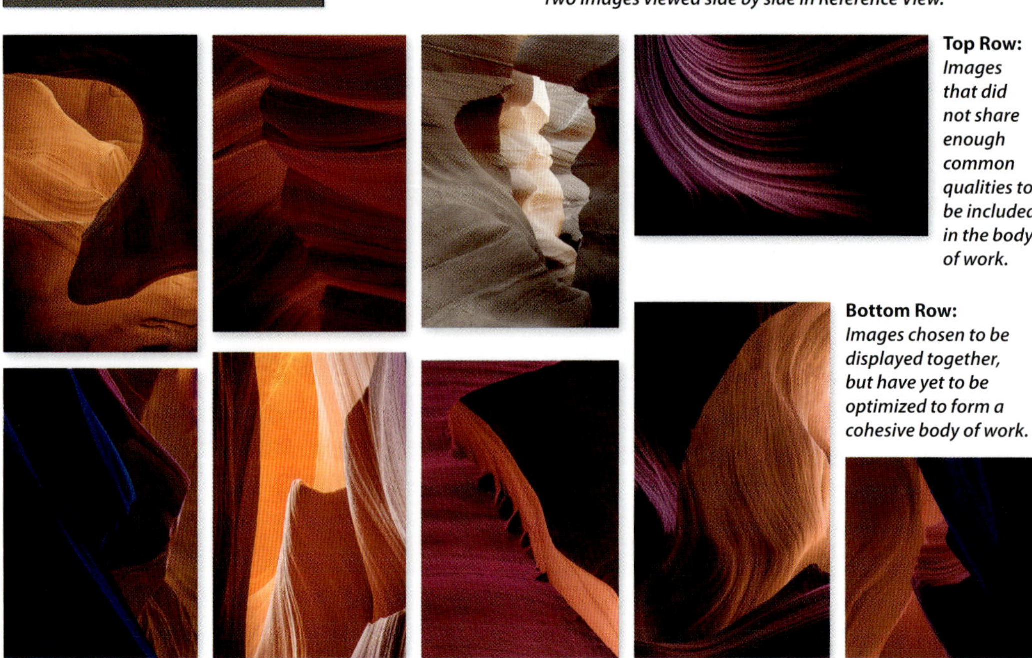

Top Row: *Images that did not share enough common qualities to be included in the body of work.*

Bottom Row: *Images chosen to be displayed together, but have yet to be optimized to form a cohesive body of work.*

Section III: Crafting a Photograph

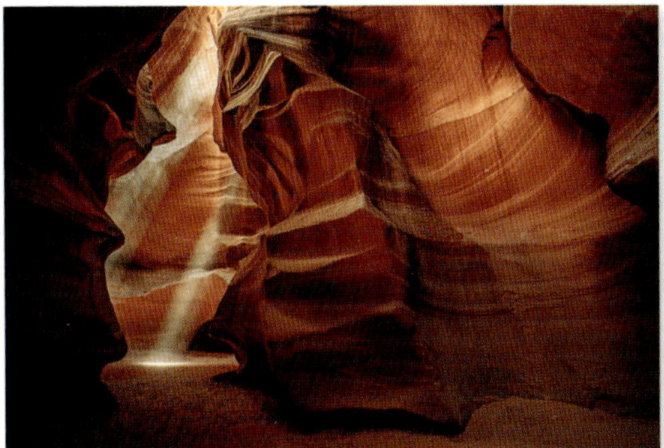

Optimized without consideration for how it would relate visually to other images that would be displayed as a group.

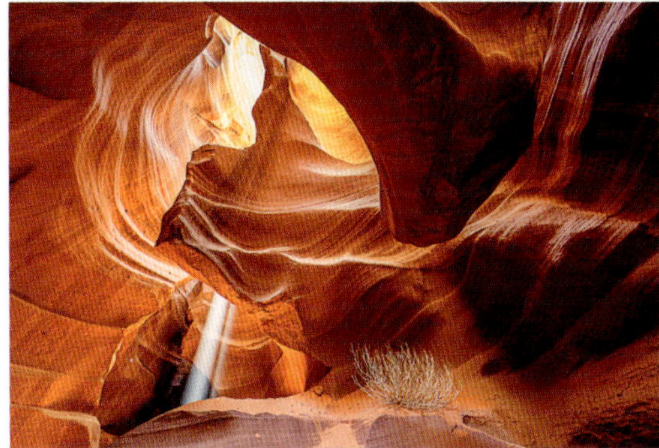

Saturation, highlight brightness, and overall color treatment differs from the image shown at left.

Uniform Brightness and Contrast: The numbers that appear below the histogram can be a useful tool for comparing the brightness of various areas between images when using **Reference View**. To do this, right-click on the histogram and choose **Show Lab Color Values**, and then inspect the **L** reading, which stands for lightness, while hovering over an area within the image.

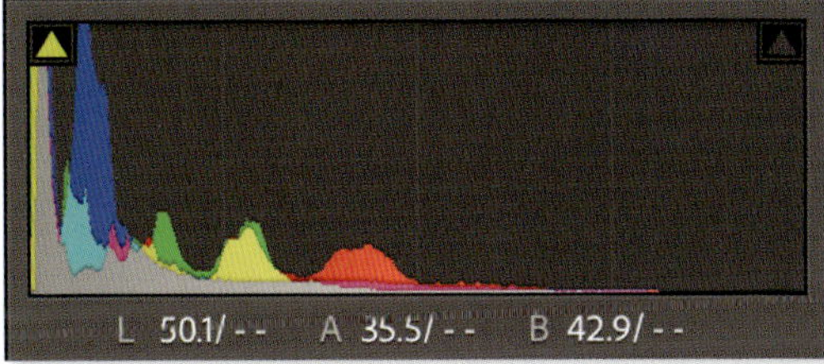

To change the brightness of an isolated area, I created a masked adjustment, clicked on the number to the right of the adjustment slider I wanted to change, and then used the up and down arrow keys to modify the setting while I watched how the change affected the **L** reading.

Take a Formulaic Approach to Effects: When stylizing an image using the techniques covered in chapter 7, it can be useful to apply them consistently across the group of images. For example, you might start with the Orton effect, followed by a conversion to black and white, and then apply a consistent **Color Grading** setting to tint all the images.

Arrange Group Based on Brightness: When displaying images as a group, consider arranging them based on where the brightest area is found within each image. This can be useful because the eye is naturally drawn to the brightest area within an image. The idea is to keep the viewer's attention within the group by preventing them from being drawn toward the outer areas where they may exit the group. Choosing **Photo>Flip Horizontal** can also be used, if needed, to flip the entire contents of an image.

The more effort you put into creating a sense of visual unity in a series of images, the more likely they will be perceived as a cohesive body of work.

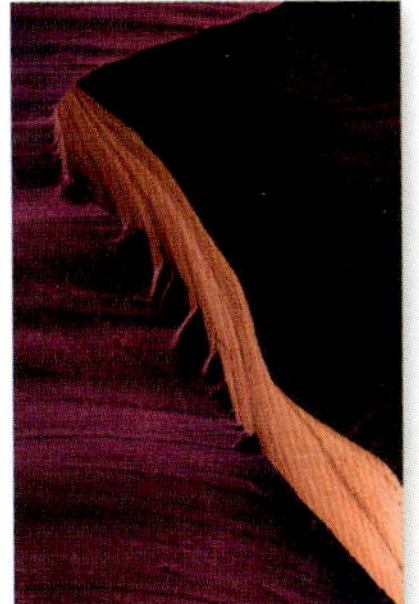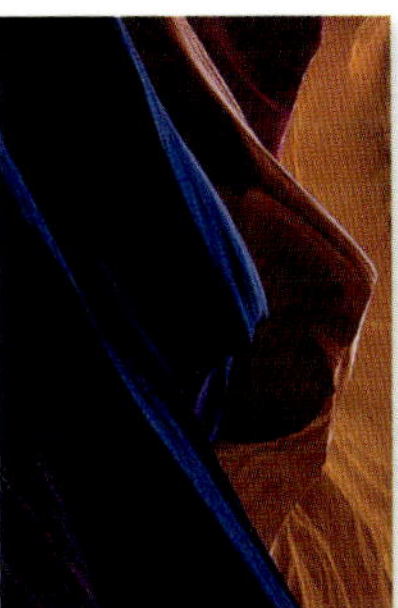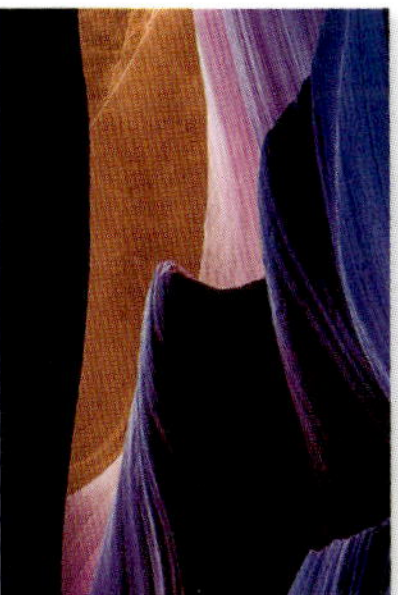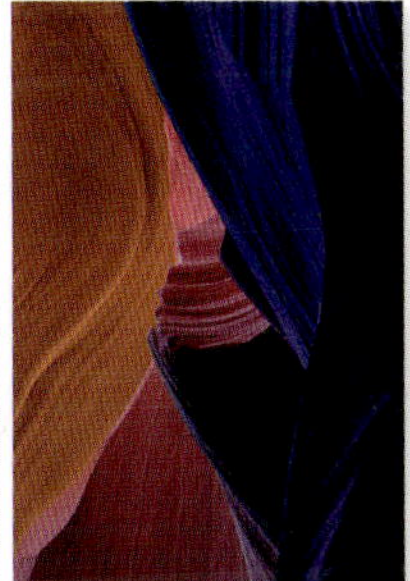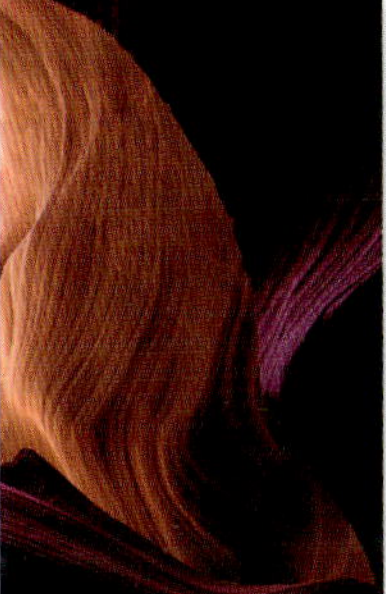

Result of cropping and optimizing the images so they share common qualities that help make them feel like a cohesive group.

Parting Thoughts

You've reached the end of this book! Before we part, here are a few closing thoughts...

Knowing When to Quit

It can be difficult to know when an image should be considered done and ready to show the public at large. It all comes down to running out of one of the following: problems, patience, or time.

When nature puts on a show and you happen to capture the moment with just the right camera settings, you might be able to produce a finished image in less than a minute using Lightroom's Develop module. A little boost of **Vibrance**, maybe a hint of **Clarity**, and a double-click of the **Blacks** slider and you're done.

Other times, an image will never really feel done. Just look at the last image in the real-world examples section earlier in this chapter—it contains over sixty layers!

I often work on images like that one while multitasking. Maybe it's listening to an audio book that I am having trouble mustering the energy to finish. Combine two things and I don't feel like my time is just being sucked away. If I don't plan on making a large print of an image, then I may call it quits when I determine it's good enough for social media.

When preparing an image for a large print, I take my time to ensure the image has been perfected. This process involves living with the image for a while and making note of any faults I notice over time. To do this, I create a small print of the image and hang it up in a visible place. I use a Sharpie marker to mark any areas that need improvement. Only with the passage of time am I able to have a fresh enough perspective that I see it anew. Once there are enough marks to fix, I make the necessary adjustments and replace the print. Sometimes I repeat the process just three or four times, but some images require more than a dozen rounds. It's only after I can live with the image for an extended period of time without marking it up that I will start to get ready to make a large print. As one final review, I zoom in and navigate around the entire image, looking for tiny imperfections before making what I hope will be my master print.

Staying Inspired

Keeping fresh is an essential part of evolving as a photographer. One way to do that is by finding inspiration in the work of others. When it comes to landscape photography, one resource that I found to be excellent is *Elements* magazine at elementsphotomag.com. This online publication is dedicated to showcasing the best in landscape photography from around the world. I have no association with the publication whatsoever. I just like what they do and think more people should know about their publication.

Finding Help Along the Way

Over the years, I have extended invitations to those who have attended my seminars to become members of a free private Facebook group. This group has since grown significantly and now boasts over 15,000 members. It is a space where people can ask questions about photography, Lightroom, and Photoshop. As many of the members have read my books or attended my seminars, they tend to be more knowledgeable than the typical photography groups found on Facebook. I make a conscious effort to regularly check the group and answer any unanswered questions that the community might have. To join the group, point your web browser to: www.facebook.com/groups/BenWillmore.

Keeping Up on My Latest Techniques

If you're looking to expand your knowledge on Lightroom and Photoshop beyond what's covered in this book, I suggest visiting my membership site at mastersacademy.com where I've been consistently posting videos for over eight years. There, you'll find a plethora of resources including over 250 hours of content covering photography, Lightroom, and Photoshop.

It is my sincere hope that you've found the ideas in this book to be of help in realizing the full potential of your photography.

Acknowledgments

While my name may be on the cover of this book, it is only because of the tremendous support and contributions of the following wonderful people that this tome exists.

My wife Karen deserves huge recognition for her support during the lengthy process of writing this book. Despite me dedicating endless hours to the project, reducing our time together, she also took on the role of initial proofreader and editor, making sure that what I turned in to my publisher as a first draft was much more polished than what came off my keyboard. I couldn't have done it without her.

Rocky Nook's team were superb to collaborate with. I must thank Scott Cowlin and Ted Waitt specifically for considering my proposal and aiding in the shaping of this book.

Thank you to my editor Jocelyn Howell, who reminded me of the darned Oxford comma, and transformed my writing into something for which I can take great pride.

There are so many people who, over the last thirty-five years of my career, have helped me along the way and it would be impossible to thank them all individually. However, a few cannot go without mention. Jay Nelson was instrumental in kick-starting my speaking career, urging me to transition from giving my own seminars to speaking at my first conference many decades ago. If it wasn't for you, my first book may have never happened, as it was at that first conference that Adobe asked me to write it. To Scott Kelby, who gave me an even larger audience by allowing me to lead seminar tours and speak at the PhotoshopWorld conference. To Lesa Snider (who happens to be Jay's better half), who introduced me to CreativeLive, which exploded my online teaching audience. To everyone who worked at CreativeLive in its heyday and made it an amazing place to teach. To Meg Bitton, for introducing me to her amazing imagery and allowing me to teach to her passionate followers.

Then there are the usual suspects, with whom I frequently cross paths with at conferences and trade shows. If you're in this group, you know who you are and your friendship has made speaking at such events one of the most rewarding and enjoyable activities I've had the pleasure to partake in.

I owe a debt of gratitude to the Adobe team, both past and present. They have sought my opinion, trusted me to test pre-release software before it was available to the public, shared valuable information with me, and been a source of support throughout the years.

I'm so grateful for my mom, who bought me my first computer, sent me to Compu-Camp, and trusted that my interest in computers might not be a passing phase. Sadly, she passed away while I was still in high school and never got a chance to see that I stuck with it.

Lastly, to all those who have attended my seminars, read my books, and watched my videos. You all have enabled me to turn my passion into my profession.

Index

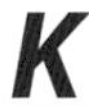

hair, selecting, 46
halos, 178–181
haze
  atmospheric, 130
  increase, 107
  reduce, 86–87
HDR images, 92–95
  artifacts, 198–201
  brightness, uneven, 198
  displays, 94
  light sources, 199
  merging files, 12
  motion artifacts, 200
  panoramas, 99
  sharpness, 201
  Smart Preview and, 111
  tone mapping, 95
Heal (LR), 30–31
Healing Brush tool (PS), 62
Healing tool (LR), 30–31
hide mask tools in LR, 24
**high-contrast scenes, 76–77,
  148–149**
highlights
  blown-out, 168–170
  clipped, 90
  increase, 121
  reduce, 72–73, 120
Highlights slider (LR), 20
  histogram, 19, 170
  clipping indicators, 169
Curves, 54
History Brush (PS), 51
horizon, crooked, 80
HSB, 57
HSL/Color panel (LR), 157
HSL/HSB plug-in, 160
hue bar, spin, 51
hue map, 165
Hue Wheel (PS), 40
Hue/Saturation (PS), 56–57

importing images (LR), 16
in-camera processing, 6
  JPEGs and, 6
Info panel (PS), 57

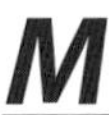

JPEG
  raw, vs., 6–7
  white balance, 152

K

keyboard shortcuts (LR), 29
keystoning, 78

L

Lab mode (PS), 158
layers (PS), 58–59
  adjustment, 41, 52, 58
  aligning, 111
  Background, 41
  Blending Options, 59
  clip, 58
  groups, 59
  lock, 41
  masks, 58–59
  non-destructive, 41
  retouching, 41
Lens Corrections panel (PS), 79
lens flare, removing, 33, 82–84
Levels, refining masks with, 189
Lighten mode (PS), 50
lighting, optimize, 122–123
Lightroom Classic, xv, 9
  basic adjustments, 20–23
  catalog, 10–11, 16–17
  delete images, 17
  exporting files, 36–37
  External Editing Preferences, 34
  File Handling, 16
  File Renaming, 16
  importing images, 16
  panels, adjusting, 29
  Photoshop, vs., 9–13
  raw files and, 9
  retouching in, 30–33
  send image to Photoshop, 34
  tips and tricks, 29
  workflow, 12–13
Linear Gradient (LR masks), 26
linear profiles, 73
linearization, 6
loading selections (PS), 50
lock layer, 41
long exposure, simulate, 140–141

Luminance Range mask
  Lightroom, 26
  Photoshop, 72
luminosity masks (PS), 43

M

mask artifacts, 182–189
  AI masks, 183
  edge fringing, 188
  halos, 185
  low-quality, 188
  noisy, 186
mask tools in Lightroom, 25–26
masks (LR), 24–28
  adjustments, 128
  AI-generated, 24–25
  combine options, 27
  disable, 27
  hide tools, 24
  manual, 25–26
  missing tools, 24
  naming, 26
  overlay, 27
  upgrade, 184
  vignette, 123
  masks (PS), 42–50
  adjustments, 129
  channel-based, 48
  combine multiple masks, 50
  depth mask, 48
  edge fringing, 188
  edge mask, 48
  edge residue, 50
  halos, 185
  issues, 185–188
  layer, 58–59
  Levels, refining with, 189
  low-quality, 188
  luminosity, 43
  noisy, 186
  Properties, 59
  refining, 50, 189
Masks panel (LR), 26–27
matching colors, 55, 57
merge
  HDR, 92–95
  panoramas, 97–102
metadata, 9
missing folders, 17
mist, reduce, 107
motion in images, 103
multi-processed raw, 76–77

N

negative elements in scene, 117
neutral elements in scene, 117
noise, 69
add, 141
color, 71
Denoise button, 71
luminance, 70
reduction, 7, 70–71
shadows and, 91

O

Object Selection tool (PS), 42
Objects mask (LR), 25
Orton effect, 132
Overlay mode (PS), 50

P

panels (LR), adjusting, 29
panoramas, 95–102
angled horizons/trees, 193
artifacts, 192–197
auto fill, 197
batch-merging, 111
find in LR catalog, 111, 196
fisheye, 192
HDR panoramas, 99
lens flares, 194
low-resolution, 196
merging, 97–102
motion blur, 192
Photoshop and, 100–102
projection method, 98
rectangular image, 98
shooting, 95
Smart Preview and, 111
parametric editor, 9
people, removing from images, 33
People mask (LR), 24
Photoshop, 8
ACR plug-in, 8
actions, 41
color issues, 40
Lightroom, vs., 8–13
Preferences, 40
revert to previous state, 51
tips and tricks, 51
workflow, 12–13, 40–41
pixel editor, 8
adjustments, 9

retouching, 9
pixels, stuck, 6
positive elements in scene, 117
posterization, 190–191
Preferences
Camera Raw, 40
Photoshop, 40
previews in Lightroom, 11
Print module (LR), 37
process version, update, 29
profiles, color, 154–155
proofing, 174
ProPhoto RGB, 34

Q

Quick Mask Mode (PS), 45
Quick Selection tool (PS), 42

R

Radial Gradient (LR masks), 26
Range (LR masks), 26
raw file, 8
JPEG, vs., 6–7
multi-process, 76–77
Photoshop and, 35
white balance, 152
rays, sun, 142–143
Refine Edge Brush tool (PS), 46
reflections, unnatural, 175
reject images (LR), 18
remote work, 11
remove object from image, 60
rename file, 16–17
after importing, 16
rename folder, 17
replace sky, 74, 108–109
reset adjustment (PS), 58
reset LR slider, 29
Reset tool (PS), 51
resolution, 34
retouching (LR), 30–33
edit prior retouching, 32
examples, 33
retouching (PS), 60–63, 119–120
Clone Source panel, 63
Clone Stamp tool, 62
Content-Aware Fill, 60
Delete and Fill Selection, 60
Healing Brush tool, 62
layer, 41
non-destructive, 119
Spot Healing Brush, 60

S

saturation, excessive, 172–175
Saturation adjustment (PS), 56
saturation map, 164
saturation mask, 160
Saturation slider (LR), 22
saving selections (PS), 50
Select & Mask (PS), 46
Edge Detection, 47
selections (PS), 42–50
brightness range, 43
color, 43–44
complex shapes, 48
depth, 48
free-form areas, 45
fur, 46
hair, 46
invert, 45
loading, 50
saving, 50
soft-edged, 47
tonal, 43
selective focus, 139
send image from LR to PS, 34
sensor, camera, 6
dust spots, 32
shadows
brighten, 121
clipped, 91, 170–171
colorful, 177
darken, 122
Shadows slider (LR), 20
sharpening, 12, 124
sky
adjustments, 109
blown-out, 74
brightening, selective, 176
gray, 74
long exposure, simulate, 140–141
replacement, 74, 108–109
sun, 177
sunrise/sunset, enhance, 162–163
unevenly lit, 176
Sky mask (LR), 24
Smart Filters (PS), 52
Smart Previews (LR), 11, 16
bypass, 29
export from, 37
snapping layers, disable, 51
Spot Healing Brush (PS), 60
Stack Mode, 106
Straighten tool (PS), 80
Subject mask (LR), 24

Index